Motivation in Education

Theory, Research, and Applications

Paul R. Pintrich
The University of Michigan

Dale H. Schunk
Purdue University

Merrill, an imprint of
Prentice Hall

Englewood Cliffs, New Jersey   *Columbus, Ohio*

Library of Congress Cataloging-in-Publication Data
Pintrich, Paul R.
 Motivation in education : theory, research, and applications/
Paul R. Pintrich, Dale H. Schunk.
  p. cm.
 Includes bibliographical references and index.
 ISBN 0-02-395621-6 (pbk.)
 1. Motivation in education. 2. Motivation (Psychology)
I. Schunk, Dale H. II. Title.
 LB1065.P52 1996
 370.15'4—dc20   95-17192
                                                         CIP

Editor: Kevin M. Davis
Production Editor: Louise N. Sette
Copy Editor: Marilyn Prudente
Design Coordinator: Jill E. Bonar
Text Designer: Ed Horcharik
Production Buyer: Deidra M. Schwartz
Electronic Text Management: Marilyn Wilson Phelps, Matthew Williams, Karen L.
 Bretz, Tracey Ward

This book was set in Dutch 823 by Prentice Hall and was printed and bound by R.R.
Donnelley & Sons Company. The cover was printed by Phoenix Color Corp.

 © 1996 by Prentice-Hall, Inc.
A Simon & Schuster Company
Englewood Cliffs, New Jersey 07632

Printed in the United States of America

10 9 8 7 6 5 4 3 2 1

ISBN: 0-02-395621-6

Prentice-Hall International (UK) Limited, *London*
Prentice-Hall of Australia Pty. Limited, *Sydney*
Prentice-Hall of Canada, Inc., *Toronto*
Prentice-Hall Hispanoamericana, S. A., *Mexico*
Prentice-Hall of India Private Limited, *New Delhi*
Prentice-Hall of Japan, Inc., *Tokyo*
Simon & Schuster Asia Pte. Ltd., *Singapore*
Editora Prentice-Hall do Brasil, Ltda., *Rio de Janeiro*

To our families,
for their motivation, love, and support

Liz and Bill
Caryl and Laura

The field of motivation has undergone many changes in recent years as psychological theories have increasingly incorporated cognitive concepts and variables. Explanations of behavior have moved away from stimuli and reinforcement contingencies and instead emphasize learners' constructive interpretations of events and the role that their beliefs, cognitions, affects, and values play in achievement situations.

Motivation involves processes that occur as individuals instigate and sustain goal-directed actions. Although many professionals feel comfortable with this cognitive perspective, there exists considerable disagreement about what processes are involved in motivation, how these processes operate, how motivation relates to learning and achievement, and how motivation can be enhanced and sustained at an optimal level.

We believe that motivation is an important quality that pervades all aspects of teaching and learning. Motivated students display interest in activities, feel self-efficacious, expend effort to succeed, persist at tasks, and typically use effective task and cognitive strategies. Motivated teachers feel that they can help students learn, put extra time into instructional planning, and work with students to help ensure their learning and mastery. When motivation declines, other educational outcomes also suffer. Teachers must not only impart knowledge and teach skills but also establish a motivating environment for learning.

This text grew from a conversation the authors had at the 1991 American Educational Research Association (AERA) convention in Chicago. At that time each of us had been active in the field of motivation for several years as researchers and teachers and specifically in the Motivation in Education Special Interest Group of AERA. In addition, both of us had been teaching graduate-level courses on motivation in education and felt the need for a textbook that would be appropriate for our courses. We wanted to write a book that would provide students with a solid theoretical and empirical grounding and illustrate how principles and research findings might be applied in education.

The primary objectives of this text are (a) to present the major motivation theories, principles, and research findings in enough detail to help students understand the complexity of motivational processes, and (b) to provide examples of motivational concepts and principles applied to educational settings in order to suggest ways of facilitating motivation in these settings. Although different perspectives on motivation are presented, the text places primary emphasis on the role of personal cognitions during teaching and learning. This focus is consistent with cognitive accounts of human behavior that view learners as active, constructive seekers and processors of information rather than as passive recipients.

To accomplish the book's objectives, the text comprises 10 chapters that are organized into three major sections. The introductory section includes the first two chapters, which introduce the study of motivation and present historical perspectives on motivation. The next section, on theoretical perspectives, includes six chapters that address the various theories and models of motivation, including attributional theory, expectancy-value theory, social cognitive theory, intrinsic motivation theory, goal theory, and models of interest and affect. The final section, on contextual influences, includes two chapters on teacher and classroom influences, and school influences on student motivations. Of course, throughout the earlier chapters we discuss contextual influences, but in the last two chapters we focus on the role of the teacher, classroom, and school and their impact on motivation.

All chapters, except the first one, are organized in a similar fashion to ensure some consistency throughout the book. Each chapter begins with a scenario that illustrates some of the processes discussed in the chapter. The chapter then discusses key theoretical principles and constructs and important research findings. We summarize basic studies testing hypothesized influences on and effects of motivation, as well as applied research investigating the operation of motivational processes in classrooms and other learning settings. Where appropriate we also address the role of developmental factors in motivation, along with such important individual difference variables as gender and ethnicity. Our intention is not to highlight differences but rather to show how personal cognitions and motivational constructs may help to explain the relation between these variables and student outcomes.

Throughout each chapter, we discuss the implications of the theory and research findings for educational practice. In addition to numerous informal examples in the text, each chapter includes detailed and specific applications with suggestions for incorporating motivational principles into instructional contexts. We gear most examples to school-age students, but we also include applications with other learners (e.g., postsecondary) and in out-of-school settings.

This book is designed for use by educational researchers and practitioners and by graduate students and advanced undergraduates who have some prior knowledge in education and psychology. The book will be appropriate in courses where motivation is covered in some depth; for example, introductory courses in learning, development, motivation, and educational psychology, as well as in specialty courses in these areas. We assume that students will have some familiarity with psychological concepts and research methods, but the text contains minimal discussion of the statistical aspects of research results.

ACKNOWLEDGMENTS

We want to thank many people for their assistance during the various phases of this project. We owe a sincere debt of gratitude to our many professional colleagues who have provided us with valuable insights into motivational processes. In particular, we have found our activities and interactions with colleagues in the Motivation in Education Special Interest Group of AERA personally rewarding and fruitful. Dale has benefited from many conversations with Barry Zimmerman and Judith Meece. At Michigan, the faculty and students in the Combined Program in Education and Psychology have provided Paul with a consistently stimulating and collegial environment for research on motivation. His faculty colleagues, Phyllis Blumenfeld, Jacque Eccles, Marty Maehr, Ron Marx, Bill McKeachie, and Carol Midgley, have consistently provided critical feedback and constructive support that have benefited him both professionally and personally. Allan Wigfield, while at Michigan and since he has been at the University of Maryland, has been a source of many great ideas, cogent advice, and stimulating conversations as a colleague and best friend for Paul. Paul also has had an excellent group of graduate students involved in his research program, including Eric Anderman, Stasia Danos Elder, Teresa Garcia, Lynley Hicks, Barbara Hofer, Allison Murphy, Helen Patrick, Tim Urdan, Scott VanderStoep, Chris Wolters, Allison Young, and Shirley Yu. This group of students from both the Competence and Commitment Project and the College Research Group has worked collaboratively with Paul on problems of motivation and learning in classrooms and has been an indispensable source of motivation and inspiration for him over the years. In addition, most of them have been students in his doctoral seminar on motivation and were the first audience for many of the ideas in this book.

We also acknowledge the several agencies who have funded our research over the years, including the Office of Educational Research and Improvement in the Department of Education, the National Science Foundation, the Spencer Foundation, the National Institute of Mental Health, The University of North Carolina, The University of Michigan, and the University of Houston. Paul was supported by a sabbatical from Michigan for the 1993-1994 academic year when much of the book was written. Besides our funding sources, we thank the administrators, teachers, and students from a number of different school districts that have collaborated with us on our research.

With respect to the book's production we thank Kevin Davis, our editor at Prentice Hall, for his support, patience, and editorial guidance. In addition, our production editor, Louise Sette, and our copy editor, Marilyn Prudente, worked with great effort and dedication to produce the book. We thank them especially for their good humor and patience with us as dilatory authors. Several reviewers provided excellent critiques of earlier portions of the manuscript. In particular, Carol Midgley from the University of Michigan and Allan Wigfield from the University of Maryland, provided excellent feedback on several chapters. We also gained valuable feedback from students at Michigan and Purdue who previewed the book in draft form. At the University of Michigan, Carol Birmingham and Loralyn Rudy assisted with word processing, indexing, and administrative requirements. Their careful and hard work made the writing process much easier.

We would also like to express our appreciation to the reviewers of this text: Myron H. Dembo, University of Southern California; James A. Middleton, Arizona State University; Samuel D. Miller, University of North Carolina; Patricia A. Pokay, Eastern Michigan University; Barbara M. Powell, Eastern Illinois University; and Janette E. Summers, University of Arkansas.

Finally, we express our heartfelt thanks to our parents, Teresa and Paul Pintrich, and the late Mil and Al Schunk, for their love and encouragement. We owe our deepest gratitude to our wives, Elisabeth De Groot and Caryl Schunk, and to our children Bill De Groot and Laura Schunk, for their patience, understanding, and support throughout this project. Although we know they became quite tired of our divided attention and a few lost weekends as we worked on "the book," they were always supportive. We also thank Liz and Caryl for several of the ideas for the applications in the book as they drew on their years of experience as teachers and principals in public schools. Lastly, we are grateful that this book project gave us many hours of stimulating conversation with each other and created a friendship that will endure over our careers.

Paul R. Pintrich
Dale H. Schunk

CONTENTS

3   The Role of Expectancy and Self-Efficacy Beliefs   67

4   Attributional Processes   105

5 Other Social Cognitive Processes   153

8 The Role of Values, Interest, and Affect   287

9 Teacher and Classroom Influences   325

10 School Culture and Organization   367

Introduction to the Study of Motivation

*K*eith Mitchell teaches seventh-grade social studies at a middle school. His fourth-period class is quite typical of those he teaches. The 12 male and 13 female students have varied socioeconomic backgrounds but most are middle class. Although they represent a range in achievement, students generally perform well in class.

The students are engaged in small-group work. As Keith takes a break from walking around and checking on the groups' progress, he scans the room. He has been studying motivation in a college class, and as his eyes settle on the following students, he thinks about each in terms of motivation.

1. *Matt*. Matt is intelligent but has little motivation for social studies. He would rather be playing his electric guitar or hanging out with friends. He *is* motivated to be a great guitar player. Keith wishes he could increase Matt's academic motivation.

2. *Sharon*. Sharon is an intelligent student who enjoys learning for its own sake. She is motivated to learn new things and enjoys the challenge. She sets goals for herself and monitors her goal progress. Keith wants to ensure that Sharon's academic motivation remains at a high level.

3. *Eric*. The main thing that seems to motivate Eric is doing better than everyone else. Eric is not content to be second best. Whenever he works on a task, he compares his work with that of others to determine how well he is performing. Keith's goal is to try to replace Eric's emphasis on beating everyone with a desire to cooperate and to find satisfaction in learning for its own sake.

4. *Deanna*. She is motivated to avoid being the slowest student in the class. Whenever the students work on a task, Deanna compares her work with that of others to make sure she is doing better than at least one other student. She wants Keith to think that she is not the dumbest student in the class. Keith wants her to stop thinking of herself in this negative fashion.

5. *Peggy*. Peggy is interested in schoolwork but has very low self-confidence for performing well. A few years ago, her older brother was an honor student who subsequently attended a prestigious university. Peggy has never considered herself to be as competent as her brother. Her low self-confidence adversely affects her motivation. She works lackadaisically on difficult tasks and gives up easily when she does not understand.

6. *José*. Unlike Peggy, José does not know what it means to give up. He is a tireless worker who believes that hard work will conquer almost any problem and lead to success. Keith appreciates his persistence but occasionally it leads to problems, such as when José works endlessly on a task he does not

understand rather than asking Keith for assistance. Through his diligent effort, José completes most of his work and earns decent grades.

7. *Kris.* Kris is a good student who works hard and makes good grades but takes little credit for her success. When she performs well she feels that she was lucky or that the task was easy. She never says that she is good in the subject area, nor does she believe that success derives from her effort. Keith is concerned because she takes little personal responsibility for her successes and failures.

These students, representative of a typical class, illustrate the various motivational patterns that present challenges for teachers. Our goals for this book are (a) to present major views and principles of motivation that will help you identify and understand these and other types of differences in student motivation and (b) to suggest ways of fostering a productive motivational climate in classrooms.

The preceding scenarios also highlight the point that motivation is an important quality that pervades all student activities. Motivated students display interest in activities, work diligently, feel self-confident, stick with tasks, and perform well. When students perform poorly, teachers may say they were not motivated to learn but that they would do better if they tried harder. Given that motivation affects all aspects of schooling and contributes to students' school success, improving students' academic motivation is viewed as a worthwhile goal of schooling. Each year, many school workshops and in-service programs are devoted to motivational topics. Teachers often list motivating students as one of their chief concerns and seek new ways to accomplish it.

Despite its intuitive importance, there is much we do not know about motivation. Professionals disagree over what motivation is, what affects motivation, how motivational processes operate, what effects motivation has on learning and performance, and how motivation can be improved. Our knowledge is further limited because many earlier research studies used people engaged in artificial tasks (e.g., ringtoss games) or laboratory animals in boxes or mazes. Such research does not capture the complexity of the operation of motivation as students think, learn, and solve problems. Fortunately, much recent research is school based and involves students engaged in academic tasks.

Our goal in this introductory chapter is to cover some basic material that you will find helpful before beginning a systematic study of motivational principles and applications in Chapter 2. We begin, therefore, by defining motivation, after which we discuss the relation of motivation to learning and performance and examine the role of theory and types of motivation research. We follow with a section on methods of assessing motivation to include indexes of motivation and research strategies. In this and the preceding section, we discuss some actual research studies to illustrate differences in research methods and tools of assessment.

MOTIVATION DEFINED

The term *motivation* is derived from the Latin verb *movere* (to move). The idea of movement is reflected in such commonsense ideas about motivation as something that gets us going, keeps us moving, and helps us get jobs done. Conversely, we know we are not motivated when we cannot seem to get out of bed or off the sofa.

Despite these commonly held ideas, definitions of motivation are numerous and varied, and there is much disagreement over the precise nature of motivation. Beginning in the next chapter, we present theoretical perspectives on motivation, and the differences between these perspectives in the nature and operation of motivation will become apparent. For now, we will simply say that motivation has been conceived of in such varied terms as involving inner forces, enduring traits, behavioral responses to stimuli, and sets of beliefs and affects.

As we will see in Chapter 2, many early views linked motivation with inner forces: instincts, volition, and will. Freud (1966) believed human behavior resulted from forces within individuals and that motivation reflected psychical energy. With respect to enduring traits, Murray (1938) identified the achievement motive and conceived of it as a personal striving to perform difficult tasks as well as possible. The achievement motive presumably was a trait that varied between persons but for any given person was relatively consistent and affected behavior on several tasks. Many conditioning theories view motivation as an increased or continual level of behavioral responses to stimuli brought about by reinforcement (reward). Skinner (1968) believed that motivation did not arise from inner forces but rather was best viewed in strictly behavioral terms. Finally, contemporary cognitive views on motivation stress the influence on motivation of individuals' thoughts, beliefs, and emotions. Beginning in Chapter 3, we cover many of these cognitive views that highlight the motivational importance of expectancies, values, perceptions of competencies, goals, and affects.

Although there is disagreement about the precise nature of motivation, we offer a general definition of motivation that is consistent with the cognitive focus of this book on learners' thoughts and beliefs and that captures the elements considered by most researchers and practitioners to be central to motivation. *Motivation* is the process whereby goal-directed activity is instigated and sustained.

Let us examine this definition in some depth. Motivation is a *process* rather than a product. As a process, we do not observe motivation directly but rather we infer it from such behaviors as choice of tasks, effort, persistence, and verbalizations (e.g., "I really want to work on this"). Various theories contend that motivation underlies much human behavior (Weiner, 1985b).

Motivation involves *goals* that provide impetus for and direction to action. Cognitive views of motivation are united in their emphasis on the importance of goals. Goals may not be well formulated and may change with experience, but the point is that individuals have something in mind that they are trying to attain (or avoid).

Motivation requires *activity*—physical or mental. Physical activity entails effort, persistence, and other overt actions. Mental activity includes such cognitive actions as planning, rehearsing, organizing, monitoring, making decisions, solving problems, and assessing progress. The activities that students engage in are geared toward attaining their goals.

Finally, we highlight that motivated activity is both *instigated* and *sustained*. Starting toward a goal is important and often difficult because it involves making a commitment to change and taking the first step. But motivational processes are critically important to sustain action. Many major goals are long-term, for example, earning a college degree, obtaining a good job, and saving money for retirement. Much of what we know about motivational processes comes from studying how people respond to the difficulties, problems, failures, and setbacks they encounter as they pursue goals over time. Throughout this book we will discuss how such motivational processes as expectations, attributions, and affects help people surmount difficulties and sustain their motivation.

In this section, we have cited different conceptions of motivation. Although there is no straightforward, agreed-upon definition, we have presented one that incorporates elements found in cognitive perspectives. We now turn to a topic of critical importance to schooling, namely, the relation of motivation to learning and performance.

RELATION OF MOTIVATION TO LEARNING AND PERFORMANCE

Keith Mitchell's perceptions of his class members exemplify our intuitive understanding of the role of motivation in classroom learning and performance. Motivation can affect both new learning and the performance of previously learned skills, strategies, and behaviors, which has important implications for schooling. Such activities as drills and review sessions involve performance of previously learned skills, but most class time is spent learning facts, beliefs, rules, concepts, skills, strategies, algorithms, and behaviors.

As an example of the effect of motivation on performance, suppose that Keith tells his class to complete some review material and that the students, being less than enthusiastic about this assignment, work lackadaisically. To boost students' motivation, Keith announces that they will have free time as soon as they complete their worksheets. Assuming that the students value free time, we would expect an increase in their motivation and work completed.

Such performance effects often are dramatic, but the role of motivation during learning also is important for schooling. Motivation can influence what, when, and how we learn (Schunk, 1991b). Students motivated to learn about a topic being discussed by a teacher are apt to engage in activities they believe will help them learn. Thus, they are likely to attend carefully to the teacher's instruction and mentally organize and rehearse the material to commit it to memory. They also are apt to take good notes to facilitate subsequent studying, to check their level of understanding frequently, and to ask for help when they realize they do not understand the material (Zimmerman & Martinez-Pons, 1992). Collectively, these activities improve learning.

In contrast, students unmotivated to learn are not apt to be as systematic in their learning efforts. They may be inattentive during the lesson and not organize or rehearse material. Note taking may be done haphazardly or not at all. They may not monitor their level of understanding or ask for help when they do not understand what is being taught. It is little wonder that their learning suffers.

It is important to realize that motivation bears a reciprocal relation to learning and performance. Just as motivation influences these outcomes, what a person does and learns influences subsequent motivation (Schunk, 1991b). When students attain their learning goals, goal attainment conveys to them that they possess the requisite capabilities for learning. These beliefs motivate students to set new challenging goals. Teachers who motivate students to learn often find that subsequent learning helps to develop intrinsic motivation in students to learn for the sake of knowledge (Meece, 1991).

MOTIVATION THEORY AND RESEARCH

In this section, we examine the role of theory in the study of motivation and in motivation research. Throughout this text we will integrate theoretical principles and show how they relate to research and practice. We believe that a good theoretical understanding of motivation and knowledge of different types of research paradigms are necessary to appreciate the role of motivation in settings involving teaching and learning.

Theory and the Study of Motivation

Like most teachers, Keith has a theory about what motivates students. He believes that his students are motivated by learning something useful or important, by feelings of progress, by performing well, and, for some students, by performing better than others. Keith's theory reflects his intuitive understanding of his students and it helps to guide his actions. Thus, he tries to point out the value of learning, show students how they are making progress, and recognize excellence when it is deserved.

Such intuitive understanding is important and benefits us in many ways. In this section, however, we discuss theory from a scientific perspective and its role in systematic empirical work. We define a *theory* as a scientifically acceptable set of principles advanced to explain a phenomenon. A theory provides a framework for interpreting environmental observations and helps link research and education (Suppes, 1974). Without a theory, research findings would be disorganized and have no common referent.

Let us consider an example that highlights the role of theory. Much research shows that students' perceptions of their capabilities relate positively to motivation. Students who feel self-confident about learning and performing well in school seek challenges, expend effort to learn new material, and persist at difficult tasks (Schunk, 1991b). Although interesting, these findings are unrelated to other knowledge about motivation and do not inform teachers about ways to raise student motivation. If we link these findings to any of the several motivation theories that stress the role of perceived capabilities in motivation, then we see how such perceptions fit into a broad motivational framework and have a better idea about what affects perceptions and how they, in turn, influence motivation.

Theories reflect environmental phenomena and generate new research through the formation of *hypotheses*, or assumptions that can be empirically tested. Hypotheses state what conditions ought to accompany or follow other variables. We could, for example, test the following hypothesis in a research study: If students' perceived capabilities improve, then they will display greater academic motivation (choice of tasks, effort, persistence). When research data support hypotheses, the theories are strengthened. Hypotheses not supported by data may necessitate revision of the theories. Scientists strive to make sense out of research results and relate them to their prior theoretical beliefs (Pintrich, Marx, & Boyle, 1993).

How this process might work in teaching can be illustrated with an example from Keith's class. From his interactions with Eric and his parents, Keith has come to an intuitive (naive theoretical) understanding that Eric's desire to outperform everyone stems from a basic insecurity. Eric is the youngest child in a family in which the older brothers and sisters have performed very well in school. Keith believes that Eric does not want to appear any less competent than his siblings. Thus, his behavior of trying to do better than everyone else represents a means of performing as well as his brothers and sisters.

Based on this understanding, Keith formulates the hypothesis that if he can make Eric see himself as a worthwhile and competent person, then Eric will become less competitive. Keith employs methods in his class that he believes will convey this impression to Eric. Keith provides Eric with ample feedback showing how his work is exemplary and how he is improving his skills. He tries to assuage Eric's fears about not performing well by encouraging Eric to work diligently. Keith structures tasks and presents material that he believes Eric can master. Keith also makes frequent use of small groups of students whereby the students work cooperatively to accomplish a task. Keith hopes that by decreasing Eric's opportunities for competition, Eric may develop greater motivation for learning. Keith will evaluate his hypothesis by observing Eric's behavior, talking with him, and gauging the reactions of his classmates.

From a scientific perspective, a good example of research data that did not support a hypothesis and required revision of the underlying theory comes from Hull's (1943) systematic behavior theory. Hull postulated that amount of reward is a critical variable for learning. Behavior is strengthened when a large reward is given immediately after goal attainment. As reward size diminishes, the strength of behavior is lessened.

Although intuitively appealing, this idea was not supported by research. Studies by Tolman and Honzik (1930) on latent learning showed that rats learn to run mazes without being rewarded (Chapter 2). Other research demonstrated that shifts in performance (e.g., speed of maze running) occur *after* the behavior has been learned and depend on changes in reward size (Crespi, 1942). The latter finding could not be due to altered strength of behavior, because learning was hypothesized to increase slowly with repeated reward.

Eventually, Hull (1952) modified his theory to include an *incentive motivation* factor. Spence (1960) explored this factor in depth and concluded that reward does not affect strength of learning but rather performance of responses and that incentive motivation is a performance variable. Although many researchers today believe that motivation affects both learning and performance, this example illustrates how theories undergo revision as a result of hypothesis testing.

Sometimes we conduct research with little theory to guide us. When that happens we may formulate objectives or questions to be answered rather than hypotheses. Regardless of whether we are testing hypotheses, addressing objectives, or answering questions, we need to state the research conditions as precisely as possible. In examining research, it is important to understand the procedure that was followed, the measures used to assess motivation and other variables, and the characteristics of the subjects. Without this information, it is difficult to adequately evaluate the research.

Motivation Research Paradigms

In this section, we discuss the typical paradigms (models) that are employed in research studies to explore motivational processes. We describe, compare, and contrast the correlational, experimental, and qualitative paradigms and then discuss the attributes, advantages, and disadvantages of laboratory and field studies. Readers who are knowledgeable in the area of research methods may wish to skip this section. We present this material for the benefit of individuals with little research background and those who are new to the field of motivation.

Correlational and Experimental Research

Researchers employ different research paradigms to investigate motivational processes (Table 1.1). For example, there is a distinction between correlational and experimental studies. *Correlational* research deals with relations that exist between variables. A researcher may hypothesize that student motivation is positively correlated with (related to) perceived capabilities such that the more confidence students have in their learning abilities, the higher is their motivation. To test this relation, the researcher might measure students' perceived capabilities and their motivation as demonstrated on a task. The researcher could statistically correlate the perceived capability and motivation scores to determine the nature and strength of their relation.

Pintrich and De Groot (1990a) conducted a correlational study that explored the relations among motivational, cognitive, and academic performance variables. Seventh-grade students completed the Motivated Strategies for Learning Questionnaire (MSLQ). This self-report instrument measured students' motivational beliefs and learning strategies. The motivational beliefs component assessed three factors: self-efficacy (perceptions of capabilities), intrinsic value (importance), and test anxiety. The learning strategies component comprised two factors: cognitive strategy use and self-regulation.

Correlations among intrinsic value, self-efficacy, strategy use, and self-regulation were positive and significant. Test anxiety showed a significant, negative correlation with self-efficacy; correlations of test anxiety with all other variables were nonsignificant. The researchers also computed correlations among these five variables and measures of academic performance: in-class seatwork and homework, quizzes and tests, essays and reports, grades. Intrinsic value, self-efficacy, and self-regulation correlated positively with all academic performance measures; strategy use correlated positively with academic measures except for seatwork (nonsignificant); test anxiety was negatively correlated with grades and quiz/test scores. This study was correlational because Pintrich and De Groot looked at the existing relations among variables and did not attempt to alter them. The results show that motivational variables relate in important ways to cognitive factors contributing to classroom success (strategy use, self-regulation) and to measures of academic performance.

In an *experimental* study, the researcher actually alters one or more variables and determines the effects on other variables. A researcher interested in the effects of perceived capabilities could conduct an experimental study by systematically altering these perceptions and gauging the effect on student

Table 1.1. Research Paradigms

Type	Qualities
Correlational	Examines relations that exist between variables
Experimental	One or more variables are altered and their effects on other variables are assessed
Qualitative	Concerned with intensive description and interpretation of meanings
Laboratory	Project conducted in controlled setting
Field	Project conducted where participants typically go to school, learn, work, and so on

motivation. For example, the researcher might have a teacher systematically praise low-achieving students to raise their perceptions of capabilities and determine if this increase enhances motivation.

Schunk (1982) conducted an experimental study that investigated how forms of effort attributional feedback (see Chapter 4) influenced students' achievement outcomes during learning. Elementary school children who lacked subtraction skills received instruction and practice opportunities over sessions. While children solved problems individually, an adult proctor periodically walked up to each child and asked on what page in the instructional packet he or she was working. For some children (prior attribution), after they replied with the page number, the proctor linked their progress with effort by remarking, "You've been working hard." For others (future attribution), the proctor stressed the value of future effort by stating, "You need to work hard." Those in a third condition (monitoring) were queried but the proctor departed without comment after the child replied. Children in a fourth (control) condition were not monitored.

This study was an experiment because Schunk altered the type of feedback children received and looked to see whether differential effects on achievement outcomes resulted. Schunk hypothesized that prior attribution would be the most effective because it supports children's perceptions of their progress in acquiring skills and conveys that they can continue to improve through effort. This prediction was supported. Prior-attribution students outperformed children in the other conditions on measures of self-efficacy and subtraction skill. Prior-attribution students also displayed higher motivation than did future-attribution and control students as assessed by the amount of problem solving during the independent practice portions of the sessions. The results of this study suggest that it is better to link students' past successes to effort than to stress the future benefits of hard work.

Each type of research has advantages and disadvantages. Correlational research helps clarify relations among variables. Correlational findings often suggest directions for experimental research. The positive correlation obtained by Pintrich and De Groot (1990a) between intrinsic value and academic performance suggests further research exploring whether increasing intrinsic value leads to higher achievement. A disadvantage of correlational research is that it cannot identify cause and effect. The positive correlation between intrinsic value and academic performance could mean that (a) intrinsic value affects academic performance, (b) academic performance influences intrinsic value, (c) intrinsic value and academic performance affect each other, or (d) intrinsic value and academic performance are each influenced by other, unmeasured variables (e.g., home factors).

Experimental research can clarify cause-effect relations. By systematically varying type of feedback and eliminating other variables as potential causes, Schunk (1982) could specify how changes in attributional feedback affect achievement outcomes. Clarifying causal relations helps us understand the nature of motivation. At the same time, experimental research is often narrow in scope. Researchers typically vary only a few variables and try to hold all others constant, which is difficult to do and somewhat unrealistic. Schunk altered only one variable—attributional feedback. Classrooms are complex places where many factors operate simultaneously. To say that one or two variables cause outcomes is probably overstating their importance. It usually is necessary to replicate experiments and examine other variables to better understand effects.

Qualitative/Interpretative Research

In recent years another type of paradigm has gained currency among researchers. The theories and methods used are referred to by various labels, including qualitative, ethnographic, participant observation, phenomenological, constructivist, and interpretive (Erickson, 1986). These approaches differ from one another but are generally characterized by intensive study, descriptions of events, and interpretation of meanings. Such a research model is not new in the social sciences, but only recently has it been applied increasingly in education.

Interpretive research is especially useful when researchers are interested in the structure of events rather than their overall distributions, when the meanings and perspectives of individuals are important, when actual experiments are impractical or unethical, and when there is a desire to search for new potential causal linkages that have not been unearthed by experimental methods (Erickson, 1986). Such research is well designed to answer the following types of questions:

1. What is happening, specifically, in social action that takes place in this particular setting?
2. What do these actions mean to the actors involved in them, at the moment the actions took place?
3. How are the happenings organized in patterns of social organization and learned cultural principles for the conduct of everyday life—how, in other words, are people in the immediate setting consistently present to each other as environments for one another's meaningful actions?
4. How is what is happening in this setting as a whole (i.e., the classroom) related to happenings at other system levels outside and inside the setting (e.g., the school building, a child's family, the school system, federal government mandates regarding mainstreaming)?
5. How do the ways everyday life in this setting is organized compare with other ways of organizing social life in a wide range of settings in other places and at other times? (Erickson, 1986, p. 121)

Research within this tradition is quite varied and can range from microanalyses of verbal and nonverbal interactions within single lessons to in-depth observations and interviews over much longer periods. Methods may include classroom observations, use of existing records, interviews, and think-aloud protocols (i.e., participants talk aloud while performing tasks). It should be noted that it is not the particular methods used that characterize this tradition; all of the preceding procedures are frequently employed in correlational and experimental studies. Rather, the hallmark is the depth and quality of analysis and interpretation of data.

An example of a study using ethnographic methods is that done by Meece (1991), who examined classroom characteristics that help to explain teacher differences in students' goal patterns. During a school year, science lessons were observed repeatedly in elementary and middle-school classes; each class was observed for an average of 600 minutes. Observers collected detailed observational records, including field notes and audiotapes. They transcribed the lessons and analyzed such activities as instructional presentations, teacher and student questioning patterns, forms of feedback, grouping practices, evaluation methods, and motivational strategies. The results are lengthy and will not be summarized here. Meece obtained evidence of important differences among teachers in the preceding activities, which, in turn, related to differences in students' goals.

Qualitative/interpretive research yields rich sources of data that are much more intensive and thorough than those typically obtained in correlational or experimental research. This research paradigm also has the potential of raising new questions and new slants on old questions that often are missed by traditional methods. Because this approach is not concerned with the aggregation of usable knowledge for teaching practice, it is not a means for providing practical answers to teaching problems (Shulman, 1986). Studies usually are conducted with few participants, which raises the issue of whether findings are reliable and representative of the population being studied (e.g., teachers, students). Another concern is that if researchers do not attempt to interpret data in light of a theoretical framework, findings may not seem linked and interpretation may prove difficult. Nonetheless, as a research model, this tradition has provided much valuable data in the study of motivation, and its influence will continue to grow.

Laboratory and Field Research

In addition to the differences among experimental, correlational, and qualitative research, another distinction exists between *laboratory* studies conducted in controlled settings and *field* studies conducted where the participants go to school, live, and work. Much early motivation research was conducted in laboratories using such infrahuman species as cats, dogs, and rats. Such research was appropriate given the influence of conditioning theories (see Chapter 2), which contended that common processes occurred in animals and humans and that controlled experiments could help isolate these processes and eliminate extraneous influences. Motivation research also has employed human subjects in controlled laboratory environments. With the increasing emphasis on schooling and other applied settings, however, most current research is conducted in field settings.

The Meece (1991), Pintrich and De Groot (1990a), and Schunk (1982) studies are examples of field studies because they were conducted in students' schools. In contrast, a study by Jagacinski and Nicholls (1990) is a laboratory study. The subjects were college students who participated in the study to satisfy a requirement for an introductory psychology course. The study was not carried out in students' actual classes; rather, subjects reported in small groups to the room where the study was conducted. They were given written scenarios in which they were asked to imagine that they were taking an intelligence test in a class and at a certain point got stuck. Their task was to evaluate possible responses to the question, "What will you do to avoid appearing to lack intelligence?"

An advantage of the experimental laboratory is that it offers a high degree of control over extraneous factors: telephones, people talking, windows to look out, and other persons in the room (unless the experiment involves group behavior). The light, temperature, and sound can be controlled. The laboratory also allows researchers to have their materials and equipment at their immediate disposal.

Such control is not possible in the field. Schools are noisy and it often is difficult to find space to work. There also are continual distractions. Students and teachers walk by, bells ring, announcements are made over the public address system, fire drills are held. Rooms may be too bright or too dark, too hot or too cold. Because rooms may be used for other purposes, researchers must bring and set up their materials and equipment each time they work. These extraneous influences can affect an experiment's results.

An advantage of field research is that results can be generalizable to similar settings because studies are conducted where students are. Generalization of laboratory findings to the field, however, is typically done with less confidence. Laboratory research has yielded many important findings on motivational processes, and researchers often attempt to replicate laboratory findings in the field.

Whether we choose the laboratory or the field depends on such factors as the purpose of the research, availability of subjects, costs, and the use we will make of the results. If we choose the laboratory, we gain control but lose generalizability, and vice versa for the field. With the latter we need to minimize extraneous influences so that we can be more confident that our results are due to the experimental factors we are studying.

ASSESSING MOTIVATION

The topic of assessing motivation is important for researchers and practitioners who are concerned with understanding the operation of motivational processes and with ways to optimize student motivation. We begin by discussing some commonly employed indexes of motivation: choice of tasks, effort, persistence, and achievement. We then discuss the measurement of motivation by direct observations, ratings by others, and self-reports. As with the preceding section, readers with research backgrounds and those familiar with motivation research may wish to omit this material.

Indexes of Motivation

We noted earlier that there is disagreement about the nature of motivation and the operation of motivational processes. At the same time, most professionals agree that we infer the presence of motivation from the behavioral indicators shown in Table 1.2. One indicator is *choice of tasks*, or interests. When students have a choice, what they choose to do indicates what they are motivated to work on. This is an important indicator for Keith. What students do (or say that they do) in and out of school when they have free time and can choose among activities indicates where their interests lie.

A good example of a research study that employed choice of tasks as a motivational index is Lepper, Greene, and Nisbett (1973). Preschoolers were observed during free play. Those who spent much time drawing were assigned to one of three conditions. In the expected-award group, children were offered a good player certificate if they drew a picture. Unexpected-award subjects were not offered the certificate, but unexpectedly received it after they drew a picture. No-award subjects were not offered the award and did not receive it. Two weeks later, children were again observed during free play when they could choose tasks to work on. Expected-award subjects chose drawing for a significantly shorter time following the study than they had prior to it, whereas the other two groups showed no significant change. That is, expected-award children chose to spend less time drawing following the study compared with the other children. The expected-award condition decreased children's motivation as assessed by their choosing to draw during free time.

Despite the intuitive appeal of choice of tasks, choice often is not a useful index of motivation in school because in many classrooms, students typically

Table 1.2. Indexes of Motivation

Index	Relation to Motivation
Choice of tasks	Selection of a task under free-choice conditions indicates motivation to perform the task
Effort	High effort—especially on difficult material—is indicative of motivation
Persistence	Working for a longer time—especially when one encounters obstacles—is associated with higher motivation
Achievement	Choice, effort, and persistence raise task achievement

have few if any choices (Brophy, 1983). A second index is *effort*. Learning often is not easy. Students motivated to learn are apt to expend effort to succeed. For motor tasks, effort is physical. When skill learning is involved, cognitive effort is an appropriate index of motivation (Corno & Mandinach, 1983). Students motivated to learn are likely to expend greater mental effort during instruction, employing cognitive strategies they believe will promote learning: organizing and rehearsing information, monitoring level of understanding, and relating new material to prior knowledge (Peterson, Swing, Braverman, & Buss, 1982; Pintrich & De Groot, 1990a). It should be noted that the usefulness of effort as an index of motivation is constrained by ability in that as ability increases, one can perform better with less effort. Many students expend high effort to learn in Keith's class—Kris, Sharon, Eric, Deanna, José— although their goals differ considerably.

Salomon (1984) assessed students' mental effort and found that it related to self-efficacy. Children judged self-efficacy for learning from television or from written text, watched a televised film or read the comparable text, judged amount of mental effort necessary to learn, and were tested on the content. Students judged mental effort greater for text and demonstrated higher achievement scores from text. For text, self-efficacy correlated positively with mental effort and achievement; for TV, it correlated negatively. Students who observed TV felt more efficacious about learning but expended less effort and achieved at a lower level. Schunk (1983a) assessed children's perceptions of how hard they worked during mathematics learning using a 10-unit scale ranging from *not hard* to *really hard*. Schunk found that providing children with feedback linking their performance to effort expenditure raised their perceptions.

A third index is *persistence*, or time spent on a task. Students who are motivated to learn ought to persist at the task, especially when they encounter obstacles. Persistence is important because much learning takes time and success may not be readily forthcoming. Persistence relates directly to the sustaining component in the definition of motivation given earlier, and greater persistence leads to higher accomplishments. In Keith's class, many students persist at tasks but José's persistence is very high.

Persistence is commonly used by researchers as a measure of motivation. Zimmerman and Ringle (1981) had children observe a model unsuccessfully attempt to solve a puzzle for either a long or short time while verbalizing statements of confidence or pessimism, after which children attempted to solve the puzzle themselves. Children who observed the high-persistent model worked longer on the task than children exposed to the low-persistent model, and children who observed the confident model persisted longer than those who observed the pessimistic model. Brown and Inouye (1978) had college students solve anagrams, after which they were told that they performed better than or the same as a model. They then observed a model fail, judged self-efficacy, and attempted the anagrams again. Telling students they were more competent than the model led to higher self-efficacy and persistence than telling them they were equal in competence.

Finally, student *achievement* may be viewed as an indirect index of motivation. Students who choose to engage in a task, expend effort, and persist are likely to achieve at a higher level (Pintrich & Schrauben, 1992; Schunk, 1991b). Many research studies obtain positive relations between achievement and motivational indexes of choice, effort, and persistence. Schunk (1983a) found that the more arithmetic problems children completed during training (which reflected effort and persistence), the more problems they solved correctly on the posttest (a measure of achievement). Most teachers, Keith included, are convinced that such effects occur in their classes.

Methods of Assessment

Motivation can be assessed in various ways, for example, by direct observations, ratings by others, and self-reports (Table 1.3). Each of these is discussed in turn.

Direct Observations

Direct observations refer to behavioral instances of choice of tasks, effort expended, and persistence. To the extent that these behaviors are straightforward and involve little inference on the part of observers, they are valid indicators of motivation. At the same time, by focusing only on overt actions, direct observations may be superficial and not fully capture the essence of motivation. Earlier, we said that motivation was inferential: We infer its presence from behaviors. Direct observations ignore the cognitive and affective processes underlying motivated behaviors. For example, Sharon, Eric, and Deanna all show relatively high levels of effort, but their reasons for trying hard differ greatly. These reasons represent important cognitive and affective processes that motivation researchers try to understand in their research.

Table 1.3.   Methods for Assessing Motivation

Category	Definition
Direct observations	Behavioral instances of choice of tasks, effort, persistence
Ratings by others	Judgments by observers of students on characteristics indicative of motivation
Self-reports	People's judgments of themselves
Questionnaires	Written ratings of items or answers to questions
Interviews	Oral responses to questions
Stimulated recalls	Recall of thoughts accompanying one's performances at various times
Think-alouds	Verbalizing aloud one's thoughts, actions, and emotions while performing a task
Dialogues	Conversations between two or more persons

Despite the latter concern, direct observations are commonly used to gauge motivation. Most of what Keith knows about the motivation of his students he has learned by observing their behaviors. When Keith says students are motivated to learn, he bases this on his observations of their persistence at tasks, the effort they expend to perform well, and how willingly they engage in tasks.

Bandura and Schunk (1981) used direct observation to assess students' intrinsic motivation in arithmetic. Students received subtraction instruction and practice over seven sessions using seven sets of material. Some children pursued a short-term goal of completing one set each session; a second group received a distant goal of completing all sets by the end of the last session; a third group was given a general goal of working productively. To assess intrinsic motivation, the researchers gave children subtraction problems of varying levels of difficulty and digit-symbol problems adapted from the Wechsler Intelligence Scale for Children (Wechsler, 1974). Children were told they could work on one or both tasks, and worked alone for 25 minutes. Observers recorded which tasks they chose, whether they changed activities, and how much work they completed. In the Lepper et al. (1973) study discussed earlier, observers recorded the length of time students engaged in the target activity as the measure of motivation.

Ratings by Others

Another way to assess motivation is to have observers (e.g., teachers, parents, researchers) rate students on various characteristics indicative of motivation (e.g., Would Tiffany rather read a book or work at the computer?, How much effort does Larry expend to solve difficult problems?). An example of a rating instrument is found in a study by Skinner, Wellborn, and Connell (1990) that focused on students' perceptions of control and engagement in academic tasks. Students' perceived control was assessed with a 50-item self-report instrument (discussed in the next section) comprising three dimensions (strategy beliefs, capacity beliefs, control beliefs); students judged each item on a 4-point scale ranging from *not at all true* to *very true*. Student engagement in activities was measured with a 10-item scale in which teachers rated children on class participation (e.g., When in class, this student participates in class discussions.) and emotional tone (e.g., When in class, this student seems happy.). The results showed that teacher reports of engagement correlated with all aspects of perceived control.

One advantage of ratings by others is that observers may be more objective about students than students are about themselves (i.e., self-reports). Ratings by others also often attempt to capture motivational processes that underlie behaviors, and thereby provide data not attainable through direct observations. At the same time, ratings by others require more inference than do direct observations. It may be difficult to judge students' levels of cognitive engagement, interest in learning, and so forth. Ratings by others also rely on observers remembering what students do. To the extent that memory is selective and constructive, ratings may not be valid indicators of student characteristics. Nonetheless, ratings by others are commonly used in motivation research and add a dimension beyond that attainable through direct observations.

Self-reports

Self-reports capture people's judgments and statements about themselves. Questionnaires, interviews, stimulated recalls, think-alouds, and dialogues—roughly ordered from least to most natural—are types of self-report instruments.

Questionnaires present respondents with items or questions asking about their actions and beliefs. Respondents may record what types of activities they engage in and how often or how long they engage in them (e.g., "What do you like to do in your free time?", "How many minutes did you study last night?"), make ratings on numerical scales corresponding to their feelings and beliefs ("On a 5-point scale ranging from 1 (low) to 5, mark how certain you are that you can learn how to add fractions with unlike denominators."), or answer open-ended questions ("How do you usually feel when you are in school?"). The Skinner et al. (1990) perceived control instrument is an example of a self-report questionnaire, as is Pintrich and De Groot's (1990a) MSLQ. For the latter, students rate each item on a 7-point scale ranging from *not at all true of me* (1) to *very true of me* (7).

A special type of questionnaire (or interview) is the *projective* measure, which involves presenting individuals with ambiguous pictures and having them respond to questions. Projective assessments are based on the assumption that people bring to situations personality characteristics and underlying motives and fantasies. Presenting them with ambiguous material may lessen their objective tendencies and allow them to subconsciously project their motives and fantasies onto the situation. Responses are recorded and scored to determine the type and strength of the underlying motives. The Rorschach test is a well-known projective measure whereby participants tell what is suggested to them by a series of inkblot designs.

The best known projective measure of achievement motivation is the Thematic Apperception Test (TAT). The TAT was developed by Murray (1938) to study personality processes. It subsequently was adapted by McClelland and his colleagues to assess the achievement motive (McClelland, Atkinson, Clark, & Lowell, 1953). Subjects are shown a series of pictures of individuals in unclear situations. They respond to four questions: "What is happening?", "What led up to this situation?", "What is wanted?", and, "What will happen?" They are given four minutes of writing time for each story. Responses are scored according to various criteria. Scores from individual stories are summed to give a total score for strength of achievement motive. The TAT has been employed in many research studies and it often bears a positive relation to achievement outcomes (Spangler, 1992). At the same time, it has been found to suffer from problems of low reliability and its correlations with other achievement measures are not always strong (Weiner, 1985b). Despite these problems, it is likely that the TAT will continue to play an important role in the assessment of achievement motivation.

An *interview* is a type of questionnaire in which the questions or points to discuss are presented by an interviewer and the respondent answers orally. Zimmerman and Martinez-Pons (1990) developed a self-regulated learning interview to assess self-regulated learning strategies (e.g., self-evaluating, organizing and transforming information, goal-setting and planning, seeking information, keeping records). The interview is conducted with students individually. During the interview, different learning contexts are described (e.g., "When taking a test in school, do you have a particular method for obtaining as many correct answers as possible?", "What if it is a difficult test question?"). For each context, students specify the methods they would employ. They are probed if they give no answer to a question. In the study, the experimenters scored students' answers, assigned answers to categories, and tallied responses within categories. The results showed that use of self-regulatory strategies was positively and significantly correlated with students' perceptions of mathematical and verbal self-efficacy.

Stimulated recalls refer to situations in which individuals work on a task and their performances are videotaped. Subsequently they watch their tapes and attempt to recall their thoughts at various points. Investigators typically stop the tapes at different times and ask questions designed to help respondents recall their thoughts. By linking thoughts to specific behaviors, stimulated recalls avoid the problem of forcing people to make judgments about their typical behaviors. At the same time, stimulated recalls rely upon respondents' memories. If the recall procedure is delayed for too long after the videotaping, people may have difficulty recalling what they were thinking about at the time they performed the activities.

A stimulated recall procedure was used by Peterson, Swing, Braverman, and Buss (1982) with fifth- and sixth-grade students during instruction. Students were videotaped during the lesson. Afterward, they were shown segments of the tape that portrayed critical incidents. Students were interviewed individually and asked such questions as "Try to remember what you were thinking about. What were you thinking about?", "Were you paying attention?", and "Were you understanding the part of the math lesson that you just saw?" Interviews were coded and scored for the presence of various cognitive processes. Students reported a high degree of effort to understand the teacher and the problems. Students who reported that they understood the material also performed well on the seatwork problems and the achievement test.

Think-alouds refer to procedures in which students verbalize aloud their thoughts, actions, and emotions while working on a task (see Ericsson & Simon, 1993). Verbalizations may be recorded by observers and scored for the presence of statements relevant to motivation. For think-alouds to be successful, subjects must verbalize, but students in school are not accustomed to verbalizing aloud while working. It may seem awkward to some students and they may feel self-conscious or otherwise have difficulty verbalizing their thoughts. Investigators must prompt students if they do not verbalize.

Diener and Dweck (1978) explored motivational processes during failure. Children were identified as mastery oriented or as learned helpless based on their attributions of failure to lack of effort or to factors beyond their control. (In Keith's class, Sharon seems mastery oriented whereas Peggy may be learned helpless.) They were presented with stimulus cards containing two figures that varied in color, form, and symbol in the center. Children had to form a hypothesis about the correct solution and choose one of the two figures for each card. They received feedback indicating their choices were wrong regardless of their answers.

Children were asked to think out loud while working. To dispel inhibitions about verbalizing, the experimenters pointed out to the children that they might think aloud about many types of things besides the task, including what they will do after school and what they will have for lunch. The experimenters were interested in how children's cognitive strategies changed as a result of continual failure feedback. Verbalizations were recorded and categorized. Helpless children showed a progressive decline in the use of good problem-solving strategies and an increase in ineffective strategies. Mastery-oriented children did not show such a decline and some actually became more sophisticated in strategy use.

Dialogues are conversations between two or more persons that are recorded and examined. A researcher may go into a classroom and record the conversation as students work on a task or as teacher and students discuss an issue. The conversation subsequently is analyzed for the presence of motivational statements. Such a procedure is commonly employed in interpretative research, as discussed earlier. Dialogues have the advantage of using actual interactions; however, they require interpretation and may be subject to problems in that regard.

Thorkildsen and Nicholls (1991) collected dialogues in a second-grade class. The following excerpt from their work shows that the youngsters were discussing motivational concerns:

> "You want a challenge," argues Jacob. . . . "You could challenge yourself to get more than someone else."
>
> "But maybe a person is trying all they can and can't get up higher," counters Joan.
>
> "Everyone learns things," answers Jacob.
>
> "But," Joan insists, "they might have done best as they can and can't get up more. . . . "
>
> "You can just keep on trying," counters Jacob. "If they just say they can't do it and quit, in a few years they'll say I don't have any money and they'll sit around saying, 'What'll I do?'"
>
> "They can just do their best," suggests Alan.
>
> "Their best is all they can do," adds Matt.
>
> Alan wants to claim more. "If you believe you can do a thing, you can." (pp. 361–362)

Thorkildsen and Nicholls relate this and the remaining dialogue to the topic under discussion and provide interpretation of children's thinking and its relation to issues of schooling.

There is no one best type of self-report measurement. The choice of instrument must match the purpose for the assessment and the research problem. Questionnaires are useful for covering a lot of material in a fairly efficient manner. Interviews are better if researchers or practitioners are interested in exploring feelings and beliefs in depth. Projective methods may allow individuals to subconsciously project their motives and fantasies onto the testing situation. Stimulated recalls ask respondents to recall their thoughts when the actions took place, whereas think-alouds examine present thoughts. Dialogues offer unique opportunities to investigate interaction patterns.

Self-report instruments typically are easy to administer, complete, and score. A problem may arise when inferences have to be drawn about students' responses. Under these conditions it is essential that the scoring system is reliable. Other concerns about self-reports are whether students are giving socially acceptable answers that do not match their beliefs, whether self-reported information corresponds to actual behavior, and whether young children are capable of self-reporting accurately. Guaranteeing confidentiality of data can help promote respondents answering truthfully. A good means of validating self-reports is to use multiple forms of assessment (e.g., self-reports, direct observations). There is evidence that beginning around the third grade, self-reports are valid and reliable indicators of the beliefs and actions they are designed to assess (Assor & Connell, 1992), but researchers need to use self-reports judiciously and design studies to minimize potential problems.

SUMMARY

Motivation refers to the process whereby goal-directed activity is instigated and sustained. Motivation is an important quality that affects all classroom activities because it can influence both learning of new behaviors and performance of previously learned behaviors. Learning and performance are related in a reciprocal fashion to motivation because what one does and learns influences one's subsequent task motivation.

Although individuals use intuitive ideas to understand motivation in themselves and others, the scientific study of motivation requires guiding theoretical principles. Motivation research proceeds by testing hypotheses, addressing objectives, or answering questions. Researchers conduct correlational studies that deal with relations existing between variables, experimental studies in which some variables are altered and their effects on other variables are determined, and qualitative studies characterized by intensive description of events and interpretation of meanings. Research studies may be conducted in experimental laboratories or in field sites (e.g., classrooms). Each type of research paradigm has advantages and disadvantages. The choice of instrument depends on the purpose of the study.

There are various indexes of motivation: choice of tasks, effort, persistence, and achievement. Motivation can be assessed through direct observations, ratings by others, and self-reports. Direct observations refer to instances of behavior. Ratings by others refer to judgments by observers of students on various characteristics indicative of motivation. Self-reports, which refer to people's judgments and statements about themselves, include questionnaires, interviews, stimulated recalls, think-alouds, and dialogues. Each method has advantages and disadvantages; the method of choice must reflect researchers' aims. The use of multiple forms of assessment is likely to provide richer data than a single measure of motivation.

In the next chapter, we turn to an examination of motivation from a historical perspective, trace some of the important themes that can be found in historical views of motivation, and show how theories reflect these themes. Much historical research was conducted in experimental laboratories using subhuman species as subjects. Many of these theoretical ideas were not applied to educational contexts, and one could question whether such applications would be appropriate. Nonetheless, knowledge of the historical background of motivation helps one understand common themes and provides a clearer perspective on current thinking.

Historical and Metatheoretical Perspectives on Motivation

*T*hree teachers were sitting in a classroom after school and talking about their students. The conversation shifted to a discussion of why students act as they do.

"It seems to me," said Jim Osgood, "that students act the way the do because of how we treat them and what we expose them to. People react to their surroundings. If we treat people well, they will treat us well in return. If we don't treat them well, we can't expect much nice from them."

"I agree with you, Jim," said Sara Wylie. "I think sometimes we create problems for ourselves. Look at competition. No wonder kids are so competitive. They're exposed to competition at home, on the playground, in school. We just make them more competitive by emphasizing grades and doing well so they can make the honor roll and get into college. That's why I think we need to stress cooperation more in school. Having kids work together should help make them more cooperative and less competitive."

A. K. Buerso was shaking her head. "You two think students are puppets. We pull the strings and they react. Since when does that happen so automatically? Aren't you forgetting about something? These kids are their own personalities. They're so different and I'm not sure we have much to do with it. I think their personalities are so heavily determined from birth. They come into the world and they're going to act certain ways. Look at so many things babies and preschoolers do. They couldn't learn them. They must be genetically determined."

"Oh sure, A. K.," said Jim. "I suppose you're going to tell me that most of what my 15-year-olds do was present at birth. Was Dora shy at birth? Mikey aggressive? Lele outgoing? How do you explain that?"

"No, not everything is present at birth," A. K. continued. "Traits come out over time, unfold so to speak. But I think many of the predispositions are present at birth. Students change, sure, but it represents more of an unfolding or maturing. My point is that I don't think we have much influence on how students behave."

"Well, there is another way to look at it," responded Sara. "How students act isn't due just to what they bring with them into the world or to how we treat them but rather a combination of the two. The characteristics that are there interact with the setting and behavior results. Put an aggressive child in an environment that does not reward aggression and the child will act less aggressively. Put the same child in an environment where aggression is encouraged and aggression will become worse. I think as teachers we can affect our students' behaviors but we always must contend with some pretty strong tendencies or dispositions that they bring with them. We succeed when what we do complements those dispositions. We have problems when what we do goes against their grain."

This discussion on the causes of behavior highlights some different views of motivation. Jim espouses the behavioral and environmental view, A. K.

stresses the role of inner causes, and Sara provides a compromise by stating that both are important.

In this chapter, we examine several important historical perspectives on motivation and we compare and contrast their explanations for motivational processes. We attempt to present a brief historical walk through the field of motivation, beginning with the early part of the twentieth century and continuing to the emergence of cognitive perspectives around 1965. We conclude the chapter by discussing *metatheoretical models*, which are models, or paradigms, of research that offer a means of organizing theories and understanding their basic assumptions.

We make no attempt to discuss theories in great depth or review all relevant historical work because such detail is beyond the scope of this book. Additional discussions of historical work appear in other chapters in this book, and interested readers can find comprehensive reviews in other sources (Heckhausen, 1991; Heidbreder, 1933; Mook, 1987; Petri, 1986; Weiner, 1985b, 1992).

Before we turn to our historical presentation, we will discuss differences between behavioral and cognitive theories of motivation. Understanding some general assumptions about theories helps to provide a better grasp of the concepts underlying human motivation and of how theoretical principles are derived.

A basic issue in the study of motivation concerns the process whereby motivation occurs. *Behavioral theories* view motivation as a change in the rate, frequency of occurrence, or form of behavior (responses) as a function of environmental events and stimuli. A response to a stimulus becomes more likely to occur as a function of how often it is paired with the stimulus or of what happens following it. Reinforcing consequences make behavior more likely to occur in the future, whereas punishing consequences make the behavior less likely to occur (Skinner, 1953). From a behavioristic standpoint, motivation is nothing more than a high rate or likelihood of behavior. Students who are motivated to learn are highly likely to engage in tasks, persist at tasks, and expend effort, all of which are behaviors.

The rise of behaviorism in psychology occurred against the backdrop of introspection (discussed later in this chapter). Behaviorism's most strident early supporter was John B. Watson (1924), who contended that if psychology was to become an objective and experimental science, it had to concern itself with observable and scientific phenomena as the physical sciences did. To psychologists, behavior was observable, whereas introspection, which dealt with subjective states that may have no basis in reality, was not observable and therefore not scientific. Watson (1914) argued that if consciousness could only be studied through introspection, then it should not be studied at all because introspection is too unreliable.

Many historical views of motivation are behavioral because they explain motivation in terms of observable phenomena. Behavioral theorists contend that explanations for motivation do not need to include thoughts and feelings but that the explanation for what motivates people lies in the environment. In the preceding scenario, Jim Osgood seems to be espousing a behavioral view.

In contrast, *cognitive theories* stress mental structures and the processing of information and beliefs. Motivation is an internal process; we do not observe it directly but rather its behavioral products. Although cognitive theorists are united in their belief of the importance of mental processes in motivation, they disagree about which specific processes are important. Some of the processes stressed by cognitive theories of motivation are attributions, perceptions of competence, values, affects, goals, and social comparisons. A. K. Buerso's comments place greater emphasis on internal processes, although she takes a more dispositional view of these processes in contrast to the more situational view of current cognitive models.

These conceptualizations of motivation have important educational implications. Behavioral theories imply that teachers should arrange the environment so that students can respond properly to stimuli. Cognitive theories emphasize learners' thoughts, beliefs, and emotions. Teachers need to consider how such mental processes may manifest themselves in the classroom and think about how instructional and social variables affect not only what students do but also their thoughts.

EARLY VIEWS OF MOTIVATION

We begin now with a largely chronological look at important historical perspectives on motivation. At the beginning of the twentieth century, motivation was not a separate topic of study as it is today but rather was ill-defined and fell under the purview of the newly emerging discipline of psychology. Views of motivation, and psychology in general, were rooted heavily in philosophy. Two prominent conceptualizations of motivation were in terms of (a) volition/will, and (b) instincts.

Volition/Will

Many early psychologists drew on the views of such philosophers as Plato and Aristotle and conceived of the mind as comprising knowing (cognition), feeling (emotion), and willing (motivation). The *will* reflected an individual's desire, want, or purpose; *volition* was the act of using the will.

Wilhelm Wundt, who studied volition and helped establish psychology as a science with the first psychological laboratory in Germany in 1879, introduced the method of *introspection*, which required subjects to verbally report their immediate experiences following exposure to objects or events. If they were shown a picture of a tree, they might report their perceptions of shape, size, color, and texture. They were to avoid labeling the stimulus ("tree") and reporting their knowledge of it and the meanings of their perceptions because labels and meanings mask the organization of consciousness. Introspection helped demarcate psychology from other sciences but often was problematic and unreliable. When viewing a tree, people naturally think of its verbal label and their knowledge about the tree. Forcing people to ignore these attributes is unnatural and does not allow studying such higher mental processes as thinking and problem solving.

Philosophers and psychologists disagreed over whether volition is an independent process or rather a by-product of other mental processes (sensations, perceptions). Wundt felt that volition is a central, independent factor in human behavior. It presumably accompanies such processes as sensation, perception, attention, and formation of mental associations, and helps translate our thoughts and feelings into action.

Wundt's ideas about volition were quite general and difficult to validate. William James, another psychology pioneer, studied volitional acts in depth (James, 1890, 1892). James believed that consciousness helps organisms adapt to their environments. Will is a state of mind in which we desire a particular action and believe that its manifestation is within our power. Volition is the process of translating intentions into actions. At times, a mental representation of the act is sufficient to motivate action, but at other times, an additional conscious element "in the shape of a fiat, mandate, or express consent, has to intervene and precede the movement" (James, 1890, p. 522).

James (1890) cites an incident of getting out of bed on a cold morning as an example of how the role of volition is minimized because a mental representation of an act can motivate action:

> Now how do we *ever* get up under such circumstances? . . . We more often than not get up without any struggle or decision at all. We suddenly find that we *have* got up. A fortunate lapse of consciousness occurs; we forget both the warmth and the cold; we fall into some revery connected with the day's life, in the course of which the idea flashes across us, 'Hollo! I must lie here no longer'—an idea which at that lucky instant awakens no contradictory or paralyzing suggestions, and consequently produces immediately its appropriate motor effects. (p. 524)

It may seem that at times action occurs automatically, but volition plays a role because it helps execute the intended action by activating a mental representation. Volition has its greatest effect when various intentions compete for action. This is the reason why so many ideas we have do not result in action. We need the type of volitional "fiat, mandate, or express consent" to translate intentions into actions and will ourselves into action.

Ach (1910) pioneered the experimental study of volition. Like many of his contemporaries, Ach conceived of volition as the process of dealing with the implementation of actions designed to attain goals—a narrow view of motivation because it does not address the process whereby people formulate goals and commit themselves to attaining them (Heckhausen, 1991). Ach referred to processes that allowed goals to be translated into action as *determining tenden-*

cies. In a series of studies that employed introspection, Ach found that determining tendencies compete with association (previously learned) tendencies to produce action even when the action conflicts with prior associations. Thus, instructions to perform a task (attain a goal) in response to a cue that conflicts with the type of task performed previously can trigger determining tendencies that allow accomplishment of the goal. Action is determined by the tendencies to attain the goal.

Ach identified four phenomenological aspects that represent reactions to obstacles encountered while attempting to attain goals: (a) *subjective aspect* (physical sensations of bodily tension); (b) *objective aspect* (ideas the individual has about performing the intended action, the goal associated with the prompting stimuli, and the appropriate time to implement the intended action); (c) *ego-related aspect* (intensifying intentions while excluding other possible actions); and (d) *state-related aspect* (the individual's awareness of the effort required to attain the goal). Ach believed that willpower and effort increase when there are more obstacles to be overcome. The more these aspects of willing are experienced, the stronger is the determining tendency.

The psychologies of Wundt, James, and Ach were concerned with motivation in the sense of volition, or a willing to action. Many of the ideas of these theories were vague and difficult to test empirically. The use of introspection often was problematic. Volition offered an incomplete perspective on motivation because volition was limited to implementing actions designed to attain goals. How people formulated goals was ignored or downplayed. Nonetheless, we will see in Chapter 5 that, in modified form, volition has recently experienced a renaissance and some historical ideas are reflected in current thinking.

Instincts

Another early perspective on motivation stressed the role of *instincts*, or innate propensities that manifest themselves in behavior. James (1890) believed that instincts could not explain all behavior but could provide a base upon which experience builds by developing habits. He thought that instinctive behavior overlaps both reflexes and learning. Sample instincts are imitation, emulation, anger, resentment, and sympathy.

McDougall (1926) hypothesized that all behavior is instinctive. Instincts are not simply dispositions to act in particular ways, but rather comprise cognitive, affective, and conative components. The *cognitive* component refers to awareness of ways to satisfy the instinct, the *affective* component denotes the emotions aroused by the instinct, and the *conative* component is the striving to attain the object (goal) of the instinct. Thus, students with the curiosity instinct will have some understanding of how to satisfy their curiosity, will feel emotionally aroused when curious, and will attempt to attain the objects of their curiosity.

McDougall believed that objects triggering instincts can be changed. By linking school activities to objects or events that elicit children's curiosity, the activities themselves eventually may trigger the curiosity instinct. Instinctive behaviors also can be changed. Infants' curiosity is satisfied by grabbing and crawling, but with experience curiosity is satisfied through reading or solving puzzles. Instincts can be altered when many are triggered at once, such that the resulting instinct represents a combination. Curiosity at school sometimes is coupled with anxiety about learning; the resulting behavior may reflect ambivalence. Instinctive behaviors can become attached to certain objects or situations: for example, students whose curiosity is not rewarded at school may display it only at home.

The instinct position is compatible with the points made by A. K. Buerso, who believes that students have dispositions that seem to be innate and that many behaviors—especially those of young children—do not reflect learning. The emphasis on instinct is seen today in various forms (e.g., the "nature-nurture" controversy over how much of human behavior is learned and how much is inherited).

Instinct theories such as McDougall's are quite compelling, but when viewed from a scientific perspective, they have problems. Classifying all behavior as instinctive downplays the role of learning. A theory of motivation needs to specify where instinct ends and learning begins. It also is true that instinctive behaviors are impacted by learning. Thus, the capacity to learn language presumably is an innate human characteristic, but language is learned through social interactions. Finally, labeling a behavior as instinctive does not explain it. A complete theory of motivation must be able to explain what causes an action, what factors interact with it, and how it can be modified.

FREUD'S THEORY

Another early theory of behavior that has relevance to motivation is that of Sigmund Freud, who is among the most influential persons in the history of psychology. Freud is well known for his theory of personality and for the psychoanalytic method of psychotherapy. We do not provide a detailed explanation of Freud's theory in this book; readers are referred to other sources (Freud, 1966; Heidbreder, 1933; Weiner, 1985b). In the following discussion, we summarize motivational principles from Freud's theory.

Freud conceived of motivation as *psychical energy*. He believed that forces within the individual are responsible for behavior. Freud's concept of *trieb*, the German word for *moving force*, bears a close resemblance to motivation. *Trieb* was translated as *instinct*, although in meaning it seems closer to *drive*.

Freud believed that people represent closed energy systems: that is, each person has a constant amount of energy although its form may change. The *psychical energy* builds up in the *id*, a personality structure devoted to attainment of basic needs. Energy develops when needs exist; needs are satisfied by channeling energy into behaviors that reduce needs. Need reduction is pleasurable because a build-up of energy is unpleasant. The aim of energy is its goal (satisfaction), its object refers to the means whereby the force is satisfied, and the source denotes bodily processes activating the energy. For example, a child neglected at home has a need for attention. The aim of the force is to satisfy the need, so gaining attention from an object (teacher) is pleasurable and reduces the source and the energy. Eventually other objects (friends) may satisfy the need for attention, or the energy may become *fixated* on a particular object (teacher) to whom the child always turns for attention.

Energy also can be *repressed*, which means that individuals resist the force to the point where it is not recognized. We resist forces when activity related to them causes more pain than pleasure. Repression does not eliminate energy; rather, repressed energy manifests itself in distorted ways (e.g., neurotic behavior). Repression may be largely unconscious; we may not be fully aware of the forces at work or why we are acting the way we are. A behavior may not represent the motive it appears to represent. For example, repressed sexual energy can disguise itself as overeating.

Freud's theory is so extensive that it makes little sense to ask whether it is correct. Some aspects have been shown to be valid; others have not received support (Weiner, 1985b). The notion of psychical energy is intuitively plausible. Many other investigators have promulgated drive theories of motivation. At the same time, many of Freud's ideas are vague and difficult to verify empirically. By assuming that motivation stems from inner forces that often are unconscious, the theory downgrades the importance of personal cognitions and environmental factors that are educationally significant. To help improve students' motivation we want to know their goals, interests, and values, how they are affected by teachers and other students, and how best to design instruction to teach and motivate. Freud's theory offers no guidance on these important points.

CONDITIONING THEORIES

Early in this century, conditioning theories became preeminent in the United States and maintained their dominance in psychology during the first half of the century. In this section, we summarize the theories of Thorndike (connectionism), Pavlov (classical conditioning), and Skinner (operant conditioning). Although these theories differ, they all are behavioral theories that emphasize the association of stimuli with responses as the mechanism responsible for behavior change. These theories are relevant to the study of motivation because at the behavioral level motivation involves the probability or rate of responding. Conditioning theories take an additive view of behavior. Complex behaviors can be reduced to a series of simpler behaviors, and behavior change is continuous and occurs by combining behaviors into larger sequences. No new principles are needed to explain complex behaviors; rather, these theories are based on a set of principles that can be applied to all aspects of behavior.

Connectionism

Thorndike (1913) presented a well-developed view of learning and behavior. He contended that learning involves the formation of associations (connections) between sensory experiences (perceptions of stimuli or events) and neural impulses that manifest themselves behaviorally. Learning often occurs by *trial and error* (selecting and connecting). Organisms find themselves in problem situations where they attempt to reach a goal. From the various responses they could perform, they select one, perform it, and experience the consequences. Learning occurs gradually; successful responses become established and unsuccessful ones are abandoned. Connections are "stamped in" or "stamped out" by being repeatedly performed or not performed.

> A central principle is the *Law of Effect*: When a modifiable connection between a situation and a response is made and is accompanied or followed by a satisfying state of affairs, that connection's strength is increased: When made and accompanied or followed by an annoying state of affairs, its strength is decreased. (Thorndike, 1913, p. 4)

The law of effect emphasizes the consequences of behavior as contributing to learning. It postulates that responses that result in rewarding consequences will be learned and those that produce punishing consequences will not be learned. Thorndike (1932) subsequently revised the law of effect because research showed that rewarding consequences strengthen connections but punishing consequences do not necessarily weaken them. Connections are weakened when alternative connections are strengthened.

In addition to the motivational consequences of rewards and punishments, another idea relevant to motivation is the *law of readiness*, which describes circumstances conducive to connections being formed.

> When any conduction unit is in readiness to conduct, for it to do so is satisfying. When any conduction unit is not in readiness to conduct, for it to conduct is annoying. When any conduction unit is in readiness to conduct, for it *not* to do so is annoying. (Thorndike, 1913, p. 2)

The law of readiness says that when an organism is prepared to act, to do so is satisfying and not to do so is annoying. Applying this motivational idea to learning, we might say that when a student is ready to learn, engaging in activities to foster that learning is satisfying and produces better learning than when the student is not ready to learn. Alternatively, when a student is forced to learn and he or she is not ready, then learning is annoying.

An important implication is that students are motivated when they are ready to work at an activity and when the consequences of engagement are pleasurable. Students should possess the prerequisites to learn and experience desirable outcomes of learning: performing new skills, recognizing the value of learning, and receiving positive feedback. At the same time, Thorndike ignored cognitive processes and believed that repeating and rewarding behaviors automatically strengthens them. This view has limited applicability to the complexities of motivation in educational settings.

Classical Conditioning

Pavlov's (1927, 1928) classical conditioning theory is important in the field of learning and can be applied to motivation. Conditioning involves presenting an *unconditioned stimulus* (UCS) to elicit an *unconditioned response* (UCR). In a prototypical experimental arrangement, a hungry dog is placed in an apparatus. The dog salivates (UCR) when presented with meat powder (UCS). Conditioning involves briefly presenting a neutral stimulus (e.g., a ticking metronome) before presenting the UCS. In the early trials, the ticking of the metronome produces no salivation. Eventually, the dog salivates in response to the ticking metronome. The metronome has become a *conditioned stimulus* (CS) that elicits a *conditioned response* (CR) similar to the original UCR (Figure 2.1). Repeated presentations of the CS alone cause *extinction*: that is, the CR diminishes in intensity and disappears.

Receipt of reinforcement (the UCS) strengthens the CS-UCS connection. Through repeated pairings with the UCS, the CS acquires the motivational potential of the UCS to generate a response (CR). Thus, neutral stimuli can

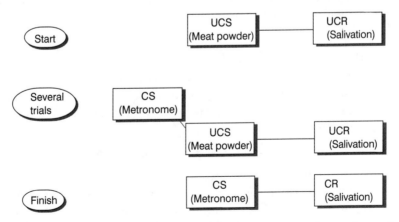

Figure 2.1. Pavlov's classical conditioning (UCS = unconditioned stimulus, UCR = unconditioned response, CS = conditioned stimulus, CR = conditioned response)

acquire motivational properties by being paired with stimuli possessing those properties. Although Pavlov believed that conditioning occurs with repeated CS-UCS pairings, research shows that conditioning is not automatic but instead depends on cognitive processes (Fuhrer & Baer, 1965). For conditioning to occur, the CS must inform individuals about the likelihood of the UCS occurring (Rescorla, 1972, 1987). The CS helps people form expectations about the time, place, quantity, quality, and so forth of the UCS. If people do not realize there is a CS-UCS link, conditioning will not occur. Even when a CS is predictive, it will not become conditioned if another CS is a better predictor. Expectations formed through conditioning apparently motivate individuals to anticipate reinforcement.

In like fashion, emotional reactions can be conditioned to neutral stimuli by pairing them with UCS's that produce reactions. In school, students may develop anxious reactions to teachers, classrooms, or buildings as a function of their being paired with aversive events (e.g., test failure). Alleviating symptoms requires *counterconditioning* the anxiety-producing cues by pairing them with stimuli that elicit pleasant feelings. If the classroom becomes an anxiety-producing cue, the teacher needs to associate the classroom with pleasant events (e.g., praise, positive feedback).

Pavlov's theory has many ideas of interest to education. The notion that learning should be accompanied by pleasurable consequences is important, and teachers generally try to make their classrooms pleasant. That conditioned emotional reactions occur is readily seen in cases of school phobia and test anxiety. But because it ignores cognitive processes, Pavlov's theory offers an incomplete account of behavior and has limited applicability to education. It also represents a passive view of learning and motivation; if conditions are right, conditioning will occur regardless of what people do. In fact, research shows that conditioning is never automatic, learners are mentally active, and they exert much control over their learning and motivation.

Operant Conditioning

B. F. Skinner's (1953) *operant conditioning* theory is an influential conditioning theory for motivation, especially in the field of education. This theory examines the external variables of which behavior is a function. The basic conditioning model is

Stimulus ➞ Response ➞ Consequence

A stimulus sets the occasion for a response to be emitted, which is followed by a consequence. The consequence is any stimulus or event that affects the future rate of responding or the probability that the response will be emitted when the stimulus is present. *Reinforcement* increases the rate or likelihood of responding. A *positive reinforcer* is a stimulus that, when presented following a response, increases the rate or likelihood of the response occurring in that situation. *Positive reinforcement* involves presenting a positive reinforcer contingent on a response. Students who work productively in class may be praised by the teacher. If students then are more likely to work productively or sustain their efforts at a high level, we would say that they were positively reinforced.

A *negative reinforcer* is a stimulus that, when removed following a response, increases the rate or likelihood of the response occurring in that situation. *Negative reinforcement* involves removing a negative reinforcer contingent on a response. In the preceding example, students who work productively may be told by the teacher that they do not have to do any homework. If students then continue their productive work, we say that homework is a negative reinforcer and that its removal is negative reinforcement.

Punishment decreases the rate or likelihood of responding. Punishment may involve either removing a positive reinforcer or presenting a negative reinforcer following a response. In the preceding example, suppose that the students are wasting time. The teacher may take away their free time or assign homework. If they then become less likely to waste time (i.e., more likely to work productively), we say that they were punished for wasting time by having a positive reinforcer (free time) removed or a negative reinforcer (homework) presented. Reinforcement and punishment are exemplified in Table 2.1.

Once a response becomes established it can extinguish. Extinction refers to a lack of responding produced by nonreinforcement of the response. Students who raise their hands in class but are never called on may stop raising their hands. Extinction depends on reinforcement history. Extinction occurs quickly if few preceding responses have been reinforced. Responding in the face of nonreinforcement is more durable with a longer reinforcement history.

Operant conditioning requires that we determine the effects of behavioral consequences. What functions as reinforcement and punishment may vary from person to person and moment to moment. Although most students are

Table 2.1.   Reinforcement and Punishment

Event	Stimulus	Response	Consequence
Positive reinforcement (present positive reinforcer)	Teacher gives student work to complete	Student studies	Teacher praises student for good work
Negative reinforcement (remove negative reinforcer)	Teacher gives student work to complete	Student studies	Teacher says student does not have to finish work
Punishment (remove positive reinforcer)	Teacher gives student work to complete	Student wastes time	Teacher takes away student's free time
Punishment (present negative reinforcer)	Teacher gives student work to complete	Student wastes time	Teacher assigns homework

reinforced by praise much of the time, at times praise does not reinforce and may actually punish (e.g., when a student does not desire teacher attention). Even valued reinforcers can change. A reinforcer applied too often can produce *satiation* and lead to decreased responding.

The *Premack principle*, which states that the opportunity to engage in a more valued activity reinforces engaging in a less valued activity, offers a systematic means for ordering reinforcers and predicting how consequences will function (Premack, 1962, 1971). Value is defined as the amount of responding or time spent on the activity in the absence of explicit reinforcers. The Premack principle predicts that (a) if the value of the contingent event is higher than the value of the instrumental event, the likelihood of occurrence of the instrumental event will increase (the reward assumption), and (b) if the value of the contingent event is lower than that of the instrumental event, the likelihood of occurrence of the instrumental event will decrease (the punishment assumption). For example, if during free time Emily often works at the computer rather than work on math, then the opportunity to work at the computer (the contingent event) will be an effective reinforcer for working on math (the instrumental event).

Operant conditioning contains no new principles to account for motivation. Motivated behavior is thought of simply as increased or continued responding produced by effective contingencies of reinforcement (Skinner, 1968). Internal processes that accompany responding (e.g., needs, drives, cognitions, emotions) are not necessary to explain behavior. The causes of an individual's behavior reside within his or her reinforcement history (what he or she has been reinforced for in the past) and the present environment (Skinner, 1953). Students display motivated behavior because they previously have been reinforced for it and because effective reinforcers for it are available in their environments.

Applying Conditioning Theories in the Classroom

Operant conditioning includes many important principles. Jim Osgood's emphasis on the role of the environment fits with this perspective. The motivational importance of reinforcement and punishment for schooling is apparent in such practices as praise, criticism, time out, free time, rules, privileges, grades, and token/point systems. The following are some common classroom applications of principles of operant conditioning and other conditioning theories:

1. *Ensure that students have the readiness to learn.* Ms. Walker, a fourth-grade teacher, needs to begin a unit on addition of fractions. Before she begins the unit, however, she checks her students to ensure that they can add whole numbers. Two students are still having problems adding whole numbers, so she spends extra time with them until they can add correctly.

Mr. Tamborina tells his fifth graders that after they learn how to divide they will be able to compute baseball players' batting averages. Midway through the school year he feels that they can divide well enough, so he teaches them how to figure batting averages (total number of hits divided by total number of times at bat).

2. *Help students form associations between stimuli and responses.* A third-grade teacher is teaching her students to put headings on papers. She has them write headings on papers in all subject areas—math, writing, spelling, and social studies. She is trying to get them to learn that as part of completing a paper (stimulus) they are to put on a heading (response).

An elementary teacher works with his students on multiplication facts by giving them brief review exercises each day. He hopes they will associate the stimuli (e.g., 9 × 7 =) with the correct responses (63).

3. *Associate learning and classroom activities with pleasing outcomes.* A fourth-grade teacher decides to start cooking in the classroom each Friday to help her students with measurement. After the students have prepared the recipes with accurate measurements, they get to cook and eat what they have made.

Ms. Kincaid, a middle school art teacher, has been working with her students on various sculpture and glazing techniques. After they have completed several small projects, the students are able to create a large piece for their own homes.

4. *Reinforce desired behaviors and extinguish undesired ones.* Mrs. Wazulski moves around the classroom and monitors students' seatwork. She comments on desirable aspects of their work (e.g., "That's good, Jim, you're working very well.") and shows students how to perform better ("That page is a bit sloppy, Mara. Look at the example here. Try to work it this way.").

Jason pushes Sam out of line. Mr. Christo spots this and immediately says, "Jason, we do not push people. You know that the penalty for pushing is no free time, so you lose your free time today." The next day, Mr. Christo notices that Jason is walking in line very well. Mr. Christo says, "Jason, you can be line leader on the way back from lunch since you are doing such a great job of walking and not pushing."

5. *Reinforce progress in learning and behavior.* Mr. Green has his high school English students keep a portfolio of their writing. Periodically, he sits down with students individually to review their work and point out the areas of improvement. They feel better knowing that they are making progress in writing.

Mr. Leland, an elementary music teacher, has a second-grade class that has been having difficulty learning six songs for the spring program. Mr. Leland makes a chart with the six songs listed. He tells his class that each time they learn a song, he will put a star on the chart. After they have earned six stars, they will get to have a popcorn party in class.

6. *Make participation at valued activities contingent on working on less-valued ones.* Al, a fifth-grade student, does not like to finish his reading assignments, but he loves to use the word processor to write stories. Mr. Willet, his teacher, tells Al that he may have extra time at the computer if he completes his reading work.

Ms. Sherrill, a high school drama teacher, tells her students that to perform in the senior play they must be present at and participate in 15 of the 20 play practices.

These practices are important, but from a scientific perspective, operant conditioning offers an incomplete account of motivation. First, operant conditioning does not distinguish motivation from learning but rather uses the same principles to explain all behavior. Although motivation and learning are related, they are not synonymous with one another (Brophy, 1983; Schunk, 1991a). Second, although reinforcement and punishment motivate students, their effects are not automatic but rather depend upon students' beliefs. Students engage in activities that they believe will be reinforced and avoid activities that they believe will be punished (Bandura, 1986). When reinforcement history conflicts with present beliefs, people are more likely to act based on their beliefs (Brewer, 1974). Research has identified many cognitive processes that motivate students (e.g., goals, social comparisons, attributions, expectancies for success). By ignoring these processes, operant conditioning cannot fully account for the complexity of human motivation.

DRIVE THEORIES

Conditioning was not the only influential perspective on learning and motivation during the first half of the twentieth century. Unlike views of conditioning, other theories emphasized the contribution of internal factors to behavior. One class of theories stresses the importance of drive. *Drives* are internal forces that seek to maintain *homeostasis*, or the optimal states of bodily mechanisms. When an organism experiences a need because of deprivation of an essential element (e.g., food, air, water), a drive is activated causing the organism to respond. Drive is reduced and the need is satisfied when the element is obtained. Originally physiological views, drive theories were broadened to include psychological needs. Drive theories focus on overt behavior but explain it in terms of inner needs. Some important drive formulations are those by Woodworth, Hull, Spence, Mowrer, and Miller.

Woodworth's Theory

Woodworth (1918) coined the term *drive* and viewed it as the force that propels behavior. Drives are activated by needs (states of deficiency) and deactivated with need satisfaction. Drives possess intensity, direction, and persistence. *Intensity* refers to the extent that a drive activates behavior. Intensity varies from too low to activate behavior to extremely high. *Direction* denotes the object or goal of the drive. When a drive is triggered, it activates behavior explicitly oriented toward satisfying the need; for example, a hunger drive leads persons to seek food rather than water. *Persistence* refers to the continuation of behavior until the goal is obtained and the need is reduced.

Woodworth's ideas were influential in early psychological research (Richter, 1927; Woodworth & Schlosberg, 1954). One problem is that much research in this tradition was conducted using laboratory animals engaged in simple behaviors. A typical experiment might vary conditions and measure the time it took for hungry or thirsty animals to run mazes to obtain reinforcement. This conception of drive may be useful to explain simple behaviors by animals and humans, but it has been found wanting as an explanation for the complex behavior that characterizes much human motivation (Weiner, 1985b).

Systematic Behavior Theory

Hull (1943) postulated that needs exist when the actual or potential survival of the individual or species is threatened. A need produces a drive to reduce the need. Drive, a motivational construct, energizes the organism toward its goal of obtaining reinforcement to satisfy a need, that is, *drive reduction*.

In addition to drive, habit strength and inhibition are important for behavior. *Habit strength*, or the strength of the stimulus-response association, increases with the number of reinforced stimulus-response pairings. Whereas drive and habit strength lead organisms to make responses, inhibition causes them to not respond. *Inhibition* refers to fatigue due to responding and to the reinforcement derived from not responding when one is fatigued.

Hull's theory expresses relations between elements in mathematical terms. *Effective reaction potential*, or the likelihood of behavior, is a function of drive (D), habit strength (H), and inhibition (I):

$$\text{Effective Reaction Potential} = D \times H - I$$

Motivation is "the initiation of learned, or habitual, patterns of movement or behavior" (Hull, 1943, p. 226). Innate behaviors usually satisfy needs and learning occurs only when innate behaviors prove ineffective. Learning represents the organism's adaptation to the environment to ensure survival. Hull also believed that much behavior is not oriented toward satisfying primary needs. Secondary reinforcers (e.g., money) acquire reinforcing power by being paired with primary reinforcement (money buys food).

As an explanation for motivation, Hull's theory seems best suited for immediate physiological needs. Drowning persons seek safety; those who are hungry seek food. One problem with Hull's theory is that needs do not always trigger drives aimed at drive reduction. Needs for food or water can be outweighed by nonphysiological needs (e.g., desire to finish important tasks). Drives can exist in the absence of biological needs. A strong sex drive can lead to promiscuity even though sex is not immediately needed for survival.

Another concern is that much human behavior is aimed at obtaining long-term goals: getting a job, obtaining a college degree, or winning a championship. People are not continuously in a high-drive state while striving for these goals. High drive is not conducive to performance over lengthy periods or on complex tasks (Broadhurst, 1957; Yerkes & Dodson, 1908). Over long periods, people typically experience high motivation intermixed with slumps. In sum, Hull's theory does not offer an adequate explanation for academic motivation.

Incentive Motivation

Hull's theory specifies that reinforcement increases habit strength and effective reaction potential. Hull (1943) postulated that large rewards lead to better learning (i.e., greater habit strength) than small rewards and that strong habits are developed when large rewards are delivered immediately after goal attainment.

These ideas were not substantiated by Tolman's research on latent learning (discussed under the heading Purposive Behaviorism), which showed that rats learn to run mazes without being rewarded. Other research demonstrated that shifts in motivation (e.g., speed of maze running) occur as a function of changes in reward size (Crespi, 1942). This finding cannot be due to altered habit strength, because habit strength presumably increases gradually with repeated reinforcements. Hull (1951, 1952) modified his position to include *incentive motivation* (K):

$$\text{Effective Reaction Potential} = D \times H \times K - I$$

Spence (1960) argued that reward does not affect habit strength but rather performance of the response and that incentive motivation is a performance rather than a learning variable. Spence postulated that incentive motivation combines additively with drive to produce a complex motivational variable:

$$\text{Effective Reaction Potential} = (D + K) \times H - I$$

The idea that reward influences behavior but not necessarily learning has been substantiated in the ensuing years (Bandura, 1986).

Mowrer's Theory

Mowrer (1960) postulated that incentive motivation is the central instigator of action. He believed that emotions are *intervening variables* that mediate the relation between stimuli and responses. Cues associated with the onset of emotion become capable of eliciting the emotion before the emotion-producing stimulus does. Such anticipatory emotion produces instrumental behavior to approach or avoid the stimulus.

There are four primary emotions: fear, relief, hope, and disappointment. *Fear* instigates behavior designed to avoid perceived danger and represents the anticipation or expectation of pain. Fear occurs from increased drive brought about by such situations as food deprivation and being shocked. *Relief* occurs when fear is reduced by a response that removes the organism from the feared situation. Relief becomes linked with stimuli present when fear cues are removed. If a light comes on in an experimental apparatus immediately before an animal may be shocked and pressing a lever turns the light off, then the sight of the lever can become conditioned to produce relief in the animal.

A decrease in drive can be accompanied by *hope*. If a hungry animal is taught to press a lever to obtain food, then obtaining food reduces drive and produces hope. Cues associated with lever pressing (e.g., a light by the lever is on when food arrives) become conditioned to elicit hope because they signal that a decrease in drive and an increase in hope are imminent. *Disappointment* occurs when hope is diminished by the consequences of a response, as when hope cues predicting a decrease in drive do not lead to drive reduction (e.g., suddenly the light goes off and lever pressing does not produce food). Disappointment, like fear, is negative and motivates organisms to remove the cues signaling disappointment. Thus, an animal may cease pressing the lever and begin making other responses to see if they produce food.

Mowrer's theory represents a plausible account of how some motivational responses are learned. The theory postulates that behaviors are motivated by emotions that become conditioned to cues. Fear, hope, relief, and disappointment are commonly seen in students in response to school situations (e.g., tests).

Mowrer's theory can account for the performance of established behaviors but not the instigation of new behaviors (Miller, 1963). Once a laboratory animal learns that cues in a maze are associated with hope because food is at the end, the animal's behaviors will continue, but the theory does not explain why the animal explores the maze the first time. Also, by emphasizing a small number of emotions, Mowrer limits the role of personal cognitions in motivation. Thus, the explanatory potential of Mowrer's theory for achievement motivation is minimal.

Acquired Drives

Hull viewed drives as innate mechanisms for ensuring survival, but drives also can be learned. Many people are highly motivated to amass wealth, material possessions, and status. Miller (1948) explored *acquired* drives in a classic experiment using a two-compartment box in which the compartments were separated by a door. Rats were shocked while in a white compartment, after which the experimenter opened the door so they could escape to a black compartment. Subsequently, rats were put into the white compartment but not shocked and could escape through the door to the black compartment. They then had to learn to turn a wheel and press a lever in the white compartment to open the door leading to the black compartment. About half of the rats learned the two responses and showed improved performance across trials. Rats not learning the responses developed habits (e.g., crouching in place) that interfered with learning.

Miller's study shows that neutral cues associated with the white compartment became associated with shock and motivated the rats to learn new, arbitrary responses (wheel turning, lever pressing) that were reinforced by the rats escaping to the black compartment. Motivation to avoid the white compartment was acquired through pairing the compartment with shock. Once acquired, the motivation helped the rats learn operant behaviors to avoid shock.

Other research shows that animals and humans will work hard to earn secondary reinforcers (Hilgard, 1963). Although drives originally were linked with survival, they can generalize to situations having little direct survival value.

PURPOSIVE BEHAVIORISM

In stark contrast to the mechanistic accounts of behavior inherent in conditioning and drive theories stands Tolman's (1932) theory of *purposive behaviorism*, which stresses the goal directedness of behavior. Environmental stimuli are means to goal attainment and must be studied in the context of behavioral sequences to understand people's actions. High school students who want to attend leading universities study hard. A focus only on the studying neglects its goal. Students study not only because they have been reinforced for studying, but also because they believe studying promotes learning and high grades, which, in turn, enhance the likelihood of college acceptance.

Tolman went beyond the stimulus-response associations of behavioral psychologists to discuss underlying mechanisms. Tolman qualified his use of cognitive terms by noting they were defined objectively. Behaviors of people and animals are goal oriented; they act "as if" they are pursuing goals and as if they choose means for goal attainment. Thus, Tolman's theory has a behavioral focus, although it alludes to cognitive mechanisms by contending that behavior must be interpreted in relation to goals that are internal processes of organisms.

Expectancy Learning

Tolman (1932) defined expectancies as involving relationships between stimuli ($S_1 - S_2$) or between a stimulus, response (R), and stimulus ($S_1 - R - S_2$). Relations between stimuli concern what stimulus is apt to follow what other stimulus; for example, If I see lightning (S_1), thunder will follow (S_2). In a three-term relation, people develop the belief that a certain response to a given stimulus will produce a result; for example, If I study (R) this book (S_1), I should make a good grade on the test (S_2).

Expectancies are learned from experiences with events. Simple stimulus-response contiguity often is sufficient to produce an expectancy. Expectancies are important because they help one attain goals. People form *cognitive maps*, or internal plans, comprising expectancies of which actions are needed to attain one's goals. Individuals follow *signs* to goals, learn *meanings* rather than discrete responses, and use cognitive maps to attain goals (Tolman, 1949).

Tolman tested his ideas in clever ways. In one study (Tolman, Ritchie, & Kalish, 1946), rats were trained to run an apparatus, after which it was replaced with one in which the original pathway was blocked. Conditioning theories predict that animals will choose a pathway close to the original one because its cues are associated with reinforcement. Instead, the most frequently chosen path was aimed toward the original location of food, which supports the idea that animals respond to a cognitive map of the food's location rather than cues based on prior responding.

Latent Learning

Additional evidence to support cognitive map learning came from experiments on *latent learning*, or learning in the absence of a goal or reinforcement. Such learning contradicts the operant conditioning principle that behavior change requires reinforced practice.

Tolman and Honzik (1930) allowed two groups of rats to wander through a maze for several trials. One group always was fed in the maze; the other group was never fed there. Fed rats reduced their time to run the maze and the number of errors; time and errors for the other group remained high. When some rats from the nonreinforced group were given food for running the maze, their times and number of errors quickly dropped to the levels of the group that always had been fed. Running times and error rates for rats who continued to be nonreinforced did not change. Rats in the nonreinforced group learned features of the maze by wandering through it without reinforcement. When food was introduced, latent learning became apparent.

Tolman's research demonstrates that learning can occur without reward or drive reduction and that incentives affect performance rather than learning (Weiner, 1990). Teachers sometimes try to motivate students to perform what they know (e.g., review sessions), but much time is spent motivating students to learn. Most researchers and practitioners currently believe that motivation is not entirely separable from learning and can affect learning in many ways. Although it offers important insights, Tolman's theory does not fully capture the complexity of influences on motivation.

AROUSAL THEORIES

A very different perspective on motivation from those we have discussed is found in theories that construe motivation in terms of level of emotional arousal. Arousal theories deal with behaviors, emotions, and other internal mechanisms. These theories are not behavioral in nature, but they are not entirely cognitive either. Some theories emphasize cognitions more than others, but all postulate that motivation depends strongly on affective processes. Researchers are increasingly showing that affects play an important role in school learning and motivation (see Chapter 8).

In this section, we discuss the James-Lange theory, ideas about optimal levels of arousal, and Schachter's theory of emotion. Readers interested in further information on arousal theories are referred to other sources (Arnold, 1968; Mook, 1987; Petri, 1986; Russell, 1970).

James-Lange Theory

Toward the end of the nineteenth century, a popular view was that emotional arousal mediates the relation between perception of a stimulus and behavior. For example, if we encounter a threatening snake outside, the perception of the snake gives rise to the emotion of fear, which leads to escape behavior. This may be depicted as

Perception ⟶ Emotion ⟶ Behavior

James (1884, 1890) and Lange (1885) independently challenged this view. The *James-Lange theory of emotion* (as it became known) stipulated that emotion is a consequence of behavior rather than an antecedent (cause) and involves perceptions of responses to arousing situations. Responses include actual behaviors as well as reactions of the autonomic nervous system—rapid heart rate, sweating, bodily pains. Emotion is the conscious experience of overt behaviors and internal responses. According to this view, we see the snake and then escape. While escaping, we realize what we are doing and we experience internal symptoms that produce the emotion or the conscious experience of fear. This causal sequence is

Perception ⟶ Behavior + Internal response ⟶ Emotion

The James-Lange theory downgrades the importance of emotion in motivation because emotion is an effect of behavior rather than a cause (Cofer & Appley, 1964). The motivation to run arises from factors other than emotions (e.g., learning that snakes are dangerous).

Cannon (1927) disputed the validity of this theory. Cannon showed that emotions can be experienced even when bodily changes that provide feedback to the brain are eliminated. He removed nerves from cats to eliminate bodily changes, but the cats still showed rage in response to barking dogs. He also demonstrated that the same bodily changes accompany the different emotions that we experience. During rage and fear, for example, blood sugar increases, pupils dilate, and heart rate accelerates. These internal responses cannot determine emotion as predicted by the James-Lange theory.

Cannon offered an alternative formulation postulating that internal responses and emotion are coeffects of perception:

Perception ⟶ Internal response + Emotion ⟶ Behavior

Emotion-provoking stimuli activate circuits in a brain structure called the *thalamus*. These circuits send messages down the spinal cord to evoke autonomic bodily arousal and up to the *cortex*, a higher brain system, to evoke emotional experience. We see the snake and simultaneously experience autonomic symptoms and emotional awareness. This view stresses the role of emotion in motivation because emotion helps determine ensuing behavior.

Optimal Level of Arousal

Different theories postulate that an optimal level of arousal is needed for bodily functioning. The notion of optimal level of arousal is highly relevant to motivation.

In Hebb's (1949) neurophysiological theory of learning, motivation results from *cell assemblies* that represent knowledge and that are gradually developed through repeated stimulation. Cell assemblies become linked into *phase sequences* that are the physiological equivalents of cognitive processes' guiding behavior.

Moderate levels of arousal are needed to keep cell assemblies and phase sequences active. When arousal is too low, sequences do not function properly; when it is too high, sequences are disrupted. It therefore is critically important that an optimal level of arousal be maintained.

Berlyne (1960, 1963) discussed the motivational functions of arousal, which he defined as roughly equivalent to drive. Berlyne postulated that exploratory activity often is accompanied by increased arousal and that *collative* properties of stimuli (e.g., novelty, ambiguity, incongruity, surprise) affect arousal. Arousal is adaptive and we attempt to maintain an optimal level. If it goes too low, boredom sets in and we become motivated to increase arousal; if it becomes too high, we are motivated to lower it. Novel or incongruous stimuli motivate behavior directed toward exploring them because they provide for a shift in arousal that is perceived as pleasant.

Hebb (1966) postulated that moderate changes in arousal are reinforcing because the brain requires activity. Hebb linked arousal to play and felt that play occurs when other needs are not active. Play can be mental as well as muscular because many games require memory of past events and rules. Play occurs as a result of boredom and provides an optimal level of arousal.

Berlyne and Hebb stress that deviations above and below an optimal level of arousal trigger motivation to return arousal to this optimal level. This view contrasts with that of Hull, who believed that motivation represents a drive to reduce arousal and return the organism to homeostasis (calm state). Berlyne and Hebb thus expanded the motivational functions of arousal.

Applying Arousal Theories in the Classroom

Teachers know the value of using novelty, uncertainty, and incongruity in the classroom to raise student interest in learning, alertness, and motivation.

Teachers routinely employ brightly colored displays, demonstrations portraying surprising results, and presentations of contradictory information (e.g., Why do pieces of metal sink but metal ships float?). At the same time, too much novelty and uncertainty can disrupt classrooms and create in students uncertainties and doubts about learning. Arousal is important for motivation and we should strive to maintain an optimal (moderate) level of student arousal. Some suggestions for applying ideas of arousal theories in the classroom follow.

1. *Maintain student motivation at an optimal level; avoid periods of boredom and high anxiety.* A new seventh-grade science teacher was concerned because many of his students finished their work quickly and then played around in class. Realizing that his students were bored, he developed several hands-on center activities for the students to do when they completed their written work. Within two days, student behavior had improved.

Mrs. Hall, a kindergarten teacher, was concerned about several of her new children who were crying each day. After conferring with the other kindergarten teachers, she realized that the cause of the crying might be that she was expecting the students to complete too many activities. Mrs. Hall adapted her plans to include fewer activities and less chaos in the classroom. All students calmed down and began to participate with more confidence.

2. *Incorporate novelty and incongruity into teaching and student activities.* A high school science teacher developed a unit where students were to learn about various substances and their reactions to certain chemicals. To make the unit more interesting, she gave each pair of students an unknown liquid and asked them to determine what the substance contained based on its reaction to the chemicals.

A third-grade teacher took his students on a field trip to a wooded area to collect various leaves and tree bark. The students used the items they had collected in a classification lesson.

3. *Develop in students positive emotions about learning rather than uncertainty.* Susan was having difficulty with long division. Her teacher, Mrs. Kush, told her, "Susan, I'll be glad to help you after school. I know you can learn how to do long division if we work together."

"Thanks, Mrs. Kush. My teacher last year told me I never was going to be able to learn anything about math," replied Susan.

Mrs. Anderson was frustrated with her resource students because they were having trouble getting their science projects finished. She suspected that they felt they were not smart enough to keep up with the students in the regular classroom. She met with children individually and helped them develop a schedule to follow so that they could finish their projects on time.

Schachter's Theory of Emotion

Schachter (1964; Schachter & Singer, 1962) contributed important ideas to the study of emotion. He proposed that emotion involves physiological arousal and a cognitive label or attribution (perceived cause). If either is absent, the emotion experienced will be incomplete.

In most situations, we can label physiological arousal because it is accompanied by cues. If someone walks up and deliberately pushes you, you experience emotional arousal and a clear cue for labeling the emotion as anger (i.e., someone deliberately pushed me). Schachter felt that cognitions determine the emotion experienced (e.g., anger, fear, rage). Cognitions arise from the present situation and are interpreted within a framework provided by prior experiences. There are times, however, when we experience arousal, but the cues for labeling the emotion are not clear. When this happens, we search the environment for an explanation.

Schachter and Singer (1962) tested these ideas in an ingenious experiment. Adult subjects were led to believe they were participating in a study on the effects of vitamin supplements on vision, but actually were given an injection of either epinephrine or a placebo. Epinephrine causes increased blood pressure, heart rate, and respiration rate, and flushing. Subjects receiving epinephrine either were correctly informed about what to expect from the injection (informed condition), were misinformed about the effects by being told it might cause numbness of the feet and itching (misinformed condition), or were told that it would have no side effects (ignorant condition). Subjects were paired with an experimental confederate, informed that the confederate also had received the vitamin shot, and told to wait for a few minutes, during which time the confederate acted in a euphoric or angry fashion. Subjects were unobtrusively observed and later completed a self-report mood measure.

Both the ignorant and misinformed subjects reported greater euphoria compared with informed subjects. The unobtrusive observations showed that misinformed subjects behaved more euphorically than ignorant subjects, who behaved more euphorically than informed subjects. Results for anger were similar although not statistically significant. Schachter and Singer proposed that informed subjects had an attribution for the bodily changes they were experiencing because they were told of the drug's effects. Both ignorant and misinformed subjects had to search their environments for cues to explain their bodily symptoms. The presence of a euphoric or angry companion apparently led subjects to label or attribute their experienced emotions as euphoria or anger. The confederate provided cues that allowed subjects to label the emotions they were experiencing.

This view is similar to the James-Lange theory except that the former adds cognitive attribution as a cause of emotion. Like Cannon, Schachter emphasizes the cognitive aspects of emotion. Schachter's formulation presents a strong case for bodily arousal and cognition being required to experience emotion.

There are some methodological problems in the Schachter and Singer (1962) procedure, and not all attempts at replication have been successful (Cotton, 1981). Debate continues in professional circles over the nature of emotion and its role in motivation. We discuss attribution theory in Chapters 4 and 8, which also highlight the role of cognition in emotion. An important implication of this work is that how students interpret events affects emotion and motivation.

FIELD THEORY

A historical chapter on motivation would seem incomplete without some coverage of field theory, an early cognitive view of motivation. *Field* refers to the idea that there is a field of conflicting forces in people's lives (Lewin, 1935, 1936). Field theory is a dynamic view that identifies forces on behavior and postulates that behavior represents a mechanism for preserving or restoring homeostasis in psychological and physical needs. Field theory stresses the interaction of individuals with their environments, as espoused by Sara Wylie in the opening dialogue.

The essence of field theory is summed up as

$$B = f(PE)$$

or, "every psychological event [*B*] depends upon the state of the person [*P*] and at the same time on the environment [*E*]" (Lewin, 1936, p. 12). The person and the environment constitute the individual's *life space*, and motivation represents the individual's efforts to satisfy needs and impose homeostasis on the field (Figure 2.2).

The outer ring of the person represents the part that interacts with the psychological environment. Sensory information enters the person and motor output proceeds outward. Needs are represented in the central portion, with more critical needs (e.g., food, water) closer to the center than less critical ones (need to watch TV). The central areas also are in contact with many other areas, thereby spreading their influence. Needs can become differentiated; the need to watch TV might become the need to watch only certain programs.

Tension exists when a potential need becomes an actual need and it motivates individuals to reduce it and restore homeostasis. There are physiological

Figure 2.2. Lewin's life space

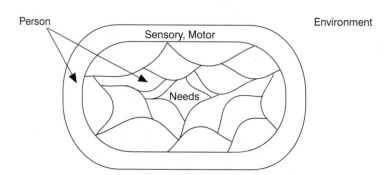

needs (e.g., food, air, water) and psychological needs (achievement, companionship). To reduce a need, the tension can be distributed from the actual need throughout the inner, personal region. This method does not satisfy the need but rather dissipates the tension. That is, the overall tension of the region increases, but areas within the region become comparable. When boundaries to a need do not allow tension to flow, inside tension cannot be evenly spread and so motivation continues. Another means of reducing tension is through *locomotion*, whereby the psychological environment helps dissipate the tension.

The *psychological environment* includes all psychological facts of which individuals are aware, or their knowledge as it exists in memory. Tension can be alleviated through locomotion from the inner, personal region to the appropriate fact that satisfies the need. The borders of the psychological environment, like those of the inner, personal region, have different permeabilities, so movement is easier through some regions than others. Facts have positive or negative *valences* that attract or repel movement.

The method for satisfying a need involves *force*, which has two properties: *magnitude* and *direction*. A particular need may impinge on an aspect of the psychological environment with varying magnitude (strength), and the particular fact imposed upon indicates the direction. When several needs are simultaneously active, individuals encounter conflicting forces. Behavior exists in a force field that determines its direction and intensity (Figure 2.2).

Lewin's theory says that to understand behavior you must understand all the forces acting on the individual. Behavior is holistic and can be understood only in its entirety. For example, if Kerry has a need to snack and a need to be socially popular, then these two needs conflict. The tension may spread throughout the inner, personal region, but eventually it must be resolved and will seek goal areas in the psychological environment. There is stored knowledge of where food is, what excess food does to weight and appearance, what her friends think of people who are overweight, and so forth. Kerry may compromise and eat nonfattening foods.

Lewin's emphasis on the whole person is intuitively appealing, but the life space idea is vague and difficult to research. The concept of psychological facts is not clearly specified, and although such facts presumably can change, the mechanism for change is not spelled out. Despite these problems, the person-situation interaction notion is valid and the holistic approach is emphasized by other perspectives, most notably humanistic views (discussed later in this chapter). Teachers trying to understand motivation in students would do well to focus on all aspects of the students' lives and not simply isolated elements.

COGNITIVE CONSISTENCY

Around the middle of the twentieth century, *cognitive consistency theories* were developed as psychological views of behavior. These theories represent a break with theories in the behavioral tradition (conditioning, drive) because they address the cognitions people have and how these cognitions affect behavior.

Cognitive consistency theories assume that motivation results from relations between cognitions and behaviors. These theories are homeostatic because, when tension occurs, there is a need to make cognitions and behaviors consistent. Cognitive consistency theories are cognitive rather than behavioral because they focus on the individual's attempts to restore internal balance. Two important views were propounded by Heider and Festinger.

Balance Theory

Heider's (1946) *balance theory* postulates a tendency for relations among persons, situations, and events to be cognitively balanced. The basic situation involves three elements with relations as positive or negative. Balance exists when all elements are positively related or when there are one positive and two negative relations. Thus, if I like Dave and Larry, and if Dave likes me and Larry, and if Larry likes me and Dave, the triad of me-Dave-Larry is balanced. Imbalance exists with one negative and two positive relations and when all elements are negatively related. An example of the former would be if I like Dave and Larry and if Dave and Larry each like me, but Dave and Larry do not like one another. The theory predicts people will not change relations when the triad is balanced but will try to resolve conflicts when imbalance exists.

That people seek to restore cognitive balance is intuitively plausible, but balance theory contains problems. It predicts when people will attempt to restore balance but not how they will do it. The theory also does not adequately take into account the importance of imbalanced relationships. We care very much when imbalance exists among people and things we value, but make no effort to restore balance when we care little about the elements. As a view of cognitive motivation, balance theory seems to be incomplete.

Cognitive Dissonance Theory

One of the most elegant consistency theories is Festinger's (1957) *cognitive dissonance theory*. Dissonance theory postulates that people attempt to maintain consistent relations among their beliefs, attitudes, opinions, and behaviors. Relations can be consonant, irrelevant, or dissonant. Two cognitions are consonant if one follows from or fits with the other (e.g., I don't like Joe and I avoid Joe). Irrelevant cognitions bear no relation to each other (e.g., I like blue and my dog's name is Fido). Dissonance is tension with drivelike properties leading to reduction. Dissonant cognitions exist when one follows from the opposite of the other (e.g., I don't like Joe and I see Joe all the time). Dissonance increases as the discrepancy between cognitions increases. The importance of the cognitions also is taken into account. Large discrepancies between trivial cognitions do not cause much dissonance, whereas even a small discrepancy between important cognitions may cause dissonance.

One way to reduce dissonance is to change a discrepant cognition. If I change my belief to I actually like Joe, dissonance will be reduced. Another way is to qualify cognitions (e.g., I see Joe all the time because I work with him). A third way is to downgrade the importance of the cognitions: It's not important that I don't like Joe because there are a lot of people I don't like. Finally, I can alter my behavior by avoiding Joe.

Dissonance theory calls attention to how cognitive conflicts can be resolved (Aronson, 1966). The idea that dissonance motivates us to reduce it is appealing. By dealing with discrepant cognitions, the theory is not confined to triadic relations as is balance theory. But dissonance theory has many of the same problems. The dissonance notion is vague and difficult to verify experimentally. To predict whether cognitions will conflict in a given situation is problematic because they must be salient and important. The theory does not predict how dissonance will be reduced. Clearly, additional factors are needed to explain human motivation.

TRAIT AND HUMANISTIC THEORIES

The final historical perspectives we consider in this chapter are trait and humanistic theories. These theories offer a direct challenge to behavioral views of motivation and provide valuable insights into why persons act the way they do. Although individuals working in these traditions differ in many ways, their theories stress mental (largely cognitive) processes.

Two influential trait theorists were Henry Murray and Gordon Allport. Murray's work is germane to achievement motivation and is discussed in Chapter 6. Allport's theory, which is covered here, stresses many ideas found in humanistic views. Two of the best known humanistic theories are those of Maslow and Rogers. Maslow's theory, which emphasizes motivation to develop one's full potential, also is discussed in Chapter 6. In this chapter, we describe the seminal work of Carl Rogers.

Allport's Functional Autonomy of Motives

Allport (1937) believed that people were best viewed as unique systems constantly evolving and striving toward goals. Traits are part of this system but are idiosyncratic and can be studied only with reference to particular individuals. Traits are unique realities within individuals that help to account for the relative consistency of behavior across situations.

Allport rejected the ideas of Freud, McDougall, and Murray that motives derive from forces in early childhood or from particular classes of needs or instincts. Rather, he proposed a *functional autonomy of motives*:

The dynamic psychology proposed here regards adult motives as infinitely varied, and as self-sustaining, *contemporary* systems, growing out of antecedent systems, but functionally independent of them. Just as a child gradually repudiates his dependence on his parents, develops a will of his own, becomes self-active and self-determining, and outlives his parents, so it is with motives. Each motive has a definite point of origin which may lie in the hypothetical instincts, or, more likely, in the organic tensions and diffuse irritability. . . . Theoretically all adult purposes can be traced back to these seed-forms in infancy. But as the individual matures the bond is broken. The tie is historical, not functional. (Allport, 1937, p. 194)

Traits (motives) can lead people to view different situations as similar or functionally equivalent, which accounts for the extensive consistency in human behavior across situations. The issue of cross-situational behavioral consistency is important and has been hotly debated in motivational circles. What it means, for example, is that persons who possess the trait of honesty will believe they should be honest and behave honestly in such diverse situations as receiving change back from purchases in stores, finding valuables belonging to others, and asking friends to perform favors. There is conflicting evidence about the extent that human behavior is consistent across situations (Mischel, 1968).

Allport's ideas were adopted by the humanistic movement in psychology with such advocates as Maslow and Rogers. His ideas are general and do not readily lend themselves to empirical testing or practical application. His major contribution to the study of motivation is that he called attention to the force of human motives as they manifest themselves in different situations.

Assumptions of Humanistic Theories

Humanistic psychology emphasizes people's capabilities and potentialities. As the *third force* in psychology (after psychoanalysis and behaviorism), humanistic psychology stresses that individuals have choices and seek control over their lives. This is an important assumption in intrinsic motivation, as we will see in Chapter 7. Humanistic psychology does not explain behavior in terms of unconscious, powerful inner forces and does not focus on environmental stimuli and responses as determinants of behavior.

Humanistic theories have many common assumptions (Weiner, 1985b). One assumption is that the study of humans is *holistic*. In order to understand people, we must study their behaviors, thoughts, and feelings. Humanists disagree with the behaviorist approach of studying individual responses to discrete stimuli. Humanists emphasize individuals' *subjective* awareness of themselves and their situations.

A second assumption is that human choices, creativity, and self-actualization are important areas to study (Weiner, 1985b). In order to understand people, researchers should not study lower organisms. The uniquely human aspect of motivation asserts itself in the study of people who are psychologically functioning and attempting to be creative and maximize their capabilities and potential. Although motivation is important for the attainment of basic needs, humans have fewer choices of ways to obtain food, clothing, and shelter as compared with ways to maximize their potential.

A third assumption concerns methodology. A goal of psychological research is to perform well-controlled studies. The literature is replete with instances of a complex methodology applied to a trivial research problem. Importance of problems must be the primary criterion used to select topics to study. From the humanistic perspective, it is better to study an important problem with a less refined methodology than a trivial problem with a complex methodology.

Rogers's Client-Centered Therapy

Carl Rogers was a famous psychotherapist whose approach to counseling became known as *client-centered therapy*. We begin by discussing his concept of the actualizing tendency and follow with sections on positive regard and applications of his ideas to education.

Actualizing Tendency

According to Rogers (1963), life represents an ongoing process of personal growth or achieving wholeness. Rogers labeled this process the *actualizing tendency* and believed it is innate. The actualizing tendency is the motivational construct in Rogers's theory (Rogers, 1963). Rogers felt that this motive was the only fundamental one and that all other motives (e.g., hunger, thirst, shelter) derive from it. The actualizing tendency is oriented toward personal growth, autonomy, and freedom from control by external forces.

> We are, in short, dealing with an organism which is always motivated, is always "up to something," always seeking. So I would reaffirm . . . my belief that there is one central source of energy in the human organism; that it is a function of the whole organism rather than some portion of it; and that it is perhaps best conceptualized as a tendency toward fulfillment, toward actualization, toward the maintenance and enhancement of the organism. (Rogers, 1963, p. 6)

Need for Positive Regard

Although the actualizing tendency presumably is innate, it is influenced by the environment. Our experiences and interpretations of them foster or hinder our attempts at growth. Rogers notes that with development individuals become more aware of their own being and functioning, or what he terms *self-experience*. This awareness becomes elaborated into a concept of self as a result of interactions with the environment and significant others (Rogers, 1959).

The development of self-awareness produces a need for positive regard. *Positive regard* refers to such feelings as respect, liking, warmth, sympathy, and acceptance. We experience positive regard for others when we have these feelings about them as a result of some interaction. We perceive ourselves as receiving positive regard when we believe that others feel that way about us as a result of some experience. These effects are reciprocal. When people perceive themselves as satisfying another's need for positive regard, they experience satisfaction of their need for positive regard.

People also have a need for *positive self-regard*, or positive regard that derives from self-experiences (Rogers, 1959). Positive self-regard develops when people experience positive regard from others, which creates a positive attitude toward themselves. That attitude then is strengthened as a result of one's experiences.

A critical element in the development of positive regard and positive self-regard is receiving *unconditional positive regard*, or attitudes of worthiness and acceptance with no strings attached. Unconditional positive regard is what most parents feel for their children. Parents value or accept ("prize") their children all the time even though they do not value or accept all of the children's behaviors. People who experience unconditional positive regard believe they are valued regardless of their actions. The actualizing tendency then can strive toward growth because individuals accept their own experiences, and their perceptions of themselves are consistent with the feedback they receive.

Problems occur when people experience *conditional regard*, that is, regard contingent on certain actions. People act in accordance with these conditions of worth when they seek or avoid experiences that they believe are more or less worthy of regard. Conditional regard can create tension, because people feel accepted and valued by others only when they behave appropriately, and can thwart the actualizing tendency and growth. Anxiety triggers defenses that people use to protect themselves. These defenses selectively perceive or distort experiences or deny their awareness.

In point of fact, people typically experience conditional regard. Society does not distinguish people from their actions. It practices conditional regard because it rewards acceptable behaviors and punishes unacceptable ones. People can function with a certain amount of conditional regard, but when conditional regard becomes excessive, people become defensive and cannot grow.

In sum, the actualizing tendency is the basic motivating force behind behavior. To be fully functioning, individuals must receive unconditional positive regard and, in turn, experience positive regard and self-regard. We grow and change when we relax our defenses and devote time to personal growth. We become defensive and stop growing when conditions are placed on our worth.

Rogers and Education

Rogers applied his theory to education in the book *Freedom to Learn* (1969). Meaningful, experiential learning has relevance to the whole person, has personal involvement (involves learners' cognitions and feelings), is self-initiated (impetus for learning comes from within), is pervasive (affects learners' behavior, attitudes, and personality), and is evaluated by the learner (according to whether it is meeting needs or leading to goals). Meaningful learning contrasts with meaningless learning, common in school, that does not lead to learners being invested in their learning, is initiated by others, does not affect diverse aspects of learners, and is not evaluated by learners according to whether it is satisfying their needs.

Rogers (1969) believes that people have a natural potential for learning, are curious about their world, and are eager to learn.

> I become very irritated with the notion that students must be "motivated." The young human being is intrinsically motivated to a high degree. Many elements of his environment constitute challenges for him. He is curious, eager to discover, eager to know, eager to solve problems. A sad part of most education is that by the time the child has spent a number of years in school this intrinsic motivation is pretty well dampened. Yet it is there and it is our task as facilitators of learning to tap that motivation, to discover what challenges are real for the young person, and to provide the opportunity for him to meet those challenges. (Rogers, 1969, p. 131)

Meaningful learning is perceived as relevant by students. They believe it will maintain or enhance their selves. The best learning occurs through active participation. Learning requires self-criticism and self-evaluation by learners and the belief that learning is important.

Learning that can be taught to others is inconsequential and has little effect on behavior. Teachers do not impart learning but rather act as *facilitators* who establish a classroom climate oriented toward significant learning and help students clarify their purposes in learning. Facilitators also arrange resources for learning to occur. Facilitators are resources and make themselves available to students by sharing their feelings and thoughts.

Providing students with the freedom to learn requires modifications. Instead of spending a lot of time writing lesson plans, facilitators should provide resources for students to use experientially to meet their needs. Individual contracts should be used rather than lockstep sequences in which all students work on the same materials for the same amount of time. Although contracts impose structure on the learning process, they also allow students considerable freedom in setting up the contract and in deciding on the goals and time lines. Freedom itself should not be imposed; students who want more teacher direction should receive it. Rogers advocates greater use of methods of inquiry, simulations, programmed instruction, and self-evaluation as ways to provide freedom.

Applying Humanistic Theories in the Classroom

Rogers's theory has seen wide psychotherapeutic application. The focus on helping people strive for challenges and maximize their potential is important, and teachers can use the principles of the theory with students. At the same time, the theory is developed only in general terms and is replete with technical constructs that are difficult to define and measure. Greater clarity is needed concerning the process whereby one's regard or self-regard affects behavior and can be improved. Another problem is that the actualizing tendency is not firmly linked with goals. Rogers emphasizes striving toward growth, but this process is vaguely defined. Much research shows that specific goals motivate individuals better than general ones (Locke & Latham, 1990). A third concern is that it is unclear how positive regard for others may influence them or how social factors (e.g., rewards, social comparisons, feedback) can affect regard and self-regard. Fortunately, research continues in the humanistic tradition that will help to clarify these concerns.

The following are some suggestions on how to use humanistic theories in the classroom:

1. *Show positive regard for students.* Mrs. Sarver, a second-grade teacher, was working with her students on a cooking project in the school's kitchen. One student was afraid of the very large oven they were using to bake the cookies they had made. Mrs. Sarver hugged the child and let that child wait for the group in the cafeteria just outside the kitchen door.

Mr. Thompson, a high school civics teacher, called for a response to a question. One student raised his hand and said, "Mr. Thompson, I don't get it. This is probably a dumb question, but could you go over that first part again?"

Mr. Thompson replied, "Steven, there are no dumb questions in this class. What you and the others have to say is important. Yes, I will review that again."

2. *Separate students from their actions; accept them for who they are rather than for how they act.* Ms. Barret received a student in her English class who was known to be one of the neighborhood gang leaders. Other teachers in the building kept telling Ms. Barret negative things about this student. Undaunted, Ms. Barret worked with and praised this student to further develop his outstanding writing ability.

Jenny, a first-grade student, continually hit other children on the playground. Mrs. Moore told Jenny, "I really like you and I'm glad you are in our class, but I don't like your behavior. You are not to hit other students."

3. *Encourage personal growth by providing students with choices and opportunities to initiate learning activities and establish goals.* Susan, a mildly handicapped fifth-grade student, was excited about moving into Mrs. Myers's class for language arts. Mrs. Myers used literature books for reading and had her students do a lot of writing. Susan loves to read and write. Mrs. Myers met privately with Susan before the class and explained the activity centers and the various reading and writing assignments. She told Susan to select those activities she felt most comfortable with at first. Then each week she could increase the number of activities to do.

A high school civics teacher gave his students a choice of participating in five different community projects. The students were to select a project and establish their own participation and completion schedule, according to what would work best with their daily personal and family commitments.

4. *Use contracts and allow students to evaluate their learning.* Mrs. Adams met with each student to develop contracts for completing a social studies unit. The contract included various readings from the class text, in-class activities, and assignments in the media center. When students completed the contract, they took a written test and wrote a report. They then graded their own test and met with Mrs. Adams to discuss the test, go over the report, and assign a grade to the overall unit.

A reading resource specialist worked with his students by developing contracts to complete several writing assignments. After the completion of each writing activity, students met with him to evaluate their work and to make a list of improvements to be incorporated into the next assignment.

5. *Facilitate learning by providing students with resources and encouragement.* A fifth-grade art teacher let his students select their own projects to complete during the last 6 weeks of school. He provided them with ample resources (e.g., clay, paint, chalk, paper, scissors) and encouraged them to work with the media they had liked best during the year. Then he moved about the room throughout the 6 weeks assisting and providing productive and positive input.

Mrs. Hagaman, a second-grade teacher, developed a unit on homes for animals. She divided her children into groups of three and let them select materials (e.g., blocks, sticks, yarn, glue) to create a make-believe animal and its home. While the students worked, she circulated in the classroom to check on progress and provide encouragement.

METATHEORETICAL MODELS AND METAPHORS

In this chapter, we have presented many important historical theories that have relevance to motivation. Being confronted with all these theories can seem overwhelming and create confusion about how they differ or which aspects are most useful in the study of motivation.

One way to distinguish theories is in terms of the larger metatheoretical models, or paradigms, of research that they reflect. Metatheoretical models offer a means of organizing theories and of understanding their basic assumptions. For example, theories may focus on overt behaviors and environmental factors as causes or more on underlying characteristics, cognitions, and affects of the individual.

Metatheoretical models also contain metaphors that can help us understand theoretical assumptions, concepts, and principles. A *metaphor* is a figure of speech with an implied comparison. A word or expression typically used in one fashion is applied in a different way. In the scenario at the beginning of the chapter, A. K.'s statement that Jim and Sara must think that students are puppets is an example of a metaphor. Metaphors are often used in science to explain unfamiliar phenomena (Leary, 1990). In the field of motivation, the metaphors have not always been precise so we need to be careful about applying them literally (Weiner, 1991). It also is true that the principles and assumptions of many theories seem to reflect more than one metaphor. A one-to-one correspondence between theory and metaphor is not always found.

In addition to providing a historical look at motivation, a second purpose of this chapter is to discuss the larger metatheoretical perspectives and metaphors that are relevant to motivation and relate them to historical views. In this section, we discuss three metatheoretical models, along with their associated metaphors, that seem to reflect the central assumptions of theoretical approaches to motivation. We will refer to these models as mechanistic, organismic, and contextual (Lerner, 1986; Overton, 1984). Table 2.2 highlights their central assumptions. We have categorized each of the theories discussed in this chapter as reflecting one of these three models; however, we will note that theories of motivation do not always neatly fit under one metatheoretical model but rather often share assumptions of two or more models. Freud's theory, for example, is mechanistic in that it treats bodily energy in a machinelike fashion, but it also is organismic because it discusses the development of personality processes.

Mechanistic Model

A fundamental assumption of the mechanistic metatheoretical model is that the laws of natural science (physics and chemistry) are the basic laws in the world and that ultimately everything is reducible to them. All matter is composed of atoms and molecules, so explanations of all phenomena involving matter eventually must include the functioning of atoms and molecules (Lerner, 1986). The mechanistic model is *reductionistic*. In a figurative sense, it contends that complex events can be reduced to simpler phenomena. Reductionism implies *continuity*. No new laws are needed to explain psychological events because they can be reduced to simpler events. Basic and advanced levels differ *quantitatively*. To move from a basic level to an advanced level, one simply adds more elements. Thus, the mechanistic model is an *additive* position because it holds that complex phenomena represent the summation of many basic phenomena.

The philosophical underpinnings of the mechanistic model predate the study of motivation and involve the mind-body problem, which referred to the question of whether there was one form of matter in the universe or two (body and mind). The body is physical and observable, whereas the mind is nonmaterial and nonobservable. If both forms exist, the question arises of how they relate to one another.

Prior to the writings of Darwin, a dualistic perspective including body and mind was used to explain human behavior, whereas a monistic system of only body was used to explain the actions of animals (Weiner, 1991). The prevalent

Table 2.2. Metatheoretical Models in the Study of Motivation

Model	Scientific perspective	Relation of complex behavior to simple behavior	Continuity between levels of behavior and stages of development	Metaphor used to explain behavior	Applicable theories
Mechanistic	Natural science: laws of natural science are basic laws of the world	Reductionistic (complex behaviors can be broken into simpler ones), additive (behaviors sum to form more complex ones)	Behavior change and development proceed in continuous fashion, levels differ quantitatively	Machine	Freudian, conditioning, drive, purposive behaviorism
Organismic	Human development: progressive changes in organisms	Nonreductionistic (complex events cannot be broken into simpler ones), multiplicative (behaviors combine to form behaviors more complex than the sum of the parts)	Behavior change and development proceed in discontinuous fashion, levels differ qualitatively	Living, growing organism (plant)	Volition/will, instincts, trait
Contextual	Interactionist: relation of person to environment	Nonreductionist and multiplicative	Mostly discontinuous	Historical event	Arousal, field, cognitive consistency, humanistic

philosophical view was that people were created by God in God's image, were rational, and possessed a soul. People had a body that served as the source of desires, but these could be controlled by the mind. Animals, in contrast, had no soul and no mind, so a monistic view could be applied to explain behavior. Behavior was a function of external stimuli (e.g., cold temperature) or internal reflexes (e.g., hunger).

This conception changed when Darwin proposed that humans and animals differed in degree along an evolutionary continuum rather than in kind. Applying a dualistic perspective to human behavior and a monistic one to animal behavior became less feasible because humans also were assumed to react to external stimuli and internal reflexes. Thus, use of a monistic system to explain all human and animal behavior became more widely adopted.

A metaphor often applied to the mechanistic model is that of a machine (Overton, 1984; Weiner, 1991). As we mentioned earlier, a metaphor relates in a relatively surprising and occasionally dramatic fashion two items that are not usually conceptualized as similar (McReynolds, 1990). Because they relate new material to what we already know by casting one thing in terms of something else, metaphors help us understand phenomena (Leary, 1990). Metaphors are common in everyday language (e.g., He had butterflies in his stomach., Love makes the world go 'round., She really blew her stack.), in literature, sport, the arts, and so forth.

The machine metaphor seems highly appropriate for the mechanistic model. Physics and chemistry are machinelike sciences because they involve physical laws at fundamental levels of analysis. Machines are reductionistic in that complex functions can be reduced to simpler operations. There is continuity because no new principles are needed to explain more complex operations. Machines also differ quantitatively. Functions can be added to provide greater complexity.

To apply the machine metaphor to people we would say that they display many of the qualities of machines in terms of input, operation, and output. Important components of machines are that they have parts and a structure, there is a desired function and the parts operate to achieve this function, actions are involuntary and performed without conscious awareness, reactions to stimuli are necessary and predetermined, and there is an interchange of force and energy such that the system stays in equilibrium (Overton, 1984; Weiner, 1991).

In the introductory teacher scenario, Jim Osgood uses a machine metaphor because he implies that people respond to forces from the environment much like machines respond to the forces that act on them (e.g., temperature, pressure, electrical current). Neither A. K. Buerso nor Sara Wylie agrees with Jim on this characterization and they suggest different perspectives for viewing students.

Among the theories we review in this chapter that reflect the mechanistic model are Freudian theory, conditioning theories, drive theories, and purposive behaviorism. Freud's theory is mechanistic because it deals with the distribution of energy in a machinelike fashion (i.e., it is dissipated or transformed via repression). We noted earlier that there is overlap of theories among categories and Freud's theory offers a good example. This theory also is organismic because it emphasizes inner processes that seem to unfold and over which individuals may have little control. We group it here as mechanistic because that theme captures its predominant characteristics.

Conditioning theories are mechanistic because they postulate a reductionistic, continuous, and additive view of behavior. Complex behavior can be reduced to many simple behaviors. Behavior change is continuous and takes place when behaviors are combined in additive fashion. Drive theories reflect a mechanistic orientation because they view the body as a machine and drives as the machinelike processes that keep the body in proper condition (homeostasis). Although Tolman's purposive behaviorism introduces cognitive processes into the theoretical formulation and is contextual in the sense that it emphasizes that behavior must be interpreted in light of goals, it remains a mechanistic theory that postulates behavioral responses to stimuli largely in machinelike fashion.

Organismic Model

A second general metatheoretical model, or paradigm, of scientific research is the organismic model (Overton, 1984). Proponents of this model reject the assumptions of the mechanistic model that phenomena can be reduced to simpler elements and that change occurs through the addition of elements. Rather, the organismic model assumes that changes in organisms often are qualitative and cannot be reduced to previous behavior. This is especially true in the area of human development, where new cognitive, physical, and social capabilities appear suddenly and bear little resemblance to previous capabilities. Lerner (1986) points out, for example, that one-year-old children display many behaviors that can be explained by stimulus-response associations. By the time children turn two, however, they have begun to develop a language capability that allows them to engage in actions they could not have performed earlier (e.g., imitate actions long after observing them). The capability for symbolic representation helps to explain many actions. Trying to reduce complex behaviors to a summation of simpler behaviors is inappropriate.

The organismic view is a discontinuous position because it assumes that changes can emerge suddenly and do not smoothly emanate from earlier behaviors. Some theorists within this tradition posit stages or phases that individuals pass through. The stages are characterized as qualitatively distinct from one another. This perspective also stresses the quality of actions and not simply the quantity (e.g., rate, frequency, likelihood). Rather than being additive, the organismic model is multiplicative. The impetus for change is activity. People interact with their environments and help to construct meanings of events. Subjective activity is critically important. New complex behaviors arise that are not simply the sum of preexisting basic behaviors.

An appropriate metaphor for this model is that of a living, growing organism like a plant (Overton, 1984). Plants grow and develop but the course of growth is uneven. Sudden growth spurts occur, followed by slower growth. Some changes are quantitative (e.g., leaves become larger), but many are qualitative (buds appear, followed by flowers and then seeds). A fully grown plant is not simply a larger version of a tiny seedling. With regard to people, similar changes occur in the areas of cognitive, linguistic, social, and emotional development.

In the opening scenario, A. K. espouses an organismic position because of her emphasis on students' predispositions and how characteristics emerge over time. Theories covered in this chapter that reflect organismic assumptions include volition/will, instincts, and trait theories. The volition/will theories of Wundt, James, and Ach are organismic in that they assume an unfolding of inner processes that may proceed without conscious awareness or direct human control. With their emphasis on inner propensities and dispositions, instinct theories are organismic in orientation. Trait theories stress the energizing role of inner motives, which, although not necessarily instinctual in nature, are internal mechanisms that develop and change in ways that are not entirely predictable from environmental events.

Contextual Model

A third general model is a *contextual* model that represents a compromise between the mechanistic and organismic positions (Lerner, 1986). This view accepts underlying organismic patterns of change but contends that environmental conditions play a greater role in such change than is admitted in a strict organismic position. Students may become developmentally ready to display new competencies, but unless the environmental conditions are conducive, the behaviors will not be displayed. Whereas the mechanistic model stresses the environment and the organismic model emphasizes the individual, the contextual model places importance on the individual in relation to, or in dynamic interaction with, the environment (Overton, 1984). This view shares many of the assumptions of the organismic model: nonreductionistic, nonadditive, and discontinuous.

An appropriate metaphor for this model is that of a historical event. Historical events do not operate in isolation; to understand events, one must know something about the dispositions of the principal individuals involved and the situation prevailing at the time. Wars, for example, are complex events. To understand the causes of a war, one must have knowledge about the leaders of countries that become involved in the war and the prevailing historical, political, economic, and social conditions. Further, an event in one domain (e.g., economics) will affect other areas (politics, daily living). Change is constant and each change produces other changes. Developmentally inspired changes in individuals affect the kinds of situations in which they find themselves, and, in turn, environmental events can stimulate developmental growth.

In the opening scenario, Sara presents a contextualistic perspective because she states that although students may have predisposing attributes, their emergence depends largely on environmental factors. Theoretical positions reflecting contextualistic assumptions are arousal, field, cognitive consistency, and humanistic theories.

Arousal theories are contextual because they highlight the interpretation of arousal in light of environmental cues or cognitive processes. There is some organismic emphasis (e.g., optimal level of arousal), but the context is essential for understanding motivation. With its emphasis on the interaction among forces within people and their environments, field theory is a highly contextual orientation. Cognitive consistency theories are contextual because efforts to restore balance or reduce dissonance depend on a person's level of cognitive development, prior experiences, and cues in the present situation; balance is not achieved automatically but is context specific. Humanistic theories are contextual because they view behavior in holistic fashion and contend that to understand people we must interpret behavior in light of personal attributes (e.g., feelings, values, thoughts) and present circumstances.

This model seems highly relevant to education. There is much emphasis today on providing experiences for students that are developmentally appropriate for their present competencies. Cognitive growth will not occur if experiences are too advanced for students. Motivation similarly suffers if material is too basic and covers skills that students already possess. By providing appropriate experiences, teachers can help facilitate cognitive, physical, and social growth in students.

In subsequent chapters, we refer to these models and metaphors to help organize general theories and approaches to motivation. We believe this approach will give readers a more unified understanding of the field of motivation than if we simply summarized theories without attempting to relate them to broader perspectives or to one another.

SUMMARY

In this chapter, we summarize some historical perspectives on motivation. Many early theories are behavioral in the sense that they define motivation in terms of overt actions and look for causes in the environment. Contemporary views tend to be cognitive, which means they examine the underlying mental processes involved in motivation and how these are affected by personal and environmental factors.

At the start of the twentieth century, motivation was not a separate field of study as it is today. Early views of motivation defined it in terms of will (desire, want, purpose) and volition (act of using the will). Another early perspective stressed the role of instincts or innate properties that manifested themselves in behavior. In the field of psychotherapy, Freud conceived of motivation in terms of psychical energy.

Learning theory perspectives are relevant to motivation. Conditioning theories emphasize the association of stimuli with responses. Prominent conditioning theories are Thorndike's connectionism, Pavlov's classical conditioning, and Skinner's operant conditioning. Drive theories stress internal forces that seek to maintain homeostasis, or optimal states of bodily mechanisms. Drive theories were formulated by Woodworth, Hull, Spence, Mowrer, and Miller. Tolman broke from the behaviorist tradition and stressed purposive behaviorism, or the goal directedness of behavior. His views on expectancies and latent learning were important precursors of cognitive theories.

Several theories construe motivation in terms of level of emotional arousal. The James-Lange theory contends that emotion is a consequence of behavior and involves perceptions of responses to arousing situations. Theories by Hebb and Berlyne postulate the importance of an optimal level of arousal for bodily functioning. Schachter proposed that emotion involves physiological arousal and a cognitive attribution.

Field theory was an important early cognitive view of behavior that emphasized the conflicting forces in people's lives. This dynamic view postulates motivation as a mechanism for preserving or restoring homeostasis. Cognitive consistency theories also are homeostatic and assume that motivation results from relations between behaviors and cognitions. Heider's balance theory and Festinger's cognitive dissonance theory are cognitive consistency theories.

Psychological trait and humanistic theories take a different stance on motivation. These theories focus on innate, qualitative differences in psychological processes that emerge with experience and development. Allport proposed a functional autonomy of motives in which motives grow out of antecedent systems but with development become independent of them. Allport's ideas are reflected in many humanistic theories. Carl Rogers formulated a well-known humanistic theory and founded the client-centered school of psychotherapy. Rogers believed that the central motivating force in people's lives is the actualizing tendency, or the ongoing process of personal growth and achieving wholeness. People have a need for positive regard and self-regard, and a critical element in developing these is receiving unconditional positive regard. With respect to education, Rogers wrote that the teacher's job consists of facilitating learning by arranging resources, helping students clarify goals, and establishing a climate of positive regard. Rogers's theory suggests the use of contracts, inquiry methods, and opportunities for self-evaluation.

Theories of motivation can be organized into larger frameworks that reflect their central assumptions. These models, or paradigms, of research have defining characteristics and metaphors used to explain behavior. The mechanistic model reflects the laws of science, is reductionistic and additive, posits continuous changes in behavior, and is exemplified by a machine metaphor. The organismic model derives from principles of human development, is nonreductionistic and nonadditive (multiplicative), assumes that changes are discontinuous, and is exemplified by a growing organism metaphor. The contextual model is based on an interaction between person and environment, is nonreductionistic and nonadditive, posits that most changes are discontinuous, and is characterized by a historical event metaphor. Contextualism is becoming increasingly influential in the field of motivation.

The Role of Expectancy and Self-Efficacy Beliefs

Several junior high students have the following conversation during lunch.

Kevin: *How are you doing in social studies? Did you think the test we just did was too easy?*

Rachel: *Well, not really. It's more just boring. I mean, who cares about what happened 300 years ago? That has nothing to do with my life.*

Kevin: *Really? I like it. It's interesting. I think what happened before does matter today, plus I'm really good at it. I think I did well on the test today. I always think that I'll do well in social studies because I always get a good grade on the tests and the reports we have to do. I've been getting good grades in social studies ever since elementary school. I might even major in social studies when I go to college.*

Sam: *Yuck, are you kidding? What a nerd! I hate it! I never seem to do well on those tests. I'm sure I flunked this one. All those true/false questions, they just confuse me. I think the teachers just make those up to trick us. Plus, do you know how hard it is to write a report? I can never think of what to say. It's too hard. I just end up copying out of the book. I'd rather play soccer. I'm really good at that. I'm not good at social studies.*

Rachel: *I hate sports, too. I'm not good at social studies or sports.*

Kevin: *Well, I'm not too good at soccer. I never do well at that, but I'm pretty good at baseball.*

At the same time, several teachers are talking in the faculty lounge.

Mr. Dearborn: *I always have a hard time getting the kids to understand photosynthesis. No matter what I do, it doesn't seem to make a difference. They just don't get it. I even expect them to have a hard time with it.*

Ms. Morgan: *Yes, that is a hard topic. I'm not sure I understand it myself, but at least you have all the top kids. I have the lower kids and you know how tough they are to handle. I just can't seem to get control of them, especially the sixth hour. It's the end of the day and we're all tired and I can't seem to get them under control. I just*

	don't think I can manage those kids, let alone teach them complex things like photosynthesis.
Ms. Rivera:	*I have some of those same low kids and I don't have that many problems with them. I have my system set up and they know I mean business and they don't dare fool around with me. I can handle just about any kid, no matter who it is or what time of day. I know it's hard, but I make sure that they understand who is boss. I never have management problems.*
Ms. Morgan:	*Well, it's easy for you. You've been doing this a lot longer than I. I'm still trying to figure out my system, get my units and lessons together, and actually teach. It's a lot harder than I thought it would be.*
Mr. Dearborn:	*Well, don't worry, you'll figure it out. I remember my first few years of teaching, I thought I would never be able to do it. I had no confidence in my ability to manage a classroom. I used to wake up every morning all anxious and worried about the day and wonder if I would get through it without a major disaster. I used to visualize all sorts of bad things happening in my rooms: fights, kids throwing things at me, everyone standing up and telling me to get lost. I look back now and realize how ridiculous some of those thoughts were. Eventually, I got more confidence in myself and figured out ways to manage my room. Now, I only worry about my instruction and the kids' understanding. The management stuff takes care of itself.*

These students and teachers are concerned with their ability to succeed at a task, whether they have the skills or knowledge to do well, and what they expect will happen if they do attempt to do the task. All of these individuals are discussing, in one way or another, a central construct in many motivation theories—the role of expectancy beliefs. The concept of expectancy represents the key idea that most individuals will not choose to do a task or continue to engage in a task when they expect to fail. They may be interested in and value a task, but if they try a task and experience repeated failure, then eventually they will not engage in the task. Accordingly, whereas most lay views of motivation stress that interest or value are the most important aspects of motivation (e.g., see Rachel's statement about not being interested in social studies vs. Kevin's statement of interest), most formal motivational models stress that the expectancy construct is very important. In fact, much of the empirical research in achievement motivation situations has focused on the role of the expectancy construct, not the value or interest constructs (Parsons & Goff, 1978).

HISTORICAL PERSPECTIVES ON THE EXPECTANCY CONSTRUCT

The use of the expectancy construct springs from a general cognitive perspective on motivation and reflects the cognitive metaphor of the individual as an active and rational decision maker in contrast to earlier behavioral models of motivation. However, even early on in experimental psychology, there were behavioral psychologists who stressed the cognitive nature of learning and utilized the expectancy construct in their models. For example, Tolman (1932) proposed that rewards did not just "stamp in" associations between stimuli and behavior, but that even animals learn expectancies about what will happen to them if they perform a certain behavior. They then come to expect the reward (or punishment) when they engage in the behavior in the situation. For Tolman, this cognitive notion of expectancy replaced the mechanistic concept of habit from Hullian drive models (Weiner, 1992).

As part of this general shift from mechanistic, behavioral models to more organismic, cognitive models, there was less of a conceptual need for postulating some *instigator* or *energizer* of behavior (i.e., an instinct, a drive, a need, a habit). When concerned with a rat in a maze, there is a place for thinking about what motivates the rat to run the maze. However, once a general cognitive model is proposed that assumes that humans are innately active learners, constantly seeking to learn and adapt to their environment (White, 1959), then the problem of what motivates behavior is not an issue, but the issue of directionality becomes paramount. Accordingly, cognitive motivational theories became concerned with how individuals make decisions about which goals or paths they will choose to pursue, about the direction in which they will focus their innate energy, curiosity, and activity.

Lewin (Lewin, Dembo, Festinger, & Sears, 1944) proposed that the construct of *level of aspiration* could capture this decision-making process. Level of aspiration is defined as the goal or standard that individuals set for themselves in a task, based on past experience and familiarity with the task. The traditional research paradigm that was used to assess level of aspiration was the ringtoss game in which individuals were asked to toss rings over a peg while standing at different distances from the peg. Distances further away from the peg were given more value because they obviously made the task more difficult. The subjects were given some experience with the game (usually 10 trials) and then asked to state their goal for the next 10 trials (How many are you going to try to get over the peg in the next 10 trials?). The combination of different distances and values allowed the experimenter and subject to estimate both expectancy (probability of success for a toss) and value (distance from peg).

A great deal of empirical research was done using this level-of-aspiration paradigm and several important findings emerged (Weiner, 1992). First, subjects were most likely to feel successful when they met the goals they set for themselves (subjective goal or level), not the actual objective level of attainment (e.g., five successful tosses). This type of situation occurs in the classroom when two different students get the same good grade of 85 out of 100 points on a test (same objective level of attainment), but one student is quite unhappy with the grade because of expectations of a higher grade, whereas the other student, who had a lower level of aspiration, is quite content with the grade. A second general finding was that level of aspiration was related to prior experience with the task and that prior success generally led to increases in level of aspiration, but failure usually decreased level of aspiration. Finally, the research found that there were individual and group differences in level of aspiration. Subjects high in ability tended to set higher aspirations than those low in ability. In addition, subjects were influenced by group goals and performance and would adjust their level of aspiration to the group norms (Weiner, 1992).

Building on these general constructs of expectancy and level of aspiration from Tolman and Lewin, Atkinson's (1957, 1964) model of achievement motivation attempted to combine the constructs of needs, expectancy, and value into a comprehensive theory. His model proposed that behavior was a multiplicative function of these three components, which he labeled *motives*, *probability for success*, and *incentive value*. Motives represented learned but stable and enduring individual differences or dispositions and included two basic achievement motives: to seek success (need for achievement or motive to approach success) and to fear failure (motive to avoid failure). These motives are affective in nature but do include an aspect of expectancy in terms of emotional anticipation (Covington, 1992). The motive for success was assumed to represent individuals' hope for or anticipation of success and reflect their "capacity to experience pride in accomplishment" (Atkinson, 1964, p. 214). If the motive for success was high, then individuals would likely approach and engage in achievement tasks. In contrast, the motive to avoid failure represents individuals' capacity to experience shame and humiliation when they fail, and when the motive is high, this would lead individuals to avoid engaging in achievement tasks.

In the voluminous research on this model, the motive for success was usually measured using the Thematic Apperception Test, TAT (Atkinson, 1958; McClelland, Atkinson, Clark, & Lowell, 1953), a projective test where individuals are asked to tell stories about a set of pictures they are shown. The pictures display people at everyday tasks (e.g., two men in a machine shop) and the stories are scored for achievement imagery (e.g., The two men are working on a new invention that will change the industry.). In contrast, the motive to avoid failure was usually measured using the Test Anxiety Questionnaire, TAQ (Mandler & Sarason, 1952), which is a more objective self-report measurement that asks people to rate their anxiety and worry about testing situations (e.g., "While taking an intelligence test, to what extent do you worry?"). The TAT has been criticized for problems of reliability and validity, although a recent meta-analysis of research on the TAT and questionnaire measures of need for achievement suggests that both types of measures show approximately the same relation to actual behavior (Spangler, 1992). There continues to be development and research on the use of the TAT and other more objective measures of the need for achievement (Smith, 1992).

In Atkinson's original model, these two motives were assumed to be orthogonal to one another, although most subsequent research usually examined the motive for success and operated as if there was a single continuum anchored by high motive for success on one end and high motive to avoid failure on the other end. Covington (1992) has suggested that the original model based on the independence of these two motives provides a more comprehensive picture of different approaches to achievement. If the two motives are conceptualized as orthogonal, a two-by-two matrix is created with four cells generated to describe four different approaches to achievement (Covington, 1992; Covington & Omelich, 1991; Covington & Roberts, 1994). This quadripolar model suggests that there are four general types of students and ways of approaching achievement tasks: success oriented, failure avoiders, overstrivers, and failure accepters (see Figure 3.1).

The *success-oriented* student who is high in motive for success and low in fear of failure would be highly engaged in achievement activities and not be anxious or worried by performance. In Chapter 1, Sharon represents this type of student because she achieves at a high level and does not worry or become anxious about doing well. A student who is a *failure avoider*, high in fear of failure and low in motive for success, would be very anxious and attempt to avoid failure by procrastinating and using other self-handicapping strategies (Covington, 1992; Garcia & Pintrich, 1994). This type of student would be very

Figure 3.1. A quadripolar model of need for achievement

From "Self-worth and College Achievement" by M. V. Covington and B. Roberts in *Student Motivation, Cognition, and Learning* (p. 160) edited by P. R. Pintrich, D. R. Brown, and C. E. Weinstein, 1994, Hillsdale, NJ: Erlbaum. Copyright © 1994 by Lawrence Erlbaum Associates. Adapted by permission.

		Motive to Approach Success	
		Low	*High*
Motive to **Avoid Failure**	*Low*	Failure acceptors	Success-oriented students
	High	Failure avoiders	Overstrivers

reluctant to even engage in academic achievement work. These two types are the most often researched and described by a simple continuum between the two motives.

The off-diagonal cells in the quadripolar model, however, suggest that there are two other types of students (Covington, 1992). *Overstrivers* are students who are high in both motives; they try to approach success but simultaneously fear failure greatly. These students work very hard at achievement tasks but also feel very anxious and stressed because of their fear of failure. In more social cognitive terms, these students are similar to defensive pessimists (Garcia & Pintrich, 1994; Norem & Cantor, 1986). Overstrivers are students who almost always do well in class, but are constantly asking the teacher about their grade and show signs of anxiety and worry about doing well. Finally, Covington labels the students who are low in both motives as *failure accepters*. These students are basically indifferent to achievement, although this indifference may be due either to lack of concern and caring or active anger and resistance to achievement values, as some have suggested is the case for minority students (Covington, 1992).

These two motives (to succeed and to avoid failure) represented the internal and personal contribution to motivation. Atkinson also included expectancy and value constructs in his model that represented the environmental side of the equation because they were assumed to be more closely tied to the situation or task. In Atkinson's model, his expectancy construct was very similar to Tolman's idea about the formation of expectancies regarding the associations between responses and rewards. In Atkinson's model and research, he used human subjects, not rats, so the construct was more cognitive in nature and reflected a person's subjective belief about the probability of success. Expectancy (or probability) for success was often measured using the same ringtoss method as developed by Lewin (e.g., How many rings will you be able to get on the peg?) or by giving subjects a set of puzzles and asking them to estimate how many they would be able to solve (Weiner, 1992). These subjective beliefs about expectancy for success, although certainly reflecting an individual's own beliefs, also were assumed to represent one of the *environmental* influences on motivation because they could reflect task difficulty (e.g., how far away from the peg the person stood, normative information about how many puzzles others solved). In this sense, the model tried to take into consideration external factors, although it is still basically an organismic model focused on the individual.

The third component of motivation in Atkinson's model was the incentive value of success. Incentive value of success was defined as an affect, specifically, pride in accomplishment. For example, the incentive value of receiving an A in a difficult course would be higher (more pride experienced) than the same grade in an easy course (Weiner, 1992). The incentive value of success was assumed to be inversely related to the probability of success (incentive value = 1.0 − probability of success). For example, as the expectation for success went up, as in an easy task, the incentive value would go down because it was assumed that the person would not value succeeding at an easy task. In the same way, for a difficult task where probability of success is low, the incentive value would be high. In Atkinson's model, incentive value was an affect, but in more general uses of the value construct, it has become a belief about the attainment value, importance, or interest in a task (Eccles, 1983). Nevertheless, the inverse relation between value and expectancy still may be applicable. For example, people may value certain careers or professions more highly and assign them more prestige and salary because of the perceived difficulty of attaining them (Weiner, 1992).

Given the inverse relation between incentive value and the probability of success, Atkinson's mathematical model predicts that motivation will be highest when tasks are of an intermediate level of difficulty. When the probability of success is .5 (the person will succeed at the task about half the time), then the incentive value of success also will be .5 (incentive value = 1.0 − .5, which is the value for probability of success). The product of multiplying the probability of success by the incentive value (as in all expectancy-value models) is greatest at this intermediate level (e.g., .5 × .5 = .25) in comparison to other conditions. For example, suppose that the probability of success is .1 (the student will succeed only 1 time out of 10), then incentive value will be high for such a difficult task (1.0 − .1 = .9) and the multiplicative product of these two numbers (.1 × .9 = .09) is lower than the number generated at the intermediate level of difficulty (.25). This is true for all values of probability of success and incentive value given the assumed inverse relation between probability of success and incentive value.

This generalization that motivation is highest at levels of intermediate task difficulty is one of the most often cited findings from achievement motivation research. Variations on this generalization are represented in behavioral theories such as Gagné's, which suggested that instruction should be designed to be within several steps of a student's prior level of competence (Gagné, 1985). Of course, in applications of Piagetian theory, it was suggested that students should only be taught concepts that were representative of the next immediate stage (+1 modeling/instruction), not concepts that were more than one stage above the students' current level. More recently, we have seen a great deal of interest in applying Vygotsky's concept of the zone of proximal development, which also represents the notion that instruction should be designed to be just beyond the students' current level of development, not too difficult to be far outside the students' capabilities or too easy to be repetitive for the students (Vygotsky, 1978). Although these theories are not conceptualized as motivational theories and tend to downplay or ignore the role of motivational constructs, the general principle that learning will be fostered when students are working at a task that is somewhat beyond their range of current capability fits with these cognitive theories as well as with most motivational theories. The real challenge is determining the students' current capabilities and the most propaedeutic difficulty level of the academic task.

Weiner (1992) summarizes the motivational research on this generalization regarding an intermediate level of difficulty and concludes that the laboratory research on task choice and persistence is supportive. However, he does note that in Atkinson's model, the third determinant of motivation, the motives for success and fear of failure, plays an important role beyond the expectancy and value components. Atkinson's model predicts that individuals high in the motive for success and low in fear of failure (what he called "high need for achievement") will be most likely to choose tasks of intermediate difficulty, whereas individuals who are high in fear failure and low in the hope for success (what he called "low need for achievement") will choose very easy or very difficult tasks. In the latter case, for individuals high in fear of failure, a choice of a very easy task ensures success, thereby minimizing fear of failure. The choice of very difficult tasks by individuals high in fear of failure does not maximize the fear of failure because there is the expectation that very few people can succeed at the most difficult tasks. Atkinson's model and reasoning here is based on the general hedonic principle of maximizing positive affect and minimizing negative affect (Weiner, 1992). However, the actual empirical findings do not support the differential predictions for individuals high in fear of failure. It appears that most people, regardless of their motives for success and failure, choose tasks of intermediate difficulty, although there is a tendency for individuals high in the motive for success to choose intermediate tasks more often than those high in fear of failure (Weiner, 1992).

Weiner and others (e.g., Trope, 1975) suggest that this choice of intermediate tasks can be explained in terms of an informational principle rather than the hedonic principle. They suggest that choosing tasks of intermediate difficulty provides the most information to individuals about their own effort and capabilities (too easy and too difficult tasks provide more information about the task than the individual). This information about personal capabilities is useful for self-evaluation and, in the long run, accurate self-information is functional and adaptive (Weiner, 1992). In any event, the finding of very little differential choice of tasks by motives and of a larger role for expectancy for success and incentive value suggests that these more cognitive and environmental constructs might be more important than the stable personality dispositions of motives.

In sum, the early research on expectancy constructs was important because of the focus on cognition and beliefs in contrast to overt behavior and the related constructs of drives, needs, and habits. These theories and models moved motivational psychology away from a dependence on a simplistic S-R psychology to a more rational and cognitive paradigm that is still dominant today. Moreover, these early cognitive models of motivation stressed the importance of the individual's perceptions and beliefs as mediators of behavior, thereby focusing motivational research on the subjective and phenomenological psychology of the individual. In particular, these early models developed the distinction between beliefs about being able to do the task (probability and expectancy for success) and beliefs about the importance, value, and desire to do the task (motives, incentive value) and posited that it is the combination of the two that results in motivated behavior. Accordingly, we may feel capable of doing a task, but if we do not value it, then we will be less likely to engage in it. In the same way, we may value a task, but if we do not feel able to do it and expect to fail, we will be less likely to engage in the task. Current research on expectancy and value constructs continue in this tradition of focusing on these two general beliefs of the individual, although they do attempt to include contextual influences in their models. In the remainder of this chapter, we will discuss students' expectancy beliefs: their perceptions of their ability to perform a task. Chapter 8 covers students' value beliefs.

CURRENT PERSPECTIVES ON THE EXPECTANCY CONSTRUCT

Although there are many current motivational theories that include some type of expectancy construct, we will focus on three general approaches that reflect current research programs that are based on academic achievement in classroom settings. The first model comes from the work of Eccles and Wigfield and their colleagues (e.g., Eccles, 1983; Eccles et al., 1989; Wigfield, 1994; Wigfield & Eccles, 1992) and is derived from and bears the closest resemblance to the early expectancy-value models of Lewin and Atkinson (for other current expectancy-value models, see Heckhausen, 1977; Pekrun, 1993). This cognitive model focuses on the role of students' expectancies for academic success and their perceived value for academic tasks and springs from a general organismic perspective based in personality and social psychology. A second related model is the research on the development of children's perceptions of competence (e.g., Harter, 1982, 1985a; Phillips & Zimmerman, 1990; Stipek, 1981). This model also derives from a general organismic perspective that focuses on the role of the individual but has a more cognitive developmental flavor, reflecting its roots in the early writings of White (1959) on competence and motivation. Finally, the third model to be discussed concerns the application of self-efficacy theory to achievement situations. Bandura (1986) has proposed a general social cognitive model of cognition and behavior that has been applied to many different domains of human behavior (e.g., depression, phobias, sports, decision making in organizations) as well as achievement contexts. Schunk (1991b) has been the most prominent researcher on the application of the self-efficacy construct in achievement contexts. Although this model focuses on the individual as in the other two organismic models, it also represents a somewhat more mechanistic metatheoretical perspective, reflecting its development from social learning theory.

A Recent Model of the Expectancy-for-Success Construct

A model that is a direct descendent from Atkinson's expectancy-value model is the one developed by Eccles and Wigfield and their colleagues (Eccles, 1983; Wigfield & Eccles, 1992). A somewhat simplified version of their elaborate model is displayed in Figure 3.2. It is clear from the figure that the two most important predictors of achievement behavior are expectancy and task value. It is important to note that these are basically two of the three components specified in Atkinson's model. In Atkinson's model, the expectancy construct was called probability for success and the task value construct was labeled incentive value. Reflecting a social cognitive and more situational approach and in line with the findings that motives don't differentially predict task choice, the current model does not include the stable and enduring personality constructs of motives for success and fear of failure. In the Eccles and Wigfield version, task value has a much more important and differentiated role to play than just being the inverse of probability for success as in Atkinson's original model. However, we will defer discussion of the task value component and the goals that lead into task value until Chapter 8. In this chapter, we will focus on the expectancy component and the constructs that lead into it.

As can be seen in Figure 3.2, achievement behavior is predicted by two general components: expectancy and value. These constructs are within the dashed lines in the figure to represent the fact that they are internal, cognitive beliefs of the individual in contrast to the achievement behaviors, which are overt and observable. In colloquial terms, the value construct refers to a student's response to the question, Why should I do this task? Responses would include those having to do with goals (I want to become a doctor.), values (I think biology is useful.), and interests (I'm interested in this topic.). Rachel's expressions of boredom and lack of care about social studies and "hate" for soccer are expressions of value beliefs. In contrast, the expectancy construct refers to the question, Am I able to do this task? (Eccles, 1983; Pintrich, 1988a, 1988b; Wigfield, 1994; Wigfield & Eccles, 1992). In Figure 3.2, expectancy refers to actual beliefs of students about their future expectancy for success; that is, whether they believe that they will do well on an upcoming test or some future event. In our example, Kevin expects to do well in social studies, whereas Sam and Rachel do not expect to do as well. This construct is usually measured by asking students to predict how well they will do in the future on some task or in some domain (see Table 3.1). Accordingly, expectancy for success is more future oriented than simple self-perceptions of competence. In a great deal of research by Eccles and Wigfield (as well as many others), higher expectancies for success are positively related to all types of achievement behavior, including achievement, choice, and persistence (Eccles, 1983; Wigfield, 1994; Wigfield & Eccles, 1992).

Referring again to the model in Figure 3.2, the next two expectancy components include students' task-specific self-concept and their perceptions of task difficulty. The self-concept belief represents students' perceptions of their com-

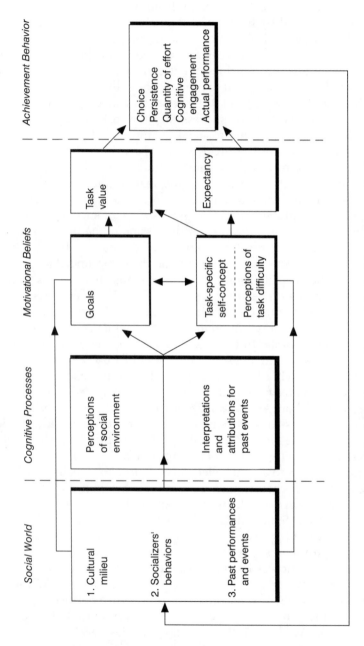

Figure 3.2. A social cognitive expectancy-value model of achievement motivation
Material drawn from Eccles et al. (1983)

petence in different domains; it is their evaluation of their ability to do a task currently (in contrast to the future orientation of expectancy for success). Eccles and Wigfield are careful to note that these self-concept beliefs can be relatively domain specific and may vary by subject area in school contexts (see also Harter, 1983, 1985a; Marsh, 1989, 1990b).

Task perceptions concern students' judgments of the difficulty of the task (not unlike Lewin's and Atkinson's models). Again, Eccles and Wigfield assume that these task difficulty perceptions are relatively domain specific. Although they have not explicitly discussed the nature of the domain boundaries, in their own empirical work they have used general school subject areas (e.g., English, math, science) as their operationalization of the domain, not unlike other self-concept researchers such as Harter and Marsh. Of course, they would allow that there may be even more domain specificity in these beliefs that could influence achievement (e.g., differential self-concept and task difficulty beliefs for algebra vs. geometry vs. calculus), but more research is needed on the level of specificity for conceptualizing domains. Specificity of domains is one of the biggest issues that needs to be resolved for any cognitive or motivational theory that proposes domain specificity of constructs. What are the boundaries of a domain and at what level—the individual task level; the project, unit, or topic level; the course level; the discipline level—do we need to specify them?

Regardless of the domain issue, the general model proposes that self-concept beliefs and task difficulty beliefs are then considered together to produce an expectancy judgment. So, for example, Kevin has a belief that he is good in social studies and that it is not that difficult a task; hence, he has high expectations for social studies. Sam, on the other hand, has a lower self-perception of his competence and thinks that social studies tasks (writing reports) are hard and, therefore, has a lower expectancy for success for future social studies tasks. Table 3.1 provides some examples of how self-concept and task difficulty perceptions are measured in this expectancy-value model.

These beliefs are influenced by two other variables in the model (see Figure 3.2). One includes another cognitive and internal process concerning how students perceive and interpret different events that happen to them. In particular, this interpretative process is driven by the types of attributions a student makes for events and actual performance. Attributions are crucial to the formation of self-perceptions of competence and expectancies and are the focus of Chapter 4 so they are not discussed here. However, it is important to note that in keeping with a general cognitive and constructivist approach, this model assumes that students' perceptions of competence and task difficulty and subsequent expectancies for success are influenced by how students perceive their social environment and what happens to them as they move through it. The other variable that influences students' beliefs is the actual culture and environment, including the general cultural and societal milieu; the nature of the students' interactions with parents, peers, and other adults (e.g., teachers); and their past performance and achievements. These final influences are represented on the far left of Figure 3.2 outside the dashed lines

Table 3.1. Different Self-Report Items Used to Measure Various Expectancy Constructs

Expectancy Constructs From Expectancy-Value Theory (Eccles, Wigfield, et al.)	Perceptions of Competence (Harter)	Self-Efficacy Beliefs (Schunk)
Rated on a 5- or 7-point Likert scale.	Harter uses a 1–4-point, forced choice scale. Children choose one side (positive statement) or the other side (negative statement) and then within that side choose a number (1,2) or (3,4).	Rated on a 0–100-point scale, 0 is no confidence in ability to do task, 100 is 100% confidence to perform task.
Expectancy for success	I remember things easily.	Shows students examples of actual arithmetic problems they will solve, so children are rating their efficacy to perform a very specific task.
How well do you think you will do on your next math test?	I'm good at schoolwork.	
Compared to other students, how well do you expect to do in math this year?	I finish my schoolwork quickly.	
How well do you think you'll do in your math course next year?	I'm just as smart as other children.	
How well do you think you will do in an advanced math course like calculus?	I understand what I read.	
	I can figure out the answers to schoolwork.	
Task-specific self-concept		
How good at math are you?		
If you were to rank all the students in your math class from worst to best, where would you put yourself?		
Compared to most of your other subjects, how good are you at math?		
How have you been doing in math this year?		
Perceptions of task difficulty		
Compared to most of your other subjects, how difficult is math for you?		

because they are assumed to be external to the student. As noted in the figure, these influences can have a direct effect on children's self-concepts and task difficulty beliefs (a direct arrow), but their main effect is mediated by the students' perceptions and interpretations of these environmental influences.

In a series of large-scale correlational field studies, Eccles and Wigfield and their colleagues (Eccles, 1983; Eccles et al., 1989; Wigfield, 1994; Wigfield & Eccles, 1992) have investigated the role of expectancy constructs in achievement. These studies have used both cross-sectional and longitudinal designs where upper elementary and junior high students are given self-report measures of their self-perceptions of ability and expectancy for success in math and English at the beginning of one school year and at the end of that same year. In some of their studies, these same students are then followed into the next grade and given the same self-report measures, again at the beginning and at the end of the school year. At the same time, the researchers also have collected data on the students' actual achievement on standardized tests and course grades. They then used path analytic models that allowed them to examine the relative effects of expectancy perceptions versus grades on subsequent perceptions and grades. These studies have consistently shown that students' self-perceptions of ability and their expectancies for success are the strongest predictors of subsequent grades in math and English, even better predictors of later grades than are previous grades. This general finding that has emerged across a number of studies highlights the importance of students' expectancies and self-perceptions of competence as mediators between the environmental context and actual achievement behavior as proposed in Figure 3.2, again demonstrating the importance of student beliefs and the constructivist nature of motivation. In addition, these studies are conducted in actual classrooms and follow students over several years, resulting in high ecological validity and increasing the generalizability of the results.

Besides actual achievement on tests and teacher-assigned grades, other researchers have linked students' expectancies and perceptions of ability to students' cognitive engagement. For example, Pintrich and his colleagues (Pintrich, 1989; Pintrich & De Groot, 1990a; Pintrich & Garcia, 1991; Pintrich & Schrauben, 1992) have investigated the relations between expectancy beliefs and students' use of various cognitive strategies, such as elaboration (paraphrasing, summarizing), and metacognitive strategies (planning, checking, monitoring work) in a series of correlational field studies. These cognitive and metacognitive strategies have been shown to result in "deeper processing" of the material to be learned and higher levels of understanding and learning. Although they have used self-report measures of both motivation and strategy use, Pintrich and his colleagues have consistently found that higher levels of expectancy and perceptions of competence are correlated with more reported use of cognitive and metacognitive strategies in both junior high and college student samples. Other researchers have found similar relations (Paris & Oka, 1986; Shell, Murphy, & Bruning, 1989) between perceptions of competence and cognitive engagement.

In contrast to these relations between expectancy perceptions and cognitive engagement and actual achievement, the findings for choice are not as clear-cut. Although earlier research by Atkinson and others showed that expectancy beliefs did relate to students' choice of distances in the ringtoss experiments, more recent research on student academic choices does not show as strong a role for expectancy beliefs. Eccles and Wigfield and their colleagues find in their field studies that the value beliefs (see Chapter 8) concerning the students' perceptions of the importance, utility, and interest in the task are better predictors of their intentions to continue to take math and of their actual enrollment decision (Wigfield, 1994; Wigfield & Eccles, 1992; also see Feather, 1982, 1988). Accordingly, from an expectancy-value perspective, it appears that expectancy beliefs are more closely tied to actual achievement and cognitive engagement but that value beliefs are more closely tied to choice behaviors that would provide the student with the opportunity to achieve in the future.

Research on Self-Perceptions of Competence and Ability

The research on students' perceptions of their own competence (Harter, 1982, 1985a, 1990) is very similar in some ways to the research on expectancy-value models. Specifically, the definition of self-perceptions of competence is isomorphic with the definition of task-specific self-concept in Eccles and Wigfield's research. Self-perceptions of competence are students' self-evaluative judgments about their ability to accomplish certain tasks (Harter, 1985a). Self-perception of competence is the more cognitive evaluation of ability in a domain (I can do math.), *not* a general measure of self-esteem or self-worth that concerns how individuals might feel about themselves (I am happy with the way I am.) (Wigfield & Karpathian, 1991). At the same time, this research on perceptions of competence springs from a more developmental perspective on the development of the self and personal identity in contrast to the focus on motivation in expectancy-value models. Given this different heritage, there are some differences in the research and theoretical underpinnings.

First, some of the research on students' perceptions of competence is closely related to the more general research on children's conceptions of their personal identity (e.g., Damon & Hart, 1988) and research on self-concept (Markus & Nurius, 1986; Marsh, 1984a, 1984b, 1990b). An important issue in the research on self-concept is the domain specificity of individuals' perceptions of themselves. Much of the early research on self-concept was not very theoretically based, good definitions of the construct were not developed, and many researchers assumed that self-concept was a rather global construct (Wylie, 1974, 1979, 1989). More recent research has focused on how children do distinguish their perceptions of competence by domain (Byrne, 1984). Although self-perceptions of competence become more differentiated with age, most researchers now accept the idea that even fairly young children (first and second graders) have self-perceptions of competence that are domain specific.

In addition, whereas there is disagreement about the levels of specificity of the domains, most researchers at least distinguish among academic, social, and physical domains of competence (Harter, 1982; Wigfield & Karpathian, 1991).

The academic domains concern students' perceptions of competence at school tasks. The perceptions of competence in Table 3.1 are from Harter's perceived competence scale (1982) and reflect a general sense of competence for schoolwork. Another self-concept measure, Marsh's *Self-Descriptive Questionnaire* (SDQI for preadolescents, SDQII for adolescents, and SDQIII for late adolescents and adults), has domains for reading, math, and all school subjects. The social domain reflects individuals' perceptions of their competence in interactions with others. Harter's revised perceived competence scale, now called the *Self-Perceptions Profile* (Harter, 1985b), and Marsh's SDQ both have separate scales for relationships with parents and relationships with peers/close friends. In addition, both Harter and Marsh have scales regarding competence for romantic relations with others for their adolescent and adult measures. The physical domain on Harter's and Marsh's measures includes perceptions of competence at physical activities like sports as well as general perceptions of physical attractiveness/appearance. Students' scores on these different domain scales show moderately positive intercorrelations, but the research does suggest that these are empirically separate domains. Accordingly, students may have differential perceptions in different domains (high in math, low in reading, high in physical ability, low in peer relations, etc.). Researchers and teachers need to be sensitive to these domain differences in perceptions of competence and not assume that students have a single global self-concept that is related to their performance in all domains.

Although the simplistic idea of a global self-concept relating to performance across many domains is not accepted, the assumption that there are domain-specific self-perceptions of competence still begs the question regarding the hierarchical nature of these self-perceptions. The issue revolves around the problem created by multiple domains and the specificity of those domains. For example, if a student has different self-perceptions of competence for different academic domains such as English, math, science, and social studies, the question becomes: Are these self-perceptions ever integrated into a general academic self-concept? This academic self-concept then might be at the same level in a hierarchy of selves as a physical self-concept (an integration of self-perceptions for different physical activities such as running, tennis, gymnastics, soccer, baseball, etc.) and a social self-concept (an integration of self-perceptions for relations with close friends, other classmates, parents, and other adults).

The research on this issue is somewhat mixed. Harter (1983, 1985a) suggests that the results of her studies with factor analysis of the domains from her student perceptions profile support a nonhierarchical model, reflecting support for the taxonomic position (Byrne, 1984). In contrast, the work of Marsh and Shavelson (Marsh, 1990b; Marsh & Shavelson, 1985; Shavelson & Bolus, 1982) suggests that the self-concept is hierarchically structured with separate domains of academic competence fitting into a global academic self-concept, although they find that the strength of the hierarchical structure differs with age (less hierarchy in older adolescents and adults). Wigfield and Karpathian (1991) suggest that these different findings may be due to developmental differences in the students and reflect a general developmental movement from nonhierarchical to hierarchical back to nonhierarchical self-concepts over time. Most of Harter's research has focused on younger students who may be less able or less motivated to integrate the different domains of their self-concept. In contrast, Marsh's early adolescents may show hierarchically organized structures because they are now able cognitively to integrate diverse information and, given the adolescent "life task" of achieving identity, be more motivated to attempt to fit together the different self-domains. Finally, Marsh and Shavelson's older adolescents and adults again may show less hierarchy because they are not actively involved in all domains (most adults are not involved in academic learning of math, science, social studies, etc.) and are less concerned with differences in domains and less upset with having multiple identities or self-concepts. Of course, as Wigfield and Karpathian (1991) point out, most of this research has been cross-sectional and there is a need for longitudinal research to examine the developmental trends and the suggested explanation of the findings.

A second important issue related to the domain specificity and hierarchical nature of perceptions of competence is the relation between perceptions of competence and global self-esteem. As already noted, after some confusion in the early research on self-concept, there is now fairly wide agreement that self-perceptions of competence and self-esteem are two theoretically and empirically distinct constructs (Wigfield & Karpathian, 1991). To reiterate, perceptions of competence are more *cognitive* judgments of personal skills and abilities, such as the belief that you are able to learn social studies, or that you can play soccer (recall Kevin, Rachel, and Sam), or that you can make friends. In contrast, self-esteem is a more global *affective* reaction or evaluation of yourself (e.g., you feel bad about yourself since you don't do well in social studies, or good about yourself because you play soccer well, or bad because you don't have many friends). Empirical research by both Harter (1985a, 1986) and Marsh (Marsh & O'Neill, 1984; Marsh & Shavelson, 1985) have shown that global self-esteem is an empirically separate dimension from self-perceptions of competence, although the two show positive moderate correlations. Obviously, perceptions of competence should be related to self-esteem, but the exact nature of this relation is unclear.

One of the early leading American psychologists, William James (1890), speculated that self-esteem was a ratio between one's "successes" and one's "pretensions" and that self-esteem would be higher to the extent that individuals were able to succeed in meeting all their goals. More recently, Harter (1985a, 1986, 1990) has made a similar argument and suggested that global self-esteem is related to both self-perceptions of competence in different domains and the importance the individual assigns to those domains (paralleling expectancy-value theory predictions). Accordingly, if students have low perceptions of competence in several academic domains, they may not necessarily have low self-esteem if they do not think those domains are that important or central to them in comparison with other domains (e.g, social relations with peers, personal physical abilities). Harter (1986) found evidence for this type of "discounting" in a sample of fifth through seventh graders where students with high self-esteem had much less discrepancy between their importance and competence ratings in comparison with those with low self-esteem. Wigfield, Eccles, Mac Iver, Reuman, and Midgley (1991) also found similar results with junior high students. Steele (1988) has suggested that many minority students, particularly African Americans, use this type of discounting strategy by lowering their value for academic domains where they have lower perceptions of academic competence in order to affirm their self-worth and self-esteem. In contrast, in a study of high school and college students, Marsh (1986) did not find that self-esteem was related to perceptions of competence and importance, but rather self-esteem was best predicted by only perceptions of competence. Developmental differences may be responsible for the different results, but clearly more research is needed on the relations between self-perceptions of competence and global self-esteem (Wigfield & Karpathian, 1991).

A third issue that arises in the research on self-perceptions of competence concerns the accuracy of children's self-evaluations. Interestingly, this issue has not been a major concern of researchers working in the expectancy-value tradition. Expectancy-value theory is built on a motivational model that stresses the subjective nature of individuals' assessments of their expectancy for success. In this case, it is not whether individuals have accurate perceptions of their future expectations (e.g., that their expectations should "match" their past performance), but rather the importance of their personal and subjective expectations, regardless of the relation to previous performance. In contrast, the developmental research on children's self-perceptions of competence has been concerned with personal and self-concept development where issues regarding the accuracy of self-beliefs are important. The issue of accuracy assumes that there is some objective indicator of children's competence that can be used as a criterion against which to assess the congruence of their perceptions of their competence. In most studies, the objective indicators in the academic domain have been standardized tests, teacher grades, or teacher ratings. In general, the research suggests that in the middle elementary grades (third, fourth grade), there is less congruence between children's self-perceptions and more objective assessments, whereas the congruence becomes much better in the later elementary grades and later junior high school (eighth and ninth grades) (Harter, 1985a). Moreover, most of the incongruence in the early grades occurs because the younger students have fairly high self-perceptions of competence. Their perceptions then become more modest as they move into the later grades (Frey & Ruble, 1987; Harter, 1985a; Stipek, 1981, 1984; Weisz, 1983), thereby making them more veridical with other, more objective assessments (Phillips & Zimmerman, 1990).

Nevertheless, in a review of various studies on the validity of self-reports of perceived competence, Assor and Connell (1992) state,

Surveys of relevant research findings clearly demonstrate that, beginning in the third and fourth grade and extending through high school, in populations ranging from upper middle-class Caucasian American youth, to lower and middle class Israeli children, to primarily poor African American adolescents, there is no empirical justification for viewing self-reported appraisals of academic competence and efficacy as invalid measures of performance affecting self-appraisals. (pp. 41–42)

Assor and Connell (1992) also note that there may be some positive advantages for having "inaccurate" self-perceptions of competence when they are higher than should be expected given actual performance. They report that these "inflated" self-reports actually are related to positive performance outcomes 2 years later in a longitudinal study of high school students. They also note that students who have inaccurate self-perceptions that are lower than they should be (deflated self-assessments) perform at much lower levels, which coincides with other studies as well (Phillips & Zimmerman, 1990). Accordingly, in line with a motivational and constructivist perspective, individuals' personal and subjective self-perceptions are important for future achievement behavior, regardless of the "accuracy" of the perceptions in terms of their match to grades, standardized tests, or ratings by adults. Researchers must still be careful, however, to get accurate perceptions that really represent childrens' beliefs about themselves, not modesty or social desirability effects.

Besides the general developmental differences in accuracy of self-perceptions, there also seem to be some individual differences in the inaccuracy of self-perceptions of competence. Inaccuracy in self-perceptions of competence can result from overestimation of competence (believing you are more competent than suggested by objective measures) and underestimation of competence (believing you are less competent than expected by objective measures). Phillips (1984, 1987; Phillips & Zimmerman, 1990) has examined three types of students in terms of their accuracy of competence perceptions. In her studies, she used samples of only high-achieving third-, fifth-, and ninth-grade students (defined in terms of a combination of standardized test scores and teacher ratings), but still found that there are overestimators (higher perceptions of competence than warranted by actual achievement), accurate perceivers (congruence between perceptions and achievement), and underestimators (lower perceptions than warranted by actual achievement). This latter group, all of whom have the "illusion of incompetence," was of particular concern to her because all of her sample students were actually achieving in the top 25% on nationally standardized tests. These underestimators were most likely to hold very low expectations for future success, to believe that their parents and teachers had low perceptions of them, to be more anxious, and to be less willing to try hard and persist on academic tasks (Phillips & Zimmerman, 1990). Accordingly, whereas most students do become more accurate in their self-perceptions of competence as they progress through school, there are still some very able children who have the illusion of incompetence and show negative motivational outcomes.

Finally, a fourth issue concerns the nature of the relation between perceptions of competence and self-concept and achievement. As noted in the section on expectancy-value theory, children's perceptions of their ability have been linked to most achievement behaviors, including effort, persistence, cognitive engagement, and actual achievement. However, within the tradition of research on self-concept, researchers have been concerned with the direction of the causal relation between self-concept and achievement. Some researchers have argued that self-concept is causally predominant over achievement, while others have taken the opposite position that achievement determines self-concept (see Byrne, 1984; Caslyn & Kenny, 1977; Hansford & Hattie, 1982; Scheirer & Kraut, 1979, for conflicting views). These different views obviously have implications for instruction. The self-concept enhancement version suggests that teachers should ensure that students believe they are capable and then their subsequent achievement will improve. The achievement-first model suggests that teachers should ensure that children have the academic skills to succeed and then their perceptions of competence will follow from their successes. The most recent view of this controversy is that "it is relatively fruitless to continue to pursue the general question of which causes which" (Wigfield & Karpathian, 1991, p. 256). Clearly, the relation is reciprocal; self-concept influences future achievement and actual achievement shapes and constrains self-perceptions of competence. Moreover, there may be individual, developmental, and contextual differences in the nature of the relations between self-concept and achievement (cf. Marsh, 1990a; Skaalvik & Hagtvet, 1990). In terms of future research and educational practice, it seems wise to realize that the relation is complex and that simple, linear models do not map onto the reality of classrooms. Future research should concentrate on understanding how self-perceptions and actual achievement work together to predict future behavior at different ages, for different students, and in different contexts. Teachers should focus on teaching their students the appropriate cognitive skills to master academic tasks and, at the same time, ensure that students have the motivational resources, including appropriate self-perceptions of competence, to engage in these tasks.

In sum, the research on self-perceptions of competence has investigated the role of children's self-evaluative judgments, a construct isomorphic with task-specific self-concept from the expectancy-value models. The research has had a decidedly developmental perspective and has investigated these self-perceptions in young children, adolescents, and adults. Current research suggests that self-perceptions of competence are domain specific, not global, although there is not agreement about the specificity of the domain. Nevertheless, it seems important for future research as well as educational practice to recognize that in the academic domain, self-perceptions of competence need to be specified at least at the level of general subject areas (i.e., English, math, science, social studies, foreign language, art, music, etc.). It probably will not be that helpful, moreover it is potentially misleading, for teachers to label children as having low self-concept as a global trait that applies across all academic, social, and physical domains. Teachers need to differentiate more carefully and recognize that children can and do differ within those domains in terms of their self-perceptions of competence and that these intraindividual differences can result in differences in motivated behavior.

A Model of Self-Efficacy Beliefs

A third general model that has examined the role of students' perceptions of competence is self-efficacy theory. Bandura (1982, 1986, 1989) has developed a social cognitive model of behavior that includes self-efficacy as a major construct. Self-efficacy theory grows out of Bandura's original social learning theory (Bandura, 1969, 1977) and, hence, has some behavioral and mechanistic aspects in contrast to the more organismic perspective on the individual represented in expectancy-value models and the research on self-perceptions of competence. Bandura and others have applied the model to a variety of domains, including mental health, such as coping with depression and phobias; health behavior, such as recovery from a heart attack and cessation of smoking; decision making and sales performance in business; athletic performance; career choices; and academic achievement. In the educational domain, Schunk (1989a, 1989c, 1991b) has been the leading theorist and researcher regarding the role of student self-efficacy in classroom settings.

In this model, *self-efficacy* is defined as "people's judgments of their capabilities to organize and execute courses of action required to attain designated types of performances" (Bandura, 1986, p. 391). In a general sense, this definition is fairly similar to the definitions of task-specific self-concept and self-perceptions of competence that have been discussed in the two previous sections. Self-efficacy does represent people's judgments of their abilities in the same way as Eccles and Wigfield represent task-specific self-concept and Harter represents self-perceptions of competence. There are, however, some important differences. First, the definition of self-efficacy includes "organize and execute courses of action," which represents the theory's more specific and situational view of perceived competence in terms of including the behavioral actions or cognitive skills that are necessary for competent performance. For example, self-efficacy in math would not be merely a self-recognition of being good in math but rather explicit judgments of having the skills for doing, say, two-digit subtraction problems (Schunk, 1991b). In fact, in assessing self-efficacy, researchers often show students the problems they will be asked to solve and then ask them to rate themselves on a scale from 1 to 100 as to how confident they are about their ability to solve the problems. This is usually done for all the problems in the set and students rate themselves for each problem, generating a series of ratings for self-efficacy for the problem set that are averaged to form a measure of self-efficacy for doing two-digit subtraction problems (see Table 3.1).

A second aspect that distinguishes self-efficacy from self-concept and self-competence is that it is used in reference to some type of goal ("attain designated types of performance"). Again, this reflects the more situational perspective of efficacy theory in contrast to the personality and developmental heritage of expectancy-value and perceptions-of-competence research. The goal may be determined by the individual or by the task conditions and environment (or their interaction), but the important point is that judgments of efficacy are in reference to this goal. One implication of the inclusion of a specific goal is that self-efficacy judgments for very similar tasks may vary as a function of intraindividual or environmental differences. For example, skilled and experienced runners may lower their efficacy judgments for maintaining their usual time for a 10-kilometer run because of a nagging muscle pull. In an academic setting, a student's self-efficacy for learning a particular topic in mathematics may be lower because of the difficulty of the material to be learned in contrast to material covered earlier in the course. In colloquial terms, these individuals have lower than usual "self-confidence" in their capabilities to perform a specific task at a certain level of competence.

Efficacy theory also proposes that outcome expectations form a second construct related to motivational behavior and affect. *Outcome expectations* are judgments or beliefs regarding the contingency between a person's behavior and the anticipated outcome. This notion of contingency between response and outcome is similar to Rotter's (1966) construct of locus of control regarding the contingency between behavior and reinforcement (see Chapter 4). In addition, in terms of the anticipation of success, it is similar to expectancy for success from expectancy-value theories. As Bandura (1986) puts it, "The belief that one can high jump six feet is an efficacy judgment; the anticipated social recognition, applause, trophies, and self-satisfactions for such a performance constitute the outcome expectations" (p. 391). In the academic domain, students would have efficacy judgments of their capabilities, skills, and knowledge to master school-related tasks, but also have outcome expectations about what grades they might receive on the tasks. Although efficacy beliefs and outcome expectations are usually positively correlated, it is possible for a student to have a relatively high efficacy belief for a task, but low outcome expectations. For example, a college student in an organic chemistry class might have relatively high efficacy beliefs about personal capability to master the material, but low outcome expectations about grades on exams due to the very high competition among premed students and the grading curve instituted by faculty to weed out the weaker students from the medical school admission process.

Although both efficacy and outcome judgments are best thought of as continuums, Bandura (1982) has suggested that a simple high/low efficacy by high/low outcome expectation comparison provides some insight into behavior and affect. Figure 3.3 shows the expected behavioral and affective reactions for individuals who vary in efficacy and outcome expectation beliefs. The expected behaviors and affects listed in the figure are assumed to apply to all aspects of life, not just academic domains. Of course, it is best to be high in both efficacy and outcome expectations. Persons in this cell would be confident and assured in their performance, would show high levels of effort, would persist, and probably would have high levels of cognitive engagement in academic tasks. Students high in efficacy but low in outcome expectations, like our organic chemistry student, would be most likely to study hard and be engaged but, at the same time, may protest and lobby for changes in the grading system. In some cases, they would leave the environment by dropping out of the premed or science program (not the class), not because their efficacy is low, but rather because they don't perceive a contingency between their learning and the outcomes, in this case grades. Bandura (1982) also notes that many social activists who lobby for changes in social policies would be in this cell, in contrast to individuals who are low in both efficacy and outcome expectations who are often the "clients" of these activists. Bandura suggests that individuals who are low in both efficacy and outcome expectations would show resignation and apathy and an unwillingness or inability to exert much effort. In the academic domain, this cell would represent students who have given up on learning and are very unwilling to exert effort. In most ways, they would be similar to learned helpless students (cf. Peterson, Maier, & Seligman, 1993, and our discussion in Chapter 4). The final cell in Figure 3.3 would include students who have low efficacy for their ability to master the task but high outcome expectations. Students low in efficacy and high in outcome expectations believe they can't do the task but are very aware (by seeing others get rewarded) that if they were able to perform, the environment would be responsive and they would be appropriately rewarded. These students would evaluate themselves very negatively and focus on themselves as the cause of all failure, in contrast to students low in both efficacy and outcome expectations who also focus on the lack of environmental responsiveness.

Although Bandura proposes both of these motivational constructs, the theory and subsequent research focus on the role of self-efficacy beliefs. Bandura (1986) suggests that outcome expectations are heavily dependent on efficacy judgments: "If you control for how well people judge they can perform, you account for much of the variance in the kinds of outcomes they expect" (p. 393). Bandura (1986) notes that outcomes are connected to actions; how one behaves largely determines the actual outcome and, in the same way, beliefs about outcome expectations are dependent on self-efficacy judgments. He gives the example that drivers who are not confident in their ability to negotiate a winding mountain road (low efficacy) will conjure up images of wreckage and injuries (one type of outcome expectation), whereas those confident in their ability will anticipate the grand views from the mountains. Recall the example of Mr. Dearborn at the beginning of this chapter. He remembers his anxiety when he began teaching and negative images about his classroom that were driven by his lack of efficacy for managing his classroom.

Self Efficacy	Outcome Expectation	
	Low outcome expectation	*High outcome expectation*
High self-efficacy	Social activism Protest Grievance Milieu change	Assured, opportune action High cognitive engagement
Low self-efficacy	Resignation Apathy Withdrawal	Self-devaluation Depression

Figure 3.3.   Behavioral and affective reactions as a function of different levels of self-efficacy and outcome expectations
From "Self-Efficacy Mechanism in Human Agency" by A. Bandura, 1982, *American Psychologist,* 37, p. 140. Copyright © 1982 by the American Psychological Association. Adapted by permission.

Similarly, in the academic domain, students' self-efficacy beliefs are very likely to be highly positively correlated with outcome expectations, represented by the top right and bottom left cells in Figure 3.3. Of course, as noted in the chemistry example, there can be occasions when students are high in efficacy but low in outcome expectations due to structural constraints in the environment such as grading curves. Another example of this high efficacy–low outcome expectation pattern would be the case of institutional discrimination on the basis of race, ethnicity, or gender. Students in the affected group (e.g., minorities in any school or classroom where they are discriminated against and women in math and science classes) might feel that they can master the material (high efficacy) but can't succeed due to the discriminatory practices in the setting. It should be noted that outcome expectations are *beliefs,* and in keeping with the general constructive perspective, students may perceive low outcome expectations due to discrimination when there may be very little actual discrimination in the setting.

This issue of accuracy in self-beliefs is even more important in terms of self-efficacy judgments. Bandura (1986), following all the other expectancy models, notes that people tend to avoid tasks and situations they believe exceed their capabilities, but they take on tasks and activities that they believe they can handle. This type of choice behavior can have a dramatic influence on personal development. His theory predicts that when self-efficacy perceptions are high, individuals will engage in tasks that foster the development of their skills and capabilities, but when self-efficacy is low, people will not engage in new tasks that might help them learn new skills. In addition, by avoiding these tasks, an individual will not receive any corrective feedback to counter the negative self-efficacy perceptions. In general, then, it is most adaptive to have self-perceptions of efficacy that slightly exceed actual skill level at any given time. Grossly optimistic efficacy beliefs that lead to tasks and situations that are far beyond the level of individual skill can result in quite aversive consequences. Consider an overly confident novice mountain climber who attempts a very difficult climb that results in a serious injury or even loss of life. In the academic domain, the consequences may not be as dire, but individuals who take on academic tasks far beyond their level of actual skill can suffer needless failure and subsequent debilitating efficacy beliefs. Individuals who grossly underestimate their efficacy, although the consequences might not be as aversive as in overestimation, will limit their potential for learning and development and, if they do undertake the task, will probably suffer from unnecessary anxiety and self-doubt that can increase the possibility of failure (Bandura, 1986).

Self-efficacy is related to choice behavior in terms of task choice, but it also has been related to career choices. For example, Betz and Hackett (1981, 1983; Hackett & Betz, 1981) have shown that although there are structural and social influences on career choices, self-efficacy is an important mediator of these external influences and has a direct bearing on career choice. In addition, they suggest that the gender differences that emerge in vocational choices are due to differences in self-efficacy; males are efficacious for all careers, whereas females are only efficacious for careers traditionally held by women and feel inefficacious for careers traditionally held by men.

Besides choice, self-efficacy has been related to the quantity of effort and the willingness to persist at tasks (Bandura & Cervone, 1983, 1986; Schunk, 1991b). Individuals with strong efficacy beliefs are more likely to exert effort in the face of difficulty and persist at a task when they have the requisite skills. Individuals who have weaker perceptions of efficacy are likely to be plagued by self-doubts and to give up easily when confronted with difficulties. However, there is some evidence that self-doubt (weak efficacy) may foster learning when students have not previously acquired the skills. As Bandura (1986) notes, "Self-doubt creates the impetus for learning but hinders adept use of previously established skills" (p. 394). Salomon (1984) found that students high in efficacy were more likely to be cognitively engaged in learning from media when the task was perceived as difficult, but they were likely to be less effortful and less cognitively engaged when the media were deemed easy.

Besides the quantity of effort, the quality of effort in terms of the use of deeper processing strategies and general cognitive engagement of learning has been strongly linked to self-efficacy perceptions (Pintrich & Schrauben, 1992). For example, Pintrich and De Groot (1990a) found that junior high students high in efficacy were more likely to report using various cognitive and self-regulatory learning strategies. In a series of experimental studies, Schunk (1982,

1983a, 1983b, 1983c, 1983d, 1984, 1987, 1991b) found that students who had stronger self-efficacy beliefs were able to master various math and reading tasks better than students with weaker efficacy beliefs. In addition, these studies showed that efficacy was a significant predictor of learning and achievement, even after prior achievement and cognitive skills were taken into consideration.

In sum, self-efficacy beliefs have been shown to be important mediators of all types of achievement behavior as well as many other types of behavior. Self-efficacy beliefs are very similar to the other expectancy constructs of task-specific self-concept and self-perceptions of competence because they all represent individuals' judgments of their capabilities. However, self-efficacy theory does differ from the other two traditions of research in assuming that self-efficacy perceptions are much more situation specific than the other expectancy beliefs. This assumption has led researchers to measure self-efficacy in a much more situationally sensitive fashion and at a much more microanalytic level (e.g., efficacy for very specific academic problems such as two-digit subtraction problems with borrowing). Related to this situational specificity, self-efficacy beliefs are assumed to be much more dynamic, fluctuating, and changeable beliefs than the somewhat more static and stable self-concept and self-competence beliefs. Self-efficacy beliefs, even for a very specific task such as subtraction problems in math, might fluctuate given the individuals' preparation on any given day, their physical condition (sickness, fatigue), and affective mood, as well as external conditions such as the nature of the task (length, difficulty, etc.) and the social milieu (general classroom conditions). In contrast, the other two traditions of research would assume a more global perception of competence (e.g., math competence) and, although they might recognize the existence of such daily shifts and fluctuations in self-perceptions of competence, would not be concerned theoretically or empirically with such microlevel instability of beliefs.

DEVELOPMENTAL AND GROUP DIFFERENCES IN EXPECTANCY CONSTRUCTS

In each of the three programs of research we discussed, there has been research on developmental and group differences. Given the similarity in the general construct of expectancy, however, we discuss developmental, gender, and ethnic differences together.

Developmental Differences

As noted in our discussion of the research on self-perceptions of competence, there has been a great deal of research on the age-related changes in children's self-perceptions of competence. There is an important distinction in this developmental literature between the level and accuracy of children's self-perceptions of competence and their definitions of ability and effort (Blumenfeld, Pintrich, Meece, & Wessels, 1982). The latter have to do with the psychological meaning of ability and effort and will be discussed in Chapter 4 on attribution theory. In this chapter, we are concerned with the level and accuracy of children's self-perceptions of competence.

The research that has examined developmental differences in children's self-perceptions of competence has consistently shown a decrease in the mean level of self-perceptions of ability as children move into adolescence (Eccles, Midgley, & Adler, 1984; Eccles & Midgley, 1989; Harter, 1990; Stipek & Mac Iver, 1989; Wigfield, Eccles, & Pintrich, forthcoming). In particular, the average level decrease seems to be the greatest when students move into junior high schools or middle schools in seventh or sixth grade, respectively (e.g., Eccles, 1993), although Marsh has found the lowest point to be in eighth or ninth grade (Marsh, 1989). Most of this research has been cross-sectional in nature, but the few longitudinal studies also show a decrease over time with age (Wigfield et al., 1991). There are a number of explanations for this age-related drop in mean level of self-perceptions.

First, there is a simple methodological explanation. Most measures of students' self-perceptions of competence use some version of a Likert-type scale whereby students rate themselves on one of several numerical scales from the *lowest level of self-perceived ability* (1) to the *highest level of self-perceived ability* (*4, 5, 7,* or *11,* depending on the scale). It may be that young children (early to middle elementary grades) are more likely to use only the endpoints of the Likert scale, especially the higher end of the scale. Although this may be the case, it is not clear that this tendency to use the endpoints on a Likert-type scale reflects a methodological artifact of Likert scales per se. Assor and Connell (1992) argue that Likert scale items are acceptable and valid measures of children's self-perceptions of competence as long as some precautions are taken in their design and administration. They do note, however, that a four-point scale may provide all the needed precision with younger children and there may not be a need for scales with a larger range.

This brings us to the second general type of explanation for the developmental differences in perceptions of ability, which is more substantive and has to do with internal psychological mechanisms. There are two issues related to a substantive explanation of the overall drop; one concerns the accuracy of perceptions and the other concerns the overall optimistic perceptions of younger children. The accuracy of perceptions usually refers to whether the children's self-perceptions match or correspond to some external, more objective criterion. In general, it is probably best for individuals to have somewhat optimistic perceptions of their competence and efficacy (Assor & Connell, 1992), although not to be too overly optimistic and certainly not too pessimistic (the illusion of incompetence as pointed out by Phillips, 1984, 1987). Nevertheless, given the general social cognitive and constructivist perspective of current motivational theories, the accuracy of these perceptions in terms of their correspondence to objective measures of achievement is not as important as the fact that these perceptions do have motivational and achievement consequences. Assor and Connell (1992) review a number of studies of both the illusion of competence (children who overrate their competence, given their actual achievement) and the illusion of incompetence (children who underrate their competence, given their actual achievement) and conclude that in both cases these perceptions have important consequences. Students who overrated their competence were more likely to be engaged and achieve at higher levels, whereas those who underrated their competence were more likely to avoid tasks, report more anxiety, and not achieve that well. Assor and Connell conclude that these inaccurate perceptions are "real" because they have real consequences in motivational and behavioral terms. Accordingly, the accuracy of perceptions in terms of a match to external criteria like teacher ratings or achievement tests is not as important a validity consideration as whether measures of children's self-perceptions actually reflect the children's own perceptions of their abilities.

Given the argument that children's perceptions are real and younger children are more likely to have higher perceptions, we still need to account for this phenomenon, not just attribute it to inaccurate or invalid measures. A cognitive psychological explanation for this is based on younger children not having the information-processing skills available to integrate the information and make the types of social comparisons necessary (Blumenfeld et al., 1982). For example, Parsons and Ruble (1977) have shown that young children have difficulty utilizing all the cues presented to them to make accurate predictions about future performance. Other researchers have shown that children do not interpret feedback about task difficulty in the same manner as adults. Meyer and colleagues (Meyer et al., 1979) found that ninth graders and adults were more likely to believe that praise after success at an easy task implied low ability and criticism for failure at a hard task indicated high ability, but that third and fifth graders used praise as an indicator of ability regardless of the task difficulty level.

Besides these differences in information processing, there are a number of studies that suggest that younger children use less comparative standards or criteria to judge ability in contrast to the more relative standards of older children and adults. For example, Blumenfeld, Pintrich, and Hamilton (1987) have shown that younger children (second graders) are more likely to use an absolute standard to judge their competence and focus on completion of the task (I can read., I can do my math.). Older students (sixth graders) were more likely to invoke comparison information (I can do my math faster than other kids.) when asked to judge their competence. Ruble and her colleagues (Ruble, 1983; Ruble & Frey, 1991) have shown that younger children do not always seek out social comparison information, let alone use it to make a judgment of their ability. The lack of interest in and failure to use social comparison information by younger children suggest that they will maintain higher perceptions of ability. If younger children do not make comparisons of their performance to others, then they will be less likely to adjust their self-perceptions downward as they see some other children do better than they do on different academic tasks.

A third explanation for the drop in ability perceptions as children grow older is contextually based and focuses not on the changing cognitive and information-processing skills of children, but on the changing developmental environments through which they move. Obviously, one of the environmental factors that changes is the nature of classrooms and schools. As a number of researchers (Blumenfeld et al., 1982; Eccles et al., 1993; Marshall & Weinstein, 1984; Rosenholtz & Simpson, 1984) have pointed out, elementary and junior high schools differ in a number of organizational and structural ways that can influence students' ability perceptions. First, the nature of the class structure changes in junior high with children moving among several different classes and teachers for subject areas instead of having one teacher for most academic subject areas as in most elementary schools. Second, the nature of evaluation changes. Most elementary classroom teachers use a simple criterion-mastery system of grading. Children are graded on their performance on worksheets, projects, tests, and so on without reference to how others perform. In contrast, in junior and senior high classrooms, teachers often use some type of relative grading system whereby students' grades are partially determined in reference to how other children performed. In these cases, children are given information about their ability relative to other children. For those who do not do as well, it is not surprising that they begin to lower their self-perceptions of ability. In addition, tracking by ability level begins to emerge in the upper grades and this can have a detrimental effect on lower ability children's perceptions of their ability (Mac Iver, 1988; Rosenholtz & Simpson, 1984). In effect, many aspects of the classroom change as the children move to junior high and most of these changes serve to increase the information available to students upon which to make relative ability judgments. Not all students lower their ability judgments (Mac Iver, 1988; Reuman, 1989), but what both the cognitive developmental and classroom/school changes seem to do is to increase the variance in students' ratings, so that all children's ratings are not clustered around a higher mean. This situation results in more dispersion of ability self-perceptions and also a lower overall mean as children get older.

Gender and Ethnic Differences

Besides the developmental differences that are found in ability self-perceptions, there also have been studies that find gender and ethnic differences. However, there are a number of problems with making broad generalizations about gender and ethnic differences in motivation. First, by concentrating on overall group differences, many of the studies ignore the more significant within-group differences among females or among minority children. Second, it is often difficult to evaluate the relative contributions of gender and ethnicity to these group differences because the influence of socioeconomic status (SES) is not considered simultaneously (Graham, 1994, Pollard, 1993). Many of these studies confound SES with ethnicity by comparing middle or upper middle income Caucasian students with lower income African American students. Moreover, as Pollard (1993) points out, there may be important interactions among gender, ethnicity, and SES on children's motivation or achievement. Studies that do not take into account the multiple statuses and roles that students can play as a function of membership in different groups can be misleading and result in simplistic conclusions being drawn about one characteristic (e.g., ethnicity) when the reality is much more complex. Third, much of the research on ethnic differences has been atheoretical in terms of conceptualizing motivation and has often relied on deficit models and compared different ethnic groups on constructs that allow for simple dichotomies between those low and high in certain characteristics (Betancourt & Lopez, 1993; Graham, 1994; Pollard, 1993). Accordingly, any generalizations about gender or ethnic differences are problematic, albeit there are some trends that should be noted.

In most cases when a gender difference is found, the difference is that females have lower self-perceptions of ability than males (Wigfield, Eccles, & Pintrich, forthcoming). This is particularly surprising since many studies that have examined actual achievement or performance (see Linn & Hyde, 1989) show that there are few gender differences and that in many cases, females actually outperform males; yet other studies still show females as having lower self-perceptions. Although this discrepancy between actual achievement and self-perceptions of ability may be due to a response bias, with boys being more self-congratulatory and girls being more modest (Eccles, Adler, & Meece, 1984; Wigfield et al., forthcoming), the difference appears often enough to be taken seriously.

Eccles and Wigfield and their colleagues have consistently found gender differences in self-perceptions of ability. Males have higher self-perceptions in math and sports, whereas females have higher self-perceptions of their ability in English (Eccles, 1983; Eccles et al., 1989; Wigfield et al., 1991). Marsh (1989) also reports gender differences in his data on self-concept. Although he finds that the gender differences only account for 1% of the variance in self-concept, he finds that males have higher self-concept scores for their self-ratings of physical appearance, physical ability, and math, whereas females have higher self-ratings for verbal and reading tasks and general school self-concept (Wigfield et al., forthcoming). Phillips and Zimmerman (1990) also found that females had lower perceptions of their competence than males, although the gender difference did not emerge with third and fifth graders, only with ninth graders. Other studies, however, have found that gender differences in ability perceptions do emerge at earlier grades. For example, studies by Entwisle and Baker (1983) and Frey and Ruble (1987) both found that even in early elementary age children, females were more likely to have lower self-perceptions of ability than males. Clearly, there is a need for more research into the nature of these differences as well as more programs to change school and classroom practices that can give rise to these gender differences (Bailey, 1993; Meece & Eccles, 1993; Kahle, Parker, Rennie, & Riley, 1993).

Much less research has been done in terms of ethnic and racial differences, and the research often confounds race and ethnicity with social class differences by comparing middle-class white children with lower class minority children (Graham, 1989, 1994; Wigfield et al., forthcoming). There are two general issues that are often addressed in research that examines ethnic differences. First, are there ethnic group differences in the mean level of self-perceptions of ability or other motivational constructs? Second, do the motivational constructs operate in the same fashion for minority group students as they do for other groups, or do we need different models of motivation for different ethnic groups?

In terms of the first question, Graham (1994) in a narrative review of published studies of African American students and their achievement motivation, finds little support for the general hypothesis that African American students should have lower expectancies for success or lower self-concepts of ability because of their poor school achievement or general economic disadvantage. In terms of expectancy for success, Graham (1994) reviews 14 experimental studies that used a common format of presenting a task to African American and Caucasian children and then asking them to predict their expectancy for success. In addition, some of the studies asked the students to make judgments of their expectancy for success after they had received either manipulated or actual success and failure. In 12 out of the 14 studies, African American students had higher expectations for success than Caucasian children. Graham (1994) also reviewed 18 studies that examined self-concepts of ability. Again, she found very little evidence for the idea that African American students have lower self-concepts of ability. Only 2 of the 18 studies reported group differences in favor of Caucasian children, 7 favored African American children, and the remaining 9 had mixed or no significant differences between the two groups. Graham (1994) interprets these "counterintuitive" findings for the deficit hypothesis for African Americans in terms of the adaptive nature of maintaining optimistic expectancies and self-concept beliefs in the face of relative social and economic disadvantage.

In terms of the second issue, some studies find that self-perceptions of ability or efficacy are linked to academic achievement in the same fashion (e.g., moderate positive correlations) for minorities and other groups (Pollard, 1993; Taylor, Casten, Flickinger, & Roberts, 1994). However, Graham (1994) notes that in many of the studies she reviewed, the actual performance measures, such as grades or standardized achievement tests, showed that African Americans had lower levels of performance, yet they had higher self-perceptions of ability. This would suggest that the relation between self-perceptions of ability and actual achievement is not as strong in African American students as it is in Caucasian students. There have been many reasons proposed to explain this weaker relation. For example, some researchers (e.g., Fordham & Ogbu, 1986; Steele, 1988, 1992) have suggested that the motivational dynamics are different for black children and that they may devalue academic achievement (a task value belief) because of their repeated school failures. In this case, they may have relatively high self-perceptions of competence (or relatively low perceptions), but perceptions of competence are not linked as closely to actual achievement as they are in Caucasian children. Other reasons include the use of different social comparison groups; for example, African Americans compare themselves to other African Americans rather than the more advantaged Caucasian group, thereby maintaining high self-perceptions (Rosenberg & Simmons, 1971). They also attribute their lower performance to external factors such as prejudice, thereby maintaining high self-perceptions (Crocker & Major, 1989). Graham (1994), however, notes that these explanations are not supported in the general motivational literature and suggests that motivational principles that are used in current theoretical work on motivation should also apply to minority students. In this sense, it may be more important to examine within-group individual differences rather than between-group differences. For example, why do some minorities or females seem to maintain their achievement even in the face of many different obstacles? Graham suggests that there is less need for a differential psychology of minority student achievement, although more minority students must be included in future research on motivation, and samples must include a range of socioeconomic levels and different groups of minorities. In any event, there is a need for more research on these issues, both to evaluate the nature of the differences in perceptions of ability between minority and other children and to evaluate the claims that different theoretical models of motivation and development are necessary to explain the linkage between minority students' motivational beliefs about competence and their actual academic achievement.

IMPLICATIONS FOR TEACHERS

The research on expectancy, competence, and efficacy beliefs provides a number of implications for teachers. These general principles reflect the research, but given that psychology and educational psychology are probabilistic sciences, not deterministic ones, the principles may not apply in all contexts and situations. That is, psychology is not like chemistry where one can predict with great precision what will happen in a new situation based on previous research. Rather, findings from psychological research can be used to appraise the probability of different events occurring in the future. In this sense, research in psychology can be used as a guide for educational practice, not as the determiner of practice. In some cases, we can say that following certain principles will most likely result in positive motivational outcomes, but there are always exceptions and problematic situations where educators must use their best professional judgment. There is disagreement in the teacher education literature about whether teachers actually can use principled knowledge in their teaching or whether their pedagogical knowledge is all case based and develops from experience. Our position is that teachers can use and benefit from principled knowledge, albeit their use of it and their representation of it may be in the form of cases. Hence, we offer the follow suggestions as a guide for teacher practice. These principles will need to be adapted to the specific classroom context, but we trust that truly professional educators will be able to apply them in a thoughtful and pedagogically sound manner.

1. Help students maintain relatively accurate but high expectations and efficacy and help students avoid the illusion of incompetence. Mr. Dearborn tries to provide positive but accurate feedback to all students on their written work. He writes on their science reports about their demonstrated level of understanding of the content as well as their level of effort (at least as perceived by him). Some students do a very hasty report and he makes sure to note this in his written comments. He often speaks with the students individually to ask them why they did not try very hard or did not do very well. Given this information, he tries to help the students see how they can increase their effort or performance. Sometimes, he shows them other students' reports (with the names removed to protect confidentiality and limit social comparison) so they can see a model of a good report. He talks to the students about how they might go about doing a report at the level of the model. At the same time, Mr. Dearborn is very careful to make sure that all students know what they did incorrectly; he does not give insincere feedback to boost self-esteem.

As the research has shown, students are motivated to engage in tasks and achieve when they believe they can accomplish the task. Teachers need to provide accurate feedback to students to help them develop reasonable perceptions of their competence but, at the same time, communicate that their actual competence and skills will continue to develop.

2. Students' perceptions of competence develop not just from accurate feedback from the teacher, but through actual success on challenging academic tasks. Keep tasks and assignments at a relatively challenging but reasonable level of difficulty. Ms. Rivera has available many different levels of classroom assignments for her junior high school science students. Over the years, she has collected a number of different projects, experiments, labs, and workbook assignments that provide her with a diversity of tasks with differing levels of challenge. All the students in her class do a common set of seventh-grade science tasks, but she also has extra-credit assignments available for those who can go beyond the basic seventh-grade material. In addition, she has other extra-credit assignments that are below grade level that she uses with students who are struggling with the content. This mixture of common and individualized tasks allows most children the opportunity to be successful and at the same time be challenged.

Although practice on easy tasks is very helpful for building automaticity of skills, children also need to be challenged by tasks in order to be motivated and to actually learn new skills. Tasks should be set at a level of difficulty where most children in the classroom can master the assignment with some effort. They should not be too easy and especially not too difficult that most children fail at the task.

3. Foster the belief that competence or ability is a changeable, controllable aspect of development. At the beginning of this chapter, three students were talking about their self-perceptions of competence for social studies. Kevin had high efficacy beliefs, whereas both Rachel and Sam had lower beliefs about their capability to do social studies. In this case, if there are many students in the classroom who have the same level of beliefs as Rachel and Sam, the social studies teacher might want to have a class discussion about how different students study for social studies tests. During the discussion, different types of study strategies might be mentioned that some children don't know about. Most likely different levels of effort and amount of time studying would be mentioned as factors that influence test performance. The social studies teacher could then use the ideas generated in the discussion to help all the students in the class see that performing well on social studies tests is something that they all can learn to do. He could do this by reemphasizing the importance of effort, the amount of time spent studying, and the use of different study strategies. In addition, he could express his belief that all students can learn to do well in social studies. This type of teacher talk about social studies would communicate to students that the teacher has high expectations for all of them and that learning in social studies is not a stable ability or trait that some students have or do not have.

The vast majority of the knowledge and skills that are taught in K–12 schools can be learned by all children who do not have serious disabilities. Of course, some children may take longer to master the knowledge or skills than others, but there are very few inherent limitations that are stable traits of students. If students come to understand that they can master the material with some effort, they will be more likely to engage in the material. The teacher needs to communicate this type of positive high expectation for all students, high and low ability, females and males, and minority and others.

4. Decrease the amount of relative ability information that is publicly available to students. Ms. Morgan, a science teacher, has one bulletin board in her room that lists all the assignments for her class and all the students' grades for each assignment. She likes having the information posted so that everyone can see it. It helps her keep track of what students have done and it helps the students see what assignments they have finished and which ones they still need to complete. In particular, she finds that it is a very effective management tool because when students are done with their assignment for the day, they can check the board and see what else they have to do without bothering her. Since she started using this system, she is not constantly being asked by students what they should do next. This freedom allows her to work closely with small groups or individuals on their hands-on science projects without too many interruptions.

Ms. Morgan also has found as the semester goes along, however, that there are always a few students who fall behind in their work, get poor grades, and seem to give up. When she asks them what is going on, they often point to the board and say things like, "Look what I have to do. There's too much. I'm too far behind. What's the use?", or, "I'm too stupid to do science. Every day I come in here, some of the nerds make fun of me. They point to the low grades I got on the board and laugh. I really hate science and anyone who is good at it is just a nerd anyway." These comments are upsetting to Ms. Morgan because she wants her students to do well and also to like and enjoy science.

Some teachers facilitate social comparison by posting all students' scores and grades on wall posters in the room or by having students call out their test scores in class while writing them down in the grade book. These types of practices can increase the amount of social comparison information available to children and help to lower some children's (those doing less well) self-perceptions of competence. In Ms. Morgan's case, her management practice with the bulletin board seems to be undermining some students' perceptions of their competence to do science. The students who are not doing so well are having negative interactions with some other students and making negative social comparisons about their ability to do science. The board presents to all students in the class, in a highly public manner, everyone's tests and assignment scores. Ms. Morgan should try to avoid these types of public practices that heighten the differences between students. She could keep the grading information private and use it in assigning final class grades, but it may not be that helpful for all students to have public access to it. If she still wanted to use the public bulletin board for management purposes, simple check marks for completion may serve just as well as the public posting of grades. On the other hand, there may be more individualized and more private ways (e.g., individual student folders or portfolios) to keep track of her students' completed work.

5. Students' perceptions of competence are somewhat domain specific and are not equivalent to global self-esteem. It is more productive for academic learning to help students develop their self-perceptions of competence rather than their global self-esteem. At the beginning of this chapter, Rachel, Kevin, and Sam all showed the domain specificity of their beliefs about school tasks and athletic tasks. Their teachers provide them with accurate feedback about their performance in their subject area. The teachers avoid global and nonspecific feedback ("You are a good person.", "You are all special in some way.", or "You should feel good about yourself.") in favor of specific feedback about their actual performance.

Although global self-esteem can be important for general mental health, in the academic domains, it is more important for students' learning that they have accurate feedback about their performance and begin to develop accurate and positive perceptions of their competence. General self-esteem improvement may not be that helpful, particularly when students can see that they can't do a certain type of math or science problem. In this case, older children from later elementary school onward will quickly surmise the insincerity of the praise and discount it in terms of their perception of ability to perform the specific task.

SUMMARY

The expectancy construct, in various guises, is one of the most important mediators of achievement behavior. Early research on expectancy constructs moved motivational psychology away from a dependence on a simplistic behavioral psychology to a more rational and cognitive paradigm that is still dominant today. Moreover, these early cognitive models of motivation stressed the importance of the individual's perceptions and beliefs as mediators of behavior, thereby focusing motivational research on the subjective and phenomenological psychology of the individual. These early theories focused on people's expectations for success and their value for the task. Current research on expectancy and value constructs continues in this tradition of focusing on these two general beliefs of the individual, although researchers do attempt to include contextual influences in their models.

There are three general research traditions on expectancy beliefs: expectancy-value theory, self-perceptions of competence research, and self-efficacy theory. Eccles and Wigfield and their colleagues have revised Atkinson's expectancy-value model by making it more social cognitive in nature to reflect the current cognitive paradigm of motivation. They have focused on students' expectancy for success and perceptions of ability for academic tasks in a number of large-scale correlational and longitudinal studies in schools. This research reflects some of the best ecologically valid studies of student motivation, given the focus on school and classroom tasks and the fact that they have followed the same students over time to actually investigate how motivational beliefs predict future behavior. They consistently find that students' expectancy beliefs about their capabilities to do a task and succeed at it are closely related to actual achievement on standardized tests as well as course grades.

The research on self-perceptions of ability has had a developmental focus and has investigated these self-perceptions in young children, adolescents, and adults. Current research suggests that self-perceptions of competence are domain specific, not global, although there is not agreement about the specificity of the domain. Self-perceptions of competence also are theoretically and empirically distinct from self-esteem. Perceptions of competence concern students' judgments of their capability in a domain and, hence, are more cognitive evaluations, whereas self-esteem is a more affective and global reaction to the self. Most students, even relatively young elementary school children, have relatively accurate self-perceptions of their own competence in specific domains. Moreover, when they are inaccurate, most children overestimate their competence, not underestimate it, although there are negative consequences for those who do underestimate their competence. Current research suggests that perceptions of competence are related in a reciprocal manner to actual achievement and performance.

Self-efficacy theory is a third model that stresses the importance of an expectancy construct for motivated behavior. Self-efficacy is based in social cognitive theory, which has its roots in the more behavioral learning theory, in contrast to the more personality-based expectancy-value theory and the developmental perspective of the perceptions-of-competence research. As such, self-efficacy theory assumes that self-efficacy is much more situation specific and defines efficacy in terms of judgments of capability to perform specific actions in light of specific goals. Research has consistently shown self-efficacy beliefs to be related to academic achievement and performance on standardized tests and actual school tasks in addition to self-report measures of cognitive engagement and self-regulated learning.

There are developmental, gender, and ethnic differences to consider in children's expectancy beliefs. In terms of developmental differences, research suggests that younger children are more likely to have relatively high perceptions of their competence and that the overall mean level of these perceptions declines with age. In particular, the research suggests that the decline is greatest when students make the transition to junior high school. There are both psychological and more sociological explanations for this drop. The psychological explanations focus on the changes in children's cognitive skills and beliefs as mediators of this age difference, whereas the more sociological explanations stress the changes in the nature of the school environment as the children move into secondary schools. The trends for gender and ethnic differences are much harder to summarize given the vagaries and confounding of gender, SES, and ethnicity in the samples or analyses in the research. Females do seem to have somewhat lower or inaccurate perceptions of competence given their performance, but there is little evidence for the idea that African Americans have lower self-perceptions of competence or lower expectations for success.

Attributional Processes

Roy and Linda are ninth graders taking algebra in a high school. Roy is an average student, not the best student in algebra, but he is passing the class. He usually gets B's and an occasional C$^+$ on the big end-of-chapter tests. On his daily homework, he might miss one or two problems, but normally he gets most of the problems correct. Linda is one of the best math students in the class. She usually gets A's and only occasionally gets a B$^+$. Her homework is almost always perfect.

The class is now studying quadratic equations and how to graph them. The whole class is having a little more difficulty than usual with this part of the course. The teacher, Mr. Kiley, spends a lot of time working through one or two examples of how to graph the problems, but doesn't stop for student questions very often. Both Roy and Linda listen hard and pay attention in class, but Linda asks questions often; Roy never asks questions.

Roy seems to be missing most of the problems on his homework on quadratic equations, but he is not sure why. When he looks at his corrected homework, he wonders to himself, What did I do wrong here? I just don't get this material. It seems so abstract and it's hard to see how this relates to anything. I just can't do this. It's too hard for me. I think I'm just not cut out to be a math person. Roy does not work as hard on this material as usual.

Linda also has been having a little more trouble, missing more problems than usual on her homework. However, when she gets back her homework, she looks it over and says to herself, I don't understand this, so I'll have to ask Mr. Kiley about this problem. Maybe I'm just not studying hard enough. I'll have to go back to the book and my notes and see what I'm doing wrong. She increases the amount of time she works on algebra.

The algebra class as a whole does not do very well on the end-of-chapter test; the overall class average is lower than usual. Roy gets a D$^-$ and Linda gets a C$^+$ on the test. Roy is very embarrassed and ashamed by the D. He wonders why he *did so poorly on this test compared to other end-of-chapter tests: I know I have been having trouble on the homework and didn't work that hard, but I didn't think I was this dumb. Maybe I just have no ability for higher level math. I think maybe I've gone as far as I can go in math given my ability for it. Roy is so ashamed of his grade, he doesn't talk to anyone about it. For the remainder of the course, Roy puts forth even less effort in algebra and spends more time on his other classes. His math grades show a drop over the course of the year, and he ends up getting a C for his overall math course grade.*

Linda's affective reaction to the C⁺ is one of shock and displeasure. She has never gotten a C before in her life on any test in any subject. She thinks to herself, Oh my god, my parents are going to kill me. I'll be grounded for sure. I studied pretty hard for this test, and it is so embarrassing to get a C⁺. I know Mr. Kiley will think I blew it off. I wonder if everyone else did poorly. I'll have to see what my friends got on the test. Maybe it was just a very hard test and that's why I didn't do so well. She talks to other kids in the class and finds out the highest grade was a B by the reigning math star. She feels better and keeps on trying hard in math. She gets an A for her final course grade.

This little case study illustrates a number of important aspects about attribution theory. We will refer back to Roy and Linda as we discuss the model in this chapter, but what is your prediction about the level of their expectancies for success and self-efficacy beliefs for math at the end of the year? What are your predictions about them in terms of their choosing to go on to take more math courses?

OVERVIEW OF THE ATTRIBUTIONAL MODEL

The preceding chapter discussed the motivational constructs of expectancy for success, perceptions of competence, and self-efficacy, and their links to achievement behaviors. Given that these expectancy constructs are very central to motivational dynamics, it is important to understand how individuals construct these beliefs and what influences the development of these beliefs. In this chapter and Chapter 5, we discuss the various psychological and social cognitive processes that help to shape the construction of individuals' expectancy beliefs. Here, we focus on attribution theory and research on the attributional processes that have a direct link to individuals' expectancy beliefs. Although there has been a great deal of research on attribution theory, the one person who has made the greatest contribution to attribution theory in achievement contexts is Bernard Weiner. Our explication of this theory and approach relies heavily on his research and writings (e.g., Weiner, 1979, 1985a, 1986, 1992).

Attribution theory is a cognitive theory of motivation and is based on a general "godlike" metaphor of the individual (Weiner, 1992) that suggests that individuals are conscious, rational, all-knowing decision makers. This metaphor is in contrast to the machine metaphor that equates human behavior with a nonconscious automaton that can produce "output," or behaviors, in reaction to stimuli in the environment or as a function of certain types of internal drives. Two general assumptions are derived from the godlike metaphor in attribution theory.

The first assumption of attribution theory is that individuals are motivated by a goal of understanding and mastering the environment and themselves. This goal is the main instigator of behavior, and the theory does not propose any other goals, needs, motives, or drives (e.g., motive for success, fear of failure, need for affiliation, need for power, intrinsic motivation). Continuing the metaphor of person as scientist, just as scientists are motivated to understand the natural world in order to predict and control future events, individuals are motivated to understand and master their own world in order to make it more predictable and controllable. As Kelley (1971) notes, "The attributor is not simply an attributor, a seeker after knowledge; his latent goal in attaining knowledge is that of effective management of himself and his environment" (p. 22). This striving for mastery and understanding has a functional value for individuals that allows them to learn and adapt to their environment.

The second assumption of attribution theory states that people are naive scientists, trying to understand their environment and, in particular, trying to understand the *causal determinants* of their own behavior as well as the behavior of others. Accordingly, as a function of their search for mastery, individuals seek to understand *why* things happen and why people say and do the things that they do. For example, in the schooling context, students may seek to understand why they failed or passed an exam, as did Roy and Linda. A teacher may attempt to understand the reasons why one student in the class can learn to read so easily and another one has difficulty. In our example, Mr. Kiley, the math teacher, probably did wonder why Linda, who usually does so well in math, got a lower grade than usual on that test. In fact, he should try to determine why all the students did so poorly on this material and if his teaching is part of the reason. In the same way, attribution theory can be applied to other aspects of everyday life, such as affiliation behaviors where individuals may try to understand why someone will not go out on a date with them. Besides these achievement and affiliation domains, the search for causes is commonplace in many other domains, such as sports (Why did your favorite team win or lose?), economics (Why did your friend lose his or her job?), and even in criminal justice (Why did this person commit this crime?), with implications for behavior and affect in these domains as well.

This search for cognitive mastery complements the general pleasure-pain principle that is the cornerstone of Freudian and drive theory models of motivation. Attribution theorists do not disavow the empirically documented fact that individuals often strive to increase pleasure and avoid pain, but rather they suggest that there are occasions when individuals will not act in accordance with this general principle. For example, rewards do not always result in increased activity, as shown in the research on intrinsic motivation and the overjustification effect (Lepper, Greene, & Nisbett, 1973). In addition, as Weiner (1986) points out, there are occasions when seeking information (i.e., how other students did on a test, what kinds of material goods your neighbors have) can result in painful negative affect (loss of self-esteem, jealousy, envy). Nevertheless, individuals often do seek out social comparison information in order to evaluate their own capabilities and performances. Linda actively asked other students about their grade on the test in order to help her figure out why she did poorly. Accordingly, we do not always operate under the pleasure-pain principle and the addition of a general goal of cognitive mastery provides another principle that is more in line with the general cognitive perspective of individuals as active and adaptive learners rather than merely passive responders.

The general attributional model is displayed in Figure 4.1, although the model can be much more complex (see Weiner, 1986). The remainder of this chapter will provide a detailed explanation of this figure, but a quick sketch of the most important points may be helpful as an advance organizer. As shown in the second and third columns of Figure 4.1, perceived causes and the causal dimensions that underlie them are the heart of the model. The perceived causes of an event will be influenced by two general types of antecedent conditions: environmental factors and personal factors (shown in column 1). The influence of these two factors on the generation of attributions is termed the *attribution process* (Kelley & Michela, 1980). Environmental factors include specific information (e.g., if the teacher told Roy and Linda that they did poorly on a test because they did not study hard enough) as well as social norms and information (e.g., how others did on the test, how math is generally perceived in the culture). Personal factors include a variety of schemas and prior beliefs individuals might hold about the test and about themselves (e.g., both Linda and Roy have perceptions of their math ability based on past experience prior to the quadratic equation test). These two general factors influence the actual attribution individuals will make in terms of whether they attribute their failure to low aptitude, bad luck, a hard test, lack of effort, a bad mood, fatigue, or just about any other reason that could be generated for failure at a test.

It is important to note that these attributions are the causes *perceived* by the individual. They may or may not be the *actual* causes. When Roy concludes that he did not do well on the test because he lacks math aptitude, then this perceived attribution is the one that produced a psychological consequence (shame) and behavioral consequence (less future effort in math), regardless of

Antecedent Conditions	Perceived Causes	Causal Dimensions	Psychological Consequences	Behavioral Consequences
Environmental factors	*Attributions for*			
Specific information	Ability	Stability	Expectancy for success	Choice
Social norms	Effort			Persistence
Situational features	Luck	Locus	Self-efficacy	Level of effort
	Task difficulty			Achievement
	Teacher	Control	Affect	
Personal factors	Mood			
Causal schemas	Health			
Attributional bias	Fatigue, etc.			
Prior knowledge				
Individual differences				
Attribution Process			**Attributional Process**	

Figure 4.1. Overview of the general attributional model
Material drawn from Weiner (1986, 1992)

the actual causes of the event (he may not have tried very hard and the test was very difficult). In this way, attribution theory is a phenomenological theory of motivation that gives precedence to the individual's construction of reality, not reality per se, in line with other constructive accounts of cognition and learning (e.g., Bruner, Piaget, Vygotsky). Accordingly, although there may be concerns about the accuracy of individuals' attributions (Nisbett & Wilson, 1977), from a motivational perspective, the accuracy of an attribution is not important in order for an attribution to have psychological and behavioral consequences.

The consequences of attributions for an individual's motivation, affect, and behavior are described as the *attributional process* (Kelley & Michela, 1980). As shown in Figure 4.1, attributions can be categorized along three dimensions (stability, locus, and control), according to Weiner's (1986) model. It is these causal dimensions that have the psychological force to influence expectancy for success and self-efficacy beliefs (see Chapter 3) as well as influence affect and actual behavior (columns 4 and 5 in Figure 4.1). These dimensions are described in more detail later in the chapter, but attribution theory assumes that even though there are an infinite number of actual attributions, they can be categorized along these three dimensions. The stability dimension refers to how stable the attribution is over time and ranges from stable to unstable. Causes can be classified as being internal or external (locus) and as controllable or uncontrollable (control).

Accordingly, in the case of Roy, the normative categorization of low aptitude would be that it is stable (his low aptitude will remain the same over time), that it is internal to Roy, and that it is not controllable by Roy (there is not much he can do to change his math aptitude). Attributional theory and research have shown that it is the stability dimension that is most closely related to expectancy for success (Weiner, 1986). In our example, Roy did poorly on a math test and attributed it to a stable cause (low math aptitude), so then he should not have a very high expectancy for success for future math tests. Conversely, if Roy had succeeded and attributed his success to high math aptitude—again, a stable cause—then he should expect to do well on the next math test. In contrast, Linda also did not do as well as in the past, but she attributed her performance to a difficult task (external) and she expects to try harder in the future, so her attribution does not seem to have the same debilitating effects. The links between the dimensions of attributions and affect are discussed in more detail in Chapter 8, but attributional theory (Weiner, 1986, 1992) suggests that esteem-related affects are related to the locus dimension (e.g., we generally feel pride when we think that something internal to us was responsible for a successful outcome) and that social-related affects such as guilt and shame are related to the controllability dimension (e.g., we often feel guilt if we fail due to something under our control or shame when it is not under our control, as in Roy's case).

These expectancy beliefs and affects are then linked to actual behavioral consequences as the final step in the model. As noted in Chapter 3, students with high efficacy and expectancies will tend to choose to pursue a task as well as try harder and persist longer at that task. This engagement should result in higher levels of actual achievement. In the same fashion, positive affects should result in more motivated behavior such as choice, effort, and persistence, whereas negative affects should lead the individual to avoid the task in the future. In our example, Roy begins to decrease his effort in the math class after the low grade and his attribution to low math ability. In contrast, Linda attributes her failure to task difficulty and increases her effort and persistence in math. In this way, attributional theory incorporates the pleasure-pain principle as a governor of the linkages between affect and behavior. Given this brief overview of the model, we now turn to a more detailed description of how attributions are formed and their psychological and behavioral consequences.

THE ANTECEDENTS OF ATTRIBUTIONS

As a cognitive model of motivation based on a metaphor of the naive scientist, attributional theory assumes that the individual will use a variety of information sources as data in order to make inferences (attributions) about the causal determinants of behavior. As noted in Figure 4.1, this information can come from two general sources: external cues and information in the environment as well as knowledge and schemas internal to the person. As the individual attempts to assign causality for an event, traditional attribution theory defines the central task of the perceiver as one of detecting covariation between causes and effects (Heider, 1958).

The Role of Environmental Factors

Specific Information and Social Norms

There are a great number of cues and sources of information presented to individuals that help them detect covariation and causality. First, there is specific information that individuals have access to that provides them with direct knowledge of the causes of their behavior. For example, in the case of Roy and Linda doing poorly on the math test, both of them know how hard they studied for the test. If they did not study or prepare for the test at all, then this lack of effort may be sufficient to cause the failure. Since both of them studied, they cannot attribute poor performance to a complete lack of effort. Interestingly, Roy and Linda have access to this information about their actual level of effort, but their teacher may not have such ready access. Accordingly, Mr. Kiley may make a different attribution for their performance, lacking the specific information about their level of effort. In fact, Linda wonders if Mr. Kiley thinks that she blew the test off; she worries that Mr. Kiley will think she didn't study for the test. This example highlights an important distinction in attribution theory between the actor (Roy/Linda) and an observer (Mr. Kiley) that we will discuss in more detail later. However, it is important to note that actors generally have more specific information about their behavior and what led up to the outcome than people who only observe the behavior and the outcome (e.g., Mr. Kiley really doesn't know how much they studied at home, but he may infer little effort for Linda, particularly given her past record of success). At the same time, this example also points out how an actor's own behavior can be external information that the actor can "read off of" to make inferences about causes. In this sense, attributional theory parallels Bem's (1972) self-perception theory and Bandura's (1986) social cognitive model where individuals make inferences about the self from observing their own behavior (see Chapters 3 and 5).

Other types of specific information that can influence an individual's attributions include specific feedback from the task or from others. One of the most direct types of information that students receive is teacher feedback. Teacher classroom feedback can influence students' perceptions of their ability and effort in a fairly straightforward manner (Pintrich & Blumenfeld, 1985). Teacher feedback usually stresses effort (I know you can do better if you try harder.), however, and few ability attributions seem to be made by teachers (see Blumenfeld et al., 1982; Blumenfeld, Hamilton, Bossert, Wessels, & Meece, 1983). If Mr. Kiley were to tell Roy specifically that he did poorly on the math exam because he lacks the aptitude for math, then Roy (in the absence of other information) may accept this attributional statement by the teacher as the major cause of his failure. This attributional feedback about lack of ability may be particularly salient given the infrequency with which teachers seem to make ability attributions. More research is needed on how students integrate the usual and frequently occurring classroom feedback with other more infrequent, yet potentially very salient, feedback (see Blumenfeld et al., 1982).

Information about the task, in particular, task difficulty, can influence the types of attributions that are generated as explanations for the outcome. Weiner and Kukla (1970) provided subjects with information about the relative success or failure of others on a task (ranging from 99% of others were successful to 1% successful). Subjects then rated whether a target person was responsible for success or failure. The results showed that subjects were likely to attribute the outcome to the task when there was consistency between the target's and others' outcome. If most everyone succeeded or failed, then the target's outcome was attributed to an easy or hard task, respectively. In contrast, if the target succeeded when most people failed or failed when most people succeeded, the attribution was made to the person (Weiner, 1992). Continuing with our example, if almost all the students in Roy's math class fail the exam, then he is not likely to attribute his failure to something about himself; rather, he will probably infer that the exam was a very difficult task. If he is the only one to fail the test and everyone else in his class does well, however, then he might see it as an easy task and attribute his failure to some personal characteristic (e.g., lack of aptitude, low skill, low effort, bad mood, etc.). This type of information about the relative difficulty of the task given other students' performance demonstrates how individuals can use social norm information to make attributions (Weiner, 1992).

Consensus, Consistency, and Distinctiveness

Although specific information and social norms do provide cues to the perceiver about what type of attributions to make, Kelley (1967) proposed that all information can be categorized according to several factors that will influence the attribution process. Kelley, working from the intuitive scientist metaphor, believed that the basic task confronting the perceiver was to assign causality to either the person or the environment, reflecting the general Lewinian principle that behavior is a function of both: $B = f(P, E)$. To answer this question, the perceiver uses a process that parallels the analysis of variance (ANOVA) model that researchers use to determine the covariation among independent and dependent variables. In the case of making attributions for an outcome (the dependent measure), there are three factors (the independent variables) that can influence the attribution process: the *distinctiveness* of the entities, the *consensus* across persons, and the *consistency* over time and situations.

The classic example from Kelley (1967) that illustrates the operation of these factors and their influence on the attribution process concerns a movie. If Anne recommends a movie to Roger, and Roger must decide whether to go see the movie, he must determine whether the movie (the entity) is good or if Anne's recommendation should be attributed to something about her (the person). If Roger knows that Anne responds differentially to some movies and not others (high distinctiveness), then Roger will probably infer that it is something about the movie (the entity) that is good. At the same time, if Roger hears from other people besides Anne that the movie is good (high consensus), then this consensus across people increases the probability that an entity attribution will be made (the entity—the movie—is good). In the same way, if Anne has gone to see the movie several times and still likes it (high consistency across time) and also has seen it in several different situations (with friends at a theater, watching a video at home alone—high consistency across situations), then Roger will tend to make an entity attribution (the movie is good). In this case of high distinctiveness, high consensus, and high consistency, an attribution to the entity—the movie—is most likely to be made. In contrast, if there is low distinctiveness (Anne likes all movies) and low consensus (other people don't like the movie), then a person attribution is most likely to be made (e.g., it is something about Anne).

These three dimensions of distinctiveness, consensus, and consistency can be applied very readily to the attribution process in classrooms. For example, Ms. Early is a seventh-grade science teacher who is trying to determine why Carla, a student in her first-period class, is misbehaving. Of course, in many situations like this, the effect (misbehavior) may be a function of the interaction between the classroom (entity) and student (person), but depending on the distinctiveness, consensus, and consistency dimensions of the information, different types of attributions may be made. If Carla only misbehaves in Ms. Early's classroom and not other classrooms (high distinctiveness) and always misbehaves in her classroom (high consistency), then it increases the probability that something about her classroom may be responsible. If Ms. Early finds that many other students in her first-period class are beginning to misbehave (high consensus across persons), then it seems likely that it is something about her class that is the causal factor. In contrast, if Carla misbehaves often in all classroom situations (low distinctiveness) and no other children misbehave in Ms. Early's class (low consensus), then an attribution might be made to Carla.

Kelley's covariation-ANOVA model is a very rational model of the attribution process and there is evidence that individuals do not always use all three types of information equally (Fiske & Taylor, 1991). In the social psychological literature it generally appears that consistency information is the most often utilized and consensus the least utilized (Kruglanski, 1977; Major, 1980; Olson, Ellis, & Zanna, 1983). In reviewing research on classroom teachers, expectancies, and attributions, Peterson and Barger (1984) suggest that consistency information is the most salient to teachers. They concluded that teachers are most likely to make attributions for a student's behavior that are consistent with prior beliefs about that individual student. For example, when a normally high-achieving student does well, the teacher is likely to attribute that performance to the students' ability, thereby maintaining prior beliefs. In contrast, if a normally low-achieving student does well on a task, this is inconsistent with prior beliefs and will be attributed to some unstable factor like luck (Clark & Peterson, 1986).

The Role of Personal Factors

The information presented to individuals obviously influences their attributions. However, given the cognitive assumptions built into attribution theory, there are a number of personal factors that also influence the attribution process. We have divided them into four general categories: (a) causal rules and schemas, (b) attributional biases (a certain type of causal schema), (c) prior knowledge, and (d) individual differences (see Figure 4.1).

Causal Rules and Schemas

Causal rules and schemas include the various principles and beliefs that individuals have about causality that they use to make attributions. These rules and schemas are assumed to be learned, stored, and represented cognitively by the individual and can be differentially activated by different situational cues in the environment. First, there are some basic principles that individuals seem to use to establish causality, and these principles seem to be established at a fairly young age, by about age 3 (Kassin & Pryor, 1985; White, 1988). Fiske and Taylor (1991) suggest that there are six general principles that individuals have learned to use to judge causality:

1. Causes must precede effects. Even children as young as 3 know that events that occur after the target event cannot be causal factors for the target event. In our example of Roy failing the math exam, the fact that he had a fight with his girlfriend 2 weeks after he took the math test cannot be a cause of his failure on the exam.

2. Events that share temporal contiguity with the target event are more likely to be seen as causal factors. If Roy had a fight with his girlfriend the night before the math exam, he might readily attribute his failure to this emotional event.

3. Events that are spatially contiguous are more likely to be linked in cause-and-effect relations. If the school band is playing outside the classroom window the day of the math exam, Roy might attribute his failure to that distraction, in contrast to the case where the band is playing on the football field, quite a distance from the classroom.

4. Perceptually salient stimuli are more likely to be seen as causal than stimuli that are in the visual background. Salient events like a fight with a girlfriend the night before an exam might be seen as more causal than mundane events like not keeping up with the daily math homework.

5. Causes resemble effects. Individuals tend to attribute "big" effects to "big" causes and "little" effects to "little" causes (Fiske & Taylor, 1991). In Roy's case, a big event like failing a final exam and failing the course might be attributed to a more traumatic event like a romantic breakup or his parent's divorce than "smaller" events like not keeping up with the work.

6. Representative causes are attributed to effects. Individuals often compare a current outcome to similar outcomes and then infer that the same cause of the related events are determinants of the current event (Fiske & Taylor, 1991). For example, Roy may have failed math exams in a previous course that was taught by a poor teacher. This leads him to infer that the teacher he has this year is also poor and that is why he failed the math test.

Besides these general causal principles that individuals might use to make attributions, there are several general causal schemas that can be used to make causal inferences. These schemas may be used when there is not complete information available in terms of the three general sources of distinctiveness, consistency, and consensus. These schemas are general beliefs individuals have that help guide their information processing in terms of attributional search and inference. In particular, they are often used when there have not been multiple occasions of the event, such as surprising events (e.g., failure at a task when success is the norm) or novel situations (Weiner, 1992). First, as Heider (1958) proposed, there is a general *compensatory* schema whereby individuals believe that one cause can compensate for the absence or weakness of another cause. In the achievement context, it is generally assumed that effort can compensate for ability and vice versa (Weiner, 1992). So, in Roy's case, most people will believe that if he has low math aptitude, then higher levels of effort should compensate for his low ability and lead to a better outcome than low effort coupled with low aptitude. Kelley (1972) proposed that there are two specific causal schemas that help individuals make causal inferences when there is not complete information available. The *multiple sufficient* and *multiple necessary* schemas can be used to determine causality and also predict effects given the existence of different causes (Weiner, 1992).

Both schemas refer to the case where there is an effect (*E*) that is related to two causes (*A* and *B*). The multiple sufficient schema describes the *disjunctive* relation between *A*, *B*, and *E*; that is, for *E* to occur, only *A or B* have to be present. In contrast, in the multiple necessary schema, both *A and B* have to be present for *E* to occur—the *conjunctive* relation. In the achievement context, aptitude and effort are often seen as two causes that can lead to success or failure. Kun and Weiner (1973) provided adult subjects with information about a target's success or failure, the ease or difficulty of the task, and the target's ability or effort level. The subjects were then asked to rate how certain they were that the "other" cause, which they did not have information about (either ability or effort level), was present or not. In success situations where the task was difficult, students who were told that the target had high ability (or high effort) also rated that the target had high effort (or high ability). In this case, the multiple necessary schema was used by the subjects; both effort and ability were seen as necessary for success on a difficult task. However, in the case of success at an easy task, subjects were unlikely to judge that the compensatory cause (effort or ability) was present. In this case, the multiple sufficient schema was invoked and the subjects assumed that just high effort (or high ability) was sufficient for success at an easy task (Weiner, 1992). For the failure outcome, the results were somewhat the reverse. If the target failed at a difficult task with low ability (or low effort), then the subjects were not likely to rate that low effort (or low ability) was present as well (multiple sufficient schema). In contrast, for failure at an easy task with low ability (or low effort), then subjects were likely to rate that low effort (or low ability) also was a cause (multiple necessary schema). As Weiner (1992) points out,

> One is reminded of the saying that a chain is only as strong as its weakest link; that is, all components must be strong for "success," and the absence of strength in any of the subparts is sufficient for "failure." It therefore appears that the attributions for success and failure might be governed by somewhat different psychological rules. (p. 242)

Attributional Biases

Research on the attribution process suggests that there are a number of schemas or inference rules that people may use to make attributions that are often incorrect or can lead to biases on the part of the perceiver (Fiske & Taylor,

1991; Nisbett & Ross, 1980). Table 4.1 lists some of the common strategies and how they might be used by both students and teachers in different situations.

1. The fundamental attribution error. This common inference error involves the attribution of others' behavior to dispositional or personal factors, ignoring situational factors that might be partially or even more causally related to the outcome (Heider, 1958; Nisbett & Ross, 1980; Ross, 1977). This bias has been documented in a large number of experimental studies where the situation clearly determines the behavior, but observers will still make an attribution to the target's personality or attitudes. For example, in the classic study by Jones and Harris (1967), subjects were asked to read essays or listen to speeches on controversial issues (defending Castro's Cuba, legalizing marijuana). The subjects were told that the writers or speakers were assigned to present one side or the other. Nevertheless, the subjects still attributed the opinions expressed in the essay or speech to the disposition of the writer or speaker, not to the fact that they had been assigned to write from that point of view (Ross & Nisbett, 1991). As shown in the examples in Table 4.1, this could easily happen in the classroom context, where teachers might be likely to attribute a student's behavior to something about the student instead of the classroom.

2. Actor-observer perspective. This bias refers to the propensity for individuals to make differential attributions depending on their perspective as an actor in the situation or as an observer and is related to the fundamental attribution error. Attribution research has shown that actors often attribute their own behavior to situational features, whereas observers will attribute actors' behavior to some personal or dispositional characteristic of the actor (Jones & Nisbett, 1972; Weiner, 1992). In a classroom situation, this bias would lead students to make dispositional attributions about the teacher and teachers to make dispositional attributions about the students (see examples in Table 4.1).

There is some empirical support for both a perceptual and an informational explanation for this bias (Fiske & Taylor, 1991). The perceptual explanation suggests that when an observer sees another person doing something, the most salient stimulus is the person acting, not the situation, which becomes background to the observer. In contrast, from the actor's perspective of the situation, what is most salient are the features of the situation, not her or his own behavior. Given these differences in perception and attention, actor-observer differences will arise (Storms, 1973). The informational explanation suggests that actors have access to a great deal of information about themselves, including their thoughts, feelings, and intentions in the situation, as well as information about how they have acted in similar situations in the past. This information allows actors to note how differences in the current situation might produce differences in their behavior. In contrast, an observer does not have access to this information and often does not see an actor across different situations and so may make a dispositional attribution (Eisen, 1979; Fiske & Taylor, 1991).

Table 4.1. Common Attributional Biases from the Student and the Teacher Perspectives

Attribution	Student Perspective	Teacher Perspective
Fundamental attribution error Attribute other's behavior to a disposition or trait	Student perceives all teacher behavior as function of a disposition "Ms. Baker is always mean." "Mr. Smith is prejudiced against minorities and women."	Teacher perceives all student behavior as a function of disposition "Sam is just a very lazy person. He never tries hard." "Sally has no aptitude for science."
Actor-observer perspective Attribute other's behavior to disposition, but own behavior to situation	Student perceives his behavior as a function of situation, but attributes teacher's behavior to a disposition "I hit him because he was bugging me, but now you are punishing me because you don't like me and always pick on me."	Teacher perceives his behavior as a function of classroom, but attributes students' behavior to disposition "You are a very aggressive boy and I'm just trying to keep control of my class."
Self-serving bias Accept personal responsibility for success, deny responsibility for failure	Student perceives her successes is due to her behavior, but attributes failures to other factors "I did well in math because I'm smart at that, but poorly in English because the teacher is terrible when she teaches English."	Teacher perceives her success as due to her behavior, but attributes failures to other factors "I did a great unit in math, but the students just aren't motivated to study English literature."
Self-centered bias Regardless of success or failure, accept more personal responsibility for a jointly determined outcome	Student will perceive that he is more responsible for an outcome, even when it is due to his and other's behavior "I did more of the work on this project than all the other students in my small group."	Teacher will perceive that he is more responsible for an outcome even when it is due to his and other's behavior "Third period class discussion was excellent. I'm a really good facilitator of discussions."
False consensus effect Assume that your beliefs and behavior are typical of most people	Student perceives that her beliefs or behavior are representative of most other students "I hate math and most girls hate it just like me." "All the other kids are cheating, so I can too."	Teacher assumes that her beliefs or behavior are representative of most other teachers "Like all the other teachers in this building, I think the biggest problem is that the kids are just not motivated."

3. Self-serving or hedonic bias. This inference error is also called the ego or self-enhancement bias, the ego-defensiveness or self-protective bias, and the beneffectance bias (Weiner, 1992). It refers to the propensity for individuals to take personal responsibility for successful outcomes (a self-enhancing bias) and deny responsibility for failure outcomes (a self-protective bias). For example, when you win at tennis, it is because you are much better than your opponent, but if you lose, it is because of bad luck or poor court conditions. This self-serving bias has been empirically demonstrated in a number of different contexts including athletics, politics, gambling, and classrooms (Mullen & Riordan, 1988; Weiner, 1992) as well as cross-culturally (Fletcher & Ward, 1988).

There may be several reasons people make these types of self-serving attributions. First, it seems likely that most individuals want to look good, and these attributions can be used to manage others' impressions of them. Second, as suggested in the hedonic bias label, these self-serving attributions can act to protect individuals' egos and sense of self-worth in keeping with the pleasure-pain principle. Finally, besides these motivational mechanisms, there are cognitive or rational explanations that suggest that most people expect to succeed (particularly the oft-tested college student who has a history of success), they also strive to succeed, and when they do succeed, are more likely to recall other instances of success when they had control and, therefore, attribute the current success to their own behavior (Fiske & Taylor, 1991; Weiner, 1992).

In the classroom context, the research is mixed regarding the propensity of teachers to make self-serving attributions (e.g., it is my superior teaching when students do well, but it is their lack of motivation when they do poorly) for their students' performance (Clark & Peterson, 1986; Peterson & Barger, 1984). A number of studies (Beckman, 1970; Brandt, Hayden, & Brophy, 1975; Johnson, Feigenbaum, & Weiby, 1964; Wiley & Eskilson, 1978) have shown that teachers do make ego-enhancing attributions. However, as Peterson & Barger (1984) have pointed out, three of these studies were experimental studies (all except Wiley & Eskilson) with preservice teachers or psychology students assigned to teach a "fictitious" student who was then either successful or unsuccessful. In contrast, studies by Ames (1975) and Ross, Bierbrauer, & Polly (1974), where college students were assigned to be teachers or students and actually interacted with each other, showed that the "teachers" were more likely to attribute success to the student and failure to their teaching, a counterdefensive attribution (see Clark & Peterson, 1986). It seems that the different results can be explained by the presence or absence of a "real" student and face-to-face interactions between teacher and student. In the presence of real students and actual interactions between teachers and students (as would be the case in classrooms), the studies show that teachers will be more likely to make a counterdefensive attribution.

There is evidence that people are more likely to make a self-enhancing attribution and accept credit for success than they are to make a self-protective attribution and deny responsibility for failure (Fiske & Taylor, 1991; Miller & Ross, 1975). In fact, attributing failure to some internal characteristic that an individual has control over can be adaptive. If the individual fails and attributes it to poor effort or lack of a learnable skill, then it is possible to actually change effort levels or attempt to learn the skill and increase the probability of success for the future. In contrast, if individuals continually protect their self-worth by making attributions for failure to external and uncontrollable events and even engage in some self-defeating behaviors (e.g., staying up late and partying before an exam), in the long run this type of attributional pattern and behavior is not adaptive. Accordingly, whereas the self-serving bias can help to maintain self-worth, it also has costs associated with it (see Covington, 1992).

4. Self-centered bias. In many situations, an outcome is jointly determined by the individual and the situation, including other people. The self-centered bias occurs when individuals take more responsibility for an outcome, regardless of the actual success or failure. For example, the self-centered bias would be operating when both husband and wife think that they do more than half of the housework or two coauthors both think they were more responsible for the research and therefore deserve to be first author on the resulting empirical article. As shown in Table 4.1, in the classroom context where most behavior is probably a function of both teacher and student, this bias would lead the teacher to believe that he was more responsible for a good discussion, rather than the fact that the students also were prepared and willing to discuss the class material. The other example in Table 4.1 may arise more frequently, given the current popularity of small-group instruction, whereby students, operating under the self-centered bias, may claim more responsibility for a group project for themselves rather than recognizing the contributions of others.

5. False consensus effect. As we have noted, one of the sources of information that individuals use in making attributions is consensus concerning others' performance or behavior. The false consensus effect occurs when individuals come to see their behavior or attitude as typical, as representing how most other people would respond in the same situation. There are a number of viable explanations of this effect, including a tendency for individuals to seek out and affiliate with others who share similar views, a propensity to focus on their own opinions and ignore or discount other, divergent views, a tendency to interpret new situations in light of previous beliefs and predetermined courses of action, and a need to see their own beliefs as good, right, and typical, and so they maintain these beliefs to preserve their self-esteem (Fiske & Taylor, 1991). In the classroom or school context, this type of bias could result in teachers who share similar views on instruction to seek each other out and reinforce for each other the "correctness" of their beliefs in contrast to those of other teachers or administrators. This particular situation could result in rather rigid beliefs about students or instructional practices that could impede school change and improvement.

Prior Knowledge and Individual Differences

Along with these biases, prior knowledge and individual differences also can influence the attribution process. Both prior knowledge and individual differences represent, to some extent, exceptions to the general "laws" or principles of attribution theory. Most social psychologists concerned with attribution theory have focused on the general principles just discussed in the previous section, whereas personality psychologists have been more concerned with the individual differences in the attribution process.

Prior knowledge and beliefs.   First, in terms of prior knowledge, the original models of the attribution process (e.g., Heider, 1958; Kelley, 1972) proposed that the various attribution processes such as use of distinctiveness, consistency, and consensus information and causal schemas were "content-free" processes that would operate in any domain. However, more recent research suggests that individuals have prior knowledge about specific domains that they use to guide the attribution process (Fiske & Taylor, 1991). Hilton and Slugoski (1986) have proposed an abnormal conditions attribution model that suggests that people only look to explain events when the outcome is unexpected. In these situations, individuals will search for the conditions that gave rise to this "abnormal" event and attribute the event to these abnormal conditions. In addition, this model assumes that people have a great deal of prior knowledge about "scripted" events, those situations where there is a fairly high degree of consensus about normal behavior in that situation (e.g., a script for eating at a restaurant in terms of the order of events). If something out of the ordinary happens that results in a deviation from the script, then observers will search for the conditions that gave rise to this unexpected deviation and attribute the outcome to these conditions.

For example, in a school context, teachers and most students, except for very young children perhaps, have a wealth of general knowledge about classrooms, instruction, and learning that they can activate to explain classroom events. This prior knowledge reduces the load on information processing by limiting the attributional search to the causes that are most likely to be operative, even though there are an infinite number of causes for any classroom event. In addition, many of the activities in a classroom are scripted and both teachers and students know what is expected. Deviations from the norms of the script can lead to an attributional search on the part of the teacher or students for the causes that give rise to an abnormal event such as a normally easy-going and pleasant teacher "losing her cool" and shouting at the students. In this abnormal case, the students may be likely to attribute the shouting to a personal problem (bad mood, bad day) of the teacher, or, perhaps, to something they actually did to deserve such behavior because the teacher does not normally shout at them. This would be in contrast to a teacher who shouts and screams at the students all the time. In this case, the students would be less likely to attribute this teacher's behavior to something they did and most likely attribute it to the teacher and his personality or usual instructional behavior.

These scripts are for general knowledge about schools, classrooms, teachers, and students. However, in a similar fashion, individuals can have personal knowledge or scripts or self-schemas about themselves that represent consistent individual differences in the way they perceive and respond to events. For example, most individuals have perceptions of their competence to do different tasks and have self-concepts about different domains, as we discussed in Chapter 3. This type of prior self-knowledge can influence the types of attributions that individuals will make in different situations (Ames & Felker, 1979). For example, if a student has a relatively high self-perception of competence in math, yet encounters a failure situation occasionally, this student may be more likely to attribute the failure to a hard task or lack of effort, not to lack of ability, in contrast to a student with a generally low perception of competence. In addition, individual differences can extend beyond personal knowledge and conscious self-schemas to particular ways individuals have of interpreting events that can lead to differences in the attribution process.

Individual differences.   One of the most consistent individual differences that is related to the types of attributions individuals might make is *locus of control* (Rotter, 1966). This construct from social learning theory refers to the tendency of some people, labeled *internals*, to perceive a contingency between their behavior and reinforcement, and others, labeled *externals*, to perceive that there is not a strong link between their behavior and reinforcement. In terms of how this individual difference might influence the attribution process, internals would be most likely to make internal types of attributions given an outcome, whereas externals would be more likely to make external types of attributions. Although there has been a great deal of research on the locus-of-control construct in general and in motivation and education specifically (e.g., Crandall, Katkovsky, & Crandall, 1965), the general locus-of-control construct has been superseded by other constructs that represent a more fine-grained analysis of the role of control beliefs (e.g., Connell, 1985; Peterson et al., 1993; Skinner, Chapman, & Baltes, 1988b). In addition, Weiner (1986) has shown in both logical and empirical analyses that the locus-of-control construct systematically confounds two dimensions that need to be separated theoretically and practically: one regarding the internality-externality and the other concerning the controllability-uncontrollability of an event. Given this more current research, there is little utility in continuing to use the general locus-of-control construct in motivational research.

A more recent formulation of the importance of controllability is learned helplessness theory and research (Peterson et al., 1993). Attribution theory, as formulated by Heider, Kelley, and Weiner, is concerned with the development of general principles of social psychology and social cognition. As such, it has not been concerned with individual differences. In contrast, the work on learned helplessness theory grows out of the interest of personality and clinical psychologists in individual differences that reliably predict adaptive behavior. The learned helplessness model assumes that individuals search for causal explanations of events (especially "bad" events like school failure, interpersonal problems with friends or lovers, poor health, loss in sports) and that these causal explanations and the dimensions that underlie them influence expectations about future events. In turn, these future expectations determine behavioral reactions such as passivity, affect, anxiety, and depression (Peterson et al., 1993). The learned helplessness model is basically the same as that displayed in the attributional model of Figure 4.1.

The main difference between the two models is that learned helplessness theory proposes that there is an individual difference construct, called *explanatory style*, formerly called *attributional style* (see Peterson & Seligman, 1984), that influences the types of causal explanations that individuals will make in different situations. Explanatory style refers to a habitual way of explaining events that is a cognitive characteristic of the individual (Peterson et al., 1993). This construct is often assessed with the Attributional Style Questionnaire (ASQ) (see Peterson, Semmel, et al., 1982) whereby individuals are asked to explain why 12 common events (6 with good and 6 with bad outcomes) might happen to them and then rate the causes in terms of internality-externality, stability-instability, and globality-specificity. The research on the ASQ suggests that there are consistent individual differences that emerge from this questionnaire, with some individuals much more likely to attribute common events to internal, stable, and global causes.

Other research has shown that these stable individual differences can then predict the types of attributions that people might make in a new situation (Peterson et al., 1993). In a learning theory sense, the individual difference of explanatory style is "generalized" to a new situation and the person interprets the new situation in terms of her explanatory style. In a cognitive, schema theoretic view, explanatory style is a particular type of prior knowledge or belief that is activated in the new situation and then guides information processing and the attribution process. In the classroom situation, if a student has an explanatory style that explains his school failures to internal, stable, and global causes (e.g., I'm just generally stupid and I can't change it.), then when he goes to a new school (transition to middle school, high school, or college) and has a failure experience, he will likely make the same attribution, even when there may be very strong situational determinants (e.g., the new school is much harder).

In sum, both environmental and personal factors influence the attribution process. Attribution theory, based in social psychology, stresses the situational nature of attributions and considers both the features of the situation and the general cognitive rules and schemas that individuals use as possible influences on the actual attributions that will be made in a specific situation. In addition, research from more of a personality and individual difference perspective has suggested that there may be stable individual differences in terms of self-beliefs and explanatory style that can influence the attribution process. We now move on to a discussion of the attributional process (see Figure 4.1) and an examination of the motivational consequences of making certain types of attributions.

THE CONSEQUENCES OF ATTRIBUTIONS

As shown in Figure 4.1, the outcome of the attribution process is an attribution about the perceived cause of the event. The model assumes that given a particular outcome for an event (success or failure on a test, winning or losing in sports, positive or negative interpersonal interaction), an individual will search for the perceived causes of the outcome. This is a crucial step in the model, because without an attribution being made regarding the perceived causes, the remaining steps in the model (see Figure 4.1) would not be followed. The attribution process we have described thus far concerns the *content* of the attribution that might be made given the various environmental and personal factors operating in a specific situation.

Conditions That Foster Spontaneous Attributional Search

The attribution process does not actually specify *if and when* an attribution might be made at all. There is some controversy over this issue of spontaneous attributional thinking in the attribution literature (cf. Smith & Miller, 1983; Weiner, 1985a, 1986). In general, critics noted that many of the studies were experimental studies that specifically asked for subjects to make attributions about an actual lab-induced event or to make attributions for an imagined or hypothetical event. The experiments used both open-ended questionnaires whereby subjects generated their own attributions and rating scales whereby specific attributions were listed by the experimenter and rated by the subjects. The critics noted that all of these studies were reactive and claimed that the attributions were elicited by the experimental procedures but did not reflect individuals' actual causal thinking about the event (Weiner, 1986). In fact, some researchers claimed that people did very little spontaneous attributional thinking in real life and that attributions were of little importance (Smith & Miller, 1983).

More recently, Weiner (1985a, 1986) has summarized the research on the spontaneous use of attributions and concludes that there is good empirical evidence that individuals do make attributions in real-life situations. He bases his conclusions on the results of studies that used methodologies quite different from the classic experimental studies where subjects were asked to rate a list of attributions. These methodologies included the analysis of written material such as newspaper articles, reports, letters, diaries, and journals for attributional statements. On any daily newspaper sports pages, it is likely that there will be at least several attributional statements about why a team won or lost or why an individual player did well or poorly. In fact, Peterson and colleagues (Peterson et al., 1993) suggest that professional athletes' attributional statements about their past successes and failures are related to their future performance, with those attributing their success to skill doing much better than those who attribute it to luck. Two other procedures are more experimental in nature and involve the coding of verbal statements from think-aloud protocols (subjects are asked to talk out loud about what they are thinking or feeling as they do a task) and indirect measures whereby students are asked to do a free recall task or a sentence completion task under the guise of a nonattributional experiment. In all three cases, there is a great deal of evidence that individuals do engage in spontaneous attributional search and make attributional statements (Weiner, 1986).

There are, however, certain conditions when individuals are more likely to engage in attributional search. As Weiner (1986) notes, if an event is unexpected, then an attributional search will often occur. In keeping with the general cognitive perspective, individuals have prior knowledge, beliefs, and expectations about what will happen in a situation in general (scripts) and what might happen to them (personal expectations). For example, after a few years in school, most students have self-perceptions of their competence about doing schoolwork and expectations about future success and failure. If these personal expectations are violated, as in the case of a usually high-achieving student failing an exam (e.g., Linda not doing well on the math exam), then it is more likely that this student will consciously search for the causes of this failure. In contrast, if the student gets a high grade as expected based on past experience, then that student is not likely to engage in attributional search. For example, a college freshmen who has had an excellent high school record enrolls at an elite university and in the first semester suddenly is getting grades of C and lower in all classes. In this situation, it is likely that this student will engage in a great deal of attributional search about personal ability to succeed at this university.

In a sports context, the expectancy disconfirmation principle also holds and there is more likely to be an attributional search when a favored team loses or an underdog wins (Weiner, 1986). In a social context, if someone violates the norms of a well-accepted script (e.g., talking out loud during a lecture), then there is a higher probability of an attributional search for why the individual did not conform than for why everyone else did follow the script. In the same way, in the context of interpersonal attraction, consider a couple who have been dating regularly every weekend for a semester. If one partner suddenly claims to not be available this coming weekend, this will probably lead to an attributional search by the other partner for the perceived causes of the rejection. In contrast, the rejected partner probably did not engage in attributional search the previous weekends when the couple did go out as usual.

Weiner (1986) also notes that the studies of spontaneous attributional search suggest that a negative outcome to an event, regardless of prior expectations, will likely lead to an attributional search. Accordingly, students are more likely to search for the perceived causes of failure than they are for the causes of success. In the same fashion, teachers are probably more likely to make an attributional search for a lesson that did not go well rather than for a lesson that went smoothly. This reaction to failure is adaptive; if individuals understand the causes for failure, then they can attempt to do something about them. Students can change their effort or study strategies, and teachers can change their lesson plans and attempt something different next time.

Besides these two general conditions for the activation of attributional search, Weiner (1986) suggests that there may be other conditions that increase the likelihood of an attributional search. There is a need for more research in general, however, and experimental research in particular to support these conditions. One condition put forth is whether an event or outcome has great interest or importance to the individual. For example, a poor grade on one of the many weekly worksheets in a math class might not generate an attributional search because it does not carry the same importance as a poor grade on the final exam for the class.

Another occasion when attributions might be more likely is in a relatively new situation where the individual does not have a great deal of prior knowledge or fully formed expectations. In this case, attribution theory would assume that a general cognitive mastery goal would be operative and the individual would be searching to understand why things are happening and searching for the causes of these events. For example, when students move to a new school or make a transition to a new school level (e.g., middle school to high school, high school to college), they might be more likely to make more attributions given their unfamiliarity with certain aspects of the new environment. One of the authors of this book has noted an increase in his own attributional searches when he travels outside the United States. He often analyzes everyday interactions with shopkeepers, waiters, and others to understand the way he was treated (Are they treating me this way because I'm an American or because of something I've done that has violated the local norms, or is this the way they treat everyone here in this culture?), whereas in the United States he doesn't give these common interactions a second thought and certainly doesn't do an attributional search to understand the interaction.

In conclusion, there is ample evidence from a number of studies employing a range of methodologies for the existence of spontaneous attributional search. Individuals do engage in a cognitive search to understand the causes of the outcomes of different events. Moreover, this attributional search is most likely to occur when the event is unexpected, negative, or important to the individual. We now move on to discuss the content of attributions.

The Content of Attributional Thinking

As Weiner (1986) points out, there is a large body of work on the types of attributions people make for any number of outcomes, including success and failure in achievement contexts (e.g., tests, sporting events, games, occupational performance) and more general situations such as interpersonal attraction (acceptance or rejection of an invitation to go to a movie), political elections, health issues, affluence and poverty, and criminal justice problems. Table 4.2 displays some of the common attributions for several different domains. These listings are not meant to cover all the possible causes of any event offered by any individual. In fact, there are probably an infinite number of possible causes for the outcome of an event. In addition, it is important to note that the causes for one domain might vary significantly from another domain (e.g., government policies as the cause of poverty is a reasonable attribution, but it is unlikely that policy would be invoked as a cause of an individual's failure on an achievement test). At the same time, there is some overlap across domains, so that poor health might be used to explain failure in an achievement situation as well as to explain interpersonal attraction or wealth/poverty (Weiner, 1986).

In terms of achievement motivation, early research on attributions often had experimental subjects rate only 4 causes—ability, effort, task difficulty, and luck—as reasons for success and failure. As more research on the role of attributions was done, experimenters began to use more inclusive lists with up to 8 or 10 attributions to be rated or used a free-response format whereby the subjects were asked to generate their own attributions. The studies that used these open-ended and more inclusive methodologies generated more potential causes of achievement success or failure, but all of them included the original four (ability, effort, task characteristics, and luck) as well as intrinsic motivation, teacher competence, and mood (Weiner, 1986). Cross-cultural studies also have found that ability and effort are perceived as common causes of success and failure in most countries. For example, Triandis (1972) found this to be the case in American, Japanese, and Greek cultures, India being the only exception of the four he examined. Miller (1984) found that Hindus in India were less likely than Americans to give dispositional or trait attributions for why people engaged in prosocial or deviant behavior. Fletcher and Ward (1988), however, in their review of cross-cultural research on attributions, suggest that the content of most attributions is somewhat similar across Western and non-Western cultures such as Japan and India. Beyond the content of attributions, what may

Table 4.2.   Summary of Perceived Causes in Different Domains

Achievement	Interpersonal Attraction	Wealth/Poverty	Health/Illness
Aptitude	Physical attractiveness	Family background	Heredity
Skill	Personal style	Intelligence	Personality
Stable effort	Physical hygiene	Effort	Family history
Unstable effort	Personality	Schooling	Life stress
Task difficulty	Status	Government policies	Fatigue
Luck	Timing and availability	Prejudice and discrimination	Good/poor habits
Interest	Health	Luck	Weather
Mood	Mood	Health	Exposure to germs
Fatigue	Wealth		Luck
Health			
Help from others			

From *An Attributional Theory of Motivation and Emotion* by B. Weiner, 1986, New York: Springer-Verlag. Copyright © 1986 by Springer-Verlag New York, Inc. Adapted by permission.

differ in Western and non-Western cultures is how these different attributions are classified in terms of the dimensions. From an attributional perspective, these dimensions are the most important for motivation.

The Motivational Dimensions of Attributions

The list of causes for success and failure provides a description of the content of attributions, but these attributions, in and of themselves, are not particularly motivational in nature. In other words, it is not clear what attributions contribute to the motivational dynamics of behavior; that is, how do attributions "motivate" behavior? In attributional theory, the motivational "push" of attributions derives from their classification into dimensions based on an analysis of the causal structure of attributions. These dimensions provide the psychological significance and meaning to the simple attributions. The properties of a dimension in terms of its stability, internality, or controllability have implications for students' expectancy beliefs, and these expectancy beliefs are implicated in almost all types of motivated behavior, as discussed in Chapter 3. In addition, the dimensional analysis of attributions has several advantages for theory building. First, if there are a small number of dimensions that capture the important aspects of attributions, there is parsimony, particularly given the infinite number of attributions. Moreover, although there are a number of different and unique attributions that can be made in different domains (i.e., achievement vs. affiliation), the dimensional analysis allows for the comparison of these "phenotypically" different attributions along "genotypically" similar lines. This increases the power of the theory as it can be shown that the dimensions work in the same ways across very different domains and given very different actual attributions.

The analysis of the causal structure of attributions has proceeded in two general ways: logical analysis and empirical analysis (Weiner, 1986). Logical analysis appeared first and was a part of the early conceptual work in this area (Weiner et al., 1971). Logical analysis was based on attributional researchers' examination of different attributions and subsequent placement of them in different categories or along dimensions (e.g., an internal vs. external cause) based on theoretical considerations. Empirical analysis appeared later in research on attributional theory and involved the use of factor analysis and multidimensional scaling to determine how individuals' ratings of attributions actually clustered together (Weiner, 1986). In both the rational and empirical analyses, a fair amount of consensus has emerged about the importance of three general dimensions of causal structure: (a) a *locus* dimension concerning how internal versus external a cause is perceived as, (b) a *stability* dimension concerning how stable versus unstable a cause is perceived as, and (c) a *controllability* dimension concerning how controllable versus uncontrollable a cause is perceived as (Weiner, 1986). Although there is some disagreement about the exact nature of these three dimensions, there is agreement that each of the dimensions has implications for individuals' motivation and affect.

The Locus Dimension

The locus-of-causality dimension concerns whether a cause is perceived as being internal or external to the individual. For example, ability and effort are both classified as internal causes, whereas task difficulty and luck would be classified as external causes. This basic distinction between causes that are internal versus external corresponds to the central question in attribution theory regarding the relative influence of personal and environmental factors on an individual's behavior (Heider, 1958).

Historically, the most common application of this dimension as a psychological construct was the work of Rotter (1966) on what he called locus of control. Rotter was a social learning theorist who was interested in individuals' perceptions of the contingency of reinforcement on their own behavior. People were classified as internals if they believed that the rewards or reinforcement they received was due to something they did (e.g., their own effort) or something about them (e.g., their ability); that is, reinforcement was contingent on their own behavior. In contrast, externals were individuals who perceived reinforcement as somehow outside their control and due to factors such as luck, fate, or other people. In the classroom setting, internal control students would believe that their grades depended on their own ability, skill, or effort, whereas external control students would believe that their grades were just a function of luck or the teacher or some other external factor. Teachers can be internal or external as well. Internal teachers would believe that their students' learning is under their control to some extent and that their skill and effort can make a difference for students. In contrast, external teachers would believe that there is little they can do to influence students' learning, that luck or chance or other external factors (e.g., parental and home environment) are the major determinants of student learning.

Research on this construct of locus of control was incredibly popular in psychology in the 1960s through the 1970s with probably thousands of studies done on both the antecedents and consequences of locus of control, not just in educational settings, but also physical and mental health, sports, business organizations, and so on. A similar construct to locus of control was proposed by de Charms (1968), who suggested that people were *origins* (internal locus of control) or *pawns* (external locus of control). More recently, in social cognitive theory, Bandura (1986) proposed a construct he labeled *outcome expectation* that is very similar to control beliefs (see Chapter 6). Connell and Skinner and their colleagues (Connell, 1985; Skinner et al., 1988a, 1988b) have revived interest in the nature of control beliefs and have specified a number of important distinctions about different kinds of control beliefs. Their work is discussed more fully in Chapter 7 on intrinsic motivation.

The Stability Dimension

The locus-of-control construct has a very intuitive appeal and can be readily applied to our own lives. However, early on in research on attribution theory,

Weiner and colleagues (Weiner et al., 1971) proposed that the locus-of-control construct really confounds two different dimensions of causality, namely, internality and stability. Weiner and his colleagues reasoned that there were some important differences regarding the stability of different internal causes. For example, ability may be seen as relatively stable, whereas effort can vary across situations. Although both ability and effort are internal causes and should have similar consequences under Rotter's theory, attribution research has shown that they do not have the same consequences (Weiner, 1986). For example, if an individual fails at a task, it is better for future expectancies to attribute it to lack of effort than to lack of ability. Both logical analysis and empirical data supported the need for a second dimension of stability beyond the locus dimension.

The stability dimension refers to whether the cause is fixed and stable or whether it is variable and unstable across situations and over time. In a personality psychology tradition, stability refers to whether the attribution would be considered a trait of the person or a more statelike or situational aspect of the person. Figure 4.2 displays how attributions could be classified according to both locus and stability. The first and original scheme (top part of Figure 4.2) was a simple classification of the four main causes investigated by attribution researchers. It can be seen that ability and effort were both classified as internal, as would be expected under Rotter's locus-of-control theory, but that these two attributions differ in terms of stability, with effort usually seen as unstable and ability as stable. In contrast, task difficulty and luck were categorized as external (as in Rotter's theory), but luck is usually perceived as unstable and task difficulty as stable. This classification scheme was the original one used by Weiner and his colleagues in their early experimental work.

It soon became clear, however, that these four general attributions, or at least their original labels, could be somewhat misleading in terms of the locus-by-stability classification scheme. More recent work suggests that the terms shown in the bottom half of Figure 4.2 are a more accurate reflection of the naive phenomenology of people (Weiner, 1986). Accordingly, *aptitude*, signifying a stable, unchangeable, internal characteristic of an individual, is a better term than ability. In contrast, *skills*, which connotes abilities that can be learned over time, is a better term to represent internal but unstable abilities. For example, some individuals might have a great aptitude for music or art or athletics that makes them outstanding in their field, but at the same time, there are skills that most people can learn over time that can influence their performance in different domains. In the same manner, individuals can put forth effort for a specific task (e.g., trying very hard on a final test for a math course) as well as be continually hard working and industrious in general for many different tasks. Of course, the opposite situation would be not trying very hard on a final math exam just this one time due to mitigating circumstances, instead of continually not putting forth effort (being lazy) for many tasks over time. Effort, depending on the type of effort involved, therefore, can be both stable and unstable, although it is always classified as internal.

Figure 4.2. Original and revised locus-by-stability classification scheme for attributions

From *An Attributional Theory of Motivation and Emotion* by B. Weiner, 1986, New York: Springer-Verlag. Copyright © 1986 by Springer-Verlag New York, Inc. Adapted by permission.

Original Scheme

Stability	Locus	
	Internal	*External*
Stable	Ability	Task difficulty
Unstable	Effort	Luck

Revised Scheme

Stability	Locus	
	Internal	*External*
Stable	Aptitude Long-term effort	Objective task characteristics
Unstable	Skills/knowledge Temporary or situational effort	Chance

The same type of clarification was done with task difficulty and luck. Most people perceive task difficulty as being relative to an individual's ability and effort levels and changeable over time. However, in the original classification scheme (see Figure 4.2), task difficulty was categorized as external and stable. Weiner (1986) now suggests that instead of task difficulty, the appropriate term for one cause that is external and stable is *objective task characteristics*, which stresses the nature of the task, independent of the individual who is attempting the task. Finally, luck is often perceived as a stable trait of some people (e.g., He is always lucky, he wins all the games he plays.), so Weiner suggests that a better term is *chance*, which reflects a focus on the opportunities presented by the environment rather than a trait of an individual.

Related to this stability dimension, is the dimension of globality as defined by researchers working with the construct of learned helplessness (e.g., Peterson et al., 1993). The dimension of stability generally refers to the attribution's changeability over time. However, implicit in our previous examples regarding short-term effort versus long-term industriousness for a variety of tasks was the notion that effort may cut across domains or situations, being more or less global in nature. Peterson and his colleagues have proposed that individuals' attributions can be classified along a global-specific dimension, paralleling the distinction between traits and situational specificity of behavior in personality theory. For example, individuals may make an attribution that they have no aptitude for all academic subjects (global), or they could make an attribution that they have no aptitude for math (fairly specific) or no aptitude for geometry (even more specific). In learned helplessness theory and research, the globality-specificity of an attribution is an important dimension, with more global causes seen as generalizing to a number of situations that can lead to learned helplessness (Peterson et al., 1993). Weiner (1986), on the other hand, notes that in almost all of the factor analytic and multidimensional scaling studies, globality-specificity has not emerged as a separate factor. Peterson and colleagues (Peterson et al., 1993) acknowledge that in their empirical work, they have only found two factors instead of the three they predicted, with locus being a separate dimension and stability and globality being highly correlated. Accordingly, pending further research, it seems that there is an important dimension concerning both the stability and the globality of an attribution, which we will subsume under the label *stability*, in line with Weiner (1986).

The Controllability Dimension

Logical and empirical analyses also have suggested that there is a third dimension of causality—controllability—which refers to how much control a person has over a cause. As noted in the label for Rotter's construct of locus of control, the dimension of controllability was included as part of his original conceptualization of internals versus externals. However, as Weiner (1985, 1986) has pointed out, the construct of locus *of* control really confounds two separate dimensions of causality: locus *and* control. For example, both aptitude and effort would be classified as representing an internal locus of control in Rotter's model, but most people see effort as something they have volitional control over, whereas aptitude (i.e., artistic ability, physical coordination) is usually perceived as something they have little control over (Weiner, 1986). Accordingly, it is important to have two separate dimensions—locus and controllability—not one construct that conflates the two dimensions.

Although the locus and stability dimensions can be crossed quite easily in a two-by-two matrix and have an entry in all the cells (see Figure 4.2), there may not be eight full cells in a locus-by-stability-by-controllability ($2 \times 2 \times 2$) matrix. In particular, there are disagreements about whether there can be causes that are external to the individual that are still controllable. Some researchers (e.g., Stipek, 1993) suggest that these cells are empty because, by definition, a cause that is external to the individual is not under that person's control. Weiner (1986), however, argues that there may be causes that are external to the individual that are not controllable by that individual but are controllable by others. For example, a student who fails a math test and believes that his failure is due to the teacher being biased against him would still hold the teacher accountable because the bias could be controlled by the teacher. The other example Weiner offers is a student failing an exam because her friends did not help her. Again, he suggests that the help of friends is controllable by the friends, although it is not controllable by the student. Figure 4.3 displays the full matrix with eight cells and common attributions classified by the three dimensions of locus, stability, and controllability. In this figure, we have included entries for external and controllable causes.

As in the discussion of the stability dimension, there is often another dimension mentioned when there is a discussion of the controllability dimension. This other dimension, intentionality, occasionally appears in the empirical factor analytic and multidimensional scaling studies. In addition, as Weiner (1986) notes, there may be good logical reasons to distinguish intentionality from controllability, although they usually covary considerably. In an achievement context, he uses the example that individuals may intentionally not exert effort, but that rarely do people intentionally use a "bad" or poor strategy to solve a problem. That is, individuals may use a bad strategy in terms of some objective criterion for solving a problem or from the perspective of an expert in contrast to a novice problem solver, but from the individuals' point of view and knowledge, they do not think it is a bad strategy. Both

Locus				
Stability	*Internal*		*External*	
	Controllable	*Uncontrollable*	*Controllable*	*Uncontrollable*
Stable	Long-term effort	Aptitude	Instructor bias/ favoritism	Ease/difficulty of school or course requirements
Unstable	Skills/knowledge Temporary or situational effort for exam	Health on day of exam Mood	Help from friends/teacher	Chance

Figure 4.3. Achievement attributions classified by locus, stability, and controllability dimensions

From *An Attributional Theory of Motivation and Emotion* by B. Weiner, 1986, New York: Springer-Verlag. Copyright © 1986 by Springer-Verlag New York, Inc. Adapted by permission.

strategy and effort are controllable (see Figure 4.3), but the intentionality of effort versus bad strategy use does add to our understanding. In fact, in the literature on the teaching of learning strategies (e.g., Weinstein & Mayer, 1986), this distinction is crucial. Most programs to teach learning strategies assume that students are not using good or effective learning strategies because they do not know about them or do not know how to use them properly, not because they intentionally decide to use poor or bad learning strategies. Besides this achievement example, Weiner (1986, p. 70) notes that intentionality is at the heart of the distinction between manslaughter and murder. A driver may not have intentionally tried to kill a pedestrian, but the driver should have been able to control the speed of the car before it hit the pedestrian.

Weiner then goes on to note that although this distinction may be useful, intentionality usually does not refer to a cause per se. For example, it is difficult to say that aptitude or effort or any other attribution is "intentional." People are intentional, or acts are intentional, but a cause is usually not considered intentional. Accordingly, if the dimensions are to describe the nature of causes and attributions, intentionality is difficult to use. Weiner (1986) suggests that intentionality be subsumed under the controllability dimension, much as the globality dimension is subsumed under the stability dimension. Future research may be able to untangle these dimensions, but for our current purposes, the three dimensions of locus, stability, and controllability are sufficient.

Linkage of Dimensions of Attributions to Expectancy Beliefs

The three dimensions of attributions can be shown to have important consequences for individuals' expectancy-for-success beliefs. Using a logical and intuitive analysis, it seems clear that if an attribution for success is made that is internal and stable (e.g., I did well on the test because I have the aptitude for it.), then the individual will expect to succeed in the future. By the same token, if an attribution for success is made that is unstable (e.g., test-specific effort or luck), then the individual will not expect to do as well in the future. For failure situations, the logic works a little differently, where the more adaptive attributions to make would be unstable and controllable. For example, if a student failed an exam, then it would be better to attribute it to not studying (lack of effort) for this specific test. The lack of studying can be changed and is controllable by the student; as long as the student puts forth the effort in studying for the next exam, he or she might expect to do better. Following this logic, a stable, internal, and uncontrollable attribution for failure (e.g., I failed because I have no aptitude for math.) would have the most detrimental consequences for future expectancies for success.

Besides the logical analysis of the relations between the dimensions and expectancies for success, there are a great many empirical studies that have linked attributions and the dimensions to expectancies for success. Weiner (1986) summarizes the many correlational and experimental laboratory studies of these relations by concluding that the stability dimension is the most closely linked to future expectancies for success, not locus as would be expected by Rotter's social learning theory. These studies show for both success and failure outcomes that the stability of an attribution is linked to expectancy change. When an outcome occurs and the attribution made is classified as stable, then the individual will expect the same outcome in the future. In contrast, if the attribution made is perceived as unstable, then the expectation for the future is that the subsequent outcome may change. Weiner (1986) summarizes this research by proposing a general principle for behavior along with three corollaries:

> *Expectancy Principle:* Changes in expectancy of success following an outcome are influenced by the perceived stability of the cause of the event.
>
> *Corollary 1:* If the outcome of an event is ascribed to a stable cause, then that outcome will be anticipated with increased certainty, or with an increased expectancy, in the future.
>
> *Corollary 2:* If the outcome of an event is ascribed to an unstable cause, then the certainty or expectancy of that outcome may be unchanged, or the future will be anticipated to be different from the past.
>
> *Corollary 3:* Outcomes ascribed to stable causes will be anticipated to be repeated in the future with a greater degree of certainty than outcomes ascribed to unstable causes. (pp. 114–115)

For example, if students attribute their success on a test or in a course to their own aptitude for the course content (a stable cause), then they will expect to do well in the future in exams or courses on that course content (higher certainty of expectancy for future success). Teachers who attribute their success in teaching to their own aptitude for teaching similarly will expect that they will be able to teach future students and classes with success. In the same way, students or teachers who fail and attribute their failure to a lack of aptitude will expect to fail in future situations (Corollaries 1 and 3). In contrast, if students ascribe their success to an unstable cause such as believing they did well on the test or in a course because of luck, then they may not expect to do well in the future, and their expectancy for success will be lower than that of someone who attributed success to a stable cause. The same would be true for beginning teachers who attribute their success in teaching to beginner's luck or to the idea that they just happened to have a really good group of students their first year. They would not necessarily expect to be as successful in their second year of teaching (Corollaries 2 and 3). It is important to note that in deriving the implications of these corollaries, there are three "variables" that are being coordinated, the outcome (success-failure), the attributional dimension (stability-instability), and the certainty of future expectancies. All three have to be considered simultaneously.

It also is important to note that in these principles and the studies on which they are based, it is the perceiver's classification of the attribution in terms of stability that has the psychological impact on future expectancies. Accordingly, although the empirical findings and normative attributional theory predict that aptitude is usually classified as stable and effort is perceived as unstable, what is most important for future expectancies is how the individual perceives the dimension of the attribution. This idiographic position is in keeping with the general phenomenological perspective of attribution theory, giving precedence to the individual perceiver and his or her construction of reality. For example, if students make an attribution to math aptitude for failure on an exam but perceive math aptitude as something that is unstable and that they can change through learning, then this attribution will not have as detrimental an influence on their expectancy for math in the future, in contrast to the normative position where math aptitude is perceived as a stable and unchanging aptitude.

In much the same fashion, cross-cultural research suggests that different cultures may classify specific attributions along different dimensions. For example, Holloway (1988) suggests that the internal-external dimension that defines causes as internal or external to the individual may operate somewhat differently in Japan, where the primary social unit may be the family or household unit in contrast to the individual as the primary social unit in the United States. In the case of Japanese culture, individuals may give what are normatively considered external attributions (i.e., I tried hard in order not to embarrass my family or disappoint my teacher.), but these attributions are not perceived as being external to the individual because the individual identifies with the social group. Similarly, Weisz, Rothbaum, & Blackburn (1984) suggest that the dimension of controllability may not operate in Japan in the same manner as in Western cultures, where the emphasis is on an individual's *primary control* of others and events as opposed to what they term *secondary control*, which involves adjusting to others and to events and being satisfied with this type of accommodation (Holloway, 1988). In contrast, Fletcher and Ward (1988) suggest that much of the empirical cross-cultural research in social psychology finds support for the classification scheme inherent in three dimensions. Clearly, there is a need for more detailed and careful research on these issues by psychologists and anthropologists from both Western and non-Western cultures. Nevertheless, a general constructivist position on attribution theory recognizes that individuals in both Western and non-Western cultures may classify attributions along the three dimensions in an idiographic manner. Given this constructivist assumption, it is most important to understand the individual's classification scheme for attributions. By combining that knowledge with the general links between expectancies and dimensions, one can understand the individual's motivation.

DEVELOPMENTAL AND GROUP DIFFERENCES IN ATTRIBUTIONS

Research on developmental and group differences in attribution theory has focused on two general issues. First, are there differences in the way young children and adults or males and females or minority and nonminority students use the various informational cues or information-processing strategies to make attributional inferences? Second, are there developmental or group differences in the content and dimensional "meaning" of attributions and their links to expectancy for success (see Blumenfeld et al., 1982)?

Developmental Differences

There is research from a developmental perspective (see Blumenfeld et al., 1982; Kassin & Pryor, 1985; Nicholls, 1990) that suggests that the findings for attribution theory may differ by age. There are a number of ways in which attribution theory can differ given developmental differences. First, there may be developmental differences in the ways younger children use informational cues, content knowledge, and reasoning schemas to form attributions (columns 1 and 2 in Figure 4.1). Second, there seem to be developmental differences in the psychological meaning of different attributions in terms of their dimensional analysis (columns 3 and 4 in Figure 4.1). These two differences represent differences in the internal, psychological, and cognitive mechanisms of attribution theory. Finally, the contexts younger children are exposed to may vary, creating differences in the attributional process.

Differences in information processing of cues are related to young children's ability to follow the six general principles of causality discussed earlier in this chapter. Kassin & Pryor (1985) suggest that even very young children (about 3 years old) do follow the ordinal priority rule that causes must precede effects when making inferences about causality. Children as young as 3 years also follow the principle of spatio-temporal contiguity where causes and effects must coincide in time and space. The third principle discussed earlier was that salient stimuli were more likely to be perceived as causes than other stimuli in the background. Of course, adults are very susceptible to this salience principle, but Kassin & Pryor (1985) suggest that young children are even more susceptible to it and may ignore other, more relevant and logical information about covariation between events to focus on the salient cues that can lead to an inaccurate attribution.

Besides these differences in the use of general information-processing strategies, children may differ in their content-specific beliefs about attributions (see Table 4.3). There has been a great deal of research suggesting that young children do not hold the same "definitions" of different attributions as adults (Blumenfeld et al., 1982; Blumenfeld, Pintrich, & Hamilton, 1986; Dweck & Leggett, 1988; Nicholls, 1990). This research suggests that the nor-

Table 4.3. Developmental Differences in Children's Concepts of Ability, Effort, Difficulty, and Luck. (Adapted from Nicholls, 1990)

Differentiating Ability and Effort	Differentiating Ability and Difficulty	Differentiating Ability and Luck
1. *Effort or outcome is ability* (3–5 years) People who try harder are smarter. People who get a higher score try harder and are smarter.	1. *Egocentric (3–5 years)* Task difficulty is relative to individuals' ability to succeed. "Hard" means "hard for me," which also means "I'm not good at it."	1. *Luck and skill are outcome are undifferentiated* (3–5 years) Luck or chance tasks are seen as easier or requiring less effort than skills tasks.
2. *Effort is the cause of outcomes* (6–8 years) People who try equally hard should have the same outcome, regardless of ability.	2. *Objective (5–6 years)* Levels of difficulty of tasks are recognized as independent of individuals' ability to succeed. Attributions for failure, however, still confound low ability and high task difficulty such that "it's hard" still means "it's hard for me," which means "I'm not smart at it."	2. *Skill and luck are partially differentiated, but basis unclear* (6–8 years) Effort is still expected to improve performance on both tasks, but a skill task is seen as more amenable to effort.
3. *Effort and ability are partially differentiated* (9–10 years) People who try equally hard may not have the same outcome because of ability, but do not follow this principle systematically.	3. *Normative (by age 7)* Ability and task difficulty are differentiated in terms of success rates of others. Tasks that fewer people succeed on are harder and require more ability, so "it's hard" is different from "it's hard for me."	3. *Skill and luck are partially differentiated, but basis is not explicit* (9–10 years) Effort is still expected to improve performance on both tasks, but a skill task is seen as more amenable to effort because individuals can compare stimuli on skill task.
4. *Ability is capacity* (12–13 years) Ability and effort are separate and can covary. Ability level acts as a capacity limitation and can constrain effort. If ability is low, there is some limit to outcome, regardless of effort level. Also, if outcome is equal, then lower effort implies higher ability.		4. *Skill and luck are fully differentiated* (12–13 years) Effort can't affect outcome on luck tasks, whereas effort can influence performance on skill tasks.

139

mative classification of different attributions such as ability, effort, luck, and task difficulty into the three general dimensions of locus, control, and stability may not hold for younger children. In effect, the psychological meanings of the attributions are different and will have different consequences in terms of expectancy-for-success beliefs and affect. These studies have involved in-depth interviews with children and experimental studies of their reactions to different vignettes.

Nicholls (1990) summarizes much of the research on the developmental differences in children's understanding of effort and ability and their covariation. The normative, adult understanding of effort and ability in Western cultures involves two distinct relations. First, most adults understand that effort and ability covary inversely. If you need to try hard at a task, it generally implies less ability for that task, and, conversely, if you have high ability, you do not need to try as hard. Second, most adults have an "ability-as-capacity" belief that suggests that the exertion of effort will help improve performance up to a certain point, but effort will not help beyond that point because their ability has set an upper limit on performance. This belief represents ability as a stable, unchanging, and uncontrollable aptitude of the individual and results in the dimensional classification as internal, stable, and uncontrollable. Young children, however, do not seem to have this belief. They tend to see ability as more incremental and changeable (Dweck & Leggett, 1988).

Nicholls and his colleagues have documented a four-level developmental pattern in the beliefs between effort and ability (see Nicholls, 1978, 1990). The first level reflects children's beliefs before the age of 6 and equates effort and outcome as ability. In this case, children do not differentiate among ability, effort, and outcomes. Success at a task means you tried hard and that you are able. In addition, if you tried hard but did not do as well as others, you are still smarter than someone who did not try as hard. The second level emerges at about the age of 6 (the beginning of school for most children) when children begin to differentiate effort and outcome. Here children expect effort and outcome to covary positively with individuals who try harder being more successful than those who don't try as hard. If individuals try equally hard, then they should receive equal outcomes. When they have equal outcomes but unequal effort, children explain by noting that the individual who worked less hard but had an equal outcome must have compensated by working really hard for awhile; those who worked harder must have misapplied their effort (worked hard and quickly but made mistakes). In the third level, which emerges at about age 9, children begin to differentiate effort and ability and believe that students who try less hard but have equal outcomes must be smarter or better. However, children at this level do not systematically follow this differentiation and still may claim that students who try equally hard may achieve the same outcome, regardless of ability. Finally, level four, which emerges at about age 13, represents the adult conception of ability as capacity, and effort and ability are clearly differentiated. Low ability can limit the effect of high effort on the outcome, and high ability combined with high effort can readily increase performance (Nicholls, 1990).

Nicholls and Miller (1983, 1985) also have shown that children's understanding of the relations between ability and task difficulty and between ability and luck change with age (see Table 4.3). The differentiation of task difficulty from ability seems to follow a developmental sequence from egocentric to objective to normative (Nicholls & Miller, 1983). In the egocentric level, approximately age 3–5 years, children see task difficulty as being relative to their ability to succeed at a task. If they can do the task, then it is "easy;" if they can't do the task, then it is "hard." Moreover, if the task is easy, then they are "smart" or good at the task, and if the task is hard, then they are not smart or good at the task. This egocentric perspective does not take into account any normative data from other children who may or may not be able to do the task. The confounding of task difficulty and ability results from children's egocentric focus on their own level of performance without taking into account what others might be able to do on the task. The objective level emerges by about 5 or 6 years old when children are able to understand that different tasks might be harder or easier depending on task characteristics (e.g., in much of this research, different puzzles are used and objectively difficult tasks are those puzzles with more pieces). However, children in the objective level still believe that their failure is due to the task being hard and that they have no ability for the task, in effect still confounding ability and task difficulty. By about age 7, children seem to be able to differentiate ability from task difficulty and also use normative information from social comparisons with other children to understand that some tasks are hard for everyone, and some tasks are hard for certain individuals. In addition, they also come to realize that if a task is harder because many people cannot do it, then it will require more ability.

The differentiation of luck and skill also seems to follow a general developmental pattern (Nicholls, 1990; Nicholls & Miller, 1985; Weisz, 1984). This research has presented children with tasks that require skill (i.e., present a standard drawing and ask children to pick from six other drawings the one that matches the standard) and those that are based on luck or chance (i.e., same task as skill task, except in the luck case, the six drawings are turned over, so the children cannot see the drawings). This work shows that at the first level, children do not distinguish luck and skill tasks and believe that effort can make a difference on both tasks. At the second level, children start to differentiate the tasks and believe that effort can help more on the skill task, but the basis for this belief is not explained in terms of the ease of comparing the six figures to the standard figure. At the third level, the children articulate that effort can help more on the skill tasks because the six figures can be visually compared to the standard figure, but they still believe that effort can help on the luck task. At the final, fourth level, which emerges at about 12 or 13 years, children clearly differentiate luck from skill tasks and do not believe that effort can make a difference on the luck tasks. It is interesting to note that this capability to differentiate luck from skill tasks emerges in early adolescence, yet many adults who play the lottery or other games of chance (slot machines) still believe that effort can make a difference in winning. As a result, adults develop very elaborate strategies for picking winning lottery numbers or pulling the handle on a slot machine and media reports about the big winners in lottery games often reveal the winner's "strategy" for picking numbers. This developmental "regression" by adults regarding luck tasks highlights the distinction between competence and performance that is important to keep in mind when interpreting developmental findings.

Besides these developmental differences in children's strategies for processing information and their different definitions and dimensional classification of attributions, the third general factor that can result in developmental differences is changes in the nature of the environment. Classrooms can influence students' perceptions and attributions directly, and if features of classrooms are changing, it may be difficult to determine if the developmental differences are due to changes in the children's internal psychological mechanisms or changes in the classroom context (see Blumenfeld et al., 1982; Rosenholtz & Simpson, 1984). For example, recent research on the nature of middle schools (see Eccles & Midgley, 1989; Eccles et al., 1993) suggests that the organization and structure of these schools can have a dramatic influence on children's motivational beliefs. Most of this research suggests that middle schools are organized and structured in ways that stress social comparison, the normative nature of ability, and offer less opportunity for student control and autonomy than elementary schools (Eccles et al., 1993). It is not surprising then that the developmental levels in the nature of children's beliefs about ability, effort, luck, and task difficulty show the most adultlike perceptions emerging at the same time as children are in middle schools. Obviously, it is some combination of both internal, psychological changes and external, environmental changes that interacts to create these developmental differences in children's attributions. We discuss the nature of the classroom influences in more detail in Chapter 9, but it is important to keep in mind that these developmental differences are not solely the children's own construction or a function of maturational differences as might be predicted by a stage model of cognitive development.

There are several implications of these developmental differences in children's beliefs about ability, effort, difficulty, and luck for attribution theory. First, these differences suggest that the normative classification of attributions along the dimensions of locus, controllability, and stability may not hold for younger children. In particular, ability is not seen as stable, which fits with a general experiential perspective on development. Young children are constantly engaging in new tasks (not just school-related ones) and, in most cases, improving their ability to do the tasks (tying shoes, drawing, riding a bike, etc.). Accordingly, it is not surprising that they perceive their abilities as incremental and changing, not entity-like (Dweck & Leggett, 1988). This difference in the stability perception of ability results in a second implication for attribution theory. If ability is not stable, but rather changeable and able to improve with time, then an attribution to ability for failure at a task does not need to have detrimental consequences for young children's future expectancies for success. In this case, ability as an unstable, controllable, and internal cause is conceptually equivalent to an attribution to lack of effort for failure (e.g., level 1 in Nicholls's model where effort and ability are equated). Young children can make an attribution to low ability for failure, but because they expect to get better with age and time, they can still expect to succeed in the future.

Gender and Ethnic Differences

In comparison to the developmental literature, there has been much less research on gender and ethnic differences. In addition, much of the research on these topics does not examine the potential interactions between gender and ethnicity. There is some research emerging (see Pollard, 1993) that suggests that minority females may not be as adversely affected as minority males. Even more important, most of the studies of ethnicity do not disentangle the effects of socioeconomic status from ethnicity. In many cases, low-income minorities are compared to middle-class white students, confounding the effects of ethnicity and class, making inferences and generalizations difficult.

The area of gender differences has a long history in psychology, and research on motivation is no exception. Differences between males and females in their motivation for achievement has often been proposed as an explanation for gender differences in achievement and, more recently, as an explanation for the smaller number of women in math and science careers in comparison to men (Meece & Eccles, 1993). One area that has been of research interest is gender differences in attributional patterns. This research, however, has produced very mixed and conflicting results. A number of studies have found gender differences in attributional patterns, with women more likely to show maladaptive patterns of attributing success to external causes (luck, ease of task) or unstable causes (effort, trying hard) and attributing failure to internal causes (lack of ability) (see review by Meece, Parsons, Kaczala, Goff, & Futterman, 1982). In contrast, other studies have not found these gender differences (e.g., Diener & Dweck, 1978; Dweck & Repucci, 1973). Eccles and colleagues (e.g., Eccles, 1983; Meece et al., 1982) conclude that it is difficult to summarize this research because of the methodological differences in the instruments used to measure attributions, the time when measures of attributions where taken (e.g., before or after feedback about success/failure in experimental studies), and the homogeneity of samples used (high vs. low achievers). Accordingly, as pointed out in Chapter 3, females in general do have somewhat inaccurate and lower expectancies, perceptions of their competence, and efficacy, but it is not clear that attributions mediate this difference.

Graham (1991, 1994) has recently summarized the research on ethnic differences in African American students' attributions. She notes that there has been relatively little research on this topic and that there is a need for more

theoretically based research. First, in terms of differences in the use of informational cues, early research seemed to suggest that blacks and whites did differ, with blacks using information about effort less often or less systematically
than whites when they evaluate hypothetical others (see Lipton & Garza,
1977; McMillan, 1980; Weiner & Peter, 1973). However, Graham (1994) notes
that more recent research on this issue has not shown these ethnic differences
(Whitehead, Smith, & Eichorn, 1982; Wong, Derlaga & Colson, 1988).

In terms of ethnic differences in the actual attributions students make for
their achievement, there have been two strands of research. First, there has
been research on the construct of locus of control, which, as we have seen,
emanates more from a personality tradition but is conceptually similar to the
locus and controllability dimensions of attribution theory. In the locus-of-control research, the general assumption is that having more internal beliefs
(believing one is in control and responsible for outcomes) is a more adaptive
motivational pattern than an external pattern. Early research on locus of control suggested that African Americans were more likely to have scores toward
the external side of the internal-external continuum, paralleling some of the
research showing that females have more external patterns of attributions and
locus of control. Graham (1994) summarizes the results from 63 studies of ethnic differences in locus of control in both children and adults by noting that
more studies do find a pattern of externality among African Americans than no
differences, and very few studies report that African Americans show more
internality than other groups. Graham (1994), however, goes on to note that
studies that examine locus of control and its relations with other achievement
related variables find no negative effect of this tendency toward externality in
African Americans. Given these findings, she suggests that this pattern of
externality and perceived uncontrollability may actually be adaptive, not maladaptive, for African Americans, but that the research in the locus-of-control
tradition has not addressed this issue.

In research from the more situational perspective of attributional theory,
where students generate attributions for their own behavior based on their
success or failure at an achievement task, Graham (1994) again notes that
early studies seemed to suggest that whites were more likely to rate internal
attributions (effort, ability) as more likely causes, whereas African Americans
rated external attributions (luck, task difficulty) higher (see Friend & Neale,
1972). More recent studies suggest that this pattern of externality among
African American students has not been replicated. Current studies either find
no differences between African American and white students (e.g, Graham &
Long, 1986; Hall, Howe, Merkel, & Lederman, 1986) in attributional patterns
or that middle-class blacks have a very adaptive attributional pattern of
attributing failure to effort in comparison to white students (Graham, 1984).
Accordingly, from a situational and attributional perspective, there seems to be
more similarity in the types of attributions African Americans and white students make. However, as Graham (1991, 1994) points out, most of this
research on ethnic differences has concentrated on the content of attributions,

but there is a great need for more research on ethnic differences in the complete attributional model, in particular, the linkages among the constructs of attributions, expectancy, and affect.

IMPLICATIONS FOR TEACHERS

Attribution theory offers teachers a specific theoretical model of how students' perceptions of the reasons for their success or failure (attributions) can influence their expectancy for success, their self-efficacy, and their actual achievement behavior. This model has been empirically validated in both laboratory and field studies and has important implications for teacher practice. The following items are some suggestions for teacher practice based on attribution theory.

1. Become a "scientist" of student behavior. In keeping with the general metaphor of attribution theory that suggests that the individual is a scientist trying to determine the causes of events, teachers should endeavor to adopt this general perspective. They should try to assess the reasons for students' behavior in a scientific manner that involves the collection and use of a variety of information. For example, there are a number of environmental cues that teachers should use as they make attributions for the behavior of their students. Teachers should seek out a variety of information about the students and attempt to examine the distinctiveness, consensus, and consistency of the information before making a final determination of the causes of the behavior. For example, if a teacher is trying to determine why a student continually acts out in her classroom, she should seek information about the specificity of the behavior in her own classroom: Does it only occur on certain types of tasks or for certain types of activities (use of distinctiveness cues)? The teacher also should look for the consistency of the student's behavior across different classrooms (ask other teachers about the child's behavior in their classrooms) as well as the consensus of different teachers' attributions for the student's problem behavior.

Another example of this general scientific perspective is the current popularity of portfolio assessment. Although often couched in more "artistic" or "humanistic" terms, the use of portfolios allows the student to present to the teacher a variety of information about his or her mastery of the course material. The teacher can examine the portfolio materials, and the diversity of the products can provide the teacher with distinctiveness, consistency, and consensus information about the student's performance. For example, the teacher might see that the student does consistently well on more structured assignments and has difficulty in reports or essays that are more open-ended. In addition, all the information in the portfolio is presented to the teacher at the same time, so she can examine all the student's work at once and avoid bias in assessment due to recency effects.

2. Avoid attributional biases. Related to the first item, attribution research also has shown that all individuals have a propensity to make biased attributions. As shown in Table 4.1, there are a variety of attributions that teachers could make that may not be accurate. In particular, teachers should be careful about making the fundamental attribution error and attributing students' behavior or performance to a disposition or trait. By assuming that most student behavior is a function of traits, teachers will be less likely to believe that they can change the behavior or have an influence on it. This belief could keep teachers from trying new or different management or instructional strategies that could lead to changes in students' behavior. It is difficult to avoid the fundamental attribution error, but one of the most basic strategies is to collect as much data as possible as often as possible about the student, rather than relying on initial perceptions of the student based on only a few interactions.

For example, Mr. Grover teaches seventh-grade math in a junior high school. He has five minority, low SES students in his sixth-period class who are not doing well. At first, he wants to attribute their failure to their lack of stable effort and what he believes are the low value and support for school by their parents. However, at parents' night, parents of two of the five students come to him and express their concern. They note that their children are not studying very hard, but the parents think math is very important and want to work with Mr. Grover to help the students do better in math. This surprises Mr. Grover and makes him rethink his attributions for all five of the students. He takes each one aside separately to talk about his or her performance in math. He finds out that two of the other three students are actually working fairly hard but are having some real difficulties understanding the material. Again, this information makes him reconsider his initial attributions. He works out a plan for helping the two who are having conceptual difficulties by staying after school and working with them. For the other three, who are not having conceptual difficulties but seem to be putting forth low effort, he works out a new accountability system (in consultation with their parents), whereby they have their homework checked every night by their parents and they turn in their notebook every day to him.

Another important aspect of avoiding biased attributions is maintaining positive beliefs about students' capabilities. Teachers should attempt to maintain their beliefs that all students can learn the knowledge and skills that are the teacher's responsibility to teach. This basically is a belief that students' capabilities are changeable. Some students will naturally take longer to reach mastery than others, but in most K–12 classrooms, the vast majority of children can learn the material. Of course, maintaining positive beliefs does not mean maintaining inaccurate ones. For example, it does not mean that the teacher should believe that all children are learning when there are clearly children who are not mastering the knowledge and skills. Rather, it suggests that teachers continue to attribute any student failure to controllable and unstable causes such as lack of effort (on either the teacher's or student's part) or a need for reteaching, rather than a dispositional trait attribution to student "stupidity." Teachers can communicate expectations through attributional statements about the students and the tasks. Obviously, teachers can lower expectations for task performance by introducing tasks with comments like, "I know that most of you will not be able to do this task, but you should try hard anyway" (an attribution to the student), in comparison to providing tasks that most students can do through effort and communicating this to students, for example, "This task may be tricky, but I think you will find it challenging" (an attribution to the task).

3. The important role of teacher feedback. There are a number of factors that can influence students' attributions, but teacher feedback can be crucial. The implications for success and failure conditions are somewhat different and further complicated by the possibility that students may not interpret the same objective event in the same way. For example, for some students, getting a B on a paper may be a success, given their past lower grades. In contrast, for other students, including many high achievers and college students, getting a B is a failure situation. Given the importance of students' perceptions of events in attribution theory, it is suggested that teachers attempt to give *accurate* feedback to the students, rather than "false" feedback designed to encourage them and maintain their self-esteem (Blumenfeld et al., 1982). In this sense, teachers will help students to make accurate attributions for their own behavior that, in the long run, will be more adaptive.

In failure situations, teachers should strive to provide accurate feedback to students about the reasons for their failure. Some researchers have suggested that teachers should attribute all failure situations to low effort and encourage students to make this low effort attribution. In many cases, this is generally good advice because it communicates to students that they can do better in future situations because effort is an unstable, internal, and controllable cause that students can change. However, there are occasions when students actually do try hard and still do poorly because they lack the skills or knowledge for the task. In these situations, the student knows he tried hard, and to be told by the teacher to keep trying harder can be frustrating and lead to a discounting of the teacher's feedback. It would be more accurate to point out to the student the skills or knowledge he lacks, communicate to him that these skills/knowledge are unstable, that he can learn them, and, perhaps, even teach him the skills/knowledge he needs to do well on the task. The attribution to lack of skills/knowledge is an important addition to the original attributional idea of ability as aptitude, which leads to the basic contrast between effort and ability. In the case of ability as aptitude that is stable, uncontrollable, and internal, then the teacher should avoid aptitude attributions for failure situations.

When students fail, attribute it to an unstable cause that can be changed (controllability). For example, Mr. Herther is teaching reading to a second-grade class. José is having some difficulty learning to recognize words and pronounce them correctly. Mr. Herther asks José to come to his desk and read to him, just the two of them. As José reads, he keeps making mistakes and says, "I can't do this, it is too hard. I wish it was in Spanish. It would be easier for me, and then my parents could teach me."

Mr. Herther responds, "Yes, it might be. It certainly is easier when your parents can help you, but you know you are still very young and you are just learning English. There are a lot of children in this room who are still learning English. The important thing is to keep trying and working at it. Every day I learn new words in English, too. It takes time. You can't give up, but you can't expect to know everything right away. If you keep trying and working with me, we can learn together. Learning takes hard work, but everyone can learn."

In the same fashion, teachers should not attribute student success to effort unless the teacher is confident that the student did actually exert effort. If students do well on a task, it may not be due to effort, but rather to an easy task. If this is the case, it would be better for the teacher to recognize this and provide more challenging tasks to the students in the future. Students who are told they tried hard on an easy task may then infer they have low ability, or they may learn to discount teacher feedback given this type of inaccuracy and, often, insincerity. On the other hand, if the task was fairly difficult and students did try hard, then attributions to effort and knowledge/skill are appropriate.

When students succeed, attribute their success to a stable cause. Mrs. Sugrue teaches fifth grade and her class is working on a science project. Kathy has just completed her project and shows it to Mrs. Sugrue.

"That is excellent, Kathy. You did a very nice job on this project and it shows a lot of work. How long did you work on it?"

"Well, not too long," replies Kathy. "It only took me two days."

"Really? That's not long at all. You must have a talent for science."

Here, Mrs. Sugrue responds to a successful performance by first determining the amount of effort put forth and then makes an ability attribution. If the student had worked hard, then an attribution to stable effort (You are always a hard worker.) would have been appropriate. This illustrates another important principle regarding teacher attributions: It is important for them to be accurate. Students will not believe teacher attributions that are not credible (e.g., praising students for hard work when they did not work hard at all). Accordingly, although attributing success to a stable cause is important, it is even more important for teachers to make accurate and valid attributions.

4. The role of attributional retraining. Besides the effect of general teacher feedback on students' everyday attributions, there has been research on the effectiveness of formal interventions designed to change students' maladaptive attributional patterns. Much of this research has assumed that students have stable attributional patterns or schemas that they invoke and use over and over again across a number of different situations. This research has developed from the learned helplessness personality tradition, rather than the general attributional model that stresses the situational nature of attributions. Given the focus on stable individual differences in attributions, the learned helplessness "change" research (see Diener & Dweck, 1978; Dweck, 1975; Dweck & Repucci, 1973) and the attributional retraining research (see Foersterling, 1985) have developed treatments to help individuals change their maladaptive attributional patterns.

The major thrust of these treatments (in both experimental studies as well as field studies) has been to have students change their attributions for success and failure to effort, but especially in the case of failure (see Foersterling, 1985). The treatment usually involves a teacher (or experimenter) working with the students individually on a task and providing effort attributions to the student after success or failure on a number of trials or attempts at a task. It is important to note that most of these treatments do not assume that a student's attributional pattern can be changed as a function of just one statement to the student (cf., however, Wilson & Linville, 1982, 1985), but that more involved interactions and repeated attributional feedback is necessary to have the students change their attributional pattern, such as that involved in scaffolded instruction. Accordingly, it may be difficult for regular classroom teachers to develop individual attributional retraining interventions for the many students in their classrooms. However, for some individual students, an attributional retraining intervention may be very useful. For example, in the area of special education, this type of attributional retraining has become fairly popular (see Borkowski, Weyhing, & Carr, 1988) because it is assumed that students with learning disabilities have had a long history of academic failure in schools and have developed maladaptive attributional patterns. In these cases, where there are more resources available to work individually with students, then attributional retraining may be a very effective technique for teachers and special educators to use.

SUMMARY

This chapter discussed the role of attributions in the formation of expectancy and efficacy beliefs. The development of attribution theory in achievement contexts has been led by Weiner. He and his colleagues have been most responsible for the explication, testing, and refinement of one of the most sophisticated and relevant models for understanding students' motivation in the classroom. In the 1980s, inspired by the work of Weiner, attribution theory was used by many educational psychologists in their own research and was probably the dominant model in research on student motivation and achievement. The research bearing on the theory has used both experimental and correlational designs and has been performed in both laboratory and classroom settings. Finally, attribution theory has relevance for understanding teacher behavior and motivation as well as student motivation.

Attributional processes are one of the most important influences for the formation of students' expectancy and beliefs. The model assumes that individuals are motivated to understand and master their world, and one outcome of this goal is that individuals will try to determine the causes of events. In an achievement context, the most important event is a success or failure, and attribution theory proposes that individuals' perceptions of the causes of their successes or failures (their attributions) will have important consequences for the formation of their expectancy beliefs and their behavior. The theory has developed two general streams of research, one that focuses on the antecedents of attributions and one that focuses on the consequences of attributions.

The antecedents of students' attributions for success and failure fall into two general categories: environmental and personal factors. Environmental factors that can influence the type of attributions that individuals make are specific information, social norms, and other situational features. Specific information can consist of a teacher's direct attribution to students for their performance (e.g., You did not try hard enough.). Other types of environmental information can include norms about the difficulty of the task (e.g., all the other students got an A on the test, which suggests that the test was easy). Situational features include the amount of consensus, consistency, and distinctiveness of the cues presented to students as they attempt to make attributions. Consensus occurs when there is high agreement across different people about the event (e.g., this teacher's math tests are always hard). Distinctiveness occurs when individuals discriminate between different situations in their reactions to the situation (e.g., a student thinks math is hard and English is easy). These features provide differential information to students that they can use to form their own attributions for their own performance on a task.

The personal factors that can influence the content of an attribution are causal schemata, attributional biases, prior knowledge, and individual differences. All of these factors concern the individuals' cognition and beliefs about themselves or about the task that can influence the type of attribution that is made. Causal schemata refer to the basic knowledge structures that people have for understanding and inferring causality from events. Attributional biases include a number of heuristics that individuals may use to infer causality from a situation that can result in misleading and incorrect attributions. Prior knowledge includes both knowledge about the self in terms of past performance on the task and general knowledge about the task. Individual differences include various styles of making attributions that are consistent across many situations. For example, there is evidence that some individuals have a consistent explanatory or attributional style whereby they always make attributions to internal, stable, and global causes.

Besides the general contextual and personal features that can influence the content of an attribution, there is some research on when students are more likely to actually make an attribution. The theory does not predict that students will make an attribution for every event that happens to them. There are many occasions when attributions are not necessary and students' motivation is more a function of their efficacy and value beliefs for the task. However, if the situation is a novel one for students, then the probability increases that they will be more likely to make attributions for their performance. A second factor that increases attributional search is when the outcome is unexpected. If a student has usually done well on a task and suddenly fails, then an attributional search is generally instigated. If the outcome is negative, then there is also a higher probability that an attributional search will be generated than if the unexpected event is a positive one. Finally, a fourth factor that can influence the attributional search process is whether the event is important to the individual. Events of high personal importance are more likely to foster an attributional search than events of low importance.

In terms of the actual content of an attribution, there are an infinite number of specific reasons that individuals can use to explain why they succeeded or failed. In many studies in achievement situations, however, the two most frequently used attributions are some form of ability and effort. Other common reasons include task difficulty, luck, teacher help, mood, and health. The important contribution of attributional theory, and its theoretical linchpin, is that these diverse attributions can be grouped along three basic dimensions of locus, stability, and controllability. It is these dimensions, which are implicitly activated once the individual has generated the attribution, that provide the psychological and motivational force in attribution theory.

The locus dimension refers to whether a cause is seen as internal or external to the person. The stability dimension concerns the changeability of the cause over time and situations from being very stable to unstable. The controllability dimension involves the perception of control and can vary from uncontrollable to controllable. Given both logical and empirical analyses, it appears that attributions can be analyzed along these dimensions and fit into one of the eight cells generated by a locus-by-stability-by-controllability ($2 \times 2 \times 2$) matrix. It is important to note, however, that although there is a normative classification of attributions into these eight cells based on the research in Western countries, there can be cultural, developmental, and individual differences in how the attributions are classified in terms of the three dimensions. Nevertheless, once classified along the three dimensions, the research is very consistent across cultures and ages about the implications of these dimensions for expectancy beliefs and behavior. The findings for the stability dimension are the most consistent and clear-cut, and Weiner proposes a general expectancy principle that reflects the findings. The general expectancy principle states that expectancy beliefs are related to the stability of a cause such that an attribution to a stable cause will increase the expectancy that the event will occur again, whereas an attribution to an unstable cause will result in the expectancy belief staying the same or decreasing. The control and locus dimensions are usually linked to affects, which are discussed in Chapter 8.

Finally, attribution theory has a number of implications for teachers both in terms of understanding their students' and their own behavior. Attribution theory can help teachers understand why some students form adaptive patterns of self-related beliefs but others use a more maladaptive pattern of attributions for their classroom performance. Teacher feedback can have an important influence on students' attributions and expectancy beliefs so teachers must be careful to provide accurate and credible feedback to students. Teachers also must realize the potential for attributional biases to influence their thinking about students' and their own behavior. Teachers need to become aware of the types of attributions they make for students' behavior, how these beliefs are formed, and how to best gather information to make appropriate attributions for student behavior.

Other Social Cognitive Processes

*M*s. Teasdale stayed late after school to set up an aquarium in an activity center at the back of her fifth-grade classroom. The next morning, the first few students to enter the room immediately spotted it and went over to investigate. As more children entered the room, they went over to the aquarium, too, and soon it was completely surrounded by children and blocked from view. When Tim, Maria, and Robert entered the room, they saw all the other children in the back of the room but did not know why *they were there. Maria said, "I wonder what's going on there. Let's go look." So they joined the group at the aquarium.*

At 8:30, Ms. Teasdale announced that they could look at the aquarium later, but that now they should go to their seats because school was ready to begin. After some introductory activities, Ms. Teasdale began a new math lesson on subtracting fractions with unlike denominators and finding lowest common denominators. Ms. Teasdale explained and demonstrated the operations while the children followed along. Afterward they practiced solving problems as a group (guided practice); Ms. Teasdale wrote problems on the board and asked different children to tell her what to do to solve them. After a few minutes, she asked children to work alone solving problems (independent practice). She circulated among students and monitored their work, providing corrective instruction to individual students as necessary.

During the independent practice time, Lisa and C. J. began to talk to each other. Ms. Teasdale noticed this but said nothing to these students because she figured it would stop. Ms. Teasdale then began to provide some corrective instruction to Bryan. The other students realized that Ms. Teasdale was busy and was letting the conversation go on. Soon the noise level in the classroom increased as more children began talking with one another. Suddenly, Ms. Teasdale stood up and said loudly, "Kerry, you know you are supposed to be working quietly. Please stop talking and get back to work." Kerry became silent, and the rest of the class quickly stopped talking as well.

Later that morning, it was time to line up to go to a computer class. The children were noisy and were pushing and shoving. Michael, a popular boy in the class, stepped out of line and said in a loud voice, "Hey, let's cut this out. You know Ms. Teasdale said if we can't line up quietly we don't get to go to the computer room. I want to go, so let's stop now." The others followed Michael's lead and the line became quiet and orderly.

These examples highlight the importance of social influences on behavior, which is the domain of social cognitive theory. People acquire knowledge, rules, skills, strategies, beliefs, and emotions by observing others. People also learn about the appropriateness of modeled actions by observing their consequences. In contrast to conditioning theories that stress reinforcement, social cognitive theory contends that individuals act based on their thoughts concerning their goals, beliefs, and values. As pointed out in the previous chapter, attributional processes play an important role in influencing individuals' behavior. In this chapter, we examine other social cognitive processes as suggested in Bandura's (1986) social cognitive theory. Although social cognitive theory contains elements of the mechanistic and organismic metatheoretical models (Chapter 2), its overall orientation is contextual because it posits that behavior represents an interaction of the individual with the environment.

This chapter focuses on Bandura's (1986) social cognitive theory. Bandura, who was influenced by Miller and Dollard's (1941) work (discussed later), conducted a series of seminal studies on modeling processes that helped to establish the theory's conceptual foundation (Bandura & Walters, 1963). Bandura felt that conditioning theories offer incomplete explanations of behavior because they do not address the influence of social models on behavior; they tend to concentrate on animal learning and human behavior in one-person situations.

Social cognitive theory distinguishes learning from performance of previously learned actions. By observing models, people learn skills and strategies that they may not demonstrate at the time of learning but rather later when they believe it would be appropriate and are motivated to act accordingly. There are countless examples of this phenomenon. A few years ago, one of the authors of this text read a newspaper article detailing how a 5-year-old boy saved a choking 6-year-old girl by applying the Heimlich maneuver (i.e., applying sudden pressure to the victim's abdomen just below the rib cage to dislodge an object caught in the throat). The boy never performed this life-saving technique previously, but learned it when he watched a TV show in which an individual applied it to someone who was choking. The 45-pound hero became motivated to use the technique when confronted with a situation in which he felt it would prove useful.

Social cognitive theory postulates that motivational processes influence both learning and performance (Schunk, 1989b), unlike some earlier theories (Chapter 2) that consider motivation to be a performance variable. Bandura expanded social cognitive theory's scope to encompass learning and performance of cognitive, social, and motor skills, strategies, and behaviors, and he integrated motivational processes with learning and self-regulation (Bandura, 1986, 1988). This expansion of the theory increases its explanatory potential and has important implications for classrooms.

Initially, we discuss important historical influences on social cognitive theory. We then explicate Bandura's theory to include key assumptions and an in-depth analysis of modeling processes. We present a model of motivated learning and show how it applies to self-regulation. Given that we discussed the roles of self-efficacy and outcome expectations in Chapter 3 and that Chapter 6 is devoted to goals, we cover these motivational processes only briefly here. We follow with a section on self-regulation and volition and present material on the motivational relevance of social comparison processes. We conclude with a section on social motivation—a related topic that further highlights the influence of the social environment.

HISTORICAL INFLUENCES

Certain social cognitive processes bear some similarity to principles of earlier theories. In Chapter 2, we discussed Tolman's theory of purposive behaviorism to include latent learning experiments. Here we address theories of imitation, Miller and Dollard's social learning of imitation, and Rotter's social learning theory.

Theories of Imitation

From the time of the ancient Greeks, imitation has been postulated as an important influence on behavior (Rosenthal & Zimmerman, 1978). The Greek word *mimesis* refers to learning through observing the actions of others and abstract models exemplifying literary and moral styles. Theories of imitation conceptualize it as an instinct, a developmental phenomenon, and a generalized response class.

Instinct

At the start of the twentieth century, a popular idea was that people possess a natural instinct to imitate the actions of others (Tarde, 1903). We noted in Chapter 2 that William James (1890) believed that imitation was an instinct:

> But the instinct of *imitating gestures* develops earlier than that of imitating sounds. . . . The various accomplishments of infancy, making "pat-a-cake," saying "bye-bye," "blowing out the candle," etc., usually fall well inside the limits of the first year. Later come all the various imitative games in which childhood revels, playing "horse," "soldiers," etc., etc. And from this time onward man is essentially *the* imitative animal. His whole educability and in fact the whole history of civilization depend on this trait. (p. 408)

James believed that the imitative instinct is pervasive and includes gestures, language, motor skills, and overt behaviors. He felt imitation is a powerful socialization influence but offered a vague explanation of why people imitate:

> A successful piece of mimicry gives to both bystanders and mimic a peculiar kind of aesthetic pleasure. The dramatic impulse, the tendency to pretend one is someone else, contains this pleasure of mimicry as one of its elements. Another element seems to be a peculiar sense of power in stretching one's own personality so as to include that of the strange person. (James, 1890, p. 409)

McDougall (1926) believed that all behavior is instinctive (Chapter 2). McDougall restricted the scope of imitation to the "copying by one individual of the actions, the bodily movements, of another" (p. 106). Within this definition, imitation may involve expressive actions sympathetically excited (e.g., children cry upon seeing their mothers cry), simple ideomotor actions (children copy the motor actions of another), and actions and gestures of someone admired. McDougall felt that imitation is an important influence on socialization, but he provided the vague explanation that observed actions of another elicit an instinct to copy them. Thorndike (1912) also considered imitation to be an instinct and believed that it is centrally important in education.

The imitation-as-an-instinct notion is vague and difficult to verify. Conditioning theorists rejected this idea because it assumes the existence of a drive or mental image that intervenes between a stimulus (actions of another person) and response (imitating the actions). Watson (1924) felt that what people labeled as instincts were actually learned behaviors.

Developmental Phenomenon

Jean Piaget (1962), a developmental psychologist, postulated that human development is characterized by the acquisition and modification of *schemas*, or cognitive structures that underlie and make possible organized thoughts and actions. Schemas determine how people react to events, reflect individuals' total knowledge, and develop through maturation and experiences slightly more advanced than individuals' existing cognitive structures. Imitation is restricted to activities corresponding to existing schemas. Children may imitate actions they understand but should not imitate actions that are far advanced from existing schemas. This view that development precedes imitation severely restricts imitation's scope and explanatory potential as a means for learning new actions.

Research has not uniformly supported Piaget's position. There is evidence that children at one stage of cognitive functioning can imitate modeled actions indicative of a higher stage of functioning, even though they never have displayed any behaviors typical of the higher stage (Rosenthal & Zimmerman, 1978). Imitation and modeling are more potent ways to influence learning and behavior than Piaget's position suggests.

Generalized Response Class

Conditioning theorists construe imitation in associationist terms. Humphrey (1921) believed that imitation is a circular reaction in which each response serves as a stimulus for the next response. Through conditioning, small reflex units form progressively more complex response chains.

Skinner (1953) views imitation in the same fashion as other behaviors and contends that it is a generalized response class (see Chapter 2). A modeled act serves as a discriminative stimulus. Imitation occurs when an observer performs the response and is reinforced. Imitation becomes established when children are reinforced for imitating adults. Once established, an imitative response class is maintained with intermittent reinforcement. Children imitate the behaviors of models (e.g., parents, peers) as long as the models remain discriminative stimuli for reinforcement.

This view limits imitation to performance of previously learned behaviors because the imitator must be able to perform the response; however, research shows that diverse types of skills and behaviors can be learned through observation (Rosenthal & Zimmerman, 1978). Another limitation concerns the necessity of reinforcement for imitated behaviors. Observers learn from models in the absence of reinforcement to models or observers. Reinforcement primarily affects observers' performance rather than original learning (Bandura, 1986).

Social Learning of Imitation

Miller and Dollard (1941) developed an elaborate theory of imitation that generated much research on modeling processes. According to their definition, imitation is "a process by which 'matched,' or similar, acts are evoked in two people and connected to appropriate cues" (Miller & Dollard, 1941, p. 10). They rejected the idea that imitation represents mimicking cues and being reinforced. Instead, they adopted a Hullian framework (Chapter 2) and proposed that imitation is instrumental behavior triggered in response to a cue and aimed at drive reduction. Imitation is instrumental because it leads to reinforcement.

There are different types of imitation. For our purposes, the most important type is *matched-dependent behavior*, which occurs when the model is older, smarter, or more skilled than the imitator. The imitator's behavior is dependent on (elicited by) behavioral cues of the model. The imitator attempts to match behavior to that of the model and need not be aware of whether the action represents a match; the model may provide feedback on the behavior's acceptability. Much classroom activity represents matched-dependent behavior: Students gradually pattern their behaviors after those of teachers, aides, and peers. Miller and Dollard believed that repeated reinforcement of imitated behavior establishes imitation as a secondary (acquired) drive, which can generalize to new situations.

Miller and Dollard's conception of imitation as learned instrumental behavior was an important advance in the study of imitation, but this view contains problems. New responses are not created through imitation; imitation represents performance of learned behaviors. This theory also cannot account for delayed imitation in which imitators perform matching responses some time after they are displayed by models or for imitated behaviors that are not reinforced (Bandura & Walters, 1963). Miller and Dollard present a narrow conception of imitation that restricts its usefulness to motivating observers to perform behaviors that correspond closely to those portrayed by models. As we discuss later, modeling is a much more powerful phenomenon that has implications for motivation and learning.

Social Learning Theory (Rotter)

Rotter's theory, which integrates learning and personality theories (Phares, 1976), "stresses the fact that the major or basic modes of behaving are learned in social situations and are inextricably fused with needs requiring for their satisfaction the mediation of other persons" (Rotter, 1954, p. 84). The theory comprises four basic variables: behavior potential, expectancy, reinforcement value, and the psychological situation (Rotter, Chance, & Phares, 1972).

Behavior potential refers to the probability that an individual will act in a certain fashion relative to alternatives. In any given situation, people may perform different actions. Behavior potential denotes the likelihood of these possibilities. Behavior includes observable and covert acts (e.g., thinking, planning) that can manifest themselves in behavior.

Expectancy is an individual's belief concerning the likelihood that a particular reinforcement will occur following a specific behavior. This is not exactly the same construct as expectancy for success that we discussed in Chapter 3, but it is related. Various outcomes may occur following an action, and each outcome has a probability of occurrence. Expectancy is subjective and need not correspond to reality. Students may believe that if they get an A on a term paper, they will make an A in the course, even though they have made low grades on every other course assignment.

Reinforcement value refers to how much individuals value a particular outcome relative to other potential outcomes. Expectancy and reinforcement value are independent; the outcome considered most likely may or may not be most valued. This construct is similar to the value component of expectancy-value theory as discussed in Chapter 8.

The *psychological situation* highlights the importance of the context of behavior. How individuals view situations affects reinforcement value and expectancy. In unpleasant situations, all potential outcomes might be viewed as negative and the least negative one as the most desirable. Behavior is situationally specific, but expectancies for reinforcement can generalize to similar situations.

Rotter's views present an expectancy-value theory (Chapters 3 and 8) contending that people form expectations about the likely outcomes of behaviors and act in accordance with these expectations and the value they place on potential outcomes. Individuals will engage in a behavior if they believe a given reinforcing outcome will occur following the behavior and if they value that outcome. Students may volunteer for a difficult project if they expect teacher praise and peer approval as outcomes and value them.

Rotter's theory offers important insights into the influences on motivation. Many of Rotter's ideas are found in Bandura's theory, but Bandura has significantly expanded Rotter's position to include greater emphasis on self-regulatory processes (e.g., goals, self-efficacy).

BANDURA'S SOCIAL COGNITIVE THEORY

Bandura's (1986) theory is based on several key assumptions that concern (a) the reciprocal nature of influence among personal, behavioral, and environmental factors; (b) the relation of learning to motivation; and (c) the enactive and vicarious sources of behavioral change.

Reciprocal Interactions

Bandura (1986) describes his framework of *triadic reciprocality* (Figure 5.1) as follows:

> In the social cognitive view people are neither driven by inner forces nor automatically shaped and controlled by external stimuli. Rather, human functioning is explained in terms of a model of triadic reciprocality in which behavior, cognitive and other personal factors, and environmental events all operate as interacting determinants of each other. (p. 18)

The behavioral-environmental link is exemplified by an instructional sequence in which a teacher presents information and directs students' attention to instructional aids. Environmental influence on behavior occurs when the teacher says, "Look here," and students direct their attention with little conscious effort. That students' behaviors alter the instructional environment can be seen when the teacher asks a question and students give wrong answers. The teacher reteaches the material instead of presenting new information.

The behavioral-personal factor interaction can be exemplified with *perceived self-efficacy*, or beliefs concerning a person's capabilities to perform actions at designated levels (Bandura, 1986; see discussion in Chapter 3). Research shows that self-efficacy—a personal factor—influences such achievement behaviors as choice of tasks, persistence, and effort (Schunk, 1989c). In turn, students' behaviors modify self-efficacy. As students work on tasks, they observe

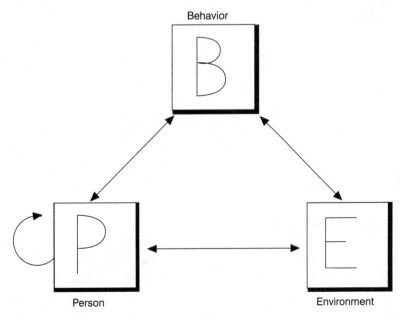

Figure 5.1.   Model of triadic reciprocality

their progress toward their goals (e.g., acquiring skills, completing material). These progress indicators convey that students are capable of learning and performing well, which enhances their self-efficacy for further learning.

An example of the personal-environmental factor interaction is found in students with learning disabilities, many of whom hold a low sense of self-efficacy for performing well (Licht & Kistner, 1986). That personal factors can influence the environment is shown with individuals who react to students with learning disabilities based on attributes typically associated with them rather than on what the students actually do. Some teachers may judge these students as less capable than nondisabled students and hold lower academic expectations for them, even in content areas where the former students are performing adequately (Bryan & Bryan, 1983). In turn, teacher feedback (environmental factor) influences self-efficacy (personal factor). The teacher statement, "You're doing great!" will have a better effect on self-efficacy than the pronouncement, "I doubt you can learn this."

The direction of influence among the three factors is not always the same; typically, one or two factors predominate. Environmental factors take precedence when classroom life is highly regimented and there are many rules and procedures. Personal factors predominate when environmental influences are weak. Students who must write a term paper and can select a topic from a list will choose one they enjoy or have an interest in.

In classrooms the three factors typically interact. As a teacher presents a lesson to the class, students think about what the teacher is saying (environment influences cognition—a personal factor). Students who do not understand a point raise their hands to ask a question (cognition influences behavior). The teacher reviews the point (behavior influences environment). Eventually, the teacher gives students work to accomplish (environment influences cognition, which influences behavior). As students work on the task, they believe they are performing it well (behavior influences cognition) and decide to ask the teacher if they can continue to work on it (cognition influences behavior).

The small loop emanating from the person factor in Figure 5.1 means that personal factors influence one another (Zimmerman, 1989). Thus, use of an effective learning strategy will promote acquisition of skills and can lead students to feel more confident about learning because they understand and can apply the strategy. In turn, higher self-efficacy may affect students' choices of strategies. Such within-person interaction is important given the complex relations possible among personal cognitions, beliefs, and emotions.

Learning and Motivation

Social cognitive theory distinguishes learning from performance of previously learned actions. People learn much by observing models, but the knowledge and skills they acquire may not be demonstrated at the time of learning (Rosenthal & Zimmerman, 1978). People will not demonstrate skills until they are motivated to display them. This motivation to perform previously learned skills may stem from the belief that the skills are appropriate in the situation and that the consequences will be positive. The learning-performance distinction is apparent in the story recounted earlier about the 5-year-old boy who saved his choking companion by applying the Heimlich maneuver. We alluded to this distinction in Chapter 2 when we noted that the contextual metatheoretical model—the appropriate framework for social cognitive theory—postulates that competence can be acquired without being displayed and addresses how the use of competence is affected by personal and situational factors.

Motivation affects performance and learning. We will present a social cognitive model of motivated learning that postulates strong links between motivational and learning processes. Although motivation can affect learning, the two are separable, which is evident in latent learning situations (Chapter 2) where motivational inducements that are weak or absent during learning become powerful later.

Enactive and Vicarious Learning

In social cognitive theory, "learning is largely an information-processing activity in which information about the structure of behavior and about environmental events is transformed into symbolic representations that serve as guides for action" (Bandura, 1986, p. 51). *Enactive learning* is learning by doing and experiencing the consequences of one's actions. Successful actions are retained; those that lead to failure are discarded. *Vicarious learning* occurs from observing live or symbolic (e.g., film) models in the absence of overt performance by learners. Vicarious learning makes possible more learning than if students have to perform every action at the time it is learned and saves students from personally experiencing negative consequences. Complex-skill learning typically occurs enactively and vicariously. Students observe teachers explain and demonstrate skills. Through observation, students may learn some components of a skill and not others. Practice allows teachers to provide corrective feedback to help students perfect their skills.

Bandura (1986) contends that behavioral consequences, whether personally experienced or modeled, inform and motivate students rather than strengthen behaviors as postulated by Skinner (1953). Consequences inform students of the likely outcomes of actions. If students fail or observe models fail, they learn that something is wrong and they may take steps to correct the problem. From a motivational perspective, students learn behaviors that they value and believe will have desirable consequences. The belief that modeled behaviors will prove useful leads people to attend to and learn from models.

MODELING PROCESSES

One of the primary contributions of social cognitive theory is its explication of modeling processes. We discuss modeling here and highlight its relevance to educational settings.

Functions of Modeling

Modeling refers to behavioral, cognitive, and affective changes that result from observing one or more models (Bandura, 1969, 1989; Rosenthal & Bandura, 1978; Schunk, 1987). Whether models are live (in person) or symbolic (pictures, TV, videotape, film), human or nonhuman (e.g., cartoon characters), modeling serves different functions: inhibition/disinhibition, response facilitation, and observational learning (Table 5.1).

Inhibition/Disinhibition

Observing a model can strengthen or weaken inhibitions. When models perform threatening or prohibited activities without negative consequences, observers may perform the behaviors themselves. Models who are punished may inhibit observers' responding. Inhibitory and disinhibitory effects result from observers' beliefs that similar consequences are likely should they act accordingly. Inhibited and disinhibited behaviors have been learned previously by observers; motivation makes them more or less likely to occur.

In the example at the beginning of this chapter, student talking during independent practice became disinhibited because Ms. Teasdale did not stop it. When Ms. Teasdale disciplined Kerry, talking among other class members ceased. Although the effects are not automatic, unpunished misbehavior can lead observers to start misbehaving themselves. Misbehavior stops when the teacher disciplines one student for misbehaving. Observers are likely to believe they, too, will be disciplined if they continue to misbehave.

Response Facilitation

Response facilitation occurs when modeled actions serve as social prompts for observers to behave accordingly. In the example earlier, response facilitation occurs when Tim, Maria, and Robert go to the back of the classroom where they see the other students gathered. The congregation of children serves as a social prompt for these three students to join them. Response facilitation is a motivational phenomenon because the behaviors reflect actions students have learned. Unlike inhibitory and disinhibitory effects, response facilitation

Table 5.1. Functions of Modeling

Function	Effect on Observers
Inhibition/disinhibition	Creates expectations of similar consequences for modeled action
Response facilitation	Social prompt causes similar behavior
Observational learning	New skills and behaviors are acquired

behaviors are socially acceptable and not accompanied by potential restraints (Bandura, 1986).

Observational Learning

Observational learning through modeling occurs when observers display new behaviors that prior to modeling had a zero probability of occurrence, even with motivational inducements in effect (Bandura, 1969; Rosenthal & Zimmerman, 1978). Observational learning expands the range and rate of learning over what could occur if each response had to be performed and reinforced for it to be learned. The students in Ms. Teasdale's class displayed observational learning when they performed fraction skills after observing her modeled demonstration. *Cognitive modeling* incorporates modeled explanations and demonstrations with verbalizations of the model's thoughts and reasons for performing actions (Meichenbaum, 1977).

Observational learning comprises four subprocesses: attention, retention, production, and motivation (Table 5.2). Rather than discuss motivation separately, we show how motivation interacts with the other three subprocesses.

Observer *attention* is necessary for modeled acts to be perceived meaningfully. At any time, there are countless cues to which one can attend. Distinctive features command attention (e.g., size, shape, color, sound, unusual location). Teachers apply this principle when they use brightly colored displays and large cutouts.

Motivation affects observer attention through the perceived functional value of modeled acts. Actions judged by observers as important and likely to lead to valued outcomes command greater attention. Students attend to teachers because of anticipated negative consequences if they do not, but also because teachers' actions are viewed as highly functional and students are expected to learn the modeled behaviors. In addition, students generally view teachers as competent, and people attend to models they believe are knowledgeable.

Retention includes coding and transforming modeled information for storage in memory and mentally rehearsing information. Observers store modeled

Table 5.2. Processes of Observational Learning

Process	Activities
Attention	Attending to distinctive features of modeled displays
Retention	Coding and transforming modeled information for storage; rehearsing information
Production	Translating visual and symbolic conceptions of modeled events into behavior
Motivation	Performing valued activities and those with expected positive consequences

displays in imaginal and verbal form. Imaginal coding is especially important for activities not easily described in words, such as motor skills performed so rapidly that individual movements are part of a smooth, larger sequence (e.g., a tennis serve). Much cognitive skill learning relies upon verbal coding of procedures or strategies.

As with attention, motivational processes influence the activities that observers retain. Modeled actions that observers believe are important are more likely to be retained; those for which observers see little value will not be learned. Retention activities clearly show the interaction of learning and motivation.

Production involves translating visual and symbolic conceptions of modeled events into behavior. Problems in production arise because information is inadequately coded or because learners experience difficulty translating coded information into behavior. Most complex skills are learned through modeling, guided practice, and corrective feedback. Learners may acquire an approximation of a complex skill by observing models and then refine their skills through practice and corrective feedback.

Individuals never demonstrate all the knowledge, skills, and behaviors they acquire through observation. Motivational inducements for action result from direct, vicarious, and self-produced experiences. People perform actions that previously have been successful for themselves or for models. They also perform activities they value and avoid those that are dissatisfying (Schunk, 1987). People forego money, prestige, and power when they judge the activities they must engage in to receive these rewards as unacceptable (e.g., questionable business practices).

Implications for Teachers

In previous chapters, we grouped implications for teachers at the end of the chapter. Because we discuss a number of different theories and constructs in this chapter, we have included implications throughout the chapter where appropriate. The following examples illustrate the application of modeling processes in the classroom.

1. Using inhibition functions of modeling. Mrs. East told her class several times if they did not finish their work they could not go to recess. It was time for recess and Mrs. East said, "Class, it is time to line up for recess." She immediately tapped on a student's desk and said, "James, you may not line up, you did not finish your work." Several other students who also had not finished their work did not line up with the class.

Mr. Taylor was checking to see if the band parade lines were straight. He was walking along the first line and adjusting students who were not in line. The students in the other parade lines began to straighten themselves.

2. Using disinhibition functions of modeling. Mrs. Jenkins told one kindergarten student several times not to pour the sand from the sand table onto the floor and that if he did it again, he would have to go to another center area. She then walked away. The little boy continued to pour sand onto the floor, but Mrs. Jenkins did nothing. Soon all the children at the sand table were pouring sand onto the floor.

A social studies teacher told his class that late work would receive a lower grade. Several students continually turned in late work, but their grade on the work was never lowered. Soon, over half of the class was submitting late work.

3. Using response facilitation functions of modeling. A physical education teacher asked the first three students who entered class to start running laps around the gym. As other students arrived, they automatically started running around the gym with the first three students.

Mr. Laird, a science teacher, brought several homemade robots to share with his class during a unit on mechanics. He had the robots operating at the back of the room when the students arrived. As the students entered, they all immediately went to the back of the room to watch the robots rather than going to their desks.

4. Using observational learning. Ms. Hagaman, a first-grade teacher, used math manipulatives to show her students how to subtract. After explaining each problem, she had the students perform the same operations with the manipulatives at their desks.

Mr. Moore, a tennis coach, demonstrated different types of tennis swings several times. After demonstrating each type, he had his students practice the swing with their rackets.

Characteristics of Effective Models

Modeling does not occur automatically when observer and model are paired. Modeled displays that are inadequately attended to or retained, as well as low motivation for observing the display, will preclude modeling. In addition, theory and research have identified characteristics of models that are important influences on modeling: competence, perceived similarity, credibility, and enthusiasm.

Competence

Perceived model competence aids observational learning because students are more likely to attend to and pattern their actions after models who perform successfully than those less competent (Schunk, 1987). Competent models also display skills correctly, which diminishes the likelihood that students will learn erroneously. This is not to suggest that models of superior competence to observers always make the best teachers. When adult models perform poorly, children may be swayed by status and try to learn anyway because they assume that the adults are not entirely at fault. Children are more likely to detect errors by peers than by teachers, especially if children are less familiar with the content demonstrated by teachers. Perceived superior competence also may not positively affect motivation. Some students who observe teachers flawlessly demonstrate complex skills may believe that they never will become that competent.

For self-evaluative purposes, the best models may be students who are equal to or slightly more competent than observers. France-Kaatrude and Smith (1985) had first and fourth graders perform a task. Children could compare their performances with a peer of higher, lower, or equal competence. Children allowed to compare with similarly performing peers compared most often and demonstrated the greatest persistence. Younger children compared more often with similar peers than did older children.

In forming self-evaluations, children routinely compare their performances with those of their peers (Schunk, 1987). Social comparisons with peers whom children judge as similar in ability can be highly motivating. When model age and competence conflict (e.g., same age but lower competence), children are swayed more by competence information. This suggests that teachers could use younger children to model skills, assuming that students believe the models are competent. Use of younger child models also could enhance observers' self-efficacy; observers may believe that if younger children can learn, they can too.

With respect to *status*, people often pattern their actions after those displayed by models of high status as defined by position, job responsibility, or social standing. In the example at the beginning of this chapter, Michael is a high-status model, as shown by the class following his directions to line up properly. Patterning one's actions after high-status models is functional and should lead to improvement so long as the models are competent and are displaying behaviors in their areas of expertise. Status becomes problematic when people model behaviors that lie outside of the areas of expertise of the models (e.g., athletes advertising personal care products).

Perceived Similarity

Similarity to models constitutes an important source of information and can be motivating (Bandura, 1986). Similarity helps observers gauge *behavioral appropriateness* and form *outcome expectations*. The more alike observers are to models, the greater is the probability that similar actions by observers are socially appropriate and will produce comparable results (Bandura, 1986; Schunk, 1987). Model attributes often predict the functional value of behavior. Similarity is especially influential when observers have little information about functional value, for example, unfamiliar tasks or those not immediately followed by consequences (Akamatsu & Thelen, 1974).

Model similarity also affects observers' self-efficacy. Observing similar others succeed can raise observers' self-efficacy and motivate them to try the task if they believe that since others can succeed, they can as well. Observing others fail can lead people to believe they lack the competence to succeed and dissuade them from attempting the task. Similarity is particularly important when students are uncertain about their performance capabilities, such as when they lack task familiarity and have little information to use in judging self-efficacy or when they previously experienced difficulties and possess self-doubts (Bandura, 1986; Schunk, 1987).

Research examining the effects of perceived similarity on students' achievement behaviors shows that children generally are not more inclined to model peers' behaviors rather than adults' (Schunk, 1987); however, model-observer similarity is a reliable cue for behavioral appropriateness. When children are unsure about what to do, they look to see what peers are doing and act accordingly. Similarity in age is less important for learning of skills, rules, and novel responses than the perceived value of the learning. Competence is important. To the extent that peers are viewed as equally competent as adults, the behaviors of each are likely to be modeled. Children model adults when peers' competence is questioned. Peers often are more effective models when children hold self-doubts about their competence. In a learning situation, viewing a peer successfully perform a task may raise children's self-efficacy more than observing an adult (Schunk & Hanson, 1985). Children may wonder if the adult possesses such a high level of competence that they will never attain it.

An important distinction is between *mastery* models who perform faultlessly and *coping* models who initially demonstrate the typical fears and deficiencies of observers, but gradually improve their performances and gain confidence (Thelen, Fry, Fehrenbach, & Frautschi, 1979). Coping models demonstrate how determined effort and positive thoughts overcome difficulties. Coping models may be especially beneficial with learners who previously encountered difficulties. To the extent that children view a coping model's initial difficulties but gradual progress as more similar to their typical performances than rapid mastery, observation of coping models might raise self-efficacy more than mastery models.

Schunk and Hanson (1985) compared the effects of peer mastery and coping models with those of adult (teacher) models and no models. Peer mastery models solved subtraction-with-regrouping problems correctly and verbalized statements reflecting high self-efficacy and ability, low task difficulty, and positive attitudes. Peer coping models initially made errors and verbalized negative statements, but then verbalized coping statements (e.g., "I need to pay attention to what I'm doing.") and eventually verbalized positive statements and performed as well as mastery models.

Peer models increased efficacy and skill better than did the teacher model or no model. Students who watched the teacher model outperformed students who watched no model. Observing models also enhanced motivation during problem solving. No differences were obtained between mastery and coping models. Although subjects' prior subtraction successes were limited to problems without regrouping, they might have drawn on these and felt that if the models could learn, they could too.

Schunk, Hanson, and Cox (1987) used a task (fractions) on which children had experienced few successes and found that observation of multiple models—coping or mastery—promoted outcomes as well as observation of a single coping model and better than observation of a single mastery model. Children who observed single models judged themselves more similar in competence to coping than mastery models. Observation of multiple models apparently exerted a strong vicarious influence on children's self-efficacy.

Research also has addressed *self-modeling*, or cognitive and behavioral changes stemming from observing oneself on tape. Schunk and Hanson (1989b) videotaped children solving problems and showed them their tapes. Self-modeling students displayed higher self-efficacy and motivation than did children who had been videotaped but did not observe their tapes and those who had not been taped. Self-model tapes may highlight progress in skill acquisition, which enhances self-efficacy and motivation.

Research on similarity in gender supports the idea that similarity is beneficial when it provides information on task appropriateness (Schunk, 1987). Seeing a same-sex child play with a toy provides the observer with sex-appropriateness information, which can have motivational effects. When children are uncertain about the gender appropriateness of behavior, they may model same-sex peers because they have been rewarded for doing so and believe the models to be good examples of their sex role. Teachers who employ peer models of both sexes to portray classroom learning activities may help alter students' preconceived ideas on sex-role appropriateness.

Credibility

Model credibility can affect the observers' motivation to model actions. Models who act consistently with the behaviors they model are more likely to be judged by observers as credible and to be emulated than are models who model one action for observers but behave otherwise themselves (Bandura, 1986). Models who practice what they preach validate their claim that the behavior is appropriate and useful. In contrast, when models say one thing and do another, they are conveying to observers that a behavior is fine for observers but not for them, and observers may wonder why.

In a classic study, Bryan and Walbek (1970) exposed elementary school children to an adult model who played a bowling game and won gift certificates, after which children played the game and won certificates. A collection box for certificates was placed on a table so that certificates won could be donated to poor children. While playing, the model preached generosity ("If I win any money today, I am going to give some to those poor children.") or selfishness ("If I win any money today, I am not going to give any to the poor children."), after which the model did or did not donate some certificates. Modeled behavior exerted stronger motivational effects on children's behavior than did verbalizations. Children exposed to a generous model were more likely to donate than those who observed a selfish model; children who heard exhortations for generosity were no more likely to donate than those who heard verbalized selfishness.

Enthusiasm

Models who present their message enthusiastically enhance observers' learning and motivational processes (e.g., self-efficacy, attributions) better than less enthusiastic models (Perry, 1985). There are numerous real-life examples of model enthusiasm ranging from TV personalities to speakers in motivational seminars. These models hope to motivate observers to act in ways they advocate.

Model enthusiasm might affect observers because people may pay better attention to enthusiastic models, which should enhance learning. Enthusiasm also might motivate observers to retain the skills and strategies being modeled. Enthusiastic models could promote observers' perceptions of task value, especially if the models practice what they preach. Enthusiasm could raise observers' self-efficacy because verbal persuasion is a source of efficacy information. To the extent that an enthusiastic model conveys a you-can-do-it attitude to observers, their self-efficacy and motivation for improving their skills should increase.

Classroom research has identified a teacher expressiveness factor that includes such attributes as enthusiasm, rapport, dynamism, and charisma (Abrami, Leventhal, & Perry, 1982; Perry, 1985). In a seminal study, Naftulin, Ware, and Donnelly (1973) had Dr. Myron L. Fox, who actually was a professional actor, give a lecture on mathematics as applied to human behavior to audiences of educators and mental health professionals. Dr. Fox delivered his talk in a distinguished and enthusiastic fashion, replete with gestures and humor; however, it made little sense and included unrelated content, double-talk, non sequiturs, neologisms, and contradictions. Afterward, the listeners judged Dr. Fox's presentation positively and felt it was thought-provoking. Naftulin and colleagues suggested that a speaker's presumed authority and a charming personality can lead students to believe they have learned in the absence of educational content, a process known as "educational seduction." In a replication study, Ware and Williams (1975) found that high-expressive instructors receive better ratings than low-expressive ones and also produce higher student achievement.

Neither of these studies directly addresses motivation, but Perry and his colleagues (Perry & Dickens, 1984; Perry, Magnusson, Parsonson, & Dickens, 1986) have found that expressive instructors enhance students' perceptions of control, internal attributions (ability, effort), self-confidence, and achievement more than low-expressive instructors. The instructors were portrayed on videotape and expressiveness was varied along the dimensions of physical movement, voice inflection, eye contact, and humor.

These findings support the idea that enthusiastic teachers help foster students' interest and motivation in learning. Of course, students can learn from unenthusiastic teachers, and overly enthusiastic teachers might be so distracting they retard student learning. There is a need for research with young children since Perry's studies were conducted with older students. In proper amount, model enthusiasm seems to be an important way to enhance student motivation and thereby increase learning.

Implications for Teachers

The following examples illustrate classroom applications of the various model characteristics.

1. Have models display skills correctly (Competence). Ms. Allen, an algebra teacher, was introducing a new concept in class. She used the overhead projector to demonstrate the process for working the problems, after which she had the students work several problems along with her. She saw that Alex was working the problems correctly, so she asked him to go to the board and solve one while the class observed.

2. Use high-status models where appropriate (Competence). Mr. Peterson, a fourth-grade teacher, was introducing a unit on map making to his class. He arranged for Mrs. Alvarez, who worked in the map section at the university library, to come to class and talk about maps. He and Mrs. Alvarez showed the students how to create a key and draw a map.

3. Use models of equal or slightly greater competence than observers (Perceived similarity). Ms. Willis introduced a new math concept to the entire class and had students work a few problems. She then formed small groups of students; each group was composed of students who were experiencing the same level of success or difficulty in mastering the concept. She circulated among the groups and worked with them on individual basis. Within each group, as some students mastered the concept, she asked them to work with the others in the group to ensure that they also learned.

4. Employ coping models with students who previously have experienced difficulties (Perceived similarity). Mr. Ankler was working with some of his students with learning problems who were having difficulty adding fractions. Mr. Ankler showed them places where it was easy to make mistakes. He said, "When I was first learning to add fractions, sometimes I would do this. It's a mistake lots of people make, but you can learn some things to help you remember the right way to work the problems. Let's work on these together and I'll show you."

5. Have students serve as their own models and gauge progress (Perceived similarity). Ms. Clayton frequently videotaped Jason, one of her remedial reading students, as he worked on a social studies assignment. Afterward, she and Jason would watch the tape together and compare his work with that portrayed on earlier tapes. They then would talk about areas in which he had made progress. Jason experienced higher self-efficacy after watching the tapes and realizing that he was learning in Ms. Clayton's class.

6. Use multiple models (Perceived similarity). A seventh-grade teacher did a lot of creative writing with her students. After students worked on a writing assignment, she would pair them to discuss and edit their work. She paired students differently throughout the writing process—pairing like abilities and then pairing differing abilities—so that various perspectives would be shared during their discussions. She also met with students individually to discuss their progress and provide productive feedback.

7. Ensure that models act consistent with behaviors they model (Credibility). Mr. Parks insisted that his students always add a column of numbers on their own. He would not let them use a calculator. Then one day when he was figuring an average for a chart they were making in class, Mr. Parks pulled out his calculator to add a column of numbers. The students commented about him using a calculator. He told them that once they had mastered the addition of a long column of numbers, they could start using calculators. Later in the spring when the class had become proficient in addition, he provided calculators for the class to use.

8. Show interest and enthusiasm in the content you are teaching and interact with students in an expressive manner (Enthusiasm). Ms. Ball, a kindergarten teacher, bubbled with enthusiasm for every activity that was done in her classroom. She was always saying something like, "Oh, children, you are going to just love what we are going to do next. It is going to be so much fun!" When interacting with the students, she would act out all the silly animals with them, laugh with them, and shout, "Wow! You are all doing such a *super* job!" Her children were always excited about being in school. Some of her students told their principal that they were the "smartest" class in the whole school.

Functions of Modeled Consequences

Modeled consequences convey information and motivate observers (Schunk, 1987). Vicarious consequences inform observers about the functional value of behaviors. Observing competent models perform actions that result in success informs observers of the sequence of actions they should use to succeed. Most social situations are structured so that the appropriateness of behaviors depends on such factors as age, gender, or status. By observing modeled behaviors and consequences, people formulate expectations concerning which behaviors are likely to be rewarded and which may be punished.

Vicarious consequences affect observers' motivation. Observing the successes, failures, rewards, and punishments of others creates expectations in observers that they are likely to experience similar outcomes for performing the same behaviors. People perform behaviors they believe will be successful and avoid those they think will fail. Students who observe another student praised for working productively are apt to believe that they also will receive praise for working diligently. Assuming the students value teacher praise, this expectation may motivate them to work.

Motivational effects of vicarious consequences may not automatically follow from outcomes but also depend on self-efficacy (Bandura, 1986). This was
shown by Zimmerman and Ringle (1981). Children observed a model who verbalized statements of confidence or pessimism while unsuccessfully attempting to solve a puzzle for a long or short time; then the children attempted the
puzzle themselves. Despite the modeled failure, observation of a model
exhibiting high persistence and confidence promoted children's motivation
(persistence). Observing a low-persistence, high-confidence model raised self-
efficacy; observing a high-persistence, high-pessimism model lowered children's efficacy. These results suggest that teachers may need to integrate into
their modeled displays statements designed to raise students' self-efficacy.

Reciprocal Teaching

An example of an instructional procedure that employs extensive use of
teacher and peer models is reciprocal teaching (Palincsar, 1986; Palincsar &
Brown, 1984; Rosenshine & Meister, 1994). *Reciprocal teaching* is an interactive model in which teacher and students take turns serving as teacher and
comprehension occurs through teacher-student and student-student dialogue.
In a typical small-group reading comprehension procedure, the teacher initially models the strategies to be learned (e.g., summarizing, questioning). The
teacher and students read the passage, after which the teacher asks a question,
summarizes the content, clarifies troublesome points, and predicts future content. Following the teacher's modeled demonstration, the teacher and students
take turns being the teacher. If at first the students have difficulty assuming
the role of teacher, the teacher may have to construct paraphrases and questions for them. As students become more familiar with the procedure, they can
implement the strategies with less teacher assistance.

Research often shows that compared with a condition in which students
receive instruction delivered in a traditional fashion, reciprocal teaching leads
to greater comprehension gains, better maintenance of skills and strategies
over time, and better generalization to classroom comprehension tasks (Palincsar, 1986; Palincsar & Brown, 1984). Students exposed to reciprocal teaching also show greater improvements in quality of summaries and questions
asked. Palincsar and Brown (1984) report the following dialogue between a
teacher (T) and student (S) in response to the text about a snake's skeleton:

> The snake's skeleton and parts of its body are very flexible—something like a
> rubber hose with bones. A snake's backbone can have as many as 300 vertebrae,
> almost 10 times as many as a human's. These vertebrae are connected by loose
> and rubbery tissues that allow easy movement. Because of this bendable,
> twistable spinal construction, a snake can turn its body in almost any direction
> at almost any point.
>
> S: Like, if a snake is turning around, he wouldn't break any bones because he
> is flexible.

T: And the reason he is so flexible is . . .

S: If someone stepped on his tail, he wouldn't be able to move unless he was flexible.

T: O.K. That explains why it would be helpful to be so flexible, but what makes a snake so flexible? I think that is an important part of the summary.

S: So he can move faster?

T: That is another reason for being flexible. Let me do a summary for you. Sara [the student] is right. The most important thing we have learned is that the snake is very flexible. The reason they can bend so easily is that they have so many little bones in their backbones and each of them can move separately, making the snake very flexible. Does that make sense? (p. 142)

Reciprocal teaching is based on Vygotsky's (1978) *zone of proximal development* (ZPD), or the difference between one's performance while working alone and while working with a more competent person. More generally, the ZPD denotes the amount of learning possible by a student given proper instructional support. As long as the teacher and peer teachers are operating in the ZPD, learning by students is possible and should be facilitated. Teachers and peers provide *scaffolding* that helps support learners until they become competent and it can be removed.

The ZPD also is closely aligned with Vygotsky's (1962) ideas about the role of *private speech*, or self-directed speech that is self-regulatory but not socially communicative (Berk, 1986, 1992). Vygotsky believed that private speech helps develop thought through its role in behavioral self-regulation. The capacity of speech to influence thought and behavior develops during the preschool years when children give themselves many self-regulatory verbal instructions. Initially such speech follows thought and behavior but develops such that it precedes them. Such private speech often is overt (aloud), but gradually becomes covert (subvocal), although it can re-emerge in overt form at any time. Vygotsky believed that private speech is essentially an intermediate step between a child's behavior being regulated overtly by others (e.g., parents) and covertly by inner speech (thought) (Behrend, Rosengren, & Perlmutter, 1992).

If private speech represents an intermediate step between regulation by others and covert self-regulation and if the ZPD represents tasks that a child is capable of mastering, then we should expect private speech to occur commonly while the child works in the ZPD (Behrend et al., 1992). This idea is captured in Meichenbaum's (1977) *self-instructional training* procedure. Meichenbaum and Goodman (1971) used the following five-step procedure to train impulsive second graders in a special education class:

1. *Cognitive modeling:* Adult tells child what to do while adult performs the task.

2. *Overt guidance:* Child performs under direction of adult instruction.

3. *Overt self-guidance:* Child performs while instructing him- or herself aloud.

4. *Faded overt self-guidance:* Child whispers instructions while performing task.

5. *Covert self-instruction:* Child performs task while guided by inner silent speech.

Self-instructional training has been used to teach various types of students different tasks (Fish & Pervan, 1985) and is especially useful for teaching students to work strategically. In the Meichenbaum and Goodman (1971) study, the following sample statements were made by an adult model for a line-drawing task to try to slow down students' performances:

> Okay, what is it I have to do? You want me to copy the picture with the different lines. I have to go slow and be careful. Okay, draw the line down, good; then to the right, that's it; now down some more and to the left. Good, I'm doing fine so far. Remember go slow. Now back up again. No, I was supposed to go down. That's okay, just erase the line carefully. . . . Good. Even if I make an error I can go on slowly and carefully. Okay, I have to go down now. Finished. I did it. (p. 117)

MOTIVATIONAL PROCESSES

In Bandura's (1986, 1989, 1993) theory, motivation is goal-directed behavior instigated and sustained by expectations concerning the anticipated outcomes of actions and self-efficacy for performing those actions. Self-efficacy and outcome expectations are discussed in Chapter 3, goals in Chapter 6. In this section, we describe these processes briefly and focus on their roles in motivated learning.

Goals, Self-Efficacy, Outcome Expectations

Goal setting refers to establishing quantitative or qualitative standards of performance (Locke & Latham, 1990). Goal setting is an important motivational process (Bandura, 1988; Schunk, 1989a). Students with a goal are apt to experience a sense of self-efficacy for attaining it and engage in activities they believe will lead to attainment: attend to instruction, rehearse information to be remembered, expend effort, and persist. Self-efficacy is substantiated as learners observe goal progress, which conveys they are becoming skillful (Elliott & Dweck, 1988). Providing students with feedback on goal progress also raises self-efficacy (Schunk & Swartz, 1993). Heightened self-efficacy sustains motivation and improves skills.

The motivational benefits of goals depend on learners making a commitment to attain the goals and on the goal properties of proximity, specificity, and difficulty. Proximal (close-at-hand) goals promote self-efficacy and motivation better than distant goals because it is easier to judge progress toward the former. For the same reason, goals incorporating specific performance standards raise efficacy and motivation better than general goals (e.g., Do your best.). From a motivational perspective, goals of moderate difficulty—those learners perceive as challenging but attainable—are most effective, although for instructional purposes, teachers may establish easy goals in the initial stages of learning and gradually increase goal difficulty as skills develop. Progress toward difficult goals raises efficacy because it conveys that students are improving.

Self-efficacy refers to "people's judgments of their capabilities to organize and execute courses of action required to attain designated types of performances" (Bandura, 1986, p. 391). Bandura (1977, 1982) hypothesized that self-efficacy affects choice of activities, effort, and persistence. People holding low self-efficacy for accomplishing a task may avoid it; those who believe they are capable are likely to participate. Especially when they encounter difficulties, efficacious students work harder and persist longer than those with doubts. People acquire information to appraise self-efficacy from their actual performances, vicarious (observational) experiences, forms of persuasion, and physiological symptoms.

Outcome expectations, or expected outcomes of one's actions (Bandura, 1986; Locke & Latham, 1990; Weiner, 1985b), are important because students anticipate outcomes for actions and act to attain the outcomes they value. Academically motivated students believe if they study diligently they will make good grades. Given that they value high grades, they are likely to study hard and thereby validate their expectations.

Model of Motivated Learning

Motivated learning is motivation to acquire skills and strategies rather than to perform tasks (Corno & Mandinach, 1983). Schunk (1989c) presented a model of motivated learning that highlights the role of self-efficacy (Figure 5.2). At the start of a learning activity, students differ in their self-efficacy to acquire the knowledge and skills. Self-efficacy varies as a function of aptitudes (e.g., abilities, attitudes) and prior experiences. Task engagement variables comprising personal factors (e.g., goal setting, information processing) and environmental factors (e.g., classroom rewards, teacher feedback) affect students while they are working. These factors make salient various efficacy cues, which signal to students how well they are learning and which students use to appraise their self-efficacy for continued learning. The perception of progress, coupled with higher self-efficacy, enhances motivation and skill acquisition.

Student Characteristics

Students enter tasks with differing aptitudes and prior experiences that influence their initial sense of self-efficacy for learning. Aptitudes include general abilities, task-specific skills, interests, attitudes, and personality characteristics (Cronbach & Snow, 1977). Students also differ in their prior educational experiences, such as schools attended, number and types of teachers, and amount of time spent on various subjects. Attitudes and prior experiences are interde-

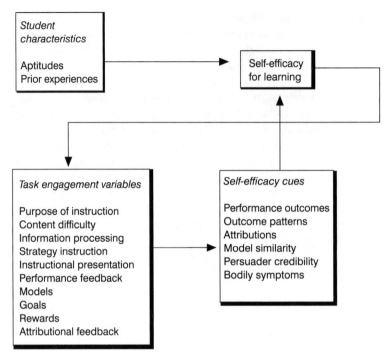

Figure 5.2. Model of motivated learning

pendent. For example, mathematical ability and interest contribute to students' classroom successes and teacher encouragement helps develop positive attitudes and interest (Schunk, 1989c).

Self-Efficacy for Learning

Aptitudes and prior experiences affect students' self-efficacy for learning. Students with high mathematical ability and who previously have performed well on mathematical tasks ought to hold higher self-efficacy for learning a new math skill than learners with lower mathematical ability and who have experienced learning difficulties. An initial sense of self-efficacy motivates students and promotes learning.

At the same time, self-efficacy is not completely determined by aptitudes and prior experiences. Collins (1982) administered standardized tests to students and identified those with high, average, and low mathematical ability. Within each ability level, she identified students of high and low mathematical efficacy and gave all students problems to solve and opportunities to rework those they missed. Ability was positively related to skillful performance; regardless of ability level, students with higher self-efficacy solved more problems correctly and chose to rework more problems they missed.

Task Engagement Variables

Task engagement variables include those factors that come into play during instruction and while students are engaged in academic activities. Some important variables are the purpose of instruction, content difficulty, information processing, strategy instruction, instructional presentation, performance feedback, models, goals, rewards, and attributional feedback.

The *purpose of instruction*, or what uses students are expected to make of the material to be learned (Marx, 1983), provides information about task value and can influence efficacy and motivation. When teachers announce that material will be on a test, students who have performed poorly on tests may experience anxiety, which could lead to low efficacy. Students who previously have earned good grades on tests should react with high self-efficacy.

Also relevant is *content difficulty*. Subject matter perceived as difficult to learn may lead to low motivation and self-efficacy for learning. Many students have qualms about solving algebraic equations. Those who believe they are competent in the component skills (multiplication, subtraction) will feel more efficacious about learning than students who doubt their capabilities.

The type of *information processing* required affects self-efficacy and motivation. Students who have difficulty processing information required by a task may conclude they have low ability and feel less certain about learning than those who believe they can process the material. Salomon (1984) found that students perceive learning from TV easier than learning from print, hold higher self-efficacy about learning from TV, and invest less mental effort in learning. For print materials, higher self-efficacy is associated with greater expended effort.

Strategy instruction can foster self-efficacy for learning. The belief that one understands and can effectively apply a strategy that aids learning leads to a greater sense of control over learning outcomes, which promotes self-efficacy and motivation to apply the strategy.

Instructional presentation affects motivation and learning. Teachers who present material in ways that students can understand engender high efficacy for learning. When assessing efficacy, students take into account how well they learn from various instructional methods. If they believe they learn best when they work in small groups and the teacher uses small groups often, they should feel more efficacious and motivated than students who believe they learn best in large groups. Brophy (1985) identified differences in how teachers introduce content. Teachers may cue positive/negative expectations by asserting that students will/will not enjoy the task and do well/poorly on it. Assuming that students view the teacher as a credible judge of their capabilities, these statements will affect their self-efficacy.

The role of *performance feedback* is minimal where students can obtain feedback on their own (e.g., mathematical problems for which students check their answers). When students cannot reliably determine how well they are learning, teacher feedback highlighting progress (e.g., That's right. You're getting better at this.) raises self-efficacy. At the same time, teachers who provide excessive assistance to students may improve their skills but not their self-efficacy because students may believe they cannot succeed on their own.

Models are important influences on self-efficacy. Although students attend to and emulate teachers despite being dissimilar in attributes and competence, observation of successful peers may exert stronger effects on efficacy, especially among learners who doubt they can attain the teacher's level of competence (Schunk, 1989c). The latter students may not feel efficacious about learning after observing a flawless teacher model, but seeing similar peers master the task may make them feel more capable and motivate them to attempt to learn.

When students set *goals*, they are apt to experience a sense of efficacy for goal attainment and higher motivation. Self-efficacy is substantiated as students make goal progress. Progress is easy to gauge with short-term and specific goals (Bandura & Schunk, 1981). Although students initially may doubt their capabilities to attain goals they believe are difficult, these goals build high efficacy because they offer more information about learning capabilities than easier goals.

Rewards are likely to enhance efficacy when they are tied to students' accomplishments. Telling students they can earn rewards (e.g., free time) based on what they accomplish instills a sense of efficacy for performing well, which is validated as they work and note their progress. Receipt of the reward further validates efficacy because it symbolizes progress. Rewards for participation regardless of performance level may motivate students but also convey that students are not expected to learn much, which negatively affects self-efficacy.

Attributional feedback that links successes and failures with causes is a persuasive source of efficacy information (see Chapter 4). Linking successes with high ability and effort and failure with low effort enhances self-efficacy and motivation (Schunk, 1989b). It is imperative that learners view the feedback as credible. Providing ability feedback (You're good at this.) when students have to struggle to succeed will not raise self-efficacy. When students believe a task is easy, teacher praise combined with effort information (That's good. You've been working hard.) signals low ability (Weiner, Graham, Taylor, & Meyer, 1983). Students who believe that the teacher does not expect much of them will doubt their capabilities.

Self-Efficacy Cues

Efficacy cues are derived from task engagement variables. Some important cues are performance outcomes (successes, failures), outcome patterns, attributions, model similarity, persuader credibility, and bodily symptoms.

Successes generally raise self-efficacy and failures lower it. With respect to outcome patterns, early learning often is fraught with failures and the perception of progress promotes efficacy. Self-efficacy is not aided much if students believe their progress is slow or their skills have stabilized at low levels.

Success attributed to great effort should raise efficacy less than if minimal effort is required, because the former implies that skills are not well developed. Self-efficacy remains high as long as learners believe they can maintain the level of effort needed to succeed. As students develop skills, ability attributions for successes enhance efficacy better than effort attributions.

Observing similar peers improving their skills conveys that students can learn as well; observed failures cast doubt on students' capability to succeed. Model similarity can be based on perceived competence or personal attributes (e.g., age, gender, ethnic background), even when the attributes have little bearing on the modeled behaviors (Rosenthal & Bandura, 1978).

Students feel efficacious when persuaded by a trustworthy source (e.g., the teacher) that they are capable of learning, whereas they may discount the advice of less credible sources. Students also may discount otherwise credible sources if they believe the sources do not understand the task demands (e.g., difficult for students to comprehend).

Bodily symptoms serve as physiological cues. Sweating and trembling may signal that students are not capable of learning. Students who notice they are reacting in less-agitated fashion to tasks feel more efficacious about learning.

Implications for Teachers

The following examples illustrate classroom applications of this model of motivated learning.

1. Make it clear that students are competent enough to learn the material being taught. A second-grade teacher has each student work with her in a small group to demonstrate how to subtract with regrouping before she assigns them a worksheet with the same type of mathematical problems.

2. Point out how the learning will be useful in students' lives. Mr. Cristopolous, a high school science teacher, links the subject matter being taught with material that students understand. For example, prior to beginning a unit on electricity, he has students discuss all the ways they use electricity in their lives. While teaching, he shows how electricity operates in these applications. The students enjoy learning about something present in so many areas of their lives.

3. Teach students learning strategies and show them how their performance has improved as a result of strategy use. Several students in Mr. Walker's fourth-grade class were having difficulty with long division. Mr. Walker worked with these students in a small group and taught them specific questions to ask themselves and steps to take when working a long division problem. He then had each student repeat the strategies aloud as they worked problems and he provided positive feedback as they successfully completed each problem.

4. Present content in ways students understand and tailor instructional presentations to individual differences in learning. Mrs. Adams explained a social studies assignment to her class. Some of the students were having difficulty understanding and remembering all the tasks in the assignment. Mrs. Adams outlined the activity and wrote the various tasks on the board.

5. Have students work towards learning goals. Mr. Seagroves told his class that he wants them to learn their 8's multiplication tables by the end of the week. He said they will practice in class each day and he wants them to study at home. Each day in class the students complete a sheet with the multiplication facts for 8 and record their progress.

6. Ensure that attributional feedback is credible. Ms. Sarver, a third-grade teacher, has a boy with emotional and behavioral disorders infused in her class. He is having difficulty concentrating and paying attention during social studies lessons. His special education teacher told Ms. Sarver to continually praise him or he would get mad and act up. Ms. Sarver decided to take a more realistic approach. She met with Neal individually and told him, "Neal, you are smart enough to learn in here, but you have to work harder and pay attention and concentrate."

Neal remarked, "Ms. Sarver, I can't believe that you really talk to me about this. Lots of others say I'm too dumb to learn. Maybe I can try to listen better."

7. Provide feedback on progress in learning and link rewards with progress. Ms. Burns has been working with Susan to learn her colors. Susan loves to work with the kindergarten games on the new computer with the color monitor. Ms. Burns tells Susan that if she learns her colors she can have extra time on the computer. Each time Susan learns a color, she and Ms. Burns color in a block on the extra-computer-time ticket (using the color just learned). After Susan learned five colors, she was given extra time at the computer.

8. Use models that build self-efficacy and enhance motivation. Mr. Prescott was working with his fifth-grade class on reducing fractions. As they worked through each problem, Mr. Prescott let several volunteers demonstrate how to complete the problem at the board. By the end of the class period, all the students in the room felt comfortable demonstrating the process on the board.

Self-Regulation and Volition

The topic of self-regulation is intimately linked with motivation. *Self-regulation* is the process whereby students activate and sustain cognitions, behaviors, and affects that are systematically oriented toward attainment of their goals (Zimmerman, 1989). Students motivated to attain a goal engage in self-regulatory activities they believe will help them (e.g., rehearse material to be learned, clarify unclear information). In turn, self-regulation promotes learning, and the perception of greater competence sustains motivation and self-regulation to attain new goals (Schunk, 1991).

In Chapter 2, we discussed early work in volition. Many current researchers define volition as part of a larger self-regulatory system that includes motivation and other cognitive processes (Corno, 1993; Snow, 1989). The conceptual basis for this current emphasis derives largely from work in action control theory by Heckhausen (1991) and Kuhl (1984), who propose differentiating *predecisional processing*, which refers to cognitive activity involved in making decisions and setting goals, from *postdecisional processing*, which denotes those activities engaged in subsequent to goal setting. In this view, predecisional analyses involve decision making and are motivational, whereas postdecisional analyses deal with goal implementation and are volitional. Volitional processes mediate the relation between one's goals and actions to accomplish them. Once students move from planning and goal setting to implementation of plans, they cross a metaphorical Rubicon in which goals are protected by self-regulatory activities rather than reconsidered or changed (Corno, 1993).

There is considerable debate whether motivation and volition are separate constructs or whether the latter is part of the former. This point notwithstanding, separating pre- from postdecisional processes seems useful. Some motivational indexes that have been used in studies of performance are not appropriate for school learning. Choice of activities is a common motivational index, yet in school students typically do not choose which activities to engage in. In school there often is little predecisional activity by students. Postdecisional activity, however, is important because there may be multiple ways to accomplish a task or many distractions to deal with while trying to perform the task. Volitional activities presumably direct and control information processing, affects, and behaviors directed toward accomplishing goals (Corno, 1993).

In sum, "volition can be characterized as a dynamic system of psychological control processes that protect concentration and directed effort in the face of personal and/or environmental distractions, and so aid learning and performance" (Corno, 1993, p. 16). Kuhl (1985) has proposed a taxonomy of volitional strategies. Corno (1993) discusses two such strategies with educational examples (see Table 5.3). *Motivation control* involves strategies students can use to regulate their motivation. *Emotion control* concerns strategies students can use to control and regulate their emotions. One problem with this volitional view is whether it is justifiable to separate goal setting from implementation when in fact research shows that individuals often adjust or set new goals during task performance (Locke & Latham, 1990). Another concern is how important processes such as self-efficacy and attributions relate to volition during task implementation. Future research undoubtedly will address these and other concerns.

SOCIAL COMPARISON

Modeling involves much *social comparison*, or comparing ourselves with others. Social comparison is an important means for learning about the appropriateness of behavior. When absolute standards of behavior are ambiguous or nonexistent, acceptability of behavior is gauged relative to what is practiced by

Table 5.3.   Examples of Volitional Control Strategies

Motivation Control	Emotion Control
Set contingencies for performance that can be carried out mentally (e.g., self-reward)	Count to 10 in your head
	Control breathing so it is slow, steady, and deep
Escalate goals by prioritizing and imagining their value	Generate useful diversions (e.g., sing to yourself)
Visualize doing the work successfully	Visualize doing the work successfully and feeling good about that (change the way you respond emotionally to the task)
Uncover ways to make the work more fun or challenging	
Immerse yourself in plans for achieving goals	
Self-instruct	Recall your strengths and your available resources
Analyze failures to direct a second try	Consider any negative feelings about the experience and ways to make it more reassuring

Material drawn from Corno (1993)

others. Social comparison also motivates observers. Seeing others act in a particular way and receive praise or recognition can instigate similar action in observers because they believe they will be rewarded. We now consider social comparison theory, how social comparison changes with development, and the role of social comparison in motivation and achievement.

Festinger's Theory

Festinger (1954) proposed that people are inherently motivated to evaluate their abilities and opinions and that they often do this by comparing themselves with others: "To the extent that objective, nonsocial means are not available, people evaluate their opinions and abilities by comparison respectively with the opinions and abilities of others" (p. 118). He also postulated that the most accurate self-evaluations derive from comparisons with individuals similar in the ability or characteristic being evaluated. In choosing people for comparison, individuals are apt to select those who are similar on the characteristics or related attributes most predictive of performance in the domain in question (Goethals & Darley, 1977). Thus, to evaluate personal math ability an individual ought to choose others who are similar in attributes relevant to math performance: age, prior math courses, math grades.

This similarity hypothesis is supported by research (Suls & Sanders, 1982) and predictions of social cognitive theory. The more alike observers are to models, the greater is the probability that similar actions by observers are socially appropriate and will produce comparable results (Bandura, 1986;

Schunk, 1987). Anticipating rewarding consequences for acting in a given fashion can motivate observers to act accordingly.

At the same time, Festinger's theory does not fully explain the motivational effects of perceived similarity because these effects depend largely on self-efficacy. Children who observe similar others accomplish a task are apt to try it themselves because they believe they will be successful. Interestingly, research also shows that perceived *dissimilarity* can motivate. Schunk and Hanson (1989a) found that average-achieving children who observed coping models learn judged their self-efficacy for learning the skills higher than did students who observed mastery models. The former children judged themselves more competent than the coping models, whereas the latter students perceived themselves similar in competence to the mastery models. The belief that one is more competent than a model enhances self-efficacy and motivation.

Development of Social Comparison

Adults employ social comparison regularly for self-evaluation, but the ability to use comparative information depends on higher levels of cognitive development and experience in making comparative evaluations (Veroff, 1969). Festinger's hypotheses may not apply to young children. Children younger than age 5 or 6 tend not to relate two or more elements in thought and are egocentric in that their "self" dominates their cognitive focus (Higgins, 1981). These characteristics do not mean that young children cannot evaluate themselves relative to others but rather that they do not do so automatically. Children become increasing interested in comparative information in elementary school. The behaviors of young children are affected by direct adult social evaluation (e.g., You're good at this., You could do better.) but by fourth grade children regularly use peer comparisons to evaluate their competence (Ruble, Boggiano, Feldman, & Loebl, 1980).

The meaning and function of comparative information changes with development and especially after entering school. Preschoolers actively compare physical characteristics (e.g., rewards they and others receive) (Ruble et al., 1980). Their comparisons determine how they are similar to and different from others (I'm 4 $\frac{1}{2}$, you're 4., We both had a birthday.) and seem to be based on a desire to be better than others without involving self-evaluation (e.g., I'm the general; that's higher than the captain.) (Mosatche & Bragonier, 1981). Less frequently, young children engage in comparison to evaluate their qualifications (I can do it, too.).

Ruble and her colleagues discuss the development of social comparison in children as a multistep process (Ruble, 1983; Ruble, Parsons, & Ross, 1976). The earliest comparisons primarily involve similarities and differences but then shift to a concern for how to perform tasks. Feldman & Ruble (1977) found that first graders engage in much peer comparison but primarily to obtain correct answers. Providing comparative information to young children may raise their motivation more for practical reasons (e.g., to finish a task) than for acquiring information about capabilities. Knowing that others are performing better will not necessarily motivate young children, and telling those who fail at a task that most other children also do poorly may not alleviate the negative impact of failure (Ruble, Parsons, & Ross, 1976). After first grade, interest increases in determining how well peers are doing and comparative information is used more often to evaluate competence.

More recently, Ruble and Frey (1991) have suggested that social comparison processes may vary not just by age, but by experience with a task. They suggest a four-phase model with social comparison playing different roles, depending on the phase. The first phase involves initial task assessment for a new task (e.g., learning to play golf) where the learner does not have much experience. In this phase, Ruble and Frey suggest that the focus is on acquiring information about the task (e.g., how to hit the ball into the air), not on performance relative to others. In addition, comparison in this phase is more likely to be with the self, given previous performance (e.g., I hit the ball better this time than last.). In the second phase, there is a shift away from just task mastery to competitive assessment via social comparison with others or with absolute standards (e.g., I can score under 100 for 18 holes of golf.). The third stage involves the confirmation or maintenance of the behavior and can include changing subgoals (getting a par on a hole) or competing with others (beating your friends). Finally, the last phase is a reassessment of overall goals and continuation of activity. Social comparison can play a role at all four phases, but the nature and function of social comparison processes may be very different.

With respect to gender differences, Ruble, Feldman, and Boggiano (1976) found that among children in kindergarten through second grade, boys showed greater interest in comparison than did girls. Spear and Armstrong (1978) found that comparative information exerted motivational effects on boys' performances on easier tasks, but not on difficult ones; no differences due to type of task were obtained for girls. Ruble, Parsons, and Ross (1976) suggest that there may be more societal pressure on boys than girls to evaluate themselves relative to others. Although much social comparison research has not yielded gender differences, the issue is important for schooling and deserves further attention.

Motivation and Achievement

Social comparison can motivate students in achievement contexts, although its effect on motivation is not automatic. Among elementary school children, Schunk (1983b) found that social comparative information promotes task motivation, academic goals enhance self-efficacy, and goals plus comparative information lead to the highest skill. In a similar study, Schunk (1983c) obtained evidence showing that difficult goals raise children's academic motivation more than easier goals, persuasive information (You can work 25 problems.) increases self-efficacy more than social comparative information, and difficult goals plus persuasive information leads to the highest skill.

These results suggest that comparative information can enhance motivation but not necessarily self-efficacy or learning. Social comparative information that focuses students on the accomplishments of similar (and average) others makes salient that they are average and therefore have no reason to feel overly competent. Direct attainment information conveys nothing about others' accomplishments; students are likely to focus on how their present performance surpasses prior attainments. The perception that one is improving is hypothesized to build self-efficacy.

SOCIAL MOTIVATION

So far we have focused on motivation for academic learning and performance, but motivation is important in the social domain as well. In this section, we discuss how motivational principles apply to socially influenced behaviors and social skills. We will see that many of the social cognitive processes explicated earlier in this chapter also are influential in social situations. Topics included in this section are social facilitation, social loafing, group motivation, and conformity and compliance. We present theory and research bearing on these topics and discuss their applicability to educational settings.

Social Facilitation

Social facilitation means that the presence of others motivates behavior. The idea dates to Triplett (1898), who found that children wound more line on fishing reels when they worked next to others who were also winding line than when they worked alone. Zajonc (1965) revived the idea and offered other examples (e.g., animals eat more in the presence of others than when alone). Social facilitation can reflect a *coaction effect*, which is a form of modeling that occurs when performance is motivated as a result of others performing the same action, or an *audience effect* that reflects the energizing of one's behavior due to the presence of observers. Social facilitation has been obtained across diverse tasks.

Zajonc (1965) explained social facilitation by postulating that the presence of others produces increased general arousal, which energizes responses that are *dominant* in the individual's repertoire (i.e., well established and highly probable). This drive theory explanation recalls Hull's (1943) theory postulating that behavior (reaction potential) is a function of drive and habit strength (Chapter 2). In Zajonc's theory, the arousal is roughly equivalent to drive, the performance reflects reaction potential, and habit strength indicates the dominance of behaviors.

Social facilitation typically does not involve new learning but rather enhanced performance due to the presence of others. In school, for example, if a student solves problems on the board after observing the teacher solve similar problems, we may label it observational learning through modeling rather than social facilitation. Social facilitation might involve a student solving problems at the board quicker when the teacher and other students watch than when he or she solves them alone.

At the same time, we know that the presence of others does not always increase performance. Sometimes people perform poorly in front of audiences even when they previously have done well. Zajonc (1965) cited the learning-performance distinction (see Chapters 1 and 2) and hypothesized that others' presence facilitates performance of previously learned behaviors because they are dominant in the performer's repertoire. When learning is occurring, however, the dominant response is incorrect or incomplete, so the presence of others can impair learning.

Another explanation is that social facilitation derives largely from concern over self-presentation (Geen, 1991). People have a need to be viewed positively. Arousal produced by the presence of others partly stems from the thought of being evaluated. When the behavior being performed is dominant, people perform well to present a positive impression, but they cannot do so when the behavior is not well established. Thus, social facilitation reflects motivation for social approval.

Social cognitive theory (Bandura, 1986) postulates that motivation stems largely from goals, self-efficacy, and outcome expectations. According to Sanna (1992), social facilitation occurs when individuals possess high self-efficacy (believe they are capable of performing well) and positive outcome expectations (believe their performances will be positively evaluated by others). Social facilitation should not occur when people hold positive outcome expectations but low self-efficacy, for example, students who doubt they can learn but believe that if they do, it will be rewarded by the teacher.

Teachers who understand social facilitation can use it wisely. Group work offers the possibility for enhanced performance by students who desire social approval by the teacher and peers. The key is to use tasks that students can perform, or if learning is involved, those that students can reasonably be expected to learn with requisite effort.

Social Loafing

Social loafing is the opposite of social facilitation and refers to a *decrease* in an individual's performance while working in a group compared to working alone. Social loafing was identified by Ringelmann (reported in Kravitz & Martin, 1986), who had workers pull on a rope alone or as part of a group. Ringelmann found that people who work alone pull the hardest and that individual performance decreases as group size increases. Ringelmann explained this effect as due to a loss of motor coordination when people work in groups.

Latane, Williams, and Harkins (1979) controlled for potential effects of coordination loss and showed that individual performance still declines as group size increases. Subsequent research has shown the effect to occur with complex tasks involving cognitive judgments and creativity (Geen, 1991). Latane and colleagues explain their results in terms of social impact: When people in a group are subjected to social forces (e.g., when subjects divide the amount of work they think they should perform or the amount of reward they expect to earn), the impact of those forces on members declines as group size increases and a corresponding decrease in output follows.

Other explanations involve equity, lack of evaluation anxiety, and inadequate standards of comparison (Geen, 1991; Latane et al., 1979). Equity means that people in groups adjust their outputs to what they perceive to be the output of others and thus attempt to achieve an equitable division of labor. Assuming that people believe others in a group will produce lower output, they adjust their work downward. Lack of evaluation anxiety occurs because group members' output is pooled to arrive at a group product that masks individual contributions. The lowered anxiety results in poorer performance. When there are no explicit standards against which to compare performances (a situation analogous to working under general goals), people can assume that any level of performance is acceptable, which retards motivation.

Sanna (1992) showed that social loafing depends on self-efficacy and evaluation. Students with high self-efficacy whose performance could not be evaluated performed worse than evaluated subjects; students with low self-efficacy who were not evaluated performed better than those who were evaluated. With high self-efficacy, evaluation raises performance, but it lowers performance when self-efficacy is low. The latter students apparently are further debilitated by anxiety arising from the performance evaluation.

Social loafing has direct relevance to education because group work is common and the loss of motivation in groups produces lower performance and less learning. We discuss group motivation next and offer suggestions on how to keep group members productive.

Group Motivation

Students spend much class time working with others. For instructional purposes, teachers routinely group students according to ability or heterogeneously. The teacher's job is to understand how to instigate and maintain group motivation at an optimal level.

Group motivation operates according to the same principles that apply to individual motivation. Factors that optimize group motivation include having a goal to attain; feeling efficacious about performing well; holding positive outcome expectations; attributing success to such factors as ability, effort, and strategy use; and receiving feedback indicating goal progress.

What distinguishes motivation in groups from individual motivation is how the task is structured and how members are rewarded. When individuals work on a task alone, they do all the work and receive all the rewards. Much work on academic group motivation has examined *cooperative learning,* in which two or more students work together to complete a task (Slavin, 1983a, 1983b). Types of task structures used in cooperative learning arrangements are task special-ization and group study. Task specialization means that each group member is responsible for completing one part of the overall task, and group study refers to the situation where group members work together and do not have separate tasks. With respect to how members are rewarded, rewards may be based on the overall group product or on the total of each individual's performance.

Reviews of research lead to several conclusions (Slavin, 1983a, 1983b). First, cooperative learning usually is effective and students often perform bet-ter in groups than working alone. Second, it is imperative that an incentive structure be in effect. In the absence of incentives, there is no evidence that group study results in higher motivation or learning compared with working alone. Third, individual accountability is necessary: Each individual's best efforts must be put forth for the group to succeed and the contribution of each member must be identifiable. Without individual accountability, one or two members can do all the work. In short, cooperative structures are ideally designed to improve performance by increasing helping and encouraging one another to work. Group methods are needed that foster these outcomes.

Another important point is whether the group succeeds or fails. Most research on cooperative groups has looked at group success in which students experience higher perceptions of ability and motivation. As Ames (1984) has shown, however, when cooperative groups fail, there is the tendency to fix blame, and typically the weaker group members receive the blame. This situa-tion adversely affects self-efficacy and motivation. When establishing small groups, teachers should select tasks at which they are relatively confident the group can succeed with diligent work, should ensure that each group member has a defined role in the group, and should hold each individual accountable for learning.

Implications for Teachers

The following examples present some ideas for using cooperative groups in the classroom.

1. Design tasks at which the group can succeed if the members work dili-gently. Group success enhances self-efficacy and motivation. Ms. Kush used recipes to help teach measurement to her fourth-grade students. After she was sure that all the students were successful with measurement activities, she divided the class into cooperative groups and gave each group recipes and ingredients to prepare an item on their own. She made sure that there were enough ingredients in each recipe so that each child would have an opportu-nity to measure and add something to the item their group was preparing.

Ms. Myers, a history teacher, assigned a mobile activity to each small group during the study of early U.S. presidents. In selecting the students for the groups, she made sure that each group had a good researcher, a good reader, a good writer, someone who printed well, an artist, and so on. She also gave each group a self-evaluation form to complete and return when they completed their mobile.

2. Ensure that each group member has some responsibility and that individual performance can be accounted for. Refocus the group if it becomes apparent that a few members are doing all the work. A homemaking teacher divided her class into four cooperative groups for each project activity. She made every effort to mix the students so that abilities and talents were equally divided. For each project, she also made sure that each student in each group had some aspect of the project to complete. As the groups worked, she observed them and rated the members on their participation.

At the beginning of the year, Mr. Harrigan assigned several social studies projects to small groups. It became apparent after the completion of the second project that some students were doing the majority of the work, whereas others were doing little or no work. Before Mr. Harrigan introduced the third project, he regrouped the students. Then he met with each group to help students select an aspect of the project they would like to do and checked with the students periodically to assess progress. At the end of the project, he met with each group to discuss participation and help them assess the quality of their project.

3. Make sure that the group has a goal and an incentive to work toward the goal. Mr. Love, a high school drama teacher, assigned each group in his senior class the task of writing a skit that would share some of their high school experiences. They were to each contribute to the skit and each student in the group was to assume a role—writing, acting, designing props, and so on. Each successful skit would be performed at the last senior class meeting.

Ms. O'Brien, a fifth-grade teacher, gave each small group the opportunity to select a science project related to their recent unit on electricity. Guidelines for selecting and completing the project were listed on each project. She met with each group after they selected their project to discuss how the guidelines applied to what they had chosen. All groups that did a good job on their projects would be allowed to take their projects to the systemwide science fair.

4. Frequently check on group progress. Provide progress and corrective feedback. Ms. Harris, an elementary art teacher, divided one of her classes into small groups to make piñatas to correlate with a unit their class was doing on Mexico. She demonstrated how to make a piñata, letting all the children assist before the groups worked on their own piñatas. Once the groups started on their projects, she circulated around the room each day to provide input regarding their progress and success.

Mr. Willet worked with a group of his resource students to complete a science project on creating a spring garden for their school. Before the students began, Mr. Willet met with them to create a chart that included all the tasks that needed to be done to produce a good garden. He helped the students select activities they wanted to do. Then he checked with the group each day to see what tasks had been completed and helped the students rate the success of the garden project.

Conformity and Compliance

Conformity and compliance often are used interchangeably to mean *obedience*. Although there are exceptions, we distinguish conformity and compliance as follows: *Conformity* involves willful obedience to a group's behaviors or mannerisms where the individual and group members are roughly equal in stature (peers), whereas *compliance* denotes obedience emanating from another's command where a difference in power or stature exists (subordinate, superior). We consider these in turn.

Conformity

Groups have rules, expectations, and pressures that, whether explicit or implicit, affect individuals' motivation. Conformity represents the desire to go along with the group regardless of one's beliefs. All of us conform to group standards on the job, in school, at home, and at social functions.

From a social cognitive perspective, conformity represents modeling of group behaviors (Bandura, 1986). Conformity may reflect any of the three forms of modeling discussed earlier. Behavior occurring in response to a prompt is response facilitation. The classroom example at the beginning of this chapter illustrates response facilitation when the children enter the room and go over to where the others are. If the chairperson of a volunteer group passes a basket for donations and each member puts in a dollar, that is a social cue for new members that a dollar is an acceptable contribution. Conformity also can represent inhibition and disinhibition. In some groups it is expected that members will not criticize senior members. Junior members conform to this standard by inhibiting their tendency to openly disagree with senior members. Disinhibition may occur when adolescents discard traditional dress and adopt an outlandish dress style to conform to that of a social group. In the example at the start of this chapter, talking initially was disinhibited because the teacher did not punish it, but then was inhibited when the teacher disciplined one student. Finally, conformity may represent observational learning. Customs and traditions of groups have to be learned. Observational learning occurs when new members demonstrate actions that they acquire from observing older members.

The power of conformity was convincingly demonstrated by Asch (1955, 1958). Asch formed groups of seven to nine adult subjects, only one of whom was a true subject (the others were confederates of the experimenter). Subjects were told the experiment involved visual judgments and that they would be comparing lengths of lines. Subjects were shown a standard line and three comparison lines, one of which was an exact match; the others differed from the standard by ¾ to 1 ¾ inches. Subjects responded individually with the line that they chose to match the standard; the naive subject responded next to last. On the first two trials, everyone agreed. Beginning on the third trial and on several subsequent ones, however, everyone up to the naive subject purposely picked a wrong line.

Under normal nonexperimental circumstances, subjects made mistakes less than 1% of the time, but Asch obtained an overall conformity rate of 37%. There were wide individual differences; some subjects never agreed with the group's erroneous judgments, whereas others sided with the majority most of the time. Other research showed that the size of the discrepancy matters. Conformity dropped as the difference between the standard line and the line chosen by the majority increased, although even when the two lines differed by 7 inches, some naive subjects still complied with the group's judgment. Asch also found that the size of the group giving erroneous judgments was important. When only one subject gave a wrong answer, the naive subject answered independently. When two subjects gave wrong answers, conformity among naive subjects increased to 14%, and with three incorrect judgments, it increased to 32%. After that, conformity changed very little with increasing group size.

What diminished conformity (to around 5–10%) was if one other member of the group gave the correct answer. In a methodological variation, group members began the trials siding with the naive subject, but gradually broke away and gave incorrect answers. Naive subjects remained independent as long as anyone sided with them, but they began to conform when they found themselves alone. That subjects have little sympathy with the loner was shown in another variation in which all subjects were naive except for one confederate who consistently gave wrong answers. Subjects reacted to the loner with amusement and laughter.

After the experiments, some subjects reported having experienced a perceptual distortion and actually believed that the group's response was correct. Other subjects distorted their judgments: They realized their judgments were different from the group's but conformed because they thought their judgments were incorrect. Some subjects distorted their actions. They realized they were different and did not necessarily feel that the group was right, but they went along in order not to appear different. Asch suggested subjects may conform to reduce dissonance (Chapter 2).

Teachers continually see the motivation to conform in students. Students, especially adolescents, usually do not want to appear to be different and this can be a problem. High-ability students who do not want to be viewed by others as studious but rather want to be socially accepted may neglect their coursework and their grades may drop.

Compliance

We introduce compliance with a famous psychological experiment by Milgram (1963), who recruited subjects for a study on the effect of punishment on learning. As each naive subject reported for the experiment, he (all subjects were men) met another subject, who actually was an experimental confederate. The naive subject was the teacher and the confederate the learner. The learner was strapped into a chair and had electrodes attached to him, after which the experimenter and teacher moved to another room. The teacher was shown the (simulated) shock generator with levels ranging from "slight" through "intense" to "XXX." The learning task was explained to the naive subject and he was told to shock the learner each time he made a mistake and to increase the shock level each time. The confederate responded incorrectly much of the time and was "shocked" each time. In fact, the switches delivered no shock, but subjects did not know that. The confederate began to pound on the wall midway through the shock series and then later quit responding. Teachers were aware of the learner's plight and were visibly nervous. Many turned to the experimenter and asked what to do. The experimenter requested them to continue, although subjects were free to leave at any time.

Prior to the experiment, Milgram questioned colleagues and students about how far they felt subjects would go in obeying the experimenter. Most felt that subjects would not obey the experimenter once the shocks presumably became painful and that only 1–2% of the subjects might deliver the most painful shock. In fact, 65% of the subjects delivered the most painful shock. Of the 35% who did not, none stopped prior to when the victim began pounding on the wall. These results were replicated by Milgram (1974) and others using different subjects and settings.

These results show that people have strong social motivation to comply with authority figures. Many of the subjects seemed to detach themselves from being responsible in the situation. Some subjects openly professed that they were not responsible for what happened to the learner, and some asked the experimenter if he would accept responsibility. In a variation of this procedure, subjects were allowed to choose how much shock to deliver and they typically chose a low level. Moving the learner into the same room as the teacher enhanced the teacher's sense of responsibility; compliance rates fell. Part of the subjects' compliance may stem from the legitimacy of the procedure. It was conducted on a university campus, the experimenter wore a gray technician's coat, and the purpose of the study sounded scientifically valid. Compliance rates fell when the experiment was conducted in a lower-class section of town. In another variation, two experimenters were present and disagreed about whether shock should be continued. Without a clear authority figure, compliance rates dropped.

Some obedience to authority is necessary because without it a society cannot function effectively. At the same time, blanket compliance with orders results in dehumanization and diffusion of responsibility. The mentality displayed by Milgram's subjects is similar (albeit on a much lesser scale) to that responsible for the Holocaust and the My Lai massacre when officers claimed they were following orders. In Milgram's studies there undoubtedly are several reasons why subjects complied, including scientific respectability, anonymity, protection against retaliation, desire to please the experimenter, assigning responsibility to the experimenter, and believing that a qualified experimenter would not allow dangerous events.

Students must behave properly, complete their assignments, and obey rules and procedures. In fact, there is evidence that when students accept responsibility for their social behavior, they also achieve better (Wentzel, 1991a). From a social cognitive perspective, other important influences on compliance are students' expectations concerning the outcomes of their actions and the value they place on those outcomes. We want students to comply with rules not because of the reasons identified by Milgram, but rather because they expect and value the positive outcomes that result from complying. Hamilton, Blumenfeld, Akoh, and Miura (1989) have shown that Japanese students are more likely to accept these responsibilities. Teachers who involve students in decision making can help to foster these beliefs. The relations among social responsibility, achievement motivation, and actual achievement in schools will be an area of increased research in the future.

SUMMARY

Social cognitive theory focuses on how people acquire knowledge, rules, skills, strategies, beliefs, and emotions through their interactions with and observations of others. Social cognitive theory is a contextual view because it posits that behavior represents an interaction of the individual with the environment. Important historical influences on social cognitive theory include theories of imitation, Miller and Dollard's (1941) social learning of imitation, and Rotter's (1954) social learning theory. Although some historical ideas bear similarity to principles of social cognitive theory, each historical view has limitations that preclude its being able to explain the scope and complexity of human motivation.

Bandura's social cognitive theory assumes triadic reciprocality among personal factors, behaviors, and environmental influences as they interact with and affect one another. The theory distinguishes learning from performance because people learn many behaviors that they do not demonstrate at the time of learning. Although learning occurs enactively (by doing), the range of human learning is greatly expanded by the capacity to learn vicariously, whereby individuals are exposed to modeled influences but do not perform the modeled behaviors.

Modeling refers to behavioral, cognitive, and affective changes that result from observing one or more models. Observing models can strengthen or weaken inhibitions (inhibition/disinhibition), serve as social prompts for observers to act accordingly (response facilitation), and lead observers to display new behaviors that prior to modeling had a zero probability of occurrence (observational learning). The latter comprises four subprocesses: attention, retention, production, and motivation. Characteristics of effective models include competence, perceived similarity, credibility, and enthusiasm. Modeled consequences of behaviors inform observers about successful sequences of actions and the likely outcomes of behaviors. Consequences also motivate observers to behave accordingly through their effects on self-efficacy and outcome expectations.

Modeling is common in classrooms. An instructional procedure that makes extensive use of teacher and peer models is reciprocal teaching. This procedure is based on Vygotsky's notion of the ZPD and relates to the self-regulatory role of private speech. The self-instructional training procedure makes extensive use of private speech that initially is overt but through training becomes internalized.

Bandura believes motivation is goal-directed behavior instigated and sustained by expectations concerning anticipated outcomes of actions and self-efficacy for performing those actions. Motivated learning is motivation to acquire skills and strategies rather than to perform tasks. Schunk's model of motivated learning postulates that at the start of a learning activity, students differ in their self-efficacy for learning, which depends on personal aptitudes and prior experiences. While working on the task, students are affected by task engagement variables that make salient cues that signal to students how well they are learning and cues that students use to appraise efficacy for continued learning. The perception of progress, along with higher efficacy, enhances motivation and skill acquisition.

Social cognitive theory has been applied to the area of self-regulation, or the process whereby students activate and sustain cognitions, behaviors, and affects, systematically oriented toward attainment of their goals. A topic assuming increasing importance in the field of self-regulation is volition. Many researchers see volitional processes as mediating the relation between goals and actions to accomplish them.

Social comparison is the process of comparing ourselves with others. Festinger proposed an elaborate theory of social comparison. Researchers have identified changes in social comparison that occur with development. Social comparison is pervasive in schools and can motivate achievement behavior.

Social cognitive processes also are influential in social situations. Social facilitation occurs when the presence of others motivates behavior. Social facilitation may depend on individuals possessing high self-efficacy and positive outcome expectations. Social loafing refers to a decrease in individual performance while working in a group compared to working alone. A key element may be the extent that individual performance can be evaluated; self-efficacy also is important.

Group motivation operates according to many of the same principles that apply to individual motivation: having goals and receiving feedback indicating goal progress, feeling efficacious about performing well, holding positive outcome expectations, and attributing success to such factors as ability, effort, and strategy use. In schools, cooperative learning is common in which two or more students work together to complete a task. Research shows that cooperative learning often is more effective for learning and motivation than when students work alone. It is important that an incentive structure be in place, that individual contributions be identified, and that groups be successful.

Conformity (modeling of group behaviors and standards) involves willful obedience where the individual and group members are roughly equal in stature (peers). Compliance denotes obedience resulting from another's commands where a difference in power or stature exists (superior and subordinate). Conformity and compliance are powerful processes that can result in dissatisfying and unethical actions. Conformity and compliance are needed in school, and it is important that teachers involve students in decisions so that students expect and value positive outcomes from willful obedience.

The Role of Goals and Goal Orientation

*F*our teachers are talking about their students. They all teach at different levels and are fascinated by the differences in their students. Karen is a kindergarten teacher, Bill is a fourth-grade teacher, Susan teaches science at the junior high, and Mal teaches tenth-grade English.

Karen: *All my children have a high need for physical activity so I have to build in time for active playing either outside or inside. They just can't sit still for 3 or 4 hours at a time. If you don't take their needs into account, you'll miss the boat.*

Bill: *Well, some of my boys are still like that, but I see many more individual differences. I think each child is unique. Some of my kids just have this real need to be the best. They are very competitive, and it is not just the boys. I have a couple of girls who always want to get the highest grades. Other kids want everyone to like them, they have a high need for approval. I have one girl who is always asking me to approve of her work before she does it and this same one worries about everyone liking her.*

Susan: *You guys have it easy. At least you don't have to deal with the raging hormones of my adolescents. These kids in junior high are off the wall because of their hormones. One day they are calm and normal, the next day they are all over the place, hyper, and teasing and fretting about the opposite sex. It drives me crazy. Sometimes I think junior high is just baby-sitting them until they calm down in high school and then you can go back to teaching them something.*

Mal: *Well, it's not any easier at the high school. Yeah, the kids are not totally off the wall like in junior high, but they all have different goals. Some of them are only concerned about finding a boyfriend or girlfriend, others are thinking about their part-time jobs and making some money to buy a car, others are only concerned about their grades and getting into college, others couldn't care less about school and just want to finish and go to work. It's not easy to motivate all these kids when they have such different goals.*

These comments all demonstrate that an approach to motivation that is concerned with personal needs or goals reflects an intuitive and lay-person account of motivation. However, there also have been a number of more formal motivational theories that have been based on the idea that people have different needs and goals and it is the search to satisfy these needs and goals that motivates behavior. In this chapter, we first review several needs-based models of motivation and then move on to more current goal theory models of motivation.

HISTORICAL PERSPECTIVE ON NEEDS AND GOALS

Goals are the current cognitive representations of a general "energy" construct that has a long-standing history in psychology, especially motivational psychology. The Latin root of the word *motive* means *to move*, and most motivational theories propose a construct such as instinct, drive, habit, needs, or goals that provide the "engine" to move organisms to act and also the direction in which to act, that is, to approach or to avoid certain objects in the environment. In the previous three chapters, we have been concerned with expectancies and attributions that do not really address the issue of what energizes behavior, even though those theories assume a general goal of mastery and understanding the environment.

Murray's Taxonomy of Needs

Although the construct of needs has fallen into disfavor given the current cognitive zeitgeist, needs served the same energizing and directional functions in earlier theories of motivation as goals do in current cognitive models. In earlier motivational theories, researchers spent a great deal of time trying to develop a taxonomy of instincts (McDougall, 1923) or needs (Murray, 1938). This taxonomic strategy is a general strategy used in biology (e.g., classification of plants and animals) as well as psychology (see Chapter 4 on classification of attributions and their dimensions and Weiner, 1986) to determine the nature of the basic elements under study, followed by research to examine the relations among the basic elements. Although McDougall's list of instincts is interesting, Murray's taxonomy of needs and his general theory show a great deal of overlap with some current models of goals, so we concentrate on his theory of needs.

Given the biological flavor of needs and instincts, it is interesting to note that Murray had a doctorate in biochemistry, not psychology. Nevertheless, during his doctoral studies in biochemistry in England he spent some time in Zurich with Carl Jung and became very interested in psychology and psychoanalysis. Upon his return to the United States, he spent a year at the Rockefeller Institute before he was recruited to Harvard to head the Psychological Clinic. The clinic was started with the purpose of studying abnormal psychology and psychoanalytic psychology, and Murray began a series of investigations to test empirically some of the ideas of psychoanalytic psychology, most often using case studies and intensive interviewing techniques. However, given his interest in a general theory of behavior, he concentrated on normal individuals in natural settings, unlike most clinical work in the psychoanalytic tradition (Hall & Lindzey, 1978). Given this background, it is not surprising to find that his theory has a biological flavor and that many of his needs have a decidedly psychoanalytic cast (e.g., his taxonomy of needs).

Murray believed needs have two aspects: a directional or qualitative aspect that specifies the objects that will satisfy the need and an energetic or quantitative aspect that influences the frequency, intensity, and duration of behavior. According to Murray (1938),

> a need is a construct (a convenient fiction or hypothetical construct) which stands for a force (the physico-chemical nature of which is unknown) in the brain region, a force which organizes perception, apperception, intellection, conation, and action in such a way as to transform in a certain direction an existing, unsatisfying situation. A need is sometimes provoked by internal processes of a certain kind . . . but, more frequently (when in a state of readiness) by the occurrence of one of a few commonly effective press (or by anticipatory images of such a press). Thus it manifests itself by leading the organism to search for or to avoid encountering or, when encountered, to attend and respond to certain kinds of press. (p. 124–124)

There are several important points to note about the theory given this definition. First, all needs are based in the physiological substrate of the brain, but are not just the viscerogenic needs for air, water, and food. More importantly, however, from a motivational point of view, needs provide the "force" for all behavior, including perception, thinking, regulation and will (*conation* in his terms), and action. Needs are assumed to operate on the classic homeostatic principle that unfulfilled needs generate tension (the unsatisfying situation noted in the quote) that leads to some approach or avoidance behavior to release the tension and satisfy the need.

Table 6.1 lists Murray's taxonomy of 20 needs that are assumed to drive all human behavior across the life span. In addition, in comparison to Hull and the other drive theorists, Murray assumed that these needs comprised stable personal characteristics that extend beyond the physical realm and involve psychological dispositions or traits. In a schooling context, the needs for achievement and understanding would be most relevant. Other researchers who developed models of motivation based on needs (e.g., Atkinson, 1964; McClelland, 1961; McClelland, Atkinson, Clark, & Lowell, 1953) focused on Murray's needs for achievement, affiliation, and dominance, although they renamed the dominance need as the need for power.

Table 6.1.   Murray's Taxonomy of 20 Needs, Listed in Alphabetical Order

1. *Abasement* (nAba)—to submit passively to external force, to admit inferiority, to seek pain, punishment, misfortune
2. *Achievement* (nAch)—to accomplish something difficult, to master, to excel, to rival and surpass others, to overcome obstacles and attain a high standard
3. *Affiliation* (nAff)—to draw near and enjoyably cooperate or reciprocate with an allied other, to adhere and remain loyal to a friend
4. *Aggression* (nAgg)—to overcome opposition forcefully, to fight, to revenge an injury, to attack, injure or kill another, to oppose forcefully
5. *Autonomy* (nAuto)—to get free, to resist coercion and restriction, to be independent and free to act, to avoid or quit activities prescribed by domineering authorities
6. *Counteraction* (nCnt)—to master or make up for a failure by restriving, to maintain self-respect and pride on a high level
7. *Defendance* (nDfd)—to defend the self against assault, criticism, and blame, to conceal or justify a misdeed, failure, or humiliation
8. *Deference* (nDef)—to admire and support a superior, to yield eagerly to the influence of an allied other, to emulate an exemplar, to conform to custom
9. *Dominance* (nDom)—to control one's human environment, to influence or direct the behaviors of others by suggestion, seduction, persuasion, or command
10. *Exhibition* (nExh)—to make an impression, to be seen and heard, to excite, amaze, fascinate, entertain, amuse, or entice others
11. *Harmavoidance* (nHarm)—to avoid pain, physical injury, illness, and death, to take precautionary measures, to escape from a dangerous situation
12. *Infavoidance* (nInf)—to avoid humilation, to quit embarrassing situations that may lead to belittlement from others, to refrain from action because of fear of failure
13. *Nurturance* (nNur)—to give sympathy and gratify the needs of a helpless object such as an infant or any object that is weak, disabled, tired, lonely, sick, dejected, to feed, help, support, console, protect, comfort others
14. *Order* (nOrd)—to put things in order, to achieve cleanliness, arrangement, organization, balance, neatness, tidiness, and precision
15. *Play* (nPlay)—to act for fun without further purpose, to seek enjoyable relaxation of stress, to like to laugh and make jokes, to participate in games and sports
16. Rejection (nRej)—to separate oneself from an object, to exclude, abandon, expel or remain indifferent to an inferior object
17. *Sentience* (nSen)—to seek and enjoy sensuous impressions
18. *Sex* (nSex)—to form and further an erotic relationship, to have sexual intercourse
19. *Succorance* (nSuc)—to have one's needs gratified by the sympathetic aid of an allied object, to be nursed, supported, protected, loved, advised, to always have a supporter
20. *Understanding* (nUnd)—to ask or answer general questions, to be interested in theory, to speculate, formulate, analyze, and generalize

From *Theories of Personality* (pp. 218–220) by C. S. Hall and G. Lindzey, 1978, New York: Wiley. Copyright © 1978 by John Wiley & Sons, Inc. Reprinted by permission of John Wiley & Sons, Inc.

As noted in the definition of needs, Murray's model proposed that needs can be evoked by internal processes in the individual, but are more likely to be linked to the environmental press of the situation. Murray was one of the first to stress the idea of environmental presses and that these features of the context can evoke and shape needs. In addition, he emphasized the importance of not mapping only the needs of an individual, but also the environmental presses in which the individual lives (Hall & Lindzey, 1978). This latter focus on the person-situation interaction is very uncharacteristic for his era, given the tendency for most psychological theories to focus either on the individual, as in psychodynamic models, or the environment, as in behavioral models. Moreover, Murray proposed that there were alpha and beta environmental presses. *Alpha presses* represented the "objective reality" of the environmental context as would be defined by others, including researchers, and *beta presses* represented the individual's own idiosyncratic perception and construction of the context. For example, a course might have a very strict grading curve that everyone could agree was operating (the alpha press). However, there still could be differential perceptions of this grading curve by different individuals (the beta presses), some students seeing this curve as something to strive to overcome and do well at (an activation of the need for achievement) and others seeing it as something to avoid and try to break out of (an activation of the need for autonomy). This distinction between actual and perceived contexts foreshadows current social cognitive and constructivist perspectives on motivation, such as goal theory (Ames, 1992b) and classroom learning and cognition (e.g., the student-mediating paradigm, Winne & Marx, 1982).

In keeping with the organismic tradition of focusing on the individual but also being sensitive to the importance of embedding the individual in the situation, Murray proposed that individual needs and environmental presses were always interacting and that a larger, more molar unit of analysis was required that linked needs and presses together in order to have a less fragmented view of behavior. He saw needs and presses integrated in a unit of analysis that he called a *thema*. This thema represented the individual's needs, the situational presses that evoked them, and the outcomes that resulted from the interaction of needs and presses (Hall & Lindzey, 1978). It is important to note that the thema construct is remarkably similar to current views of the person-in-situation construct of interactional psychology (Magnusson, 1990), behavior episode schemas in goal theory (M. Ford, 1992), and the person-operating-with-mediational-tools notions (Wertsch & Tulviste, 1992) from a Vygotskian perspective that all attempt to create a larger unit of analysis by embedding the individual in the context.

According to Murray, the psychologist's task was to describe and understand the themas that defined an individual's life. To accomplish this task, Murray developed the Thematic Apperception Test (TAT), which asked individuals to react to a series of ambiguous pictures by telling a story about what they thought was going on in each picture. These stories were then analyzed in terms of the needs expressed in the stories, the presses seen operating (beta presses in this case since it is the individual's perceptions), and themas that characterized the interactions of needs and presses. The TAT was probably the most used instrument to measure motivation up through the 1970s, although it was adapted and most often used to measure just three needs—for achievement, for affiliation, and for power (see Chapter 3)—as McClelland's and Atkinson's theories of motivation superseded Murray's theory.

Maslow's Hierarchy of Needs

Another theory that stressed needs that have since been reformulated as goals in current cognitive goal theories is Maslow's hierarchy of needs. Maslow's theory (Maslow, 1954) grew out of his interest in developing a "third force" in psychology that was not based in clinical studies of neuroses and psychopathology (psychodynamic psychology) or studies of infrahuman subjects (behavioral psychology), but rather focused on normal human growth and development. Although there were a number of aspects of his humanistic theory, the one that generated the most attention and is still relevant today is his hierarchy of needs (see Table 6.2). Maslow believed that the classification of individual motives and the attempts to develop comprehensive taxonomies of all the needs (as had Murray and McDougall) was of little theoretical value (Heckhausen, 1991). He developed a list of needs that classified all needs into five general groups, and, most importantly, asserted that there was a hierarchy of these five groups of needs in terms of their importance for human development. The higher, or growth, needs at the top of the hierarchy in Table 6.2, such as self-actualization, were most important for the development of personality. However, these higher needs could not be satisfied until the lower needs (or deficiency needs), such as the physiological needs and safety needs (see Table 6.2), were satisfied, or if two different needs were in conflict, the lower need would dominate. In addition, the hierarchy of needs paralleled develop-

Table 6.2. Maslow's Hierarchy of Needs

Higher needs (growth needs)	5.	Self-actualization needs—growth through the realization of one's potential and capacities; the need for comprehension and insight
	4.	Esteem needs—need to achieve, to gain approval and recognition
	3.	Needs for belongingness and love—need for love, affection, security, social acceptance; need for identity
	2.	Safety needs—need for security and protection from pain, fear, anxiety, and disorganization; need for sheltering, dependency, order, lawfulness, and rules of behavior
Lower needs (deficiency needs)	1.	Physiological needs—hunger, thirst, sexuality, and so on, as homeostatic and organismic needs

mental tasks in life-span development (Erikson, 1963) with the physiological needs most important for infants, safety needs for young children, followed by the belongingness and esteem needs in later childhood, and the need for self-actualization not becoming prepotent until adolescence and adulthood (Heck-hausen, 1991).

These needs function much the same way that Murray's needs operate to influence behavior. A need that is unsatisfied generates behavior that is designed to satisfy the need. The same general homeostatic tension-release model is followed, whereby a need creates the behavior to satisfy the need and once the need is satisfied, there is homeostasis and the behavior is no longer required. Of course, Maslow also noted that the environment played a role, although his model of needs was not as interactionist as Murray's needs-press-thema interaction model. For Maslow, the environment provided the opportunities for satisfaction of the needs and if the environment did not allow the needs to be satisfied, then growth and development would not occur in the most propaedeutic fashion. For example, a family environment that did not provide for the basic physiological and safety needs for a child would not foster the most positive development. Although Maslow's hierarchy of needs may not be explicitly cited, many of the school reform plans that now offer a full range of social and health services to school children including not just lunch, but breakfast, after-school care, health care, dental care, and the like, are implicitly based on this general idea that if children are hungry and in poor health, then it is unlikely they will be able to learn. Of course, the importance of dealing with problems of school violence that threaten not just children's safety, but also the faculty and staff of schools, would fit into Maslow's hierarchy as safety needs are the second level of needs. Without those being met, higher levels such as esteem and self-actualization needs cannot be satisfied.

Deficiencies of Murray's and Maslow's Needs Models

There are some serious conceptual problems with the construct of needs as it has been used in these models. First, it seems to be difficult to develop a manageable list of needs that provides both predictive power and parsimony. Murray's list seems rather long and unparsimonious, whereas McClelland's and Maslow's lists seem to be rather short to be used to explain all behavior. This same problem plagued research on "instincts," where instincts represent unlearned wants or urges that all people have (Weiner, 1992). Freud, of course, was one of the most important psychologists to propose that these urges (such as the son's desire to sleep with his mother) drove behavior. McDougall (1923) also proposed an elaborate theory of instincts that propelled all behavior. As the idea was elaborated, however, it became clear that there was no scientifically acceptable way to determine what an instinct was and how it was linked to behavior. Instinct theory was eventually discarded when the list of instincts became so large (one researcher put it at over 2,500) that researchers recognized the construct did not have much scientific utility.

Moreover, the logic of using constructs like needs and instincts to explain behavior eventually becomes tautological. The most common use of the construct as an explanatory mechanism is to observe a behavior and then infer that the person must have a need to do that behavior. For example, a child acts out in a classroom and ends up hitting the teacher. A simple explanation is that the child has an aggressive urge or need that is being expressed in this behavior. Another student is quiet, not too social, and seems to enjoy spending time alone, while yet another child is very social and talks to everyone and tries to make as many friends as possible. The former child would be said to have a need to be alone, whereas the latter student would be high in social or belongingness needs. At this point, almost any behavior can be referenced to a need as the cause of the behavior and, in turn, when someone has these needs, they cause the behavior. The logic is circular and does not provide any real explanation of the behavior. Given these serious problems with needs, especially the long lists like Murray's, the need construct is not used much in current research. However, there are more social cognitive theories that recast needs as goals that do represent an improvement on traditional needs models. We turn to those cognitive models now.

CURRENT SOCIAL COGNITIVE PERSPECTIVES ON GOALS

There are a number of goal theories that reflect a general social cognitive model of motivation, but we will focus on three general models. In this section, we will examine the goal-setting theory of Locke and Latham (1990) and the motivational systems theory of M. Ford (1992). In the next section of this chapter, we will present the various goal orientation theories that have been used most often in developmental and educational psychology (e.g., Ames, 1992b; Dweck & Leggett, 1988; Nicholls, 1984).

Goal-Setting Theory

Locke and Latham (1990) have proposed a goal-setting theory for task performance. Although they are organizational psychologists mainly concerned with the motivation and performance of individuals in work settings, their theory does have some important implications for education. As Brophy (1983) has noted, schools and classrooms do have some similarities to work settings and the application of motivational constructs from organizational psychology might provide some insights into student and teacher behavior and the nature of classroom organizations. Of course, the school-as-work metaphor is not without problems (see Marshall, 1988), but it does have some utility. Moreover, in current research on social cognition and self-regulated learning in classrooms, the role of goals, goal setting, and goal commitment has become very important; many of the researchers in self-regulated learning explicitly or implicitly use a goal construct in much the same way as Locke and Latham.

Locke and Latham's (1990) definition of goals represents a social cognitive perspective that defines a goal as something the individual is consciously trying to attain, but the thing being sought is outside the individual (p. 7). They make a distinction between goal-related constructs that are internal to the individual and conscious and goal-related constructs that are external to the individual or nonconscious. Table 6.3 displays a table from Locke and Latham (with some additions from us to provide educational examples) that places many of the various goal-related constructs such as needs, drives, motives, and goals in perspective. The main distinction represented in the columns is whether the construct stresses the internal (to the individual) conscious and psychological elements or focuses on the external, or nonconscious aspects.

There are three columns in Table 6.3 suggesting a continuum from internal to external, with the middle column representing the intersection and interaction of the internal and external elements. In the first row, the focus is on describing behavior or action. They would place theories such as Fishbein & Ajzen's (1975) model of intentions and behaviors in this row. *Intentions* are the individuals' own beliefs about what actions they plan to take in a specific situation. For example, the following are all examples of specific intentions: I

Table 6.3. Locke and Latham's Classification of Goal Concepts

Focus of construct	Internal/external and consciousness/nonconscious dimension		
	Internal and conscious	Intersection of internal and external	External and/or nonconscious
Focus on behavior or action	Intention	Norm	Actual task Academic work
Emphasis on the end or aim of action	Level of aspiration General life goals	Personal goal Aim Objective Personal standard	Teacher-assigned goal Task-defined goal Time deadline Quota/task requirements
Emphasis on underlying motivation	Motive Value Attitude Psychological needs Desire Wish		Drive Instinct Biological needs

From *A Theory of Goal Setting and Task Performance* by E. A. Locke and G. P. Latham, 1990, Englewood Cliffs, NJ: Prentice Hall. Copyright © 1990 by Prentice Hall. Reprinted by permission.

intend to mail this application to college today, I intend to take this course in math, I intend to study hard for this upcoming test. In this way, they would be similar to the intentions in Kuhl's (1984) and Heckhausen's (1991) model of motivation and volition.

Norms represent the intersection of the internal and external because the norms are defined by groups of people (external to the individual), but the individual must perceive and understand them and perhaps eventually internalize the norms. For example, Blumenfeld and colleagues (Blumenfeld, Hamilton, Bossert, Wessels, & Meece, 1983; Blumenfeld, Pintrich, & Hamilton, 1987) have discussed how students come to understand the academic conventional norms of classrooms regarding work (e.g., finish on time, do your own work) and the social conventional norms of classrooms (e.g., be quiet, do not talk when the teacher is talking). It appears that an important aspect of adapting to classroom life is for students to understand these norms and, if not internalize them, then at least abide by them behaviorally. Finally, in the last column in row 1 of Table 6.3, the actual task procedures the individual must perform are an external element that can shape the individual's behavior and action. This is certainly true in work settings, but many classroom researchers have also noted how the different features of classroom academic tasks can influence students' cognition, motivation, and actual behavior (see Blumenfeld, Mergendoller, & Swarthout, 1987; Blumenfeld et al., 1991; Doyle, 1983; Pintrich, Marx, & Boyle, 1993).

In the next row, Locke and Latham place constructs that focus on the goal or aim of the action, not the behavior. They classify level of aspiration as an internal and conscious construct that refers to the level of performance one is hoping to attain on a task, and this maps onto Lewin's level-of-aspiration construct discussed in Chapter 3. This level of aspiration is a more subjective, individualized goal that an individual wishes to strive for on a task (e.g., I want to toss the rings from this distance., I want to have the highest score in this class on the spelling test.). Locke and Latham then locate their own goal construct in the next cell in Table 6.3. Goals are placed at the intersection of the internal and external elements. Goals represent the individual's personal goal for a specific task, but also incorporate the goals that are assigned by others or that are inherent in the task. For example, a salesperson is assigned to sell 100 units of a product (the assigned goal), but that salesperson's personal goal is to sell 10% more than this company quota. In the same fashion, students are given tasks by the teacher that have assigned goals inherent in them (e.g., learn how to do quadratic equations), but students also may have personal goals for the task (e.g., to just complete the task, to do it faster than everyone else, to get more correct than anyone else) that can influence their behavior. Principals and teachers also can have goals assigned to them by school superintendents, such as increasing student achievement on standardized tests, but also can adopt personal versions of these goals (e.g., to increase the mean level of performance for the school building, to help the lower achieving students in the classroom do better).

It is important to note that in this framework, goals are very situation specific, not general life or career goals (cf. Schutz, 1991, 1994) or more general psychological goals such as mastery, superiority, or belongingness goals (cf. M. Ford, 1992; Maehr & Braskamp, 1986). For Locke and Latham, these goals are usually proximal goals, not distal or more global life goals (cf. Schunk, 1991b). Finally, as already suggested, the external elements in this row represent the external constraints that individuals operate under as they attempt a variety of tasks. So, quotas and time lines do influence the nature of the work people do and the types of personal goals they may adopt for tasks. In the same way, students operate under constraints of the specific tasks as well as more general classroom features such as time deadlines that can influence the goals they adopt and the type of learning that may result (see Pintrich, Marx, & Boyle, 1993).

In the last row in Table 6.3, Locke and Latham place the various motivational constructs such as internal and conscious constructs like values, motives, and attitudes as well as the various unconscious instincts or drives that can give rise to various goals. They are very explicit in their theory that personal goals may arise from an interaction between the assigned goals of a task and other "deeper" psychological constructs such as the need for achievement (a motive). For example, Locke and Latham note that the previously mentioned salesperson may want to increase sales by 10% to please his or her boss, to get promoted, to demonstrate successfulness to parents, to get a larger bonus, and so on. In the same way, students may have different motives for adopting their personal goals, including pleasing their teacher or parents, to get very good grades, to best the other students, or to master the material. Similarly, principals and teachers can have different motives for their personal goals that reflect parallel motives about pleasing authority figures, receiving rewards, and mastery. Nevertheless, Locke and Latham think that this deeper level of analysis is not as useful as their first level of analysis that focuses on the situated, immediate, conscious, personal goals of the individual. This reflects their very cognitive approach that eschews more psychodynamic or needs-based models of motivation. Accordingly, in their theory, they do not develop an analysis of this deeper level; they focus on describing how people develop their personal goals in different situations and how these cognitive goals then influence individuals' subsequent behavior. However, we will discuss some of these other deeper motives or rationales for behavior in a later section of this chapter on goal orientation and in Chapter 7 on intrinsic motivation.

The Formation of Goals

In Locke and Latham's theory, there are two important aspects of goals: goal choice and goal commitment. *Goal choice* refers to the actual goal individuals are trying to obtain and the level at which they are trying to attain it. Earlier, we gave an example of goal choice by noting how students can select a variety of levels of goals they want to pursue on classroom tasks, including getting all the questions right on an exam, getting enough correct to get a good grade, or getting enough correct to pass the test. The important issue for Locke and Latham is that each individual chooses a personal goal level, although there also may be an "assigned" or expected goal (i.e., most teachers expect that children should try to get all the answers correct on a test).

Goal commitment represents how strongly individuals are attached to the goal, how enthusiastic they are about the goal, or how determined to achieve the goal (Locke & Latham, 1990, p. 125). Although Locke and Latham note that there have been both theoretical and methodological problems distinguishing between goal commitment and goal acceptance, especially for externally assigned goals, they still propose that the general term—goal commitment—is a useful one to reflect the strength of an individual's endorsement of a goal. They note that goal commitment would usually be assessed by asking individuals to respond to the following types of questions or rating items: "How committed are you to attaining the goal?"; "To what degree did you adopt the goal?"; "It is hard to take this goal seriously." (reversed scored); "I don't care if I achieve this goal or not." (reversed scored); "I am strongly committed to trying to achieve this goal." (Locke & Latham, 1990, p. 126).

In addition, they note that goal commitment may be assessed through behavior and action because the simple selection of a goal is often not enough to spur action. There must be a volitional element to goal commitment (see Corno, 1993). As Locke and Latham (1990) state,

> *Believing* that a goal is desirable and reachable does not automatically force an individual to act. The individual must *choose* to put his or her judgment in action. Individuals who simply wait for their conscious and subconscious estimates of a situation to "turn them on," more often than not find themselves doing nothing or drifting without any sustained purpose. (p. 127)

They go on to give the example of having the goal of writing their book on goal-setting theory, and although they both thought the goal was desirable (goal level) and possible to achieve (self-efficacy), there was still a volitional choice they had to confront every day—to sit down and write—that reflected their commitment to the goal. This description certainly applies to us as authors, and we are sure that it rings true for anyone who has attempted to write a book, an article, a dissertation, a report, or even a class paper. In this sense, the willingness and commitment to enact a goal is very similar to the volitional phases in Heckhausen's (1991) and Corno's (1993) models where the individual "crosses the Rubicon" in terms of goal acceptance and then tries to obtain that goal through volitional strategies (see Chapter 5).

What factors are related to goal choice and goal commitment? Table 6.4 displays a partial list of the factors that Locke and Latham have identified as influencing the choice of a personal goal as well as an individual's commitment to that goal. The first category includes a number of personal factors. Most importantly, previous performance and actual ability/skill level will influence goal choice and commitment. Individuals are most likely to try to attain goals that they have had some success at previously (e.g., good students trying to attain high grades), whereas it is unlikely that people will try to attain goals that are very much beyond their actual skill level or previous performances (e.g., a slow runner setting a goal of under 9 seconds in a 100-meter run; a student with a long history of very poor grades setting a goal of earning all A's). In Locke and Latham's theory, self-efficacy is one of the most important positive influences on personal goal setting. People who have higher efficacy set higher goals for themselves. In addition, they note that even when previous performance or ability was partialled out, or controlled for, self-efficacy still had a direct influence on the level of the goal set. Moreover, self-efficacy also has a positive linear relation to goal commitment, with commitment being stronger when efficacy is high. Locke and Latham also note that causal attributions can play a role in goal setting; for example, attributing failure to unstable causes (bad luck, low effort) led to setting higher goals on subsequent tasks. This is exactly the pattern that would be expected under attribution theory (see Chapter 4).

Two other personal factors that can influence goal setting are valence and mood. In Locke and Latham's terms, *valence* often refers to the monetary incen-

Table 6.4. Factors Influencing Goal Choice and Goal Commitment in Locke and Latham's Model

Personal-individual factors

    Previous performance
    Actual ability/skill level
    Self-efficacy
    Causal attributions
    Valence/values
    Mood

Social-environmental factors

    Group factors
        Group norms, normative information
        Group goals
        Peer group

    Role modeling

    Reward structure
        Nature of rewards
        Competition

    Nature of authority and goal assignment
        Authority is legitimate
        Authority is knowledgeable

    Nature of feedback
        Conveys efficacy information
        Fosters sense of achievement and mastery
        Implies opportunities for self-development

tives an individual would receive upon accomplishing the goal, which would be an external factor. However, they also note that individuals' personal value beliefs about the importance of the goal, which may be based on interest, utility, or attainment value beliefs (see Eccles, 1983), can influence goals and goal commitment. According to Locke and Latham's model, goal choice and goal commitment are outcomes of the traditional expectancy (efficacy)-by-value components, so that goals are dependent on value and efficacy beliefs (cf. Wigfield & Eccles, 1992). In this case, values determine goals, whereas in the Eccles-Wigfield model, goals precede task value. Finally, *mood* can be related to goal choice, with positive moods leading to higher goals (Locke & Latham, 1990).

In terms of the external or more situational factors, Locke and Latham's model, because it has been developed and tested in organizational and work settings, places much more emphasis on the importance of external factors than do many other motivational models. In addition, Locke and Latham do not find detrimental effects for various external factors like competition as do other intrinsic motivation or mastery goal models (e.g., Ames, 1992b; Deci & Ryan, 1985; Maehr & Braskamp, 1986). This is partially due to Locke and Latham's focus on the very cognitive and situational construct of personal goals as well as their emphasis on actual job performance or behavior in contrast to more cognitive outcomes such as cognitive engagement and learning or more affective or motivational outcomes such as intrinsic motivation, goal orientation, personal investment, satisfaction, and attitudes. Nevertheless, it is interesting to note the differences in their perspective in comparison to those of other motivational researchers.

First, group norms and normative information seem to have a generally positive effect on goal setting; higher group norms lead to individuals setting higher personal goals for themselves (see Table 6.4). However, if individuals are assigned very high, almost unreachable goals by someone else and are also told that very few people reach these goals (normative information), then personal goals are likely to be lowered in this case (Locke & Latham, 1990). Second, group goals (a goal for the group or a two-person partnership) also can have a positive effect on personal goals, although it is important to have individual goals as well. Finally, the general peer group can exert pressure on members of the group that can result in the raising or lowering of goals, depending on the group support. For example, if the group does not support the assigned goal (the teacher-assigned or task-explicit goal), then individuals in the group will be less personally committed to the goal. This can happen in cooperative groups in classrooms when the small group undermines the teacher's goal for the task with the subsequent detrimental effect on the individuals in the group in terms of task engagement. In contrast, if the group does support the goal and exert pressure or encourage members of the group to work at the assigned goal, then personal commitment to the goal should be higher. This should be one of the positive effects of cooperative groups in classrooms where a small group of students can help a recalcitrant student become more engaged in the classroom task through encouragement and peer pressure.

Related to this peer-group support factor, Locke and Latham also review studies that show that positive role modeling of goal setting by others influences individuals to set higher goals for themselves. In the classroom, this would involve children watching or hearing other children set high but attainable goals for classroom work (e.g., I'm going to read the next two stories in this book and then write a report about them.) and then trying to set similar goals for themselves. This finding of positive role models for goal setting is parallel to the self-efficacy literature where positive role models (including both mastery and coping models) can have positive influences on other children's self-efficacy (Schunk & Hanson, 1985, see Chapter 5). Accordingly, it seems that positive role models can influence both goal setting and the efficacy to reach those goals.

Another external factor that can affect the goals that individuals adopt is the reward structure. Locke and Latham (1990) note that the actual rewards and incentives offered to individuals can influence goals, although the relation is complex. Some of the studies they review suggest that there is a positive relation between monetary incentives and bonuses and goals, whereas others find negative effects. Although they call for more research on this topic, they do suggest that there may be an interaction with goal difficulty. When assigned goals are very difficult or almost impossible, then the awarding of bonuses or incentives does not seem to increase performance. When goals are relatively easy to moderate, however, these extra incentives do seem to have a positive influence on performance. Besides the actual rewards, Locke and Latham also suggest that competition can have a positive influence on the level of goals set but not the commitment to the goals, with some competition resulting in the setting of higher goals in contrast to a no-competition treatment.

The two final factors in Table 6.4 regarding the influences on goal level and goal commitment concern the role of an authority and the type of feedback. Locke and Latham (1990) review research by organizational and industrial researchers that suggests there are a number of characteristics of an authority figure (e.g., a supervisor or manager in business, whose role is not unlike one of the roles of a teacher in a classroom) that can influence both goal level and goal commitment. In most of these studies, the authority figure is assigning goals to workers so the positive effects of these studies are somewhat counter to the research on self-set or participatively set goals. In fact, Locke and Latham suggest that participatively or self-set goals that allow for individual control do not necessarily have a positive effect over and above assigned goals. However, they do propose that the manner in which the goals are assigned by the authority figure is most important, rather than just whether they are assigned or self-set. They suggest that individuals will be more committed to the goals when the authority figure is seen as legitimate, supportive, physically present, trustworthy, knowledgeable, likable, providing a convincing rationale for the goal, and exerting reasonable pressure. In addition, the nature of the feedback is crucial. Most important are the provision of positive self-efficacy information and feedback that stresses challenge, mastery, self-improvement, and achievement. When presented in this manner, assigned goals and the accompanying feedback can have positive results and are not in direct conflict with intrinsic motivation theory (Deci & Ryan, 1985) or other writers on academic motivation (see Brophy, 1983). A recent meta-analysis of the role of rewards on intrinsic motivation also suggests a positive relation between informational feedback and motivation (Cameron & Pierce, 1994). For Locke and Latham, self-efficacy to reach the goal is a crucial mediator and if feedback (including rewards) provides positive efficacy information, then there should be a positive effect of using this type of feedback. This is basically the same argument that intrinsic motivation theorists make regarding the positive influence of informational feedback about competence and progress in contrast to the negative effect of controlling feedback (Cameron & Pierce, 1994; Deci & Ryan, 1985; Morgan, 1984).

In sum, goal level and goal commitment can be influenced by a number of personal and environmental factors. Many of these factors seem to work in a similar fashion to that predicted by self-efficacy theory (Bandura, 1986) or attribution theory (Weiner, 1986). However, Locke and Latham (1990) propose that several external factors, most notably competition, assigned goals, and the use of rewards, can have positive influences on goal level and goal commitment, which is quite contrary to goal orientation theory (Ames, 1992b; Maehr & Midgley, 1991) and intrinsic motivation theory (Deci & Ryan, 1985). There are several reasons for these different interpretations. First, Locke and Latham are discussing research based on experimental studies or field studies in work settings. Work settings place much more emphasis on worker productivity and actual performance output than do school settings that, although concerned with student productivity in terms of achievement, emphasize more cognitive outcomes like learning and cognitive engagement as well as affective outcomes like intrinsic motivation and attitudes.

In addition, Locke and Latham stress a very cognitive goal construct having to do with a specific task or performance, whereas school motivation researchers often are more concerned with more global constructs like overall academic achievement, goal orientation, self-determination, continuing motivation, and life-long learning. Given these differences, there are still some parallels in the findings and conclusions between the different literatures that suggest that teachers can have a positive influence on students' goals and their commitment to those goals through the proper use of their authority and appropriate management of the classroom environment to facilitate students' actual academic performance, their value for the class work, and their motivation (see Blumenfeld et al., 1983; Brophy, 1983; Brophy & Good, 1986).

The Influence of Goal Level and Commitment on Performance

Locke and Latham (1990) also review the organizational literature on how goal level and goal commitment influence actual performance. They propose that "goals are immediate, though not sole, regulators of human action" (p. 27) and, as such, should have a substantial and consistent relation to performance. There are several important relations between goal level and performance. First, Locke and Latham review a number of studies and meta-analyses (over 100 studies with over 7,000 cases) that show that the relation between goal difficulty and performance is basically a positive linear function with harder, more difficult goals leading to better performance. Of course, they note that the relation may level off at very high levels of goal difficulty that are beyond the individual's actual skill or ability level. However, within the normal range of the person's ability, more difficult goals usually result in better performance. This relation between goal level difficulty and performance is goal-setting theory's version of the ZPD from Vygotskian theory that suggests the same idea between tasks that push students to do their best within the range of their skill level. Locke and Latham explain the goal difficulty–performance function by suggesting that difficult but attainable goals lead to greater effort and persistence that, in turn, lead to better performance. In addition, they note that difficult goals make self-satisfaction contingent on a higher level of performance, so individuals are less likely to stop performing because they have become satisfied too quickly, as may be the case with easy goals.

The second core finding regarding goals and performance is that specific and difficult goals lead to higher levels of performance than vague and global goals such as doing one's best or no assigned goals (Locke & Latham, 1990). Locke and Latham note that in many cases when there are no assigned goals, individuals often interpret this as a do-your-best situation and operate under this assumption. Again, Locke and Latham base this conclusion on a review of studies from organizational settings and meta-analyses of this literature. They attribute this finding of more support for specific goals over do-your-best goals to the possibility that individuals operating with do-your-best goals can use a number of different standards to evaluate their performance and that this range of standards will result in some people being satisfied with rather low standards for performance. In contrast, those operating under specific but difficult goals have a rather high and single standard by which to evaluate their performance and should continue to try to reach that performance level.

The findings for goal commitment are not as strong or as straightforward as goal level, according to Locke and Latham (1990). They note that many of the studies of goal commitment have had difficulty generating variance in commitment in experimental studies. Nevertheless, they conclude that when there is some variance in goal commitment, performance is generally higher when individuals report being more committed to the goal than less committed or rejecting the goal. At the same time, Locke and Latham note that goal commitment and goal level might interact to influence performance. They suggest that when commitment is high, then the linear relation between goal level and performance should be maintained; that is, more difficult goals should lead to better performance when people are committed to the goals. In contrast, they suggest that when commitment is low, then performance will be low, regardless of the goal level difficulty. They point out the need for more research on this interaction between goal level and commitment, but they do conclude that goal commitment is an important component of motivated behavior and performance.

Locke and Latham (1990) also report that these general findings have been identified in a number of different studies that used a variety of different tasks with nearly 40 thousand individuals from a number of other countries besides the United States. Many of the studies have used very simple tasks such as listing nouns, doing arithmetic problems, or performing clerical tasks, but also have included more complex tasks such as reading, doing coursework, assembling objects, management or production simulations, or bargaining/negotiation tasks. They also report few differences in the goal-setting studies by age, race, gender, or educational level, although not many studies have examined these potential moderators. In general, Locke and Latham's theory does seem to have some generalizability, although it does need to be tested more directly in actual classroom situations. Nevertheless, the basic principles of goal setting and goal commitment and the factors that influence goals can be used by educators in their classrooms.

Implications for Teachers

Locke and Latham's (1990) theory has been used in many organizations to improve employee motivation and performance. There are four principles based on their theory that can be applied to the classroom setting:

1. Set clear and specific goals. Teachers should specify clear and unambiguous goals for all students in the class. Locke and Latham's work shows that having this type of goal is much more beneficial than setting no goals or encouraging individuals to do their best.

Ms. Shapiro asks her high school English students to read four books each semester. The students may choose their four books from a large reading list that Ms. Shapiro provides.

2. Goals should be challenging and difficult, but not outside the range of students' capabilities. This principle is the same as any number of goal theories (see the discussions on motivational systems theory and goal orientation theory that follow) as well as intrinsic motivation theory and Vygotskian theory. Basically, students should spend most of their time working on tasks that challenge them but are not so far beyond their skill level that the tasks frustrate them.

Mr. Washington, an elementary school teacher, pushes his students hard in math and, over the years, he has built up a very clear idea about what his fifth-graders can do. He presents them with many different kinds of problems to work on, but he does not give them any problems they can't master.

3. Set both proximal and distal goals for students. Locke and Latham report that the research is mixed on the relative effectiveness of proximal goals over distal goals. However, Bandura (1986) suggests that setting proximal goals can have positive effects on self-efficacy and performance. Teachers can help students set proximal goals by designing contracts with them that specify a series of subgoals that lead to larger distal goals.

Ms. Yu, a junior high science teacher, requires lab reports and science term papers. However, she divides large reports and projects into a series of subgoals, giving students a due date for an outline, a due date for research notes, a due date for the first draft, and so on, thereby helping her students set proximal goals.

4. Provide feedback that increases students' self-efficacy for obtaining the goal. This suggestion is obviously the same as would be suggested by efficacy theory (see Chapter 5 for specific examples). The most important aspect for Locke and Latham is that any rewards or verbal feedback that are given provide efficacy information to individuals that encourages them to continue working toward goal attainment. Locke and Latham do favor the use of extrinsic rewards in contrast to other motivational theorists, but this view can be reconciled with intrinsic motivation theory by noting that even intrinsic motivation theory allows for the positive effect of rewards when they are informational, not controlling. Accordingly, teachers should not be afraid to use extrinsic rewards, but should use them in a way that makes them contingent on actual academic performance, not as ways to control general behavior or as bribes to comply with the teacher (see Cameron & Pierce, 1994).

The Role of Goals in M. Ford's Motivational Systems Theory

M. Ford (see M. Ford, 1992; M. Ford & D. Ford, 1987; M. Ford & Nichols, 1991) has proposed his Motivational Systems Theory (MST) as a comprehensive model of motivation for human behavior. As M. Ford (1992) notes, MST is an integrative theory that attempts to organize the various motivational constructs from different theories into one model and is "generally compatible with existing theories of motivation and does not try to replace them" (p. 11). The model is based in the living systems framework of D. Ford (D. Ford, 1987; M. Ford & D. Ford, 1987), which represents an organismic-contextual model of human development (see Lerner, 1986). This framework focuses on the individual as the unit of analysis, but it embeds the individual in the biological, social, and environmental contexts that are crucial for development. Following a biological metaphor, it attempts to describe the development of the whole person-in-context, much the same way a biologist might describe an individual plant and its relation to its immediate ecological niche as well as the larger ecosystems in which it resides.

Following this metaphor, M. Ford proposes a simple mathematical formula that attempts to represent all these factors in one model. The formula for effective person-in-context functioning is:

$$\text{Achievement or competence } = \text{(Motivation} \times \text{Skill) / Biology} \times \text{Responsive environment}$$

This formula proposes that actual "achievement and competence are the result of a motivated, skillful, and biologically capable person interacting with a responsive environment" (M. Ford, 1992, p. 70). We will describe motivation in more detail later, but *skill* represents the various cognitive and information-processing functions as well as the actual behaviors necessary for competent action. *Biology* is defined in terms of the person's physical and biological capabilities that can enhance or constrain performance. *Responsive environment* includes the various contexts (home, school, community, etc.) that individuals move through that must provide positive opportunities for development.

As an example of how these components work together, consider that a highly motivated and skilled basketball player with excellent coaching (the responsive environment) will probably not be able to play professional basketball if he is only 5 feet tall (the biological component acts as a constraint). In the same way, another individual may actually have much better physical capabilities (height, speed, good eye-hand coordination) to play basketball well, but if not provided with a responsive environment in terms of good coaching and opportunities to play, he may not achieve his potential either. This scenario can also apply to academic learning because even when students are motivated, have the prerequisite skills, and no physical constraints are operating, if they are not provided with a responsive school environment, they will usually not achieve well.

The model attempts to provide a comprehensive theory of motivation and proposes that motivation is a "psychological, future-oriented (anticipatory) and evaluative (rather than instrumental) phenomenon" (M. Ford, 1992, p. 248). This means that motivation provides the energy and direction for behavior (the future-oriented function) as well as the evaluation of behavior in terms of whether to continue or stop (persistence), whereas other cognitive and behavioral components actually provide the means for action (the instrumental function that is represented by skill in the preceding formula). There are three main components of motivation such that:

$$\text{Motivation} = \text{Goals} \times \text{Emotions} \times \text{Personal agency beliefs}$$

This triarchic model of motivation assumes that goals, emotions, and personal agency beliefs interact to determine motivation, and the mathematical formula with multiplicative terms also implies that if any of these three components are missing, then individuals will not be motivated in that situation. That is, if they do not have a goal activated or have very negative inhibitory affect or have a very low belief in their personal capabilities, motivation will be very low and the behavior will likely be terminated for that situation (M. Ford, 1992).

In our summary of the theory, we will concentrate on the goals component. However, personal agency beliefs in M. Ford's model are basically the same construct as self-efficacy and control beliefs that were discussed in Chapter 4. Emotions are the various affects that are generated through interactions with the context and serve to energize behavior as well as provide evaluative information in order to regulate behavior. Affect is discussed more fully in Chapter 8.

Goal Content

In M. Ford's theory, there are two important aspects of goals: goal content and goal processes. *Goal content* refers to the desired or undesired consequences of a particular goal. Goal content would be assessed by asking people what they want, what they are trying to accomplish, and why they did something (M. Ford, 1992). M. Ford has classified the contents of goals into a taxonomy that has 24 general categories (see Table 6.5). This taxonomy was developed through both empirical and clinical work with students, clients, and profes-

Table 6.5. M. Ford and Nichols's Taxonomy of Human Goals

I. Desired Within-Person Consequences
   A. Affective goals
      1. *Entertainment*—experiencing excitement, arousal; avoiding boredom, stressful inactivity (cf. Murray's 15. nPlay in Table 6.1)
      2. *Tranquility*—feeling relaxed and at ease; avoiding stressful overarousal
      3. *Happiness*—experiencing joy, satisfaction; avoiding emotional distress
      4. *Bodily sensations*—experiencing pleasure associated with physical sensations, movement, or body contact; avoiding unpleasant bodily sensations (cf. Murray's 17. nSen and 18. nSex in Table 6.1)
      5. *Physical well-being*—feeling healthy, energetic; avoiding feelings of lethargy, weakness, or ill-health

   B. Cognitive goals
      6. *Exploration*—satisfying curiosity about personally meaningful events; avoiding a sense of being uninformed
      7. *Understanding*—gaining knowledge; avoiding misconceptions (cf. Murray's 20. nUnd in Table 6.1)
      8. *Intellectual creativity*—engaging in original thinking, using novel ideas; avoiding mindless or familiar way of thinking
      9. *Positive self-evaluations*—maintaining a sense of self-confidence, pride, or self-worth; avoiding feelings of failure, guilt, or incompetence (cf. Murray's 6. nCnt and 12. nInf in Table 6.1).

   C. Subjective organization goals
      10. *Unity*—experiencing a profound or spiritual sense of connectedness, harmony with people, nature, or a greater power; avoiding feelings of psychological disunity or disorganization
      11. *Transcendence*—experiencing optimal or ordinary states of functioning; avoiding feeling trapped within the boundaries of ordinary experience

sionals. These 24 goal categories are assumed to represent classes of goals at a fairly abstract level of analysis. Individuals may conceive of their own personal goals in a myriad of idiosyncratic ways, but at an abstract level, the idiographic goals of an individual should fit into the 24 categories. The taxonomy of goals has a great deal of overlap with Murray's taxonomy of needs (see Table 6.1 and notes in Table 6.5 that attempt to match Murray's needs and M. Ford's goals), but Ford suggests that his taxonomy is not as tautological as Murray's because he attempts to distinguish between goals and the behavior patterns that might be generated by the goals. In addition, Ford's taxonomy has a more social cognitive emphasis than the psychodynamic flavor of Murray's taxonomy. Finally, Ford suggests that his taxonomy and the goals listed in it are more specific and less global than Murray's taxonomy, yet also represent

---

II. Desired Person-Environment Consequences
  A. Self-assertive social relationship goals
    12. *Individuality*—feeling unique, special, or different; avoiding similarity or conformity with others
    13. *Self-determination*—experiencing freedom to make choices; avoiding feelings of being pressured, constrained, or coerced (cf. Murray's 5. nAuto in Table 6.1)
    14. *Superiority*—comparing favorably to others in terms of winning, status, or success; avoiding unfavorable comparisons
    15. *Resource acquisition*—obtaining approval, support, advice, or validation from others; avoiding social disapproval and rejection (cf. Murray's 19. nSuc in Table 6.1)
  B. Integrative social relationship goals
    16. *Belongingness*—building and maintaining attachments, friendships, intimacy, or a sense of community; avoiding feelings of social isolation (cf. Murray's 3. nAff in Table 6.1)
    17. *Social responsibility*—keeping interpersonal commitments, meeting social role obligations, conforming to social and moral rules; avoiding social transgressions and unethical and illegal conduct (cf. Murray's 8. nDef in Table 6.1)
    18. *Equity*—promoting fairness, justice, or equality; avoiding unjust or unfair actions
    19. *Resource provision*—giving approval, support, advice, or validation to others; avoiding selfish or uncaring behavior (cf. Murray's 13. nNur in Table 6.1)
  C. Task goals
    20. *Mastery*—meeting a challenging standard of achievement or improvement; avoiding incompetence, mediocrity, or decrements in performance (cf. Murray's 2. nAch in Table 6.1)
    21. *Task creativity*—engaging in activities involving artistic or creative expression; avoiding tasks that do not provide opportunities for creative action
    22. *Management*—maintaining order, organization, or productivity in daily life tasks; avoiding sloppiness, inefficiency, or disorganization (cf. Murray's 14. nOrd in Table 6.1)
    23. *Material gain*—increasing amount of money or tangible goods one has; avoiding loss of money or material possessions
    24. *Safety*—being unharmed, physically secure, safe from risk; avoiding threatening, depriving, or harmful circumstances (cf. Murray's 11. nHarm in Table 6.1)

---

a more comprehensive list of goals than Maslow's 5 needs (see Table 6.2) or McClelland's 3 needs (need for achievement, power, and affiliation).

There are several other aspects to note about the taxonomy. First, M. Ford does not propose that there is a hierarchy to the goals in the taxonomy, unlike Maslow. Ford does not assume that any of the 24 goals are more important or more fundamental than any of the other goals. He notes that some goals may end up being more important or more compelling than others (e.g., happiness, physical well-being, belongingness), but that this is an empirical question, not a theoretical assumption of the model (M. Ford, 1992). Second, Ford assumes that behavior is usually guided by multiple goals simultaneously, so that the activation of one goal does not preclude the activation of other goals. Finally, the 24 goals may combine into larger units or "themes" (cf. Murray's themas) that represent the merging of several goal categories. For example, Ford suggests that friendship goals may reflect belonging, resource acquisition, and resource provision concerns and that need for achievement may represent both mastery and superiority goals (M. Ford, 1992). Refer to Table 6.5 as you read the following text discussion. Specific goals as listed in the table are referenced by number in parentheses.

The taxonomy (see Table 6.5) has two main categories: goals that are intrapersonal and reflect desired within-person consequences and goals that represent desired outcomes of a person's interactions with the environment. In terms of the intrapersonal goals, there are three main categories: affective, cognitive, and subjective organization. *Affective goals* are feelings and emotions that individuals want to experience or avoid. For example, entertainment goals (1) reflect our desire to be aroused and stimulated and to avoid repetitive, boring activities, whereas tranquility goals (2) represent our need to avoid very stressful stimulation. The equilibrium between these two goals of entertainment and tranquility would be similar to Berlyne's (1960) notion of optimal arousal (M. Ford, 1992). In terms of the classroom, this would suggest that students would like to have activities that are interesting and spark their curiosity, but not so different or difficult as to be overly stressful. Happiness (3) is usually high in most individuals' goal hierarchies and also can play a regulatory function as an indicator of progress toward other goals (most people are satisfied when they reach a personal goal). The final two affective goals (4 and 5) have to do with physical sensations in terms of specific or transitory physical states (I wish I could take a nice, hot shower now—a bodily sensation goal) and with longer term physical goals (I want to be in good shape aerobically so I can have more energy and live longer—a physical well-being goal) (M. Ford, 1992).

The *cognitive goals* include four kinds of goals (see Table 6.5) with the first three representing three different levels of cognitive engagement. The first level is exploration (6) and reflects a person's desire to "change the unknown into the known by acquiring new information" (M. Ford, 1992, p. 90) through attention to relevant information in the environment (e.g., what's going on in the news today). In the classroom context, students operating with this goal would seek out new information in books, worksheets, lectures, and labs and attempt to remember it for later use. In contrast, an understanding goal (7) represents a desire for a deeper level of comprehension that goes beyond just the discovery and observation processes that might accompany an exploration goal to the use of reasoning, thinking, interpretation, and analysis processes to help the individual create a meaningful understanding (e.g., wondering why people think a certain way). This type of goal is the goal most often proposed as important for conceptual change learning and constructivist classroom teaching (Pintrich, Marx, & Boyle, 1993). Most teachers want students to go beyond just an exploration goal and to attempt to gain a deep understanding of the content area. M. Ford (1992) also notes that this understanding goal is often attractive to scholars, philosophers, highly educated people, and people who prefer reading to watching television. Finally, the third level, intellectual creativity (8), reflects a desire to engage in mental activities or create mental products that are evaluated in terms of their novelty, cleverness, or elegance, in contrast to the understanding goals that are usually evaluated in terms of truth, accuracy, validity, or persuasiveness. Intellectually creative goals would be pursued by creative writers, humorists, or musicians in contrast to the task creativity goals (see goal 21 in Table 6.5), which would be pursued by artists and architects as well as young children (M. Ford, 1992). Teachers would want to encourage all three of these goals, but certainly the first two would seem to be essential for learning. In fact, Pintrich, Marx, and Boyle (1993) suggest that students are often not pursuing understanding goals in the classroom and this hinders conceptual change learning and instruction. The final cognitive goal is the protection of self-worth or the self in general (9). This is the same goal proposed by many other motivational theorists and includes the motive to protect self-worth or self-esteem (see Covington, 1992; Harter, 1990).

Subjective organization goals represent a complex mix of both affective and cognitive states. Unity goals (10) refer to feelings of being connected to a larger power or force in nature (e.g., God), not just a feeling of belongingness to a group or community (which is goal 16) and avoiding a sense of psychological disunity (I'm too fragmented, I've got to get myself together.). Transcendence goals (11) involve feelings of optimal functioning that is quite out of the ordinary. This would be similar to a high level of self-actualization in Maslow's theory or the "flow" state in Csikszentmihalyi's (Csikszentmihalyi & Rathunde, 1993) theory of optimal experience (see Chapter 7). In more colloquial sports terms, it is often referred to as "being in the zone" where distractions are gone, time seems to slow down, and the individual is able to focus completely and very competently on the task at hand. It is important to keep in mind that in M. Ford's theory, this feeling of flow is a transcendent goal that a person strives to attain; it is not the actual behaviors that might lead to this feeling. This is true for all the goals in Ford's theory. They represent something the person is trying to attain, not the actual behaviors, although descriptions of them may describe the behaviors used to attain the goals as well.

The second large set of goals is the *desired person-environment consequences*. The first eight goals in this set (12–19) include *self-assertive goals*

(12–15) where the individual is most prominent and *integrative goals* (16–19) where the group or others are more prominent. Each of the self-assertive goals are paired with an integrative goal to reflect the general tension between individuality and the group. Goal 12, individuality, reflects the person's desire to be unique and different from others, whereas goal 16, belongingness, represents a need to be part of a larger group or community. During adolescence these two goal are often both quite high in students' goal hierarchies as they struggle with their own identity as well as with becoming accepted into a peer group. The next two goals, self-determination (13) and social responsibility (17), reflect our desires to experience freedom in making choices, which parallels the need for self-determination in intrinsic motivation theory (Deci & Ryan, 1985). These goals also reflect our need to conform to certain rules and social obligations in general and in the classroom (cf. Blumenfeld et al., 1983; Blumenfeld, Pintrich, & Hamilton, 1987).

Superiority goals (14) represent individuals' needs to best others, to win, to achieve success at a level better than others (positive social comparison) as well as avoid negative social comparisons with others. This would be similar to a general ego orientation in Nicholl's (1984) goal theory, a performance orientation in Dweck's model (Dweck & Leggett, 1988), and an ability focus in Ames's (1992b) goal model. The countervailing goal in M. Ford's model would be an equity goal (18) where the emphasis is on justice, equality, and fairness. The last two goals, resource acquisition (15) and resource provision (19), represent our need to acquire help and support from others (recall the supportive environment aspect of the theory) as well as to provide help and mentoring to others and should be reciprocally related. Teachers should be high in resource provision goals in order to support their students' optimal development.

The final category of goals outlined in Table 6.5 is *task goals*, which refer to how we choose to relate to different types of tasks we confront in our lives. Mastery goals (20) reflect a desire to meet challenging standards or to show personal improvement. This goal is identical to the mastery goals of Dweck, the task goals of Ames, and the task-involved goals of Nicholls. Task creativity goals (21) represent a goal to engage in activities where creative expression can be evoked and to avoid tasks that do not allow for creativity. M. Ford notes that mastery and task creativity goals are in the same relation to each other as understanding and intellectual creativity goals discussed earlier. Mastery goals are usually evaluated in terms of more objective standards of excellence and/or personal improvement, whereas task creativity goals are more likely to be evaluated in subjective terms. Management goals (22) reflect people's desire to maintain order and organization in their daily life and tasks. Material gain (23) is a goal of accumulating wealth or material goods and avoiding the loss of these goods. Finally, safety goals (24) are the same as Maslow's safety goals and represent our need to be secure from harm and deprivation.

These 24 goals represent the broad, general categories of goals, but individuals will always have personalized representations of these goals depending on both the individual and the contexts the individual encounters over time.

Accordingly, M. Ford points out that it is important to assess the nature of goals within an individual using idiographic methods that allow for comparison between the different types of goals that might be pursued, but the comparisons are made within the individual. For example, within this individual, does he rate belongingness or individuality goals as more important, not comparing his ratings of these two goals with other people (see M. Ford & Nichols, 1991)? The model also allows for people to pursue multiple goals simultaneously. In fact, this model is one of the few current goal theories that highlights the idea that people can and do pursue multiple goals within any one situation. Most goal theories stress the importance of pursuing intrinsic or mastery goals instead of extrinsic or performance goals (see Chapter 7 and the next section in this chapter on goal orientation).

Given this notion of multiple goals, M. Ford proposes that there are *goal hierarchies* that help the individual set priorities and coordinate the multiple goals that might be evoked in any situation. Ford proposes that within any one situation, there might be a larger overall goal (e.g., to obtain an A in the course, a mastery goal in Ford's theory) as well as many subgoals or proximal goals (to get an A on the midterm, final exam, term paper, etc.) (see Chapter 5) that help the individual evaluate her progress and maintain her overall direction to the larger target goal. In addition, Ford notes that there may be goal conflict and goal alignment within these hierarchies. For example, the student who wants to obtain an A in the course and has subgoals of getting A's on the various tests and papers in the course has these goals in alignment and her motivation should be fairly high. However, another student might have goals that conflict with one another, such as wanting to get an A (a mastery goal) and also wanting to be with friends (a belongingness goal). To the extent that the behaviors and subgoals that serve the overall goal of wanting to be with friends (e.g., talking with them during class; getting together with them to study for the course, but spending most of the time talking about other things) conflicts with the goal of getting an A, then the student's motivation will be diverted into these multiple goals and performance will suffer. Wentzel (1989, 1991a) has shown that high school students with low GPAs (D+ or lower) report having fun and making friends as more important goals for them than mastery/learning goals in comparison to high achievers. Although these ideas of multiple goals, hierarchies for multiple goals, and the coordination and alignment of multiple goals are very important, there is little research on these processes in the classroom context. Wentzel and others have shown the existence of multiple goals and their relation to achievement, but it is not clear how individuals actually construct hierarchies or align their goals. Much more research is needed on these important processes.

Goal Processes

The 24 categories of goals just discussed represent the content of the goals individuals are trying to achieve in different situations. Besides the content of a goal, M. Ford (1992) also proposes that there are different methods or styles that individuals use to conceptualize a goal. Within any one situation, what he calls a behavior episode, there are various *goal-setting strategies* that individuals might use to actually represent the content of the 24 goals. These goal-setting strategies in Ford's model are basically the same as those discussed in the research of Locke and Latham presented earlier. These strategies include setting very specific goals that can help guide and regulate cognition and action better than a vague or do-your-best goal (see Locke & Latham, 1990). Ford also notes that the strategy of setting a difficult but attainable goal has positive consequences (cf. Csikszentmihalyi, 1975; Deci & Ryan, 1985; Locke & Latham, 1990). Finally, M. Ford (1992) notes that a goal-setting strategy that aligns a mastery goal (performance on a specific task) with other goals such as material gain, social responsibility, or resource acquisition can facilitate performance. For example, a student who has a mastery goal for a math exam but also has other nonconflicting goals for that task, such as obtaining a reward from parents, might do better on the exam. The basic notion is that if multiple goals are aligned and do not conflict with one another, they can have a synergistic effect on behavior.

Besides the goal-setting processes that work within a specific behavior episode, M. Ford (1992) also proposes that there are goal orientations that are more general, personality-like styles that cut across different situations and behavior episodes. There are a number of different types of goal orientations in his model. For example, M. Ford and Nichols (1991) have shown that there are three general dimensions along which individuals might differ in terms of their orientation to goals.

The first dimension is an *active-reactive style* where an active orientation refers to an individual being more involved in initiating, directing, and planning behavior, in contrast to a reactive style where behavior is more a function of the situational features of the context. The active style tends to be associated with more personal meaning and coherence because individuals are directing their behavior and are not as subject to the whims of situational constraints and influences. In the classroom, students with an active style would show more self-initiative and self-directed learning, whereas those with a more reactive style would be more passive and wait for the teacher to tell them what to do.

The *approach-avoidance style* describes individuals who tend to conceptualize goal content (see Table 6.5) in terms of approaching desired consequences (e.g. for the mastery goal in Table 6.5, seeking and meeting a challenge) instead of avoiding undesired consequences (e.g., for the mastery goal, avoiding incompetence). This is not unlike the difference in McClelland's (1961) theory between those individuals who have a motive for success in contrast to those who have a motive to avoid failure (M. Ford, 1992). More recently, Covington and Roberts (1994) have suggested that this approach-avoidance orientation can be crossed with success-failure to form a matrix of four types of orientations to achievement. Obviously, students with an approach style would seek out new tasks, be more likely to take risks, and not be afraid of failure, in contrast to the avoidance style students who would be anxious about trying new tasks and always seek to avoid failure.

The final style of M. Ford and Nichols (1991) is *maintenance-change,* which refers to people actively seeking to maintain their general goals and behavior in contrast to those individuals who are continually seeking to change and improve their goal levels and themselves. Students with a maintenance style would be self-satisfied with their level of performance, whereas change-orientated individuals would be interested in learning new things and increasing their level of achievement.

M. Ford (1992) notes that other researchers have discussed three other types of goal orientation styles. First, Winell (1987) and many clinical psychologists have distinguished a coping-thriving orientation. Ford sees this pattern as being a more global orientation that combines his (M. Ford & Nichols, 1991) three dimensions into one pattern. Individuals with a general coping orientation would be reactive, avoidant, and focused on maintenance. In contrast, those with a thriving orientation would be active, focused on approaching goals, and seeking positive change. A second general orientation is the action versus state orientation of Kuhl (1985, 1992). Kuhl has investigated this general style in a number of studies in academic, organizational, and clinical settings. Generally, a state orientation is a way of thinking about goals that interferes with action, such as ruminating about potential negative events, procrastinating before starting the task, difficulty in concentrating on the task while doing it, and having a more passive, reactive style. In contrast, an action orientation describes individuals who work in a directive, active, and self-regulatory fashion toward their goals. The final type of goal orientation that Ford mentions is the general mastery-task-learning orientation as opposed to the ego-performance-ability orientations (see Ames, 1992b; Dweck & Leggett, 1988; Nicholls, 1984). Given that this construct has been the focus of a great deal of research in educational settings, we will discuss it in detail in the next section of this chapter.

In sum, M. Ford's theory of motivation represents a comprehensive organismic-contextual model of motivation. It includes three general components of motivation that interact to result in overall motivation. Goals are one of the three components that we have focused on here; personal agency beliefs and emotions are similar to constructs we have covered or will discuss in other chapters. The theory has been applied in educational, work, and clinical settings and does have implications for teachers.

Implications for Teachers

M. Ford (1992) has proposed a series of principles for motivating people based on his theory. There are 17 general principles that apply to all situations, including motivating students in classrooms, but his theory also can be used to motivate individuals in work settings, to promote social responsibility and caring, and to lead a generally healthy and emotionally satisfying life. One general assumption underlies all these principles. The assumption is that facilitation, not control, should be the guiding idea in attempts to motivate people. Facilitation should focus on the individuals' goals, personal agency, and emotions and not on direct control of individuals' behavior. Accordingly, highly controlling strategies such as threats, strong punishments, controlling (not informational) rewards, and forced competition can have immediate short-term positive effects (they increase wanted behavior, decrease unwanted behavior), but in the long run, when used repeatedly or continuously, these types of direct control strategies can have negative consequences. They can adversely affect people's goals, agency beliefs, and emotions that, in turn, will mediate future behavior. M. Ford (1992) suggests that motivational strategies that can facilitate the attainment of individuals' goals, increase their agency beliefs, and engender positive emotions will have more positive long-term and more durable effects.

1. The Principle of Unitary Functioning This principle, in keeping with the organismic perspective of the theory, states that the unit of analysis is always the *whole person* and that motivational interventions will always need to take into account what the individual brings to the situation in terms of prior personal and developmental history and also that the situation and the person will interact in complex ways to influence behavior patterns. Given this principle, M. Ford (1992) notes that it is important to keep in mind that each individual is unique and that all motivational interventions will not work in similar ways with all individuals. This implication is the same basic idea behind aptitude-treatment interaction (ATI) research (see Corno & Snow, 1986). Ford also notes that another implication of this unitary functioning principle is that changes in one motivational parameter can produce changes in other parts of the person-in-context system. For example, using cooperative groups may help to motivate children because it allows them to meet their belongingness goal, but it also can result in some poor instructional practices, as may be the case where students who know very little about a topic or have misconceptions attempt to teach their misconceptions to others. This type of outcome (increased motivation, but perhaps sharing of misinformation) is an example of Ford's third implication of this principle that sometimes motivational changes can have unanticipated consequences.

2. The Motivational Triumvirate Principle This principle refers to the idea that behavior is influenced by all three motivational constructs—goals, personal agency beliefs, and emotions—as they interact with each other. Accordingly, interventions to improve individuals' motivation must consider all three of these constructs at the same time instead of just focusing on one of the three. For example, a teacher who wants to encourage more females to continue in math should not concentrate only on improving their efficacy beliefs (which are often lower than males even though they get higher grades; see Eccles, 1983), but also try to get them to adopt goals that encourage them to continue in math as well as increase their positive affect toward math (see Eccles, 1983; Miura, 1987).

3. The Responsive Environment Principle This principle concerns the nature of the environment that is created by a teacher, an environment that should be responsive to the individual. M. Ford (1992) suggests that there are four dimensions that can be used to judge the responsiveness of the environment. First, he believes that there should be an alignment between the individual students' personal goals and the general goals that are part of the classroom environment. For example, if a student has mainly task creativity goals and a teacher has mainly management goals (see Table 6.5), then there is not much alignment and that student's motivation will probably suffer. However, aligning goals for all students in a class of 20 to 30 children may be very difficult for a teacher. There would have to be some type of assessment of the students' goals and, given the diversity that would probably emerge, then there would probably have to be a great deal of individualized instruction, which is not always the easiest type of instruction to implement with the fairly large class sizes and one-teacher arrangement commonly found in schools.

The other dimensions are probably somewhat more easily attained in classrooms. The second is the idea that the environment must be responsive to the students' biological, transactional, and cognitive capabilities; that is, the physical space, the curriculum, and the nature of instruction should take into account the students' capabilities. For example, the nature of instruction to teach first graders early reading skills should take into account their developmental cognitive level and will most likely be different from instruction for high school students in a social studies class, given their cognitive capabilities. The third dimension is that the objectives for the tasks to be accomplished are realistic and appropriate given both the materials and resources available. Essentially, the second and third dimensions parallel the general principle of the ZPD from Vygotskian theory where the environment is challenging but supportive by providing activities still within the range of the individual's competence. The final dimension of a supportive environment is that the emotional climate of the classroom be supportive and foster a feeling of trust between the students and teacher.

4. The Principle of Goal Activation This principle is basic to any goal theory (cf. Locke & Latham, 1990; Maehr & Braskamp, 1986) and it refers to the necessity of activating a relevant goal for the completion of a task. In terms of implications, it means that the task to be accomplished must provide opportunities for attainment of personally relevant goals. For example, students who are high in belongingness goals will benefit from cooperative learning groups because the activity allows them to work with other students and may help them attain their goal of building friendships. A classroom that has a variety of tasks and activities and allows students different procedures for accomplishing them will increase the probability that personally relevant goals will be activated by this diversity as opposed to a classroom that does not allow for much diversity in tasks or procedures.

5. *The Principle of Goal Salience* Beyond simply activating relevant goals, teachers should try to ensure that the goals that are activated are clear, compelling, and presented in such a way that students understand what they need to do to accomplish them. Strategies for accomplishing this goal include setting very specific "targets" for performance (see Harackiewicz & Sansone, 1991; Locke & Latham, 1990) and setting proximal subgoals that help students monitor their progress (Bandura & Schunk, 1981). As noted in the previous section, teachers use these strategies when they help students break up a large task like a major paper or report into subparts (outline, research notes, first draft, final draft, etc.) that have specific due dates. Dividing the larger task into smaller subparts makes the task seem more manageable for the students and the specific due dates help both the teacher to monitor progress and the students to self-regulate their behavior toward completion of the task.

6. *The Multiple Goals Principle* This principle invokes the idea that behavior can be related to multiple goals and, in fact, students who are most successful in classroom settings (at least in terms of a high GPA) are more likely to pursue multiple goals (Wentzel, 1989, 1991a, 1991b). Accordingly, teachers should try to activate multiple goals for students. For example, they can provide a number of rationales for why doing a particular task is important (mastery of the task, to obtain rewards, to avoid punishment) (cf. Brophy, 1983) in the hope that these rationales will activate multiple goals within any one student as well as increase the possibility that one of these goals will be activated in all students.

7. *The Principle of Goal Alignment* This principle complements the principle of multiple goals and concerns the importance of having goals that are aligned, not conflicting with each other. It may be good to have multiple goals, but they also need to be coordinated so that by trying to achieve one goal, other goals are not short-circuited. For example, a proximal goal of completing a section of a report or paper by a certain date (a management goal) may conflict with the more distal goal of intellectual creativity in terms of expressing one's ideas in new or different ways. Teachers also may want to encourage or facilitate intellectual or task creativity goals, but they have management goals as well in terms of classroom order. If the management goal is implemented in too strict or rigid a fashion, that can inhibit the attainment of the creativity goals.

8. *The Feedback Principle* This principle, basic to all motivational and most general psychological theories, purports that relevant feedback is crucial for continued progress toward a goal. Feedback provides information that can be used to judge progress, repair mistakes, and redirect efforts. It also can influence personal agency beliefs and emotions in positive ways that can facilitate motivation. There are a number of guidelines for effective feedback for teach-

ers, including those put forth by Brophy (1981). Chapters 5 and 9 also offer some suggestions.

9. The Flexible Standards Principle This principle refers to the idea that individuals should have flexible and adaptive standards when evaluating their work or progress. For example, a college student who does poorly on a midterm, thereby eliminating the possibility of attaining an overall A for the course (the original standard), should not become completely discouraged, anxious, and self-doubting, which can lead to withdrawal of effort. The student should instead adjust his standard from getting an A in the course to something more attainable or make his new standard simply an improvement in grade from the midterm. This flexibility and adaptability will help to maintain his motivation because his personal agency beliefs about being able to attain the new standard will be higher and his affect will be less depressed. In addition, Ford notes that it is important to remember that this flexible standard principle does *not* mean that standards should be vague or "loose." Rather, the standards should be flexible enough to change given the context, but the new standard should be just as clear, attainable, and challenging as any goal (cf. Locke and Latham, 1990).

10. The Optimal Challenge Principle This principle also is well-represented in most motivation theories (see Bandura, 1986; Berlyne, 1960; Csikszentmihalyi, 1975; Deci & Ryan, 1985; White, 1959) and concerns the importance of providing tasks that are difficult and challenging, but not beyond the individual's range of competence (cf. the ZPD from Vygotsky). Implementation of this principle is often difficult in classrooms because of the heterogeneity in levels of competence, even when children are in age-graded classrooms. Of course, one avenue around this problem is to individualize the curriculum for groups of children who share the same levels of competence. This can be very time-consuming and fraught with problems both ethical (e.g., within-classroom grouping or tracking) and practical (how to assess the levels of competence). Nevertheless, this principle is a general goal for teachers to strive for as they think about the general level of tasks that they will present to all students in their classrooms.

11. The Principle of Direct Evidence This principle is one of the most interesting and important for teachers to consider, given the current interest in school programs to increase general self-esteem. Basically, the principle suggests that interventions should be focused directly on a specific problem of personal agency rather than vague and very general platitudes about building self-esteem, creating trust, or boosting confidence. M. Ford (1992) suggests that many of these self-esteem programs are too broad and general to have a direct impact on specific problems students may have (e.g., inability to read, difficulty in math, lack of cognitive and regulatory strategies). He suggests that efforts should be targeted at the specific problems and opportunities should be provided for the students to experience success at real academic tasks, rather than just chanting a mantra like, "I'm a good person," without learning the actual academic skills required in schools. The actual success that comes from learning a specific skill and being able to overcome a problem will provide the direct evidence that the student has learned the appropriate skills and will do much more to increase personal agency than empty platitudes. Bandura (1986) has shown that this type of guided instruction can be very helpful in the treatment of a number of psychological problems from phobias to depression. Schunk (1991b) has shown that this type of direct and targeted intervention can be very successful in academic settings.

12. The Reality Principle This principle follows directly from this last point. M. Ford (1992) suggests that in many cases, a motivational intervention that is targeted at personal agency, goals, or emotions may not be sufficient to change behavior. In these instances, it may be more realistic to actually try to change the problem behavior directly rather than try to change the motivation for the behavior. For example, for children with low efficacy for academic skills, rather than encouraging them to change their efficacy perceptions, teachers should teach them the skills they need, and efficacy perceptions will change as a function of this increase in skilled behavior. These two principles (11 and 12) stress the need to consider both motivational and cognitive/behavioral components of school learning in any intervention designed to help students academically (cf. Pintrich, 1989, 1991, 1994; Pintrich & Garcia, 1991).

13. The Principle of Emotional Activation Just as the other principles discuss the importance of activating relevant goals and personal agency beliefs, this principle suggests that activating appropriate emotions will facilitate motivation. Teachers can do this by providing simulations that emotionally involve students in an experience. For example, a junior high teacher one of us has worked with uses a role-playing activity when teaching about medieval history and the relations between royalty and serfs. One student is appointed king and this student then selects other students to be knights and other royalty. Other students are then assigned to be serfs and peasants. The role play then progresses as the royalty are given a great deal of freedom and control of resources, while the serfs are restricted greatly in their movements and access to resources. The affect and emotions that are generated in this role play are quite intense as the serfs become increasingly angry with the undemocratic system. All the students are involved in the role play and it seems to be a motivating experience. Nevertheless, as Ford cautions, the activation of emotions can be delicate and there is always the possibility that they can get out of control. The medieval role play has resulted in some very heightened emotions for some of the students and must be used with care.

14. The "Do It" Principle This idea is not borrowed from a Nike shoe advertisement, but it does stress the importance of having people actually engage in the desired behavior, especially when they are having a great deal of difficulty beginning the activity. The idea is supported by the general notion from cognitive behavioral research (see Bandura, 1986; Meichenbaum, 1977) that suggests that people's negative cognitions and motivational beliefs are often so inhibiting that they never attempt the desired behavior. If an individual can engage in the behavior and not suffer the expected negative consequences but instead have a positive experience, this type of feedback and engagement will increase the probability that the behavior will be attempted again. Teachers use this strategy quite often when they work individually with students to help them engage in a task.

15. The Principle of Incremental Versus Transformational Change This principle suggests that change is more likely to come in small, incremental steps, a more classic evolutionary pattern, than in large, dramatic, or revolutionary steps (a more punctuated equilibrium view). Accordingly, teachers should not attempt large, dramatic changes in the environment or in their teaching strategies unless absolutely necessary. Instead, smaller, more incremental changes will be easier for the students to adapt to and may lead to more change in the long run.

16. The Equifinality Principle This principle is based on the idea that there are multiple pathways to a goal, that there is no one best or right answer to the problems of motivating students. In addition, different students will require different motivational strategies. Teachers should be wary and skeptical of any instructional, management, or motivational program that offers to solve all their problems with a simple plan or system. Education is not a deterministic science; it is a probabilistic human endeavor. Consequently, teachers will need to be active decision makers as they use different kinds of information about students' motivation, including these 17 principles, to make informed choices about what they will do in their own classrooms to motivate their own students.

17. The Principle of Human Respect This final principle in M. Ford's (1992) theory is the one he considers the most important and basic. He feels that people should always be treated with respect and as unique individuals who possess a variety of skills and goals. This principle parallels the basic ideas of humanistic psychology from Rogers and Maslow and can be particularly important in classrooms. Teachers are often overwhelmed with large numbers of students, especially secondary school teachers who often have over 100–150 students to teach every day, and it can be difficult to act on this principle. Ford is simply reminding all of us about the importance of respect in our interactions with others.

Goal Orientation Theories

In comparison to the two previous goal theories that deal with human behavior more broadly, goal orientation theories, for the most part, were developed specifically for explaining achievement behavior. They were created by developmental and educational psychologists to explain children's learning and performance on academic tasks and in school settings. As such, they are the most relevant and applicable goal theory for understanding and improving learning and instruction. There are a number of different variants of goal orientation theories for achievement behavior, but the main construct that is involved is *goal orientation*, which concerns the purposes for engaging in achievement behavior. In contrast to Locke and Latham's (1990) goal-setting theory that focuses on specific goals (e.g., get 10 problems correct), goal orientation theory is concerned with why individuals want to get 10 problems correct and how they approach this task. Goal orientation represents an integrated pattern of beliefs that leads to "different ways of approaching, engaging in, and responding to achievement situations" (Ames, 1992b, p. 261). In addition, goal orientation can reflect a type of standard by which individuals will judge their performance or success, which then has consequences for other motivational beliefs such as attributions and affect as well as actual performance and behavior. There may be a number of different goal orientations, but the two that are always represented in the different goal orientation theories have been labeled *learning* and *performance* goals (Dweck & Leggett, 1988; Elliott & Dweck, 1988), or *task-involved* and *ego-involved* goals (Nicholls, 1984), or *mastery* and *performance* goals (Ames, 1992b; Ames & Archer, 1987, 1988), or *task-focused* and *ability-focused* goals (Maehr & Midgley, 1991). There is some disagreement among these researchers about whether all these goal pairs represent the same constructs (see Nicholls, 1990), but there is enough conceptual overlap to treat them in similar ways in a textbook such as this one. Accordingly, we will use the terms *mastery* and *performance* goals to refer to the two general goal orientations.

The distinction between mastery and performance goals parallels to some extent the distinction between intrinsic and extrinsic motivation (see Chapter 7). The focus in goal orientation theories, however, is on a more specific cognitive goal that is more situational and context dependent than the general, more personality-like intrinsic and extrinsic motivation constructs that come from a more organismic, not contextual, perspective. If a student adopts a mastery goal orientation, then she should be focused on learning, mastering the task according to self-set standards, developing new skills, improving her competence, trying to accomplish something challenging, and trying to gain understanding or insight (see Ames, 1992b; Dweck & Leggett, 1988; Maehr & Midgley, 1991; Nicholls, 1984; and cf. Harter, 1981b). Table 6.6 shows how this construct of mastery goal orientation has actually been operationalized by different researchers. Most often, both mastery and performance goals have been measured with self-report instruments that ask students to rate on a Likert-type scale (from 1 to 4, from 1 to 5, from 1 to 7) how much they agree or disagree with a particular description. It seems clear from Table 6.6 that there is quite a bit of overlap, at least in terms of measurement, between the different labels of mastery, learning, and task orientation.

A performance goal orientation, in contrast to a mastery orientation, represents a focus on relative ability and how ability will be judged, for example, trying to surpass normative performance standards, attempting to best others' performance (I got a better grade than everyone else in the classroom.), and seeking public recognition of this performance level (Ames, 1992b). Although there is overlap among the different items that have been used to measure a

Table 6.6. Different Items Used to Assess Mastery and Performance Orientations

Dweck	Ames	Maehr and Midgley	Nicholls
Learning goal I like problems that I'll learn something from, even if they're so hard that I'll get a lot wrong.	*Mastery goal* I work hard to learn. Making mistakes is part of learning.	*Task focused* The main reason I do my schoolwork is because I like to learn. Understanding the work in school is more important to me than the grade I get. I feel most successful in school when I learn something I didn't know before.	*Task orientation* I feel successful when I learn something interesting. I feel successful when something I learn makes me want to find out more. I feel successful when something I learn makes me think about things.
Performance goal I like problems that aren't too hard, so I don't get too many wrong. I like problems that are hard enough to show that I'm smart.	*Performance goal* I work hard to get a high grade. I really don't like to make mistakes.	*Performance focused—extrinsic* The main reason I do my schoolwork is because we get grades. The main reason I do my schoolwork is because I would get into trouble if I didn't. An important reason why I do my schoolwork is to get rewards or special treatment from my teachers. *Performance focused—relative ability* I like to show my teacher I'm smarter than other kids. I would feel successful in school if I did better than the other students in my class. I feel good if I am the only one who can answer the teacher's questions in class.	*Ego orientation* I feel successful when I'm the smartest. I feel successful when I know more than other people. I feel successful when I have the highest test scores. *Work avoidant* I feel successful when I don't have to try hard. I feel successful when I don't have anything tough to do. I feel successful when I can goof off.

performance orientation (see Table 6.6), there may be less consistency in the definition of a performance orientation than in mastery orientation. For example, Maehr and Midgley and their colleagues (see Midgley, Maehr, & Urdan, 1993) have distinguished theoretically and empirically among three types of performance orientation: extrinsic, relative ability, and effort avoidance. An extrinsic performance orientation is similar to Harter's (1981b) extrinsic orientation and Pintrich and his colleagues (Pintrich, Smith, Garcia, & McKeachie, 1993) extrinsic goal orientation where the focus is on getting grades, doing schoolwork to get rewards, special privileges, or to avoid getting into trouble. Students with a relative ability performance goal orientation would be concerned about ability, doing better than others, trying to show that they are smarter than all the other students. Finally, students with a work avoidant performance orientation are those who try only to complete the work as quickly as possible without exerting too much effort. Meece, Blumenfeld, & Hoyle (1988) found students who had a work avoidant orientation besides the two other mastery and performance orientations. Nicholls, Cheung, Lauer, and Patashnick (1989) and Duda and Nicholls (1992) also proposed a third work avoidant orientation along with their ego- and task-involved orientations.

As can be seen in Table 6.6, there is a great deal of overlap in how these two goal orientation constructs have been measured. There are some differences, however. First, Dweck, Ames, and Maehr and Midgley all attempt to measure students' general approach to tasks, their reasons for doing a task, or their general purpose when doing a task. Nicholls, in contrast, begins all his items with the stem, "I feel most successful when," (cf. Table 6.6; Maehr and Midgley also begin some of their items with this same stem) and then adds descriptors that are very similar to the other items in Table 6.6. Nevertheless, Nicholls's approach asks students at what point they feel most successful when doing a task, a somewhat different perspective on goals. This perspective reflects a concern with students' general theories of classroom success and as part of his research, Nicholls also has included measures of students' beliefs about what causes success, which are basically attributions for the causes of success (see Chapter 3). In his model, Nicholls proposes that individuals' goal orientation will be related to their beliefs about the causes of success. Moreover, Nicholls assumes that the goal orientation an individual adopts will become the general standard for judging success and, therefore, goal orientation should predict beliefs about the causes of success. For example, students who adopt a task-involved orientation focused on learning will be more likely to give as a cause for student success responses such as "they try to understand instead of just memorizing" or "they try to figure things out." Students who adopt an ego-involved goal orientation will be concerned with their ability and besting others and will be more likely to cite as reasons for success in school that "they are better than others at taking tests" or "they try to beat others" (see Duda & Nicholls, 1992).

In contrast to this position, Dweck and her colleagues (e.g., Dweck & Elliott, 1983; Dweck & Leggett, 1988; see Table 6.7) suggest that goal orientation is a function of different theories about the nature of intelligence. In this model, theories of intelligence are defined as students' perceptions about how ability and intelligence change over time. In essence, this belief is isomorphic with the stability dimension for the classification of ability attributions in attribution theory (see Chapter 3). This stability dimension of attributions is not at the same level as the construct Nicholls uses—beliefs/attributions for the causes of success or failure— but as we saw in Chapter 3, attributions can be classified into these higher order dimensions that have motivational implications. Dweck proposes that there are two basic implicit theories of intelligence: incremental and entity theories. *Incremental theories* of intelligence reflect students' beliefs that their intelligence and ability can change and can increase with time and experience. In contrast, *entity theories* of intelligence represent the belief that ability is fixed, stable, and unchanging so students think they will not be able to increase their ability or intelligence over time.

In Dweck's research, these two beliefs are usually operationalized as opposite sides of a dichotomous variable and students should have one or the other implicit theory. The model, however, suggests that there may be a continuum between entity and incremental beliefs and that individuals may show mixed theories of beliefs about intelligence. These beliefs should be somewhat stable over time once the students are older than 12 or 13 years. Accordingly, these theories of intelligence are more traitlike than many other more contextual models of goals, although theories of ability/intelligence may vary by domain. For example, you may have an entity belief about your ability in mathematics, but you may have an incremental theory of ability for English coursework. This does not just apply to academic domains, however. Individuals may have

Table 6.7. Dweck's Model of Goal Orientation

Theory of Intelligence	Goal orientation	Confidence in intelligence	Behavior pattern
Entity theory (intelligence is fixed)	Performance goal (to gain positive judgments of competence)	If High ⟶	Mastery Oriented Seek challenge High persistence
		but	
		If Low ⟶	Helpless Avoid challenge Low persistence
Incremental theory (intelligence is malleable)	Learning goal (to increase competence)	If High or Low ⟶	Mastery oriented Seek challenge (fosters learning) High persistence

From "A Social-Cognitive Approach to Motivation and Personality" by C. Dweck and E. Leggett, 1988, *Psychological Review*, 95(2), p. 259. Copyright © 1988 by the American Psychological Association. Adapted by permission.

an entity theory of ability to play basketball because of their short height, but may be incrementalists in terms of their ability to play tennis or to learn how to do their job.

In Dweck's model, these theories about the stability of intelligence and ability create a schema for interpreting and evaluating information about the self. In effect, they become the criteria and standards by which goals, outcomes, and behavior are judged. Dweck assumes, therefore, that these theories of intelligence drive the type of goal orientation students will adopt (see Table 6.7), and her empirical research seems to support this view (see summary in Dweck & Leggett, 1988). Although they are examining somewhat different constructs, this causal link between theories of intelligence and goal orientation in Dweck's model is just the opposite causal relation proposed by Nicholls, who assumes goal orientation influences beliefs about success. In Dweck's model, if a student has an entity theory of intelligence and believes that his ability is generally stable, then he will be most likely to adopt a performance goal when engaged in a task. This student, because of the stable conception of ability, will be most concerned with how his performance is evaluated, how it compares to others, and with trying to best others. In contrast, the incrementalist theorist believes that ability can be increased and she is more likely to be focused on mastery goals such as trying to increase her competence and judging her success at reaching this goal by using criteria focused on self-improvement, not social comparison with others.

Goal Orientation and Other Motivational and Cognitive Outcomes

Regardless of the conflicting relations between goal orientation and theories of intelligence or beliefs about the causes of success or failure, goal orientation is an important influence on a number of motivational outcomes as well as achievement behaviors. Table 6.8 summarizes the definitions of mastery and performance goal orientations and their relations to other motivational and cognitive variables. First, goal orientation has been associated with patterns of attributions in a number of studies. In general, the research shows that a mastery goal orientation is linked to a positive, adaptive pattern of attributions, whereas a performance goal orientation is linked to a maladaptive, helpless pattern of attributions (Ames, 1992b; Dweck & Leggett, 1988).

When operating under a mastery goal orientation, students are concerned with learning and mastery of a task and increasing their ability. This schema seems to lead students to interpret outcome feedback in different ways than those following a performance goal orientation where the focus is on maintaining or enhancing their ability and there is a concern with how ability is assessed. In the mastery goal orientation, students are more likely to see a strong link between their effort and the outcome and make more effort attributions for both success and failure. In addition, students with a mastery goal orientation see effort linked in a positive manner with ability, that is, that more effort means more ability.

In contrast, a performance goal orientation seems to lead to using ability attributions for both success and failure, and it is well known that ability attributions for failure (when ability is conceived of as stable) are maladaptive and can lead to learned helpless patterns of behavior (Dweck & Leggett, 1988; Weiner, 1986; see Chapter 3). In addition, students with a performance goal tend to see effort and ability as inversely related as opposed to the positive relation under a mastery goal. The performance-oriented students tend to think that the harder they try, the less ability they have, and this belief can lead them to be at risk for avoiding effort in order to protect their ability and self-worth (Covington & Omelich, 1979). It is important to note that in Dweck and Leggett's model (see Table 6.7), this helpless pattern will emerge if students have a performance orientation and low confidence or efficacy in their intelligence. If students have a performance orientation but high confidence in their intelligence, then a performance orientation can lead to a mastery pattern of adaptive attributions and adaptive behavior like seeking challenges and persistence.

Besides these attributional patterns, mastery and performance goals also have been associated with various affective outcomes. Given the attribution-affect link specified in attributional theory, it is not surprising that mastery goals seem to lead to pride and satisfaction when successful and guilt when not successful (Ames, 1992b; Jagacinski & Nicholls, 1984, 1987). These affective outcomes are usually generated by attributions that stress the controllability of behavior (such as effort), and if mastery goals lead to more effort attributions, then these emotions would be expected to follow by attribution theory (Weiner, 1986). Mastery goals also have been associated with reports of more intrinsic interest in and positive attitudes toward learning tasks (Ames, 1992b; Butler, 1987; Meece et al., 1988; Stipek & Kowalski, 1989). In general, although many of these studies were correlational, which makes it difficult to infer causality, it appears to be fairly well established empirically that the adoption of a mastery goal is associated with an adaptive pattern of attributions and positive affect that will help a student try hard, persist, and ultimately do better on academic tasks.

In fact, there have been other studies that have linked mastery and performance goals to more quantitative academic behaviors like effort and persistence as well as the quality of engagement. Again, mastery goals are linked to more time spent on learning tasks and more persistence at these tasks in comparison to performance goals (Ames, 1992b; Butler, 1987; Elliott & Dweck, 1988). Moreover, there are a number of studies that have shown that mastery goals, in contrast to performance goals, lead to more cognitive engagement, especially the use of deeper processing strategies and self-regulated learning strategies. For example, Pintrich & De Groot (1990a) showed that junior high students who adopted an intrinsic goal focused on learning were more likely to report using cognitive strategies like elaboration (summarizing, paraphrasing) and self-regulatory strategies like comprehension monitoring. Pintrich

Table 6.8. Goal Orientation and Other Motivational and Cognitive Outcomes

Definitions/outcomes	Mastery goals	Performance goals
Goal definitions		
Success defined as	Improvement, progress, mastery, creativity, innovation, learning	High grades, better performance than others, higher achievement on standardized tests, winning at all costs
Value placed on	Effort, attempting challenging tasks	Avoiding failure
Reasons for effort	Intrinsic and personal meaning of activity	Demonstrating one's worth
Evaluation criteria	Absolute criteria, evidence of progress	Norms, social comparison with others
Errors viewed as	Informational, part of learning	Failure, evidence of lack of ability or worth
Outcomes associated with different goals		
Attributional patterns	Adaptive, failure attributed to lack of effort, outcome is seen as contingent on personal effort	Maladaptive, failure attributed to lack of stable ability
Affect	Pride and satisfaction for effortful success Guilt associated with lack of effort Positive attitudes toward learning Intrinsic interest in learning	Negative affect following failure
Cognition	Use of "deeper" processing strategies Use of self-regulatory strategies including planning, awareness, and self-monitoring	Use of more surface or rote learning strategies
Behavior	Choice of more personally challenging tasks More risk-taking, open to new tasks Higher levels of achievement	Choice of easier tasks Less willing to take risks, try new tasks Lower levels of achievement

Material drawn from Anderman and Maehr (1994), Ames (1992b), and Maehr and Midgley (1991)

240

and his colleagues also have found this same relation in college students (see Pintrich, 1989; Pintrich & Garcia, 1991, 1993; Pintrich & Schrauben, 1992; Pintrich, Smith, Garcia, & McKeachie, 1993). Ames and Archer (1988) also have found a relation between a classroom focus on mastery goals and student reports of deeper cognitive engagement. In addition, in more experimental laboratory studies, both Graham and Golen (1991) and Nolen (1988) have found that mastery goals lead to more cognitive engagement in terms of the use of more cognitive strategies and also better actual performance on learning tasks such as memory for words and text comprehension.

Given that mastery goal orientation can have a positive influence on students' cognition, affect, and behavior, how does the classroom context shape students' goal orientation? The research on goal orientation has often conceptualized students' goal orientation as a context dependent or classroom situated construct that is very amenable to change, depending on the environmental cues and presses. This research has used both experimental designs where goal orientations seem to be quite easily induced through certain kinds of instructions to the subjects and correlational field studies where characteristics of the classroom are observed and then linked to students' goal orientations. This work has been summarized by Ames (1992b) and she organizes the research findings around three dimensions of classrooms: (a) tasks and learning activities, (b) evaluation practices and use of rewards, and (c) distribution of authority and responsibility. It should be noted that, although these three dimensions are discussed individually in terms of different features that can facilitate the adoption of a mastery orientation, given the reality of classrooms, these features are not orthogonal to one another and they will overlap in the classroom.

Tasks and learning activities are important influences on student motivation and cognition (Blumenfeld, Mergendoller, & Swarthout, 1987; Doyle, 1983). There are several features of classroom tasks that can encourage students to adopt a mastery orientation according to Ames (1992b). First, the amount of variety and diversity in tasks can help maintain student interest and, by decreasing the amount of public comparability and opportunities for social comparison regarding performance, help students adopt a mastery goal orientation (Marshall & Weinstein, 1984; Nicholls, 1989; Rosenholtz & Simpson, 1984). A second feature of tasks concerns how they are introduced and presented to students. If the teacher can help students see the personal relevance and the meaningfulness of the content for their own learning, then this can facilitate an adoption of a mastery goal orientation (Brophy, 1987; Meece, 1991). A third feature concerns the level of difficulty of the task. As do most motivational theories we have discussed previously (and those in Chapter 7), goal orientation theory suggests that tasks that offer an optimal level of challenge for students—tasks that can be mastered with effort but are neither easy enough to produce boredom nor hard enough to produce anxiety—can facilitate a mastery goal orientation (Ames, 1992b; Lepper & Hodell, 1989; Malone & Lepper, 1987). Finally, Ames (1992b) notes that tasks that are structured to highlight specific, short-term, or proximal goals can help students marshall their efforts toward these goals and feel efficacious as they accomplish these goals. This latter feature represents the same implication regarding task design that would be derived from self-efficacy theory (Schunk 1991b) as well as goal-setting theory, which we discussed earlier in this chapter (Locke & Latham, 1990).

In terms of the evaluation practices and reward systems, goal orientation theory suggests that there are several factors that can facilitate a mastery goal (Ames, 1992b). First, the publicness of the evaluation practices can increase the salience of social comparison information, which can foster a performance orientation on the part of students. For example, disclosing students' grades for all classwork on bulletin boards, displaying only a select group of papers or tests in public spaces, or calling out test grades in public can provide social comparison information to all students about their relative performance and ability and can foster a performance orientation (Ames, 1992b; Marshall & Weinstein, 1984; Rosenholtz & Simpson, 1984). The use of within-classroom ability grouping that is made salient to students can also influence students' social comparison behavior and their perceptions of ability (Reuman, 1989), although the relation can be mediated by the degree of heterogeneity of student ability levels in the classroom (Mac Iver, 1988). A third factor concerns the general type of feedback that is provided to students about their performance and what criteria are used to evaluate the students' performance. Ames (1992b) suggests that feedback that communicates that mistakes are a part of learning and that effort is important will help students adopt a mastery goal orientation. In addition, she notes that when evaluation criteria allow for assessment of individual improvement, progress, and mastery rather than normative comparisons, then students will be more likely to focus on learning and mastery than on competition and performance goals.

The last dimension that Ames (1992b) discusses concerns the authority structure of the classroom. The general principle is that students should be given some choice and control in the classroom setting, the same principle that intrinsic motivation theorists (Deci & Ryan, 1985) propose as important for intrinsic motivation (see Chapter 7). Research from both goal theory and intrinsic motivation theory suggests that the provision of some control and choice for students increases their interest in the task and their cognitive engagement in the task (Ames, 1992b). This can include having students participate in the decision making for the classroom, such as setting priorities for *when* work will be done, not *what* work will be done; that is, the content of the curriculum is still under the teacher's control. Other aspects can include giving students opportunities to set the pace of learning or how the task will be accomplished. These types of opportunities can provide students with real choices and encourage them to develop personal responsibility for their own learning. At the same time, as Corno and Rohrkemper (1985) point out, students must have the necessary cognitive and self-regulatory skills to be able to cope with this type of responsibility. It may be that very young children or students with learning problems may not have the self-regulatory skills that would enable them to adapt to a classroom situation that allows a great deal of choice. If the students are unable or unwilling to regulate their own behavior in line with classroom opportunities for choice and control, then it is unlikely that these opportunities will have a positive influence on students' motivation and achievement (Ames, 1992b).

These three general dimensions often overlap; classrooms may have some or all of the positive features to facilitate a mastery orientation. It is possible that classrooms may have some task structure features (interesting tasks) that will facilitate a mastery orientation but have evaluation (public display of grades) or authority structures (little student choice or control) that are not very mastery oriented. As both Ames (1992b) and Blumenfeld (1992) point out, there is very little research on how students perceive and react to this type of diversity in classroom structures. It could be that certain dimensions are more salient to all the students in terms of their perceptions of classroom mastery orientation. For example, in a classroom where there is a great deal of emphasis on public evaluation and social comparison, this evaluation dimension may result in students perceiving the classroom as more performance oriented, even if the task and authority structures are more mastery oriented. A second possibility is that there may be individual differences in students in terms of what they perceive as more salient, with some focusing on the evaluation structures and others focusing on the task or authority structures. This is an important unresolved issue in goal theory and there is a need for more classroom-based research to investigate these and other possibilities.

This matter regarding how students perceive and react to differential classroom structures also brings up several other unresolved issues in goal orientation theory. First, as noted earlier, there is disagreement among goal orientation theorists about the conceptual definitions of mastery and performance goal orientations. Different researchers espouse different labels for these two general goals, different definitions, and, of course, different ways of measuring the goals. Second, beyond the definitions of the two goals, there are varying models regarding the issue of whether goal orientation is more situated and contextual or is more of a personal predisposition or individual difference variable. If one adopts a more situated view, then classrooms can have a stronger influence on students' goal orientation. This is a more optimistic view of student motivation because it suggests that teachers can structure classrooms in such a way to increase the mastery orientation of all students. In contrast, a more individual difference perspective on goal orientation suggests that it may be harder for teachers to change students' goal orientation. It may be that the solution to this matter regarding the stability of goal orientation will involve the adoption of a strategy used in social and personality psychology that assumes that both situational and personal conceptualizations are important and the issue is to specify how they interact (Mischel, 1990). Possibly there are personal dispositions for certain types of goal orientations that situational features can override. For example, it may be that when the situational features and cues in a classroom stress a performance orientation, then most students may adopt this orientation regardless of their initial level of a mastery orientation. In the absence of strong environmental cues, personal goal orientations may take precedence. In addition, there may be developmental differences such that younger elementary students may not have formed stable goal orientations and so are more susceptible to the classroom context, whereas older students in secondary classrooms have formed more stable goal orientations and are less likely to be influenced by the classroom context.

Related to the idea that goal orientations may be somewhat stable over individuals is a third issue concerning multiple goals. The goal theories of Locke and Latham (1990) and M. Ford (1992) that were discussed earlier in this chapter both assume that individuals can adopt and pursue multiple goals at the same time. Goal orientation theorists have not been clear about this issue. Some propose that mastery and performance goals are opposite ends of one continuum, thereby suggesting that individuals are basically pursuing either a mastery or a performance goal (Dweck & Leggett, 1988). Others (Meece & Holt, 1993; Nicholls et al., 1989) find that these goals can be orthogonal to one another and that it is possible for individuals to have a mixture of different goals that they report they are pursuing at the same time. In addition to this issue of the theoretical relations between the two types of goals, goal orientation researchers are still struggling with the best way to operationalize these multiple goals in their research. One strategy would be to specify the multiple goals in terms of orthogonal dimensions (e.g., a classification of individuals into a two-by-two matrix of high–low mastery and high–low performance goals) and another strategy would be to examine the intraindividual patterns of goals using cluster analysis (see Meece & Holt, 1993). Beyond this specification of multiple goals, there is still a need for more research on how these multiple patterns of goals then influence students' cognition and achievement. It appears that having a higher mastery goal orientation and a lower performance orientation results in the best level of cognitive engagement and achievement (Meece & Holt, 1993; Pintrich, 1989; Pintrich & Garcia, 1993), but in the absence of a mastery goal, then at least some concern with grades and performance seems to be helpful for cognitive engagement and performance (Pintrich, 1989).

Developmental and Group Differences in Goal Orientation Beliefs

It appears from a large number of studies done in both classroom and laboratory settings that a mastery goal can have a very positive influence on other motivational outcomes as well as cognition and actual achievement behavior. However, there are some important developmental differences that emerge in this research. Dweck and Elliott (1983) suggest that younger children generally have an incremental theory of intelligence, whereas older children (about 10–12 years old) will start to develop more entity-like theories of intelligence. In Dweck's model, these two different theories of intelligence would then lead to different goal orientations, with the younger children more likely to adopt a mastery goal orientation and the older children a performance orientation. Eccles and her colleagues (e.g., Eccles & Midgley, 1989) suggest that as children make the transition to junior high school, they tend to endorse an entity theory of ability and intelligence.

This research suggests that most adults have entity views of general intelligence, although they also may have incremental theories of ability for certain domains. For example, most adults may have a view of general intelligence as consisting of verbal ability, general thinking and problem-solving skills, and social competence (see Sternberg, 1990) but only think that the verbal ability and problem-solving components are actually entity-like, whereas social competence (ability to get along with others, be on time for appointments, etc.) can be more incremental. If teachers have a more entity-like view of intelligence and ability, then they would be more likely to believe that children who are achieving at lower levels would be less able to change their performance. This could result in teachers having lower expectations for these children and subsequently treating them differentially (see Brophy & Good, 1974; Eccles & Wigfield, 1985).

Nicholls and his colleagues (see Nicholls, 1978, 1990; Nicholls & Miller, 1983, 1984a, 1984b, 1985) also have shown that there are developmental differences in students' theories of ability, in particular what ability is and how it is related to beliefs about luck, skill, difficulty, and effort (see Chapter 4). Nicholls has followed a developmental perspective in these studies and his work has revealed that there are general levels of development in students' understandings of these concepts. Although Nicholls discusses the development of these concepts in terms of age-related levels of development, he is not advocating a strong stage model of development in a Piagetian or structuralist manner. These levels are descriptive of children's thinking about ability and are age related but they are context sensitive and not necessarily dependent on larger shifts in cognitive development (e.g, a shift from preoperational to concrete operational thinking).

In this research, Nicholls and his colleagues have found that young children, about 5 years old or younger, generally do not differentiate the concepts of luck, skill, ability, and effort in the same way that adults do. For example, young children do not distinguish luck from skill and believe that effort can make a difference on tasks that are essentially determined by chance. It is not until children are about 12 years old that they fully distinguish luck from skill and realize that effort will not make any difference on tasks determined by chance, but effort can make a difference on skill tasks. Of course, adults may suspend this belief about effort being unrelated to chance tasks. As anyone who has ever watched people playing slot machines knows, the players often expend a great deal of effort and have a number of strategies they use to help them win, no matter how illusory the link is between their effort and their winnings.

Nicholls and his colleagues also have found that young children (preschoolers) have different conceptions of the relations between task difficulty and ability than older children. There seem to be three levels in terms of this relation: the egocentric, objective, and normative levels (see Table 4.3 in Chapter 4). At the first level, labeled *egocentric* by Nicholls, all judgments about task difficulty are in reference to the child's own competence, so that a hard task is one that is hard for the child, not necessarily for anyone else. The second level, called the *objective level*, occurs when the child can recognize that there is a continuum of difficulty levels that requires different levels of ability. However, the child still cannot distinguish between low ability or high difficulty in a failure situation. In the final level, the *normative level*, which occurs at about 6 or 7 years old, children can distinguish between a task that is hard for everyone, which is a hard task, and a task that is hard just for them, which means they have low ability. This differentiation may come about because children at this age start to become aware of and actually use social comparison and normative information from peers to make ability, effort, and difficulty judgments (Ruble & Frey, 1991).

Finally, Nicholls also has shown that young children confound ability and effort or, at least, do not share the normative, adultlike definitions of ability and effort. This relation appears to be divided into four levels. Again, children 5 years and younger tend to merge the concepts of ability, effort, and outcome together, so that a person who tries hard is automatically smarter and someone who is smart also tries hard, regardless of actual outcome. At the second level, which emerges at about 6 or 7 years old, while they begin to develop the normative conception of ability and task difficulty, children begin to differentiate effort from outcome but think effort should determine outcome. They believe that equal effort should lead to equal outcomes. In cases where the outcome is the same and effort differs, the children will have difficulty reconciling this and invent reasons for why those who did not try as hard still did as well (they tried really hard for a short time) or for those who tried harder but still achieved at the same level (they went too fast and made mistakes). In the third level, the notion that ability can interact with effort to influence outcome begins to develop, although it is not applied systematically. Children at this level will begin to understand that if they try hard but do not do as well as others, then they may lack some ability. However, children at this level may still state that equal effort should lead to equal outcomes. The fourth and final level, achieved at about 12 or 13 years of age, reflects the normative adult conception of ability and effort as distinct and often covarying. In particular, ability is conceived of as capacity and ability can therefore limit the effect of effort. For example, students at this level believe that if they have low ability, then high effort will only be able to improve their performance to a certain level. Conversely, if students have high ability and combine that with high effort, then they should be able to achieve at a very high level. In addition, students at this level will likely believe that effort and ability covary, such that if an individual has high ability, then lower effort is required for most tasks.

These developmental differences in children's beliefs about intelligence, ability, skill, effort, difficulty, and luck imply that younger children, particularly preschool and early elementary age children, will more likely be mastery oriented than older children. As students begin to see that ability is capacity or that intelligence is entity-like, they will become concerned about their ability and how their performance reflects on their ability. This focus on ability is in line with a performance orientation, not a mastery goal orientation. The source of these developmental differences appears to be both cognitive-developmental as well as contextual. Nicholls (1990) and Ruble and Frey (1991) both argue that these developmental differences come about because of changes in young children's cognitive capabilities in understanding and using a variety of sources of information in the environment. In contrast, Rosenholtz and Simpson (1984) and Weinstein and Marshall (1984) argue that cognitive/structural changes are not the cause of these differences but rather the nature of the contexts the children move through, in particular, the classroom context. Eccles and her colleagues (e.g., Eccles & Midgley, 1989) as well as Maehr and his colleagues (e.g., Anderman & Maehr, 1994; Maehr & Midgley, 1991) suggest that the organization and structure of junior high schools influence students' motivational beliefs, rather than developmental differences alone. We discuss the contextual changes in more detail in Chapters 9 and 10, but it is clear that the classroom environment can have a major impact on children's goals and beliefs about ability and intelligence.

In terms of gender and ethnic differences, there is very little empirical research on differences in goal orientation by gender or ethnicity. Although Graham (1994) notes the dire need for more research on ethnic differences in attributions and self-perceptions of ability, at least there are some empirical studies on ethnic differences and those motivational constructs in contrast to the void in research on ethnicity and goal orientation. Clearly, given the importance of goal orientation to a variety of other motivational and cognitive outcomes, we need research that examines goal orientation beliefs and their relations to these outcomes for diverse groups of students.

In terms of gender differences, some of the original research by Dweck on learned helplessness (Dweck, Davidson, Nelson, & Enna, 1978) showed gender differences, with females having a less adaptive pattern of attributions. It was this early research that led Dweck to reformulate her ideas in terms of theories of intelligence and goal orientation beliefs (Dweck & Leggett, 1988) in which theories of intelligence and goals are the causal determinants of attributions, affect, and behavior. Following the logic of this model and working backward from the early findings of gender differences in attributions, then it might be predicted that females would be more performance oriented and more likely to endorse entity theories of ability (Henderson & Dweck, 1990). That is, if entity theories lead to performance goals and these goals lead to more maladaptive patterns of attributions, then the reverse should hold as well for individuals who use more maladaptive patterns of attributions (see Table 6.7). However, the research on gender differences in attribution patterns is not clear at all; many studies do not find maladaptive patterns among females (Eccles, 1983), so it is not clear that females would be less mastery oriented and more performance oriented. Henderson & Dweck (1990) do report on one study that showed that bright females were twice as likely to endorse an entity theory as opposed to bright males. In most of the empirical studies on goal orientation, however, gender differences have not been reported as significant, so there may not be large differences in goal orientation associated with gender. In fact, it might also be proposed that males are more performance oriented. If the stereotypical pattern of males being more competitive than females is assumed, then males might be more likely to adopt goals of besting others and trying to achieve the highest grades. Again, there is a need for more research on gender differences in these motivational beliefs about ability, goal orientation, and subsequent attributional, affect, and behavioral patterns before any strong conclusions can be drawn about the role of gender in students' goal orientation.

Implications for Teachers

Mastery and performance goals have been conceptualized as both individual difference constructs and more contextually sensitive beliefs. It appears that students will adopt the goal orientations that are stressed in their classroom (Ames, 1992b; Ames & Archer, 1988; Maehr & Midgley, 1991). Given that mastery goal orientations are related to better motivational outcomes as well as cognitive outcomes, what can teachers do to facilitate the adoption of mastery goals? Ames (1992) and Maehr and Midgley (1991) have suggested a number of strategies that teachers might use in their classroom.

1. Focus on meaningful aspects of learning activities. Teachers should stress how the academic tasks that are done in the classroom are relevant and "authentic" tasks that have meaning in the real world. For example, Mr. Herther, a tenth-grade biology teacher, has students involved in a project on local water quality. Students go out into the field and take samples of water from local streams and the main river in the area, perform tests for water quality, and then discuss the implications of their findings for water use in terms of drinking, sanitation, and overall water pollution.

2. Design tasks for novelty, variety, diversity, and interest. Teachers should attempt to provide a wide variety of tasks for students to engage in and ensure that the tasks have some novel, interesting, or surprising features that will engage the students. Ms. Donovan, a third-grade teacher, uses her one classroom computer to help students practice their math skills. She has acquired a number of different math software programs that embed arithmetic skills in games and fantasy-like environments. Even though they are basically drill-and-practice activities on a computer, she finds that her children, especially some of the low achievers, really enjoy working on the computer rather than doing math worksheets.

3. Design tasks that are challenging but reasonable in terms of students' capabilities. Again, Ames (1992b) suggests the same basic principle as Locke and Latham (1990) and M. Ford (1992) as well as the general Vygotskian principle regarding the ZPD. Given the diversity of student capabilities in the classroom, this suggestion to individualize instruction is often difficult to implement. However, it does not mean that every individual student needs to have different types of tasks, but that a range of tasks are offered for students. For example, Ms. Nelson, a sixth-grade English teacher in a middle school, teaches the whole class certain aspects of literacy in terms of reading and writing. All the students have some core projects, papers, and assignments that have to be in their individual portfolios. However, she does individualize by providing a range of extra required assignments that must be included in the students' portfolios. These extra assignments include creative writing tasks as well as basic grammar and spelling assignments. Students can choose which of these extra tasks they are going to engage in, but Ms. Nelson guides students to work on areas where they can improve. Accordingly, some children have more grammar assignments in their portfolios, whereas others have more reading comprehension assignments. This system also allows Ms. Nelson to give reading and writing tasks that are at different grade levels without using highly public within-classroom grouping practices.

4. Provide opportunities for students to have some choice and control over the activities in the classroom. This does not mean that the teacher should give up all decision making about the curriculum or tasks. In fact, it is probably shirking professional responsibility and ethics for a teacher to turn over the curriculum to the students. Teachers are in their role because they supposedly have some knowledge and skills about their content areas and instruction in general that can help students to learn. However, it is possible for teachers to provide opportunities for students to do different activities within a range of activities that fit the curriculum. For example, Mr. Wolters, a junior high social studies teacher, allows students some choice in topics for reports or papers. He constrains the general topic (e.g., the era of the American Revolution) and students' papers have to fit within one of the general themes of the unit (e.g., military, economic, political, social, cultural, geographical), but the students are allowed to pursue their own interests within these constraints.

5. Focus on individual improvement, learning, progress, and mastery. Teachers in both their daily verbal feedback and in the rewards they give should focus students on their improvement. Ms. Prescott, a fourth-grade teacher, provides individual feedback to students on worksheets and their daily work that focuses on how the students are mastering the skills or knowledge required and their improvement from previous days or weeks. In addition, she has students compile their work in folders that she periodically reviews with them individually. In these conferences with the students, she tries to help the students see how they are progressing in terms of growth in their own skills and knowledge.

6. Strive to make evaluation private, not public. Although it is impossible to make all evaluation private (after all, classrooms are public places), teachers can minimize public evaluations. Mr. Martin, a seventh-grade English teacher, used to have students call out their spelling test scores to save time, but he eventually found that it promoted a lot of social comparison and contests among students because it provided very public information about who is doing well and who is not doing well. The students who did well seemed to thrive on the competition, but after a while, the students who did not perform well consistently began to resist taking the spelling tests. They would be slow to get ready for the test, they would often drift off and stare out the window when Mr. Martin was calling out the words, and they would not even try to write them down. He also used a big bulletin board to display all the students' grades on all assignments, tests, and papers that everyone in the class could see. Although these management procedures were helpful to him, Mr. Martin found that they led to some very negative feedback and teasing from the higher achieving students toward the students who were not doing so well. At the end of the first marking period, he stopped using both of these procedures and had students turn in their papers to him and he kept all their grades in a record-keeping spreadsheet on his computer. This took some time to set up and enter students' grades, but it allowed him to keep evaluations more private and did not foster as much negative social comparison. In addition, the spreadsheet program allowed him to print out individual student records, so he could give each student a copy of his or her own performance over the term.

7. Recognize student effort. Although effort cannot and should not be the sole criteria for judgments regarding the quality of work, there are ways to build effort into the evaluation. Ms. Danos, a high school English teacher, gives separate scores or grades for content and effort on major papers. She tries to help her students see that the effort they put in is linked to the overall quality of the paper, but also recognizes that there still may be differences in content due to knowledge and skill differences. Nevertheless, she wants to encourage students who are trying hard by giving them a high mark for effort, although they may need more work on their grammar and overall writing skills.

8. Help students see mistakes as opportunities for learning. Teachers, through their feedback and grading practices, can encourage the view that mistakes are indicators of a students' ability or that mistakes happen to everyone regardless of ability and really represent an opportunity to learn. How teachers treat wrong answers in a class recitation can send strong messages about the nature of mistakes and their role in learning. In order to foster a mastery orientation, teachers need to be careful to recognize mistakes (that is, don't just let mistakes go by without comment) but treat them in a way that encourages students to see them as positive and fruitful for learning. For example, Ms. Garcia, a high school algebra teacher, has students work problems on the board. She sends up teams of two or three students to work on different problems and the whole class works at the board during this time. When the students are done, they return to their seats, then each team goes up individually and explains how they worked the problem. Ms. Garcia and the students can ask the team questions about their methods to see if there are difficulties and where they are in the problem solution. Errors are treated as a way to learn as the class sees and discusses the process by which the team came to use the method they chose for the problem. In addition, since the students work in teams of two or three, no one student ever feels that it is his or her sole responsibility for the problem.

These are just a few of the strategies that different goal theorists have suggested to foster a mastery goal orientation in the classroom. In addition, Maehr and Midgley (1991) suggest that schools, not just classrooms, can adopt many of these same strategies. In fact, their work suggests that it is difficult for one teacher in a school to adopt many of these mastery strategies without support from other teachers in the building and the school principal. They have worked with whole school buildings to incorporate these strategies schoolwide in order to ensure that there is consistency throughout the building. We will discuss these school strategies in Chapter 10 of this book.

SUMMARY

In this chapter, we have reviewed a number of different need and goal theories that have been proposed to explain personal motivation. The early need theories of Murray and Maslow were much more global and encompassing theories of human motivation. These theories were designed to explain all of human behavior, not just the achievement motivation of students in classrooms. Both theories developed a taxonomy of needs that were assumed to provide the instigation for action as well as the direction of action. Murray's list of needs included 20 needs, whereas Maslow's hierarchy of needs included 5 different levels of needs. Although needs have an intuitive appeal for explaining motivated behavior, there are serious conceptual and theoretical problems associated with the construct, particularly difficulties in avoiding a tautological argument between needs and behavior and in specifying a parsimonious number of needs.

Most current research on motivation has focused on goals, a more social cognitive construct that does not have some of the same conceptual difficulties as needs. We discussed three general goal theories and their implications for student motivation and achievement in the classroom. The first theory discussed was Locke and Latham's (1990) theory of goal setting. This theory was developed in organizational psychology to explain individuals' achievement behavior in work settings, although it can be applied to school settings if used carefully and thoughtfully. Goal-setting theory proposes that goals represent the very situation specific and conscious intentions or purposes that an individual is pursuing or trying to attain. A student who consciously sets a goal of getting 75% of the words correct on a spelling test reflects the level of specificity of goals in Locke and Latham's theory. This theory is very compatible with self-efficacy theory (see Chapter 3) and, in fact, self-efficacy is one of the major influences on goal setting and goal attainment in Locke and Latham's theory. Research on the theory suggests that setting very specific, proximal goals and setting relatively high goals have a positive influence on motivation and achievement. In addition, research in this tradition suggests that the level of commitment to the goal has a positive influence on subsequent achievement. The theory proposes that the level of goal setting is influenced by both personal and contextual factors. Most importantly, the research suggests that rewards do not have to undermine motivation and achievement; when rewards provide important feedback about progress and performance as well as efficacy information, they can have a positive influence on achievement.

The second theory presented was M. Ford's (1992) Motivational Systems Theory (MST). This theory represents an attempt to synthesize a number of different motivational theories into one comprehensive system. As such, it includes goals, personal agency beliefs (efficacy and control), and emotions as the three defining motivational constructs. The functions of agency beliefs and emotions are similar to those in other motivational theories such as self-efficacy theory, but the definition of goals is somewhat different from that in other goal theories. Ford proposes that there are 24 general goals that individuals can be striving to attain. The taxonomy of 24 goals is derived from empirical work with individuals not only in school settings, but in many other institutional settings such as work organizations and clinical settings. These goals are much more global and psychological in nature than the very specific task goals that are central to Locke and Latham's goal-setting theory. These 24 goals are similar in many ways to Murray's 20 needs, but they are more specific and less psychodynamic than Murray's and they are not assumed to be hierarchical as in Maslow's theory. In addition, these 24 goals can be combined in a number of ways, which allows individuals to pursue multiple goals. The theory has been developed to explain human motivation in many settings, and it does have relevance for educational settings. MST proposes 17 general principles for the facilitation of motivation that are directly applicable to classrooms and schools.

The final goal theory discussed in this chapter is goal orientation theory. Of all the current goal theories, this one has the most direct applicability to classrooms and student motivation. It was developed to explain achievement behavior specifically and has been tested in many experimental and classroom field studies with both children and adults as they perform various learning tasks. Currently, it is probably the most active area of research on student motivation in classrooms and it has direct implications for students and teachers. The theory proposes that there are two general goal orientations that students can adopt toward their academic work: a mastery orientation with the focus on learning and mastery of the content and a performance orientation with the focus on demonstrating ability, getting good grades or rewards, or besting other students. These two goal orientations have been linked to a number of cognitive, affective, and behavioral outcomes in a number of empirical studies. Generally, the research suggests that a mastery goal orientation leads to adaptive attributional patterns, positive affect and interest, higher levels of cognitive engagement, more effort and persistence, and better performance. In contrast, a performance goal orientation often leads to maladaptive patterns of attribution, higher levels of anxiety, lower value for tasks, less cognitive engagement, withdrawal of effort and failure to persist, and lower levels of performance. Besides these links to student outcomes, goal orientation theory and research has shown that the task, authority, and evaluation structures of classrooms can help to create mastery and performance orientations in students. Given these findings, there are a number of instructional strategies that teachers can use in their classrooms to make changes in the task, authority, and evaluation structures to make classrooms more mastery oriented.

Intrinsic Motivation

255

*J*on Crocker, a high school English teacher, sat at home planning his week's lessons. His students were studying nineteenth-century American writers (e.g., Emerson, Hawthorne, Poe, Thoreau), and their assignment was to write a critical analysis of a literary work by one of the figures of the period. Jon was planning whole-class, small-group, and individual activities, including time to do library research on the students' topics.

Jon loved literature and teaching. He recalled how excited he became when he was in high school and studied great literature. He had a couple of dynamic teachers who made literature come alive and showed how issues and events of long ago related to contemporary happenings. For Jon, class was only the beginning. He read more books and did more work in his English classes than was required because of his love for learning literature rather than because it was something to be done. He always earned good grades, but they were less important to him than the excitement he derived from studying literature.

Jon's challenge was to try to recreate that excitement among his students. So far the results were disappointing; the students seemed interested in everything but literature. For example, Todd talked with Jon the other day and said that he really needed to make an A in the course to improve his grade point average so he *could get admitted to college. Todd asked what he could do to ensure that he would get an A in the class. Alex complained about having to take the class and hoped that she could stay awake in there. Tina announced in front of the class that all this "literature stuff" seemed like a waste of time because it didn't pertain to living in today's world. Mark was less candid but made the same point when he said that he hoped more time could be spent on authors who understand young people better. Lisa was an exception. She seemed truly interested in literature and displayed some of the excitement that Jon felt. A couple of other students seemed similarly intrinsically motivated, but Jon thought that only 3 highly interested students out of 23 seemed pretty dismal.*

Jon considered the problems he faced. His was a required course; students needed it to graduate. They had no control over who taught the course, the topics were pretty well set, and the assignments did not offer much latitude. Many students were concerned about their grades. At a minimum, they did not want to appear to be stupid. They also likely did have a legitimate problem relating historical material to their own lives.

Jon thought about some ways he might enhance intrinsic motivation for literature among the students. The term papers were a good start because students could choose their own topics and pursue a format mutually agreed upon by themselves and by him. He decided to spend more time relating themes and events in literature to contemporary happenings. He knew the students enjoyed small-group work and discussions, so he decided to plan more of those. Some discussion time could focus on how literature related to current events and students' own lives. He decided to try some role playing where students would assume the role of characters and act out scenes. He planned one session where he would come to class dressed as Poe and talk about his life and writings. Jon realized that he could not change many things (e.g., students' concern about grades), but he believed that collectively these activities would make the class more interesting and that maybe students would feel more of a sense of personal involvement.

Like most teachers, Jon is concerned about his students' intrinsic motivation for learning. *Intrinsic motivation* refers to motivation to engage in an activity for its own sake. People who are intrinsically motivated work on tasks because they find them enjoyable. Task participation is its own reward and does not depend on explicit rewards or other external constraints. In contrast, *extrinsic motivation* is motivation to engage in an activity as a means to an end. Individuals who are extrinsically motivated work on tasks because they believe that participation will result in desirable outcomes such as a reward, teacher praise, or avoidance of punishment.

It is tempting to think of intrinsic and extrinsic motivation as two ends of a continuum such that the higher the intrinsic motivation, the lower the extrinsic motivation, but, in fact, there is no automatic relation between intrinsic and extrinsic motivation. For any given activity, an individual may be high on both, low on both, medium on both, high on one and medium on the other, and so forth. It is more accurate to think of intrinsic and extrinsic motivation as separate continuums, each ranging from high to low.

Another point is that intrinsic and extrinsic motivation are contextual. They characterize people in relation to activities, and the same activity can be intrinsically or extrinsically motivating for different people. Jon's English class is extrinsically motivating for Todd but intrinsically motivating for Lisa. As another example, assume that Sammy and Rhonda play the banjo. Sammy's intrinsic motivation is high because he plays for enjoyment, whereas his extrinsic motivation is low. In contrast, Rhonda's extrinsic motivation is high because she plays largely as a means to the end of playing well enough to earn money in a Dixieland band. Rarely does she play for intrinsic reasons.

Because intrinsic motivation is contextual, it can change over time. Many things that young children find interesting (e.g., "Sesame Street") gradually lose their appeal as they become older. Sudden changes in level of intrinsic motivation are not uncommon. Sammy may become extrinsically motivated to play the banjo well if he has financial problems and decides to play the banjo to earn money.

Aside from the fun that people have while engaging in activities they enjoy, we can ask whether intrinsic motivation bears any relation to learning. Do students learn better when they enjoy the content, or can they learn just as well if their goal is to please the teacher, earn good grades, or stay out of trouble with parents? We can all remember times when we were intrinsically and extrinsically motivated to learn. Students still learn for intrinsic and extrinsic reasons. Nonetheless, working on a task for intrinsic reasons is not only more enjoyable, there also is evidence that intrinsic motivation facilitates learning and achievement (Gottfried, 1985). These benefits presumably occur because students who are intrinsically motivated engage in activities that enhance learning; they attend to instruction, rehearse new information, organize knowledge and relate it to what they already know, and apply skills and knowledge in different contexts. In turn, learning promotes intrinsic motivation. As students develop skills, they perceive their progress and feel more efficacious about learning. Heightened self-efficacy and positive outcome expectations (see Chapters 3 and 5) raise intrinsic motivation and lead to further learning (Bandura, 1986, 1993).

In this chapter, we examine intrinsic motivation from several perspectives: effectance motivation, incongruity, mastery motivation, personal causation and control, self-determination, self-perception and overjustification, and emergent motivation. Despite some differences, there are common themes running through these views. Lepper and Hodell (1989) identify four major sources of intrinsic motivation: *challenge, curiosity, control,* and *fantasy*. Intrinsic motivation may depend on students finding activities challenging, as when goals are of intermediate difficulty and success is uncertain. Intrinsic motivation also may depend on learners' curiosity being piqued by activities that are surprising, incongruous, or discrepant with their existing ideas. Intrinsic motivation derives in part from students experiencing a sense of control over their learning and task participation. And, finally, activities that help learners become involved in make-believe and fantasy may enhance intrinsic motivation.

EARLY VIEWS OF INTRINSIC MOTIVATION

Early work on intrinsic motivation explained it in terms of a developmental phenomenon or as dependent upon arousal and incongruity. We discuss these perspectives, then turn our attention to contemporary views.

White's Effectance Motivation

In a classic paper, White (1959) discussed *effectance motivation* as

> fitness or ability, and the suggested synonyms capability, capacity, efficiency, proficiency, and skill. It is therefore a suitable word to describe such things as grasping and exploring, crawling and walking, attention and perception, language and thinking, manipulating and changing the surroundings, all of which promote an effective—a competent—interaction with the environment. . . . The behavior . . . is directed, selective, and persistent, and it is continued not because it serves primary drives . . . but because it satisfies an intrinsic need to deal with the environment. (pp. 317–318)

White argued that people have an inherent need to feel competent and interact effectively with the environment. The goal of effectance motivation is a feeling of personal mastery or efficacy. This need is present early in life, as seen in babies who grab objects that catch their attention. As children get older, they examine objects, turn them over, push them away, and pull them back—all of which actions are part of their efforts to control the environment. The effectance motive does not include reflexes or well-learned behaviors and it exerts itself only when such homeostatic motives as the need for food, air, and water are satisfied. The effectance motive has evolutionary value because it helps organisms competently deal with environmental forces. It also may contribute to learning, although that is not its primary function. A child who opens a kitchen cupboard learns there are cookies inside, and this knowledge eventually may be used to satisfy hunger.

White suggested that effectance motivation is undifferentiated in young children; that is, it is global and directed toward environmental features that capture their attention. Toddlers may engage in the same action repeatedly (turning a light switch on and off). Parents may not understand such actions, but they serve an important developmental function. With development, effectance motivation becomes specialized. Once students enter school, they may direct effectance motivation toward mastery of certain school subjects. School achievement and other outcomes (e.g., mastery in art and music) are hypothesized to derive from effectance motivation. In adults the motive is further specialized and manifested in mastery of job skills.

White's contention that people possess an effectance motive that propels them toward competence and is satisfied by feelings of mastery is intuitively appealing. Although it is tempting to say that a global construct of effectance motivation explains diverse phenomena, the construct's generality limits its ability to explain and predict events. Specification and assessment of the construct are needed to determine the circumstances in which it is valid and the types of factors that might affect it. The idea of effectance motivation is found in many other perspectives on intrinsic motivation and most clearly in work on mastery motivation (the next primary topic in this chapter).

Arousal and Incongruity

Recall that Berlyne's (1960, 1963) theory (Chapter 2) postulates that an optimal level of physiological arousal (stimulation to the nervous system) is adaptive. If it becomes too low, individuals are intrinsically motivated to increase arousal. Conversely, if arousal becomes too great, they are motivated to reduce it. Berlyne also felt that collative properties of stimuli involving their novelty, ambiguity, incongruity, and surprise affect arousal and motivate people to explore the objects.

Hunt (1963) argued that intrinsic motivation, which gives rise to exploratory behavior and curiosity, stems from incongruity between prior experiences and new information. People extract information from the environment and compare it with memory. When incongruity exists between inputs and knowledge, people become intrinsically motivated to reduce the incongruity (a notion somewhat akin to cognitive dissonance, see Chapter 2). Hunt believed that individuals require an optimal level of incongruity. Too much incongruity is frustrating and triggers a drive to reduce it.

Hunt's incongruity is conceptually similar to Berlyne's arousal. Although Hunt's and Berlyne's ideas seem intuitively sensible, the notion of optimal level of incongruity or arousal is vague and it is not clear how much is needed to stimulate intrinsic motivation (Deci, 1975). From a practical perspective, we know that use of novelty, surprise, and incongruity in the classroom are popular ways to enhance student interest in learning. But the notion of an optimal level is important. When arousal or incongruity becomes too great, people may become frustrated and attempt to escape from the situation or diminish level of arousal.

MASTERY MOTIVATION

Contemporary perspectives on effectance motivation stress the individual's goals and attempts to master environmental challenges. Here we discuss the views of Harter and Dweck.

Harter's Theory of Effectance Motivation
Theoretical Predictions

Harter (1978, 1981a) attempted to specify the antecedents and consequences of effectance motivation. She assumed that effectance motivation was best viewed in a developmental framework where the content and operation of the motive change with development. Although White focused on the effects of success on effectance motivation, Harter believed that the effects of failure also are relevant. Further, the degree of challenge of tasks is a potentially important mediator of the effects of outcomes. The roles of socializing agents and rewards in the environment also need to be considered. How children internalize mastery goals and develop a self-reward system is relevant as well. Finally, the important correlates of effectance motivation (e.g., perceived competence, perceived control) need to be identified.

In the reformulated model of effectance motivation shown in Figure 7.1, the left side portrays success experiences and is similar to White's original formulation. Beginning at the top, we see that effectance motivation can trigger mastery attempts. White postulated that the motive is generic, but Harter suggests differentiating it according to domain (school performance, peer relationships, athletic accomplishments). Most behaviors are likely to involve optimally challenging tasks (not too easy and not too hard), which also should yield maximum pleasure. Successes should produce intrinsic pleasure and perceptions of competence and control, and these in turn should strengthen effectance motivation.

The bottom left part of Figure 7.1 highlights the role played by socializing agents. Harter believed that some positive reinforcement for mastery attempts is necessary for children to develop and maintain effectance motivation. Much of this reinforcement presumably comes from primary caregivers in the child's early years. With sufficient reinforcement children gradually internalize a self-reward system and mastery goals. The self-reward system allows children to reinforce themselves for mastery attempts. Through observational learning

Figure 7.1.   Harter's model of effectance (mastery) motivation

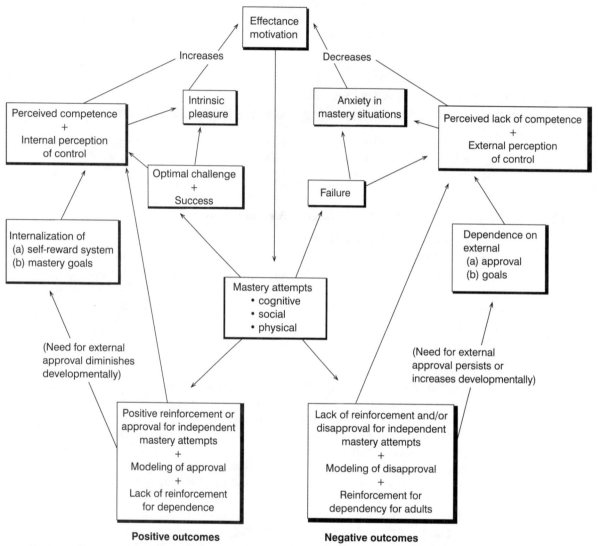

and reinforcement, children acquire mastery goals from caregivers. With development comes greater internalization and less dependence on others as models and reinforcing agents.

The left side of Figure 7.1 portrays the positive outcomes that might result when children's social environments cooperate with their natural desires. In contrast, the right side of the figure portrays negative outcomes, or what might lead to extrinsically oriented individuals. Mastery attempts that result in failure, coupled with an environment that does not model or reward mastery, can result in children developing perceptions of low competence and of outcomes as controlled by external agents, as well as anxiety in achievement situations. Effectance motivation is diminished as children increasingly depend on others to set their goals and reinforce their efforts.

A critical variable in the model is perceived competence, which Harter believes applies to specific areas rather than being generic in nature. She developed the Perceived Competence Scale for Children (Harter, 1982), which assesses perceptions of competence in three areas (cognitive, social, physical) and includes a fourth scale to measure self-worth (see Chapter 3). Harter (1981b) also developed a measure of intrinsic and extrinsic classroom motivational orientation, which assesses such dimensions as curiosity, challenge, and mastery. The latter scale is based on the assumption that intrinsic motivation includes the following five aspects (Harter & Connell, 1984):

1. Preference for challenge rather than for easy work
2. Incentive to work to satisfy one's own interest and curiosity rather than working to please the teacher and obtain good grades
3. Independent mastery attempts rather than dependence on the teacher
4. Independent judgment rather than reliance on teacher's judgment
5. Internal criteria for success and failure rather than external criteria

Research Evidence

Research supports many of the hypothesized relations among variables in Harter's model. For example, intrinsic motivation relates positively to perceived competence and internal control (Harter, 1981a; Harter & Connell, 1984). Students who believe they are competent enjoy tasks more and display greater intrinsic motivation than do students who judge their competence lower (Boggiano, Main, & Katz, 1988; Gottfried, 1985, 1990). With respect to level of difficulty, children judge their competence higher and obtain greater pleasure from succeeding on more difficult tasks compared with easier tasks (Harter, 1978, 1981a). Models and reinforcement affect children's mastery attempts and internalization of mastery goals and self-rewards (Bandura, 1986). On the negative side, students with learning problems often fail and believe they lack the competence to do well, which lowers their intrinsic motivation (Licht & Kistner, 1986; Schunk, 1989b). Such children may be held in low esteem by peers, and their parents may have low academic expectations for them (Bryan & Bryan, 1983). Motivation suffers when families do not reward mastery attempts and students do not associate with mastery-oriented peers.

Harter postulated that the effectance motive should operate across different developmental levels but that its corresponding behaviors may change with development (Harter, 1978). In one study (Harter, 1975), 4-year-old and 10-

year-old children participated in a discrimination task in which they were presented with colored disks and had to choose one; a marble was released if they chose the correct disk. The results showed that older children were motivated to succeed to obtain correct answers, whereas younger children were motivated for sensorimotor reasons (e.g., pushing buttons that made lights go on and off, causing marbles to be released). This point supports White's (1959) contention that effectance motivation becomes more focused with development.

Harter's theory addresses the development of intrinsic motivation and its links to other variables. The model has generated much research and many hypotheses have been supported. At the same time, Harter relies on models and rewards from socializing agents as primary influences on students' internalization of mastery goals and development of self-reward systems. These influences are important, but motivational research shows the importance of other ways to foster mastery behavior, including setting learning goals, providing attributional feedback linking outcomes to effort and strategy use, and teaching self-regulatory activities (Ames, 1992a; Pintrich & Schrauben, 1992; Schunk, 1991; Zimmerman, 1989). Another potential concern is that little attention has been paid to the educational implications of the theory. We might ask whether and how students can be taught to adopt an intrinsic orientation toward school learning. In Chapters 3 and 5, for example, we discuss ways to enhance students' perceptions of self-efficacy and control. It appears that Harter's theory needs to be broadened to include the role of these educational influences.

Implications for Teachers

Although Harter's theory may need to be broadened, there are a number of implications for developing a mastery orientation in the classroom.

1. Foster in students a preference for challenge rather than for easy work assigned. A kindergarten teacher said to Joey, "Why don't you work on this puzzle today? You put those easy ones together so quickly yesterday. I know you can work this harder one."

Mr. Hopkins, an eighth-grade social studies teacher, was assigning student projects. He listed several activities that could be done with each project. The more activities that students selected to complete, the higher the grade they could earn.

2. Develop in students an incentive to satisfy interests and curiosity rather than to please the teacher and obtain good grades. Ms. Burns, a fifth-grade teacher, was working with a group of students in selecting topics for a research paper. She told the students she wanted them to pick a topic they really wanted to learn something about. She worked with each student throughout the research, compiling, and writing processes. When the paper was complete, she met with them to assign a grade based on effort, how much they felt they learned, and quality of the completed product.

Every Friday a third-grade teacher set up various activity centers (math, writing, reading, science, social studies, art, music) in the classroom. The students selected one or more activities to participate in for the entire morning.

3. Encourage independent mastery attempts rather than dependence on the teacher. Mr. Petersen worked with each of his fourth-grade math students at the beginning of each 6 weeks to select five learning goals. The students then kept their own records on mastering the skills and concepts to accomplish the goals. Each student met with Mr. Petersen periodically to discuss progress.

A high school science teacher gave her students a list of objectives and activities for each unit of study. Students completed the tasks independently and took written and laboratory tests to demonstrate mastery of the unit objectives.

4. Have students exercise independent judgment rather than relying on the teacher's judgment. Mr. Sampson, a seventh-grade language arts teacher, had his students work through the writing process for each writing assignment. Students used a checklist to assess progress and improvement over previous drafts. During the final phase of each assignment, he met with students individually and discussed the process, improvement, and final grade.

Ms. Chambers, a second-grade teacher, listed six to eight independent activities on the board each morning. She then had students individually decide which four of the activities they wanted to do and the order in which they wanted to complete them.

5. Get students to apply internal criteria for success and failure rather than external criteria. Mr. Laird, a basketball coach, continually worked with his team members on mastery of various skills. While reviewing game videotapes with the team, he asked the members to evaluate their performances and the reasons for their successes and failures. They talked about what they did and what they might have done differently.

Ms. Appleton, a high school civics teacher, planned various units throughout the year that included different activities and independent and group projects. For each unit, she had students write a couple of paragraphs that expressed what they had learned from the unit, what contributed to their success or failure on the unit, and how their new knowledge and insights would affect their lives.

PERCEIVED CONTROL

The concept of perceived control over task engagement and outcomes is central to many views of intrinsic motivation. In the introductory scenario, Jon felt that a lack of perceived control by students may be contributing to their low intrinsic motivation. We discuss two important perspectives on control: Rotter's locus of control and de Charms's personal causation.

Locus of Control

Rotter (1966) expanded his social learning theory (Chapter 5) to include *locus of control*, which is a generalized belief about the extent to which behaviors influence outcomes (successes, failures). People with an external locus of control believe their actions have little impact on outcomes and there is little they can do to alter them, whereas those with an internal locus of control believe that outcomes are contingent on their actions and largely under their control. As Rotter (1966) states,

> When a reinforcement is perceived by the subject as following some action of his own but not being entirely contingent upon his action, then, in our culture, it is typically perceived as the result of luck, chance, fate, as under the control of powerful others, or as unpredictable because of the great complexity of the forces surrounding him. When the event is interpreted in this way by an individual, we have labeled this a belief in *external control*. If the person perceives that the event is contingent upon his own behavior or his own relatively permanent characteristics, we have termed this a belief in *internal control*. (p. 1)

Locus of control is postulated to affect learning, motivation, and behavior. Students who believe they have control over whether they succeed or fail should be more motivated to engage in academic tasks, expend effort, and persist on difficult material than students who believe their actions have little effect on outcomes. In turn, these motivational effects should raise learning. Research supports the hypothesized positive relation between internal locus of control and motivation and achievement in school (Phares, 1976).

Internal locus of control bears some similarity to White's (1959) effectance motive. Individuals with an internal locus of control make greater efforts to attain mastery over their environment (Phares, 1976), which is indicative of intrinsic motivation. Locus of control presumably is a generalized expectancy that affects behavior across different settings, but other investigators have noted that locus of control varies with the situation (Phares, 1976). For example, a student may hold an internal locus in math class and an external locus in English. Although locus of control is important, there is a need to specify the conditions that can affect it and the extent to which it generalizes across tasks and settings. Moreover, as we noted in Chapter 4, attributional theory has reformulated locus of control into two separate dimensions of locus and control, which can have different influences on motivation and achievement.

Personal Causation

Origins and Pawns

The role of personal causation in intrinsic motivation is highlighted by de Charms (1968, 1984). *Personal causation* is an individual's initiation of behavior intended to alter the environment. De Charms postulated that people strive to be causal agents and that a primary motivation is to produce changes in the environment. As Rotter distinguished internal from external locus of control, de Charms (1968) differentiated *origins* and *pawns* in terms of personal causation:

> We shall use the terms "Origin" and "Pawn" as shorthand terms to connote the distinction between forced and free. An Origin is a person who perceives his behavior as determined by his own choosing; a Pawn is a person who perceives his behavior as determined by external forces beyond his control. We hypothesize . . . that feeling like an Origin has strong effects on behavior as compared to feeling like a Pawn. The distinction is continuous, not discrete—a person feels *more* like an Origin under some circumstances and *more* like a Pawn under others. (pp. 273–274)

Origins have strong feelings of personal causation and attribute changes in their environments to their actions. They believe they are responsible for their behavior, and feedback showing they have produced effects reinforces these feelings. The perception of personal causation motivates behavior. Origins engage in activities they value and they believe that outcomes will be consistent with their expectations. In contrast, pawns believe that causes of behavior are beyond their control and reside in external forces or the behaviors of others. Pawns typically have feelings of powerlessness and ineffectiveness and perceive situations as threatening. A low perception of personal causation inhibits behavior. Pawn feelings are self-fulfilling; low motivation leads to avoidance of activities, and the lack of involvement retards development of skills that help people deal better with environmental events.

Similar to Rotter's internal-external distinction, origin feelings reflect intrinsically motivated behavior, whereas pawn perceptions place the locus of causality outside of oneself. Origins set realistic goals for themselves, know their strengths and weaknesses, determine actions that they can take to accomplish their goals, and assess their goal progress. One problem with the origin-pawn distinction is that it oversimplifies the explanation of intrinsic motivation. People typically are not wholly one or the other, but rather may shift their perceptions depending on the context. This point notwithstanding, de Charms's principles are highly germane to classrooms. We now discuss some programs that have been used to help people develop origin beliefs.

Personal Causation Training

De Charms (1976) describes a longitudinal program in which teachers were trained in ways to foster origin behaviors in students. Teacher training included self-study of academic motivation, realistic goal setting, development of concrete plans to accomplish goals, and evaluation of goal progress. Following the training, teachers worked with students. Methods to induce origin behaviors were integrated with academic activities. Classroom exercises were designed to enhance achievement motivation, self-concept, realistic goal setting, and personal responsibility. For example, teachers taught realistic goal setting by having students choose easy, moderate, or difficult words to learn to spell. To teach personal responsibility, teachers had students write imaginative achievement motivation stories from supplied skeleton plots (e.g., write a story about a hero trying to do something better than she or he did it before).

Students demonstrated significant increases in origin behaviors as a consequence of the training and this increase was maintained over time. In contrast, control students who received the regular curriculum from nontrained teachers demonstrated no change in origin behaviors. Over a 2-year period, training stopped the trend among low achievers to fall increasingly behind peers in school achievement. The training also reduced student absenteeism and tardiness and positively affected teachers' motivation. De Charms (1984) reports similar results from other efforts to enhance origin behaviors in students.

Alderman (1985) applied goal setting and self-evaluation to a senior high girls' physical education class. Students evaluated their health, physical fitness status, competence, and interest in different activities, and also set fitness goals. Weekly self-tests were given in aerobics, flexibility, strength, and posture. At the end of the first grading period, students set goals for the final exam. Students had some choices of ways to accomplish the aerobic goal (running, walking, jumping rope). The teacher met with students to assess goals and made suggestions if these did not seem realistic. Students established practice schedules of at least three times a week for 9 weeks and kept a record of practices. Following the final exam, students completed a self-evaluation of what they had learned.

Several points can be gleaned from these interventions. First, fostering origin behaviors in students requires that teachers believe they themselves are origins and that they can stimulate similar behaviors in students (de Charms, 1984). Another point is that origin training requires teacher structure. Teachers need to present students with possibilities and have students make choices, but teachers must decide what the range of choices will be. An origin classroom is not an unstructured classroom where students decide what they will work on and when they will do it. A third point is that personal responsibility must be developed. Once students make a choice, they must live with the consequences of that choice. One means of teaching personal responsibility is by helping students place greater emphasis on effort as a cause of outcomes and not to blame others when they fail or to believe they were lucky when they succeed. As students experience success, they should develop higher self-efficacy and believe they have control over the attainment of their academic goals.

Implications for Teachers

The following examples illustrate a number of strategies that can be used in the classroom in order to teach personal responsibility.

1. Model personal responsibility and believe you can develop it in students. Ms. Smith always organizes books and materials, cleans the board, picks up trash, and straightens her desk at the end of each class period. Her room looks neat and it is easy for students to find books and materials that are needed for each activity. She also works with her students to straighten and organize their own materials for each activity.

Mr. Anderson was working with his debate class to foster open, active group discussions. He wanted to encourage a free exchange of ideas and eliminate the need to raise hands. He never interrupted a student who was sharing and he accepted each student's response as a valuable contribution.

2. Provide students with options to choose from and have them consider the consequences of each choice. A high school counselor was working with small groups of students on course selections for the next semester. She explained the demands of each class and reviewed grade points and unit totals necessary for graduation. She had each student select three possible class loads and then meet with her to discuss the pros and cons of each option.

Mr. Elledge, a middle school principal, was working with a student to develop a program to help him with his aggressive behavior. First, Mr. Elledge asked the student to share some of the problems he was having in the classroom. Then they discussed various ways to handle those situations and what the consequences of each solution might be.

3. Foster internal attributions. Do not allow students to blame others for their failures or attribute successes to luck. Mr. Love meets with his students individually to go over the results of each unit test. While looking at each section of the test, he discusses with the students why they felt they had done well or poorly and what they might have done differently to have prepared and performed better.

Ms. Valentine had a kindergarten student who loved to work with blocks, but when he built something and it fell over, he always started crying and told her someone had knocked it down. Ms. Valentine had him talk to her while he was building. If the structure fell over, she would ask him why he thought it fell and help him figure out how he might build it next time to keep it from falling. When he succeeded with a structure, she praised him, letting him know his hard work and persistence had helped him.

4. Have students set goals, periodically evaluate their progress, and decide if a change in strategy is necessary. Mr. Rhoads, a high school geometry teacher, uses small-group instruction, computer programs, and activity packets in his classroom. At the beginning of each geometry unit, Mr. Rhoads has each student list areas that need to be worked on from the previous unit and the new goals for the current unit. The last activity for each class period is for all students to complete an individual checklist that includes the progress they are making and how well they are doing with each computer assignment or class activity. Mr. Rhoads reviews the checklists each afternoon, makes comments related to progress, and sets up individual meetings with students who are having difficulty and need additional assistance or a change in activities.

Ms. Long has been working with one of her first-grade students to complete her work during the allocated time. Before Jill starts on her independent work each day, Ms. Long talks with her and they decide how much of each written assignment Jill thinks she can complete (trying to increase the amount every few days). Toward the end of each working period, Ms. Long checks with Jill to see how much she has done and if adjustments to the amount to be completed are needed. At the end of each period, Jill and Ms. Long record the goal and accomplishment for the day.

SELF-DETERMINATION

The views of de Charms (1968), Rotter (1966), White (1959), and Harter (1978) stress that motivation derives in part from the belief that individuals can exert control over their environment. A related perspective, which has been advanced by Deci, Ryan, Connell, and Skinner, postulates that humans have a need to be autonomous and engage in activities because they want to. In this section, we discuss this *self-determination* (autonomy) view of intrinsic motivation.

Assumptions

Deci and his colleagues (Deci, 1980; Deci & Ryan, 1985, 1991) distinguish self-determination from will. *Will* is "the capacity of the human organism to choose how to satisfy its needs" (Deci, 1980, p. 26). *Self-determination* is "the process of utilizing one's will" (Deci, 1980, p. 26). Self-determination requires that people accept their strengths and limitations, be cognizant of forces acting on them, make choices, and determine ways to satisfy needs. Will and self-determination are linked: To be self-determining, people have to decide how to act on their environment. Individuals would not be content if all their needs were automatically satisfied without them having choices and deciding how to attain those choices.

Intrinsic motivation is "the human need to be competent and self-determining in relation to the environment" (Deci, 1980, p. 27). The need for intrinsic motivation energizes people's wills, and the will uses the energy of intrinsic motivation to satisfy needs, resolve conflicts among competing needs, and hold needs in check. Intrinsic motivation is satisfied when an individual acts willfully. It is the *process* of self-determination that is intrinsically motivating rather than the underlying need of the manifested behavior. A person may have an inherent need to learn and may manifest it by reading books. Intrinsic motivation is satisfied when that person decides which books to read and when to read them, although the actual reading may provide further satisfaction. Deci's position reflects an organismic perspective because it postulates that these needs are present at birth and evolve with development.

Motivational Processes

Intrinsic motivation leads people to seek out and master challenges, which satisfies their needs to be competent and self-determining (Deci & Porac,

1978). Challenges need to be within students' reach. If challenges are too easy, they will seek more difficult ones; if too difficult, they may abandon their efforts. Intrinsic motivation will suffer when individuals cannot exercise self-determination. They want to feel responsible for their actions and free to make choices. Unfortunately, in many classrooms students have few choices about what to do and when and how to do it. Self-determination theory also predicts that intrinsic motivation will be diminished when individuals believe their actions are extrinsically determined (i.e., they are rewarded for engaging in an activity). We discuss the effects of rewards on intrinsic motivation later.

Perceived control is an important determinant of intrinsic motivation. Skinner, Wellborn, and Connell (1990) distinguish three types of beliefs that contribute to perceived control and that are important in school (see also Chapter 1). *Strategy beliefs* are expectations about factors that influence success in school, such as ability, effort, others, luck, or unknown factors (e.g., The best way for me to get good grades is to work hard.). *Capacity beliefs* refer to an individual's personal capabilities with respect to ability, effort, others, and luck (e.g., I can't seem to try very hard in school.). *Control beliefs* are expectations about an individual's likelihood of doing well in school without reference to specific means (e.g., I can do well in school if I want to.). Skinner and colleagues (Skinner et al., 1990) found that perceived control influences academic performance by promoting or decreasing active engagement in learning and that teachers contribute to students' perceptions of control by providing contingency (clear and consistent guidelines and feedback) and involvement (interest in and dedication of resources to students).

Research Evidence

Research has explored the relation of self-determination to intrinsic motivation (Ryan, 1993). Ryan and Grolnick (1986) had children complete de Charms's (1976) Origin Climate Questionnaire and measures of perceived competence, perceived control, and mastery motivation. The de Charms instrument measures perceptions of the origin (autonomy) versus pawn (control) orientation of the teacher and classroom. Children perceiving the environment as more origin-like reported greater internal control over outcomes and higher perceived competence and mastery motivation.

Research shows that choice affects intrinsic motivation (Swann & Pittman, 1977; Zuckerman, Porac, Lathin, Smith, & Deci, 1978). In the Zuckerman (Zuckerman et al., 1978) study, college students either chose puzzles to solve or were assigned puzzles that had been selected by other subjects. Students who chose puzzles displayed greater intrinsic motivation than did no-choice subjects. Swann and Pittman (1977) found that leading children to believe they had choice over play activities increased their intrinsic motivation.

Glass and Singer (1972) report experiments showing that when individuals feel they have control over their environment, they tolerate aversive stimuli better and perform at a higher level. Adults worked on tasks and periodically were exposed to a loud irritating noise. No-control subjects could not control the sound. Perceived direct-control subjects were told they could terminate the noise by pressing a button, but were advised not to press the button unless they needed to. Perceived indirect-control subjects were told that pressing a button would signal a confederate who could terminate the noise. The experimenter also advised these subjects not to press the button unless they needed to. Perceived control (direct or indirect) led to significantly longer persistence and fewer errors compared with no perceived control. Perceived-control subjects judged the noise as less aversive than did no-control subjects. In an interesting study, Rodin, Solomon, and Metcalf (1978) found that subjects who stood in front of an elevator's control panel reported feeling less crowded than subjects who stood away from the control panel, even though the elevator was equally crowded in the two conditions.

Deci and Ryan (1987) have summarized the research on the contextual features that support or curtail self-determination and intrinsic motivation. These features include the element of providing rewards that are controlling, such as rewards given to merely engage in an activity, which seem to decrease self-determination. Threats and deadlines also can curtail self-determination as they become more controlling and individuals feel compelled by the deadline rather than by interest in the activity. A third negative feature is evaluation and surveillance. Although a common characteristic of classrooms, in experimental studies, evaluation and surveillance have been shown to decrease interest and intrinsic motivation (Deci & Ryan, 1987). Two positive features that support self-determination are the amount of choice allowed and positive feedback regarding competence and efficacy. These five contextual features are all part of everyday life in classrooms and teachers need to be sensitive to how they can affect students' self-determination and intrinsic motivation, although it is unlikely that teachers can remove them completely.

Development of Self-Determination

Intrinsic motivation is an innate human need and begins in infants as an undifferentiated need for competence and self-determination (Deci & Porac, 1978). This organismic position is quite similar to that of White (1959). As children develop, the need differentiates into such specific areas as the need to achieve in academics, athletics, or manual activities. Which activities assume children's interest will depend on environmental interactions. "A child who is surrounded by artist-painters and is supported for engaging in various art endeavors is more likely to become intrinsically motivated toward art than is a person who has had no exposure to art until college" (Deci & Porac, 1978, p. 153).

An important aspect of development concerns the internalization of social values and mores (Deci & Ryan, 1991; Ryan, Connell, & Deci, 1985). In school, there are extrinsic structures, controls, and rewards that may not fit with the child's quest for self-determination but help to produce good behavior and desirable social functioning. Eventually, these extrinsic motivators may become internalized and part of the self-regulation process.

Deci and his colleagues (Rigby, Deci, Patrick, & Ryan, 1992) have recently conceptualized motivation along both intrinsic and extrinsic dimensions. Intrinsic motivation concerns activities that are *autotelic*—engaged in for their own sake—which by definition are self-determined. Extrinsic motivation involves a progression from behaviors that originally were extrinsically motivated but became internalized and now are self-determined. The first level includes what Deci and his colleagues call *external* regulation. For example, students initially may not want to work on math but do so to obtain teacher rewards and avoid punishment. There is very little self-determination in this situation. At the next level of extrinsic motivation, students may engage in a task because they think they should and may feel guilty if they don't do the task (e.g., study for an exam). Deci and his colleagues call this *introjected* regulation because the source of motivation is internal (feelings of "should," "ought," guilt) to the person but not self-determined since these feelings seem to be controlling the person. The third level is called *identified* regulation and here individuals engage in the activity because it is personally important to them. For example, a student may study hours for tests in order to get good grades to be accepted into college. This behavior represents the student's own goal, although the goal has more utility value (see Wigfield & Eccles, 1992; Chapter 8) than intrinsic value such as learning. The final level of extrinsic motivation is *integrated* regulation, whereby individuals can integrate various internal and external sources of information into their own self-schema and engage in behavior because of its importance to their sense of self. This final level is still instrumental, rather than autotelic as in intrinsic motivation, but integrated regulation does represent a form of self-determination and autonomy. As such, both intrinsic motivation and integrated regulation will result in more cognitive engagement and learning than external or introjected regulation (Rigby et al., 1992).

Deci and his colleagues' (Rigby et al., 1992) position is thought-provoking, has generated much research, and has important implications for educational practice. Many points in the self-determination model are not clearly specified, but researchers increasingly are conducting studies that are adding to our understanding of how this theory can be applied in the classroom.

EXTRINSIC REWARDS AND INTRINSIC MOTIVATION

Earlier we mentioned four sources of intrinsic motivation (Lepper & Hodell, 1989): challenge, curiosity, control, and fantasy. The perspectives on intrinsic motivation we have discussed support the importance of these sources. Despite their differences, the various perspectives contend that intrinsic motivation is a strong and positive force in people's lives.

We typically think of intrinsic motivation as growing and developing, but it also can diminish. Much research has shown that engaging in an intrinsically interesting activity to obtain an extrinsic reward can undermine intrinsic motivation (Lepper & Greene, 1978). This finding is distressing and has important implications for education because of the prevalence of rewards. In this section, we examine the theory and research and discuss ways that rewards can be used productively to enhance and maintain student motivation.

Experimental Findings

An early study by Lepper, Greene, and Nisbett (1973) provided evidence for the detrimental effects of rewards on intrinsic motivation. The subjects were preschool children who spent a high percentage of time drawing during free play. The experimenter took children individually and asked them to draw. Expected-award children were shown a good player certificate and told they could win one by drawing. After they drew, they were told they had done well and were given the certificate. Unexpected-award subjects were not informed about the certificate, but after they drew, they were given the same feedback and certificate. This condition controlled for any effect due to receiving a reward. No-award children drew with no mention of a certificate and were not given one at the end, which controlled for any effect due to drawing. Two weeks later, children again were observed during free play to determine the percentage of time spent drawing.

Expected-award children spent less time drawing during the postexperimental phase compared with the pretest baseline phase; pretest-to-posttest changes of the other groups were nonsignificant. Compared with the other conditions, expected-award subjects spent less time drawing during the postexperimental phase. The investigators also rated the quality of the drawings children made during the experimental session. The three conditions did not differ in number of pictures drawn, but the quality of expected-award subjects' pictures was lower than the quality of pictures drawn by children in the other conditions. Similar results have been obtained in several studies using different subject populations (children, adolescents, adults), types of rewards (monetary, social), and target activities (Lepper & Greene, 1978).

The *salience* of the reward also may be important. Ross (1975) offered preschoolers a prize for playing a drum (an intrinsically interesting activity). For some subjects, no further mention was made of the reward, others (salient reward condition) were told that the reward was in a nearby box and they could have it at the conclusion of the study, and control children were neither offered nor given a reward. Salient-reward subjects displayed less subsequent interest in playing the drum compared with the other two conditions. In a second study, preschoolers were promised a reward for playing with drums. Some subjects were told to think about the reward as they engaged in the activity (salient condition), others were told to think about something else (distraction condition), and those in a control condition were not given thinking instructions. Relative to the salient and control conditions, distraction subjects showed more interest in playing with drums.

Overjustification

To explain the preceding findings and other similar ones, Lepper and his colleagues advanced the *overjustification* hypothesis: Working at an intrinsically interesting task under conditions that make it clear that the activity is a means to an end can diminish subsequent intrinsic motivation (Lepper, 1981, 1983; Lepper & Greene, 1978; Lepper & Hodell, 1989). When people work on a task to obtain a reward, they are likely to view their behavior as extrinsically motivated. Offering people a reward to work on a task they enjoy provides more than adequate justification for (overjustifies) their participation. When the reward contingency is no longer in effect, people lose their justification and motivation for working on the task. When people work in the absence of external conditions that could explain their participation, they should believe their actions reflect their interests. They engage in the task because they want to, not because they have to. Rather than being a means to an end, the task is an end by itself. Such intrinsic motivation is likely to sustain itself in the future.

This overjustification explanation derives from cognitive dissonance theory (Chapter 2). Cognitive dissonance research often explored reactions of subjects who were led to act in ways that contradicted their beliefs. Studies showed that the less clear or powerful the external pressures put on individuals to behave contrary to their beliefs, the more likely they are to internalize the contrary behavior and alter their beliefs (Lepper & Greene, 1978). Cognitive dissonance research findings were reinterpreted by Bem (1967, 1972), who emphasized self-perception (or self-attribution; see Chapter 4). Bem postulated that people's attitudes toward an activity are determined in part by their perceptions of why they are engaging in it. Individuals are likely to attribute their actions to external factors when those factors are clear and sufficient to explain the actions and to internal factors when external forces are unclear or insufficient to explain actions. From an attributional standpoint, students attribute their actions to rewards when they are offered for performance and to their own desires when extrinsic rewards are absent or too weak to justify task participation.

Cognitive Evaluation Theory

Whether the overjustification hypothesis best explains the negative effects of offering rewards on intrinsic motivation is debatable. An alternative explanation, which overlaps somewhat with the overjustification view, derives from cognitive evaluation theory (Deci, 1975; Deci & Porac, 1978). According to Deci (1975),

Every reward (including feedback) has two aspects, a controlling aspect and an informational aspect which provides the recipient with information about his competence and self-determination. The relative salience of the two aspects determines which process will be operative. If the controlling aspect is more salient, it will initiate the change in perceived locus of causality process. If the informational aspect is more salient, the change in feelings of competence and self-determination process will be initiated. (p. 142)

All rewards have the potential to control and to inform and the relative salience or weight of each aspect determines the effect on intrinsic motivation. Rewards control behavior when they are given contingent on individuals accomplishing a given task or performing at a certain level. Thus, teachers tell students they can have free time after they finish their work, supervisors tell employees they will get a pay raise if they boost company profits, parents tell children they can have dessert once they eat all of their dinner. When people view rewards as controlling their behavior (they believe they are acting the way they are in order to earn the reward), they attribute their actions to factors outside of themselves (e.g., the reward) and they lose a sense of self-determination. Once the reward contingency is no longer in effect, there is nothing compelling them to work at the activity so their interest declines.

Rewards also convey information about one's skills or competence when they are linked to actual performance or progress, such as when teachers praise students for learning new skills or acquiring new knowledge, supervisors give workers merit raises for performing better than others, and parents buy children toys for keeping their room neat. People who derive such performance information from rewards feel efficacious and experience self-determination. Interest is sustained even when the reward contingency is removed because people place the locus of causality of behavior inside themselves (e.g., desire to learn).

Research studies have shown that such factors as task-contingent rewards (rewards given for working on tasks regardless of level of performance), offers to receive good player awards, deadlines, imposed goals, avoidance of unpleasant stimuli, surveillance, and social evaluation can diminish intrinsic motivation (Cameron & Pierce, 1994; Deci & Ryan, 1991; Morgan, 1984). In contrast, intrinsic motivation is maintained or enhanced when people are offered choices or allowed to work in an environment perceived as supporting autonomy rather than as controlling (Deci & Ryan, 1991). Positive feedback that enhances perceived competence also raises intrinsic motivation (Deci, Vallerand, Pelletier, & Ryan, 1991).

Schunk (1983d) tested the idea that reward structure affects self-efficacy, motivation, and skill acquisition. Some children were offered rewards based on their level of problem solving (performance-contingent rewards), others were offered rewards for working on the task regardless of level of performance (task-contingent rewards), and children in a control group were not offered rewards. Performance-contingent rewards led to the highest skill, motivation, and self-efficacy. Task-contingent rewards resulted in no benefits compared with not offering rewards.

Enhancing Intrinsic Motivation

The preceding discussion focuses on the detrimental effects of rewards on high intrinsic motivation, but in school there are many students who have low intrinsic motivation and an important goal for teachers is to raise motivation. Enhancing motivation requires that rewards be linked with the development of students' competencies. Rewards tied to skill acquisition (e.g., points given based on mastery of skills) inform students that they are developing competence and raise self-efficacy (Cameron & Pierce, 1994; Morgan, 1984; Schunk, 1991b).

Such other classroom factors as goals and attributional feedback also convey information about capabilities and raise self-efficacy and motivation, as we discussed in preceding chapters. Investigators increasingly are exploring how to structure instructional and social factors to optimize intrinsic motivation. To enhance intrinsic motivation, attention must be given to the four sources mentioned at the beginning of this chapter: challenge, curiosity, control, and fantasy (Lepper & Hodell, 1989).

Challenge.   Activities that challenge students' skills may be intrinsically motivating (Deci, 1975; Harter, 1978; White, 1959). Challenging activities are intermediate in level of difficulty, and as students develop skills, difficulty level must be adjusted upward to maintain this intermediate level. Attainment of challenging goals conveys to learners that they are becoming more competent, which raises self-efficacy and perceived control over outcomes. In turn, learners are apt to set new challenging goals, which serves to maintain intrinsic motivation.

Curiosity.   Curiosity is elicited by activities that present students with information or ideas that are discrepant from their present knowledge or beliefs and that appear surprising or incongruous (Berlyne, 1960, 1963; Hunt, 1963; Lepper & Hodell, 1989). Such incongruities prompt students to seek information and resolve the discrepancy. As with challenge, moderate discrepancies are most effective because they are easily incorporated into an individual's mental framework; large discrepancies may be rapidly discounted.

Control.   Activities that provide students with a sense of control over their academic outcomes may enhance intrinsic motivation (de Charms, 1968; Deci, 1980). Allowing students choices in activities and a say in establishing rules and procedures fosters perceptions of control. In contrast, students are not motivated to engage in activities when they believe their actions bear little relationship to outcomes. A perceived lack of control is associated with learned helplessness (Chapter 4).

Fantasy.   Intrinsic motivation can be promoted with activities that involve learners in fantasy and make-believe through simulations and games that present them with situations not actually present (Lepper & Hodell, 1989). By identifying with fictional characters, students can derive vicarious pleasure not ordinarily available to them. As shown in Figure 7.2, gamelike elements can add meaning to what might otherwise be a boring activity. Fantasy may portray out-of-school situations to which school learning can be applied and thereby reinforce teachers' instructions to students about the usefulness of learning. Students who place greater value on learning are likely to be more intrinsically motivated in the activity.

There also is evidence that fantasy can enhance learning compared with instruction presented without fantasy elements. Parker and Lepper (1992) conducted two studies with third- and fourth-grade students. In one study, students were taught computer graphics programming whereby they received instruction both in straightforward fashion and embellished with fantasy contexts involving pirates, detectives, or astronauts. Students preferred the fantasy to the traditional context. In a second study, children received computer instruction and were assigned to an individualized-fantasy, assigned-fantasy, or no-fantasy condition. The two fantasy conditions had fantasy elements incorporated into instruction. Individualized-fantasy students selected their fantasy context; assigned-fantasy students had their contexts assigned by the experimenter in the same proportion as fantasies chosen by children in the individualized group. The results showed greater learning by students in the

Figure 7.2.   Fractions task presented in traditional format (*top*) and gamelike format (*bottom*)

$$1/2 + 1/4 = ?$$

Note: Player 1 dribbles ball from end to mid-court and passes ball to player 2. Player 2 dribbles ball to where player 3 is and passes to player 3, who shoots basket. Down what fraction of the court did the players dribble?

fantasy conditions compared with children assigned to the no-fantasy condition. Fantasy contexts also produced generalization; these students showed better general understanding of geometric concepts.

Lepper and Malone (1987) discuss mechanisms whereby greater interest in learning activities may translate into better learning. These mechanisms involve focusing the learner's attention on relevant features of the learning context and increasing cognitive effort in the learning activity. By their very nature, many fantasy elements ought to focus learners' attention and increase mental effort. A caveat is in order, however, because it is imperative that motivational embellishments be relevant to the task and not overly distracting (Lepper & Hodell, 1989). Nonrelevant features or those that distract will not enhance students' mental effort in relevant task features and may convey that students lack control over outcomes, both of which do not enhance intrinsic motivation. Computer programs with such motivational enhancements as lights and noises that are only loosely linked to what learners do quickly lose their motivational appeal and are distracting. If the enhancements are contingent on learner progress in skill acquisition, then they convey that learners are developing competence, which builds intrinsic motivation.

Implications for Teachers

The following examples illustrate a number of strategies that can be used to incorporate sources of intrinsic motivation in classroom activities.

*1. **Challenge:** Challenge students' skills with activities of intermediate difficulty. Ensure that students do not become bored with easy tasks or reluctant to work on tasks perceived as overly difficult.* Ms. Logan, a middle school math teacher, pretests all of her students at the beginning of each unit. After analyzing the results of the test, she plans small-group and individual activities that will challenge each student but are attainable.

Mr. Armstrong uses cooperative groups often in his sixth-grade social studies class. When he places students in the group initially and works with each group to assign various tasks, he makes sure that each child is involved and responsible for a challenging yet attainable task.

*2. **Curiosity:** Present ideas slightly discrepant from learners' existing knowledge and beliefs. Incorporate surprise and incongruity into classroom activities.* Mrs. Watkins, a high school teacher, told her history class that she wants them to develop their own test for the next unit. As they read through the assigned reading for the unit, they are to develop relevant activities and make a list of possible questions for the end-of-unit test. Each student contributes to developing the unit and the test, working individually, in small groups, and as a whole class.

Mr. Adams, a sixth-grade science teacher, had each group of students in his class build a replica of a volcano out of clay, mud, and twigs. Then he gave each group the correct proportions of baking soda and vinegar to simulate the eruption. After each group experimented with their volcanoes, he introduced a unit on mixing and reactions of various substances and chemicals. At the end of the unit, each group repeated the project and explained why the volcano had erupted.

3. ***Control:*** *Allow students choices in activities and a voice in formulating rules and procedures. Foster attributions to causes over which they have some control.* At the beginning of each school year Mr. Tilley helps his fourth-grade class develop the classroom rules and create a list of rewards and consequences for following or breaking the rules.

Mrs. Hicks, a middle school assistant principal, worked with the Student Council to develop extracurricular spectator rules of conduct. She let the students work in groups of three to brainstorm areas that each group felt should be addressed. The entire Student Council then evaluated each group's suggestions and developed overall guidelines and consequences.

4. ***Fantasy:*** *Engage students in make-believe activities, games, and simulations. Ensure that the motivational embellishments are task relevant and not too distracting.* Mr. Hopkins, a fifth-grade teacher, portrays presidents from the past with costume and voice. He periodically dresses as one of the former presidents (e.g., Washington, Lincoln) and tells about his life as if he were that president. He makes sure that he does an outstanding job of portraying the character so that the students learn about the life of the individual and are not just fascinated with the costume and voice.

Mrs. Littlejohn, a second-grade teacher, often uses cooking in the classroom to reinforce skills in measurement and following directions. She always emphasizes the importance of both to ensure that the students are learning and not just playing during the activity.

EMERGENT MOTIVATION

Perspectives on intrinsic motivation emphasize such qualities as perceived control, the desire for autonomy, and the need to master the environment. A perspective on intrinsic motivation closely aligned with these others has been advanced by Csikszentmihalyi (1975; Csikszentmihalyi & Rathunde, 1993) and is referred to as *emergent motivation*, which denotes motivation stemming from the discovery of new goals and rewards as a consequence of interacting with the environment. As Csikszentmihalyi (1978) states,

> When small children begin to play with building blocks, they rarely have a plan or a goal to guide their actions. They will place the blocks more or less randomly next to or on top of each other until some combination of shapes suggests a particular form that the children will then seek to approximate—at this point we

might say that they have a "goal" or plan to direct their actions. This goal will typically change with every new block they place along the others, as new possibilities are suggested by the developing structure. The reward that keeps the children going is the feedback that tells how closely they are able to match what they do with what they want to do. . . . Neither the goal nor the rewards could be specified in advance, because both emerge out of the interaction. (p. 207)

Csikszentmihalyi believes that behavior is governed by intrinsic and extrinsic motivational forces. Extrinsic forces are preprogrammed biologically (e.g., food, sleep) or derive from the reward structure in which the individual is socialized (money, prestige). Intrinsic forces grow out of the individual's belief that a given outcome is worth striving for.

Intrinsic Rewards and Flow

Csikszentmihalyi (1985) studied individuals who engaged in intrinsically motivating activities and found that their experiences reflected complete involvement with the activities. This involvement, or *flow*, is defined as "the holistic sensation that people feel when they act with total involvement" (Csikszentmihalyi, 1985, p. 36). The relation of flow to other human motives is shown in Figure 7.3. The dimensions in this two-by-two classification are closed- versus open-system goals and intra- versus interindividual processes. Closed goals are those determined by genetics (needs) or socialization; open goals develop as a result of experience and cannot be explained by pre-existing factors.

Figure 7.3. Relation of emergent motivation to other motives. (Adapted from Csikszentmihalyi, 1985)

	Primarily intra-individual processes	*Primarily inter-individual processes*
Primarily closed systemic goals	*Needs* Hunger Thirst Safety Optimal activation, etc.	*Socialization* Sex Affiliation Achievement Presented life theme
Primarily open systemic goals	*Emergent Motives* Intrinsic motivation Flow Self-development Discovered life theme	*Cultivation* Values Social goals Identification Ideologies, etc.

Interindividual processes are social in nature, whereas intraindividual processes refer to the person. Flow is a personal process and reflects open systemic goals. It is analogous to Maslow's growth motivation and Rogers's concept of the fully functioning individual (see Chapters 2 and 6).

Individuals experiencing flow are so intensely involved with a task that they may lose awareness of time and space. They also seek a flow experience for itself rather than for anticipated rewards. Although flow can be experienced with any activity, it is more likely to occur with activities that allow for free expression and creativity such as games, play, and art. De Charms's (1968) origin state shares many elements with flow. In extreme form, individuals forsake a traditional lifestyle and most contingent material rewards to engage in activities that provide flow.

Figure 7.4 portrays a model of the flow state. Flow represents a state of equilibrium between the amount of challenge in activities and an individual's capabilities. People feel bored when their perceived skills exceed their opportunities for using them; they become anxious when they believe that challenges exceed capabilities. Flow can vary in intensity, with the critical variable being the ratio of challenge to skill. The portrayed relations presumably hold for peak as well as everyday experiences.

Research on Flow

Despite being nebulous, the notion of flow makes intuitive sense. Csikszentmihalyi (1982) describes a research study in which the Experience Sampling Method was employed (a self-report measure; see Chapter 1). Adults carried beepers that sounded several times a week, at which time subjects rated themselves on two dependent variables: affect (comprising items "happy," "cheerful," "sociable") and activation (comprising "active," "alert," "strong"). Subjects also judged their situation for challenges present and skills available. The amount of time individuals judged themselves to be in flow (defined as challenges and skills present and equal to one another) was related positively to affect and activation.

Figure 7.4. The flow state
From "Toward a Psychology of Optimal Experience" by M. Csikszentmihalyi in *Review of Personality and Social Psychology* (Vol. 3, p. 17) edited by L. Wheeler, 1982, Beverly Hills, CA: Sage Publications. Copyright © 1982 by Sage Publications, Inc. Reprinted by permission of Sage Publications, Inc.

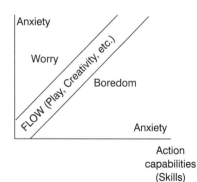

Mayers (reported in Csikszentmihalyi, 1982) had high school students rate school subjects and activities on challenge and skill (Figure 7.5). Favorite activities fell into the flow area (challenge = skill): TV and music listening (low on each); friends (moderate); and arts, such as drama or ballet, and sports (high on each). Skills were judged to exceed challenges in humanities and social sciences, resulting in boredom. Challenges were rated as exceeding skills in mathematics and the sciences, resulting in anxiety.

Other research compared the flow experiences of three groups of adolescents. One group attended a select public school in Italy, a second group attended a typical suburban high school near Chicago, and a third group comprised talented math students from a top Chicago public school (Csikszentmihalyi, 1985). Students used the Experience Sampling Method. The Italian teens reported more flow experiences than U.S. teens, especially those talented in math. Among U.S. teens, those attending the typical school reported more time in flow than the talented ones. The talented U.S. sample reported the most amounts of boredom (skills exceed challenges) and anxiety (challenges exceed skills). Interestingly, the talented group scored significantly lower than the other two samples in apathy, defined as skills and challenges in sync but below average (e.g., watching TV, listening to music). In sum, experiences are comparable for average and above average students across cultures, whereas for talented U.S. teens, flow and apathy are rarer and boredom and anxiety more common.

These findings have implications for teaching and learning because they highlight the importance of ensuring that challenges and skills are in balance and sufficiently high to counter apathy. Unfortunately, many school activities do not challenge students. The suggestions given in this chapter of ways to enhance students' choices, challenges, and perceived capabilities are relevant. Flow will suffer when students have few opportunities to structure their environments in ways that might maximize flow, such as by establishing challenging goals and mastering difficult tasks that build beliefs in their capabilities.

Figure 7.5. Ratings of school subjects and activities on challenges and skills

From "Toward a Psychology of Optimal Experience" by M. Csikszentmihalyi in *Review of Personality and Social Psychology* (Vol. 3, p. 18) edited by L. Wheeler, 1982, Beverly Hills, CA: Sage Publications. Copyright © 1982 by Sage Publications, Inc. Reprinted by permission of Sage Publications, Inc.

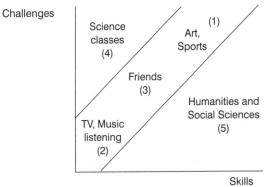

SUMMARY

Intrinsic motivation is motivation to engage in an activity for its own sake; extrinsic motivation is motivation to engage in an activity as a means to an end. Intrinsic motivation is contextual and refers to how people view activities, and it can vary over time and with changes in circumstances. Different levels of intrinsic and extrinsic motivation can exist within individuals at a given time. The constructs are not conceptually distinct and each may range on separate continuums from high to low. There is evidence that intrinsic motivation can promote learning and achievement better than extrinsic motivation.

Early views of intrinsic motivation explained it in terms of a developmental phenomenon or as dependent upon arousal and incongruity. White discussed effectance motivation to feel competent and interact productively with the environment. The effectance motive presumably is undifferentiated in young children but becomes specialized with development. Berlyne believed that people are intrinsically motivated to maintain an optimal level of arousal. Hunt felt that intrinsic motivation stemmed from incongruity between prior and new experiences. These views are important but are too general in nature to be applicable to school settings.

Harter formulated a theory of mastery motivation that refined the effectance motivation construct and specified its antecedents and consequences. Harter believed that the content and operation of the mastery motive change with development. Harter's model also considers success and failure experiences. Important variables are degree of challenge of tasks, rewards, socializing agents, need for approval, perceived competence, and internalization of mastery goals. Harter believes that intrinsic motivation comprises a preference for challenge, incentive to work to satisfy one's curiosity, independent mastery attempts, independent judgment, and internal criteria for success and failure.

Many perspectives stress the role of perceived control over outcomes as an integral component of intrinsic motivation. Rotter proposed that people differ in locus of control, or whether they believe that outcomes generally occur independently of how they behave (external control) or usually are contingent on their behaviors (internal control). De Charms discussed personal causation, or an individual's initiation of behavior intended to alter the environment. According to de Charms, people can act like origins, who perceive their behavior as determined by their own choosing, or as pawns, who believe that behavior is determined by external forces beyond their control.

A related perspective postulates that humans have a need to be autonomous and engage in activities they desire. This self-determination view of Deci and his colleagues postulates that individuals have a need to make decisions about how to act. Intrinsic motivation leads them to seek and master challenges that are optimal given their capabilities. Motivation suffers when people cannot exercise self-determination. Perceived control—comprised of strategy, capacity, and control beliefs—is an important determinant of intrinsic motivation. Intrinsic motivation is an innate need and differentiates with development through internalization of values and self-regulatory influences.

Much educational research has explored the role of extrinsic rewards on intrinsic motivation. Although there are exceptions, the general finding is that the offer of a reward to perform an intrinsically interesting task leads to a decrease in intrinsic motivation. Lepper and his colleagues formulated the overjustification hypothesis: Engaging in an intrinsically interesting activity under conditions that make it obvious that the activity is a means to an end can diminish subsequent intrinsic interest because offering a reward justifies task participation. When the reward contingency is no longer in effect, people lose their motivation. Deci postulates that every reward has controlling and informational aspects. Rewards control behavior when they are given contingent on individuals accomplishing a given task or performing at a certain level. Controlling rewards lead people to attribute their behaviors to external factors and to lose a sense of self-determination. Rewards are informational when they are linked to actual level of performance or progress. Informational rewards lead to feelings of self-efficacy and a sense of self-determination, both of which enhance intrinsic motivation.

Students' intrinsic motivation can be affected by four sources: challenge, curiosity, control, and fantasy. Activities are intrinsically motivating when they challenge students' skills, present information or ideas that are discrepant from students' present knowledge and beliefs and that appear surprising or incongruous, provide students with a sense of control over outcomes, and involve learners in fantasy and make-believe through simulations and games that present situations not actually present.

A perspective on intrinsic motivation highly relevant in education is Csik-szentmihalyi's emergent motivation, which refers to motivation stemming from the discovery of new goals and rewards as a consequence of interacting with the environment. Emergent motivation grows out of the belief that an outcome is worth striving for. The ideal state is flow, or the holistic sensation that people feel when they act with total involvement. People experiencing flow are so intensely involved with a task that they may lose awareness of time or space. Flow is often found with activities allowing for free expression and creativity, and it represents a state of equilibrium between the amount of challenge in activities and an individual's capabilities. Unfortunately, many students feel bored in classes because their perceived skills exceed their opportunities for using them.

The Role of Values, Interest, and Affect

*S*everal high school teachers are talking in the lunch room about one of their favorite topics—student motivation. The teachers have somewhat different views about motivation, but they all are concerned that their students just do not have much motivation for schoolwork.

Ms. Garcia: *I'm really worried. None of my students have any interest in math. They just don't care about anything to do with school. They just don't have the right values. All they care about are their girlfriends or boyfriends, MTV, and having a good time partying. I really think that song about sex, drugs, and rock and roll describes kids pretty accurately when they get to the high school.*

Mr. Anderman: *Well, I don't know. I have some kids who at least care about their grades. They might not be too interested in math, but they do think it's important to get good grades so they can go to college.*

Mr. Lopez: *Well, at least you have those high-track kids. They would care about things like grades. The kids I have in the lower track math classes are not interested and don't think it's that important. But, I do try to show them that math can be useful to them in their own lives. I talk about computing interest rates on new car loans or how taxes can affect their paychecks. They at least see the utility of some of what I'm trying to teach. They start to value some of this basic business math when I can make the connections for them.*

Mr. Anderman: *Yes, but sometimes some of my kids get so wound up about going on to college and making sure they get into the best one that they get so nervous they bomb the test. You can just see them getting all anxious before the test, and then during the test, you can see them wriggling around, sweating, looking all panicky. Some of them make themselves sick with nerves. Some of my best students have trouble on the tests. They will do great on the homework but then really blow it on the test. I don't know what to do with them.*

Ms. Garcia: *Well, I have some like that, too. They don't seem too interested in the math, but they do get anxious for a test. I just try to make them feel good about themselves. You know that is the biggest thing for all adolescents—they need all the positive strokes and self-esteem we can give them. They are dealing with so many things, it's no wonder they have self-esteem problems. I just wish they would get more interested in school.*

Mr. Lopez: *Well, I don't know if that's all there is to it. I think self-esteem is important, but there is more to motivation than that. I used to be really nervous before tests, too. I would think I was prepared because I could do the problems correctly on homework assignments, but then once I started on the test, it seemed like I couldn't do the problems. I would start to think, Oh no, I'm going to fail this test, I'm going to flunk out, my parents will really be mad at me then. I would look around and everyone else seemed to be just working away, doing fine, which would just make me more nervous. It was so hard to concentrate. Eventually, I had a teacher who helped me. He showed me some tricks to help me control my nerves. He also helped me see that if I did do poorly, it was not due to being a stupid Latino, like some of the other teachers used to say. He helped me see that I did have the ability to do math. In fact, he's probably the reason I went on to be a math teacher. Now, I try to help my students the same way he helped me and it is not just by giving them positive strokes, or warm fuzzies, or trying to raise their self-esteem. I have high standards and try to make sure my students have the skills to meet them. They will feel better about themselves if they can actually do the math problems than if I just tell them how great they are. They can spot a phony right away and they think, just like Holden Caulfield, that most adults are phonies, so they don't need their teachers to be that way.*

The research discussed in this chapter concerns a variety of motivational constructs that have been linked to student learning and achievement. We will discuss the various values that students can have toward schoolwork. We will also discuss one of the most common explanations for motivation—the role of interest. Finally, although many motivational models do not include emotions and affect, we discuss anxiety, self-worth, and attributionally driven emotions in the last sections of this chapter. Given the diversity of constructs, this chapter is not organized around one theoretical perspective like many of the other chapters in this book, but it includes most of the current models of values, interest, and affect.

VALUES IN EXPECTANCY-VALUE ACHIEVEMENT MOTIVATION MODELS

As evidenced by the comments of Ms. Garcia and Mr. Anderman, one of the most common and intuitive notions of motivation involves values, the idea that people will only be motivated when they are interested in or care about the activity or believe it is important to them or their goals. In earlier motivational models such as Lewin's (1935), the term *valence* was used to signify the value a person attached to an object in the environment. In Lewin's theory, an object acquired valence because it satisfied a need of the person given the range of other objects in the environment. For example, if a person is hungry, then food objects will have more positive valence than other objects in the environment (TV, work, books, other people) because food will satisfy the current need (Weiner, 1992). In the same fashion, in a classroom setting, the company of other students might have more positive valence for an individual who has high social interaction "needs" than would academic work. This highly social individual would tend to approach other students more and avoid the academic work. Once the social needs had been satisfied, then other objects might acquire a positive valence and the student would tend to approach them.

Building on Lewin's notion of valence, Atkinson (1957, 1964) included a term for value in his mathematical model of achievement motivation, which he called *incentive value*. Recall that in Atkinson's model, the motivation to approach success was defined as

$$\text{Motive for success} = \text{Achievement motive} \times \text{Probability of success} \times \text{Incentive value}$$

In earlier chapters, we noted that the achievement motive was defined as a stable, relatively enduring personal trait of striving for success and taking pride in accomplishments. In Chapter 3, we discussed the expectancy construct—probability of success—which was assumed to be more situation specific and represented the individual's expectation for success at a task, given the overall difficulty of the task. Incentive value also was assumed to be more situation specific and reflect the attractiveness of the task and pride taken in doing the task as a function of task difficulty. Tasks that are too easy usually do not generate much pride in accomplishment or seem very attractive, whereas difficult but manageable tasks do seem attractive and generate more pride and self-worth when individuals are successful (Weiner, 1992; Wigfield & Eccles, 1992). Thus, incentive value covaries inversely with task difficulty. In addition, probability of success covaries inversely with task difficulty, obviously with easy tasks having higher probability of success than harder tasks. Given these relations, Atkinson was able to logically define incentive value as 1.0 minus the probability for success. This relation means that incentive value will be higher for tasks where probability of success is lower; that is, people will tend to value more difficult tasks in comparison to easier tasks.

Although this inverse relation between incentive value and probability of success is logical and also makes intuitive sense, by defining incentive value as 1.0 minus probability of success, Atkinson made probability of success the component that had to be determined in his mathematical model (along with motive for success, of course). In effect, as Wigfield and Eccles (1992) point out, this equation "removed" incentive value from the model and researchers did not have to measure incentive value as long as they could determine the probability of success. Incentive value would simply be 1.0 minus whatever the probability of success was determined to be. This convention led to the long-standing focus on probability and expectation for success in most research on achievement motivation. Incentive value was ignored in empirical research for the most part until relatively recently (Parsons & Goff, 1978; Wigfield & Eccles, 1992).

Several researchers working within the expectancy-value tradition, however, did examine the value component of motivation in early work. Battle (1965, 1966) developed the term *attainment value* and defined it as "the importance to the individual of achievement in a given task . . . [that] should determine the length of his persistence in working at it" (Battle, 1965, p. 209). Battle also distinguished between absolute attainment value, which referred to the importance of the task overall, and relative attainment value, which referred to the importance of the task relative to other tasks (Wigfield & Eccles, 1992). Battle (1965) found that both expectancies and attainment value were positively related to persistence on a math task in a sample of junior high school students. Crandall, Katkovsky, and Preston (1962) found that attainment value predicted early elementary students' choice of intellectual activities, especially for girls. In a second study that examined junior high students' actual performance in math and English, Battle (1966) showed that expectancies were more strongly related to performance than to relative attainment value or overall attainment value. This pattern of expectancies relating to actual performance and attainment value being more closely linked to choice or persistence also has been found in more recent research by Wigfield and Eccles and their colleagues (Wigfield & Eccles, 1992). However, Battle (1966) did show, contrary to Atkinson's model, that expectancy and attainment value were positively correlated with each other, not inversely related as suggested by the formula of incentive value being equal to 1.0 minus the probability of success. Accordingly, it seems that students tend to value tasks they expect to do well on and expect to do well on those tasks that they think are important (Wigfield & Eccles, 1992).

Feather (1982, 1988) also has been one of the main researchers in the expectancy-value tradition who has been concerned with the value side of the model. His model of values integrates Rokeach's (1979) general values with the more traditional achievement motivation expectancy-value constructs. Rokeach (1979) proposed a general model of values that defined values as "core conceptions of the desirable within every individual and society" (p. 2). These values guide cognition, motivation, and behavior by serving as general beliefs and standards against which to make judgments about which behaviors are desirable and should be approached and, by implication, which opposing values and behavior are undesirable and should be avoided. Rokeach (1979) discussed 18 terminal values, such as sense of accomplishment, wisdom, freedom, self-respect, comfortable life, mature love, world peace, inner harmony, and national security, that he believed represent life's ultimate goals. These terminal values are similar in many ways to the general needs and goals that were discussed in Chapter 6. He also proposed that there were 18 instrumental values, such as being ambitious, honest, intelligent, independent, courageous, loving, helpful, polite, obedient, clean, and self-controlled, that are modes of conduct for achieving the terminal values. It is interesting to note that the recent interest in teaching virtues in education (see Bennett, 1993) proposes some of the same values as Rokeach's instrumental values.

In Feather's (1982, 1988) expectancy-value model, personal values are the larger, more general values based on Rokeach's instrumental values. These personal values are assumed to determine the values individuals have for specific tasks, called *task value* in Feather's model. Task value is similar in function to incentive value in Atkinson's model and, along with expectation for success, should determine achievement behaviors like choice, persistence, and actual performance. Feather (1988) found that college students' enrollment in either a humanities, social sciences, or science course of study was related to both expectations and task value for math and English. Students who had higher task value for math and higher perceptions of their ability in math were more likely to enroll in science. Similarly, students who had higher task value and perceptions of their ability in English were less likely to enroll in a science course of study and more likely to enroll in humanities. Moreover, Feather found that task value for math and English were related to different types of personal values based on Rokeach's instrumental values. Students who were high in restrictive control personal values (high importance ratings of clean, obedient, polite, responsible, and self-controlled personal values) were more likely to have higher task value for math. In contrast, students who were high in prosocial concern (high importance ratings of forgiving, helpful, and loving personal values) were more likely to have higher task value for English. These personal values of restrictive control and prosocial concern did not have a direct relation to course enrollment; their effect was through math and English task values. It seems that these more general personal values do influence specific task values, but the specific task values are what relate more closely to achievement behavior, at least in terms of choice of a course of study. Feather (1988) also found that expectations were positively correlated with task value, similar to Battle (1966) and counter to the theoretical assumptions of Atkinson about the inverse relation between expectancy for success and incentive value.

The Eccles-Wigfield Model of Achievement Task Values

Most recently, Jacque Eccles and Allan Wigfield and their colleagues (see Eccles, 1983; Eccles, Adler, & Meece, 1984; Eccles & Wigfield, in press; Parsons & Goff, 1978; Wigfield, 1994; Wigfield & Eccles, 1992; Wigfield et al., 1991) have developed the most comprehensive model of the value components in an expectancy-value framework. This model has its roots in traditional expectancy-value models such as Lewin's, Tolman's, and Atkinson's, but it is much more social cognitive in nature and assumes that both expectancies and values are cognitive beliefs that are related to the conscious decisions and choices individuals make about their achievement (Wigfield & Eccles, 1992). Besides these older models of achievement motivation, Eccles and Wigfield's conceptualization of achievement task values also incorporates more recent social cognitive research on intrinsic and extrinsic motivation (e.g., Deci & Ryan, 1985).

Components of Task Value

Eccles and Wigfield define achievement task value in terms of four components, each of which can influence achievement behaviors such as choice, persistence, and actual achievement. The four components and sample items that are often used to measure them (see Eccles & Wigfield, 1995; Pintrich, Smith, Garcia, & McKeachie, 1993) are displayed in Table 8.1. Three of these four (attainment value, intrinsic interest, and extrinsic utility value) have been shown to be empirically separable constructs in confirmatory factor analyses (see Eccles & Wigfield, 1995).

In this model, *attainment value* (or, more simply, *importance*) is defined as the importance of doing well on a task, similar to Battle's (1965, 1966) definition. At the beginning of the chapter, Mr. Anderman notes how some of the students in her class have high importance for math because of their goals of col-

Table 8.1.Sample Self-Report Items Used to Measure Components of Task Value

Subjects are asked to respond to items using a Likert scale that ranges from 1 to 7 (or 1 to 5) with anchors at the endpoints such as *not very important* (interesting, useful) to *very important* (interesting, useful) or *not at all true of me* to *very true of me.*

Sample attainment value or importance items

> How important is it to you to get good grades in math? (1 = not very important, 7 = very important)
> I feel that being good at solving problems that involve math or reasoning mathematically is (1 = not very important, 7 = very important)
> It is important to me to learn the course material in this class (1 = not at all true of me, 7 = very true of me)
> Understanding the subject matter in this course is very important to me. (1 = not at all true of me, 7 = very true of me)

Sample intrinsic interest items

> In general, I find working on math assignments (1 = very boring, 7 = very interesting)
> How much do you like doing math? (1 = not very much, 7 = very much)
> I am very interested in the content area of this course. (1 = not at all true of me, 7 = very true of me)
> I like the subject matter of this course. (1 = not at all true of me, 7 = very true of me)

Sample extrinsic utility value items

> How useful is high school math for what you want to do after you graduate and go to work? (1 = not very useful, 7 = very useful)
> How useful is what you learn in high school math for your daily life outside school? (1 = not at all useful, 7 = very useful)
> I think I will be able to use what I learn in this course in other courses. (1 = not at all true of me, 7 = very true of me)
> I think the course material in this course is useful for me to learn. (1 = not at all true of me, 7 = very true of me)

Sample perceived costs items

> Is the amount of effort it will take to do well in your math course this year worthwhile to you? (1 = not very worthwhile, 7 = very worthwhile)
> How much does the amount of time you spend on math keep you from doing other things you would like to do? (1 = takes away no time, 7 = takes away a lot of time)

lege admission. In addition, attainment value is defined as the extent to which a task allows individuals to confirm or disconfirm salient or central aspects of their self-schema (Wigfield & Eccles, 1992). For example, doing well at an athletic event may be very important for a student because an important aspect of her self-identity is her concept of herself as a good athlete. In this case, her attainment value for most athletic events would be very high. For another student, her academic self-concept may be more central to her identity and, hence, academic tasks would be likely to have higher attainment value. As Wigfield & Eccles (1992) point out, other values, such as the importance of masculinity and femininity values, may be more or less salient in an individual's self-schema and to the extent that tasks allow these more general values to be expressed, then attainment value would be higher for these tasks. For example, if mathematics is stereotyped as a "masculine" activity and at odds with "feminine" values, then girls who have these feminine values would have a low attainment value for mathematics and be less likely to engage in it. By linking these more global personal values such as masculinity and femininity to attainment values, Wigfield and Eccles (1992) attempt to incorporate the more general values of Rokeach (1979) and Feather (1982, 1988) into their model.

The second component of task value is *intrinsic interest value*, defined as the enjoyment people experience when doing a task or as their subjective interest in the content of a task (Wigfield & Eccles, 1992). Ms. Garcia noted that many of her students have little interest in math. In this sense, intrinsic interest value is more concerned with the means of doing a task, not the end result of the task. It is conceptually similar to intrinsic interest in the intrinsic motivation theory of Deci & Ryan (1985) and interest in Csikszentmihalyi (1978), which was discussed in Chapter 7, as well as the more recent work on personal interest discussed in the next section of this chapter (see Renninger, Hidi, & Krapp, 1992; Schiefele, 1991; Tobias, 1994). When intrinsic interest value is high, individuals will be more engaged in the task, persist longer, and be intrinsically motivated for the task (Wigfield & Eccles, 1992).

The third component of task value is *extrinsic utility value*. Utility value is defined as the usefulness of the task for individuals in terms of their future goals, including career goals. It is related more to the ends in a means-ends analysis of a task. For example, a college student may not have much intrinsic interest in organic chemistry, but because she wishes to become a medical doctor, this course has a high utility value for her. In this sense, utility value is similar to some of the extrinsic reasons for doing a task in Deci and Ryan's (1985) model. Mr. Lopez was concerned with the utility value of math for his students in terms of how they could use it outside school.

The fourth and final component of the model is the *cost* attached to engaging in the task. This component has not been researched as much by Eccles and Wigfield, but it is defined as the perceived negative aspects of engaging in the task (Wigfield & Eccles, 1992). When individuals engage in one task, it usually means they cannot engage in other tasks at the same time. Accordingly, along with any choice of one specific task, there are some costs associated with it. Eccles and Wigfield assume that costs include the perceived amount of effort required for the task as well as anticipated emotional states (e.g., performance anxiety, fear of failure). For example, a college student might not choose to continue in science or math because he perceives that the costs in terms of the effort required are too much for him to bear at this time. If these courses require too much effort and study time, they take time away from other activities such as dating, sports, and social events. In terms of the anticipated emotional costs influencing behavior, a researcher may not participate often in conference presentations because of his performance anxiety about speaking in front of large groups and his fear of failure.

These four components of task value are assumed to operate together to determine the achievement value a task might have for an individual. Accordingly, individuals will generally have perceptions of the attainment value, interest, and utility value of a task as well as the costs associated with a task. In this sense, this model is a rational decision-making model of motivation, not unlike other expectancy-value models and goal theory models (Locke & Latham, 1990) discussed earlier and does fit under the godlike metaphor suggested by Weiner (1992). However, in their empirical work, Eccles and Wigfield and their colleagues have focused on how these value components combine with expectancy beliefs to influence student achievement behavior in actual school settings. Given this high level of ecological validity, their research is very relevant to understanding student motivation in K–12 schools in comparison to laboratory studies of college students or field studies done in business settings.

Research Studies

Most of Eccles and Wigfield's empirical research on values has focused on late elementary through secondary school students' values and expectancies for math and English. The studies have been correlational and longitudinal in design and have used survey methodology with large samples of students. The general pattern has been to survey students about their values and expectancies at one point in time and then examine the predictive power of these motivational beliefs for subsequent achievement in terms of grades and performance on standardized tests at a later point in time. Because they have been interested in choice behavior—in particular, student decisions about whether to continue taking math courses—these researchers have asked junior high students about their intentions to keep on taking math in high school and college. In addition, in longitudinal studies, they have actually followed the students over time and collected data on actual math enrollment decisions as well as the values and expectancies of the students.

The main effects of these studies are fairly easy to summarize. Expectancy beliefs, including self-concepts, ability perceptions, and expectancy for success, seem to predict actual achievement in terms of grades and performance on standardized tests. Values are positively correlated with actual achievement, but when both expectancy beliefs and values are used to predict achievement, expectancy beliefs are significant predictors and values are not significant predictors. In contrast, in terms of intentions to take future courses and actual enrollment in those courses (choice behavior), value beliefs, including attainment value, intrinsic interest, and extrinsic utility value, are better predictors than expectancy beliefs (see Eccles, 1983; Meece, Wigfield, & Eccles, 1990; Wigfield & Eccles, 1992). It appears that achievement values may be more important for choice behaviors and be responsible for students enrolling in courses, but once in the course, values are not as important for actual performance as are expectancy beliefs. This implies that it may be more important for teachers to encourage appropriate expectancy and self-competence beliefs in order to improve students' classroom achievement than to worry about increasing students' value and interest in the course material. Of course, increasing the value and interest levels may result in students electing to continue on in the subject area at a later point and, given the positive correlation of values with achievement, will not have detrimental effects on actual classroom achievement.

There are several other consistent findings in this program of research that bear on the theoretical and conceptual relations among the constructs in expectancy-value models. First, in their construct validity studies using confirmatory factor analyses, Eccles and Wigfield have found that the different expectancy constructs such as self-concept, self-perceptions of ability, and expectancy for success are not differentiated into separable factors empirically (Eccles & Wigfield, 1995). Accordingly, although self-concept of ability may be distinguished theoretically from expectancy for success in terms of the former being considered somewhat more stable and general and the latter being more task and situation specific, it appears that students do not make these distinctions, at least in their responses to a self-report questionnaire. Second, their research has shown that the three value components of attainment value, intrinsic interest, and extrinsic utility value are empirically distinct from one another and from the expectancy component. It appears that students do make differential judgments about importance, interest, and utility and that there can be intraindividual variability on these dimensions for the same task. For example, students may be intrinsically interested in English but report low levels of importance or utility value for it. Moreover, Eccles and Wigfield's research shows that these value components are positively correlated with an expectancy component, such that students tend to value those activities in which they think they do well and vice versa (Eccles & Wigfield, 1995). These results, taken together with Battle's (1966) and Feather's (1988) findings, offer strong empirical support for the idea that expectancy and value components are positively related to one another, not inversely related as originally proposed by Atkinson (1964). Although expectancy and value beliefs have been shown to be positively related to one another, Eccles and Wigfield do note that at this point in their research, which is causally predominant is still an open question. That is, it is still not clear whether children develop competence at a task and then begin to value it or whether value leads to more time spent doing the task and, hence, competence develops out of this increased engagement. Their future work will examine this issue, but it does bring up questions of development.

Developmental and Individual Differences in Achievement Task Values

One of the hallmarks of Eccles and Wigfield's research on task values has been the focus on how these values develop over time in school settings and the role of gender differences. In fact, the original study that spawned their program of research was concerned with the more pragmatic question of why elementary and junior high female students don't continue on in upper level math courses in senior high or college when their actual math achievement in the early grades is remarkably similar to males. As developmental and motivational psychologists, Eccles and Wigfield approached this problem in terms of examining how expectancy and value beliefs are developed over time, situated in home and school contexts, and how these motivational beliefs then influence future achievement behaviors.

In terms of developmental differences, there are several issues that Eccles and Wigfield and their colleagues have addressed in their research. First, they have examined the differentiation of the different value constructs over the course of development. In general, they find that 5th through 12th graders do distinguish among the three components of importance, interest, and utility (Eccles & Wigfield, 1995). However, Wigfield and Eccles (1992) report that children in the early elementary grades do not reliably distinguish the three components of task value. In confirmatory factor analytic studies, they find only two value components, interest and utility/importance. It appears that the development of task value beliefs follows the general orthogenetic principle of Werner (1957) with task value beliefs becoming more differentiated with age and experience. As children have more experience with a variety of tasks and activities that engage their interest and ideas of importance differently, then they will begin to differentiate these components of task value beliefs. Although task value beliefs may not be differentiated into the three principal components in early elementary school, Eccles and Wigfield have consistently found that expectancy and task value beliefs are distinguished from one another in the early elementary grades (Eccles, Wigfield, Harold, & Blumenfeld, 1993; Wigfield & Eccles, 1992). Moreover, these same studies found that young children did distinguish between expectancy and value beliefs for different domains such as math, reading, computers, music, social activities, and sports. Accordingly, even very young children in the early elementary grades can make distinctions about what they like or think is important to them versus their perceptions of competence in different domains (Wigfield, 1994; Wigfield & Eccles, 1992).

The second issue that is of developmental importance concerns the change in the level of children's achievement task values. The general finding for academic task value beliefs is fairly easy to summarize: Older children's ratings of interest, importance, and utility for school subjects decline in comparison to the mean levels of younger children's (Eccles & Midgley, 1989; Wigfield, 1994; Wigfield & Eccles, 1992). There are some domain differences with students in upper elementary grades rating mathematics as more important, interesting, and useful in comparison to students in junior and senior high schools. In addition, this same research showed that students' task value beliefs for English increased across the elementary to high school samples (Wigfield & Eccles, 1992). Other research in this tradition has shown that the transition from elementary school to junior high school is marked by a significant decrease in students' interest and importance ratings of math and English (Eccles et al., 1989; Wigfield et al., 1991). In contrast, research on developmental changes within elementary schools using a sample of first, second, and fourth graders has found that math task value ratings did not decline across grade, although math was not rated very highly in comparison to other subjects or activities (Eccles, Wigfield, et al., 1993). The ratings of reading, music, and computer activities were lower in older children, and these children rated sports as more interesting and important to them. In a follow-up longitudinal study of these same children, Wigfield, Eccles, and their colleagues found that within subjects, only reading and music task value ratings declined, whereas interest in math and sports did not decline within individuals over time. As Wigfield (1994) points out, these findings highlight the importance of examining task value beliefs by domain and activity as well as by age of the child. Accordingly, although children's general task value beliefs decline with age, there are important domain and developmental differences in this generalization.

There are two general explanations for the decline in children's task value beliefs. The developmental explanation focuses more on internal changes in children's strategies and beliefs (Blumenfeld et al., 1982; Wigfield & Eccles, 1992). For example, as children get older, their beliefs about the nature of ability change (see Chapter 3) from a more incremental view of ability as malleable to a more entity-like view of ability as stable and unchanging (Dweck & Leggett, 1988). If students do poorly in certain school areas, such as math, and attribute this poor performance to low ability that will remain stable, then they may lower their perceptions of the value of math to protect their overall self-worth (Steele, 1988; Wigfield & Eccles, 1992). In addition, as students get older, they become more interested in social comparison with others as well as more able to integrate social comparison information with their own beliefs (Blumenfeld et al., 1982; Ruble & Frey, 1991). These developmental changes in ability to use social comparison also can lead to lower perceptions of ability, as we discussed earlier in Chapter 3. In any event, given the generally positive relations between ability perceptions and task value beliefs, if ability perceptions decline with age, then value perceptions will also.

The second explanation for the decline in task value beliefs reflects a more experiential and situated argument about the power of the classroom context to shape students beliefs. Eccles and her colleagues have proposed that in most junior high schools, there is a developmental mismatch between beliefs and developmental needs of the students entering the school and the structure and organization of the school. They suggest that students entering junior high school are likely to have high needs for autonomy and control and also the cognitive skills to exercise self-control and regulation. The researchers go on to note, however, that in most junior high and senior high schools, there is actually little opportunity for student autonomy and control. Rather, the students encounter lower cognitive level tasks, more emphasis on normative and comparative grading practices, and less criterion-referenced grading. This mismatch between the students and the school results in a significant decrease in young adolescents' motivation for school (see Eccles et al., 1984; Eccles & Midgley, 1989; Eccles, Midgley, et al., 1993; Eccles, Wigfield, et al., 1993; Wigfield & Eccles, 1992). This argument is similar to the proposal made by Rosenholtz & Simpson (1984) in Chapter 3 regarding the decline in children's ability perceptions. As we suggested in that chapter, an integration of these two positions represents the most viable explanation. There are both internal cognitive and motivational changes as well as environmental changes that reciprocally interact with each other that are responsible for the decline in students' motivation for school. Accordingly, we need to develop models that incorporate both types of changes in order to explain student motivation.

There has been little research on ethnic differences in task values, but Eccles and Wigfield have examined gender differences. Their empirical research shows some gender differences, but the findings vary across studies and age groups (Wigfield & Eccles, 1992). They found that male and female adolescents do differ in the relative value they attach to various subjects such as math (males value more) and English (females value more), although these gender differences did not always emerge with younger children. In fact, Wigfield and Eccles found no differential valuing of math or computer activities by gender in a study of elementary school students, although boys reported more value for sports activities and girls valued reading and music more (Wigfield & Eccles, 1992). There is a need for more research on how these gender differences emerge in the context of classrooms and how these gender differences may then moderate the relation between value beliefs and other motivational outcomes such as choice, persistence, and actual achievement.

RESEARCH ON SITUATIONAL AND PERSONAL INTEREST

If you asked most laypersons and teachers for their definition of motivation, they would probably provide an answer that refers to some aspect of interest. For example, at the beginning of this chapter, Ms. Garcia talks about how her students are just not interested in learning. Many parents will explain their children's lack of motivation and poor performance in school as due to a lack of interest. Intuitive views of motivation and general folk psychology usually propose interest as an important aspect of motivation that causally influences attention, learning, thinking, and performance. In addition, most people believe that they know what interest is and that they understand how it operates to influence learning. The popularity of these intuitive notions about interest has sometimes hindered the development of careful psychological research on interest.

As noted in the previous section, the construct of interest is basically the same construct that Eccles and Wigfield have called intrinsic interest. However, research on interest, broadly defined, has been pursued by researchers from a number of different perspectives, beyond specific expectancy-value models and motivational theories in general. As pointed out by Krapp, Hidi, and Renninger (1992), interest in the construct of interest has waxed and waned in psychology and education over the years. Krapp and colleagues (Krapp et al., 1992) note that early in the nineteenth century, Herbart developed a model of interest and that both James and Dewey also discussed the role of interest in learning early in the twentieth century. These models usually owed more to philosophical perspectives than psychological theories and there was often little empirical research to support the models. Of course, during the heyday of behaviorism, there was very little research on interest in the United States, although related concepts such as curiosity (Berlyne, 1960) and attitudes (Evans, 1971) were examined (Krapp et al., 1992). However, with the development of cognitive and constructivist models of learning and development, research on interest became more popular in the 1980s and 1990s. Currently, there are a number of active programs of research on the role of interest in learning and development that include researchers from around the world. The book on interest edited by Renninger, Hidi, and Krapp (1992) still represents the best introduction to this burgeoning area of research. Nevertheless, current theoretical and empirical work on the construct of interest is still rather young in comparison with the traditions of expectancy-value theory, attribution theory, self-efficacy theory, and intrinsic motivation theory.

Three Definitions of Interest

One of the issues that has plagued research on interest is the theoretical and conceptual definition of the construct. There has been recent research on interest by motivational psychologists, developmental psychologists, educational psychologists, and reading and literacy researchers, all of whom have used somewhat different definitions of interest. However, Krapp, Hidi, and Renninger (1992) have proposed that there are three general definitions of interest that can help us understand this diverse body of research. The three definitions cover personal interest, situational interest, and interest as a psychological state. Each of these three definitions is explained in the following text along with its relations to the other two general definitions of interest.

Personal Interest

Researchers who have investigated *personal interest* have conceptualized it as a personality trait or a personal characteristic of the individual that is a relatively stable, enduring disposition of the individual (Krapp et al., 1992). In addition, this personal interest is usually assumed to be directed toward some specific activity or topic (a particular interest in sports, science, music, dance, computers, etc.) in contrast to curiosity, which is assumed to be a characteristic of the person that is more diffusely directed (e.g., someone who is generally curious about many things). For example, much of the vocational education and career choice literature is based on assessing individuals' interests in different activities and careers. In the previous section, Eccles and Wigfield's concept of intrinsic interest would be conceptually similar to personal interest. Other researchers (see review by Schiefele, Krapp, & Winteler, 1992) have measured personal interest as a preference for certain topics (e.g., I prefer math to science.), a general liking for the subject area (e.g., I like math.), personal enjoyment (e.g., I enjoy working on math problems.), and sometimes importance or personal significance of the topic (e.g., Math is important to me.). Of course, in Eccles and Wigfield's model, this last aspect would be a separate construct of importance or attainment value, not interest. Given these definitions, this work has focused on individual differences in personal interest and how these individual differences are related to learning and performance.

Situational Interest

In contrast to the more personality or traitlike characteristic of personal interest, *situational interest* has been defined by researchers as interest that is generated mainly by environmental conditions (Krapp et al., 1992). The researchers who have studied situational interest have often been reading researchers who have been investigating text-based interest and trying to understand how different aspects of texts can generate and sustain interest on the part of readers. There are many different features of texts that can generate interest, such as novelty, surprise, complexity, ambiguity, and inclusion of certain types of themes (e.g., death, sex). Given this situated perspective, researchers have tended to ignore individual differences and have looked for general principles to describe how the features of the environment (classrooms, media, computers, textbooks) can generate interest. Hidi and Anderson (1992) note, however, that situational interest is different from just arousal or curiosity (cf. Berlyne, 1960) because situational interest may be tied to very specific content (e.g., a story about space travel), not only structural features (novelty, surprise) of the text or environment, and it may last longer than simple arousal and may develop into a personal interest.

Interest as a Psychological State

The third construct of interest, *interest as a psychological state*, reflects an interactive and relational perspective on interest whereby an individual's personal interest interacts with the interesting environmental features to produce the psychological state of interest in the person (Krapp et al., 1992). For example, a student may have a fairly high level of personal interest in science-related topics and, in her reading class, she occasionally gets to read expository texts about science topics. On these occasions, she experiences a heightened psychological state of interest in contrast to other occasions during reading class when she reads about other topics. There has been less research on this relational construct in comparison to the work on personal and situational interest, although in many studies of the other two constructs, individuals have experienced a psychological state of interest.

Renninger (1990, 1992; Renninger & Wozniak, 1985) has been one of the researchers most involved with developing a research program on interest that reflects this relational construct of interest as a psychological state. She has conceptualized interest not just in terms of a personal preference or liking for an activity or topic, but as occurring only when the individual has both high value for an activity (choosing to do it, thinking it is important) and high stored knowledge about the activity or topic. It is only under these conditions that Renninger would label the state as interest (see Figure 8.1). The argument is that if individuals have very little knowledge of an activity or topic, then it is hard for them to judge their interest in it. In addition, individuals usually have more knowledge about activities that have a high level of interest and value for them. Accordingly, if a person has a high value for an activity but low knowledge of the activity, then Renninger does not consider this interest; she labels this state as *attraction*. *Noninterests* are defined by high stored knowledge for an activity but low value for the activity. Renninger (1992) does not label the fourth cell in this two-by-two matrix of knowledge and value, which would represent the low value and low knowledge cell, but the psychological state would be unconcern, indifference, and ignorance about the topic (see Figure 8.1).

Figure 8.1. Contrasting models of the relations between interest and knowledge

Renninger's Model of the Relations

		Value for Activity	
		Low	High
Prior Knowledge	Low	Ignorance	Attraction
	High	Noninterest	Interest

Tobias' Model of the Relations

		Personal Interest	
		Low	High
Prior Knowledge	Low	1	2
	High	3	4

This position that interest is only evoked when an individual has both high value and high knowledge of an activity or topic has not been accepted by all interest researchers. For example, Alexander, Kulikowich, and Jetton (1994) and Tobias (1994) have argued that interest/value is orthogonal to prior knowledge. They assume that individuals can have high interest and high knowledge (cell 4 in Figure 8.1), which would be similar to Renninger's interest cell. However, these researchers assume that individuals can have high interest in a topic even though they may have low knowledge about it (cell 2 in Figure 8.1). Tobias (1994) does not label his cells explicitly, but notes that the low knowledge–high personal interest cell (cell 2) may not be found often in adults, but that there could be domains where children would be interested in the content but have little knowledge or expertise in that domain. Accordingly, Tobias (1994) suggests that this state of high interest–low knowledge (cell 2) would be transitory over the course of development. He notes that cells 1 and 3 would be similar to the ignorance and noninterest cells in Renninger's matrix. It seems intuitively possible that individuals could have high interest and low knowledge, but Renninger's (1992) logic about this state representing only attraction also seems plausible. This controversy over the relation between prior knowledge and interest/value reflects the theoretical and conceptual difficulties in research on interest. We still need better theoretical models and more empirical research on the construct of interest. Fortunately, this work is currently under way and promises to be an important area of research in motivation theory.

Measures of Interest and Research Findings

Related to the fact that there are various definitions and theories of interest, there have been a number of different methods used to measure student interest. In contrast to the research on students' perceptions of ability and efficacy, which has mainly used self-reports (see Chapter 3), the research on interest has used self-reports and other measures. Research on personal interest has often used self-report instruments like questionnaires that ask students to rate various topics or activities on Likert-scaled items. Items are rated in a number of different ways, depending on the theoretical framework for personal interest, including general attitude toward the activity, specific preference for or liking the activity, enjoyment of the activity, personal importance or significance of the activity to the individual, intrinsic interest in the content of the activity, and reported choice of or participation in the activity (see Schiefele et al., 1992; Wigfield, 1994; Wigfield & Eccles, 1992). Students' responses to these various aspects of interest are then used to create scales that reflect different levels of interest in different activities (e.g., math vs. English, academics vs. sports). These scales represent individual differences in interest (i.e., some people will have high interest for academics, others will have high interest for sports) that are then used to predict various outcomes such as choice to do an activity in the future, persistence, level of effort or engagement in the activity, and actual performance. Although these self-reports of interest can be used quite easily and efficiently, there remain validity problems with using them because they require some metacognition or self-awareness on the part of individuals responding to them. This is not just a problem with interest self-report items; it may be difficult for some individuals (young children) to accurately report on their interests.

Besides self-report measures, Renninger (1990, 1992; Renninger & Wozniak, 1985) has used actual observations of the play of young children to measure interest as a psychological state. Students were observed during 240 minutes of free play and interest was coded for objects that the children (a) returned to play with repeatedly, (b) spent more time with than other objects, (c) played with in solitary play, and (d) played with in other than manipulative play (Renninger, 1992). Objects could then be classified as high or low interest in *relation* to the individual child's actual behavior with the object. This allowed for a very sensitive measure of interest for each individual, rather than just assuming, for example, that all boys are interested in trucks and all girls are interested in dolls. The results clearly showed that play objects that were of high interest to some children were not of much interest to other children (e.g., some boys had a high interest in trucks, but other boys did not). This type of behavioral measure also allowed Renninger to examine interest without having to ask children specifically about their own interests. Accordingly, this type of measure does not assume that individuals have to be metacognitively aware of their interests as do explicit questionnaire items that ask about personal interest. Actual observations allow for the investigation of interest in young children who may be lacking in the verbal, cognitive, or metacognitive skills to answer questionnaire items. Moreover, by focusing on behavior, observational measures do not introduce the term *interest* and avoid the validity problems associated with invoking participants' prior conceptions of interest that they then might use to interpret questionnaire items differently than the researcher intended.

Finally, the situational interest researchers, who have mainly been concerned with the influence of text-based interest on students' learning, have used a number of different measures of interest (Alexander et al., 1994). They have used self-report questionnaires of students' interest in the general domain of the reading (e.g., science) and the specific topic of the reading (space travel) in much the same way as noted in the research on personal interest. These researchers also have used students' personal ratings of the interestingness of the text (e.g., text on space travel written in an interesting style) as well as specific details of the text (e.g., walking on the moon or living in outer space). The research on text-based interest also has used ratings of the text by others in terms of interest and then assigned students to high and low interest groups based on these ratings by others (e.g., Hidi & Anderson, 1992). Of course, this strategy assumes that one can normatively classify a text as generally interesting or uninteresting without considering how an individual student will perceive the text. This methodology also raises questions of validity concerning the normative and idiographic measurement of interest, another problem that will have to be resolved in future research.

Although there are problems in both the theoretical conceptions of interest and in the measurement of interest, the research has revealed fairly consistent results regarding how interest is related to other cognitive and achievement outcomes. First, in terms of cognitive outcomes, interest is generally related positively to measures of memory, attention, comprehension, deeper cognitive engagement, and thinking (Schiefele, 1991; Tobias, 1994), as suggested in most lay or folk psychology theories on the role of interest in learning. For example, Renninger and Wozniak (1985) have shown that preschoolers' interest in different activities predicts their attention, recognition, and recall memory for these objects at a later point in time. Schiefele (1991), using both experimental and correlational designs, has shown that college students' personal interest was positively related to the use of deeper cognitive processing strategies such as elaboration, seeking information when confronted with a problem, engagement in critical thinking, and self-reported time and effort investment. In addition, Schiefele (1991) reported that personal interest was negatively related to the use of a more surface processing strategy, rehearsal. Pintrich and his colleagues (Pintrich, 1989; Pintrich & Garcia, 1991; Pintrich & De Groot, 1990a) have shown that personal interest and task value measures are correlated positively with deeper processing strategies such as the use of elaboration and organizational strategies as well as reports of critical thinking and time and effort regulation strategies in both college and junior high samples. The research on situational interest and text-based learning shows basically the same pattern of relations (Alexander et al., 1994; Hidi & Anderson, 1992; Tobias, 1994), although the findings are somewhat more complicated by the type of text involved (narrative vs. expository text, linear vs. nonlinear text) and levels of student prior knowledge.

Given these generally consistent positive findings on the role of interest in learning, future research will probably be more likely to address the issue of *how* interest has an influence on learning, not *whether* it does have an effect (Hidi, Renninger, & Krapp, 1992). One of the traditional mechanisms through which interest was hypothesized to have an effect on learning was attention. Higher levels of interest were supposed to lead to greater attention to the task, which in turn would lead to better memory or learning. Although this selective attention explanation does have empirical support (see Shirey, 1992), others (e.g., Hidi, 1990) have argued that interest may actually result in less conscious attention given to the task. Hidi (1990; Hidi & Anderson, 1992) suggests that when interest is high, there does not have to be as much effortful selective attention, that, in fact, interest could result in more spontaneous attention and less cognitive effort, but still have a positive influence on learning. Tobias (1994) also suggests that high interest might make it easier for students to activate a richer network of prior knowledge about the topic or activity that would make memory and learning easier. High levels of personal interest might also decrease the demands for self-regulation of time and effort (i.e., students trying to maintain their effort level in the face of a boring task) and thereby free up more cognitive capacity for actual learning of the task content, rather than self-regulation. Current research is examining these and other possibilities to help us understand just how interest can influence learning.

Developmental and Individual Differences in Interest

In comparison to the research on task values, there has not been as much research on developmental and group differences in interest. First, in terms of developmental issues, the research does suggest that even fairly young (3–4 years old) preschool children do have relatively stable interests and that these interests are related to their choice of activities and their learning (Renninger, 1992). There has been little research, however, on how interests develop over time and experience. Second, interest may play a larger role in directing and guiding the behavior of younger children for a larger number of tasks than it does for older children and adults. Older children and adults very often have to engage in tasks that do not really interest them and they often have no choice over these tasks (e.g., tasks in school, job-related tasks). In these situations, interest may have a more differential effect, depending on the task and content area, than the diverse effect it has for younger children on many tasks (Krapp et al., 1992). For example, Hidi and Anderson (1992) found that situational interest had a stronger effect in reading tasks for upper elementary school children than it did in writing tasks. It seems that the functional role of interest in learning may vary depending on the age of the child. Finally, in terms of developmental differences in levels of interest, research clearly shows that students' interest in school and school tasks does decline with age and that interest in math and science may drop the most (see Kahle et al., 1993; Wigfield, 1994; Wigfield & Eccles, 1992). Clearly, there is a need for more research on the domain and developmental differences in the role of interest in learning and development.

In terms of ethnic differences, there is very little research, but gender differences in interest have been found in the research. First, Renninger (1992) found gender differences in the nature of preschool boys' and girls' play with objects of interest to them. Girls were more likely to use their interest objects in a number of different ways in their play, whereas boys showed more play actions only when using their objects to mimic the real-world use of the object. In addition, Renninger (1992) found gender differences in the role of interest in elementary school students' solution of arithmetic problems. Boys were more likely to make errors on uninteresting math problems, whereas the girls made more errors when they worked on interesting math problems. Renninger interprets this gender-by-interest interaction by suggesting that interest facilitates boys' problem solving because it helps them to understand and work on the interesting problems. In contrast, interest seems to interfere and becomes a distraction for girls on the interesting math problems. Schiefele, Krapp, and Winteler (1992) also found that the interest-achievement linkage was stronger for males; about 12% of the variance in achievement for males was accounted for by interest, whereas the variance was only 6% for females.

RESEARCH ON TEST ANXIETY

At the beginning of this chapter, both Mr. Anderman and Mr. Lopez discussed the problem of test anxiety and how it can have a negative influence on student performance on tests. Test anxiety can be a major problem in the classroom at all levels, from elementary through postsecondary classrooms. It represents a type of emotion that can have a negative effect on learning, in contrast to the positive affect that is generated by interest. In addition, unlike the recent resurgence of empirical research on interest, test anxiety research has been ongoing since at least the 1950s (Tryon, 1980). In fact, there is a professional organization devoted to research on test anxiety (International Society for Test Anxiety Research), separate journals that are devoted to research on test anxiety (*Anxiety, Stress, and Coping: An International Journal*), and a number of edited books on the problems of anxiety and stress (e.g., Hagtvet & Johnsen, 1992; Schwarzer, van der Ploeg, & Spielberger, 1989). Given all the research on test anxiety, we do not attempt to provide a detailed discussion of the construct and how it can influence classroom performance but will highlight some important issues about test anxiety.

Defining Text Anxiety

In terms of the definition of test anxiety, there are a number of important issues to consider. First, a general definition of *anxiety* is "an unpleasant feeling or emotional state that has physiological and behavioral concomitants, and that is experienced in formal testing or other evaluative situations" (Dusek, 1980, p. 88). In addition, most theories of test anxiety distinguish between a cognitive component, usually called the worry component, and the emotionality, or affective, component of test anxiety (Liebert & Morris, 1967; Wigfield & Eccles, 1989). The *cognitive, or worry, component* refers to the cognitions that accompany anxiety, such as worrying about flunking the test, thinking about the consequences of failing the test (parents being upset, having to drop out of college), worrying about being unable to finish the test, thinking about items that one can't answer, and thinking about being embarrassed because of a low grade. These are just some of the thoughts that can run through a highly test anxious person's mind as he or she tries to take a test.

The *emotionality component* refers to the actual physiological and emotional arousal that individuals experience as they take a test. This arousal can become a classically conditioned affective reaction to evaluation situations (Wigfield & Eccles, 1989). It should be noted that most people do feel some anxiety when put in a performance situation. For test anxious individuals, however, the anxiety becomes overwhelming and interferes with their ability to actually perform a task they have mastered in another nonevaluative situation. In the example at the beginning of this chapter, Mr. Lopez recalled how he could do the math problems on the homework (nonevaluative situation) but had difficulties during tests. Many performers (musicians, actors) and athletes also can show debilitating effects of anxiety during a performance in contrast to rehearsals or practice. The emotionality component can include physiological symptoms like sweaty palms, upset stomach, faster than usual heartbeat, and pervasive negative affects such as fear and general unease or uncomfortableness.

A second issue related to the definition of test anxiety concerns the stability of test anxiety. Most models of test anxiety propose that there is both a trait of test anxiety and a state of test anxiety (Covington, 1992; Spielberger, 1972). This dichotomy parallels the distinction between personal interest as a relatively enduring trait of the individual and a more situational interest fostered by external conditions. *Trait test anxiety* represents a stable traitlike individual difference; some individuals are much higher on test anxiety across many different situations in comparison with those low on test anxiety. Highly test anxious individuals tend to experience anxiety in most testing or evaluative situations. In contrast, *state test anxiety* is more situation specific and may be experienced by many or most people in certain stressful situations. For example, taking a college or graduate school admissions test (i.e., the SAT , the ACT, the GRE, the medical or law school exam), which has high importance for most people, will probably generate state test anxiety in many of the test-takers. Bedsides these high-stakes testing situations, some classrooms (see Hill & Wigfield, 1984) in which testing, grading, and competition are emphasized can generate high levels of state test anxiety in many students. Of course, most test anxiety models also predict that people who are high in trait test anxiety will be even more anxious in these types of anxiety-arousing situations.

Effects on Learning and Performance

The empirical research on the negative effects of anxiety on academic performance is quite large and consistent. Hembree (1988), in a meta-analysis of 562 studies that related test anxiety and academic achievement, found that test anxiety does cause poor performance, is negatively related to self-esteem, and is directly related to students' defensiveness and fear of negative evaluation. Hill and Wigfield (1984) report that studies have found correlations up to –.60 between test anxiety and achievement, suggesting that anxiety and achievement share significance variance. Moreover, Hill and Wigfield estimate that in most classrooms, about 10% of the children will have a relatively high level of trait anxiety, which translates into about 2–3 children per classroom. By their estimates, between 4 and 5 million children in elementary and secondary schools in the United States will have to cope with high test anxiety. Hill and Wigfield also suggest that another 10–15% of the children in any classroom, although not in the top 10% of the population in test anxiety, will experience some anxiety. Taken together, this resulting estimate that 25% of the children in classrooms will have some problems with anxiety means that approximately 10 million children in the United States could be affected by test anxiety. Accordingly, there is a need to understand how test anxiety works and what can be done about it in classrooms (Wigfield & Eccles, 1989).

There are a number of mechanisms that have been suggested by researchers to explain how anxiety influences learning and performance. Given that many empirical studies have shown that the worry component is more closely linked to performance decrements than the emotionality component (Covington, 1992; Tryon, 1980), explanations have tended to focus on the role of the worry component. Tobias (1985) has provided a model that integrates two explanations of the effects of test anxiety. One explanation has been that anxiety interferes with attention (see Wine, 1971) because all the negative thoughts and worry distract the individual from the task. Given the limited capacity of working memory, these distracting thoughts take up cognitive resources that could be used to work on the task at hand (the test). The other explanation has been that highly test anxious students have deficits in general cognitive learning strategies or test-taking strategies; that is, they don't know how to study very well, don't know how to take a test strategically, and are often not well-prepared for the test. Tobias (1985) has suggested that these two models are complementary given our limited cognitive capacity. He suggests that when students do have good study skills and test-taking strategies, then more working memory capacity will be freed up to cope with any negative thoughts and worry generated by high test anxiety. In contrast, if students don't have those skills, then the worry generated by high test anxiety does interfere with attention and cognitive processing and there is a concomitant drop in performance. Much research needs to be done to tease apart these different explanations, but research that focuses on the interactive nature of anxiety and cognition, learning and coping strategies, and self-regulation is promising.

In terms of how the classroom situation can create state anxiety, Hill and Wigfield (1984) and Wigfield and Eccles (1989) discuss a number of features of the classroom that can heighten anxiety for children. First, they note that many classroom and standardized achievement tests have time limits that create pressure on students to finish within a certain amount of time. The lack of time (or perceived lack of time) can increase students' anxiety, particularly if anxious students spend part of the testing time worrying about their performance. This distraction will not only reduce cognitive attentional capacity, it will reduce the amount of overall time spent thinking about the test. In addition, these tests are often introduced or discussed in terms of students' relative ability, which can heighten social comparison and anxiety. Finally, Hill and Wigfield (1984) note that the format and mechanics of the tests can be unfamiliar to students or more difficult than their usual schoolwork.

Wigfield and Eccles (1989) note that classrooms that have overly high standards for evaluation are associated with higher levels of anxiety (cf. Helmke, 1988; Zatz & Chassin, 1985). Research on aptitude-treatment interactions

(ATIs) suggest that organized instruction and fairly easy tasks can help anxious students learn better, whereas less organized and student-centered instruction may not work as well with anxious students (Cronbach & Snow, 1977; Tobias, 1980; Wigfield & Eccles, 1989). Moreover, general changes in grading practices as students move into secondary schools, where grading systems are more normative and stricter, can increase student anxiety over testing and evaluation. Finally, standardized testing and grades do become more salient and have greater real consequences in later grades in secondary schools, thereby increasing anxiety (Wigfield & Eccles, 1989).

Interventions

Hill and Wigfield (1984) summarize a number of studies that attempted to change school or classroom use of tests and report cards. These studies suggest that very simple things like removing time constraints from classroom tests can help anxious students perform better. Of course, this may not be easy when classes are only 45–50 minutes long as in secondary classrooms compared to elementary classrooms, but teachers can develop creative ways to change their test format to ensure that all students have enough time to demonstrate their mastery. If demonstrating mastery of the material is the most important aspect of the assessment, then the amount of time taken to do so should not be an issue, particularly given individual differences in students' speed and ability to perform. In addition, Hill and Wigfield suggest that reducing the amount of importance that teachers place on tests as a sign of ability and decreasing the opportunities for social comparison of report card grades and test grades (no public displays of grades) can help to create a less anxious classroom climate.

Of course, besides changing the classroom climate and structure, there have been a large number of studies that have attempted to change students' coping strategies for dealing with anxiety (Wigfield & Eccles, 1989). These interventions would include the "tricks" that Mr. Lopez said that his math teacher taught him. Some of these intervention or treatment studies have mainly addressed the emotionality component, others have addressed the cognitive or worry component, and some have attempted to address both components (Tryon, 1980). Treatments aimed at the emotionality component usually attempt some type of desensitization to the negative affect generated in the situation, similar to what is done with desensitization of phobics in behavioral therapy. Some studies have also used self-directed relaxation techniques to help students cope with the negative affect and anxiety. Tryon (1980) suggests that these studies have had mixed success and it may be due to the fact that by addressing only the emotionality component, they are not considering the worry component, which is more closely associated with actual decrements in performance.

Interventions that have been aimed at the worry component have included direct study and strategy skills training, cognitive behavioral self-regulation to control the unwanted and distracting thoughts, and motivational or attributional training to help students control and manage their anxiety. These more cognitive treatments have shown somewhat stronger positive effects on reducing anxiety and improving performance, but both Tryon (1980) and Hill and Wigfield (1984) suggest that interventions need to address both emotionality and worry components through a diversity of methods. For example, Hill and Wigfield outline a school-based anxiety reduction program that includes training in both study and test-taking skills as well as motivational and attributional training. It seems likely that these types of ecologically valid programs that address the multiple aspects of anxiety in the classroom will be more successful than single treatment or more simple interventions. Wigfield and Eccles (1989) note that these anxiety intervention programs need to become more integrated into the school curriculum, be sensitive to developmental differences, and develop strategies targeted to help the different problems that different types of test-anxious students have (skills training vs. anxiety control).

RESEARCH ON SELF-WORTH

The construct of *self-worth*, or as it is more often called in popular views, *self-esteem*, concerns individuals' affect toward or evaluation of themselves. At the beginning of this chapter, Ms. Garcia invokes self-esteem as an explanation for some students' motivational problems. Although it is often confounded in popular views with self-perceptions of ability, self-esteem should *not* be confused with individuals' perceptions of their own competence or efficacy, which are more cognitive appraisals or beliefs about the self (see Chapter 3). In contrast, the research on self-esteem usually suggests that self-esteem is a more affective or emotional reaction to the self. It can mean taking pride in yourself and your behavior and having a general positive image of yourself. In addition, self-esteem is usually a more diffuse and less specific reaction to the self than a specific appraisal of personal ability to do a specific task or of competence in a specific domain (Harter, 1985a, 1990). Accordingly, a person could believe that he is not very good at tennis (a low perception of tennis competence), but this would not necessarily influence his overall positive or negative feeling toward himself as a person, as long as tennis is not that important to him. Harter (1985a, 1990) has proposed that self-worth can be linked differentially to a number of different domains across the life span rather than linked to all domains in a global and diffuse fashion.

This distinction is often lost in the popular views of self-esteem, not just in schools but in many domains of life, much to the detriment of our understanding of motivation and how self-beliefs can play a role in influencing behavior. For example, on many TV talk shows or in many popular self-help books, high self-esteem is offered as the major panacea for all individual problems. The basic argument is that poor or low self-esteem is the root of all problems, whether they be child abuse, spouse abuse, substance abuse, weight or body image problems, marital infidelity, delinquency, personal unemployment, criminality, learning problems, or just personal unhappiness and depression. Given this assumption, it then follows that increasing self-esteem will result in the remediation of these problems. As Lazarus (1991) notes, this logic leads people to believe that they will avoid these problems by rehearsing simple positive statements about the self (i.e., I'm a good person, student, or worker.) or having others give them the same type of noncontingent positive feedback. Of course, any view this simplistic is absurd in the face of the complexity of these problems.

The difficulty is that in U.S. schools today, many teachers do subscribe to this simplistic view, reflecting the emphasis it receives in our popular culture. Teachers are often afraid to say anything negative to students about their performance because they believe it will hurt the students' self-esteem. There are schools and classrooms that engage in self-esteem programs whereby children are asked to chant positive statements about themselves in order to enhance self-esteem (cf. Ms. Garcia's comments at the beginning of this chapter). In contrast to these popular views of self-esteem, Covington (see Covington, 1992; Covington & Beery, 1976) has proposed a model of self-worth that is based on current theoretical views of student motivation and has developed a program of empirical research that helps us understand self-worth in school contexts.

Covington (1992) proposes that the need for self-worth is a basic need of all individuals. This need is represented in the universal search for self-acceptance. Covington notes that in our society, worth for school-age children is often determined by their academic achievements. To the extent that children internalize or accept this general societal value, their self-worth will depend on their school achievement. Covington then suggests that the need for self-worth will generate a number of different patterns of motivational beliefs and behaviors. First, Covington (1992) shows that children and adults will often want to make attributions to ability for their successes because that increases self-worth more than attributions to hard work. In this case, the need for self-worth is driving the types of attributions individuals make in a situation, an important addition to the standard model of attribution theory, which does not really include the possibility that personal needs can influence the attribution process (see Chapter 4). In fact, Covington suggests that individuals will often try to hide how much effort they put forth on a task in order that others will think they simply have high ability. For example, some students will not tell their peers that they studied hard for a test. If they then do well, the usual attributional logic is that they must have high ability since they did not study hard (Covington, 1992).

In addition, Covington (1992) has shown that students will often engage in self-handicapping patterns of behavior in order to protect their self-worth. For example, students will often procrastinate on studying for an exam or doing a paper or project for a class. If they wait until the last minute to do the work, it is likely that they will not be as successful as they could be, and over the long run, this behavior is self-handicapping because performance is lower than possible. However, from a self-worth and attributional perspective, procrastination can have a positive motivational effect. If the students do poorly, then they can attribute their performance to lack of effort, thereby protecting their self-worth because they do not have to conclude they lack ability. At the same time, if they end up doing well, even with the procrastination, they can make an attribution that they must have high ability. Otherwise, how could they explain success with a low level of effort? On the other hand, if they do try hard and don't procrastinate and still do poorly, then it's likely that the students will conclude they lack ability and their self-worth will suffer. By combining his self-worth perspective with constructs from attribution theory, Covington shows us that the dynamics of self-worth are much more complicated than simple self-esteem models would have us believe. The role of affect and self-worth is explored in more detail in the next section on emotions and attributions.

EMOTIONS AS OUTCOMES OF THE ATTRIBUTIONAL PROCESS

Earlier in this chapter, we began with a description of Eccles and Wigfield's expectancy-value model and discussed the role of values in achievement choice and behavior. Another model that fits within the same general expectancy-value paradigm is attribution theory (Weiner, 1986; see Chapter 4 in this text). In Chapter 4, we discussed how attributions influence expectancy beliefs, but we did not discuss the "value" side of the equation for attribution theory. In contrast to the traditional definition of value as set forth by Atkinson and extended by Eccles and Wigfield to include students' beliefs about interest, importance, and utility, Weiner (1986) does not include these constructs in his attribution theory of motivation and emotion. In his view, *value* is defined by the emotions, such as pride, shame, guilt, and pity, that are generated by the attributional process. These emotions, combined with expectancy beliefs as in any expectancy-value theory, are then predictive of choice, persistence, and achievement behavior.

Attribution theory as developed by Weiner (1986) is one of the few social cognitive theories of motivation that explicitly incorporates emotions into the motivation-achievement behavior process. As in most social cognitive models of motivation, cognitions (attributions in this case) are one of the most important determiners of affect. That is, in this model, emotions are basically outcomes of the cognitive process of making attributions, or, to put it more colloquially, how we *think* influences how we *feel* (Weiner, 1986). This view of emotions as being dependent on a cognitive appraisal process is consistent with other cognitive models of emotions (e.g., Lazarus, 1991; Ortony, Clore, & Collins, 1988; Schachter & Singer, 1962). It is quite different, however, from psychodynamic models where emotions arise from unconscious processes and from behavioral models where emotions are represented as drives or outcomes of reinforcement contingencies. Of course, as Weiner (1986) points out, this cognitive approach to emotions does not deny that there can be emotions without cognitive appraisal, such as in the case of classically conditioned emotions (e.g., a child's ongoing fear of dogs due to an earlier dog bite) or emotions linked to physiological changes (e.g., hormonally induced depression). Weiner also recognizes that emotions can influence cognitions, as when a depressed person consistently uses a particularly explanatory or attributional style (Peterson et al., 1993), but, nevertheless, assumes that one of the main influences on emotions is how we perceive and think about what happened to us (Weiner, 1986).

Of course, attribution theory recognizes that some emotions are not a function of cognitive appraisal processes. These emotions are labeled *outcome dependent emotions* and are a function of the outcome, success or failure, of a task. In general, these outcome dependent emotions are relatively simple, or primitive, positive or negative emotions that are linked to the outcome. For example, individuals feel generally happy when they have done well on a test, been successful on the job, or performed well in an athletic situation, and they feel sad or frustrated when they have performed poorly in those situations. Accordingly, these simple emotions can be generated by the actual outcome without any cognitive appraisal on the individual's part. In attribution theory, however, the more complicated emotions are not really experienced until the individual engages in an attributional analysis.

Self-Evaluations

Figure 8.2 shows the basic attributional model for the linkages among attributions (causal dimensions), affects, and behavior outcomes. Recall from Chapter 4 that the attributions an individual makes can be categorized into three basic dimensions—locus, stability, and controllability. In a number of experimental studies, Weiner and his colleagues have shown that these dimensions are then linked to the various types of affect individuals will report. Many of these studies were laboratory studies in which individuals were asked to read vignettes or stories about a situation and then report how they would feel or how they think others would feel if in that situation. In some of the studies, individuals were asked to think of a time when they felt anger, pity, guilt, or pride and then asked to rate these self-generated events in terms of how the causal dimensions apply to the events (Weiner, 1986). It should be noted that these studies are more cognitive in nature; they may not evoke the actual emotions but simply the memory of the emotions and the accompanying cognitions. In contrast to the research on the accuracy of attributions and their link to future expectancies, as discussed in Chapter 4, questions regarding the validity of the emotions in these laboratory studies are appropriate. Accordingly, the links between attributions and affect may not be as straightforward as those between attributions and future expectancy beliefs. There is a clear need for more research in general and for more ecologically valid research specifically on the relations between attributions and emotions.

The Locus Dimension

Nevertheless, the research does demonstrate empirical linkages between attributions and affect that are logical and intuitive as well as in line with psychological and, perhaps, evolutionary theory (Weiner, 1986, 1994). As suggested in Figure 8.2, the studies have shown that the locus dimension is generally related to feelings of pride and self-esteem or self-worth. If individuals experience a success and attribute it to an internal cause, they are likely to take some pride in the success and experience an increase in self-worth. A failure that is attributed to internal causes, however, usually results in a lowering of self-esteem. Weiner (1986) notes that even Kant was aware of the link between locus and pride by suggesting that everyone at a meal could enjoy it, but only the cook could experience pride. Teachers may help to manage a student's self-esteem by suggesting that the student's failure on a task was not due to something about the student, but that the task was too hard. Failure in athletic events often generates a similar type of external attribution by the participants or others, such as coaches or parents (e.g., It was really windy. That's why you misjudged and dropped that fly ball to right field.), that helps the individual maintain self-esteem. In the same way, Weiner (1986) summarizes attributional studies of affiliative situations (e.g., asking a person for a date) by noting that most individuals are well aware of the potential damage to another person's self-esteem if rejection for a date is predicated on an internal attribution (e.g., I won't go out with you because you are very unattractive physically.). In fact, Weiner notes that many people will not tell the "truth" in this situation

Figure 8.2.   Relations among causal dimensions, affect, and behavior. (Adapted from Weiner, 1994)

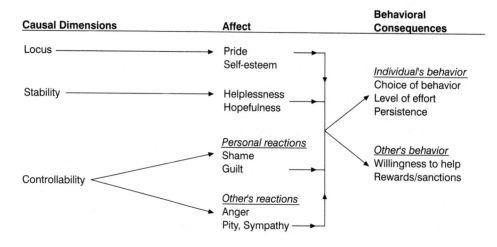

but rather provide some other excuse for affiliative rejection in order to protect the rebuffed individual's self-esteem.

The Stability Dimension

The stability dimension has been linked to feelings of hopefulness or hopelessness, paralleling the findings for the link between stability and future expectancy for success. Recall from Chapter 4 that Weiner (1986) proposed the expectancy principle such that attributing an outcome to a stable cause will result in an expectation that the outcome will occur again in the future and that attributing an outcome to an unstable cause will lead to an expectation that future outcomes will be different than earlier outcomes. Following this logic and applying it to emotion, Weiner suggests that attributions to stable causes for failure should result in feelings of hopelessness. For example, if a student fails an exam and attributes it to a traitlike lack of ability, then he may experience a feeling of hopelessness about being able to perform better in the future since he believes his ability cannot change. In contrast, an athlete who fails in a competition but attributes her failure to poor training and preparation can still feel hopeful about the future competitions because training and preparation can be changed. Weiner, Russell, and Lerman (1978) found some support for this linkage between feelings of helplessness, depression, and hopelessness and causal attributions to both internal and stable causes for failure. However, Weiner (1986) notes that not as much research has been conducted on the links between the stability dimensions and emotions in comparison to the links between controllability and emotions.

The Controllability Dimension

The research on the controllability dimension and emotions has focused on both personal reactions experienced by individuals as they react to their own performance and the affect experienced by others as they evaluate or react to an individual. In terms of the personal reactions of individuals to their own performance, the research suggests that personal controllability is associated with shame-related emotions and guilt (Weiner, 1986). Weiner (1994) argues that controllability is related to personal responsibility. If a cause is seen as controllable, then the individual is deemed responsible, whereas uncontrollable causes generate a perception of less personal responsibility for the outcome. The attribution-emotion sequence for a failure situation when an attribution is made to ability (which is normatively classified as uncontrollable) is that the individual will feel shame, embarrassment, or humiliation (Brown & Weiner, 1984; Covington & Omelich, 1979). Moreover, these negative shame-related emotions will probably lead to disengagement in the task and performance decrements (see Figure 8.2).

For example, a student who fails an exam in science and thinks it is due to his lack of ability, which he believes is not controllable, will likely be embarrassed by his failure. These feelings of embarrassment could lead to the student not choosing to take science courses in the future and also have an adverse effect on his performance in his current science course. In contrast, if a person fails and attributes it to lack of effort, which is controllable and under her personal responsibility, then she is likely to feel guilty (or experience guilt-related affects such as regret or remorse) about her lack of effort and poor performance (Weiner, 1994). This guilt can be harnessed to increase effort for the next exam and the increased effort should lead to better performance for the student. Of course, students may not feel guilty even if the cause of their performance is seen as personally controllable, but Weiner (1986) suggests that if guilt is experienced, then some element of personal responsibility is usually present as well. For example, students may feel guilty that they are letting their parents down when they do poorly on an exam, or feel guilty when they are caught cheating on an exam, or feel remorse when they are caught in a lie, but these situations are usually perceived as personally controllable (Weiner, Graham, & Chandler, 1982; Graham, Doubleday, & Guarino, 1984).

The reactions of others as they evaluate an individual's performance are also shown in Figure 8.2, but are represented by the paths from controllability to the emotions of anger and pity and then on to the behavioral consequences. The attributional analysis of how evaluators might feel and react as they judge a target person's performance corresponds directly to the teacher-student interaction when the teacher evaluates and reacts to the student's performance. In fact, many of the attributional laboratory studies have asked the participants to imagine that they are teachers. The participants are presented with vignettes about hypothetical students who demonstrate different levels of performance and are then asked to make judgments about these hypothetical students, report on their affect toward these students, and report their behavioral reactions to the students.

These laboratory studies have shown that the emotional and behavioral reactions of the evaluators are linked to the controllability dimension (Weiner, 1986). For example, if a teacher believes that a student's failure is due to lack of ability (an uncontrollable cause), then that teacher is likely to feel pity or sympathy for that student. The reasoning is that the student is perceived as not being responsible for the poor performance due to lack of ability. This link between uncontrollable causes and the emotions of sympathy and pity aroused in others is complementary to the personal reactions of shame when failure is due to an uncontrollable cause (Weiner, 1994). In addition, lab studies have shown that teachers also are likely to report that they will not punish a student who, as perceived by them, is not at fault for not doing well (Weiner, 1986). Moreover, Brophy and Rohrkemper (1981), in a study with actual teachers reacting to vignettes about different types of problem students (e.g., defiant students, hyperactive students), showed that the teachers were much more likely to offer more help, instruction, and support when the cause of the problem was seen as uncontrollable for the student. When the problem behavior was seen as controllable by the student (e.g., defiance), however, the teachers were less likely to report that they would offer help and more likely to react with threats or punishment. Other studies of helping behavior (e.g., Barnes, Ickes, & Kidd, 1979; Weiner, 1980a, 1980b) have shown the same pattern with peer help. College students are more likely to offer their class notes to a student who missed class due to illness (uncontrollable cause) than to a student who missed class to go to the beach (controllable cause).

In contrast to the positive emotions generated (sympathy) and the positive behavioral reactions (no punishment, more help) when another's failure is perceived as uncontrollable, if the failure is seen as controllable, the evaluator usually reacts with negative emotions and behavior. For example, if a student fails and the teacher or parent attributes the failure to a lack of effort, then the emotion most often expressed in the vignette studies is anger (Weiner, 1986). The teacher or parent perceives the student's lack of effort as under the student's control and as the personal responsibility of the student and feels angry that the student did not try harder on the task. This link between a controllable cause and an evaluator's emotional reaction of anger complements the personal reaction of guilt felt by an individual who did not try hard. The research on behavioral reactions of evaluators to a failure due to controllable causes also shows that evaluators will be more likely to punish the student for lack of effort (Weiner & Kukla, 1970; Weiner, 1986). As already noted, the student will be less likely to get help from others when they perceive that the student has not tried hard or has control over the problem.

These linkages among the dimensions of an attribution, the emotions experienced, and the subsequent behavioral reactions can help us understand both student and teacher affect and behavior in the classroom. Although there is a need for more research on attributions and affect in actual classroom settings, the linkages are supported by empirical research and also make sense theoretically, logically, and intuitively. Many teachers have experienced anger when a student is able to do a task but does not try hard and then performs poorly. Even more so than teachers, many parents, especially those with adolescents, may experience anger when their sons and daughters clearly have the ability to do well in school yet do not put forth any effort for academic work. Many of us, as either teachers or students, have probably felt guilty when we have performed poorly due to low effort. By using attribution theory, we can help students and teachers understand their emotional reactions. As they become more aware of how these attributional-emotional dynamics may work, they will be better prepared to cope with their emotions and regulate their behavior. This is especially important for teachers because their behavioral reactions to students in terms of help, instruction, and support is crucial for student learning and development.

In closing, it is important to note that these linkages among attributions, dimensions of control and personal responsibility, emotions, and behavioral consequences apply to many domains of everyday life, not just to teachers, students, and classrooms. Weiner (1986, 1992) has pointed out that judgments of personal responsibility and the behavioral consequences that are generated from these judgments underlie many domains. For example, discussion of the provision of welfare or unemployment benefits often turns on the perception of controllability and personal responsibility. More liberal individuals in the United States are inclined to favor the wide provision of government benefits because they are likely to attribute an individual's need for benefits to factors that are not controllable by that person, such as macroeconomic structural factors, poor educational institutions, persistent race and class discrimination, and so on. In contrast, conservatives are more likely to attribute the problem to controllable factors, such as lack of personal effort, habitual laziness, or unwillingness to learn. By branding welfare mothers or the chronically unemployed as lazy and not motivated to get a job, control and responsibility are shifted to the individual, which leads to the conclusion that it is really up to the individual to remedy the problem, not the government through welfare benefit programs.

Weiner (1986, 1992) also has shown that these dynamics regarding controllability and personal responsibility can play a role in parole decisions, medical decisions, reactions to AIDS patients, reactions to obesity or alcoholism, and marital distress. For example, individuals' reactions to AIDS patients, obese individuals, or alcoholics were more positive when the cause of the condition was perceived as uncontrollable (e.g., AIDS due to blood transfusion, obesity due to a thyroid problem, a genetic predisposition to alcoholism) than when the cause was perceived as controllable (unsafe sex, overeating and lack of exercise, personal choice of excessive drinking). Following this logic, Weiner (1992) notes that often medical doctors treat patients when their condition is perceived as personally uncontrollable, whereas mental health professionals often treat those patients who are seen as personally responsible for their condition. In a marriage, negative events (being late for dinner, missing an important family engagement) can generate discord if the cause is seen as controllable (choosing to work late) rather than uncontrollable (being stuck in rush-hour traffic).

IMPLICATIONS FOR TEACHERS

The different constructs and models we have discussed in this chapter lend themselves to a number of implications for teachers. Some of them overlap greatly with the suggestions offered in Chapter 7. Moreover, given the diversity of constructs discussed in this chapter and Chapter 7, all the implications will not necessarily be congruent with other suggestions. As we have noted previously, teachers must make difficult decisions about their goals for students and the different instructional strategies they might use to reach those goals.

1. Teachers should offer rationales for schoolwork that include discussion of the importance and utility value of the work. As noted in the beginning of this chapter, Mr. Lopez does try to communicate to his students how math can help them in their everyday life. Brophy (1983) has noted how seldom teachers actually do this in the course of instruction.

Ms. Brennan, a seventh-grade science teacher, discusses with her class how important science is, not just for understanding life outside school, but for keeping certain career options open. She points out how engineers and medical doctors need to take a great many science courses in both high school and college.

2. Activate personal interest through opportunities for choice and control. Although it can be very difficult, impractical, and probably unnecessary to develop a wholly child-centered curriculum based on students' individual interests, teachers can provide opportunities for students to exercise some choice and control over their learning.

Ms. Wong has collected a very large number of reading books and stories for her fourth-grade classroom. These books and stories range from first grade to junior high reading level (range of difficulty levels) and cover a great many different topics. She allows her students to choose their own reading books based on their interest in the topics and their own perception of the difficulty level of the books. She finds that most students are fairly good at picking out books that match their level of reading competence. Moreover, she scaffolds her instruction by helping those who pick books that are too hard and encourages students to try harder books if they seem to perseverate on choosing books that are too easy.

3. Create situational interest in the schoolwork and tasks. Given the difficulties in adapting instruction to diverse personal interests, it may be easier for teachers to attempt to create situational interest. There are any number of ways to create situational interest, as noted in Chapter 7.

Mr. Urdan, a high school American history teacher, uses a number of different texts and sources in his class, not just the textbook. These texts include more detailed scholarly books as well as original source material. The students find these materials more interesting than the rather dry textbook.

Ms. Murphy, a high school biology and chemistry teacher, consciously tries to model her own interest in the science material she is teaching by talking about her own learning of it and how it interests her. In addition, she attempts to create surprise and disequilibrium by having students predict what will happen in different experiments and then showing that the students' predictions are wrong when she does the model experiment. She then spends the remainder of the class talking about how the students derived their predictions and how the experiment and related theory disprove their predictions.

4. Reduce test anxiety in the classroom. Mr. Walters, an eighth-grade math teacher, makes arrangements for some students to have a longer period of time to complete his end-of-unit tests. He knows his tests usually take about 40–45 minutes of his 50-minute period for most students. However, there are several students who need more time to take the tests because of their test anxiety. He allows them to continue to work on the test into the next class period. His next class is not disrupted because they also are taking the same end-of-unit test. Mr. Walters always explains to the other teachers why some of the students will be a little late to their next class. Mr. Walters does not post grades in public places for everyone to see. He also tries to communicate that the tests reflect students' effort and their learning, not a stable traitlike math ability.

5. *Develop self-worth in the classroom.* There are many ways to help students develop self-worth in the classroom. Covington (1992) discusses a number of different strategies that can be used; however, he does emphasize the importance of contingent teacher feedback for actual student performance, not just noncontingent and insincere teacher feedback.

Ms. Garcia tries to praise her math students all the time, regardless of their actual performance. She believes this will help their self-esteem, but she doesn't understand why so many of her students still lack math skills and still believe they can't do math. Mr. Lopez, on the other hand, gives feedback that is contingent on actual math performance. If the students don't get the problems correct, he tells them so but accompanies his comments with feedback about how and why their approach to the math problems went wrong.

6. *Develop appropriate attributions for student behavior and manage affect.* Ms. Hofer, a third-grade teacher, is very careful in making attributions about students' ability and effort in her classroom. She knows that she can get very angry when a student who clearly has the ability does not try hard and this makes her want to punish the student. She tries to understand this pattern of affect and behavior, to understand why the student is not trying and still try to help the student increase his or her effort, even though her first reaction is to be angry and to punish the student.

SUMMARY

This chapter has covered a great deal of material from a number of different theories and models on the role of values, interest, and affect in the classroom. We began with a discussion of Eccles and Wigfield's four-component model of task values that includes importance, utility, interest, and cost. These four components of task value have been empirically validated in a large number of correlational studies. This research suggests that values are more likely to be related to choice behavior such as choosing to take more math classes, whereas expectancy and efficacy perceptions are probably more related to actual achievement.

Personal and situational interest are two different types of interest that can influence learning and performance. Personal interest is a more stable, personality or individual difference variable. Personal interests are directed at specific activities or topics but there is a great deal of variability in what activities or topics will become of personal interest to any one individual. In contrast, situational interest is a more situated view of interest, where interest is generated by the features of the immediate environment. Situational interest can be increased by the use of interesting texts, media, presentations, and the like, and is generally assumed to be relatively consistent across individuals. Both personal and situational interest are positively related to choice of future activities, memory, attention, deeper cognitive processing, and actual achievement and performance.

Test anxiety has two general components, a worry and an emotionality component. The worry component refers to the cognitions or thoughts that individuals have when they worry during a test-taking situation. The emotionality component involves both physiological (sweaty hands, rapid heartbeat) and emotional arousal (fear and negative affect) that are often generated in evaluative situations. Paralleling the distinction between personal and situational interest, test anxiety is often divided into both trait and state anxiety. Trait anxiety represents a more stable personality characteristic of an individual, whereas state anxiety is a more situational arousal of anxiety due to stressful testing circumstances. Test anxiety has been consistently shown to have a negative effect on academic learning and performance.

Self-esteem and self-worth are emotional reactions to the self. Popular views of self-esteem are too simplistic to offer much help in our attempts to understand student achievement in the classroom. Covington's (1992) self-worth theory represents an important discussion of the role of self-worth in school learning because of his use of current theoretical models of motivation, such as attribution theory. In addition, his research is based on empirical research with students, not just popular opinions about the role of self-esteem.

Attribution theory can help us understand some of our more complicated emotions and our behavioral reactions to others in the classroom. When teachers perceive that a student's failure was controllable due to low effort, they will often feel anger and be likely to punish the student. In contrast, if the student's failure is due to causes that are not under the student's control (low ability), then the teacher may be likely to feel sympathy and be more willing to help the student. These motivational dynamics among attributions, emotions, and behavioral reactions are very useful for understanding classroom life.

Teacher and Classroom Influences

*L*isa McMahan was beginning her sixth year of teaching and she could never remember feeling so discouraged. After 2 months of school, she was ready to give up on her fourth-grade class. Part of her problem undoubtedly stemmed from her move this past summer to a new community and going to work at an unfamiliar school. But a larger part was due to her interactions—or lack thereof—with her students. She thought she might be experiencing burnout.

Lisa recalled the day she was at school about a week before classes started to get her room ready for her children. Betty, an experienced teacher, came by to see how things were going. She sat down and proceeded to give Lisa the rundown on the students she would have in her class, and it was quite a cast. Betty told her *that Preston was caught stealing over the summer, Mike had an abusive father, Doris's mother was a drug addict, Kip's brother was in prison, Lele's father was an alcoholic, Todd ran with an older crowd that some people thought were part of a gang, and so forth. Betty said, "You really can't expect much from them. Do your best but don't go out of your way because they have too many problems to do well in school. No one will blame you." Betty also told Lisa the names of a few good students worth working with.*

When Lisa finally met each of the children, all she could think about was what Betty had told her. During the first few weeks of school, Lisa acted in accordance with her expectations for the students created by what Betty had said. Previously she had taught average classes; now in her lesson planning she "dumbed down" the instruction to a level she thought students could handle. She introduced lessons by noting that the material was tough and some students might have trouble learning it. When she interacted with students, she asked harder questions of those who she felt were brighter and easier ones of students who she thought would have trouble learning. When she grouped students, she separated the slower ones from the brighter ones.

Not surprisingly, the scenario played out according to her expectations. The students she expected would learn did learn, the ones she expected would not learn did not. As her low achievers fell farther behind, Lisa felt less motivated to try to help them improve. Discipline problems increased. No wonder she felt discouraged!

Lisa was enrolled in a master's degree program at a local university and one of the classes she was taking had a unit on motivation. Included in that unit was a discussion of the role that teacher expectations and classroom factors play in student motivation. Lisa read with fascination how research showed that teachers' expectations for students can become self-fulfilling prophecies: If teachers expect little, then students perform worse than when teachers expect more from them. Lisa shared her teaching experiences with her university class and a lively discussion ensued. She became so interested in the topic she chose to write a term paper on it for the class.

Lisa decided to make some changes in her own teaching. First, she stopped differentiating students and instead assumed that they all could learn. She planned lessons around this new higher standard of achievement. She introduced units by stating that all students could learn the material if they were will-

ing to work diligently. When she grouped students, she mixed students of different ability levels and ensured that each student in the group had some responsibility for the group's success. She challenged all students based on her perceptions of what would motivate them.

Changes in the class became readily apparent. Some of the students who Betty said could not learn in fact were quite bright and learned easily. Students were more motivated to learn and there were fewer discipline problems in class. Students who had fallen behind began to catch up. And Lisa decided not to give up on the class and realized that this year might not be so bad after all!

Few people would argue with the contention that teachers can affect student motivation. Lisa McMahan's story illustrates some of the ways this can happen. In their planning of instruction and interactions with students, teachers can structure classroom events to have different effects on student motivation. Despite this seemingly powerful influence of teachers, however, only recently have researchers identified the many ways that teachers can affect student motivation. Historically, the function of teachers as motivators was viewed in a narrow sense. Their primary means to motivate students was to dispense such rewards as grades, privileges, praise, prizes, and stickers. This view, which derived from operant conditioning theory (Chapter 2), placed the locus of motivation in the environment. The ultimate goal of an operant system was to have students engage in much independent learning. The teacher arranged materials and students responded and received reinforcement. Learning could occur with little interaction with teachers (Keller, 1968).

Evidence from various sources has altered this role of the teacher to one in which virtually everything the teacher does has potential motivational impact on students. This includes not only the more obvious ways that teachers attempt to influence student motivation (e.g., by setting goals, rewarding good performances) but also teacher activities typically associated with instruction (grouping students, questioning strategies) and teacher attempts at classroom management and methods for minimizing and dealing with disciplinary problems. In many of the previous chapters, we have outlined some of the ways various teacher behaviors can influence student motivation.

Another recent development concerns the reciprocal nature of influence between teachers and students. Many early studies of teaching effectiveness assumed that teachers' actions affected student motivation, but there was little effort to determine how students' behaviors influenced teachers (Dunkin & Biddle, 1974). In recent years, increasing evidence supports the notion that students do influence teachers' thoughts and actions. Teachers' planning and instructional activities affect student cognitions and learning and, in turn, teachers' thoughts and behaviors are influenced by how students react to classroom activities. This point brings to mind Bandura's (1986) emphasis on reciprocal interactions among cognitions, behaviors, and environmental factors (Chapter 5).

We begin this chapter by discussing motivational processes associated with traditional teacher functions of planning and instruction. We then discuss teacher-student interactions and the influence of teacher beliefs. The next area covered, which is receiving increased research emphasis, is how teacher expectations for student learning and performance affect student motivation. We conclude by discussing classroom management and the role of classroom structural factors in motivation.

TEACHER PLANNING AND DECISION MAKING

Planning and decision making are integral components of teaching. Instructional models incorporate these aspects and relate them to student achievement. Planning and decision making also are relevant to motivation. We discuss models of planning and decision making, followed by the important topic of grouping for instruction.

Models of Planning and Decision Making

Many models of teacher planning are prescriptive and spell out what teachers should do to foster student learning (Clark & Yinger, 1979). They include such steps as specifying learning objectives, selecting teacher and student activities, organizing activities, and delineating evaluation methods. These models are linear and rational in the sense that they assume that planning requires orderly thinking concerning ways to attain objectives. A second type of planning model conceives of planning as beginning with teacher decisions about the types of learning activities to be used. Within this context, objectives arise and are integrated with activities. The means and ends of teaching become integrated, so goals are not specified initially.

Current advances in learning theory and research methodology have led some researchers away from these types of models and toward exploring teachers' thought processes prior to, during, and after teaching (Clark & Yinger, 1979). In this view, planning and decision making are not confined to the preinstructional aspects of teaching but rather occur during all phases of teaching, including while lessons are being conducted. This view is based on information-processing and cognitive theories, which stress the reception, organization, and encoding of information in memory (Anderson, 1990; Gagné, Yekovich, & Yekovich, 1993). To explore teachers' thought processes, researchers rely on such methods as self-reports through interviews and questionnaires, think-aloud protocols whereby teachers verbalize aloud while planning, and stimulated recall procedures in which teachers comment on their thought processes while planning and teaching as they watch videotapes of their performances (see Chapter 1).

Teachers' planning is strongly influenced by the characteristics of their students, such as needs, abilities, and motivation (Clark & Peterson, 1986; Clark & Yinger, 1979). Teachers are concerned with not only how to foster attainment of objectives given the abilities and competence of the students but also how much the instruction and activities will appeal to students' interests. When teachers take interest value into account, it is often the case that student activities do not follow logically from specification of objectives and that the latter is not always an important component of planning (Zahorik, 1975).

Motivational concerns are important in teachers' decision making. Clark and Yinger (1979) report a study in which elementary school teachers rated potential language arts teaching activities in terms of how likely they were to use each activity in their classrooms. For those activities rated highly, teachers listed features that contributed to their decisions. The most frequently mentioned category involved students; within this the activity feature contributing most strongly to positive judgments was motivation and student involvement.

Similar importance of motivation is found in studies examining teachers' decisions while they are engaged in instruction. In one study (Clark & Yinger, 1979), teachers viewed videotaped segments of their teaching and were asked to recall what they were thinking about at that particular time. Some important findings were that teachers considered using alternative teaching strategies only when the instruction was not working well and that the main cue teachers used to determine how well instruction was proceeding was the involvement and participation of their students. Thus, teachers considered changing approaches when they noticed that student motivation was lagging. Other research supports the point that teachers' decisions during teaching are heavily influenced by their inferences about students' cognitive and affective processes relevant to motivation (Clark & Yinger, 1979).

In sum, teachers often do not follow a rational planning model because they do not begin planning in relation to specific objectives or goals (Clark & Yinger, 1979). Teachers often begin planning by considering the setting and content to be taught, after which they shift their attention to motivational concerns (i.e., student participation and involvement). With respect to decisions during teaching, teachers typically deviate little from their plans, but when they do, it often is because of motivational concerns (student interest is lagging). There exists a reciprocal influence between teachers and students. Teachers affect student motivation and learning through their planning, but student reactions to instruction cause teachers to take stock of the situation and implement strategies that they believe will have a better effect on motivation and learning.

Instructional Grouping

A critical component of planning is deciding what activities students will work on, which also involves deciding how students will be grouped. Much research has examined the effects of grouping on student motivation (see Chapter 5). We examine the effects of three types of structures: competitive, cooperative, and individualistic. *Competitive* situations are those in which the goals of individuals are negatively linked such that if one person attains his or her goal, the chances of others attaining theirs are lessened. *Cooperative* situations are those in which the goals of the group members are positively linked such that one individual can attain his or her goal only if others attain theirs. In *individualistic* situations, there is no link between the goals of individuals; accomplishment or nonaccomplishment of one person's goal has no effect on goal attainment of others (Deutsch, 1949; Johnson & Johnson, 1974; Slavin, 1983a). Table 9.1 presents descriptions and examples of the three types of grouping.

Structures affect student motivation in large part by the cues they provide that inform students about their capabilities (Ames, 1984; Johnson & Johnson, 1985). Competitive structures accentuate the importance of ability and social comparisons of one person's work with that of others. Motivation is enhanced when students believe they are performing better than others but is weakened for those students who perceive their work as inferior to that of others. In competitive situations, it commonly happens that a few students receive the rewards most of the time. These situations obviously may not motivate many students in the class. In individualistic structures, rewards are based on self-improvement (Ames, 1984). Rather than comparing personal performance with that of others, students compare their present outcomes with their prior performances. Students who notice that they are improving are apt to feel a sense of self-efficacy for learning and be motivated to continue to improve (Schunk, 1989c). In cooperative structures, students share in the successes or failures as a function of their collective performance. The group outcome affects students' perceptions of their capabilities.

Ames (1981) compared competitive and cooperative structures for their effects on children's self-evaluations. In the competitive condition, students

Table 9.1.   Instructional Grouping

Arrangement	Description	Example
Competitive	Students' goals negatively linked: One attains one's goal only if others do not attain theirs	Teacher grades "on the curve" and gives 15% of the students A's, 25% of the students B's, and so on
Cooperative	Students' goals positively linked: One attains one's goal only if others attain theirs	Teacher forms small group to work on project; each student is responsible for completing a part and all students put parts together to form final product
Individualistic	Students' goals not linked: Attainment or nonattainment has no effect on goal attainment by others	Students work on computer software programs individually and record completion on their progress sheets

were paired and told that the winner would receive a prize; in the cooperative condition, both group members were informed that they would receive prizes if they attained a specific performance goal. Performance outcome was manipulated such that one child in each pair outperformed the other; within the cooperative condition, groups either did or did not attain their goal. The results showed that in cooperative groups, the group outcome had a direct effect on students' perceptions of their ability and feelings of satisfaction. Group success also alleviated negative self-perceptions resulting from poor individual performance, and group failure lowered positive self-perceptions of students who performed well. This and other research (Ames, 1984) shows that failure in competitive settings has more deleterious effects on self-perceptions than does failure in noncompetitive ones. In cooperative groups, low achievers share in the group success as much as high achievers. At the same time, however, when cooperative groups fail, dissatisfaction can run high regardless of one's individual performance. For low achievers, successful cooperative groups can help to build efficacy, but unsuccessful ones can have the same type of negative effect on self-efficacy as does failure under competitive conditions (Ames & Felker, 1979).

INSTRUCTIONAL PRACTICES

In addition to their planning efforts, how teachers deliver instruction and monitor student performance has an important impact on student motivation. In this section, we review the literature on the influence of teaching practices on student motivation.

Effective Teaching

Much research has investigated how teaching practices affect student achievement. In several studies, some teachers were trained to implement various instructional practices in their classrooms and others were not trained but continued to teach in their regular manner. Research generally is consistent in showing that teachers trained to implement effective teaching practices raise student achievement more so than untrained teachers (Brophy & Good, 1986).

Rosenshine and Stevens (1986) reviewed research on how effective teachers teach structured content where the objectives are to attain knowledge or master skills that can be taught in step-by-step fashion or to acquire general rules that students might apply to new problems or content. Examples are arithmetic facts and computation, decoding skills, grammar and vocabulary, musical notation, map reading, solving algebraic equations, mechanics of letter writing, and factual aspects of history and science. Their findings are summarized in Table 9.2.

Table 9.2.   Effective Teaching Practices for Structured Content

---

- Begin lessons with a short review of prerequisite learning and a statement of goals.
- Present new material in small steps and give students practice after each step.
- Give clear, detailed instructions and explanations.
- Provide students with high levels of active practice.
- Ask questions, check for student understanding, and obtain responses from all students.
- Guide students during initial practice.
- Provide systematic feedback and corrective instruction.
- Provide explicit instruction and practice for seatwork exercises; monitor students during seatwork.

Material drawn from Rosenshine and Stevens (1986)

These findings are consistent with principles of contemporary cognitive theories of learning (Anderson, 1990; Gagné et al., 1993; Schunk, 1991a). For example, by beginning lessons with short reviews of prior relevant material and stating learning objectives, teachers help to activate information in students' long-term memories and provide them with a cognitive structure for encoding the new material. Information processing is easier for students as they integrate new information with the prior learning and thereby build better organized mental networks of knowledge. Presenting material in small steps and allowing student practice ensures that students' information processing capabilities are not overloaded and that the students can effectively process information and store it in memory before more material is presented. Practice is a form of rehearsal, which helps to organize and store information in memory. With repeated practice, material is learned and skills can be executed with little conscious attention, which frees space in working memory for new learning. Clear explanations and demonstrations ensure that students understand the content and do not engage in complex mental processing to determine what the teacher has said. Asking students questions, checking for understanding, monitoring students' work, and providing corrective feedback ensure that learning has occurred properly and serve to correct errors before faulty knowledge is acquired.

Some steps are more important for certain learners and types of content (Rosenshine & Stevens, 1986). For example, use of small steps helps young children, who have their developmental limitations in information-processing capability, students with learning problems, and all learners during the early stages of learning. Presenting material in small steps ensures that students are not mentally overloaded with information, which could result in faulty learning. Younger students may need more practice and feedback. With development, the amount of presentation time can increase relative to practice because older students rehearse and encode information more effectively. All of these points apply best to material that is hierarchically ordered, such that more advanced skills build on mastery of basic skills, and to difficult material for which a small-step approach and much student practice facilitate learning.

By integrating learning research with research on teaching, Rosenshine and Stevens (1986) developed the following list of fundamental instructional functions:

1. Review, check previous day's work, reteach as necessary
2. Present new material
3. Give students guided practice, check for understanding
4. Provide feedback, reteach if needed
5. Give students independent practice
6. Review at spaced (weekly, monthly) intervals

These instructional procedures should promote student motivation and achievement. The review of previous material helps prepare students for new learning and creates an initial sense of self-efficacy for learning. Students are apt to believe that since they understand prerequisite material, they will be able to learn the new material. Presenting new material, especially in small steps, allows them to be successful, and successful performances constitute an important means for sustaining student motivation to learn (Schunk, 1991a). Teacher feedback is another source of efficacy information. Teachers who tell students they are performing well or give corrective information help substantiate students' initial sense of efficacy for learning. Independent practice increases efficacy; students who can succeed on their own feel efficacious about learning and are motivated to continue to improve. Periodic reviews in which students perform well convey that students have learned and retained the information, which enhances motivation for further learning because it validates students' beliefs about their competence (Schunk, 1989c).

Use of Models

Models are important influences on student motivation (Bandura, 1986; Schunk, 1987; see Chapter 5). Teachers as models are a vicarious source of self-efficacy information for students. Students who observe teachers explain and demonstrate concepts and skills are apt to believe that they are capable of learning. As students follow teacher explanations and mentally rehearse operations, they may believe that they are learning the material, especially if teachers present material in manageable units and provide clear explanations.

Teachers also provide persuasive information to students. Consider the following example of how a teacher might introduce a lesson:

Today we are going to learn how to add fractions with like denominators. For the past few days, we have been discussing fractions and you all know how to add numbers. We will see that adding fractions with like denominators requires you to do things that you already can do. So I know that we all will be able to learn how to add fractions.

This introduction should lead students to believe they are capable of learning. Their self-efficacy is validated as they work on the task and experience success. Teachers also enhance motivation through the use of interesting displays and presentations that capture and hold student attention. Attention is a critical component of learning and the interest generated is motivational. Finally, teachers often provide information about why learning is important. Teachers who inform students about why learning is important and how it will help them on different tasks motivate students to attend to material, organize and rehearse information to be remembered, and use the material as needed.

Peers as models also impact student motivation (Schunk, 1987; see Chapter 5). Observing a similar peer performing a task well instates a sense of self-efficacy. Students believe that if peers can succeed, they can as well. This sense of efficacy motivates students to work on the task productively and is validated as students experience success. An important variable in modeling is the number of models used (Schunk et al., 1987). Compared with a single model, multiple models increase the probability that observers will perceive themselves as similar to at least one of the models (Thelen et al., 1979). Students who might discount the successes of a single model due to dissimilarity in important characteristics (e.g., abilities) may be influenced by observing several peers accomplishing a task.

Another way to raise efficacy is to use *coping models*, who initially demonstrate the typical fears and deficiencies of observers but gradually improve their performance and gain confidence. Coping models show how effort and positive self-thoughts overcome difficulties. In contrast, *mastery models* demonstrate faultless performance and high confidence from the outset (Schunk, 1987). Coping models enhance perceived similarity and self-efficacy among students who view the coping models' initial difficulties and gradual progress as more similar to their typical performances than the rapid learning of mastery models.

TEACHER-STUDENT INTERACTIONS

Classrooms are active places where teachers and students constantly interact with one another. Teachers ask questions, provide feedback, administer rewards and punishments, praise and criticize, respond to students' questions and requests for help, and offer assistance when students experience difficulties. In this section, we discuss how these interactions affect student motivation.

Teacher Feedback

Teacher feedback is a major teaching function (Rosenshine & Stevens, 1986) and we present the different types of teacher feedback in this section. They also are summarized in Table 9.3.

Performance Feedback

Performance feedback is feedback on the accuracy of work and may include corrective information. Performance feedback is an important influence on student learning. Teachers give performance feedback following four types of student responses (Rosenshine & Stevens, 1986): a correct answer given quickly and firmly, a correct answer given hesitantly, an incorrect answer reflecting a careless error, and an incorrect answer suggesting lack of knowledge of facts or a process.

Students are likely to respond correctly in a quick and firm fashion during the later stages of learning and during reviews. Teacher feedback conveying accuracy of the response (e.g., Right.) is informative. Research suggests that teachers should then ask a new question and maintain the momentum of the lesson. Student responses that are correct but hesitant are more likely during the earlier stages of learning—during guided or independent practice and when teachers check for understanding. Teachers need to provide confirma-

Table 9.3.   Teacher Feedback

Type	Description	Examples
Performance	Provides information on accuracy of work; may include corrective information	"That's correct." "The first part is right but then you need to remember to bring down the next number."
Motivational	Provides information on progress and competence; may include social comparisons and persuasion	"You've really gotten much better at this. You're doing a great job." "I know you can do this."
Attributional	Links student performance with one or more attributions	"You're good at this." "You've been working hard and you're doing well."
Strategy	Informs students about how well they are applying a strategy and how strategy use is improving their work	"You got it right because you used the steps in the right order." "You're really using the five-step method well and it's helping you do better."

tory feedback (Correct., Good.), and may need to provide feedback covering the process used to arrive at the correct answer. This process feedback also informs other students who still may be unsure of what they are doing (Rosenshine & Stevens, 1986).

When students make careless errors, teachers should provide corrective feedback but not explain the process again (Rosenshine & Stevens, 1986). Student errors indicating lack of knowledge of facts or the process are likely during the early stages of learning. In this circumstance, teachers either can provide students with prompts to lead them to the correct answer or can reteach the material to the students who do not understand. If the teacher is leading the class, it seems helpful to attempt to lead the student to the correct answer with hints or simple questions; however, such interactions are most effective if they remain brief (30 seconds or less). Longer personal contacts tend to lose the attention of the rest of the class. If the student cannot be guided to a correct answer through a brief contact, it is necessary to reteach the content to that student and others who do not understand, for example, when the other students engage in independent practice.

Reteaching and leading students to the correct answer are effective ways to promote learning (Rosenshine & Stevens, 1986). Asking simpler questions and giving hints are useful when the contact can be kept short (Anderson, Evertson, & Brophy, 1979). Reteaching is helpful when errors are made by many students during a lesson (Good & Grouws, 1979). With a small group, the teacher will reteach the entire group. With a large group when only some of the students require assistance, the teacher should reteach when the others are engaged with the material (Arlin & Webster, 1983). Alternatively, reteaching can be scheduled during breaks (lunch, recess) and peers can reteach the material in groups.

Feedback informing students that answers are correct motivates because it indicates that the students are becoming more competent and are capable of further learning (Schunk, 1989c). Feedback indicating an error also can build motivation and efficacy if followed by corrective information showing the student how to perform better. Such feedback engenders the belief that students will perform better by using the method demonstrated by the teacher. The belief of individuals that they are capable of learning raises motivation and leads to better skill acquisition.

Motivational Feedback

Teachers often provide students with feedback designed to motivate rather than to inform about accuracy of answers. One type of motivational feedback provides *social comparative information* about capabilities of other students. A teacher might remark to Kevin, "See how well Mark is doing. Why don't you try to work like that?" Another common type of motivational feedback is *persuasive* and takes the form of such statements as, "I know you can do this," and, "Keep up the good work." Although both forms of feedback indirectly convey information about competence, their primary function is to get students to work on tasks and maintain productive task engagement.

The vicarious information provided with social comparisons and persuasive feedback are important sources of self-efficacy information (Bandura, 1986; Schunk, 1989c; see Chapter 3). Observing similar others succeed raises observers' self-efficacy and motivates them to persevere at the task. Once students become engaged in the task and experience success, this initial sense of efficacy is substantiated and motivation improves. Similarity is especially influential in situations where individuals have experienced difficulties and hold doubts about performing well. Positive persuasive feedback also creates feelings of efficacy. Students experience high efficacy when told they are capable of learning by a trustworthy source such as the teacher but may discount the advice of less credible sources. Students also may discount otherwise trustworthy sources if they believe the sources do not fully understand the task demands (e.g., difficult for students to comprehend) or contextual factors (room is too noisy or too warm).

The effects of vicarious and persuasive sources on self-efficacy generally are weaker than those due to actual performances, so it is imperative that increases in self-efficacy derived from vicarious and persuasive sources be confirmed by subsequent performance successes. Information derived from these sources that is not confirmed loses its impact.

Attributional Feedback

Attributional feedback links student performance with one or more attributions (perceived causes of outcomes) in an attempt to facilitate motivation (Schunk, 1989c; see Chapter 4). Some students who have difficulty during the early stages of learning attribute the difficulty to low ability. Students who believe they lack the ability to perform well may work in a lackadaisical fashion and give up readily. These negative motivational effects retard learning. Teachers may train students to attribute their difficulties instead to controllable factors (e.g., low effort, improper strategy use).

The role of effort has received special attention. If students believe they fail because of low ability, they may not expend much effort to succeed, but if they attribute failure to low effort, they may work harder because effort is controllable and they may believe that more effort will lead to better outcomes. Several research studies show that students can be taught to attribute outcomes to effort and that effort feedback produces beneficial effects on self-efficacy, motivation, and skills (Andrews & Debus, 1978; Dweck, 1975; Relich, Debus, & Walker, 1986; Schunk, 1982; Schunk & Cox, 1986; Schunk & Rice, 1986). Linking children's prior achievements with effort (e.g., You've been working hard.) enhances motivation, self-efficacy, and skills better than linking future achievement with effort (You need to work hard.) or not providing effort feedback. Effort feedback must be perceived by recipients as credible; that is, students realistically need to work hard to succeed, as in the early stages of learning or when working on difficult material.

Effort feedback may be especially useful for students with learning problems. When students must work hard to succeed, effort feedback for success is credible and likely to raise self-efficacy for skill acquisition (Schunk & Cox, 1986). Effort feedback also is highly credible and motivating for young children, who tend to attribute successes to effort. Around the age of 9, however, they begin to form a distinct conception of ability (Nicholls, 1978, 1979; see Chapters 4 and 6). Ability attributions become increasingly important with development, whereas the influence of effort declines (Harari & Covington, 1981). Schunk (1983a) found among average-achieving elementary school children that ability feedback for prior successes (You're good at this.) enhances self-efficacy and skill better than effort feedback or effort-plus-ability feedback. Combining the two types of feedback may lead children to discount some of the ability information in favor of effort. Children may think that if they have to work hard to succeed, then their ability cannot be too high. Schunk (1984) found that ability feedback given for initial learning successes enhances achievement outcomes better than effort feedback regardless of whether ability feedback is continued later on.

Strategy Feedback

Strategy feedback informs learners about how well they are applying a strategy and how strategy use is improving their performance (Pressley et al., 1990). Strategies help learners attend to tasks, focus on important features, organize material, and maintain a productive psychological climate for learning (Weinstein & Mayer, 1986). Because it leads to better performance, strategy use raises self-efficacy and motivation. Use of strategies relates positively to achievement and self-efficacy (Borkowski, Carr, Rellinger, & Pressley, 1990; Pintrich & De Groot, 1990a; Zimmerman & Martinez-Pons, 1992).

Of course, simply teaching students a strategy does not ensure they will use it. Failure to employ a strategy may result from the belief that the strategy, although useful, is not as important as such other factors as time available or effort expended. *Strategy value information* is information about the usefulness of a strategy as an aid to performance (Paris, Lipson, & Wixson, 1983; Pressley et al., 1990). Teachers who provide students with strategy value feedback help engender the belief that they are learning a useful strategy, which can raise self-efficacy and motivate learners to continue applying it (Schunk, 1989c). Strategy value feedback promotes achievement outcomes and strategy use better than instruction alone (Borkowski et al., 1988; Kurtz & Borkowski, 1987; Paris, Newman, & McVey, 1982).

Schunk and Rice (1987) taught a reading comprehension strategy to children with low reading skills. Children given multiple forms of strategy value information stressing both the general usefulness of the strategy as an aid to performance and its specific value for the task at hand developed higher self-efficacy and skill than did students who received either type of information alone. Schunk and Rice (1987) also found that combining specific strategy value information with feedback linking students' improved performance with strategy use (e.g., You got it right because you followed the steps in the right order.) led to higher self-efficacy and skill compared with providing either specific information or strategy feedback. Schunk and Swartz (1993) found that strategy feedback benefited students' self-efficacy and writing skills.

Strategy feedback actually is a type of attributional feedback because it conveys strategy attributions by linking outcomes with use of the strategy's steps. Strategy feedback can be combined effectively with effort feedback (e.g., That's correct. You're working hard and using the steps properly.).

Rewards

Teachers dispense a variety of rewards to students for good behavior and academic performance: grades, privileges, honors, free time, points or tokens exchangeable for other things, stickers, and stars. Rewards hold a prominent place in motivation. In Skinner's (1953) operant conditioning theory (Chapter 2), rewarding (reinforcing) the consequences of behavior influences the likelihood of future occurrence of the behavior. Responses to stimuli that are reinforced will be repeated; those that are punished will not.

Bandura (1986) challenged this view as an incomplete perspective on how rewards affect motivation. It is not the reward itself that is important, but rather the individual's belief about the consequences of behavior. Based on personal experiences and observations of models, people develop beliefs about likely outcomes of actions (see Chapter 5). Rewards are motivational because people expect that behaving in a given fashion will be rewarded. This belief, coupled with perceived importance or value of the reward, leads people to act in ways they believe will result in reward attainment.

Perceived similarity can enhance motivational effects. Observers who see models rewarded become motivated to act accordingly. These motivational effects depend in part on self-efficacy (Chapter 3). Observing similar others succeed raises observers' self-efficacy and motivates them to perform the task. Such motivational effects are common in classrooms. Students who observe other students performing a task well may become motivated to try their best.

Rewards also can inform learners about their progress in skill acquisition and thereby sustain motivation. Rewards given contingent on students' actual accomplishments are likely to enhance self-efficacy. Telling students that they can earn rewards based on what they accomplish instills a sense of self-efficacy for performing well, which is validated as they work on the task and perceive they are making progress. Receipt of the reward further validates self-efficacy because it symbolizes progress. When teachers reward students for time spent working regardless of how well they perform, rewards may convey negative efficacy information and be detrimental to motivation (Morgan, 1984). Students might infer that they are not expected to learn much because they lack the ability. During mathematics instruction, Schunk (1983d) found that giving students rewards commensurate with their actual performances enhanced motivation, self-efficacy, and skill, whereas offering rewards for participation at the task led to no benefits.

In Chapter 7, we discussed the deleterious effect on intrinsic interest of offering students rewards for performing tasks they enjoy (Lepper & Greene, 1978). Less has been written about ways to help students develop interest. The development of interest depends in part on an enhanced sense of competence for the activity (Lepper & Hodell, 1989). Performance-contingent rewards may raise interest when they promote students' perceptions of learning progress and self-efficacy (Schunk, 1989c).

Classroom Climate

Classroom climate refers to the atmosphere of the classroom—its social, psychological, and emotional characteristics (Dunkin & Biddle, 1974). The importance of classroom climate as it relates to motivation derives from the notion that teaching is leadership intended to affect classroom behavior. Classroom climate is often described using such terms as warm, cold, permissive, democratic, autocratic, and learner-centered. The climate in the classroom is largely established through teacher-student interactions.

A classic study by Lewin, Lippitt, and White (1939) shows how different forms of leadership affect motivation and behavior. Although this study was not conducted in a school, the results have classroom implications. Adult leaders supervised 10-year-old boys as they worked on group construction projects (e.g., making masks). The boys were exposed to three different forms of leadership. The *authoritarian* (autocratic) leader was cold and harsh, took control and told the boys what to do, assumed full responsibility, and did not allow the boys to make contributions. The *democratic* (collaborative) leader worked with the boys cooperatively, stimulated them about how to complete the projects, posed questions, and had them share ideas. Although the leader assumed ultimate responsibility for the outcomes, he encouraged problem solving and decision making by the boys. The *laissez-faire* (permissive) leader used a hands-off approach and let the boys work on tasks with minimal supervision. He did not take responsibility for the tasks and did not provide structure, suggestions, or assistance in completing the projects.

Group productivity was highest with the authoritarian and democratic styles. Under the authoritarian leader, the boys followed the instructions and completed the tasks. Although effective, this group was characterized by anxiety and tension, submission, and overt rebellion. When the leader was present, productivity was high, but when the leader was absent, productivity dropped and aggression and destructive behavior resulted. The laissez-faire group showed the lowest productivity because it essentially was leaderless. The boys did not achieve consensus on their goals and worked individually without being organized. They seemed to enjoy their work but there was hostility and scapegoating and little was accomplished.

The boys preferred the democratic style of leadership. The democratic leader produced a group that was task oriented, cooperative, and friendly. The boys displayed a high degree of independence and initiative, continued to work productively in the leader's absence, and endured frustration well. They showed a slight loss in efficiency compared with the authoritarian group—probably due to the time spent solving problems and seeking consensus—but this was minor and more than compensated for by the improvement in group atmosphere. This leadership style seemed to produce the benefits of the other two styles without the negative features.

The classroom implications are obvious. Laissez-faire leadership creates chaos and uncertainty; authoritarian leadership leads to high performance but also to frustration, aggression, and a negative group atmosphere; and democratic leadership allows learners to reach their goals without producing frustration and aggression. Democratic leadership has the added benefit of teaching the group to collaborate on projects and function independently in the leader's absence.

These styles are quite general and include many qualities, which makes it difficult to determine the critical variables. In attempting to apply these findings to classrooms, researchers have suggested that one critical variable is the degree of emotional support or warmth provided by the leader (Dunkin & Biddle, 1974). A second critical dimension may be the extent that the leader directs the group's activities, with the middle ground being preferred. The following suggestions can be used to apply democratic leadership principles in the classroom.

1. Foster collaborative relationships through cooperative groups. When Mr. Burns divides his students into cooperative groups for social studies, he groups students with varying abilities and talents. He tries to rotate students so that the same students do not continually end up in the same groups.

Ms. Linklater, a high school drama teacher, forms three-student groups to write and perform a television ad. The students select their own product and write and produce their ad. All three students in each group receive grade points based on their average score. Each student is encouraged to help his or her teammates complete difficult portions of the assignment.

2. Question students and have them share ideas on ways to complete projects. While introducing a history unit, a teacher has his students brainstorm ideas about projects that would be appropriate for the unit. The class then selects three projects to complete and each student chooses one of the three to do individually. Each student is able to generate his or her own list of activities that will be included in the project. The project grade is based on originality and completion of the activities.

Ms. Henessey asked her second-grade students to identify what geometric shapes they saw in various objects placed throughout the room. After the students played with the objects and were able to identify all the shapes, she gave each student copies of the same shapes made out of construction paper, which the students then used to make a picture.

3. Encourage problem solving and decision making by students. Mr. Moore, a math teacher, started each unit with a different "teaser" (a question for students to solve that required using the math skills to be taught in the new unit). Students were able to work in pairs the last 10 minutes of each class to make decisions about how to solve the problem. The students kept notes on the steps they used to solve the teaser.

Ms. Vaughn, an elementary teacher, was introducing a review unit on linear measurement. She divided her students into groups of three and gave each group a 12-inch ruler, a yardstick, a ball of string, a notepad, and pencils. She asked each group to find three objects in the school building that they could measure with the items they had. The students were to sketch the objects and label their measurements. At the end of the activity, each group shared their sketches with the entire class and explained how they selected and measured the items.

4. Make sure students understand that the teacher bears the ultimate responsibility for classroom activities. Mr. Kerr, a high school teacher, let his students select their own science projects. After each student selected a project, he or she completed a proposal sheet defining and outlining the project. Mr. Kerr then met with each student individually to discuss the project. At that time, Mr. Kerr accepted or revised the student's proposal or worked with the student to develop a new proposal.

Mrs. Patrick, a third-grade teacher, worked with her students to establish classroom rules. Before they began setting rules and consequences, she discussed one rule that she said must be included in the list and stated that she must approve all rules and consequences that the class formulated.

Praise and Criticism

Teacher-student interactions often include praise and criticism for students. There is an extensive literature on the effects of these variables on student behavior. We examine next the relation of praise and criticism to student motivation.

Praise

Praise is positive feedback given to students that expresses approval or commendation. It goes beyond simple feedback indicating that behavior is appropriate or that answers are correct because it conveys positive teacher affect and provides information about the worth of students' behaviors (Brophy, 1981). When a teacher says to a student, "That's correct. You're doing so well," the first part of the statement (That's correct) is feedback on performance, whereas the last part is praise. As a type of positive reinforcer, praise given following a student behavior should make that behavior more likely to be repeated (Skinner, 1953). O'Leary and O'Leary (1977) note that to be effective as a reinforcer, praise must be delivered contingent on performance of the behavior to be reinforced, be specific about which aspects of the behavior are being reinforced, and be viewed by students as sincere and credible. Teachers praise students when they display good classroom behavior and progress in learning in the hope that the praise will reinforce the desirable behavior and students will repeat it.

Brophy (1981) reviewed research on teacher praise and found that praise does not always function as a reinforcer because it frequently is not delivered following student responses. It often is infrequent, noncontingent, general in nature rather than linked to specific behavior, and dependent more on teachers' perceptions of students' need for praise than on students' actual behaviors (Wittrock, 1986). There also is evidence that praise does not relate well to student achievement (Brophy, 1981). Correlations between praise and student achievement are weak and mixed in direction (Dunkin & Biddle, 1974). The effects of praise may be moderated by such variables as grade level, socioeconomic status, and ability. At the early elementary level, praise correlates weakly but positively with achievement among low-socioeconomic and low-ability students and correlates weakly but negatively or not at all with achievement among high-socioeconomic and high-ability students (Brophy, 1981).

Bandura (1986) disputed Skinner's notion that reinforcers operate as response strengtheners. Rather, reinforcement serves to inform and motivate. Reinforcement informs individuals about the desirability and accuracy of responses. It also can motivate; students who expect and value reinforcement for acting in a given fashion are likely to behave accordingly. Wittrock (1986) notes that these informational and motivational functions also pertain to teacher praise. Overall, the evidence suggests that praise is a weak reinforcer, especially after the first few grades in school (Brophy, 1981). Up to around age 8 children desire to please adults, so praise effects are more powerful. But praise can have unintended effects. Because praise conveys information to students about teachers' beliefs, teachers who praise students for success at easy tasks may send the message that they do not expect the students to learn much. Students believe the teacher thinks they have low ability, which negatively affects motivation (Weiner et al., 1983).

From an attributional perspective (see Chapter 4), praise conveys information to students about the teacher's beliefs about their ability (Pintrich & Blumenfeld, 1985). Praise given for success and progress in learning substantiates students' beliefs that they are learning and raises self-efficacy for learning. Praise used indiscriminately carries no information about capabilities and has little effect on behavior. Good and Brophy (1987; see also Brophy, 1981; Brophy & Good, 1986) present guidelines for using praise effectively (Table 9.4). As these guidelines make clear, effective praise is contingent on successful performances and is aimed at boosting students' perceived competencies and motivation for learning.

Table 9.4.   Guidelines for Using Praise Effectively

- Make praise simple and direct, deliver it in a natural voice, and avoid theatrics.
- Use straightforward, declarative sentences rather than gushy exclamations and rhetorical questions.
- Specify the accomplishment being praised and recognize noteworthy effort, care, and persistence. Call attention to progress and the development of skills.
- Use a variety of phrases in praising students.
- Back up verbal praise with nonverbal communication of approval.
- Avoid ambiguous statements (e.g., You were really good today.) and make it clear that praise is for learning rather than for compliance.
- Praise individual students privately to avoid public embarrassment.

Material drawn from Good and Brophy (1987)

Criticism

Criticism refers to teacher disapproval of student behavior through verbal feedback or gestures. Criticism is distinguished from performance feedback because it provides information about undesirability of students' behaviors. The statement, "Alex, that's wrong. I'm disappointed that you didn't do better," contains performance feedback (first part) and criticism (second part).

We intuitively might expect that criticizing students is bad and lowers performance and motivation; however, the research evidence is mixed. Studies have shown that criticism is unrelated to student achievement, that it relates negatively to achievement, and that it relates to achievement in a curvilinear fashion such that moderate criticism may be motivating but effects diminish as criticism increases and decreases (Dunkin & Biddle, 1974). The effects of criticism on performance are tempered by other variables. Criticism is more frequently given to boys than to girls, to black students than to white students, to students for whom teachers hold low expectations than to those for whom they hold high expectations, and to students of lower social status (primarily boys) than to higher status students (Brophy & Good, 1974). Clearly, the reasons are complex why teachers criticize some students more often than others.

Whether criticism increases, decreases, or has no effect on student motivation should depend on the extent that it involves motivational processes. Thus, criticism should motivate students when it conveys they are competent and can perform better with more effort or better use of strategies, informs students about the value of the learning, provides information on progress toward goals, and so forth. A statement such as, "I'm disappointed in you. I know that you can perform better," contains persuasive self-efficacy information and may motivate students to try harder, whereas the statement, "I'm disappointed in you. You probably never will figure this out," may lower self-efficacy and motivation in students. Teachers who use criticism should try to incorporate positive motivational features and use it judiciously in situations where other motivational techniques have been ineffective and they believe that the student might respond.

Unsolicited Help

Providing unsolicited help is another way that teachers interact with students. Unsolicited help is best viewed against the background of classroom life in which teachers routinely provide assistance to students in the form of corrective feedback and instruction. During guided and independent practice, teachers stay on the lookout for student problems and attempt to correct them. Students also ask for help when they are baffled about what to do. Recent research shows that seeking help is an important self-regulatory strategy that relates positively to motivation and achievement (Newman & Schwager, 1992). Although such help is well intended and generally serves to enhance learning, under certain conditions, it can have an undesirable effect on motivation.

First, let us consider the benefits of providing help. Teachers who provide corrective feedback to students having difficulty are likely to help students learn. As a consequence of such assistance, students should observe that they are making progress in learning, which raises self-efficacy and motivates them to continue to improve. While providing assistance, teachers also may praise correct performance (e.g., You're doing great on this part.) and persuasive efficacy information (I know that you can learn to do this.). These comments also raise efficacy and motivation.

The downside to unsolicited assistance is that it conveys information about the recipient's ability. According to attribution theory (Chapter 4), unsolicited assistance reflects the perceived cause of the recipient's problems (Weiner, 1985a). Help is most likely forthcoming when the perceived cause is a factor beyond the recipient's control, such as low ability (Weiner et al., 1983). If the causal factors appear to be within the recipient's control (e.g., low effort), then the recipient is held personally responsible and help is not given. As a consequence of helping, the recipient may infer the help-giver's intentions. The recipient may believe that help was provided because the help-giver felt the recipient's ability was low. The recipient may attribute difficulty to low ability, which negatively affects perceptions of competence and motivation.

Teachers can alleviate potential negative effects of assistance by casting it in a positive light. Comment on what the student is doing well, what needs improvement, and what the student needs to do to perform better. Giving help with words of encouragement (I know that you can do this.) should benefit motivation.

TEACHER EXPECTATIONS

An important process influencing student motivation involves the expectations that teachers hold for student learning and performance. Research on teacher expectations in the past 25 years has addressed such issues as how teachers form expectations, how they communicate them to students, and how these expectations affect student outcomes (Braun, 1976; Cooper & Good, 1983; Cooper & Tom, 1984; Dusek, 1985; Jussim, 1986, 1991). Practitioners are equally concerned about expectation effects; recall the story of Lisa McMahan at the beginning of this chapter.

We begin by discussing a famous study that instigated interest in the role of teacher expectations. We then present models formulated to explain expectation effects and how expectations are formulated. We conclude by discussing ways that teachers communicate expectations and by providing a critique of this controversial phenomenon.

The Pygmalion Study

In 1968, Rosenthal and Jacobson conducted the classic study *Pygmalion in the Classroom* (Rosenthal & Jacobson, 1968). The researchers gave elementary school children (grades one through six) a test of nonverbal intelligence at the start of the academic year. Teachers were told that this test predicted which students would bloom intellectually during the year. Actually, the researchers randomly identified 20% of the school population as intellectual bloomers and gave the names of these students to their teachers. Teachers were not aware of the deception: The test did not predict intellectual blooming and the names they were given bore no relation to test scores. Teachers taught in their usual fashion and students were retested after 1 semester, 1 year, and 2 years. For the first two tests, students were in the classes of teachers who had been given the names of the bloomers; for the last test, students were in new classes with different teachers who had not been given the bloomers' names.

After the first year, there were significant differences in intelligence between the bloomers and control students (students who had not been identified as bloomers) and the differences were greater among students in grades one and two. During the subsequent year, these younger bloomers lost their advantage, but bloomers in the upper grades showed an increasing advantage over control students. Differences were greater among average achievers than they were among high and low achievers. In reading grades, bloomers gained significantly more than control students; these differences were greater among average and younger students. It should be noted that overall the differences between bloomers and control students were small both in reading and on the intelligence test.

Rosenthal and Jacobson concluded that teacher expectations can act as self-fulfilling prophecies because student achievement comes to reflect the expectations. (The name *Pygmalion* comes from George Bernard Shaw's play, in which others' expectations concerning the heroine influence how they perceive and treat her). With regard to the grade-level differences, the researchers suggested that younger children's advantage may stem from their close personal contact with teachers and that the advantage disappears when students lose this contact with the influencing teacher. Older students may function better autonomously after they move to a new teacher.

These conclusions are controversial. The Rosenthal and Jacobson study has been criticized on conceptual and methodological grounds (Elashoff & Snow, 1971; Jensen, 1969). There have been several attempts to replicate the Pygmalion study and not all have been successful (Cooper & Good, 1983). In an interesting series of studies, Schrank (1968, 1970) told some teachers that they had students of high learning potential and other teachers that their classes had low learning potential, when in fact the groups had been randomly assigned to conditions. Students of teachers in the high-potential condition learned more than students of teachers in the low-potential group. In a follow-up replication study, teachers knew that students had been grouped randomly rather than by ability level but Schrank asked teachers to teach the groups as if they had been grouped by ability. No differences in learning between the groups were obtained. Collectively, these two studies highlight the potential influence of teacher beliefs on student learning.

Models of Teacher Expectation Effects

Various explanations exist for teacher expectation effects. Brophy and Good (1974) describe a process whereby teacher expectations may be formed, conveyed to students, and affect student behavior. Early in the school year, teachers form expectations based on initial interactions with students and information from school records. Teachers then begin to treat students differently consistent with their expectations. Teacher behaviors are reciprocated; for example, teachers who show warm interaction with students are likely to have that warmth returned. Thus, student behaviors begin to complement and reinforce teacher behaviors and expectations. The differential teacher behaviors may spread to such areas as opportunities for learning, type of feedback provided, and leadership roles assumed. Effects will be most pronounced for expectations that are rigid and inappropriate. Where expectations are appropriate, or inappropriate but flexible, student behavior may substantiate or redefine expectations. But when expectations are inappropriate and not easily changed, student performance may decline and become consistent with expectations.

Another model is described by Cooper and Tom (1984). Students enter learning settings differing in abilities and backgrounds and teachers have initial beliefs for individual students that are formed based on prior experiences with students and knowledge of their intelligence and abilities from school records. A critical variable is the teacher's perception of control over student performance, where control refers to the teacher's ability to influence the content, timing, and duration of interaction with students. Control beliefs vary with the context; some settings allow the teacher greater control than others. Control beliefs influence teachers' decisions about providing student feedback (e.g., praise, criticism) and the type of socioemotional climate to create for the student. Different climates and types of feedback affect students' beliefs about their performance capabilities and the value of effort in producing good performance. Capability and effort beliefs, in turn, affect student motivation and achievement.

Braun (1976) developed a model to explain the origin of teacher expectations. Some possible sources of expectations are intelligence and ability scores, gender, information from previous teachers, medical and psychological information on records, ethnic background, knowledge about older siblings, physical characteristics, prior achievement, socioeconomic status, and actual behaviors of the students. Research supports the potential influence of these factors (Brophy & Good, 1974). Teachers often hold higher expectations for students of higher intelligence or ability compared with students of lower ability. Teachers expect fewer behavior problems from girls and, at least at the elementary level, expect girls to perform better academically; however, beginning in middle school, many teachers expect girls to perform worse than boys in mathematics and the sciences (Eccles, 1983). Teachers generally hold higher expectations for upper- and middle-class students than for lower-class ones, as well as for white compared with black students (Brophy & Good, 1974). Expectations also vary according to achievement level, with teachers expecting more from students who have demonstrated high achievement in the past. Other research shows that teachers may believe physically attractive students are more intelligent than unattractive students and hold correspondingly higher expectations for them (Brophy & Good, 1974). Teachers' expectations also are influenced by information they obtain from records and previous teachers and by their knowledge of older siblings. To Braun's (1976) list of sources of expectations, we might add speech characteristics. Children who speak in nonstandard English tend to be perceived negatively by teachers who hold lower expectations for their performances (Brophy & Good, 1974).

Differential Teacher Behaviors

Once teachers form expectations, how are they communicated to students and translated into teacher behaviors? Expectations may translate into behaviors in four areas: socioemotional climate, verbal input, verbal output, and feedback (Rosenthal, 1974). *Socioemotional climate* includes such verbal and nonverbal behaviors as smiles, head nods, eye contact, and supportive and friendly actions. In general, teachers provide a warmer socioemotional climate for students for whom they hold high expectations than for those for whom expectations are lower (Cooper & Tom, 1984). *Verbal input* denotes opportunities to learn new material and the difficulty of material. High-expectation students may have more opportunities to interact with and learn new material and be exposed to more difficult material compared with low-expectation learners (Cooper & Tom, 1984). *Verbal output* refers to the number and length of academic interactions. Teachers engage in more academic interchanges with high- than with low-expectation students (Brophy & Good, 1974). High-expectation students (highs) initiate more contacts with teachers compared with low-expectation students (lows). Teachers have more public interactions with highs and more private or individual interactions with lows (Cooper & Tom, 1984). They also are more persistent with highs; if highs fail to answer a question, teachers are apt to repeat or rephrase the question or provide prompts. Teachers may devote more time to brighter students, allow them longer to respond before redirecting questions, and pay closer attention to their answers compared with slower students. *Feedback* refers to use of academic praise and criticism. Teachers praise highs more and criticize lows more (Cooper & Tom, 1984). Each of these factors is genuine and operates in classrooms (Cooper & Tom, 1984). At the same time, there are differences among teachers. Few teachers will behave differently in all four areas, and some teachers may not treat students differently at all. The best conclusion is that many teachers occasionally act in accordance with one of these factors.

Critique

Expectations are normal, usually reasonable, and based upon observations. Most beliefs that teachers hold about students are accurate because they are based on multiple observations of performance (Jussim, 1991). Because teacher expectations generally reflect actual student behaviors, the effects of teacher expectations on student performances typically are weak and affect student achievement minimally (Jussim, 1991). Where effects are found, they usually are negative; holding positive expectations for students does not seem to raise performance as much as holding negative expectations lowers it (Brophy & Good, 1974; Cooper & Tom, 1984; Good & Brophy, 1987).

Rosenthal and Jacobson (1968) found that expectation effects were stronger among young children and became weaker with development. The stronger effects among early elementary children may be due to the close teacher-student interaction that typically is found in those grades. Such close interactions allow ample opportunities for teachers to behave differently in the preceding areas (Rosenthal, 1974). As students progress through grades, teacher-student interactions become less frequent and less personal.

Some expectations are appropriate and instructionally sound. Because expectations usually result from student performance rather than cause it (Brophy & Good, 1974), teachers typically hold higher expectations for students who perform better. It may make instructional sense to present high achievers with more difficult material, question them more extensively about it, and move them through a sequence of instruction more quickly. In short, expectations may have instructional benefits when they are appropriate (based on student performances) and flexible (capable of changing to reflect changes in student performances). Expectations become a problem when they are inappropriate and rigid such that teachers hold firm beliefs about what students can and cannot do that bear little relation to students' actual behaviors (Brophy & Good, 1974).

Let us reiterate that expectation effects do not always occur. Smith (1980) found that expectation effects were stronger in reading than in mathematics.

This may result because reading typically is taught in small groups with much teacher-student interaction, whereas mathematics usually is a large-group and individual activity and the frequency of teacher-student interactions is less.

Expectation effects typically are not obtained when expectations are highly inaccurate. Teachers who hold low expectations about bright students are likely to raise their expectations rather than lower them (Cooper & Tom, 1984). Grossly distorted expectations are not credible. Mild self-fulfilling prophecies reflecting a small distortion between expectations and student behavior may be more common, which helps explain why expectation effects typically are small and in a negative direction. Although teacher expectation effects are real and can affect student performance, the scope and size of their effects have probably been distorted, which has led to more concern than warranted (Jussim, 1991). Some suggestions for handling expectations in the classroom follow.

1. Enforce rules fairly and consistently. Ms. Jacobs, a new kindergarten teacher, worked with her students at the beginning of the year on classroom rules. She reviewed the rules and consequences and made sure she enforced the rules fairly and consistently. She corrected each child who did not follow one of the rules so that all the children were aware that the rules applied to everyone.

Mr. Adams was having discipline problems in his second-period physical education class. He asked a department member, Ms. Lourcey, to observe the class and give him feedback. After observing, Ms. Lourcey told him that he always corrected the same five boys for not following the classroom rules but did not say anything to eight other students who were doing the same thing. She suggested that he try harder to apply the rules to everyone. After Mr. Adams worked on being more consistent, student misbehavior became less frequent.

2. Assume that all students can learn and convey that expectation to them. Ms. Ball, a kindergarten teacher, told her class that she was very excited because they had learned their colors. Ms. Ball said, "I am so proud of you. I know that you are the smartest class in the whole school. Now we are all going to learn our shapes. I know we can."

A high school English teacher greeted his new class by stating, "I look forward to getting to know all of you. We are going to have a great time in this class as we improve our writing, and we all can improve it if we try. I am going to work with each of you, and I know by the end of the semester, each of you will be writing well."

One student replied, "I can hardly write a sentence. I don't know how you'll make a writer out of me."

"Well, sentences are a great place to start," countered the teacher.

3. Do not form differential student expectations based on qualities (e.g., gender, ethnicity, parents' background) unrelated to performance. Mr. Willett, a special education resource teacher, was always quick to defend his students. He had several boys who were from a rough neighborhood and were known to be involved in gang activities. Some teachers ignored the boys in their classes and did not try to help them when they had difficulty learning. Mr. Willett worked with these boys and did everything he could to help them succeed.

A sixth-grade teacher planned several projects that included activities for her students to do with their parents. There were two students whose parents never participated in school activities or did anything with their children. She met with these students privately and told them she would be glad to work with them on the parent activities after school each day. This would allow them to complete as many activities as the others in the class.

4. Do not accept excuses for poor performance. Justin kept telling Ms. Hagaman that he could not complete his social studies assignment because he could not read as well as the other students. "After all, I'm in reading resource," said Justin.

Ms. Hagaman said, "I know you are in reading resource, but you also are a very good social studies student. You are always sharing in the class and can answer all the questions during discussion time." Ms. Hagaman offered to help Justin read any of the words or selections that he felt were too difficult.

Mr. Leeland assigned homework in his history class every evening. Kyle, a capable but lazy student, usually complained about completing homework. He said he did not have any supplies at home. Mr. Leeland gathered up several items (paper, pens, pencils, resource books) and sent them home with Kyle. Mr. Leeland told Kyle he expected him to complete all of his homework from now on.

5. Realize that upper limits of student ability are unknown and not relevant to school learning. Mr. Willis, a third-grade teacher, was helping one of his students with her math.

"Emily, let's try some regrouping in subtraction since you have been doing such a wonderful job with all your other subtraction problems. It's time for you to try something harder."

Emily said, "I'm not smart enough to try those. They're too hard."

"That's not true, Emily. I know you can do them, just give it a try," replied Mr. Willis.

Ms. Harlow, a university English teacher, introduced a poetry unit to her class. She told the students at the end of the unit they were going to write their own poetry. Carla said, "I can't write poetry, I'm not smart enough to do that."

Ms. Harlow replied, "Carla, I know that with my help you will be able to write at least one poem. There are many different styles of poetry and I know that one of those styles will be something you can build on."

CLASSROOM MANAGEMENT

Among the more important classroom processes are those involving classroom management. Few would dispute that how teachers manage students' behaviors affects learning. Teachers who are effective classroom managers establish rules and procedures and organize activities to help keep students productively engaged. These teacher activities prevent discipline problems. When problems occur, effective teachers deal with them quickly and fairly so they are stopped and do not interfere with other students (Doyle, 1986). Collectively, these efforts make the classroom more productive for learning. Teacher activities designed to prevent, minimize, and deal with problems also affect student motivation. Even bright, task-oriented students who enjoy learning are not motivated to work diligently in noisy and disruptive environments. Students who engage in misbehavior and receive punishment are likewise not motivated to concentrate on academic material.

In this section, we consider the role of classroom management in motivation and will distinguish between proactive and reactive teacher processes. *Proactive* processes are those teacher activities designed to prevent disciplinary problems from occurring, and *reactive* processes are designed to deal with problems when they occur and attempt to quickly return misbehaving students to academic work and minimize disruption to others. Both processes are critical to good classroom management and student motivation. Initially, we discuss Kounin's (1977) research on effective classroom management. We then show how proactive and reactive processes can affect motivation and suggest ways to incorporate these into classrooms.

Kounin's Research

Kounin (1977) conducted an extensive analysis of dimensions of group management in elementary school classrooms to determine what factors contributed to student work involvement and diminished misbehavior. The research done by Kounin (1977) was prompted by a fortuitous incident:

> I was teaching a course in Mental Hygiene. . . . While lecturing, I glanced around the room and noticed a student in the back row intently reading a newspaper that he was holding completely unfolded in front of himself. Contrary to what I advocated in the course, I angrily reprimanded him without diagnosis or understanding. . . . The reprimand succeeded. He stopped reading the newspaper, or at least did not hold it completely unfolded in midair. But, the major observable impact seemed to be upon *other* members of the class. Side glances to others ceased, whispers stopped, eyes went from windows or the instructor to notebooks on the desks. The silence was heavy, as if the students were closing out the classroom and escaping to the safety of a notebook. I believe that if I had sneezed they would have written the sound in their notes. (p. 1)

What Kounin observed was a *ripple effect*, or how a teacher's handling of misbehavior by one student affects the behaviors of other students who are witnesses to, but not participants in, the event. The ripple effect is actually a form of modeling (Chapter 5); this incident illustrates inhibition of student misbehavior brought about by disciplining one offender. The term *desist* refers to the teacher's actions to stop misbehavior. In the preceding incident, the teacher's desist had a ripple effect. In four settings (kindergarten, high school, college, summer camp with children ages 7 to 13), Kounin tested the hypothesis that a teacher's desist would have a ripple effect. Support was obtained in all four settings, although the most powerful effects were obtained with the kindergartners. The ripple effect was more pronounced early in the school year and diminished as the year progressed.

In the kindergarten study, Kounin (1977) explored whether the qualities of desists—clarity, firmness, and roughness—made a difference among observing children. *Clarity* is the extent to which the desist named the misbehaving student, specified the unacceptable behavior, and gave the reasons for the desist. *Firmness* refers to how well the desist conveyed an I-mean-it attitude with follow-through until the misbehavior ceased. *Roughness* is the extent to which the desist included threats, anger, physical handling, and punishment. Greater clarity increased conformity among observing students, firmness increased compliance only in students who also were misbehaving or were inclined toward misbehavior, and roughness did not improve behavior and tended to promote emotional upset among observers. Examples of these qualities are given in Table 9.5.

Interestingly, Kounin (1977) found no relationship between these qualities of desists and success in handling a deviancy.

> For any one teacher, neither the degree of clarity, firmness, or intensity of her desist effort; nor whether she focuses on the misbehavior; . . . nor whether she treats the child positively, negatively, or neutrally; makes any difference for how readily a child stops his deviancy or gets with the prescribed task. (p. 70)

Thus, qualities of desists influence observing students' behaviors but not the behaviors of misbehaving students. Kounin (1977) concluded that the tech-

Table 9.5. Qualities of Desists

Quality	Description	Example
Clarity	Extent that desist names the misbehaving student, states the unacceptable behavior, and gives the reason for the desist	"Karen, stop bothering Alex. You know that you are to be working alone. Please get back to work on your math."
Firmness	Extent that desist conveys I-mean-it attitude with follow-through until misbehavior ceases	"Luis, we do not push in the line. If you cannot behave in line you will not get to go to recess."
Roughness	Extent that desist includes threats, anger, physical handling, punishment	"A.J., you are so lazy. You're worse than your brother and look where he ended up. You make me furious. I wish you weren't in this class."

niques of dealing with misbehavior are not good predictors of how well children behave in classrooms or whether misbehavior spreads to other students. Intuitively, it seems puzzling that how teachers react to misbehavior makes little difference in the overall work involvement of the classroom. We need to consider this in light of the earlier distinction between proactive and reactive disciplinary techniques. Teachers' efforts to prevent disciplinary problems are more important than techniques for handling problems. Kounin (1977) identified some proactive teacher activities, which we will discuss separately, that relate positively to group management:

> *Withitness*—demonstration by teachers that they know what is going on at all times; having "eyes in the back of their heads"
>
> *Overlapping*—ability of teachers to attend to more than one issue simultaneously
>
> *Movement management*—strategies designed by teachers to initiate, sustain, and alter activity flow in the classroom
>
> *Group focus*—extent to which teachers keep students attentive to the learning task
>
> *Programming to avoid satiation*—how well teachers minimize boredom due to repetition of material

Withitness

Withitness is "a teacher's communicating to the children by her actual behavior (rather than by simple verbal announcing: 'I know what's going on.') that she knows what the children are doing, or has the proverbial 'eyes in back of her head'" (Kounin, 1977, pp. 80–81). For example, a teacher may be writing on the board with his or her back to the class, yet observe a child misbehaving. The teacher may remark (perhaps without turning around), "Shawn, stop bothering your neighbor and pay attention to what I'm doing." Shawn probably will be surprised that his teacher knew about his misbehavior even without looking at him. This teacher action communicates the teacher's withitness to Shawn.

Kounin identified two types of errors in teacher desists that are designed to convey withitness. *Target errors* are instances where the teacher identifies the wrong student for a desist (e.g., teacher utters a desist to Shawn even though Shawn's neighbor Kim is bothering Shawn and Shawn is trying to get Kim to stop). Another type of target error is when the teacher overlooks a more serious deviancy and utters a desist designed to stop a less serious one. For example, a teacher tells two children to stop talking while in another part of the room two students are pushing and shoving one another. *Timing errors* are those in which the deviancy spreads to more students or becomes more serious before the teacher intervenes.

Kounin found that withitness was a significant predictor of good classroom management. Studies showed that withitness correlates positively with student work involvement and with freedom from deviancy, both during student recitation periods and while students are engaged in seatwork. Although these results do not imply causality, they do show that the higher the level of a teacher's withitness, the better that teacher's classroom is managed and the more productive the learning environment.

Overlapping

A second important teacher characteristic is *overlapping*, defined as what teachers do when they have two matters to deal with simultaneously (Kounin, 1977). Overlapping occurs when teachers are occupied with students at a task at the same time a deviancy occurs. For example, a teacher may be working with a small group of students on reading while the rest of the class is engaged in seatwork. Suddenly, two students in the class start talking to one another and become distracted from their work. These are overlapping situations: attending to the reading group and issuing a desist to stop the talking. In some cases, a teacher might exit the reading group, move over to the talking students, and utter a desist. In other cases, the teacher might stay with the reading group and keep them on task while simultaneously uttering a desist to the offending students. Teachers overlap well when they attend to two issues at once.

Overlapping correlates positively with work involvement and freedom from deviancy both during recitation and seatwork, although its correlations are stronger with freedom from deviancy than with encouraging work involvement. Interpreting these results is a bit difficult because some correlations of overlapping may result from withitness because the two often go together. Highly with-it teachers generally can attend to two issues simultaneously. Data analyses using partial correlations (taking out the effects of some variables to determine how other variables correlate by themselves with student outcomes) showed that withitness alone correlates more strongly with managerial success than does overlapping alone in both recitation and seatwork settings.

Movement Management

A third important attribute, *movement management*, reflects how smoothly teachers keep lessons moving and make transitions between activities. It is important to keep a smooth classroom pace, maintain momentum, and avoid jerkiness in transitions. Two kinds of mistakes that teachers make involve jerkiness and slowdowns. Jerkiness occurs when teachers suddenly announce a change in activities that catches the students by surprise, or when a teacher temporarily or permanently leaves one activity unfinished and moves to another. Slowdowns (delays that waste time) occur when teachers spend too much time giving directions and explanations or when they unnecessarily fragment a task by breaking it into many small tasks when it could be accomplished easily as a whole.

Kounin (1977) found that momentum (the absence of slowdowns) correlates positively with work involvement and freedom from deviancy during recitation but less so during seatwork. It seems that momentum is more highly related to students' behaviors during recitation. Smoothness correlates positively with both indexes during recitation and seatwork. In addition, momentum and smoothness correlated positively with each other.

Group Focus

Group focus, which refers to the teacher's efforts to keep students on task, consists of three dimensions. The first, *group alerting*, refers to the extent that the teacher maintains student attention during a group activity. For example, a teacher may call on students in random order. *Accountability*, the second dimension, means that each student in the group is responsible for learning the concepts being taught. Thus, a teacher may not let students move to new material until they have mastered basic concepts. The third dimension of group focus, *format*, involves grouping students in such a way to facilitate active participation by all students. For example, during a recitation lesson when one student is reciting, what does the teacher do to keep the other students involved?

Of these three dimensions of group focus, accountability and group alerting correlated positively with each other and with dimensions of classroom behavior. Accountability was correlated with work involvement and freedom from deviancy in recitation settings only; it is important during recitations for teachers to ensure that all students are learning the material. Alerting correlated in recitations with work involvement and freedom from deviancy, and weakly but positively with freedom from deviancy during seatwork. Keeping children alert and focused on the task is important during recitations. Format did not relate to any outcome, suggesting that how teachers conduct classes with different formats is more important for classroom management and motivation than the formats themselves.

Programming to Avoid Satiation

Kounin (1977) examined teachers' efforts to minimize *satiation*, defined as the change of value of an activity due to repetition. Repetition creates boredom and changes activities from positively valued (liked) to disliked. Kounin found that satiation does not occur, or occurs slowly, when students experience feelings of progress and do not believe that the work is repetitious. Other variables that minimize satiation and boost motivation are variety and challenge. *Variety* means greater numbers or types of activities per unit of time. *Challenge* derives from the teacher showing enthusiasm, remarking about the positive valence of the activity (e.g., This next one will be fun. I know you'll like it.), and discussing the challenge (e.g., This is a tough one but I know you can figure it out.).

Summary

Kounin (1977) found that classroom management does not depend on how teachers react to disciplinary problems. What distinguishes classrooms with few problems and where students are involved in academic work from classrooms with more problems and less work involvement are techniques teachers use to prevent problems. Effective classroom managers are with-it, attend to more than one issue at a time, keep classroom activities moving well, keep students focused on the task, and minimize boredom. Effective managers make the work environment more productive and give students little opportunity to misbehave.

Expectations and Rules

Effective teachers establish a good classroom environment. The beginning of the school year is the time to establish this environment, because it is then that students learn rules and procedures to follow for the year. A major goal is to obtain student cooperation in following rules and procedures and successfully completing assignments. Teacher expectations for student behavior are conveyed to students through rules and procedures that need to be taught (Evertson, Emmer, Clements, Sanford, & Worsham, 1984). Evertson and colleagues (Evertson et al., 1984) recommend a three-step sequence for doing so: (a) describe and demonstrate desired behaviors to students, (b) have students practice behaviors repeatedly, and (c) provide students with feedback on whether they performed behaviors correctly and suggest improvement where needed.

These ideas are supported by a series of studies that examined third-grade classrooms (Emmer, Evertson, & Anderson, 1980). Researchers observed classrooms at the start of the school year and at other times during the year. They then compared what teachers did during the first 3 weeks of school to determine what distinguished good classroom managers from poor ones. A major difference was how teachers handled rules and routines. Effective classroom managers established clear rules for conduct (e.g., Be prepared for class.). They also set up routines for conducting tasks (e.g., going to the bathroom). An important priority was to teach students rules and procedures during the first few days of the year. In contrast, ineffective managers did not have clear rules and procedures. In some cases, they had none; in others, the rules were vague (e.g., Be in the right place at the right time.). They often introduced rules casually without clear explanations.

This research highlights the importance of teachers establishing high expectations for classroom behavior and conveying those expectations to students. They expect students to obey rules and do not tolerate excuses for disobeying them. The research by Emmer and Evertson substantiates Kounin's finding that the teacher's proactive efforts to create a productive classroom are critical in establishing good management. Rules, procedures, and expectations are proactive techniques designed to prevent problems. Teachers who use them wisely and devote adequate time at the start of the year to instill them in students will not regret the time spent, but rather will find that they benefit student motivation.

CLASSROOM ORGANIZATION AND STRUCTURE

The preceding discussion makes it clear that teachers can influence student motivation through their planning, scheduling, organization, management, and interactions. That is not surprising, but only recently have researchers examined how classroom factors influence motivation and the process whereby these effects occur. A particularly intriguing area of research addresses the role of classroom structure and organization, specifically, how activities are set up, how students are grouped, how work is evaluated and rewarded, how authority is established, and how time is scheduled. Marshall and Weinstein (1984) contend that classrooms are complex places, that to understand student motivation one must consider many factors, and that factors interact such that one factor may enhance or lessen the impact of another factor. Thus, a democratic classroom may have its motivational impact negated by a system of strict ability grouping. As another example, much has been written about how social comparisons with students of higher ability can have a negative effect on other students' self-efficacy, but such social comparisons also identify who is competent in an area and that tells students whom to seek out for help in completing work (Marshall & Weinstein, 1984). We address classroom organization in the next section and follow this with a discussion of other structural factors.

Classroom Organization

An important aspect of classroom organization is *dimensionality* (Rosenholtz & Simpson, 1984), a basic distinction being between unidimensional and multidimensional classrooms. *Unidimensional* classrooms have a few classroom activities that tap a limited range of student abilities. Classrooms become *multidimensional* when there are more activities that allow for diversity in student abilities and performances. There are four specific characteristics of classrooms that indicate dimensionality (see Table 9.6): differentiation of task structure, student autonomy, grouping patterns, and salience of formal performance evaluations. Unidimensional classrooms have undifferentiated task structures; all students work on similar tasks and a small number of qualitatively similar materials and methods are used during instruction (Rosenholtz & Simpson, 1984). The more undifferentiated the structure, the more likely the daily work will produce consistent performances from each student and the greater the opportunities for social comparisons for students to determine how well they are performing. Negative comparisons can have deleterious effects on the low-performing students. Structures become more differentiated (classrooms become multidimensional) as students work on different tasks at the same time. Social comparisons are less likely to occur and student motivation may be greater.

Student autonomy refers to the degree of choice that students have about tasks and when and how to perform them. Classrooms can be unidimensional to the extent that autonomy is low, which can stifle student motivation. Multidimensional classrooms motivate by giving students choices of work and times and places to perform it. Greater autonomy also can enhance intrinsic motivation because it takes individuality into account and provides students with a measure of control.

Unidimensional classrooms are characterized by social comparisons among students, which become more likely when students work in whole-class activities or are grouped by ability. Comparisons are not as straightforward when students work individually or in groups not formed on the basis of ability. Grouping patterns contribute to the multidimensionality of the classroom and have profound implications for motivation. Grouping also has long-term effects if groups remain intact and students realize they are bound to those groups regardless of their level of performance.

Salience of formal performance evaluations refers to the public nature of grading. Unidimensional classrooms are characterized by students being graded on the same assignments and grades being made public so students know the grades of others. Those who receive low grades are not motivated to improve. As grading becomes less formal or as grades are assigned for different projects (as in multidimensional classes), grading can motivate more students, especially if they are making progress and grades are improving.

Unidimensional classrooms also are characterized by high visibility of performance (Rosenholtz & Rosenholtz, 1981). This situation may motivate the high achievers but often has negative effects on students who typically per-

Table 9.6.   Dimensionality Characteristics of Classrooms

Characteristic	Unidimensional class	Multidimensional class
Differentiation of task structure	Undifferentiated: Students work on same task simultaneously	Differentiated: Students work on different tasks simultaneously
Student autonomy	Low: Students have little choice about what to do, when, and how to do it	High: Students have greater choice of activities, time, place, and method used to complete them
Grouping patterns	Whole-class activities; small groups formed based on ability	Individual work; small groups formed not on the basis of ability
Performance evaluations	Students graded on same assignments; grades are public; much social comparison	Students graded on different assignments; social comparisons less likely because grades reflect progress

form worse. Multidimensional classrooms motivate more students because they introduce greater differentiation, increase student autonomy, minimize ability grouping, and reduce the extent of public grading of assignments.

Classroom Factors

Several motivation researchers have focused on factors that can affect students' mastery goal orientations (and thereby motivation). Although this work is based on goal theory (Chapter 6), it is relevant to classroom structure. Epstein (1989) identified six dimensions of classrooms that affect motivation and that are modifiable: task design, distribution of authority, recognition of students, grouping arrangements, evaluation practices, and time allocation. The acronym TARGET has been used to represent these dimensions (*t*ask, *a*uthority, *r*ecognition, *g*rouping, *e*valuation, *t*ime).

TARGET

Task.   The task dimension concerns the design of learning activities and assignments. Various motivational strategies involve ways to structure tasks to develop a mastery goal orientation in students. These strategies include making learning interesting, using variety and personal challenges, helping students set realistic goals, and developing in students organizational and management skills and effective task strategies (Ames, 1992a, 1992b). Task structure helps to distinguish unidimensional from multidimensional classes. In unidimensional classes, students use the same materials and have the same assignments, so ability differences have motivational impact. In multidimensional structures, students work on different tasks, and there is less opportunity for negative social comparisons.

Authority.   This dimension involves the degree of opportunity that students have to take leadership roles and develop a sense of independence and control over learning activities. Authority is fostered by allowing students to participate in decisions, giving students choices and leadership roles, and teaching them skills that allow them to take responsibility for learning. Students' perceptions of competence tend to be higher in classrooms where they are given greater autonomy (see Chapter 7).

Recognition.   Recognition relates to the formal and informal use of rewards, incentives, and praise, which have important consequences for students' motivation to learn. To develop a mastery goal orientation, Ames (1992a, 1992b) recommends that teachers recognize student effort, progress, and accomplishments; give all students opportunities to earn rewards; and use private forms of recognition and reward so their value is not derived at the expense of others.

Grouping.   The grouping dimension focuses on students' ability to work effectively with others. To develop an atmosphere where differences in ability do not translate into differences in motivation, teachers should provide opportunities for heterogeneous cooperative groups and peer interaction. Small-group work is especially useful for low achievers who share in the group success and feel more efficacious about performing well. Group work allows students to assume more responsibility for their learning. Individual work also is important, however, because it allows for a clear portrayal of individual progress.

Evaluation.   Evaluation involves methods used to monitor and assess student learning. Some evaluation strategies that effectively enhance motivation are to evaluate students for individual progress and mastery, give students opportunities to improve their work (e.g., revise compositions for a higher grade), vary methods of evaluation, and use private evaluation. Teachers must be careful about normative grading systems where students are compared to one another; such normative comparisons can lower feelings of efficacy among students who do not compare favorably to their peers.

Time.   Time encompasses the appropriateness of workload, the pace of instruction, and the time allotted for completing work (Epstein, 1989). Time relates closely to design of tasks. Effective strategies for enhancing mastery goal orientation are to adjust time or task requirements for students having trouble completing work and to allow students to plan their work schedules and timetables for progress. These effective strategies also may allay student anxiety about learning, which can raise perceptions of competence and motivation.

Implementing TARGET in the Classroom

Collectively, these six dimensions we have discussed contribute to the motivational climate of the classroom. Suggestions for implementing them follow.

   1. Task. Make learning interesting; use variety and personal challenges; help students set realistic goals; develop in students organizational and management skills and effective task strategies. Mr. Sarver, a middle school teacher, used activity centers for each social studies and science unit. At the beginning of each unit, he let students help develop the activities to be included. After developing the activities, students selected those they wanted to complete and kept records of their progress. At the end of each unit, students took mastery tests and rated their performance on unit activities.

   2. Authority. Allow students to participate actively in decisions; give students choices and leadership roles; teach students skills that allow them to take responsibility for learning. Ms. Park, a fourth-grade teacher, involved her students in planning class activities and developing guidelines for participation. At the beginning of each reading, social studies, and science unit, she shared the unit objectives with the class. Then she had the students brainstorm activities that might be done to attain the objectives. Once activities were decided on, students were allowed to select those activities that they wanted to complete.

3. **Recognition.** *Recognize student effort, progress, and accomplishments; give all students opportunities to earn rewards; use private forms of recognition and reward whenever possible.* Ms. Harris, a high school art teacher, kept portfolios of each student's work. At the end of each week, she met individually with each student to discuss the work and to point out growth in techniques. She regularly wrote notes to students in which she commented on positive aspects of their artwork. She believed that every student should have the opportunity to include work in the spring art show, so at the end of the winter quarter, she met with each student and together they selected the piece that would be displayed.

4. **Grouping.** *Use heterogeneous cooperative groups to foster peer interaction; use individual work to convey progress.* Mr. Myers, a fifth-grade teacher, used cooperative grouping for all his social studies and science units. He changed groups with each unit, making an effort to group students according to abilities and talents related to the skills and creativity needed to complete the selected activities. Students were forced to participate actively by being given responsibilities. At the conclusion of each unit, students were graded on their performance on the mastery test and their participation in group activities.

5. **Evaluation.** *Evaluate students for individual progress and mastery; give students opportunities to improve their work; vary methods of evaluation; use private evaluation.* Mr. Cox, a university history teacher, kept portfolios on each student's work. In determining a grade for each unit, he used a variety of assignments (multiple choice tests, essay questions, creative essays based on feelings the students had while working on the unit, projects, research papers, homework assignments that included reading and reflecting activities). Throughout the unit, Mr. Cox met individually with students, wrote notes on their written work, and gave them the opportunity to review and edit their essays and papers. At the conclusion of each unit, Mr. Cox met with students individually and discussed improvement over their performance on prior units and made suggestions for further growth.

6. **Time.** *Adjust time on task requirements for students having trouble completing work; allow students to plan work schedules and timelines for progress.* Ms. Chambers had several students with learning problems in her class. Initially, the students had difficulty completing assigned work in the allotted time. Ms. Chambers met with each student and together they adjusted the amount of work to complete for each assignment. She told students that she expected them to eventually be able to complete all of the work. She met with each student and allowed each of them to set goals for the amount of work to complete each day, with the overall goal being total completion at the end of 6 weeks.

SUMMARY

Teachers can affect student motivation in many ways. An important means is through planning and decision making. Some models of teacher planning are prescriptive and state what teachers should do to foster student learning. Other models conceive of planning as beginning with teacher decisions about the types of learning activities to be used. Objectives arise and are integrated with activities. Currently, many researchers are exploring teachers' thought processes prior to, during, and after teaching. In this view, planning and decision making are not confined to the preinstructional phase of teaching but instead occur throughout all phases of teaching. Teachers often do not use a rational planning model, but instead begin by considering the setting and content to be taught. Teacher planning is strongly influenced by student characteristics, and motivational concerns are important in decision making. A critical component of planning is deciding on what activities students will work, which involves decisions about grouping. Types of grouping structures are competitive, cooperative, and individualistic. Structures affect student motivation largely by the cues they provide that inform learners about their capabilities. Competitive structures highlight the importance of ability and increase the likelihood of social comparisons with others. In individualistic structures, rewards are based on self-improvement. Cooperative structures allow students to share the rewards as a function of the group's collective performance.

Research exploring the effects of teaching practices on student achievement shows that when teachers teach well-structured content, they engage in practices that are consistent with principles of contemporary cognitive theories of learning (e.g., begin with a short review of prior relevant material, present material in small steps). These practices also are likely to enhance motivation because they help to ensure student learning and provide for success. Another important influence on student motivation is the use of models. Models provide a vicarious source of information about learners' self-efficacy, which motivates them to try the task themselves. Multiple models and peers as models can impact student motivation; for some students, portraying behaviors designed to cope with difficulties is useful.

Teacher-student interactions are critical influences on motivation. A major teaching function is providing different forms of feedback: performance, motivational, attributional, and strategy. Another function involves dispensing rewards. Rewards enhance motivation when they are linked to progress in learning and thereby inform learners about their competencies. Classroom climate affects motivation. The best effects on motivation and performance derive from the democratic (collaborative) classroom leader, who works with students cooperatively and encourages their problem solving and decision making. Laissez-faire (permissive) leadership creates chaos and uncertainty; authoritarian (autocratic) leadership leads to high performance but also to frustration, aggression, and a negative group atmosphere. Teacher-student interactions often involve praise and criticism. Praise is a type of positive reinforcer. Although praise usually facilitates motivation, teachers often do not deliver praise contingent on good performance, but rather give it infrequently and noncontingently. After the first few grades in school, praise often is a weak reinforcer. Moderate criticism may motivate but the effects diminish when criticism is high. Providing unsolicited help is another way teachers interact with students. Help can correct problems and inform students of their progress, which raises motivation.

Much research has examined the influence of teacher expectations on student learning and performance. The Pygmalion study found that teacher expectancies acted as self-fulfilling prophecies because student achievement came to reflect the expectations. This conclusion is controversial and research has not always demonstrated expectation effects. Various models have been proposed to explain how teachers form expectations and convey them to students and how, in turn, student motivation and achievement are affected. Much of the time expectations are realistic and based upon observations. They become problematic when they are inappropriate and inflexible.

Teacher activities relating to classroom management, which are designed to prevent, minimize, and deal with problems, also affect student motivation. Kounin identified several key variables, including the ripple effect, the qualities of desists, withitness, overlapping, movement management, group focus, and programming to avoid satiation. Kounin found that good classroom management depended on the teacher's proactive efforts to prevent disciplinary problems; how teachers reacted to misbehavior and the techniques they used to deal with it made little difference. Productive classrooms are those with expectations and rules, which are best established at the start of the school year and enforced consistently and fairly.

Much recent work has examined the role of classroom structure and organization in motivation. An important organizational aspect is dimensionality. Unidimensional classrooms have a few activities that tap a limited range of student abilities; multidimensional classrooms have more activities that allow for greater diversity in student abilities and differences in student performances. Unidimensional and multidimensional classrooms differ in task structure, student autonomy, grouping patterns, and salience of formal performance evaluations. Other researchers have identified TARGET aspects of classrooms that affect motivation and are modifiable: task design, distribution of authority, recognition of students, grouping arrangements, evaluation practices, and time allocation.

School Culture and Organization

Shirley, Chris, and Stasia are students at a big urban high school. They are talking about their school as they walk to school in the morning.

Shirley: *I really hate going to this place. It really gets to me. I mean, you have to show up here every day and all these teachers do is just talk at you. They never listen to you. It's like they just don't care about us, all they really care about is getting through the books and for us to get high scores on the stupid state tests. I don't think some of them even know my name.*

Chris: *Aw, c'mon, Shirl, it's not that bad. They try hard but they have so many of us and so little time to do anything but teach.*

Shirley: *Well, they could at least act like they cared about us sometimes.*

Stasia: *Yeah. Chris, I think you think it's okay because you do well and no one bothers you. You're a guy and they leave you alone. We get picked on all the time. I'm scared half the time when I go to the bathroom. I won't even go to that bathroom on the second floor at the end of the hallway.*

Shirley: *Oh, yeah, that one. That's where all the losers hang out, those kids in the low track. I'm afraid of them, too. I think they would just as soon beat you up as look at you. I won't go there either.*

Chris: *What are you talking about? Come to the boys' gym sometime, then you'll see pure fear. Half the kids won't even look at anyone else because they don't want to act like they disrespect anyone. That could be dangerous and it sure makes it hard to play basketball if no one will even look at each other. At least in my neighborhood we know each other. There are fights and all, but we know we belong there. Here you never feel like you belong to anything. I just keep to myself and try to do well in my classes. I can't wait to get out of here and get to college.*

Stasia: *Yeah, but the thing that gets to me is that these kids never get in trouble. They break the rules all the time, get into fights, and the teachers never do anything about it.*

Shirley: *Oh, I don't know. I think those kids always get into trouble. The teachers seem to be just waiting for them to screw up and then they nail them. People like Chris who brownnose the teacher, they can get away with murder. Those other kids, they just won't play the game and they get killed.*

Chris: *Hey, that's not fair! I just do my work and stay out of trouble.*

Others: *Yeah, right!*

At the same time, several teachers are talking in the faculty lounge, waiting for the day to start.

Ms. Strobel: *Well, another day at the salt mines. It is so hard to keep going. Most of the kids are not motivated, and the rest of the kids are just troublemakers. I think they love to see how far they can push the rules. Then, if you do call them on it, they raise a stink and the principal doesn't even back you up.*

Mr. Lin: *What, are you dreaming? Half the teachers don't even believe in the rules. That's one of the problems around here, the staff can't even agree on what the rules should be, let alone what we should be doing in our classrooms.*

Mr. De Groot: *Yes, I went to this workshop about teaching for conceptual understanding a few weeks ago and thought it would be good to try some of the ideas in my classroom, but most of my colleagues in the math department just laughed when I told them about it. They said who cares about those kinds of things, the only thing that matters is that the kids do well on the standardized tests. They're not going to change their ways.*

Ms. Strobel: *Well, I'd like to hear about those ideas. It's a big thing in science, this conceptual change stuff, but I don't really understand how you're supposed to do it and still cover the curriculum. I sure could use some new ideas, though. It might motivate me. But when could we do it? You have fourth hour free and I have second hour. There really isn't much time to talk about this.*

Mr. Lin: *There's the bell! Off to another day in the trenches.*

These students and teachers are talking about different aspects of a school's culture and organization. In the previous chapter, we discussed how characteristics of the classroom can influence students' motivation. In this chapter, we turn to a larger unit of analysis, the school level, and show how schools can influence student motivation. A focus on schools as the unit of analysis has not been adopted by many psychologists interested in motivation, but there are a few exceptions (see Maehr & Midgley, 1991, forthcoming; Mac Iver, Reuman, & Main, 1995; Sarason, 1990). Psychologists, given their disciplinary traditions, have tended to focus on individuals and have been concerned with how individuals' motivational beliefs, perceptions, needs, goals, and so on can influence motivation and behavior. In many ways, the psychological theories and basic and applied research described in Chapters 3 through 8 took this perspective. Of course, in Chapter 9 specifically, and in most of the other chapters, we have contextualized our discussion of the theories and research in terms of what they mean for student motivation and teacher behavior in classrooms. At the same time, as will become clear in this chapter, many of the psychological ideas regarding individual motivation are relevant to a school-level analysis.

Nevertheless, a move to a discussion of school influences involves a shift from a more psychological perspective to a more sociological and cultural perspective. In fact, much of the research and theory we will draw on in this chapter comes from the sociology of education and school effectiveness literature, rather than the educational and motivational psychology literature. As such, some of this sociological literature has been more concerned with overall student achievement and academic performance on standardized tests, not with student motivation as we have conceptualized it in this book. Moreover, when concerned about social outcomes, this literature has tended to use more broadly defined constructs such as commitment and engagement, not the more specific and narrowly defined motivational constructs used by psychologists. These more global constructs are surely related to the types of motivational beliefs such as attributions, self-efficacy, goals, intrinsic motivation, values, and interest that we have been discussing in this book, but the empirical research on school-level effects has not necessarily focused on them. Given this gap in the literature, some of our discussion of school effects on student motivation in this chapter will be more speculative and general than in previous chapters. In addition, most of the research is correlational, so it is difficult to make strong causal statements. Of course, there are some motivational psychologists (e.g., Eccles & Midgley, 1989; Maehr & Midgley, 1991, forthcoming) who have been concerned with the effects of school culture and organization on specific motivational beliefs. When relevant, we will rely heavily on their work in this chapter.

Figure 10.1 displays the general conceptual framework that we will use as a heuristic to help us organize this chapter. This figure is based on the overview of school effects in Lee, Bryk, and Smith (1993) and Maehr and Midgley (1991). The component at the top of the figure displays the various external constraints and opportunities that can have an influence on school culture and organization as well as on teachers and students. The main focus of discussion in this chapter will be the next component in the figure, school culture and organization. As in the previous chapter on classrooms, the TAR-

GET framework that was developed by Epstein (1989) and has been applied to classrooms and schools (see Maehr & Midgley, 1991) serves as the main organizer for our treatment of school culture and organization. Finally, Figure 10.1 shows that school culture and organization can have an influence on teacher and student motivation and behavior. We will focus on the school culture and organization component first, sketching out how it can influence teacher and student motivation and behavior. Then, paralleling the organization of the previous chapters where we discussed developmental and individual differences, we will discuss how the various external constraints and opportunities might moderate the general relations between school culture and organization and teacher and student outcomes.

Figure 10.1. A conceptual model for school culture and organization

External Constraints/Opportunities

- Type of students
- School size/number of students
- Parental/community involvement
- District level constraints/opportunities
- State level constraints/opportunities

School Culture and Organization

- Norms, values, and shared beliefs
- Climate
- Task and work structures
- Authority and management structures
- Recognition and reward structures
- Grouping practices
- Evaluation practices
- Time use

Teacher Outcomes

- Goal orientation
- Self-efficacy
- Effort
- Persistence
- Satisfaction

Student Outcomes

- Goal orientation
- Self-efficacy
- Effort
- Persistence
- Achievement

SCHOOL CULTURE AND ORGANIZATION

The eight dimensions listed in Figure 10.1 under the school culture and organization component represent various features of schools that can have an influence on teacher and student outcomes. These eight dimensions are listed separately only for expository purposes in this chapter. In the reality of schools, they are overlapping, interdependent, and interactive dimensions that help to create the overall culture of the school building. In many ways, the first two listed—school norms, values, and shared beliefs and school climate—which are more perceptual and constructive dimensions, will be reflected and instantiated in the other six TARGET dimensions. At the same time, the six TARGET dimensions, which are more directly observable, will help to create the norms and climate of the school. Accordingly, to discuss them as separate dimensions is somewhat misleading given how they combine to constitute school culture, but for the didactic purposes of this chapter, it is a necessary rhetorical strategy.

Norms, Values, and Shared Beliefs

There are any number of ways from psychology, sociology, and anthropology to theoretically define and conceptualize norms, values, and shared beliefs. We will not detail these different theoretical perspectives, but rather for our purposes in this book, we will use a fairly broad and global definition. If one thinks of a school building as having a culture, just as different countries have a culture, then the individuals in the school building will share some common values and core beliefs about the organization, its function, its students, and its teaching and learning practices. These core beliefs and values are constructed by the individuals and can be consciously held, as in the case of a list of school goals, or implicit beliefs that are reflected in the daily practices that guide teacher and student behavior. There should be some tacit consensus among individuals within a school about these beliefs because they are partially created by the school structure and organization, but there is always the possibility that there will be subcultures of individuals within a building that do not necessarily endorse the beliefs of the larger group. In any event, as one talks to individuals in schools and observes the practices and organization of the school, it is possible to come to an understanding of the norms, values, and shared beliefs of a school.

It is important to note that the effects these beliefs might have on students must be mediated through the actual practices that teachers engage in as they interact with the students. Accordingly, whereas it is valuable to acknowledge the role of shared beliefs, it will become even more significant to discuss the actual practices that teachers use, which we do later in this chapter. The shared beliefs become very important, however, when there are efforts made to change teacher or school practices because the beliefs can act as a constraint on the reform efforts. These shared beliefs can be seen as analogous to the entrenched beliefs and knowledge that individual students have about science concepts in the conceptual change literature (Pintrich, Marx, & Boyle, 1993). In the same way, the shared beliefs at the school level can act as an ecology of school-level thinking that can accept, adapt to, or resist change. Changing the shared beliefs of a building is analogous to the difficulty of the conceptual change process at the individual level (Maehr & Midgley, forthcoming).

There are a number of aspects of these shared beliefs that could have an influence on both teachers and students. However, in terms of our interest in motivational outcomes, we will focus on four general beliefs. These four beliefs can influence the types of instructional practices that teachers will engage in and how they will interact with their students. In turn, these practices can influence student motivation and learning. The first general belief concerns a very global belief about the character of human nature. Are students basically good, motivated to learn, and intrinsically interested in schoolwork or are they basically bad, not motivated to learn, and in need of control or coercion to do their schoolwork? At some level, these beliefs hark back to the general metatheoretical positions and metaphors we discussed in Chapter 2 as organizing principles for motivational theories. These very general beliefs will obviously have some influence on the types of discipline and management practices that are put into place at the school (Maehr & Midgley, forthcoming). In turn, we know from goal orientation theory (Chapter 6) and intrinsic motivation theory (Chapter 7) that certain types of practices where students have less control and choice (Chapter 9) may result in students who will be less mastery oriented and less intrinsically motivated.

The second aspect of beliefs concerns the malleability or stability of student learning and ability. At a general school level, teachers can believe that the students can learn and that students can increase their knowledge and ability to do well in school (an incremental belief about learning and intelligence, Dweck & Leggett, 1988) or the teachers can have an entity belief about student learning and ability that assumes that students have a set amount of ability and that it will not change much. This belief about the malleability of student ability is related to the idea from the effective schools literature that teachers should have high expectations for all students (Brookover, Beady, Flood, Schweitzer, & Wisenbaker, 1979; Edmonds, 1979; Purkey & Smith, 1983; Rutter, Maughan, Mortimore, Ouston, & Smith, 1979). This literature on school effectiveness has proposed that one of the tenets of an effective school is the shared belief among staff that all students can learn and therefore teachers should have high expectations for all students regarding their ability to learn and master the material (see Chapter 9). Good and Brophy (1986) point out, however, that it is difficult in many of the school effectiveness studies to assess causality between school practices, such as setting high expectations for the building, and student achievement given the correlational designs used. Nevertheless, current motivational theories about incremental and entity beliefs and goal orientation (Ames, 1992b; Dweck & Leggett, 1988; Maehr &

Midgley, 1991) and the stability of attributions (Weiner, 1986; see Chapter 4) suggest that having a general incremental belief about the malleability of student learning at the school level would lead to positive school practices regarding instruction. For example, if teachers believe that all students can learn and that students' ability is not stable, then they might be more willing to use instructional practices like reciprocal teaching (see Rosenshine & Meister, 1994) that require more teacher effort and support of students.

A third aspect of the shared beliefs system that could have an influence on teacher practices and, in turn, on student motivation essentially relates to shared beliefs and norms about teaching and instruction. At one level, the content of these beliefs can refer to norms about how instruction is supposed to occur in classrooms. For example, school norms about the need for quiet classrooms where students work silently and individually at their seats as a sign of good instruction or of a good teacher may not be most conducive to student motivation and cognition given current constructivist views of teaching and learning. Of course, if these are the norms for the building and they are enforced by the principal and other teachers directly (warnings from principal) or indirectly (faculty lounge discussions, see beginning of chapter), then it may be difficult to use cooperative groups, discovery learning, or project-based learning, which require more interaction and discussion among students and teachers.

At a more psychological level, beliefs about teaching can refer to the perceptions of controllability and efficacy that teachers have about instruction (Ashton & Webb, 1986). That is, do teachers in the building share the belief that their instructional actions can make a difference in student motivation or learning, or do they assume that student change is beyond their control? If these beliefs about lack of control and efficacy of instruction become very rigid and stable, teachers may develop a sense of learned helplessness about their efforts. For example, teachers in a large urban school that serves children with many life stresses may begin to see their instructional efforts as fruitless. Of course, as we have already seen in Chapter 3 in our discussion of attribution theory, this type of attributional pattern of helplessness will not be conducive to change in behavior, exertion of effort, or persistence. Teachers with this pattern of beliefs will be unlikely to try to engage in much innovative instruction and in some cases of severe teacher helplessness and burnout, even much of any kind of instruction. In these cases, it seems clear that student motivation and learning will suffer. In fact, Midgley, Feldlaufer, and Eccles (1989a) in a longitudinal study of the transition from elementary school to middle school found that students who moved from having high-efficacy elementary math teachers to low-efficacy middle school math teachers had the lowest level of expectancy beliefs for math performance in comparison to other students.

The last aspect of the belief system that could have an influence on teachers and students concerns the shared goals or purposes of the school. The effective schools literature (Brookover et al., 1979; Good & Brophy, 1986; Edmonds, 1979; Purkey & Smith, 1983; Rutter et al., 1979) has stressed the importance of a school having an agreed upon set of clear goals and purposes (a mission statement for the school). The related literature on the principal as an instructional leader (e.g., Leithwood & Montgomery, 1982; Manassee, 1985) also has stressed the importance of the principal as an instructional leader who helps a school building staff develop and strive for a set of clearly articulated goals. A set of clear and shared goals that are consistently enforced would certainly help guide teachers and students as they make choices about their behavior (recall Ms. Strobel's comment about behavior at the beginning of this chapter). In fact, Good and Brophy (1986) summarize this research by noting that schools with clear goals had higher teacher morale, fewer classroom disruptions, less student misbehavior, more time-on-task, and lower student absenteeism, all positive teacher and student outcomes (see Figure 10.1).

Although clear goals are undoubtedly important for a school, Lee, Bryk, and Smith (1993) have pointed out that much of this research has not examined the content of the goals in an effective school. They note that this research has often used what they call a *rational-bureaucratic* model to conceptualize school organization. They suggest that it can be misleading to ignore the content of the goals that are put forth by a school. First, they note that there can be multiple goals operating at different levels in a school (e.g., between departments in a secondary school regarding teaching all students vs. preparing the academic elite; or teaching to the test vs. teaching for conceptual understanding, see Mr. De Groot's comments) and that the content of these goals may not be compatible. Second, they suggest that even if the organizational goals are clear and shared, there may be some disagreement about the desirability of these goals. Lee and colleagues (Lee et al., 1993) provide examples of two organizations that have very clear and shared goals, a medical school (see Becker, Geer, & Hughes, 1961) and a fundamentalist academy (see Peshkin, 1986), yet point out that the culture in these two organizations may not be the most adaptive or democratic. They note that the medical school had very clear goals and common activities but the result was a very competitive environment with low personal support. The fundamentalist academy also had clearly articulated goals, but the goals did not encourage tolerance of diversity and hence were antithetical to some basic democratic values (Lee et al., 1993). Lee and colleagues (Lee et al., 1993) suggest that a communitarian perspective regarding goals, where the emphasis is on social and personal relations, on creating a community, and on a shared ethos, may be more adaptive for schools than a rational-bureaucratic model.

Maehr and Midgley (forthcoming) also raise this issue regarding the importance of the content of the shared goals, not merely having consensus about any goals. Given their work on the role of achievement goals at the school level (Anderman & Maehr, 1994; Maehr & Midgley, 1991; Midgley & Wood, 1993), they suggest that schools should adopt goals that are in line with a general mastery goal orientation. As pointed out in Chapter 6 (see Table 6.8), this goal orientation defines success as individual improvement, growth, and mastery. Value is placed on effort, evaluation criteria are absolute and based on progress toward these standards, and errors are viewed as informational and part of learning. In contrast, a performance goal orientation defines success as besting others on tests and grades and winning at all costs. Value is placed on avoiding failure, evaluation criteria are normative and force comparisons between teachers and students, and errors are viewed as failures to be avoided at all costs. At the school level, these different goal orientations would be reflected in the staff position on standardized test scores, the public display of grades and honors (bulletin boards displaying only some students' work), competitions for academic performance (numbers of books read in a month without concern for comprehension), grouping and teaching practices, and differential and salient rewards for winning competitions of academic performance (special field trips awarded to top 10% of students in a schoolwide ranking of performance), all of which can have important influences on student outcomes (Mac Iver et al., 1995).

These school-level beliefs and the practices that are derived from them can, in turn, create individual goal orientations (Anderman & Maehr, 1994; Maehr & Midgley, forthcoming). As we have already shown in Chapter 6, a personal goal orientation toward mastery, in comparison to performance goals, has a strong link to a number of positive motivational and cognitive outcomes, including better self-efficacy, more effort and persistence, more cognitive engagement, and better achievement. Whereas we stressed the importance of individuals' personal goal orientations in Chapter 6, the research on school context suggests that these personal goals are created, supported, and maintained by both the classroom and school context. Accordingly, if a school wishes its students to be mastery oriented at the individual level, then the content of the school's goals should reflect the same type of mastery orientation at the building level (Maehr & Midgley, forthcoming).

Climate

The climate of a school building also can have an influence on teacher and student outcomes. The construct of school climate has been defined in many different ways using a number of different typologies and theories and, not surprisingly, has been researched using a number of different methodologies (Anderson, 1982; Moos, 1979). In some ways, the construct of school climate has been incorporated into research on school culture, reflecting a general shift away from simple psychological models of climate to more complex sociological and anthropological perspectives on school culture. Most of the six TARGET dimensions listed in Figure 10.1 as part of school culture and organization would have been included in various models of school climate as well as the dimension of norms, values, and shared beliefs just discussed (see Anderson, 1982). However, we will single out three affective aspects of school climate and discuss them in this section as part of climate rather than as part of the other seven dimensions listed in Figure 10.1. The three we will present are (a) a sense of community and belongingness, (b) warmth and civility in personal relations, and (c) feelings of safety and security.

A sense of community is a rather vague construct, but it would include individuals' feelings that they belong to the group or organization (recall comments by Chris at the beginning of the chapter), that they are committed to the organizations' goals and values (see preceding discussion), and that there is some reciprocity in the relation such that the organization or representatives of the organization care about and are concerned about the individual group member. Lee and colleagues (Lee et al., 1993) stress the importance of a communitarian perspective on school organization that explicitly focuses on the quality of the social relations among the individuals in the organization. They note that schools where the administration, faculty, and students seem to demonstrate mutual respect and concern for each other are linked to positive outcomes for teachers and students (see Figure 10.1). Noddings (1992) has proposed that caring for others is an important component that should be present in all relations in a school as well as explicitly taught in the curriculum. The student dropout and at-risk student literature also suggests that the absence of teacher concern and care (recall Shirley's comments) is a major factor mentioned by students who leave school (Bryk, Lee, & Holland, 1993; Calabrese & Poe, 1990; Lee et al., 1993; Natriello, 1986). Deci and Ryan (1985) also propose that all individuals have a basic need to feel a sense of belongingness or relatedness and that organizational structures that support or satisfy this need will result in more intrinsic motivation and engagement. Skinner and Belmont (1993) have shown that students' feelings of relatedness are sensitive to contextual aspects of the classroom and are connected to their future motivation and involvement. Given these few examples that reflect the results from both sociological and psychological research, it seems important, at least from a motivational perspective, that teachers and students feel a sense of community in their schools.

The second dimension of climate also reflects the affective life of the school in terms of the warmth and civility expressed in the relations among individuals in the building. At the teacher and staff level, Lee and colleagues (Lee et al., 1993) have noted that research from both the rational-bureaucratic and the communitarian perspectives has shown that civil and collegial relations between teachers and administrators are associated with positive outcomes in terms of organizational effectiveness. The effective schools literature also stresses the importance of collegial relations for school effectiveness (Purkey & Smith, 1983). In addition, these researchers (Lee et al., 1993) note that friendly and collegial relations among teachers helps them personally in terms of easing the isolation of teaching and is associated with more teacher satisfaction.

In terms of teacher-student relations, certainly a feeling of concern, care, support, and respect for students and positive teacher-student interactions would be associated with positive motivational outcomes (see Calabrese & Poe, 1990; Eccles, Midgley, et al., 1993; Midgley, Feldlaufer, & Eccles, 1989b;

Natriello, 1986). Bryk, Lee, and Holland (1993) in their study of Catholic schools suggest that a concern for the welfare of others or the creation of a caring community can have very positive effects for all students, even those from populations that would be at risk for school failure. The literature on middle schools suggests that they are more bureaucratic, less personal, and engender fewer positive teacher-student interactions than elementary schools. These differences have been linked to declines in student motivation as the students make the transition to middle schools (Eccles, Midgley, et al., 1993; Midgley et al., 1989b). In their review of the process-product research on teaching, Brophy and Good (1986) note that the emotional climate of the classroom (as defined by teacher criticism and teacher and student negative affect) can be associated with student achievement. However, they note that although a very negative emotional climate can have negative consequences for achievement, a warm emotional climate is not necessarily associated with better achievement. They suggest that neutral climates are just as supportive of achievement as warm climates. At the same time, it should be noted that these classroom studies only focused on student achievement on standardized tests for the most part and motivational constructs were not usually examined. Nevertheless, it seems clear that positive teacher-student interactions at the school level can create a positive climate for all members of the school community.

The last dimension of climate refers to the teachers' and students' feelings of personal safety and security (see students' comments at the beginning of the chapter). In one sense of psychological climate, these perceptions could refer to individuals' feelings about taking risks and feeling secure in expressing different ideas and opinions. However, in many schools today, this aspect of climate refers to feelings of physical safety and being free from the fear and anxiety of physical harm. There is no real need to document the harmful effects and problems that school violence can create in a school building, although the school effectiveness literature has demonstrated the importance of this decision. For example, Lee and Bryk (1989) have shown that schools that offer a safe and orderly environment have higher achievement, especially for minority students. As common sense will tell us, and as Maslow's (1954) hierarchy of needs suggests (see Chapter 6), if individuals are concerned about basic survival and safety needs, then it is difficult to achieve other goals. Accordingly, it is important for schools to offer a safe and secure environment for all staff and students.

Task and Work Structures

The remaining six dimensions of school culture and organization reflect the TARGET dimensions that were introduced in Chapter 9 on classroom structure. These same dimensions can be applied to the larger unit of school organization in terms of its impact on both students and teachers (Lee et al., 1993; Maehr & Midgley, 1991). The first dimension, task and work structures, can refer to the nature of the activities and curriculum that students and teachers engage in as they enact the school curriculum in the classroom. Work structures can also refer to how the school is organized in terms of teachers' work and role differentiation. As far as the nature of the curriculum and tasks is concerned, Maehr & Midgley (1991) suggest that a mastery-oriented school will focus the curriculum and academic tasks in such a way to foster student value and interest in learning, rather than merely provide coverage of the curriculum to meet assessment or bureaucratic needs. This can be done by encouraging the use of authentic tasks and meaningful activities that link the content of the curriculum to real-world problems and to the backgrounds and experiences of the students. These tasks also should be challenging to students, but not beyond their level of competence. A mastery-oriented curriculum also can include the use of programs that encourage learning in nonschool settings, such as internships in work settings, field experiences, and cocurricular activities (Maehr & Midgley, 1991). This emphasis on the value of learning along with these types of activities should support the adoption of a personal mastery goal orientation that should then have positive outcomes for students.

In terms of the work structures of the school, Lee and colleagues (Lee et al., 1993) note that several work design features of large bureaucratic schools may act against some of the positive outcomes for teachers and students listed in Figure 10.1, although the actual empirical evidence is limited. For example, departmentalization and specialization of teachers' roles can create the possibility that students' interactions with teachers will be relatively transient, that is, limited to a 45- to 60-minute class period once a day with four to six teachers, as in most large secondary schools, in contrast to the 4–6 hours per day contact with one teacher possible in elementary schools. This lack of interaction obviously can create barriers to the development of personal relations between teachers and students (see previous section on climate) as well as increase the problems of student alienation (Lee et al., 1993; Newmann, 1981). In fact, some of the recommendations for the reform of middle schools (e.g., Carnegie Council on Adolescent Development, 1989) have suggested that there be structures set in place that allow for teachers to work with smaller groups of students in order to form more close personal relations. Bryk, Lee, and Holland (1993) found that the small, more communally organized Catholic schools they examined are structured in such a way that there is not as much teacher role specialization and departmentalization, thereby providing more opportunities for the development of personal relations between teachers and students.

Authority and Management Structures

The second dimension in the TARGET framework refers to the authority and management structures that guide both teacher and student participation in school and classroom activities. At the teacher level, there is a great deal of literature on the need for teacher control, teacher empowerment, and teacher participation in shared decision making and school management (e.g., Bolin,

1989; Duke, Showers, & Imber, 1980; Shedd & Bacharach, 1991), although the empirical base for this research is not strong (Lee et al., 1993). From a motivational perspective involving both goal orientation theory (Ames, 1992b; Maehr & Midgley, forthcoming) and intrinsic motivation theory (Deci & Ryan, 1985), teachers' perceptions of control and autonomy over aspects of their work environment should be associated with positive outcomes.

At the student level, Maehr & Midgley (1991, forthcoming) suggest that allowing student participation in learning and school decisions will help to develop a mastery orientation. At the classroom level, as discussed in Chapter 9, allowing students some autonomy, choice, and control can have beneficial effects on their motivation and learning as well as on their development of self-regulation strategies. Finally, these opportunities for participation in decision making can help students develop responsibility, independence, and leadership skills. Of course, no one is suggesting that school staff and teachers give up their authority to students, but rather that there are some areas where the authority structure can be expanded so that students can exercise some control. For example, school councils can have student members who are allowed to play an active role in school decision making. School discipline can be a matter that is determined by the staff with little input from students, or efforts can be made to include students in the discussion and clarification of the values that guide group and institutional behavior. Students can be given opportunities for some choice in instructional settings, or they can be forced to take certain types of curricula without much control over the decision. Schools can foster choice and participation in cocurricular and extracurricular activities for all students or limit these activities to certain types of students (Maehr & Midgley, 1991).

Recognition and Reward Structures

This dimension concerns how students are recognized for their work and performance and, given the recognition criteria used, who then gets recognized. Maehr and Midgley (1991) note that the operation of school-level recognition structures was the first school-level dimension that convinced them they could not simply try to reform schools by acting at the classroom level. They were working with classroom teachers to help the teachers make their classrooms more mastery oriented. A large part of this effort involved building classroom recognition and reward structures that were based on student progress, mastery, individual improvement, and effort, not social comparison, competition, and extrinsic rewards. However, as they worked with the teachers, the teachers noted that the school's honor roll did not recognize these types of mastery-oriented criteria, but in fact recognized normative criteria that could increase social comparison among students and foster an orientation to just "getting good grades" rather than learning. Besides the honor roll, the school also participated in a book-reading program in which the students who read the most books would receive rewards (free pizzas). Maehr and Midgley report that this program often resulted in students reading the greatest number of the easiest and shortest books they could find, without regard for challenge or difficulty level, let alone comprehension and learning. Needless to say, the mismatch between the classroom efforts to increase mastery-based criteria for recognition and the school-level recognition structures did not support the teachers' efforts to change their classroom reward structures.

Accordingly, although it is important to have classroom recognition and reward structures that are focused on mastery, progress, and individual improvement, it is also important that the school-level recognition structures be aligned and support these criteria. In addition, if school recognition structures are based solely on normative and competitive criteria, then there is always the chance that only certain types of students will be able to be recognized. For example, the same group of high-achieving students could always be the ones who win all the academic awards, suggesting that good academic performance can't be attained by others and that it is a stable, entity-like trait. These types of messages can discourage other students from even trying to attain reasonable levels of academic performance.

Maehr and Midgley (1991) suggest that schools provide opportunities for all students to be recognized, such as fostering "personal best" awards and recognition procedures. They suggest that there are schoolwide strategies and policies that can help teachers and students focus on progress in goal attainment, not just comparative levels of achievement. For example, Mac Iver, Reuman, and Main (1995) review several schoolwide programs designed to help teachers implement recognition and reward structures that are based on personal improvement. These programs assume that there may be some students who do need rewards to at least begin their schoolwork. Moreover, if the rewards are informational about their skills and increase their efficacy, they can have a positive influence on the students' behavior (Cameron & Pierce, 1994; Morgan, 1984). Finally, Maehr and Midgley (1991) note that schools can recognize efforts in a number of domains and learning activities by recognizing and publicizing achievements in different domains (e.g., science fairs, debating clubs, artistic and musical accomplishments, school-community relations), not just overall academic achievement based on GPA.

Grouping Practices

As Maehr and Midgley (1991) characterize this dimension, it has to do with the structures that allow for certain types of student interaction and the development of social skills in students. At the classroom level, grouping practices can involve the use of within-classroom grouping (e.g., high and low reading groups in first grade) as well as the use of cooperative groups and other alternatives to whole-group instruction. At the school level, one aspect of grouping practices would involve the support for alternatives to whole-group instruction. There is a wealth of research that supports the use of small groups and cooperative groups as long as they are designed and implemented properly, not just used to throw students together and let them interact without guidance and support (see Bossert, 1988; Cohen, 1994; Johnson, Maruyama, Johnson, Nelson, & Skon, 1981; Rosenshine & Meister, 1994; Sharan, 1980; Slavin, 1983a, 1983b, 1995). If school policies and practices undermine the appropriate use of small groups at the classroom level, then teachers will have a difficult time using them as one of their instructional strategies.

Beyond the use of small-group instruction within the classroom, the grouping dimension at the school level involves the use of between-classroom tracking. The literature on the effects of tracking is extensive and can't be easily summarized in a chapter of this scope. For more detail, see the articles and books by Alexander, Cook, and McDill (1978); Bowles and Gintis (1976); Gamoran and Berends (1987); Heyns (1974); Jencks and Brown (1975); Lee and Bryk (1988); Mac Iver, Reuman, and Main (1995); Oakes (1985); Rosenbaum (1976, 1980); Sorensen (1987); and Sorensen and Hallinan (1986) to name just a few. Rather, we will focus our comments on some general considerations for school-level policies that can lessen the negative effects of between-classroom tracking.

First, Lee and colleagues (Lee et al., 1993) point out that there is some evidence that in many schools in the United States today there are not the clear and well-defined two or three tracks within a school (i.e., academic, business, vocational) that may have been the norm in earlier research. They note that there is much more flexibility and variance in individual course-taking patterns of students and that there is often a much wider range of course offerings for students to choose from than in earlier times, especially in large comprehensive high schools. Accordingly, they suggest that it may be more important to examine differential course taking by students and what learning and instructional opportunities and resources are offered in these different courses than to examine the effects of nominal track designations per se.

Mac Iver, Reuman, and Main (1995) point out in a review on the social structures of schools that access to these different types of courses can offer either positive opportunities or negative constraints for students. They note that many schools do not offer equal access to college preparatory courses for all students, even though these courses usually offer more academic content and are necessary for college admission. They do suggest, however, that often restrictions in scheduling and resources at the school level and lack of information at the teacher, counselor, or student level can be responsible for enrollment decisions, not intentional decision making on the part of the school personnel. Nevertheless, the types of courses taken by students (e.g., advanced academic courses) correlate very highly with achievement, holding other student background variables constant and without even taking into account the quality of instruction (Lee et al., 1993).

Second, besides access to general college preparatory courses, there are a number of studies that show that access to advanced or accelerated math courses (e.g., algebra in the eighth grade) has very positive effects on student achievement in math. For example, in one study (Lee & Bryk, 1988), the correlation between taking advanced math courses and senior year achievement was .65, and this relation remained strong even after student background, attitudes, and behaviors were considered (Lee et al., 1993). Finally, Mac Iver and colleagues (Mac Iver et al., 1995) note that access to courses that are focused on teaching for understanding (a current suggestion for quality instruction) is often limited to those upper level or upper track courses within a school (cf., Oakes, 1985; Page, 1990; Raudenbush, Rowan, & Cheong, 1993). Although there may not be a great deal of teaching for understanding even in these upper track courses, it seems clear from current constructivist models of motivation and cognition that this type of instruction can have positive benefits for students.

Given these findings, it is important for schools to offer opportunities for all students to have access to academic track courses. Lee and colleagues (Lee et al., 1993) note that in their research on Catholic schools (Bryk et al., 1993), a much higher percentage of the students enroll in the academic courses, partially because there are not as many other types of courses offered and partially because it is the general norm of the school that most students will take these academic courses. Beyond the types of classes, equal access to quality instruction is important. Maehr and Midgley (1991) suggest that schools offer all students opportunities for group learning, problem solving, and decision making of the kind that could be provided when small-group instruction is used. In much the same way, if teaching for understanding is deemed to be an exemplar of quality instruction, then all groups and tracks should have access to it. Given that some form of tracking will probably exist in many large high schools for bureaucratic reasons, Maehr and Midgley also encourage the development of subgroups (teams, families, schools within a school) in large schools that will provide more opportunities for positive teacher-student and student-student interaction. They also suggest that there should be encouragement of multiple group membership to increase the range of peer interaction across groups.

Evaluation Practices

Evaluation practices concern the nature and use of student evaluation and assessment procedures. As with the grouping dimension, there can be two levels of school influences on evaluation practices. First, some school buildings might have fairly standard grading policies regarding the distribution of grades. For example, the school policy might be that there should be some distribution of grades from A's to F's in a course, with fewer A's and F's, more B's and D's, and a large number of C's (i.e., an approximation of a normal curve distribution). If this is the policy of the school, then mastery-oriented classroom evaluation systems that focus on personal effort, improvement, and progress will be difficult for teachers to implement (Maehr & Midgley, 1991). Accordingly, general school building policies regarding grades and evaluation can support or undermine what teachers may try to do in their classroom in terms of changing the evaluation practices.

In addition, the evaluation policies of the school can have a direct impact on student motivation. For example, if the evaluation procedures stress normative comparisons among students (e.g., class rankings of students), then it is likely that social comparisons will be made and, at least for those who are not doing well, students' perceptions of competence and efficacy may suffer. The types of schoolwide assessment programs also can influence what teachers come to stress in their instruction and what students come to believe is important to learn (Maehr & Midgley, 1991). Of course, if the assessments are designed to reflect important and valued goals, then this may not be a problem. However, many of the assessments that are used at the school, district, or statewide levels mainly represent factual knowledge assessments, not assessments for conceptual understanding or higher level thinking. In these cases, it is not surprising that many teachers don't teach for conceptual understanding, as we noted in the previous section. Moreover, it is unlikely that students will see the utility or value of these large-scale assessments for their own learning given that they are often not connected to the regular classroom activities or to any meaningful tasks (Paris, Lawton, Turner, & Roth, 1991).

Schools can help decrease these potentially negative influences of evaluation practices by reducing the emphasis on normative social comparisons that are highly public. They also can establish procedures by which students can assess their own progress toward their own goals. For example, portfolios offer one assessment procedure that can help students reflect on their own strengths and weaknesses in a particular course (see Paris & Ayres, 1994). Portfolios also can help teachers to individualize instruction and assessment to meet individual students' needs. They can be used by teachers to gauge student progress and improvement as well. However, portfolios are a fairly new assessment tool for most schools, classrooms, and teachers and there are still many problems with their reliability and validity that need to be resolved. There also are practical implementation problems in terms of time to evaluate and use portfolios across teachers, classes, and grades/year in school. Nevertheless, they do offer one type of assessment that can be used to foster many of the goals suggested by mastery goal orientation researchers (Ames, 1992b; Maehr & Midgley, 1991, forthcoming).

Time Use

The final TARGET dimension concerns how time is used at the school level. Many of the current suggestions for increasing mastery goals, for improving instruction to facilitate conceptual understanding and critical thinking, and for creating shared norms and a climate of collegiality will require more time from teachers and students or a change in the way time is currently used. Yet in many schools in the United States, teachers do not have time for many of the suggestions we have been making throughout this chapter and in the book as a whole. Stevenson and Stigler (1992) point out that in Japanese schools, teachers usually have much more time set aside for planning, for consulting with colleagues, and for grading and evaluating student work because they do not teach as many hours per school day as their counterparts in the United States. This time away from teaching, but spent at the school building involved with other teachers, helps to facilitate the collegial climate and consultation among teachers seen in Japan. It also allows more opportunity for teachers to discuss their goals and their teaching practices, which can help to build a consensus about the norms and goals for the school. Although it is unlikely that there will be a major change in how most U.S. schools structure outside class time use by teachers due to financial constraints, it seems important to find ways for teachers to work together and to collaborate on school and instructional improvement without making it extra work that is taken on after an entire day of teaching (see Maehr & Midgley, forthcoming).

In terms of time use by students, there are a number of ways that schools can help students develop appropriate time management skills. For example, some flexibility in when students do their work during the day or during the week can increase student control and responsibility. Of course, students need to be taught and guided in their time management, but these kinds of opportunities can help to increase student intrinsic motivation and mastery goal orientation (Deci & Ryan, 1985; Maehr & Midgley, 1991). Another strategy is to provide students with opportunities to set proximal and long-term goals (see Chapters 5 and 6) regarding the completion of their work. Students will have to be scaffolded and monitored by the teacher at first, but eventually these opportunities can help the students become self-regulating in terms of assessing goal progress, implementing their plans to reach their goals, and monitoring their time use on different goals (Zimmerman, Greenberg, & Weinstein, 1994).

EXTERNAL CONSTRAINTS AND OPPORTUNITIES

Although it has been implicit in our discussion to this point, it seems clear that these eight dimensions of school culture and organization are created, shaped, and exist within a larger context. As shown in Figure 10.1, this context includes a number of different features that can act as constraints to limit the development of the school culture and organization or as opportunities to facilitate the development of an adaptive school culture and organization. There are many different features of the larger school context that can influence school culture and organization, but we focus on a few of the most salient. In general, much of the research on these external features has linked them directly to teacher and student outcomes. However, in this chapter, we focus on how these external features have an indirect effect on these outcomes through their influence on school culture and organization (Lee et al., 1993).

Type of Students

There are many ways to characterize students, but we will focus on general ability or achievement level, race, social class, and age. In terms of ability composition, it appears that effective schools have at least a core group of academically motivated and engaged students (Rutter et al., 1979), a situation that can help facilitate the development of a school culture that is focused on academic learning and mastery. In contrast, if a school has too many students who present serious problems and are alienated from school, then it is more difficult to create and maintain an ethos focused on academic concerns. Just as a teacher and a classroom can be constrained by a preponderance of low-achieving and difficult students (Barr & Dreeben, 1983), schools can be constrained in a similar way (Lee et al., 1993). At the same time, most of this data is correlational, so it is possible that positive school and classroom cultures will help to create a core of motivated and engaged students.

In terms of race, there has been a great deal of research on racial composition, school integration, and achievement (see Rossell and Howley, 1983), which is too extensive to be summarized in this chapter. In terms of our analysis of school culture that focuses on shared values and a climate of good social relations, however, there is evidence that intergroup relations were somewhat better in schools that had a higher percentage of minority students (Schofield & Sager, 1983). Nevertheless, there is also evidence based on case study data (Cusick, 1983; Metz, 1978) that intergroup problems between students of different races in forced integrated schools contributed to a breakdown of community and cohesion with a concomitant drop in the academic focus of the school (Lee et al., 1993). Accordingly, the racial heterogeneity of schools can be an opportunity for multicultural learning, but it can also act as a constraint on building a school culture of shared values and a climate of social community if the groups do not actually interact and work together (Eyler, Cook, & Ward, 1983; Grant, 1988).

Social class may not act in such a marked manner as race, but Lee and Bryk (1988) have found that the average SES level of a school is related to overall achievement of the school. Moreover, research in the effective schools tradition has found that there are differences in how schools with low and high social class students implement the various tenets of effective schools (Hallinger & Murphy, 1986). For example, principals of effective schools with a mainly lower class population were likely to exert more direct control and authority than principals of effective schools with higher SES levels (Lee et al., 1993). Of course, given our analysis of school culture from mastery goal theory, higher levels of direct control by the principal could act as a constraint in the implementation of some of the changes suggested by Maehr and Midgley (1991, forthcoming).

In terms of age, there may be different school structures and organizations that provide a better fit or match for students of different ages. For example, the literature on the transition to middle schools (Anderman & Maehr, 1994; Braddock & McPartland, 1993; Eccles, Lord, & Midgley, 1991; Eccles & Midgley, 1989; Eccles, Midgley, et al., 1993) documents large decrements in children's achievement, motivation, and engagement as they make the move from elementary schools to middle schools. Traditionally, psychologists have attributed some of these changes to cognitive-developmental processes such as the increase in metacognition and the ability to use social comparison processes (cf., Anderman & Maehr, 1994; Ruble & Frey, 1991). However, the most recent research suggests that this drop is due to a developmental mismatch between the students' needs and capabilities and the structure and organization of middle schools.

For example, junior high school students are developmentally able to exercise greater choice and control, are better able to engage in more self-regulated learning, and are cognitively able to engage in more critical thinking and metacognition (Eccles & Midgley, 1989; Simmons & Blyth, 1987). However, middle schools are often structured with stricter rules and discipline systems that provide fewer opportunities for these students to have choice and control in comparison to elementary schools. In addition, the classroom tasks and instructional procedures often do not allow for much self-regulation or critical thinking (Anderman & Maehr, 1994; Eccles, Midgley, et al., 1993; Midgley, Anderman, & Hicks, 1995; Urdan, Midgley, & Wood, 1995). Given these types of developmental mismatches, it is not surprising that many motivated and engaged elementary students become less motivated and engaged middle school students.

These kinds of developmental differences suggest that the effects of the school culture and organizational dimensions on student outcomes may vary depending on the age of the students. Many of the issues we discussed in the previous section may be especially salient and important at the middle school level (Midgley et al., 1995; Urdan et al., 1995). Certainly, they can be important at the high school level, but the salience may not be as great as in the middle schools. Many high school students may have adapted to the bureaucratic structures of middle schools and have an easier time adjusting to a similar culture at the high school level. Nevertheless, given our analysis of school culture, we still believe it is important to work to improve school culture and organization at the high school level. At the elementary level, there may not be as much urgency as at the middle school level because the students are still developing their beliefs, knowledge, skills, and motivation. Moreover, many elementary schools, due to their smaller size and more cohesive norms and structures, may have relatively positive school cultures (Maehr & Midgley, forthcoming; Midgley et al., 1995).

School Size

As we have just noted, school size can operate as a facilitator of changes in school culture and organization or as a constraint in a number of ways. Lee and colleagues (Lee et al., 1993) note three problems that are generated by very large bureaucratic schools. First, the role differentiation is increased in large schools and there can be a diffusion of responsibility or loyalty to the school in favor of other subunits, especially the academic department in high schools. Second, in a large school, it is harder to communicate with all members of the staff, thereby lowering the opportunities for the development of shared values and a climate of collegial and personal relations. Finally, norms and goals can become more formalized (e.g., written lists of school goals), but given the large size and lack of opportunity to interact among all staff members, members' individual beliefs and goals may not be represented in the formalized mission statement or list of school goals. This can result in individuals holding goals and beliefs that are in opposition to the formalized school goals and hinder any efforts to work toward those goals or to change the school goals.

Maehr and Midgley and their colleagues (Maehr & Midgley, 1991, forthcoming; Urdan et al., 1995) present a case study of many of these problems as they struggled to reform both an elementary and a middle school to bring them more in line with a mastery goal orientation. They had a fair amount of success at the elementary school level for many of the reasons just enumerated. At the junior high school, however, they were less successful at first. Some of the department chairs formally and forcefully blocked the recommended changes and the principal was not able to develop strategies to involve all the faculty in the changes. Obviously, size was not the direct cause of the successes and failures of the project, but the smaller, more manageable size of the elementary school allowed for more sustained interaction and the development of a coherent plan for school reform. In contrast, at the junior high school, size operated as a constraint; there were many more individuals involved and it was difficult to build a consensus for reform. Nevertheless, some of the junior high teachers banded together in smaller teams and continued to implement changes. Urdan, Midgley, and Wood (1995) discuss some of the special constraints and challenges involved in reforming middle schools.

Parental and Community Involvement

There is a wealth of evidence that parental involvement in schools can have a positive influence on the school in general as well as on the students and teachers (Becker & Epstein, 1982; Chubb, 1988; Comer, 1980; Epstein, 1986, 1987, 1995; Lee et al., 1993). Hence, it seems important to involve parents in schools and classrooms. At the same time, however, it should be noted that parental and community involvement or control of schools can increase the probability that there will be conflict between the professional judgment and expertise of school personnel and the parents' and community's interests and goals (Lee et al., 1993). This does not mean that there is necessarily an automatic conflict between school personnel and the community, but suggests that there is a need for negotiation of common interests, values, and goals, just as we have suggested is necessary for school personnel to do within the school building.

For example, in terms of the types of reforms and changes that we discussed in the earlier section on fostering a mastery goal orientation at the school building level, parents may support these changes or they may not see them as compatible with their goals. Some parents may see a mastery goal orientation and the accompanying changes as important and work with the school staff to implement these changes (see Maehr & Midgley, forthcoming; Urdan et al., 1995). In contrast, other parents may not believe that a general mastery goal orientation will prepare their children for competition in the "real world" and work to block or constrain any changes along these lines. Accordingly, parental and community involvement can act as a moderator of school culture and organization and, in particular, facilitate or constrain school reform efforts.

District- and State-Level Constraints and Opportunities

Schools operate within a community, a state, and, of course, a national context. All of these contexts can influence the dimensions of school culture and organization. We note only a few of the possible influences of the district and state levels. First, there are always fiscal constraints and opportunities. Given the vagaries of local and state school funding practices, some school districts have much more funding than other school districts. This allows the wealthier districts many more opportunities to develop school reforms along some of the lines we have discussed in this chapter. For example, we mentioned time as an important dimension of school organization. Districts with more funds can afford more staff and allow them some flexibility in time use and staffing patterns.

For example, one local district we know of that has a fairly high level of funding has had a middle school staffing arrangement that provides the teachers time to meet individually with students and other teachers. These teachers teach fewer class hours and the nonteaching periods are used to develop closer relations with their students and their colleagues (in line with the 1989 Carnegie report on improving middle schools). However, recent budget cuts have forced the school district administration to cut back on these periods and require the teachers to teach more hours per day. Interestingly, this did not only upset the teachers, but the middle school students were so angry about the changes that they organized strikes at school and demonstrations at the school board meetings. This anecdote serves to illustrate the problems of school finance and how these problems can constrain school reform.

Another type of district or state constraint that can operate on schools concerns assessment practices. Standardized testing at the district or state level can have a great influence on teacher beliefs, the nature of the curriculum, the general goals that a school adopts, and the nature of instruction. If the tests are designed to reflect mainly the acquisition of knowledge, then it seems likely that curriculum and instruction decisions will follow from this type of assessment. There could be a focus on coverage of the curriculum and drill-and-practice in factual knowledge, instead of teaching for conceptual understanding or critical thinking. Moreover, if the tests are "high-stakes" tests with funding decisions contingent on performance, then assessment can have even a greater impact on the school culture and organization.

IMPLICATIONS FOR SCHOOL STAFF

The research reviewed in this chapter has a number of implications for school staff. Moreover, there are any number of suggestions for school reform that are being put forth by educational researchers and policymakers currently (see Muncey & McQuillan, 1993; Perkins, 1992; Sizer, 1992; and just about any recent issue of *Educational Leadership* and *Phi Delta Kappan*). We do not pretend to discuss all of the suggestions or even do justice to the ones we do discuss. School reform is a difficult, time-consuming, and nonalgorithmic task. If there were one simple "magic bullet" of school reform that could be enacted with positive consequences for all, then it seems likely that schools would have adopted it and there would be no need for us to make suggestions (Cuban, 1990; Newmann, 1993; Sarason, 1990). However, just as changing a classroom is a difficult task and involves personal judgment, so is school reform. We offer the following suggestions as guidelines for thinking about changes in schools. These guidelines reflect a concern for student motivation first and foremost, in keeping with the focus of the book. Nevertheless, they should also be related to better student achievement and more positive teacher outcomes. In fact, Lee and Smith (in press) have found that schools that were at least attempting some reforms had better achievement levels than those that were not trying to change their culture and organization, even after controlling for various differences in the schools.

   1. Develop common school norms, values, and shared beliefs. As we have already noted, schools that have shared beliefs and goals seem to function better and are more effective. Although it is difficult and time-consuming, there must be opportunities for teachers and staff to work together, to collaborate, and to develop a shared vision for their school. For example, Sizer's Coalition of Essential Schools (see Muncey & McQuillan, 1993; Sizer, 1992) proposes nine common principles that should guide school organization, curriculum, and staff. These principles are fairly general and reflect many of the ideas we have discussed in this chapter. At the same time, it is recognized that the nine principles will be adapted and implemented in relation to the local school context, staff, and resources available. Accordingly, there will have to be substantial time available for school staff to discuss how these nine principles can be enacted at their school. Maehr and Midgley and their colleagues (see Maehr & Midgley, 1991, forthcoming; Urdan et al., 1995) also describe a school reform process where considerable time, energy, and resources were devoted to the development of a school-level commitment to creating a mastery goal-oriented school.

2. Develop a school climate of good collegial and personal relations. Related to the first suggestion, schools seem to work better when the personal relations among staff and students reflect a mutual trust and concern for the school community. Of course, given the various constituencies and personal differences in staff, this type of climate is not easy to create in any school. However, the principal can help model appropriate behavior and, as Sizer (1984, 1992) points out in his anecdotes about teachers and schools, if school staff are engaged in a common task of school reform that is taken seriously and has some chance of making real changes, then respectful and trusting relations can develop among the staff.

3. Design task and work structures to foster engagement. Students are more likely to be engaged in tasks that take advantage of their backgrounds, interests, and experiences. There are many ways that teachers can develop tasks and activities that provide for authentic and meaningful work. For example, Paris and Ayres (1994) describe how portfolios can be used in elementary classrooms to provide a range of literacy tasks, including journals, letters, self-portraits, peer conferencing, and self-evaluation of artifacts, that can motivate students and facilitate the development of self-regulation. Sizer (1992) also provides a number of suggestions for "exhibitions," which are tasks that require students to demonstrate the products of their learning in meaningful ways. Recent calls for project-based instruction (e.g., Blumenfeld et al., 1991) also suggest ways that teachers and schools can involve students in meaningful and authentic activities.

4. Design authority and management structures that allow for some control. Mastery goal theory and intrinsic motivation theory both suggest that individuals who have some choice and control over their activities within an institution will be more motivated, be more engaged, try harder, persist longer, and actually perform better. Almost all the current school reform efforts stress the importance of involving teachers in the decision making for the school (*school-based management* or *site-based management* are the terms often used). This process can take place in many ways, including school reform or restructuring committees headed by and staffed with teachers, school improvement teams made up of teachers who are charged with different tasks, schools-within-schools that have their own curriculum and planning committees headed by teachers, and university-school collaborations in which teachers play an active role. Of course, as we have noted throughout this chapter, merely giving control to teachers or local school staffs is not enough. Close attention must be paid to the content of the goals developed by the teams and committees and how the goals or policies adopted might influence student motivation and learning. Nevertheless, involving school staff, teachers, parents, and students in school decision and policy making can have important benefits for school reform when it is seen as a continuing process, not as an outcome in itself (Midgley & Wood, 1993).

5. *Provide opportunities for all students to be recognized and rewarded.* Schools can develop programs that reward and recognize all students for their progress and improvement, not just for normative achievement. Although it is difficult to envision alternative reward structures, many school improvement programs are implementing different types of grading and recognition practices. Sizer (1992) describes how a school can use exhibitions whereby students actually demonstrate their knowledge and skills. These exhibitions can then be judged in terms of absolute standards that are set by a team of teachers, not norm-referenced comparisons. Portfolios also allow for the development of standards and evaluation criteria that focus on student improvement and effort as well as criterion-referenced standards rather than norm- or group-referenced standards.

6. *Provide grouping arrangements that foster student interaction.* The use of small groups within the classroom can foster student-student interaction. Between-classroom grouping, or tracking, should be minimized. In addition, many schools that are constrained by their large size are instituting schools-within-school arrangements or forming teams of teachers and students. These differential teacher staffing and student grouping structures can promote more and better teacher-student and student-student interactions because they can provide more opportunities for the individuals involved to get to know one another.

7. *Evaluation practices should focus on progress and improvement.* Alternative assessment tools, like portfolios, can help teachers and students judge their progress and evaluate their strengths and weaknesses. This practice might be better implemented at the classroom level than the school level, but schoolwide grading policies can influence teacher practices. Report cards can be changed to reflect an emphasis on mastery and improvement. Actual letter grades don't have to be used, nor do percentages (e.g., 88%) need to appear on report cards. Of course, letter grades can be used to represent mastery and improvement, but this type of individually referenced system is not usually implied by an A–E letter grading system.

8. *Time use should be managed to facilitate changes in the culture and organization of the school.* Schools can use a number of different strategies for differentiated teaching patterns that can provide the needed time for school reform efforts. Maehr and Midgley and their colleagues (Maehr & Midgley, forthcoming; Urdan et al., 1995) note that the rigidity of the schedule of the middle school they worked with was an extremely difficult constraint to overcome. Sizer (1992) also notes that time use and daily schedules can constrain many school reform efforts. However, block scheduling (e.g., two class periods of 45 minutes each are combined into a 90-minute instructional period) can provide more time for teachers and students to work on sustained activities and projects. Schools-within-school structures can allow for more flexible scheduling because the number of teachers and students to coordinate is smaller.

SUMMARY

In this chapter, we have discussed the various aspects of a school's culture and organization that can influence student and teacher outcomes. We have relied heavily on the work of both sociologists of education and educational psychologists.

We proposed a model of eight dimensions of school culture and organization. The first two dimensions were more perceptual and constructive dimensions of culture that are reflected in teachers' beliefs about their school. Norms, values, and shared beliefs represent the notions about human nature, the stability of learning, the controllability of teaching, and the extent of the consensus about these beliefs. The climate of the school was defined in terms of the collegial and professional relations among staff as well as the warmth and civility of the building for all staff and students.

The next six dimensions of school culture and organization were taken from the TARGET framework of Epstein (1989) as elaborated by Maehr and Midgley (1991). Task and work structures concern how the work is designed and accomplished in schools. Authority structures refer to the nature of the relations between teachers and students regarding how much choice and control is allowed. Recognition and reward structures involve the criteria by which rewards are distributed and who actually receives the rewards. Grouping practices refer to both the use of alternative ways of grouping for instruction within classrooms and between-classroom tracking. Evaluation practices relate to how students are evaluated in terms of tests and assignments. Time, the last dimension, involves the use of time in the school building.

These eight dimensions make up the internal culture and organization of schools, which can have a direct influence on teacher and student outcomes. However, there also are external factors that can operate as opportunities or constraints on the school culture. The composition of the school's student body in terms of achievement, race, social class, and age can facilitate the development of a positive school culture or it can act to constrain this development. School size is another external factor; large school size generally has a negative effect on school culture in comparison to smaller school sizes. Parental and community involvement can support or hinder the development of school culture. Finally, district- and state-level factors can have a dramatic influence on school culture and organization.

REFERENCES

Abrami, P. C., Leventhal, L., & Perry, R. P. (1982). Educational seduction. *Review of Educational Research, 52,* 446-464.

Ach, N. (1910). *Uber den Willensakt und das Temperament.* Leipzig, Germany: Quelle & Meyer.

Akamatsu, T. J., & Thelen, M. H. (1974). A review of the literature on observer characteristics and imitation. *Developmental Psychology, 10,* 38-47.

Alderman, M. K. (1985). Achievement motivation and the preservice teacher. In M. K. Alderman & M. W. Cohen (Eds.), *Motivation theory and practice for preservice teachers* (pp. 37-51). Washington, DC: ERIC Clearinghouse on Teacher Education.

Alexander, K., Cook, M., & McDill, E. (1978). Curriculum tracking and educational stratification: Some further evidence. *American Sociological Review, 43,* 47–66.

Alexander, P., Kulikowich, J., & Jetton, T. (1994). The role of subject-matter knowledge and interest in the processing of linear and nonlinear texts. *Review of Educational Research, 64,* 201–252.

Allport, G. W. (1937). *Personality: A psychological interpretation.* New York: Henry Holt.

Ames, C. (1981). Competitive versus cooperative reward structures: The influence of individual and group performance factors on achievement attributions and affect. *American Educational Research Journal, 18,* 273-287.

Ames, C. (1984). Competitive, cooperative, and individualistic goal structures: A cognitive-motivational analysis. In R. Ames & C. Ames (Eds.), *Research on motivation in education* (Vol. 1, pp. 177-207). New York: Academic Press.

Ames, C. (1992a). Achievement goals and the classroom motivational climate. In D. H. Schunk & J. Meece (Eds.), *Student perceptions in the classroom* (pp. 327-348). Hillsdale, NJ: Erlbaum.

Ames, C. (1992b). Classrooms: Goals, structures, and student motivation. *Journal of Educational Psychology, 84,* 261-271.

Ames, C., & Archer, J. (1987). Mothers' beliefs about the role of ability and effort in school learning. *Journal of Educational Psychology, 79,* 409–414.

Ames, C., & Archer, J. (1988). Achievement goals in the classroom: Students' learning strategies and motivation processes. *Journal of Educational Psychology, 80,* 260–267.

Ames, C., & Felker, D. (1979). An examination of children's attributions and achievement-related evaluations in competitive, cooperative, and individualistic reward structures. *Journal of Educational Psychology, 71,* 413-420.

Ames, R. (1975). Teachers' attributions of responsibility: Some unexpected nondefensive effects. *Journal of Educational Psychology, 67,* 668–676.

Anderman, E., & Maehr, M. L. (1994). Motivation and schooling in the middle grades. *Review of Educational Research, 64,* 287–309.

Anderson, C. (1982). The search for school climate: A review of the research. *Review of Educational Research, 52,* 368–420.

Anderson, J. R. (1990). *Cognitive psychology and its implications* (3rd ed.). New York: Freeman.

Anderson, L. M., Evertson, C. M., & Brophy, J. E. (1979). An experimental study of effective teaching in first-grade reading groups. *Elementary School Journal, 79,* 193-222.

Andrews, G. R., & Debus, R. L. (1978). Persistence and the causal perception of failure: Modifying cognitive attributions. *Journal of Educational Psychology, 70,* 154-166.

Arlin, M., & Webster, J. (1983). Time costs of mastery learning. *Journal of Educational Psychology, 75,* 187-195.

Arnold, M. B. (1968). *The nature of emotion.* Middlesex, England: Penguin.

Aronson, E. (1966). The psychology of insufficient justification: An analysis of some conflicting data. In S. Feldman (Ed.), *Cognitive consistency: Motivational antecedents and behavioral consequences* (pp. 109-133). New York: Academic Press.

Asch, S. E. (1955). Opinions and social pressure. *Scientific American, 193*(5), 31-35.

Asch, S. E. (1958). Interpersonal influence. In E. E. Maccoby, T. M. Newcomb, & E. L. Hartley (Eds.), *Readings in social psychology* (3rd ed., pp. 174-183). New York: Holt.

Ashton, P., & Webb, R. (1986). *Making a difference: Teachers' sense of efficacy and student achievement.* New York: Longman.

Assor, A., & Connell, J. P. (1992). The validity of students' self-reports as measures of performance affecting self-appraisals. In D. H.

Schunk & J. L. Meece (Eds.), *Student perceptions in the classroom* (pp. 25-47). Hillsdale, NJ: Erlbaum.

Atkinson, J. W. (1957). Motivational determinants of risk-taking behavior. *Psychological Review, 64,* 359–372.

Atkinson, J. W. (1958). *Motives in fantasy, action, and society.* Princeton, NJ: Van Nostrand.

Atkinson, J. W. (1964). *An introduction to motivation.* Princeton, NJ: Van Nostrand.

Bailey, S. M. (1993). The current status of gender equity research in American schools. *Educational Psychologist, 28,* 321–339.

Bandura, A. (1969). *Principles of behavior modification.* New York: Holt, Rinehart & Winston.

Bandura, A. (1977). Self-efficacy: Toward a unifying theory of behavioral change. *Psychological Review, 84,* 191-215.

Bandura, A. (1982). Self-efficacy mechanism in human agency. *American Psychologist, 37,* 122-147.

Bandura, A. (1986). *Social foundations of thought and action: A social cognitive theory.* Englewood Cliffs, NJ: Prentice Hall.

Bandura, A. (1988). Self-regulation of motivation and action through goal systems. In V. Hamilton, G. H. Bower, & N. H. Frijda (Eds.), *Cognitive perspectives on emotion and motivation* (pp. 37-61). Dordrecht, The Netherlands: Kluwer.

Bandura, A. (1989). Social cognitive theory. In R. Vasta (Ed.), *Annals of child development* (Vol. 6, pp. 1-60). Greenwich, CT: JAI Press.

Bandura, A. (1993). Perceived self-efficacy in cognitive development and functioning. *Educational Psychologist, 28,* 117-148.

Bandura, A., & Cervone, D. (1983). Self-evaluative and self-efficacy mechanisms governing the motivational effects of goal systems. *Journal of Personality and Social Psychology, 45,* 1017-1028.

Bandura, A., & Cervone, D. (1986). Differential engagement of self-reactive influences in cognitive motivation. *Organizational Behavior and Human Decision Processes, 38,* 92-133.

Bandura, A., & Schunk, D. H. (1981). Cultivating competence, self-efficacy, and intrinsic interest through proximal self-motivation. *Journal of Personality and Social Psychology, 41,* 586-59.

Bandura, A., & Walters, R. H. (1963). *Social learning and personality development.* New York: Holt, Rinehart & Winston.

Barnes, R., Ickes, W., & Kidd, R. (1979). Effects of perceived intentionality and stability of another's dependency on helping behavior. *Personality and Social Psychology Bulletin, 5,* 367–372.

Barr, R., & Dreeben, R. (1983). *How schools work.* Chicago: University of Chicago Press.

Battle, E. (1965). Motivational determinants of academic task persistence. *Journal of Personality and Social Psychology, 2,* 209–218.

Battle, E. (1966). Motivational determinants of academic competence. *Journal of Personality and Social Psychology, 4,* 634–642.

Baumeister, R. F., & Scher, S. J. (1988). Self-defeating behavior patterns among normal individuals: Review and analysis of common self-destructive tendencies. *Psychological Bulletin, 104,* 3-22.

Becker, H., & Epstein, J. (1982). Parent involvement: A survey of teacher practices. *Elementary School Journal, 83,* 85–102.

Becker, H., Geer, B., & Hughes, E. (1961). *Boys in white: Student culture in the medical school.* Chicago: University of Chicago Press.

Beckman, L. (1970). Effects of students' performance on teachers' and observers' attributions of causality. *Journal of Educational Psychology, 61,* 76–82.

Behrend, D. A., Rosengren, K. S., & Perlmutter, M. (1992). The relation between private speech and parental interactive style. In R. M. Diaz & L. E. Berk (Eds.), *Private speech: From social interaction to self-regulation* (pp. 85-100). Hillsdale, NJ: Erlbaum.

Bem, D. J. (1967). Self-perception: An alternative interpretation of cognitive dissonance phenomena. *Psychological Review, 74,* 183-200.

Bem, D. J. (1972). Self-perception theory. In L. Berkowitz (Ed.), *Advances in experimental social psychology* (Vol. 6, pp. 1-62). New York: Academic Press.

Bennett, W. J. (1993). *The book of virtues: A treasury of great moral stories.* New York: Simon & Schuster.

Berk, L. E. (1986). Relationship of elementary school children's private speech to behavioral accompaniment to task, attention, and task performance. *Developmental Psychology, 22,* 671-680.

Berk, L. E. (1992). Children's private speech: An overview of theory and the status of research. In R. M. Diaz & L. E. Berk (Eds.), *Private speech: From social interaction to self-regulation* (pp. 17-53). Hillsdale, NJ: Erlbaum.

Berlyne, D. E. (1960). *Conflict, arousal, and curiosity.* New York: McGraw-Hill.

Berlyne, D. E. (1963). Motivational problems raised by exploratory and epistemic behavior. In S. Koch (Ed.), *Psychology: A study of a science* (Vol. 5, pp. 284-364). New York: McGraw-Hill.

Betancourt, H., & Lopez, S. (1993). The study of culture, ethnicity, and race in American psychology. *American Psychologist, 48,* 629–637.

Betz, N. E., & Hackett, G. (1981). The relationship of career-related self-efficacy expectations to perceived career options in college women and men. *Journal of Counseling Psychology, 28,* 399–410.

Betz, N. E., & Hackett, G. (1983). The relationship of mathematics self-efficacy expectations to the selection of science-based college majors. *Journal of Vocational Behavior, 23,* 329–345.

Blumenfeld, P. (1992). Classroom learning and motivation: Clarifying and expanding goal theory. *Journal of Educational Psychology, 84,* 272-281.

Blumenfeld, P., Hamilton, V. L., Bossert, S., Wessels, K., & Meece, J. (1983). Teacher talk and student thought: Socialization into the student role. In J. Levine & M. Wang (Eds.), *Teacher and student perceptions: Implications for learning* (pp. 143–192). Hillsdale, NJ: Erlbaum.

Blumenfeld, P., Mergendoller, J., & Swarthout, D. (1987). Task as a heuristic for understanding student learning and motivation. *Journal of Curriculum Studies, 19,* 135-148.

Blumenfeld, P., Pintrich, P. R., & Hamilton, V. L. (1986). Children's concepts of ability, effort and conduct. *American Educational Research Journal, 23,* 95–104.

Blumenfeld, P., Pintrich, P. R., & Hamilton, V. L. (1987). Teacher talk and students' reasoning about morals, conventions, and achievement. *Child Development, 58,* 1389–1401.

Blumenfeld, P., Pintrich, P. R., Meece, J., & Wessels, K. (1982). The formation and role of self-perceptions of ability in the elementary classroom. *Elementary School Journal, 82,* 401-420.

Blumenfeld, P., Soloway, E., Marx, R. W., Krajcik, J. S., Guzdial, M., & Palincsar, A. (1991). Motivating project-based learning: Sustaining the doing, supporting the learning. *Educational Psychologist, 26,* 369–398.

Boggiano, A. K., Main, D. S., & Katz, P. A. (1988). Children's preference for challenge: The role of perceived competence and control. *Journal of Personality and Social Psychology, 54,* 134-141.

Bolin, F. (1989). Empowering leadership. *Teachers College Record, 91,* 81–96.

Borkowski, J. G., Carr, M., Rellinger, E., & Pressley, M. (1990). Self-regulated cognition: Interdependence of metacognition, attributions, and self-esteem. In B. F. Jones & L. Idol (Eds.), *Dimensions of thinking and cognitive instruction* (pp. 53-92). Hillsdale, NJ: Erlbaum.

Borkowski, J. G., Weyhing, R. S., & Carr, M. (1988). Effects of attributional retraining on strategy-based reading comprehension of learning-disabled students. *Journal of Educational Psychology, 80,* 46-53.

Bossert, S. (1988). Cooperative activities in the classroom. In E. Rothkopf (Ed.), *Review of Research in Education* (Vol. 15, pp. 225–250). Washington, DC: American Educational Research Association.

Bowles, S., & Gintis, H. (1976). *Schooling in capitalist America: Educational reform and the contradictions of economic life.* New York: Basic Books.

Braddock, J., & McPartland, J. (1993). Education of early adolescents. In L. Darling-Hammond (Ed.), *Review of educational research* (Vol. 19, pp. 135–170). Washington, DC: American Educational Research Association.

Brandt, L., Hayden, M., & Brophy, J. (1975). Teachers' attitudes and ascription of causation. *Journal of Educational Psychology, 67,* 677–682.

Braun, C. (1976). Teacher expectation: Sociopsychological dynamics. *Review of Educational Research, 46,* 185-213.

Brewer, W. F. (1974). There is no convincing evidence for operant or classical conditioning in adult humans. In W. B. Weimer & D. S. Palermo (Eds.), *Cognition and the symbolic processes* (pp. 1-42). Hillsdale, NJ: Erlbaum.

Broadhurst, P. L. (1957). Emotionality and the Yerkes-Dodson law. *Journal of Experimental Psychology, 54,* 345-352.

Brookover, W., Beady, C., Flood, P., Schweitzer, J., & Wisenbaker, J. (1979). *School social systems and student achievement: Schools can make a difference.* New York: Praeger.

Brophy, J. (1981). Teacher praise: A functional analysis. *Review of Educational Research, 51,* 5-32.

Brophy, J. (1983). Conceptualizing student motivation. *Educational Psychologist, 18,* 200-215.

Brophy, J. (1985). Teacher-student interaction. In J. B. Dusek (Ed.), *Teacher expectancies* (pp. 303-328). Hillsdale, NJ: Erlbaum.

Brophy, J. (1987). On motivating students. In D. Berliner & B. Rosenshine (Eds.), *Talks to teachers* (pp. 201-245). New York: Random House.

Brophy, J., & Good, T. L. (1974). *Teacher-student relationships: Causes and consequences.* New York: Holt, Rinehart & Winston.

Brophy, J., & Good, T. L. (1986). Teacher behavior and student achievement. In M. C. Wittrock (Ed.), *Handbook of research on teaching* (3rd ed., pp. 328-375). New York: Macmillan.

Brophy, J., & Rohrkemper, M. (1981). The influence of problem ownership on teachers' perceptions of and strategies for coping with problem students. *Journal of Educational Psychology, 73,* 295–311.

Brown, I., & Inouye, D. K. (1978). Learned helplessness through modeling: The role of perceived similarity in competence. *Journal of Personality and Social Psychology, 36,* 900-908.

Brown, J., & Weiner, B. (1984). Affective consequences of ability versus effort ascriptions: Controversies, resolutions, and quandaries. *Journal of Educational Psychology, 76,* 146–158.

Bryan, J. H., & Bryan, T. H. (1983). The social life of the learning disabled youngster. In J. D. McKinney & L. Feagans (Eds.), *Current topics in learning disabilities* (Vol. 1, pp. 57-85). Norwood, NJ: Ablex.

Bryan, J. H., & Walbek, N. H. (1970). Preaching and practicing generosity: Children's actions and reactions. *Child Development, 41,* 329-353.

Bryk, A., Lee, V., & Holland, P. (1993). *Catholic schools and the common good.* Cambridge, MA: Harvard University Press.

Butler, R. (1987). Task-involving and ego-involving properties of evaluation: Effects of different feedback conditions on motivational perceptions, interest, and performance. *Journal of Educational Psychology, 79,* 474–482.

Byrne, B. M. (1984). The general/academic self-concept nomological network: A review of construct validation research. *Review of Educational Research, 54,* 427–456.

Calabrese, R., & Poe, J. (1990). Alienation: An explanation of high dropout rates among African-American and Latino students. *Educational Research Quarterly, 14*(4), 22–26.

Cameron, J., & Pierce, W. D. (1994). Reinforcement, reward, and intrinsic motivation: A meta-analysis. *Review of Educational Research, 64,* 363–423.

Cannon, W. B. (1927). The James-Lange theory of emotion: A critical examination and an alternative theory. *American Journal of Psychology, 39,* 106-124.

Carnegie Council on Adolescent Development. (1989). *Turning points: Preparing American youth for the 21st century.* New York: Carnegie Foundation.

Caslyn, R., & Kenny, D. (1977). Self-concept of ability and perceived evaluations by others: Cause or effect of academic achievement? *Journal of Educational Psychology, 69,* 136–145.

Chubb, J. (1988). Why the current wave of school reform will fail. *The Public Interest, 90,* 28–49.

Clark, C. M., & Peterson, P. (1986). Teachers' thought processes. In M. C. Wittrock (Ed.), *Handbook of research on teaching* (3rd ed., pp. 255-296). New York: Macmillan.

Clark, C. M., & Yinger, R. J. (1979). Teachers' thinking. In P. L. Peterson & H. J. Walberg (Eds.), *Research on teaching: Concepts, findings, and implications* (pp. 231-263). Berkeley, CA: McCutchan.

Cofer, C. N., & Appley, M. H. (1964). *Motivation: Theory and research.* New York: Wiley.

Cohen, E. (1994). Restructuring the classroom: Conditions for productive small groups. *Review of Educational Research, 64,* 1–35.

Collins, J. (1982, March). *Self-efficacy and ability in achievement behavior.* Paper presented at the meeting of the American Educational Research Association, New York.

Comer, J. (1980). *School power: Implications of an intervention project.* New York: The Free Press.

Connell, J. P. (1985). A new multidimensional measure of children's perceptions of control. *Child Development, 56,* 1018-1041.

Cooper, H. M., & Good, T. L. (1983). *Pygmalion grows up: Studies in the expectation communication process.* New York: Longman.

Cooper, H. M., & Tom, D. Y. H. (1984). Teacher expectation research: A review with implications for classroom instruction. *Elementary School Journal, 85,* 77-89.

Corno, L. (1993). The best-laid plans: Modern conceptions of volition and educational research. *Educational Researcher, 22*(2), 14-22.

Corno, L., & Mandinach, E. B. (1983). The role of cognitive engagement in classroom learning and motivation. *Educational Psychologist, 18,* 88-108.

Corno, L., & Rohrkemper, M. (1985). The intrinsic motivation to learn in the classroom. In C. Ames & R. Ames (Eds.), *Research on motivation in education* (Vol. 2, pp. 53–90). New York: Academic Press.

Corno, L., & Snow, R. (1986). Adapting teaching to individual differences among learners. In M. C. Wittrock (Ed.), *Handbook of research on teaching* (3rd ed., pp. 605–629). New York: Macmillan.

Cotton, J. L. (1981). A review of research on Schachter's theory of emotion and the misattribution of arousal. *European Journal of Social Psychology, 11*, 365-397.

Covington, M. V. (1992). *Making the grade: A self-worth perspective on motivation and school reform.* New York: Cambridge University Press.

Covington, M. V., & Beery, R. G. (1976). *Self-worth and school learning.* New York: Holt, Rinehart, & Winston.

Covington, M. V., & Omelich, C. L. (1979). Effort: The double-edged sword in school achievement. *Journal of Educational Psychology, 71*, 169–182.

Covington, M. V., & Omelich, C. L. (1991). Need achievement revisited: Verification of Atkinson's original 2 × 2 model. In C. D. Spielberger, I. G. Sarason, Z. Kulcsar, & G. L. Van Heck (Eds.), *Stress and emotion: Anxiety, anger, and curiosity* (Vol. 14, pp. 85-105). Washington, DC: Hemisphere.

Covington, M.V., & Roberts, B. (1994). Self-worth and college achievement: Motivational and personality correlates. In P. R. Pintrich, D. R. Brown, & C. E. Weinstein (Eds.), *Student motivation, cognition, and learning: Essays in honor of Wilbert J. McKeachie* (pp. 157-187). Hillsdale, NJ: Erlbaum.

Crandall, V. C., Katkovsky, W., & Crandall, V. J. (1965). Children's beliefs in their own control of reinforcements in intellectual-academic achievement situations. *Child Development, 36*, 91–109.

Crandall, V. J., Katkovsky, W., & Preston, A. (1962). Motivational and ability determinants of young children's intellectual achievement behavior. *Child Development, 33*, 643–661.

Crespi, L. P. (1942). Quantitative variation of incentive and performance in the white rat. *American Journal of Psychology, 55*, 467-517.

Crocker, J., & Major, B. (1989). Social stigma and self-esteem: The self-protective properties of stigma. *Psychological Review, 96*, 608–630.

Cronbach, L. J., & Snow, R. (1977). *Aptitudes and instructional methods.* New York: Irvington.

Csikszentmihalyi, M. (1975). *Beyond boredom and anxiety.* San Francisco: Jossey-Bass.

Csikszentmihalyi, M. (1978). Intrinsic rewards and emergent motivation. In M. R. Lepper & D. Greene (Eds.), *The hidden costs of reward: New perspectives on the psychology of human motivation* (pp. 205-216). Hillsdale, NJ: Erlbaum.

Csikszentmihalyi, M. (1982). Toward a psychology of optimal experience. In L. Wheeler (Ed.), *Review of personality and social psychology* (Vol. 3, pp. 13-36). Beverly Hills, CA: Sage.

Csikszentmihalyi, M. (1985). Emergent motivation and the evolution of the self. In D. A. Kleiber & M. L. Maehr (Eds.), *Advances in motivation and achievement* (Vol. 4, pp. 93-119). Greenwich, CT: JAI Press.

Csikszentmihalyi, M., & Rathunde, K. (1993). The measurement of flow in everyday life: Toward a theory of emergent motivation. In J. E. Jacobs (Ed.), *Nebraska symposium on motivation 1992* (Vol. 40, pp. 57-97). Lincoln: University of Nebraska Press.

Cuban, L. (1990). Reforming, again, again, and again. *Educational Researcher, 19*, 3–30.

Cusick, P. (1983). *The egalitarian ideal and the American high school.* New York: Longman.

Damon, W., & Hart, D. (1988). *Self-understanding in childhood and adolescence.* Cambridge: Cambridge University Press.

de Charms, R. (1968). *Personal causation: The internal affective determinants of behavior.* New York: Academic Press.

de Charms, R. (1976). *Enhancing motivation: Change in the classroom.* New York: Irvington.

de Charms, R. (1984). Motivation enhancement in educational settings. In R. Ames & C. Ames (Eds.), *Research on motivation in education* (Vol. 1, pp. 275-310). New York: Academic Press.

Deci, E. L. (1975). *Intrinsic motivation.* New York: Plenum.

Deci, E. L. (1980). *The psychology of self-determination.* Lexington, MA: D. C. Heath.

Deci, E. L., & Porac, J. (1978). Cognitive evaluation theory and the study of human motivation. In M. R. Lepper & D. Greene (Eds.), *The hidden costs of reward: New perspectives on the psychology of human motivation* (pp. 149-176). Hillsdale, NJ: Erlbaum.

Deci, E. L., & Ryan, R. M. (1985). *Intrinsic motivation and self-determination in human behavior.* New York: Plenum.

Deci, E. L., & Ryan, R. M. (1987). The support of autonomy and the control of behavior. *Journal of Personality and Social Psychology, 53,* 1024–1037.

Deci, E. L., & Ryan, R. M. (1991). A motivational approach to self: Integration in personality. In R. A. Dienstbier (Ed.), *Nebraska symposium on motivation 1990* (Vol. 38, pp. 237-288). Lincoln: University of Nebraska Press.

Deci, E. L., Vallerand, R. J., Pelletier, L. G., & Ryan, R. M. (1991). Motivation and education: The self-determination perspective. *Educational Psychologist, 26,* 325-346.

Deutsch, M. (1949). A theory of cooperation and competition. *Human Relations, 2,* 129-152.

Diener, C. I., & Dweck, C. S. (1978). An analysis of learned helplessness: Continuous changes in performance, strategy, and achievement cognitions following failure. *Journal of Personality and Social Psychology, 36,* 451-462.

Diener, C. I., & Dweck, C. S. (1980). An analysis of learned helplessness: II. The processing of success. *Journal of Personality and Social Psychology, 39,* 940-952.

Doyle, W. (1983). Academic work. *Review of Educational Research, 53,* 159-199.

Doyle, W. (1986). Classroom management. In M. C. Wittrock (Ed.), *Handbook of research on teaching* (3rd ed., pp. 392–431). New York: Macmillan.

Duda, J., & Nicholls, J. (1992). Dimensions of achievement motivation in schoolwork and sport. *Journal of Educational Psychology, 84,* 290–299.

Duke, D., Showers, B., & Imber, M. (1980). Studying shared decision making in schools. In S. B. Bacharach (Ed.), *Organizational behavior in schools and school districts* (pp. 220–268). New York: Praeger.

Dunkin, M. J., & Biddle, B. J. (1974). *The study of teaching.* New York: Holt, Rinehart & Winston.

Dusek, J. B. (1980). The development of test anxiety in children. In I. G. Sarason (Ed.), *Test anxiety: Theory, research, and applications* (pp. 87–110). Hillsdale, NJ: Erlbaum.

Dusek, J. B. (1985). *Teacher expectancies.* Hillsdale, NJ: Erlbaum.

Dweck, C. S. (1975). The role of expectations and attributions in the alleviation of learned helplessness. *Journal of Personality and Social Psychology, 31,* 674-685.

Dweck, C. S. (1986). Motivational processes affecting learning. *American Psychologist, 41,* 1040-1048.

Dweck, C. S. (1991). Self-theories and goals: Their role in motivation, personality, and development. In R. A. Dienstbier (Ed.), *Nebraska symposium on motivation 1990* (Vol. 38, pp. 199-235). Lincoln: University of Nebraska Press.

Dweck, C. S., Davidson, W., Nelson, S., & Enna, B. (1978). Sex differences in learned helplessness: II. The contingencies of evaluative feedback in the classroom. III. An experimental analysis. *Developmental Psychology, 14,* 268–276.

Dweck, C. S., & Elliott, E. S. (1983). Achievement motivation. In P. H. Mussen (Ser. Ed.) & E. M. Heatherington (Vol. Ed.), *Handbook of child psychology: Vol 4. Socialization, personality, and social development* (4th ed., pp. 643-691). New York: Wiley.

Dweck, C. S., & Leggett, E. L. (1988). A social-cognitive approach to motivation and personality. *Psychological Review, 95,* 256-273.

Dweck, C. S., & Repucci, N. (1973). Learned helplessness and reinforcement responsibility in children. *Journal of Personality and Social Psychology, 25,* 109–116.

Eccles, J. (1983). Expectancies, values and academic behaviors. In J. T. Spence (Ed.), *Achievement and achievement motives* (pp. 75-146). San Francisco: Freeman.

Eccles, J., Adler, T., & Meece, J. (1984). Sex differences in achievement: A test of alternate theories. *Journal of Personality and Social Psychology, 46,* 26-43.

Eccles, J., Lord, S., & Midgley, C. (1991). What are we doing to early adolescents? The impact of educational contexts on early adolescents. *American Journal of Education, 99*, 521–542.

Eccles, J., & Midgley, C. (1989). Stage-environment fit: Developmentally appropriate classrooms for young adolescents. In C. Ames & R. Ames (Eds.), *Research on motivation in education* (Vol. 3, pp.139–186). San Diego: Academic Press.

Eccles, J., Midgley, C., & Adler, T. (1984). Grade-related changes in the school environment: Effects on achievement motivation. In J. Nicholls (Ed.), *Advances in motivation and achievement: The development of achievement motivation* (Vol. 3, pp. 283–331). Greenwich, CT: JAI Press.

Eccles, J., Midgley, C., Wigfield, A., Buchanan, C., Reuman, D., Flanagan, C., & Mac Iver, D. (1993). Development during adolescence: The impact of stage-environment fit on young adolescents' experiences in schools and families. *American Psychologist, 48*, 90-101.

Eccles, J., & Wigfield, A. (1985). Teacher expectancies and student motivation. In J. B. Dusek (Ed.), *Teacher expectancies* (pp. 185–226). Hillsdale, NJ: Erlbaum.

Eccles, J., & Wigfield, A. (1995). In the mind of the actor: The structure of adolescents' achievement task values and expectancy-related beliefs. *Personality and Social Psychology Bulletin, 21*, 215–225.

Eccles, J., Wigfield, A., Flanagan, C., Miller, C., Reuman, D., & Yee, D. (1989). Self-concepts, domain values, and self-esteem: Relations and changes at early adolescence. *Journal of Personality, 57*, 283–310.

Eccles, J., Wigfield, A., Harold, R., & Blumenfeld, P. (1993). Age and gender differences in children's self- and task perceptions during elementary school. *Child Development, 64*, 830–847.

Edmonds, R. (1979). Effective schools for the urban poor. *Educational Leadership, 37*, 15–24.

Eisen, S. V. (1979). Actor-observer differences in information inference and causal attribution. *Journal of Personality and Social Psychology, 37*, 261–272.

Elashoff, J. D., & Snow, R. (1971). *Pygmalion reconsidered.* Worthington, OH: Jones.

Elliott, E. S., & Dweck, C. S. (1988). Goals: An approach to motivation and achievement. *Journal of Personality and Social Psychology, 54*, 5-12.

Emmer, E. T., Evertson, C. M., & Anderson, L. M. (1980). Effective classroom management at the beginning of the school year. *Elementary School Journal, 80*, 219-231.

Entwisle, D. R., & Baker, D. P. (1983). Gender and young children's expectations for performance in arithmetic. *Developmental Psychology, 19*, 200–209.

Epstein, J. (1986). Parents' reactions to teacher practices of parent involvement. *Elementary School Journal, 86*, 277–294.

Epstein, J. (1987). Toward a theory of family-school connections: Teacher practices and parent involvement. In K. Hurrelmann, F. Kaufmann, & F. Losel (Eds.), *Social intervention: Potential and constraints* (pp. 121–136). Hawthorn, NY: Aldine de Gruyter.

Epstein, J. (1989). Family structures and student motivation: A developmental perspective. In C. Ames & R. Ames (Eds.), *Research on motivation in education* (Vol. 3, pp. 259-295). San Diego: Academic Press.

Epstein, J. (1995). School/family/community partnerships: Caring for the children we share. *Phi Delta Kappan, 76*, 701–712.

Erickson, F. (1986). Qualitative methods in research on teaching. In M. C. Wittrock (Ed.), *Handbook of research on teaching* (3rd ed., pp. 119-161). New York: Macmillan.

Ericsson, K., & Simon, H. (1993). *Protocol analysis: Verbal reports as data* (2nd ed.). Cambridge, MA: MIT Press.

Erikson, E. (1963). *Childhood and society.* New York: Norton.

Evans, K. (1971). *Attitudes and interests in education.* London: Routledge & Kegan.

Evertson, C. M., Emmer, E. T., Clements, B. S., Sanford, J. P., & Worsham, M. E. (1984). *Classroom management for elementary teachers.* Englewood Cliffs, NJ: Prentice-Hall.

Eyler, J., Cooke, V., & Ward, L. (1983). Resegregation: Segregation within desegregated schools. In C. Rossell & W. Howley (Eds.), *The consequences of school desegregation* (pp. 126–162). Philadelphia: Temple University Press.

Feather, N. (1982) Human values and the prediction of action: An expectancy-valence analysis. In N. T. Feather (Ed.), *Expectations and actions: Expectancy-value models in psychology* (pp. 263-289). Hillsdale, NJ: Erlbaum.

Feather, N. (1988). Values, valences, and course enrollment: Testing the role of personal values within an expectancy-value framework. *Journal of Educational Psychology, 80,* 381–391.

Feldman, N. S., & Ruble, D. N. (1977). Awareness of social comparison interest and motivations: A developmental study. *Journal of Educational Psychology, 69,* 579-585.

Festinger, L. (1954). A theory of social comparison processes. *Human Relations, 7,* 117-140.

Festinger, L. (1957). *A theory of cognitive dissonance.* Stanford, CA: Stanford University Press.

Fish, M. C., & Pervan, R. (1985). Self-instruction training: A potential tool for school psychologists. *Psychology in the Schools, 22,* 83-92.

Fishbein, M., & Ajzen, I. (1975). *Belief, attitude, intention, and behavior: An introduction to theory and research.* Reading, MA: Addison-Wesley.

Fiske, S., & Taylor, S. (1991). *Social cognition.* New York: McGraw-Hill.

Fletcher, G., & Ward, C. (1988). Attribution theory and processes: A cross-cultural perspective. In M. H. Bond (Ed.), *The cross-cultural challenge to social psychology* (pp. 230–244). Newbury Park, CA: Sage.

Foersterling, F. (1985). Attributional retraining: A review. *Psychological Bulletin, 98,* 495–512.

Ford, D. H. (1987). *Humans as self-constructing living systems: A developmental perspective on personality and behavior.* Hillsdale, NJ: Erlbaum.

Ford, M. (1992). *Motivating humans: Goals, emotions, and personal agency beliefs.* Newbury Park, CA: Sage.

Ford, M., & Ford, D. H. (1987). *Humans as self-constructing living systems: Putting the framework to work.* Hillsdale, NJ: Erlbaum.

Ford, M., & Nichols, C. W. (1991). Using goal assessments to identify motivational patterns and facilitate behavioral regulation and achievement. In M. L. Maehr & P. R. Pintrich (Eds.), *Advances in motivation and achievement: Goals and self-regulation* (Vol. 7, pp. 51–84). Greenwich, CT: JAI Press.

Fordham, S., & Ogbu, J. (1986). Black students' school success: Coping with the burden of "acting white." *Urban Review, 18,* 176–206.

France-Kaatrude, A., & Smith, W. P. (1985). Social comparison, task motivation, and the development of self-evaluative standards in children. *Developmental Psychology, 21,* 1080-1089.

Freud, S. (1966). *The complete introductory lectures on psychoanalysis* (J. Strachey, Trans.). New York: Norton.

Frey, K., & Ruble, D. N. (1987). What children say about classroom performance: Sex and grade differences in perceived competence. *Child Development, 58,* 1066–1078.

Friend, R., & Neale, J. (1972). Children's perceptions of success and failure: An attributional analysis of the effects of race and social class. *Developmental Psychology, 7,* 124–128.

Fuhrer, M. J., & Baer, P. E. (1965). Differential classical conditioning: Verbalization of stimulus contingencies. *Science, 150,* 1479-1481.

Gagné, E. D., Yekovich, C. W., & Yekovich, F. R. (1993). *The cognitive psychology of school learning* (2nd ed.). New York: Harper Collins.

Gagné, R. M. (1985). *The conditions of learning* (4th ed.). New York: Holt, Rinehart, & Winston.

Gamoran, A., & Berends, M. (1987). The effects of stratification in secondary schools: Synthesis of survey and ethnographic research. *Review of Educational Research, 57,* 415–435.

Garcia, T., & Pintrich, P. R. (1994). Regulating motivation and cognition in the classroom: The role of self-schemas and self-regulatory strategies. In D. H. Schunk & B. J. Zimmerman (Eds.), *Self-regulation of learning and performance: Issues and educational applications* (pp. 127-153). Hillsdale, NJ: Erlbaum.

Geen, R. G. (1991). Social motivation. *Annual Review of Psychology, 42*, 377-399.

Glass, D. C., & Singer, J. E. (1972). *Urban stress: Experiments on noise and social stressors.* New York: Academic Press.

Goethals, G. R., & Darley, J. M. (1977). Social comparison theory. In J. M. Suls & R. L. Miller (Eds.), *Social comparison processes: Theoretical and empirical perspectives* (pp. 259-278). Washington, DC: Hemisphere.

Good, T., & Brophy, J. (1986). School effects. In M. C. Wittrock (Ed.), *Handbook of research on teaching* (3rd ed., pp. 570–602). New York: Macmillan.

Good, T., & Brophy, J. E. (1987). *Looking in classrooms* (4th ed.). New York: Harper & Row.

Good, T., & Grouws, D. A. (1979). The Missouri mathematics effectiveness project. *Journal of Educational Psychology, 71*, 355-362.

Gottfried, A. E. (1985). Academic intrinsic motivation in elementary and junior high school students. *Journal of Educational Psychology, 77*, 631-645.

Gottfried, A. E. (1990). Academic intrinsic motivation in young elementary school children. *Journal of Educational Psychology, 82*, 525-538.

Graham, S. (1984). Communicating sympathy and anger to black and white students: The cognitive (attributional) antecedents of affective cues. *Journal of Personality and Social Psychology, 47*, 40–54.

Graham, S. (1991). A review of attribution theory in achievement contexts. *Educational Psychology Review, 3*, 5-39.

Graham, S. (1994). Motivation in African Americans. *Review of Educational Research, 64*, 55-117.

Graham, S., Doubleday, C., & Guarino, P. (1984). The development of relations between perceived controllability and the emotions of pity, anger, and guilt. *Child Development, 55*, 561–565.

Graham, S., & Golan, S. (1991). Motivational influences on cognition: Task involvement, ego involvement, and depth of information processing. *Journal of Educational Psychology, 83*, 187-194.

Graham, S., & Long, A. (1986). Race, class, and the attributional process. *Journal of Educational Psychology, 78*, 4–13.

Grant, G. (1988). *The world we created at Hamilton High.* Cambridge, MA: Harvard University Press.

Hackett, G., & Betz, N. E. (1981). A self-efficacy approach to the career development of women. *Journal of Vocational Behavior, 18*, 326–339.

Hagtvet, K., & Johnsen, T. B. (1992). *Advances in test anxiety research* (Vol. 7). Amsterdam: Swets & Zeitlinger.

Hall, C. S., & Lindzey, G. (1978). *Theories of personality.* New York: Wiley.

Hall, V., Howe, A., Merkel, S., & Lederman, N. (1986). Behavior, motivation, and achievement in desegregated junior high school science classes. *Journal of Educational Psychology, 78*, 108–115.

Hallinger, P., & Murphy, J. (1986). The social context of effective schools. *American Journal of Education, 94*, 328–355.

Hamilton, V. L., Blumenfeld, P., Akoh, H., & Miura, K. (1989). Citizenship and scholarship in Japanese and American fifth grades. *American Educational Research Journal, 26*, 44–72.

Hansford, B., & Hattie, J. (1982). The relationship between self and achievement/performance measures. *Review of Educational Research, 52*, 123–142.

Harackiewicz, J., & Sansone, C. (1991). Goals and intrinsic motivation: You *can* get there from here. In M. L. Maehr & P. R. Pintrich (Eds.), *Advances in motivation and achievement: Goals and self-regulation* (Vol. 7, pp. 21–49). Greenwich, CT: JAI Press.

Harari, O., & Covington, M. V. (1981). Reactions to achievement behavior from a teacher and student perspective: A developmental analysis. *American Educational Research Journal, 18*, 15-28.

Harter, S. (1975). Developmental differences in the manifestation of mastery motivation on problem-solving tasks. *Child Development, 46*, 370-378.

Harter, S. (1978). Effectance motivation reconsidered: Toward a developmental model. *Human Development, 21*, 34-64.

Harter, S. (1981a). A model of mastery motivation in children: Individual differences and developmental change. In W. A. Collins (Ed.), *Aspects on the development of competence: The Minnesota symposia on child psychology* (Vol. 14, pp. 215-255). Hillsdale, NJ: Erlbaum.

Harter, S. (1981b). A new self-report scale of intrinsic versus extrinsic orientation in the classroom: Motivational and informational components. *Developmental Psychology, 17*, 300-312.

Harter, S. (1982). The perceived competence scale for children. *Child Development, 53*, 87-97.

Harter, S. (1983). Developmental perspectives on the self-system. In P. H. Mussen (Ser. Ed.) & E. M. Heatherington (Vol. Ed.), *Handbook of child psychology: Vol. 4. Socialization, personality, and social development* (4th ed., pp. 275–386). New York: Wiley.

Harter, S. (1985a). Competence as a dimension of self-evaluation: Toward a comprehensive model of self-worth. In R. Leahy (Ed.), *The development of the self* (pp. 55–121). New York: Academic Press.

Harter, S. (1985b). *The Self-Perception Profile for Children: Revision of the Perceived Competence Scale for Children* (Manual). Denver, CO: University of Denver.

Harter, S. (1986). Processes underlying the construction, maintenance, and enhancement of the self-concept in children. In J. Suls & A. C. Greenwald (Eds.), *Psychological perspectives on the self* (Vol. 3, pp. 137–181). Hillsdale, NJ: Erlbaum.

Harter, S. (1990). Causes, correlates, and the functional role of self-worth: A life-span perspective. In R. J. Sternberg & J. Kolligian (Eds.), *Competence considered* (pp. 67–97). New Haven, CT: Yale University Press.

Harter, S., & Connell, J. P. (1984). A comparison of children's achievement and related self-perceptions of competence, control, and motivational orientation. In J. G. Nicholls (Ed.), *Advances in motivation and achievement: The development of achievement motivation* (Vol. 3, pp. 219-250). Greenwich, CT: JAI Press.

Hebb, D. O. (1949). *The organization of behavior.* New York: Wiley.

Hebb, D. O. (1966). *A textbook of psychology* (2nd ed.). Philadelphia: Saunders.

Heckhausen, H. (1977). Achievement motivation and its constructs: A cognitive model. *Motivation and Emotion, 1*, 283–329.

Heckhausen, H. (1991). *Motivation and action.* Berlin: Springer-Verlag.

Heidbreder, E. (1933). *Seven psychologies.* Englewood Cliffs, NJ: Prentice Hall.

Heider, F. (1946). Attitudes and cognitive organization. *Journal of Psychology, 21*, 107-112.

Heider, F. (1958). *The psychology of interpersonal relations.* New York: Wiley.

Helmke, A. (1988). The role of classroom context factors for the achievement-impairing effect of test anxiety. *Anxiety Research, 1*, 37–52.

Hembree, R. (1988). Correlates, causes, effects, and treatment of test anxiety. *Review of Educational Research, 58*, 47–77.

Henderson, V., & Dweck, C. S. (1990). Motivation and achievement. In S. Feldman & G. Elliott, (Eds.), *At the threshold: The developing adolescent* (pp. 308–329). Cambridge, MA: Harvard University Press.

Heyns, B. (1974). Social selection and stratification within schools. *American Journal of Sociology, 79*, 1434–1451.

Hidi, S. (1990). Interest and its contribution as a mental resource for learning. *Review of Educational Research, 60*, 549-571.

Hidi, S., & Anderson, V. (1992). Situational interest and its impact on reading and expository writing. In K. A. Renninger, S. Hidi, & A. Krapp (Eds.), *The role of interest in learning and development* (pp. 215-238). Hillsdale, NJ: Erlbaum.

Hidi, S., Renninger, K. A., & Krapp, A. (1992). The present state of interest research. In K. A. Renninger, S. Hidi, & A. Krapp (Eds.), *The role of interest in learning and development* (pp. 433–446). Hillsdale, NJ: Erlbaum.

Higgins, E. T. (1981). Role taking and social judgment: Alternative developmental perspectives and processes. In J. H. Flavell &

L. Ross (Eds.), *Social cognitive development: Frontiers and possible futures* (pp. 119-153). Cambridge: Cambridge University Press.

Hilgard, E. R. (1963). Motivation in learning theory. In S. Koch (Ed.), *Psychology: A study of a science* (Vol. 5, pp. 253-283). New York: McGraw-Hill.

Hill, K. T., & Wigfield, A. (1984). Test anxiety: A major educational problem and what can be done about it. *Elementary School Journal, 85*, 105–126.

Hilton, D. J., & Slugoski, B. R. (1986). Knowledge-based causal attribution: The abnormal conditions focus model. *Psychological Review, 93*, 75–88.

Holloway, S. (1988). Concepts of ability and effort in Japan and the United States. *Review of Educational Research, 58*, 327–345.

Hull, C. L. (1943). *Principles of behavior: An introduction to behavior theory.* New York: Appleton-Century-Crofts.

Hull, C. L. (1951). *Essentials of behavior.* New Haven, CT: Yale University Press.

Hull, C. L. (1952). *A behavior system: An introduction to behavior theory concerning the individual organism.* New Haven, CT: Yale University Press.

Humphrey, G. (1921). Imitation and the conditioned reflex. *Pedagogical Seminary, 28*, 1-21.

Hunt, J. McV. (1963). Motivation inherent in information processing and action. In O. J. Harvey (Ed.), *Motivation and social interaction: Cognitive determinants* (pp. 35-94). New York: Ronald.

Jagacinski, C., & Nicholls, J. (1984). Conceptions of ability and related affects in task involvement and ego involvement. *Journal of Educational Psychology, 76*, 909–919.

Jagacinski, C., & Nicholls, J. (1987). Competence and affect in task involvement and ego involvement: The impact of social comparison information. *Journal of Educational Psychology, 79*, 107–114.

Jagacinski, C., & Nicholls, J. G. (1990). Reducing effort to protect perceived ability: "They'd do it but I wouldn't." *Journal of Educational Psychology, 82*, 15-21.

James, W. (1884). What is an emotion? *Mind, 9*, 188-205. (Reprinted in K. Dunlap (Ed.), *The emotions* (pp. 11-30). Baltimore: Williams & Wilkins, 1922.)

James, W. (1890). *The principles of psychology* (Vol. 2). New York: Henry Holt.

James, W. (1892). *Psychology: Briefer course.* New York: Henry Holt.

Jencks, C., & Brown, M. (1975). Effects of high schools on their students. *Harvard Educational Review, 45*, 273–324.

Jensen, A. (1969). How much can we boost IQ and achievement? *Harvard Educational Review, 39*, 1-123.

Johnson, D., & Johnson, R. (1974). Instructional goal structure: Cooperative, competitive, or individualistic. *Review of Educational Research, 44*, 213-240.

Johnson, D., & Johnson, R. (1985). Motivational processes in cooperative, competitive, and individualistic learning situations. In C. Ames & R. Ames (Eds.), *Research on motivation in education* (Vol. 2, pp. 249-286). New York: Academic Press.

Johnson, D., Maruyama, G., Johnson, R., Nelson, D., & Skon, L. (1981). Effects of cooperative, competitive, and individualistic goal structures on achievement: A meta-analysis. *Psychological Bulletin, 89*, 47–62.

Johnson, T. J., Feigenbaum, R., & Weiby, M. (1964). Some determinants and consequences of the teacher's perceptions of causation. *Journal of Educational Psychology, 55*, 237–246.

Jones, E. E., & Harris, V. A. (1967). The attribution of attitudes. *Journal of Experimental Social Psychology, 3*, 1–24.

Jones, E. E., & Nisbett, R. (1972). The actor and the observer: Divergent perceptions of the causes of behavior. In E. E. Jones, D. E. Kanouse, H. H. Kelley, R. Nisbett, S. Valins, & B. Weiner (Eds.), *Attribution: Perceiving the causes of behavior* (pp. 79–94). Morristown, NJ: General Learning Press.

Jussim, L. (1986). Self-fulfilling prophecies: A theoretical and integrative review. *Psychological Review, 93*, 429–445.

Jussim, L. (1991). Social perception and social reality: A reflection-construction model. *Psychological Review, 98*, 54–73.

Kahle, J., Parker, L., Rennie, L., & Riley, D. (1993). Gender differences in science education: Building a model. *Educational Psychologist, 28,* 379–404.

Kassin, S., & Pryor, J. (1985). The development of attribution processes. In J. Pryor & J. Day (Eds.), *The development of social cognition* (pp. 3–34). New York: Springer-Verlag.

Keller, F. S. (1968). Good-bye, teacher. . . . *Journal of Applied Behavior Analysis, 1,* 79-89.

Kelley, H. H. (1967). Attribution theory in social psychology. In D. Levine (Ed.), *Nebraska symposium on motivation* (Vol. 15, pp. 192–238). Lincoln: University of Nebraska Press.

Kelley, H. H. (1971). *Attributions in social interactions.* Morristown, NJ: General Learning Press.

Kelley, H. H. (1972). Causal schemata and the attribution process. In E. E. Jones, D. E. Kanouse, H. H. Kelley, R. Nisbett, S. Valins, & B. Weiner (Eds.), *Attribution: Perceiving the causes of behavior* (pp. 151–174). Morristown, NJ: General Learning Press.

Kelley, H. H., & Michela, J. (1980). Attribution theory and research. *Annual Review of Psychology, 31,* 457–501.

Kounin, J. S. (1977). *Discipline and group management in classrooms.* Huntington, NY: Krieger.

Krapp, A., Hidi, S., & Renninger, K. A. (1992). Interest, learning, and development. In K. A. Renninger, S. Hidi, & A. Krapp (Eds.), *The role of interest in learning and development* (pp. 3-25). Hillsdale, NJ: Erlbaum.

Kravitz, D. A., & Martin, B. (1986). Ringelmann rediscovered: The original article. *Journal of Personality and Social Psychology, 50,* 936-941.

Kruglanski, A. (1977). The place of naive contents in a theory of attribution: Reflections on Calder's and Zuckerman's critique of the endogenous-exogenous partition. *Personality and Social Psychology Bulletin, 3,* 592–605.

Kuhl, J. (1984). Volitional aspects of achievement motivation and learned helplessness: Toward a comprehensive theory of action control. In B. A. Maher (Ed.), *Progress in experimental personality research* (Vol. 13, pp. 99-171). New York: Academic Press.

Kuhl, J. (1985). Volitional mediators of cognition-behavior consistency: Self-regulatory processes and action versus state orientation. In J. Kuhl & J. Beckmann (Eds.), *Action control: From cognition to behavior* (pp. 101-128). New York: Springer-Verlag.

Kuhl, J. (1992). A theory of self-regulation: Action versus state orientation, self-discrimination, and some applications. *Applied psychology: An international review, 41,* 97-129.

Kun, A., & Weiner, B. (1973). Necessary versus sufficient causal schemata for success and failure. *Journal of Research in Psychology, 7,* 197–207.

Kurtz, B. E., & Borkowski, J. G. (1987). Development of strategic skills in impulsive and reflective children: A longitudinal study of meta-cognition. *Journal of Experimental Child Psychology, 43,* 129-148.

Lange, C. G. (1885). One leudsbeveegelser (I. A. Haupt, Trans.). In K. Dunlap (Ed.), *The emotions* (pp. 33-90). Baltimore: Williams & Wilkens, 1922.

Latane, B., Williams, K., & Harkins, S. (1979). Many hands make light the work: The causes and consequences of social loafing. *Journal of Personality and Social Psychology, 37,* 822-832.

Lazarus, R. (1991). *Emotion and adaptation.* Oxford: Oxford University Press.

Leary, D. E. (1990). Psyche's muse: The role of metaphor in the history of psychology. In D. E. Leary (Ed.), *Metaphors in the history of psychology* (pp. 1-78). Cambridge: Cambridge University Press.

Lee, V., & Bryk, A. (1988). Curriculum tracking as mediating the social distribution of high school achievement. *Sociology of Education, 61,* 78–94.

Lee, V., & Bryk, A. (1989). A multilevel model of the social distribution of high school achievement. *Sociology of Education, 62,* 172–192.

Lee, V., Bryk, A., & Smith, J. (1993). The organization of effective secondary schools. In L. Darling-Hammond (Ed.), *Review of research in education* (Vol. 19, pp. 171–267). Washington, DC: American Educational Research Association.

Lee, V., & Smith, J. (in press). Effects of high school restructuring and size on gains in achievement and engagement for early secondary school students. *Sociology of Education.*

Leithwood, K., & Montgomery, D. (1982). The role of the elementary school principal in program improvement. *Review of Educational Research, 52*, 309–339.

Lepper, M. R. (1981). Intrinsic and extrinsic motivation in children: Detrimental effects of superfluous social controls. In W. A. Collins (Ed.), *Aspects of the development of competence: The Minnesota symposia on child psychology* (Vol. 14, pp. 155-214). Hillsdale, NJ: Erlbaum.

Lepper, M. R. (1983). Extrinsic reward and intrinsic motivation: Implications for the classroom. In J. M. Levine & M. C. Wang (Eds.), *Teacher and student perceptions: Implications for learning* (pp. 281-317). Hillsdale, NJ: Erlbaum.

Lepper, M. R., & Greene, D. (1978). Overjustification research and beyond: Toward a means-ends analysis of intrinsic and extrinsic motivation. In M. R. Lepper & D. Greene (Eds.), *The hidden costs of reward: New perspectives on the psychology of human motivation* (pp. 109-148). Hillsdale, NJ: Erlbaum.

Lepper, M. R., Greene, D., & Nisbett, R. E. (1973). Undermining children's intrinsic interest with extrinsic reward: A test of the "overjustification" hypothesis. *Journal of Personality and Social Psychology, 28*, 129-137.

Lepper, M. R., & Hodell, M. (1989). Intrinsic motivation in the classroom. In C. Ames & R. Ames (Eds.), *Research on motivation in education* (Vol. 3, pp. 73-105). San Diego: Academic Press.

Lepper, M. R., & Malone, T. (1987). Intrinsic motivation and instructional effectiveness in computer-based education. In R. E. Snow & M. J. Farr (Eds.), *Aptitude, learning, and instruction* (Vol. 3, pp. 255-296). Hillsdale, NJ: Erlbaum.

Lerner, R. M. (1986). *Concepts and theories of human development* (2nd ed.). New York: Random House.

Lewin, K. (1935). *A dynamic theory of personality: Selected papers* (D. K. Adams & K. E. Zener, Trans.). New York: McGraw-Hill.

Lewin, K. (1936). *Principles of topological psychology* (F. Heider & G. M. Heider, Trans.). New York: McGraw-Hill.

Lewin, K., Dembo, T., Festinger, L., & Sears, P. (1944). Level of aspiration. In J. McV. Hunt (Ed.), *Personality and the behavioral disorders* (Vol. 1). New York: Ronald.

Lewin, K., Lippitt, R., & White, R. K. (1939). Patterns of aggressive behavior in experimentally created "social climates." *Journal of Social Psychology, 10*, 271-299.

Licht, B. G., & Kistner, J. A. (1986). Motivational problems of learning-disabled children: Individual differences and their implications for treatment. In J. K. Torgesen & B. W. L. Wong (Eds.), *Psychological and educational perspectives on learning disabilities* (pp. 225-255). Orlando, FL: Academic Press.

Liebert, R., & Morris, L. (1967). Cognitive and emotional components of test anxiety: A distinction and some initial data. *Psychological Reports, 20*, 975–978.

Linn, M., & Hyde, J. (1989). Gender, mathematics, and science. *Educational Researcher, 18*, 17–19, 22–27.

Lipton, J. P., & Garza, R. T. (1977). Responsibility attribution among Mexican-American, Black, and Anglo adolescents and adults. *Journal of Cross-Cultural Psychology, 8*, 259–272.

Locke, E. A., & Latham, G. P. (1990). *A theory of goal setting and task performance.* Englewood Cliffs, NJ: Prentice Hall.

Mac Iver, D. (1988). Classroom environments and the stratification of pupils' ability perceptions. *Journal of Educational Psychology, 80*, 495–505.

Mac Iver, D., Reuman, D., & Main, S. (1995). Social structuring of the school: Studying what is, illuminating what could be. *Annual Review of Psychology, 46*, 375–400.

Maehr, M. L., & Braskamp, L. A. (1986). *The motivation factor: A theory of personal investment.* Lexington, MA: Lexington Books, D.C. Heath.

Maehr, M. L., & Midgley, C. (1991). Enhancing student motivation: A schoolwide approach. *Educational Psychologist, 26*, 399–427.

Maehr, M. L., & Midgley, C. (forthcoming). *Transforming school cultures.* Boulder, CO: Westview Press.

Maehr, M. L., & Pintrich, P. R. (1991). *Advances in motivation and achievement: Vol 7. Goals and self-regulatory processes*. Greenwich, CT: JAI Press.

Magnusson, D. (1990). Personality development from an interactional perspective. In L. A. Pervin (Ed.), *Handbook of personality: Theory and research* (pp. 193–222). New York: Guilford Press.

Major, B. (1980). Information acquisition and attribution process. *Journal of Personality and Social Psychology, 39*, 1010–1023.

Malone, T., & Lepper, M. R. (1987). Making learning fun: A taxonomy of intrinsic motivations for learning. In R. Snow & M. Farr (Eds.), *Aptitude, learning, and instruction* (Vol. 3, pp. 223-253). Hillsdale, NJ: Erlbaum.

Manassee, A. (1985). Improving conditions for principal effectiveness: Policy implications of research. *Elementary School Journal, 85*, 439–463.

Mandler, G., & Sarason, S. (1952). A study of anxiety and learning. *Journal of Abnormal and Social Psychology, 47*, 166–173.

Markus, H., & Nurius, P. (1986). Possible selves. *American Psychologist, 41*, 954-969.

Marsh, H. (1984a). Relations among dimensions of self-attribution, dimensions of self-concept, and academic achievements. *Journal of Educational Psychology, 76*, 1291–1308.

Marsh, H. (1984b). The relationship between dimensions of self-attribution and dimensions of self-concept. *Journal of Educational Psychology, 76*, 3–23.

Marsh, H. (1986). Global self-esteem: Its relation to specific facets of self-concept and their importance. *Journal of Personality and Social Psychology, 51*, 1224–1236.

Marsh, H. (1989). Age and sex effects in multiple dimensions of self-concept: Preadolescence to early adulthood. *Journal of Educational Psychology, 81*, 417–430.

Marsh, H. (1990a). Causal ordering of academic self-concept and academic achievement: A multivariate, longitudinal panel analysis. *Journal of Educational Psychology, 82*, 646–656.

Marsh, H. (1990b). The structure of academic self-concept: The Marsh/Shavelson model. *Journal of Educational Psychology, 82*, 623–636.

Marsh, H., & O'Neill, R. (1984). Self-description questionnaire III: The construct validity of multidimensional self-concept ratings by late adolescents. *Journal of Educational Measurement, 21*, 153–174.

Marsh, H., & Shavelson, R. (1985). Self-concept: Its multifaceted hierarchical structure. *Educational Psychologist, 20*, 107–123.

Marshall, H. (1988). Work on learning: Implications of classroom metaphors. *Educational Researcher, 17*, 9–16.

Marshall, H., & Weinstein, R. S. (1984). Classroom factors affecting students' self-evaluations: An interactional model. *Review of Educational Research, 54*, 301-325.

Marx, R. W. (1983). Student perception in classrooms. *Educational Psychologist, 18*, 145-164.

Maslow, A. (1954). *Motivation and personality*. New York: Harper.

McClelland, D. (1961). *The achieving society*. Princeton, NJ: Van Nostrand.

McClelland, D., Atkinson, J. W., Clark, R. A., & Lowell, E. L. (1953). *The achievement motive*. New York: Appleton-Century-Crofts.

McDougall, W. (1923). *Outline of psychology*. New York: Scribner.

McDougall, W. (1926). *An introduction to social psychology* (Rev. ed.). Boston: John W. Luce.

McMillan, J. H. (1980). Children's causal attributions in achievement situations. *Journal of Social Psychology, 112*, 31–39.

McReynolds, P. (1990). Motives and metaphors: A study in scientific creativity. In D. E. Leary (Ed.), *Metaphors in the history of psychology* (pp. 133-172). Cambridge: Cambridge University Press.

Meece, J. (1991). The classroom context and students' motivational goals. In M. L. Maehr & P. R. Pintrich (Eds.), *Advances in motivation and achievement* (Vol. 7, pp. 261-286). Greenwich, CT: JAI Press.

Meece, J., Blumenfeld, P. C., & Hoyle, R. H. (1988). Students' goal orientation and cognitive engagement in classroom activities. *Journal of Educational Psychology, 80*, 514-523.

Meece, J., & Eccles, J. (1993). Introduction: Recent trends in research on gender and education. *Educational Psychologist, 28*, 313–319.

Meece, J., & Holt, K. (1993). A pattern analysis of students' achievement goals. *Journal of Educational Psychology, 85*, 582–590.

Meece, J., Parsons, J., Kaczala, C., Goff, S., & Futterman, R. (1982). Sex differences in math achievement: Toward a model of academic choice. *Psychological Bulletin, 91*, 324–348.

Meece, J., Wigfield, A., & Eccles, J. (1990). Predictors of math anxiety and its influence on young adolescents' course enrollment intentions and performance in mathematics. *Journal of Educational Psychology, 82*, 60–70.

Meichenbaum, D. (1977). *Cognitive behavior modification: An integrative approach.* New York: Plenum.

Meichenbaum, D., & Goodman, J. (1971). Training impulsive children to talk to themselves: A means of developing self-control. *Journal of Abnormal Psychology, 77*, 115-126.

Metz, M. (1978). *Classrooms and corridors: The crisis of authority in desegregated secondary schools.* Berkeley: University of California Press.

Meyer, W., Bachmann, M., Biermann, U., Hempelmann, M., Plöger, F., & Spiller, H. (1979). The informational value of evaluative behavior: Influences of praise and blame in perceptions of ability. *Journal of Educational Psychology, 71*, 259–268.

Midgley, C., Anderman, E., & Hicks, L. (1995). Differences between elementary and middle school teachers and students: A goal theory approach. *Journal of Early Adolescence, 15*, 90–133.

Midgley, C., Feldlaufer, H., & Eccles, J. (1989a). Change in teacher efficacy and student self- and task-related beliefs in mathematics during the transition to junior high school. *Journal of Educational Psychology, 81*, 247–258.

Midgley, C., Feldlaufer, H., & Eccles, J. (1989b). Student/teacher relations and attitudes toward mathematics before and after the transition to junior high school. *Child Development, 60*, 981–992.

Midgley, C., Maehr, M. L., & Urdan, T. (1993). *Patterns of adaptive learning survey (PALS).*

Ann Arbor, MI: University of Michigan, Combined Program in Education and Psychology.

Midgley, C., & Wood, S. (1993). Beyond site-based management: Empowering teachers to reform schools. *Phi Delta Kappan, 75*, 245–252.

Milgram, S. (1963). Behavioral study of obedience. *Journal of Abnormal and Social Psychology, 67*, 371-378.

Milgram, S. (1974). *Obedience to authority: An experimental view.* New York: Harper & Row.

Miller, D. T., & Ross, M. (1975). Self-serving biases in the attribution of causality: Fact or fiction. *Psychological Bulletin, 82*, 213–225.

Miller, J. G. (1984). Culture and the development of everyday social explanation. *Journal of Personality and Social Psychology, 46*, 961–978.

Miller, N. E. (1948). Studies of fear as an acquirable drive: I. Fear as motivation and fear-reduction as reinforcement in the learning of new responses. *Journal of Experimental Psychology, 38*, 89-101.

Miller, N. E. (1963). Some reflections on the law of effect produce a new alternative to drive reduction. In M. R. Jones (Ed.), *Nebraska symposium on motivation* (Vol. 11, pp. 65-112). Lincoln: University of Nebraska Press.

Miller, N. E., & Dollard, J. (1941). *Social learning and imitation.* New Haven, CT: Yale University Press.

Mischel, W. (1968). *Personality and assessment.* New York: Wiley.

Mischel, W. (1990). Personality dispositions revisited and revised: A view after three decades. In L. Pervin (Ed.), *Handbook of personality: Theory and research* (pp. 111–134). New York: Guilford Press.

Miura, I. T. (1987). A multivariate study of school-aged children's computer interest and use. In M. E. Ford & D. H. Ford (Eds.), *Humans as self-constructing living systems: Putting the framework to work* (pp. 177–197). Hillsdale, NJ: Erlbaum.

Mook, D. G. (1987). *Motivation: The organization of action.* New York: Norton.

Moos, R. (1979). *Evaluating educational environments.* San Francisco: Jossey-Bass.

Morgan, M. (1984). Reward-induced decrements and increments in intrinsic motivation. *Review of Educational Research, 54,* 5–30.

Mosatche, H. S., & Bragonier, P. (1981). An observational study of social comparison in preschoolers. *Child Development, 52,* 376-378.

Mowrer, O. H. (1960). *Learning theory and behavior.* New York: Wiley.

Mullen, R., & Riordan, C. A. (1988). Self-serving attributions for performance in naturalistic settings: A meta-analytic review. *Journal of Applied Social Psychology, 18,* 3–22.

Muncey, D., & McQuillan, P. (1993). Preliminary findings from a five-year study of the Coalition of Essential Schools. *Phi Delta Kappan, 74,* 486–489.

Murray, H. A. (1938). *Explorations in personality.* New York: Oxford University Press.

Naftulin, D. H., Ware, J. E., & Donnelly, F. A. (1973). The Doctor Fox lecture: A paradigm of educational seduction. *Journal of Medical Education, 48,* 630-635.

Natriello, G. (1986). *School dropouts: Patterns and policies.* New York: Teachers College Press.

Newman, R. S., & Schwager, M. T. (1992). Student perceptions and academic help-seeking. In D. H. Schunk & J. L. Meece (Eds.), *Student perceptions in the classroom* (pp. 123-146). Hillsdale, NJ: Erlbaum.

Newmann, F. (1981). Reducing student alienation in high schools: Implications of theory. *Harvard Educational Review, 51,* 546–564.

Newmann, F. (1993). Beyond common sense in educational restructuring: The issues of content and linkage. *Educational Researcher, 22,* 4–13.

Nicholls, J. (1978). The development of the concepts of effort and ability, perception of academic attainment, and the understanding that difficult tasks require more ability. *Child Development, 49,* 800-814.

Nicholls, J. (1979). Development of perception of own attainment and causal attribution for success and failure in reading. *Journal of Educational Psychology, 71,* 94-99.

Nicholls, J. (1984). Achievement motivation: Conceptions of ability, subjective experience, task choice, and performance. *Psychological Review, 91,* 328-346.

Nicholls, J. (1989). *The competitive ethos and democratic education.* Cambridge, MA: Harvard University Press.

Nicholls, J. (1990). What is ability and why are we mindful of it? A developmental perspective. In R. Sternberg & J. Kolligian (Eds.), *Competence considered* (pp. 11–40). New Haven, CT: Yale University Press.

Nicholls, J., & Miller, A. (1983). The differentiation of the concepts of difficulty and ability. *Child Development, 54,* 951–959.

Nicholls, J., & Miller, A. (1984a). Development and its discontents: The differentiation of the concept of ability. In J. Nicholls (Ed.), *Advances in motivation and achievement: The development of achievement motivation* (Vol. 3, pp. 185–218). Greenwich, CT: JAI Press.

Nicholls, J., & Miller, A. (1984b). Reasoning about the ability of self and others: A developmental study. *Child Development, 55,* 1990–1999.

Nicholls, J., & Miller, A. (1985). Differentiation of the concepts of luck and skill. *Developmental Psychology, 21,* 76–82.

Nicholls, J., Cheung, P., Lauer, J., & Patashnick, M. (1989). Individual differences in academic motivation: Perceived ability, goals, beliefs, and values. *Learning and Individual Differences, 1,* 63–84.

Nisbett, R., & Ross, L. (1980). *Human inference: Strategies and shortcomings of social judgment.* Englewood Cliffs, NJ: Prentice-Hall.

Nisbett, R., & Wilson, T. (1977). Telling more than we can know: Verbal reports on mental processes. *Psychological Review, 84,* 231–259.

Noddings, N. (1992). *The challenge to care in schools.* New York: Teachers College Press.

Nolen, S. (1988). Reasons for studying: Motivational orientations and study strategies. *Cognition and Instruction, 5,* 269-287.

Norem, J. K., & Cantor, N. (1986). Defensive pessimism: Harnessing anxiety as motivation. *Journal of Personality and Social Psychology, 51,* 1208-1217.

Oakes, J. (1985). *Keeping track: How schools structure inequality*. New Haven, CT: Yale University Press.

O'Leary, K., & O'Leary, S. (1977). *Classroom management: The successful use of behavior modification* (2nd ed.). New York: Pergamon.

Olson, J., Ellis, R., & Zanna, M. (1983). Validating objective versus subjective judgments: Interest in social comparison and consistency information. *Personality and Social Psychology Bulletin, 9*, 427–436.

Ortony, A., Clore, G., & Collins, A. (1988). *The cognitive structure of emotions*. Cambridge: Cambridge University Press.

Overton, W. F. (1984). World views and their influence on psychological theory and research: Kuhn-Lakatos-Laudan. In H. W. Reese (Ed.), *Advances in child development and behavior* (Vol. 18, pp. 191-226). Orlando, FL: Academic Press.

Page, R. (1990). The lower track curriculum in a college-preparatory high school. *Curriculum Inquiry, 20*, 249–282.

Palincsar, A. S. (1986). Metacognitive strategy instruction. *Exceptional Children, 53*, 118-124.

Palincsar, A. S., & Brown, A. L. (1984). Reciprocal teaching of comprehension-fostering and comprehension-monitoring activities. *Cognition and Instruction, 1*, 117-175.

Paris, S., & Ayres, L. (1994). *Becoming reflective students and teachers with portfolios and authentic assessment*. Washington, DC: American Psychological Association.

Paris, S., Lawton, T., Turner, J., & Roth, J. (1991). A developmental perspective on standardized testing. *Educational Researcher, 20*, 12–20.

Paris, S., Lipson, M. Y., & Wixson, K. K. (1983). Becoming a strategic reader. *Contemporary Educational Psychology, 8*, 293-316.

Paris, S., Newman, R. S., & McVey, K. A. (1982). Learning the functional significance of mnemonic actions: A microgenetic study of strategy acquisition. *Journal of Experimental Child Psychology, 34*, 490-509.

Paris, S., & Oka, E. (1986). Children's reading strategies, metacognition, and motivation. *Developmental Review, 6*, 25-56.

Parker, L. E., & Lepper, M. R. (1992). Effects of fantasy contexts on children's learning and motivation: Making learning more fun. *Journal of Personality and Social Psychology, 62*, 625-633.

Parsons, J., & Goff, S. (1978). Achievement and motivation: Dual modalities. *Educational Psychologist, 13*, 93–96.

Parsons, J., & Ruble, D. N. (1977). The development of achievement-related expectancies. *Child Development, 48*, 1075–1079.

Pavlov, I. P. (1927). *Conditioned reflexes* (G. V. Anrep, Trans.). London: Oxford University Press.

Pavlov, I. P. (1928). *Lectures on conditioned reflexes* (W. H. Gantt, Trans.). New York: International Publishers.

Pekrun, R. (1993). Facets of adolescents' academic motivation: A longitudinal expectancy-value approach. In M. L. Maehr & P. R. Pintrich (Eds.), *Advances in motivation and achievement: Motivation in adolescence* (Vol. 8, pp. 139–189). Greenwich, CT: JAI Press.

Perkins, D. (1992). *Smart schools: From training memories to educating minds*. New York: The Free Press.

Perry, R. P. (1985). Instructor expressiveness: Implications for improving teaching. In J. G. Donald & A. M. Sullivan (Eds.), *Using research to improve teaching* (pp. 35-49). San Francisco: Jossey-Bass.

Perry, R. P., & Dickens, W. J. (1984). Perceived control in the college classroom: Response-outcome contingency training and instructor expressiveness effects on student achievement and causal attributions. *Journal of Educational Psychology, 76*, 966-981.

Perry, R. P., Magnusson, J. L., Parsonson, K. L., & Dickens, W. J. (1986). Perceived control in the college classroom: Limitations in instructor expressiveness due to noncontingent feedback and lecture content. *Journal of Educational Psychology, 78*, 96-107.

Peshkin, A. (1986). *God's choice: The total world of a fundamental Christian school*. Chicago: University of Chicago Press.

Peterson, C., Maier, S., & Seligman, M. (1993). *Learned helplessness: A theory for the age of personal control.* New York: Oxford University Press.

Peterson, C., & Seligman, M. (1984). Causal explanations as a risk factor for depression: Theory and evidence. *Psychological Review, 91,* 347-374.

Peterson, C., Semmel, A., Von Baeyer, C., Abramson, L. Y., Metalsky, G. I., & Seligman, M. (1982). The attributional style questionnaire. *Cognitive Therapy and Research, 6,* 287-300.

Peterson, P., & Barger, S. (1984). Attribution theory and teacher expectancy. In J. Dusek (Ed.), *Teacher expectancies* (pp. 159–184). Hillsdale, NJ: Erlbaum.

Peterson, P., Swing, S. R., Braverman, M. T., & Buss, R. (1982). Students' aptitudes and their reports of cognitive processes during direct instruction. *Journal of Educational Psychology, 74,* 535-547.

Petri, H. L. (1986). *Motivation: Theory and research* (2nd ed.). Belmont, CA: Wadsworth.

Phares, E. J. (1976). *Locus of control in personality.* Morristown, NJ: General Learning Press.

Phillips, D. (1984). The illusion of incompetence among academically competent children. *Child Development, 55,* 2000–2016.

Phillips, D. (1987). Socialization of perceived academic competence among highly competent children. *Child Development, 58,* 1308–1320.

Phillips, D., & Zimmerman, M. (1990). The developmental course of perceived competence and incompetence among competent children. In R. Sternberg & J. Kolligian (Eds.), *Competence considered* (pp. 41–66). New Haven, CT: Yale University Press.

Piaget, J. (1954/1981). *Intelligence and affectivity.* Palo Alto, CA: Annual Reviews, Inc.

Piaget, J. (1962). *Play, dreams and imitation.* New York: Norton.

Piaget, J. (1985). *The equilibration of cognitive structures.* Chicago: University of Chicago Press.

Pintrich, P. R. (1988a). A process-oriented view of student motivation and cognition. In J. Stark and L. Mets (Eds.), *Improving teach-ing and learning through research: New directions for institutional research* (Vol. 57, pp 65–79). San Francisco: Jossey-Bass.

Pintrich, P. R. (1988b). Student learning and college teaching. In R. Young and K. Eble (Eds.), *College teaching and learning: Preparing for new commitments: New directions for teaching and learning.* (Vol. 33. pp. 71–86). San Francisco: Jossey-Bass.

Pintrich, P. R. (1989). The dynamic interplay of student motivation and cognition in the college classroom. In C. Ames & M. L. Maehr (Eds.), *Advances in motivation and achievement: Motivation enhancing environments* (Vol. 6, pp. 117-160). Greenwich, CT: JAI Press.

Pintrich, P. R. (1991). Current issues and new directions in motivational theory and research. *Educational Psychologist, 26,* 199–205.

Pintrich, P. R. (1994). Continuities and discontinuities: Future directions for research in educational psychology. *Educational Psychologist, 29,* 137–148.

Pintrich, P. R., & Blumenfeld, P. (1985). Classroom experience and children's self-perceptions of ability, effort and conduct. *Journal of Educational Psychology, 77,* 646–657.

Pintrich, P. R., Cross, D. R., Kozma, R. B., & McKeachie, W. J. (1986). Instructional psychology. *Annual Review of Psychology, 37,* 611-651.

Pintrich, P. R., & De Groot, E. (1990a). Motivational and self-regulated learning components of classroom academic performance. *Journal of Educational Psychology, 82,* 33-40.

Pintrich, P. R., & De Groot, E. (1990b). *Quantitative and qualitative perspectives on student motivational beliefs and self-regulated learning.* Paper presented at the American Educational Research Association conference, Boston.

Pintrich, P. R., & Garcia, T. (1991). Student goal orientation and self-regulation in the college classroom. In M. L. Maehr & P. R. Pintrich (Eds.), *Advances in motivation and achievement: Goals and self-regulatory processes* (Vol. 7, pp. 371-402). Greenwich, CT: JAI Press.

Pintrich, P. R., & Garcia, T. (1993). Motivation and self-regulation in the college classroom. *Zeitschrift für Pädagogische Psychologie, 7,* 99–107.

Pintrich, P. R., Marx, R. W., & Boyle, R. (1993). Beyond "cold" conceptual change: The role of motivational beliefs and classroom contextual factors in the process of conceptual change. *Review of Educational Research, 63,* 167–199.

Pintrich, P. R., Roeser, R., & De Groot, E. (1994). Classroom and individual differences in early adolescents' motivation and self-regulated learning. *Journal of Early Adolescence, 14,* 139–161.

Pintrich, P. R., & Schrauben, B. (1992). Students' motivational beliefs and their cognitive engagement in classroom tasks. In D. Schunk & J. Meece (Eds.), *Student perceptions in the classroom: Causes and consequences* (pp. 149-183). Hillsdale, NJ: Erlbaum.

Pintrich, P. R., Smith, D. A. F., Garcia, T., & McKeachie, W. J. (1993). Reliability and predictive validity of the Motivated Strategies for Learning Questionnaire (MSLQ). *Educational and Psychological Measurement, 53,* 801–813.

Pollard, D. S. (1993). Gender, achievement, and African-American students' perceptions of their school experience. *Educational Psychologist, 28,* 341–356.

Premack, D. (1962). Reversibility of the reinforcement relation. *Science, 136,* 255-257.

Premack, D. (1971). Catching up with common sense or two sides of a generalization: Reinforcement and punishment. In R. Glaser (Ed.), *The nature of reinforcement* (pp. 121-150). New York: Academic Press.

Pressley, M., Woloshyn, V., Lysynchuk, L. M., Martin, V., Wood, E., & Willoughby, T. (1990). A primer of research on cognitive strategy instruction: The important issues and how to address them. *Educational Psychology Review, 2,* 1-58.

Purkey, S., & Smith, M. S. (1983). Effective schools: A review. *Elementary School Journal, 83,* 427–452.

Raudenbush, S., Rowan, B., & Cheong, Y. (1993). Higher order instructional goals in secondary schools: Class, teacher, and school influences. *American Educational Research Journal, 30,* 523–553.

Relich, J. D., Debus, R. L., & Walker, R. (1986). The mediating role of attribution and self-efficacy variables for treatment effects on achievement outcomes. *Contemporary Educational Psychology, 11,* 195-216.

Renninger, K. A. (1990). Children's play interests, representation, and activity. In R. Fivush & J. Hudson (Eds.), *Knowing and remembering in young children* (pp. 127–165). Cambridge: Cambridge University Press.

Renninger, K. A. (1992). Individual interest and development: Implications for theory and practice. In K. A. Renninger, S. Hidi, & A. Krapp (Eds.), *The role of interest in learning and development* (pp. 361-395). Hillsdale, NJ: Erlbaum.

Renninger, K. A., Hidi, S., & Krapp, A. (1992). *The role of interest in learning and development.* Hillsdale, NJ: Erlbaum.

Renninger, K. A., & Wozniak, R. H. (1985). Effect of interest on attentional shift, recognition, and recall in young children. *Developmental Psychology, 21,* 624-632.

Rescorla, R. (1972). Informational variables in conditioning. In G. H. Bower (Ed.), *The psychology of learning and motivation* (Vol. 6, pp. 1-46). New York: Academic Press.

Rescorla, R. (1987). A Pavlovian analysis of goal-directed behavior. *American Psychologist, 42,* 119-129.

Reuman, D. (1989). How social comparison mediates the relation between ability-grouping practices and students' achievement expectancies in mathematics. *Journal of Educational Psychology, 81,* 178–189.

Richter, C. P. (1927). Animal behavior and internal drives. *Quarterly Review of Biology, 2,* 307-343.

Rigby, C. S., Deci, E. L., Patrick, B. C., & Ryan, R. M. (1992). Beyond the intrinsic-extrinsic dichotomy: Self-determination in motivation and learning. *Motivation and Emotion, 16,* 165–185.

Rodin, J., Solomon, S. K., & Metcalf, J. (1978). Role of control in mediating perceptions of density. *Journal of Personality and Social Psychology, 36,* 988-999.

Rogers, C. R. (1959). A theory of therapy, personality, and interpersonal relationships, as developed in the client-centered framework. In S. Koch (Ed.), *Psychology: A study of a science* (Vol. 3, pp. 184-256). New York: McGraw-Hill.

Rogers, C. R. (1963). The actualizing tendency in relation to "motives" and to consciousness. In M. R. Jones (Ed.), *Nebraska symposium on motivation* (Vol. 11, pp. 1-24). Lincoln: University of Nebraska Press.

Rogers, C. R. (1969). *Freedom to learn*. Columbus, OH: Merrill.

Rokeach, M. (1979). *Understanding human values*. New York: Free Press.

Rosenbaum, J. (1976). *Inequality: The hidden curriculum of high school tracking*. New York: Wiley.

Rosenbaum, J. (1980). Track misperceptions and frustrated college plans: An analysis of the effects of track and track perceptions in the NLS. *Sociology of Education, 53,* 74–88.

Rosenberg, M., & Simmons, R. (1971). *Black and white self-esteem. The urban school child*. Washington, DC: American Sociological Association.

Rosenholtz, S. J., & Rosenholtz, S. H. (1981). Classroom organization and the perception of ability. *Sociology of Education, 54,* 132-140.

Rosenholtz, S. J., & Simpson, C. (1984). The formation of ability conceptions: Developmental trend or social construction? *Review of Educational Research, 54,* 31-63.

Rosenshine, B., & Meister, C. (1994). Reciprocal teaching: A review of the research. *Review of Educational Research, 64,* 479–530.

Rosenshine, B., & Stevens, R. (1986). Teaching functions. In M. C. Wittrock (Ed.), *Handbook of research on teaching* (3rd ed., pp. 376-391). New York: Macmillan.

Rosenthal, R. (1974). *On the social psychology of the self-fulfilling prophecy: Further evidence for Pygmalion effects and their mediating mechanisms*. New York: MSS Modular Publications.

Rosenthal, R., & Jacobson, L. (1968). *Pygmalion in the classroom*. New York: Holt, Rinehart & Winston.

Rosenthal, T. L., & Bandura, A. (1978). Psychological modeling: Theory and practice. In S. L. Garfield & A. E. Bergin (Eds.), *Handbook of psychotherapy and behavior change: An empirical analysis* (2nd ed., pp. 621-658). New York: Wiley.

Rosenthal, T. L., & Zimmerman, B. J. (1978). *Social learning and cognition*. New York: Academic Press.

Ross, L. (1977). The intuitive psychologist and his shortcomings: Distortions in the attribution process. In L. Berkowitz (Ed.), *Advances in experimental social psychology* (Vol. 10, pp. 174–221). New York: Academic Press.

Ross, L., Bierbrauer, G., & Polly, S. (1974). Attribution of educational outcomes by professional and nonprofessional instructors. *Journal of Personality & Social Psychology, 29,* 609–618.

Ross, L., & Nisbett, R. (1991). *The person and the situation*. New York: McGraw-Hill.

Ross, M. (1975). Salience of reward and intrinsic motivation. *Journal of Personality and Social Psychology, 32,* 245-254.

Rossell, C., & Howley, W. (1983). *The consequences of school desegregation*. Philadelphia: Temple University Press.

Rotter, J. B. (1954). *Social learning and clinical psychology*. New York: Prentice Hall.

Rotter, J. B. (1966). Generalized expectancies for internal versus external control of reinforcement. *Psychological Monographs, 80*(1, Whole No. 609).

Rotter, J. B., Chance, J. E., & Phares, E. J. (1972). *Applications of a social learning theory of personality*. New York: Holt, Rinehart & Winston.

Ruble, D. N. (1983). The development of social-comparison processes and their role in achievement-related self-socialization. In E. T. Higgins, D. N. Ruble, & W. Hartup (Eds.), *Social cognition and social development* (pp. 134-157). New York: Cambridge University Press.

Ruble, D. N., Boggiano, A. K., Feldman, N. S., & Loebl, J. H. (1980). Developmental analysis of the role of social comparison in self-evaluation. *Developmental Psychology, 16,* 105-115.

Ruble, D. N., Feldman, N. S., & Boggiano, A. K. (1976). Social comparison between young children in achievement situations. *Developmental Psychology, 12,* 192-197.

Ruble, D. N., & Frey, K. (1991). Changing patterns of comparative behavior as skills are acquired: A functional model of self-evaluation. In J. Suls & T. Wills (Eds.), *Social comparison: Contemporary theory and research* (pp. 79–113). Hillsdale, NJ: Erlbaum.

Ruble, D. N., Parsons, J., & Ross, J. (1976). Self-evaluative responses of children in an achievement setting. *Child Development, 47,* 990-997.

Russell, W. A. (1970). *Milestones in motivation: Contributions to the psychology of drive and purpose.* New York: Appleton-Century-Crofts.

Rutter, M., Maughan, B., Mortimore, P., Ouston, J., & Smith, A. (1979). *Fifteen thousand hours: Secondary schools and their effects on children.* Cambridge, MA: Harvard University Press.

Ryan, R. M. (1993). Agency and organization: Intrinsic motivation, autonomy, and the self in psychological development. In J. E. Jacobs (Ed.), *Nebraska symposium on motivation 1992* (Vol. 40, pp. 1-56). Lincoln: University of Nebraska Press.

Ryan, R. M., Connell, J. P., & Deci, E. L. (1985). A motivational analysis of self-determination and self-regulation in education. In C. Ames & R. Ames (Eds.), *Research on motivation in education* (Vol. 2, pp. 13-51). New York: Academic Press.

Ryan, R. M., & Grolnick, W. S. (1986). Origins and pawns in the classroom: Self-report and projective assessments of individual differences in children's perceptions. *Journal of Personality and Social Psychology, 50,* 550-558.

Salomon, G. (1984). Television is "easy" and print is "tough": The differential investment of mental effort in learning as a function of perceptions and attributions. *Journal of Educational Psychology, 76,* 647-658.

Sanna, L. J. (1992). Self-efficacy theory: Implications for social facilitation and social loafing. *Journal of Personality and Social Psychology, 62,* 774-786.

Sarason, S. B. (1990). *The predictable failure of school reform: Can we change course before it's too late?* San Francisco: Jossey-Bass.

Schachter, S. (1964). The interaction of cognitive and physiological determinants of emotional state. In L. Berkowitz (Ed.), *Advances in experimental social psychology* (Vol. 1, pp. 49-80). New York: Academic Press.

Schachter, S., & Singer, J. E. (1962). Cognitive, social, and physiological determinants of emotional state. *Psychological Review, 69,* 379-399.

Scheirer, M. A., & Kraut, R. E. (1979). Increasing educational achievement via self-concept change. *Review of Educational Research, 49,* 131–149.

Schiefele, U. (1991). Interest, learning, and motivation. *Educational Psychologist, 26,* 299-323.

Schiefele, U., Krapp, A., & Winteler, A. (1992). Interest as a predictor of academic achievement: A meta-analysis of research. In K. A. Renninger, S. Hidi, & A. Krapp (Eds.), *The role of interest in learning and development* (pp. 183–212). Hillsdale, NJ: Erlbaum.

Schofield, J., & Sagar, H. (1983). Desegregation, school practices, and student race relations. In C. Rossell & W. Howley (Eds.), *The consequences of school desegregation* (pp. 58–102). Philadelphia: Temple University Press.

Schrank, W. (1968). The labeling effect of ability grouping. *Journal of Educational Research, 62,* 51-52.

Schrank, W. (1970). A further study of the labeling effect of ability grouping. *Journal of Educational Research, 63,* 358-360.

Schunk, D. H. (1982). Effects of effort attributional feedback on children's perceived self-efficacy and achievement. *Journal of Educational Psychology, 74,* 548-556.

Schunk, D. H. (1983a). Ability versus effort attributional feedback: Differential effects on self-efficacy and achievement. *Journal of Educational Psychology, 75,* 848-856.

Schunk, D. H. (1983b). Developing children's self-efficacy and skills: The roles of social comparative information and goal setting. *Contemporary Educational Psychology, 8,* 76-86.

Schunk, D. H. (1983c). Goal difficulty and attainment information: Effects on children's achievement behaviors. *Human Learning, 2,* 107-117.

Schunk, D. H. (1983d). Reward contingencies and the development of children's skills and self-efficacy. *Journal of Educational Psychology, 75,* 511-518.

Schunk, D. H. (1984). Sequential attributional feedback and children's achievement behaviors. *Journal of Educational Psychology, 76,* 1159-1169.

Schunk, D. H. (1987). Peer models and children's behavioral change. *Review of Educational Research, 57,* 149-174.

Schunk, D. H. (1989a). Self-efficacy and achievement behaviors. *Educational Psychology Review, 1,* 173-208.

Schunk, D. H. (1989b). Self-efficacy and cognitive achievement: Implications for students with learning problems. *Journal of Learning Disabilities, 22,* 14-22.

Schunk, D. H. (1989c). Self-efficacy and cognitive skill learning. In C. Ames & R. Ames (Eds.), *Research on motivation in education* (Vol. 3, pp. 13-44). San Diego: Academic Press.

Schunk, D. H. (1989d). Social cognitive theory and self-regulated learning. In B. J. Zimmerman & D. H. Schunk (Eds.), *Self-regulated learning and academic achievement: Theory, research, and practice* (pp. 83-110). New York: Springer-Verlag.

Schunk, D. H. (1991a). *Learning theories: An educational perspective.* New York: Merrill/Macmillan.

Schunk, D. H. (1991b). Self-efficacy and academic motivation. *Educational Psychologist, 26,* 207-231.

Schunk, D. H., & Cox, P. D. (1986). Strategy training and attributional feedback with learning disabled students. *Journal of Educational Psychology, 78,* 201-209.

Schunk, D. H., & Hanson, A. R. (1985). Peer models: Influence on children's self-efficacy and achievement. *Journal of Educational Psychology, 77,* 313-322.

Schunk, D. H., & Hanson, A. R. (1989a). Influence of peer-model attributes on children's beliefs and learning. *Journal of Educational Psychology, 81,* 431-434.

Schunk, D. H., & Hanson, A. R. (1989b). Self-modeling and children's cognitive skill learning. *Journal of Educational Psychology, 81,* 155-163.

Schunk, D. H., Hanson, A. R., & Cox, P. D. (1987). Peer-model attributes and children's achievement behaviors. *Journal of Educational Psychology, 79,* 54-61.

Schunk, D. H., & Rice, J. M. (1986). Extended attributional feedback: Sequence effects during remedial reading instruction. *Journal of Early Adolescence, 6,* 55-66.

Schunk, D. H., & Rice, J. M. (1987). Enhancing comprehension skill and self-efficacy with strategy value information. *Journal of Reading Behavior, 19,* 285-302.

Schunk, D. H., & Swartz, C. W. (1993). Goals and progress feedback: Effects on self-efficacy and writing achievement. *Contemporary Educational Psychology, 18,* 337-354.

Schutz, P. (1991). Goals in self-directed behavior. *Educational Psychologist, 26,* 55–67.

Schutz, P. (1994). Goals as the transactive point between motivation and cognition. In P. R. Pintrich, D. R. Brown, & C. E. Weinstein (Eds.), *Student motivation, cognition, and learning: Essays in honor of Wilbert J. McKeachie* (pp. 135–156). Hillsdale, NJ: Erlbaum.

Schwarzer, R., van der Ploeg, H., & Spielberger, C. D. (1989). *Advances in test anxiety research* (Vol. 6). Amsterdam: Swets & Zeitlinger.

Sharan, S. (1980). Cooperative learning in small groups: Recent methods and effects on achievement, attitudes, and ethnic relations. *Review of Educational Research, 50,* 241–271.

Shavelson, R., & Bolus, R. (1982). Self concept: The interplay of theory and methods. *Journal of Educational Psychology, 74,* 3–17.

Shedd, J., & Bacharach, S. B. (1991). *Tangled hierarchies: Teachers as professionals and the management of schools.* San Francisco: Jossey-Bass.

Shell, D., Murphy, C., & Bruning, R. (1989). Self-efficacy and outcome expectancy mechanisms in reading and writing achievement. *Journal of Educational Psychology, 81,* 91-100.

Shirey, L. (1992). Importance, interest, and selective attention. In K. A. Renninger, S. Hidi, & A. Krapp (Eds.), *The role of interest in learning and development* (pp. 281–296). Hillsdale, NJ: Erlbaum.

Shulman, L. S. (1986). Paradigms and research programs in the study of teaching: A contemporary perspective. In M. C. Wittrock (Ed.), *Handbook of research on teaching* (3rd ed., pp. 3-36). New York: Macmillan.

Simmons, R., & Blyth, D. (1987). *Moving into adolescence: The impact of pubertal change and school context*. Hawthorn, NY: Aldine de Gruyter.

Sizer, T. (1984). *Horace's compromise: The dilemma of the American high school*. Boston: Houghton Mifflin.

Sizer, T. (1992). *Horace's compromise: Redesigning the American high school*. Boston: Houghton Mifflin.

Skaalvik, E.M., & Hagtvet, K. (1990). Academic achievement and self-concept: An analysis of causal predominance in a developmental perspective. *Journal of Personality and Social Psychology, 58*, 292–307.

Skinner, B. F. (1953). *Science and human behavior*. New York: Free Press.

Skinner, B. F. (1968). *The technology of teaching*. New York: Appleton-Century-Crofts.

Skinner, E. A., & Belmont, M. (1993). Motivation in the classroom: Reciprocal effects of teacher behavior and student engagement across the school year. *Journal of Educational Psychology, 85*, 571–581.

Skinner, E. A., Chapman, M., & Baltes, P. (1988a). Children's beliefs about control, means-ends, and agency: Developmental differences during middle childhood. *International Journal of Behavioral Development, 11*, 369-388.

Skinner, E. A., Chapman, M., & Baltes, P. (1988b). Control, means-ends, and agency beliefs: A new conceptualization and its measurement during childhood. *Journal of Personality and Social Psychology, 54*, 117-133.

Skinner, E. A., Wellborn, J. G., & Connell, J. P. (1990). What it takes to do well in school and whether I've got it: A process model of perceived control and children's engagement and achievement in school. *Journal of Educational Psychology, 82*, 22-32.

Slavin, R. (1983a). *Cooperative learning*. New York: Longman.

Slavin, R. (1983b). When does cooperative learning increase student achievement. *Psychological Bulletin, 94*, 429-445.

Slavin, R. (1995). *Cooperative learning*. Boston: Allyn and Bacon.

Smith, C. P. (1992). *Motivation and personality: Handbook of thematic content analysis*. New York: Cambridge University Press.

Smith, E. R., & Miller, F. (1983). Mediation among attributional inferences and comprehension processes: Initial findings and a general method. *Journal of Personality and Social Psychology, 44*, 492–505.

Smith, M. L. (1980). Meta-analysis of research on teacher expectations. *Evaluation in Education, 4*, 53-55.

Snow, R. (1989). Cognitive-conative aptitude interactions in learning. In R. Kanfer, P. L. Ackerman, & R. Cudeck (Eds.), *Abilities, motivation, and methodology* (pp. 435-473). Hillsdale, NJ: Erlbaum.

Sorensen, A. (1987). The organizational differentiation of students in schools as an opportunity structure. In M. Hallinan (Ed.), *The social organization of schools* (pp. 103–129). New York: Plenum Press.

Sorensen, A., & Hallinan, M. (1986). Effects of ability grouping on growth in academic achievement. *American Educational Research Journal, 23*, 519–542.

Spangler, W. D. (1992). Validity of questionnaire and TAT measures of need for achievement: Two meta-analyses. *Psychological Bulletin, 112*, 140-154.

Spear, P. S., & Armstrong, S. (1978). Effects of performance expectancies created by peer comparison as related to social reinforcement, task difficulty, and age of child. *Journal of Experimental Child Psychology, 25*, 254-266.

Spence, K. W. (1960). *Behavior theory and learning: Selected papers*. Englewood Cliffs, NJ: Prentice-Hall.

Spielberger, C. D. (1972). Anxiety as an emotional state. In C. D. Spielberger (Ed.), *Anxiety: Current trends in theory and research* (pp. 23–49). New York: Academic Press.

Steele, C. (1988). The psychology of self-affirmation: Sustaining the integrity of the self.

In L. Berkowitz (Ed.), *Advances in experimental social psychology* (Vol. 21, pp. 261–302). New York: Academic Press.

Steele, C. (1992). *Addressing the challenges of increasing and varied minority populations.* Paper presented at the annual meeting of the American Educational Research Association, San Francisco.

Sternberg, R. (1990). Prototypes of competence and incompetence. In R. Sternberg & J. Kolligian (Eds.), *Competence considered* (pp. 117–145). New Haven, CT: Yale University Press.

Stevenson, H., & Stigler, J. (1992). *The learning gap.* New York: Summit Books.

Stipek, D. (1981). Children's perceptions of their own and their classmates' ability. *Journal of Educational Psychology, 73,* 404–410.

Stipek, D. (1984). Young children's performance expectations: Logical analysis of wishful thinking? In J. Nicholls (Ed.), *Advances in motivation and achievement: The development of achievement motivation* (Vol. 3, pp. 33–56). Greenwich, CT: JAI Press.

Stipek, D. (1993). *Motivation to learn: From theory to practice.* Boston, MA: Allyn & Bacon.

Stipek, D., & Kowalski, P. (1989). Learned helplessness in task-orienting versus performance-orienting testing conditions. *Journal of Educational Psychology, 81,* 384–391.

Stipek, D., & Mac Iver, D. (1989). Developmental change in children's assessment of intellectual competence. *Child Development, 60,* 521–538.

Storms, M. D. (1973). Videotape and the attribution process: Reversing actors' and observers' points of view. *Journal of Personality and Social Psychology, 27,* 165–175.

Suls, J., & Sanders, G. S. (1982). Self-evaluation through social comparison: A developmental analysis. In L. Wheeler (Ed.), *Review of personality and social psychology* (Vol. 3, pp. 171-197). Beverly Hills, CA: Sage.

Suppes, P. (1974). The place of theory in educational research. *Educational Researcher, 3,* 3-10.

Swann, W. B., & Pittman, T. S. (1977). Initiating play activity of children: The moderating influence of verbal cues on intrinsic motivation. *Child Development, 48,* 1128-1132.

Tarde, G. (1903). *The laws of imitation* (2nd ed.). New York: Holt.

Taylor, R., Casten, R., Flickinger, S., & Roberts, D. (1994). Explaining the school performance of African-American adolescents. *Journal of Research on Adolescence, 4,* 21–44.

Thelen, M. H., Fry, R. A., Fehrenbach, P. A., & Frautschi, N. M. (1979). Therapeutic videotape and film modeling: A review. *Psychological Bulletin, 86,* 701-720.

Thorkildsen, T. A., & Nicholls, J. (1991). Students' critiques as motivation. *Educational Psychologist, 26,* 347-368.

Thorndike, E. L. (1912). *Education: A first book.* New York: Macmillan.

Thorndike, E. L. (1913). *Educational psychology: Vol. 2. The psychology of learning.* New York: Teachers College Press.

Thorndike, E. L. (1932). *The fundamentals of learning.* New York: Teachers College Press.

Tobias, S. (1980). Anxiety and instruction. In I. G. Sarason (Ed.), *Test anxiety: Theory, research, and applications* (pp. 289-309). Hillsdale, NJ: Erlbaum.

Tobias, S. (1985). Test anxiety: Interference, defective skills, and cognitive capacity. *Educational Psychologist, 20,* 135–142.

Tobias, S. (1994). Interest, prior knowledge, and learning. *Review of Educational Research, 64,* 37–54.

Tolman, E. C. (1932). *Purposive behavior in animals and men.* New York: Appleton-Century-Crofts. (Reprinted 1949, 1951, University of California Press, Berkeley)

Tolman, E. C. (1949). There is more than one kind of learning. *Psychological Review, 56,* 144-155.

Tolman, E. C., & Honzik, C. H. (1930). Introduction and removal of reward, and maze performance in rats. *University of California Publications in Psychology, 4,* 257-275.

Tolman, E. C., Ritchie, B. F., & Kalish, D. (1946). Studies in spatial learning. I. Orientation and the short-cut. *Journal of Experimental Psychology, 36,* 13-24.

Triandis, H. C. (1972). *The analysis of subjective culture.* New York: Wiley-Interscience.

Triplett, N. (1898). The dynamogenic factors in pacemaking and competition. *American Journal of Psychology, 9,* 507-533.

Trope, Y. (1975). Seeking information about one's ability as a determinant of choice among tasks. *Journal of Personality and Social Psychology, 32,* 1004–1013.

Tryon, G. S. (1980). The measurement and treatment of test anxiety. *Review of Educational Research, 50,* 343–371.

Urdan, T., Midgley, C., & Wood, S. (1995). Special issues in reforming middle level schools. *Journal of Early Adolescence, 15,* 9–37.

Veroff, J. (1969). Social comparison and the development of achievement motivation. In C. P. Smith (Ed.), *Achievement-related motives in children* (pp. 46-101). New York: Russell Sage Foundation.

Vygotsky, L. S. (1962). *Thought and language.* Cambridge, MA: MIT Press.

Vygotsky, L. S. (1978). *Mind in society: The development of higher psychological processes.* Cambridge, MA: Harvard University Press.

Ware, J. E., & Williams, R. G. (1975). The Dr. Fox effect: A study of lecturer effectiveness and ratings of instruction. *Journal of Medical Education, 50,* 149-156.

Watson, J. B. (1914). *Behavior: An introduction to comparative psychology.* New York: Henry Holt.

Watson, J. B. (1924). *Behaviorism.* New York: Norton.

Wechsler, D. (1974). *Wechsler intelligence scale for children: Form R.* New York: The Psychological Corporation.

Weiner, B. (1979). A theory of motivation for some classroom experiences. *Journal of Educational Psychology, 71,* 3–25.

Weiner, B. (1980a). A cognitive (attributional)-emotion-action model of motivated behavior: An analysis of judgments of help-giving. *Journal of Personality and Social Psychology, 39,* 186–200.

Weiner, B. (1980b). May I borrow your class notes? An attributional analysis of judg-ments of help-giving in an achievement-related context. *Journal of Educational Psychology, 72,* 676–681.

Weiner, B. (1985a). An attributional theory of achievement motivation and emotion. *Psychological Review, 92,* 548-573.

Weiner, B. (1985b). *Human motivation.* New York: Springer-Verlag.

Weiner, B. (1986). *An attributional theory of motivation and emotion.* New York: Springer-Verlag.

Weiner, B. (1990). History of motivational research in education. *Journal of Educational Psychology, 82,* 616-622.

Weiner, B. (1991). Metaphors in motivation and attribution. *American Psychologist, 46,* 921-930.

Weiner, B. (1992). *Human motivation: Metaphors, theories, and research.* Newbury Park, CA: Sage.

Weiner, B. (1994). Integrating social and personal theories of achievement striving. *Review of Educational Research, 64,* 557–573.

Weiner, B., & Kukla, A. (1970). An attributional analysis of achievement motivation. *Journal of Personality and Social Psychology, 15,* 1–20.

Weiner, B., Frieze, I., Kukla, A., Reed, L., Rest, S., & Rosenbaum, R. (1971). *Perceiving the causes of success and failure.* Morristown, NJ: General Learning Press.

Weiner, B., Graham, S., & Chandler, C. (1982). Pity, anger, and guilt: An attributional analysis. *Personality and Social Psychology Bulletin, 8,* 226–232.

Weiner, B., Graham, S., Taylor, S., & Meyer, W. (1983). Social cognition in the classroom. *Educational Psychologist, 18,* 109-124.

Weiner, B., & Kukla, A. (1970). An attributional analysis of achievement motivation. *Journal of Personality and Social Psychology, 15,* 1–20.

Weiner, B., & Peter, N. (1973). A cognitive-developmental analysis of achievement and moral judgments. *Developmental Psychology, 9,* 290–309.

Weiner, B., Russell, D., & Lerman, D. (1978). Affective consequences of causal ascriptions. In J. Harvey, W. Ickes, & R. Kidd

(Eds.), *New directions in attribution research* (Vol. 2, pp. 59–88). Hillsdale, NJ: Erlbaum.

Weinstein, C. E., & Mayer, R. (1986). The teaching of learning strategies. In M. C. Wittrock (Ed.), *Handbook of research on teaching* (3rd ed., pp. 315-327). New York: Macmillan.

Weisz, J. (1983). Can I control it? The pursuit of veridical answers across the life-span. In P. Baltes & O. Brim (Eds.), *Life-span development and behavior* (Vol. 5, pp. 233–300). New York: Academic Press.

Weisz, J. (1984). Contingency judgments and achievement behavior: Deciding what is controllable and when to try. In J. Nicholls (Ed.), *Advances in motivation and achievement: The development of achievement motivation* (Vol. 3, pp. 107–136). Greenwich, CT: JAI Press.

Weisz, J., Rothbaum, F., & Blackburn, T. (1984). Standing out and standing in: The psychology of control in America and Japan. *American Psychologist, 39,* 955–969.

Wentzel, K. (1989). Adolescent classroom goals, standards for performance, and academic achievement: An interactionist perspective. *Journal of Educational Psychology, 81,* 131–142.

Wentzel, K. (1991a). Social and academic goals at school: Motivation and achievement in context. In M. L. Maehr & P. R. Pintrich (Eds.), *Advances in motivation and achievement: Goals and self-regulatory processes* (Vol. 7, pp. 185–212). Greenwich, CT: JAI Press.

Wentzel, K. (1991b). Social competence at school: Relation between social responsibility and academic achievement. *Review of Educational Research, 61,* 1–24.

Werner, H. (1957). *Comparative psychology of mental development.* New York: International Universities Press.

Wertsch, J., & Tulviste, P. (1992). L. S. Vygotsky and contemporary developmental psychology. *Developmental Psychology, 28,* 548–557.

White, P. (1988). Causal processing: Origins and development. *Psychological Bulletin, 104,* 36–52.

White, R. W. (1959). Motivation reconsidered: The concept of competence. *Psychological Review, 66,* 297-333.

Whitehead, G., Smith, S., & Eichorn, J. (1982). The effect of subject's race and other's race on judgments of causality for success and failure. *Journal of Personality, 50,* 193–202.

Wigfield, A. (1994). Expectancy-value theory of achievement motivation: A developmental perspective. *Educational Psychology Review, 6,* 49–78.

Wigfield, A., & Eccles, J. (1989). Test anxiety in elementary and secondary school students. *Educational Psychologist, 24,* 159–183.

Wigfield, A., & Eccles, J. (1992). The development of achievement task values: A theoretical analysis. *Developmental Review, 12,* 265-310.

Wigfield, A., Eccles, J., Mac Iver, D., Reuman, D., & Midgley, C. (1991). Transitions during early adolescence: Changes in children's domain-specific self-perceptions and general self-esteem across the transition to junior high school. *Developmental Psychology, 27,* 552–565.

Wigfield, A., Eccles, J., & Pintrich, P. R. (forthcoming). Development between 11 and 25. In D. Berliner & R. Calfee (Eds.), *Handbook of educational psychology.* New York: Macmillan.

Wigfield, A., & Karpathian, M. (1991). Who am I and what can I do? Children's self-concepts and motivation in achievement situations. *Educational Psychologist, 26,* 233-262.

Wiley, M., & Eskilson, A. (1976). Why did you learn in school today? Teachers' perceptions of causality. *Sociology of Education, 51,* 261–269.

Wilson, T., & Linville, P. (1982). Improving the academic performance of college freshmen: Attribution therapy revisited. *Journal of Personality and Social Psychology, 42,* 367–376.

Wilson, T., & Linville, P. (1985). Improving the performance of college freshmen with attributional techniques. *Journal of Personality and Social Psychology, 49,* 287–293.

Wine, J. (1971). Test anxiety and direction of attention. *Psychological Bulletin, 76,* 92–104.

Winell, M. (1987). Personal goals: The key to self-direction in adulthood. In M. E. Ford & D. H. Ford (Eds.), *Humans as self-constructing living systems: Putting the framework to work* (pp. 261–287). Hillsdale, NJ: Erlbaum.

Winne, P. H., & Marx, R. W. (1982). Students' and teachers' views of thinking processes for classroom learning. *Elementary School Journal, 82,* 493-518.

Wittrock, M. C. (1986). Students' thought processes. In M. C. Wittrock (Ed.), *Handbook of research on teaching* (3rd ed., pp. 297-314). New York: Macmillan.

Wong, P., Derlaga, V., & Colson, W. (1988). The effects of race on expectancies and performance attributions. *Canadian Journal of Behavioral Science, 20,* 29–39.

Woodworth, R. S. (1918). *Dynamic psychology.* New York: Columbia University Press.

Woodworth, R. S., & Schlosberg, H. (1954). *Experimental psychology* (Rev. ed.). New York: Henry Holt.

Wylie, R. C. (1974). *The self-concept* (Vol. 1). Lincoln: University of Nebraska Press.

Wylie, R. C. (1979). *The self-concept* (Vol. 2). Lincoln: University of Nebraska Press.

Wylie, R. C. (1989). *Measures of the self-concept.* Lincoln: University of Nebraska Press.

Yerkes, R. M., & Dodson, J. D. (1908). The relation of strength of stimulus to rapidity of habit-formation. *Journal of Comparative Neurology and Psychology, 18,* 459-482.

Zahorik, J. A. (1975). Teachers' planning models. *Educational Leadership, 33,* 134-139.

Zajonc, R. B. (1965). Social facilitation. *Science, 149,* 269-274.

Zatz, S., & Chassin, L. (1985). Cognitions of test-anxious children under naturalistic test-taking conditions. *Journal of Consulting and Clinical Psychology, 53,* 393–401.

Zimmerman, B. J. (1989). A social cognitive view of self-regulated academic learning. *Journal of Educational Psychology, 81,* 329-339.

Zimmerman, B. 422J., Greenberg, D., & Weinstein, C. E. (1994). Self-regulating academic study time: A strategy approach. In D. H. Schunk & B. Zimmerman (Eds.), *Self-regulation of learning and performance: Issues and educational applications* (pp. 181–199). Hillsdale, NJ: Erlbaum.

Zimmerman, B. J., & Martinez-Pons, M. (1990). Student differences in self-regulated learning: Relating grade, sex, and giftedness to self-efficacy and strategy use. *Journal of Educational Psychology, 82,* 51-59.

Zimmerman, B. J., & Martinez-Pons, M. (1992). Perceptions of efficacy and strategy use in the self-regulation of learning. In D. H. Schunk & J. L. Meece (Eds.), *Student perceptions in the classroom* (pp. 185-207). Hillsdale, NJ: Erlbaum.

Zimmerman, B. J., & Ringle, J. (1981). Effects of model persistence and statements of confidence on children's self-efficacy and problem solving. *Journal of Educational Psychology, 73,* 485-493.

Zuckerman, M., Porac, J., Lathin, D., Smith, R., & Deci, E. L. (1978). On the importance of self-determination for intrinsically-motivated behavior. *Personality and Social Psychology Bulletin, 4,* 443-446.

Paul R. Pintrich is Associate Professor in the Combined Program in Education and Psychology at the University of Michigan, Ann Arbor. He has a M.A. in developmental psychology from the University of Michigan and received his Ph.D. from the Combined Program in Education and Psychology in 1982. He has published over 50 journal articles and book chapters on student motivation, self-regulated learning, and social and personal development in school contexts. He is co-editor with Martin Maehr of the motivation research book series, *Advances in Motivation and Achievement*, published by JAI Press, and is currently editor of the journal *Educational Psychologist*, an American Psychological Association (APA) publication for Division 15 (Educational Psychology). He has been a Spencer Fellow of the National Academy of Education and has received an award for overall excellence in undergraduate teaching from both the College of Literature, Science and Arts and the School of Education at the University of Michigan.

Dale H. Schunk is Head of the Department of Educational Studies and Professor of Educational Psychology at Purdue University. He received his Ph.D. in educational psychology from Stanford University in 1979. He is author of *Learning Theories: An Educational Perspective* (Merrill, 1991). With Barry J. Zimmerman he is editor of *Self-Regulation of Learning and Performance: Issues and Educational Applications* (Erlbaum, 1994) and of *Self Regulated Learning and Academic Achievement: Theory, Research and Practice* (Springer-Verlag, 1989); with Judith Meece he is editor of *Student Perceptions in the Classroom* (Erlbaum, 1992). He has published over 55 journal articles and book chapters, has been on the editorial boards of six journals, and served as editor for a special section on motivation and efficacy for the *Journal of Educational Psychology* in 1990. In 1989 he received the Albert J. Harris Research Award from the International Reading Association, and in 1982 he was honored with an Early Contributions Award from Division 15 (Educational Psychology) of the American Psychological Association. His research investigates the relations among students' achievement beliefs, learning, motivation, and self-regulation.